PRAISE FOR *THE CANADIAN WAR ON QUEERS*

"Compelling personal stories illuminate this impeccably researched analysis of the use of national security legislation to wage a war against lesbian and gay Canadians during the Cold War years. As if that wasn't enough to accomplish in a single book, the authors employ this history to lay bare the current government's use of national security legislation to silence critics of corporate power and justify a litany of human rights abuses in today's 'war on terror.' A profound and extremely readable contribution to both queer history and the politics of fear that masquerade as straightforward policy concerns."

> — Lynne Fernie, filmmaker, co-director of *Forbidden Love:*
> *The Unashamed Stories of Lesbian Lives* and *Fiction and Other*
> *Truths: A Film about Jane Rule*

"*The Canadian War on Queers* is destined to be a landmark book in the study of Canadian state security apparatuses and an important contribution to Canadian history and LGBT studies."

> — Barry Adam, author of *The Rise of a Gay and Lesbian Movement*

THE CANADIAN WAR
ON QUEERS

Sexuality Studies Series

This series focuses on original, provocative, scholarly research examining from a range of perspectives the complexity of human sexual practice, identity, community, and desire. Books in the series explore how sexuality interacts with other aspects of society, such as law, education, feminism, racial diversity, the family, policing, sport, government, religion, mass media, medicine, and employment. The series provides a broad public venue for nurturing debate, cultivating talent, and expanding knowledge of human sexual expression, past and present.

Other volumes in the series are:

Masculinities without Men? Female Masculinity in Twentieth-Century Fictions, by Jean Bobby Noble

Every Inch a Woman: Phallic Possession, Femininity, and the Text, by Carellin Brooks

Queer Youth in the Province of the "Severely Normal," by Gloria Filax

The Manly Modern: Masculinity in Postwar Canada, by Christopher Dummitt

Sexing the Teacher: School Sex Scandals and Queer Pedagogies, by Sheila L. Cavanagh

Sapphistries: A Global History of Love between Women, by Leila J. Rupp

Gary Kinsman and Patrizia Gentile

THE CANADIAN

NATIONAL SECURITY AS SEXUAL REGULATION

WAR ON QUEERS

UBCPress · Vancouver · Toronto

Library and Archives Canada Cataloguing in Publication

Kinsman, Gary
    The Canadian war on queers : national security as sexual regulation /
Gary Kinsman and Patrizia Gentile.

(Sexuality studies series, ISSN 1706-9947)
Includes bibliographical references and index.
ISBN 978-0-7748-1627-4

    1. Homosexuality – Government policy – Canada – History. 2. Internal security – Canada – History. 3. Gay rights – Canada – History. 4. Homosexuality – Law and legislation – Canada – History. 5. Subversive activities – Government policy – Canada. I. Gentile, Patrizia, 1970 II. Title. III. Series: Sexuality studies series

HQ76.3.C3K54 2010   323.3'2640971   C2010-903770-X

Canadä

UBC Press gratefully acknowledges the financial support for our publishing program of the Government of Canada through the Book Publishing Industry Development Program (BPIDP), and of the Canada Council for the Arts, and the British Columbia Arts Council.

This book has been published with the help of a grant from the Canadian Federation for the Humanities and Social Sciences, through the Aid to Scholarly Publications Programme, using funds provided by the Social Sciences and Humanities Research Council of Canada.

Cover photo credits: Montreal demonstrations against Olympic "clean-up," June 19, 1976, CLGA 1986-032_08P (28) 01P (front); Ottawa conference demonstration, June 30, 1975, CLGA 1986-032_02P (40) 01 (back).

UBC Press
The University of British Columbia
2029 West Mall
Vancouver, BC V6T 1Z2
604-822-5959 / Fax: 604-822-6083
www.ubcpress.ca

This book is dedicated to all those
who resisted the Canadian war on queers
and for those
who continue to resist the national security campaigns
today.

Contents

Illustrations

Preface
National Security Wars – Then and Now

National security campaigns are very much in the news as we put the finishing touches to this book. Under the guise of the "war on terror," "evidence" provided by Canadian security police resulted in the extradition (i.e., rendition) of Maher Arar to Syria, with the knowledge that he would be tortured.[1] We have seen the indefinite detention of Muslim- and Arab-identified "non-citizens" under the so-called national security certificates as well as the racial profiling and targeting of people identified as Arabs and Muslims.[2] Under cover of national security, we have seen the mobilization of racism and the continued denial of human and civil rights. The targets of these most recent national security campaigns are once again defined as enemies of Canada, are denied citizenship, and are identified as national security risks. At times, allegations of "national security risk" and even "terrorism" have been directed towards global justice and anti-poverty activists who challenge the injustice and misery that capitalist social relations have produced in the lives of people around the globe.[3]

In all this we hear the echoes of earlier national security campaigns against suspected lesbians and gay men – campaigns that took place across the Canadian state from the 1950s into the late 1990s and that, in some ways, continue today. These earlier campaigns live on in the current national security war, which is now directed at new targets. We therefore reject current national security campaigns, and we support those who have been tortured and imprisoned for no reason other than their perceived country of origin or their assumed religious and/or political commitments. In resisting this current national security war, we must critically examine earlier national security campaigns both within the Canadian state and elsewhere. There is much to be learned by linking the earlier story of national security wars against queers with current campaigns against Arabs and Muslims. We cannot view the injustices of these campaigns as simply "mistakes" or "excesses" committed by a few overzealous security operatives; rather, these injustices are an integral part of the ideology and practice of national security itself. There is something very dangerous at the heart of national security, and we need to challenge and resist it.

While we have been working on this book in our historical present, during the so-called war on terror, we have been surprised to find that, since 9/11, the relatively constant generation of fear and crisis over security issues has not resulted in major attempts to learn from earlier national security campaigns against "others." It is as if we are so mesmerized by the spectacle of 9/11 that we have forgotten the earlier history of national security and its wars on "subversion." In part, this is because the ideology of the war on terror works through ahistorical decontextualization, which results in the forgetting of how national security operated long before September 2001. Given this context, we hope *The Canadian War on Queers* succeeds in linking this past to our historical present.

In this book we provide a detailed and critical examination of the social organization of the national security campaigns against lesbians and gay men from the 1950s until the present. This is not simply a sad and depressing story about injustices committed against those identified as lesbian and gay; it is also very much a story of how this experience was lived by the people most directly affected and how, even in extremely difficult circumstances, there was always resistance. For instance, even in the restrictive atmosphere of the 1960s, it was possible for people involved in lesbian and gay networks to force security police to alter their tactics.

The Canadian War on Queers has been a long time coming. In 1998, we released a preliminary research report on national security campaigns against lesbians and gay men, focusing on the late 1950s and the 1960s.[4] Since then we have done a great deal more research, especially on the national security surveillance of the lesbian and gay activist movement in the 1970s and developments in the 1980s and 1990s. We hope this book is well worth the wait, although, given the urgency of the questions it raises, we are pained by how long it has taken for it to see the light of day.

Most of this book is a duet; however, since Gary was personally involved in some of the events that we describe, his particular voice comes through at times, and this is signalled by a sans serif font. The following vignette is an example of this.

TOWARDS A GENEALOGY OF "COMMIE PINKO FAG" – NATIONAL SECURITY AND ME

My life history as a gay man and an activist is interwoven with a number of the stories told in this book. I am, therefore, very interested in this critical interrogation of national security for multiple personal, political, and social/historical reasons.

"Commie, pinko, fag." This used to be scrawled on my locker and was used as a greeting in the halls when I was a student at Victoria Park Secondary School in Don Mills in the early 1970s. I was involved in the radical left as a member of the Young Socialists and, later, of the Revolutionary Marxist Group, so the "commie" part made some sense to me. I never understood where the "pinko" came from. The sole basis for the "fag" part seemed to be my refusal to laugh at the anti-gay jokes that were all-pervasive at my school.[5] A certain type of "cutting out" operation was mobilized against me, much as George Smith describes, as I was socially cut out of regular forms of "normal" heterosexual interaction.[6] I do remember some of the school jocks squirming when I pointed out to them that they spent all their time hanging out with other guys. It was during these years that I was beginning to explore my sexuality and starting to come out to myself and to others as gay. So I did become an anti-Stalinist "commie fag."

My interest in national security campaigns against queers flows from my continuing interest in exploring where this association between commies and fags, which has been integral to my experience, has come from historically and socially. And this particular association was forged in important ways during the years of the national security campaigns against gay men and lesbians, and also through the very real connections of some queer activists with sections of the left.[7]

I made an Access to Information request for my personal files in 1999 in preparation for this book, only to be disappointed by the RCMP's response. I received a letter saying that no such files existed. I know they should have had information on me since I knew they did surveillance work on the Revolutionary Marxist Group. When my father's workplace was taken over by the government for a period of time he was even asked a security-related question about me. I have been involved in the left since 1971 and in the gay movement since 1972. I have been present at many of the events, demonstrations, and conferences at which the RCMP conducted surveillance in the 1970s, and I was at the Young Socialist convention, where the RCMP put letters on everyone's chairs during the lunch break (this is referred to in Chapter 8).

THE HISTORICAL PAST, THE HISTORICAL PRESENT

In contrast to the historical past, which involved the general national security campaigns against lesbians and gay men from the late 1950s through the 1990s, the historical present finds us in a rather different position with regard to lesbian and gay rights.[8] Although the national security campaigns against queers are not over, especially for those of us deemed to be in the closet or to have something to hide, and for those of us who are people of colour (specifically those identified as Arab and Muslim), the lesbian and gay movements have made remarkable progress with regard to human rights.[9] We have won important human rights victories and have been able to utilize the shift in Canadian state legal formation signalled by Section 15 (the equality rights section) of the Canadian Charter of Rights and Freedoms, which was enacted in the 1980s. For example, there has been significant progress on basic human rights protection, spousal rights, family recognition rights, and same-sex marriage rights. This has led some to view the existing federal form of the Canadian state, and particularly the Charter, as crucial to queer liberation.[10]

At the same time, major forms of sexual censorship remain, as do issues relating to the criminalization of our consensual sexualities, and many queer people experience poverty, racism, sexism, and class exploitation. Although the December 2005 Supreme Court decision regarding "swingers" clubs in Montreal expanded the ability of heterosexuals to engage in sexual activities in sex clubs, such freedom has not been extended to gay men in bathhouses and sex clubs, and queer sex can still be defined as "acts of indecency."[11] This shapes the contradictory situations queer people now face. On the one hand, lesbians, gay men, and bisexuals have won recognition of our individual human rights; we have established our formal equality with heterosexuals in a number of realms. On the other hand, we have yet to establish substantive social equality with heterosexuals, and major forms of marginalization, exclusion, violence, and hatred continue to exist.[12] Legal acceptance of our rights has done little to create full social acceptance of our sexualities and lives. Grudging acceptance of rights for queer people can still easily give way to expressions of hatred and violence. *The Canadian War on Queers* thus reminds us of the heterosexist past and the ways in which it continues in the historical present as a central part of Canadian state and social formation.

For example, the current federal Conservative government – supported by the Liberals and most of the NDP – raised the age of sexual consent from fourteen to sixteen without proposing a comparable reduction in the current age of consent from eighteen to sixteen for anal sex (often homosexualized in official discourse) outside Ontario, Quebec, and British Columbia. This change will have a major impact on queer young people, and young people more generally, decreasing their ability to gain access to sexual and safe sex information.

In 2009, our right to marry has been established through federal legislation, even though it has been contested by the current Conservative government.[13] The present government cannot overturn the legislation; however, by raising the issue, it continues to create opportunities for moral conservative organizing and anti-queer bigotry. More moderate forces in our communities and movements, as well as much of the media, view winning the right to marriage as an end point of our struggles.[14] It is suggested that, in winning the right to marry, we have achieved full equality (really full integration) and that our oppression will soon be over. Although, as queer authors and activists, we welcome this victory and support the fight for formal equality, in our view this legal victory has neither magically eliminated our oppression nor encouraged discussion of developing forms of relationships based on equality and democracy outside institutionalized marriage.[15] The focus on our right to marry has been tied up with strategies for integrating us into the existing capitalist, patriarchal, and racist social order and with strategies for how we can perform social "respectability" and "responsibility."[16] We need to challenge existing social forms such as marriage, which have historically been based on our exclusion and marginalization as well as on the oppression of women, and we need to focus more on how to transform oppressive social relations and how to build social alternatives.

Some queers – but only some – are now being included in the fabric of the "nation" and the "national security" mobilized in its defence. In the context of the national security state and the war on terror, some queers (usually white, middle-class men) are now defending national security against a series of "others" (including people of Arab descent and Muslims in Canada), against global justice and anti-capitalist protesters, against people living in poverty, against prostitutes and hustlers, and against groups of queer people such as queers of colour, queers living in poverty, and young queers. It is for these reasons that we must proceed with caution in our fight for legal "victories," as these may well continue to perpetuate social exclusions based on class, race, gender, and sexuality.

This strategy of integration and normalization is tied up with the emergence of stronger professional, managerial, and middle-class social strata within gay and lesbian communities. The people who occupy these strata share a number of social commitments with the broader middle class. They are not interested in questioning the social relations of capitalism and raise only those queer issues that do not challenge these relations.[17] They are invested in the commercialization and commodification of capitalist society.[18] Such people often suggest that existing Canadian state formation and, especially, the equality rights section of the Charter of Rights and Freedoms are the royal road to our liberation.[19] Although the use of Section 15 has been crucial to our struggles, including those against the national security regime during the 1980s and 1990s, it has not brought about our liberation. And the strategy of integration, which is premised on the desirability of being incorporated within the heterosexually defined nation, leads to a reconciliation with the forces of national security. We come back to some of the limitations of this strategy in Chapters 11 and 12. The analysis developed in this book is directed not only at locating resources for our current battles against national security but also at providing ways for queer activists in the historical present to reignite a more radical movement – one that gets at the root of the problem and resists a strategy of integration that would see us buy into a "normality" and a "respectability" that includes support for national security.

Acknowledgments

The Canadian War on Queers has been a very long time coming. Since 1993, many people have been invaluable to the making of this book. We are grateful to Cynthia Wright, who convinced Gary to embark on this project, and Dean Beeby, whose work leading to the release of security regime documents related to the campaigns against queers made our work seem possible. The chapter on the surveillance of gay and lesbian groups in the 1970s is inspired by Steve Hewitt's generous gift of security documents. These documents extended our research and, we believe, made this a better book.

Books are always collective endeavours because they are much more than the product of individual research, writing, and conceptualization, especially when they are a collaborative project. Ultimately, they are about friendship, support, and community. Many people assisted us along the way, including Aerlyn Weissman, A.K. Thompson, Amy Gottlieb, Becki Ross, Brian Drader, Cathy Jones, Corinne Gaudin, Dan Irving, Daniel J. Robinson, David Kimmel, David Pepper, Deborah Brock, Dieter Buse, Dino Zuccarini, Elise Chenier, Greg Kealey, the late Greg Pavelich, the late Jennifer Keck, Joan Kinsman, Kaili Beck, Karen Pearlston, Kevin Crombie, Kim Tomczak, Larry Hannant, Laurent Gagliardi, Len Scher, Lesbians Making History, Lisa Steele, Lorna Weir, Lynne Dupuis, Lynne Fernie, Maureen Fitzgerald, Mercedes Steedman, Nancy Nicol, Paul Jackson, Richard Goreham, Robin Metcalfe, Ross Higgins, Scott Neigh, Steven Maynard, Svend Robinson's office, and Terry Pender.

We are indebted to the invaluable work of the Canadian Lesbian and Gay Archives (CLGA) and, especially, to Harold Averill and Paul Leatherdale, who helped us with the wonderful photographs that animate this book. Many of the CLGA photographs originally appeared in the *Body Politic*, and were taken by a number of its contributors, including Gerald Hannon. Many thanks also to Harriet Fried from the City of Ottawa Archives, who assisted us in procuring images. Patti Harper at the Carleton University Archives helped us with photos and institutional files on F.R. Wake, for which we are also grateful. Kim Foreman from the National Archives of Canada helped us muddle through the Access to Information requests for documents regarding the gay liberation movement and organizations. Rhonda Hinther of the Museum of Civilization helped us with leads on the "fruit machine" housed at the Canadian War Museum in Ottawa.

The Canadian War on Queers could never have been written, however, without the contributions of all those who spoke to us and shared their experiences and stories, including Albert, Andrew, Arlene, Barbara, Barry Deeprose, Bernie, Blair Johnston, Bob, Brenda Barnes, Brian Waite, Bruce Somers, Charles Hill, David, David Garmaise, Dorothy Kidd, Doug Sanders, Ellen Skinner, Frank Letourneau, the late George Hislop, Hank, Harold, Hector Mackenzie, the late Herbert Sutcliffe, Jake, the late Jim Egan, Joan, the late John Grube, John Sawatsky, John Wilson, Josh, Lois, Marie Robertson, Marielle, Marty, Marvin, Merv, Michael, Morgan, Patrick, Paul-François Sylvestre, Peaches Latour, Peter, Pierre, Robert, Sam, Shawn, Simon, Steve, Sue, Svend Robinson, and Tom Warner.

Without the work of Heidi McDonell and Treanor Mahood-Greer (in an earlier period) and Grace Irving, Tracy Gregory, Oren Howlett, and Ander Reszczynski (in the present), *The Canadian War on Queers* would have taken even longer to complete. Wendy Atkin did editing work at an early stage, and Ellen Vincer copyedited a version of the manuscript. Grace Irving was an endless source of support for us as we prepared the manuscript in its last stages. The critical work of helping with the research, editing, and formatting of this book was not always fun, but it was indispensable, and we are very thankful for the time and effort we received from these individuals.

We thank Jean Wilson (the book's grandmother), Darcy Cullen, Ann Macklem, Joanne Richardson (the copy editor), Melissa Pitts, and UBC Press for persevering during this extended research and writing journey. We also thank the two anonymous reviewers who provided many useful suggestions for improving *The Canadian War on Queers*. Needless to say, these individuals bear no responsibility for any errors found in the book you now hold in your hands.

This research was funded by the Social Sciences and Humanities Research Council grant #410-94-1609, a Laurentian University Research Fund Grant for 1995-96, an emerging researcher grant at Laurentian University for 1996-97, and a research start-up fund provided by Carleton University. This financial support was critical, and we are thankful to the institutions listed above.

Gary thanks his partner, Patrick Barnholden, and their wonderful son, Mike, for love and support. Patrizia is thankful for the comfort and love provided by Pauline Rankin.

Abbreviations

AIM	American Indian Movement
APEC	Asia Pacific Economic Co-operation
ASK	Association for Social Knowledge
ATIP	Access to Information Program
BEAVER	Better End to All Vicious Erotic Repression
CBC	Canadian Broadcasting Corporation
CBNRC	Communication Branch of the National Research Council
CCRH	Canadian Council on Religion and the Homosexual
CF	Canadian Forces
CFAO 19-20	Canadian Forces Administrative Order 19-20 (1967 and 1976)
CGAA	Canadian Gay Activists Alliance
CGRO	Coalition for Gay Rights in Ontario
CHAR	Comité homosexuel anti-répression/ Gay Coalition against Repression
CHAT	Community Homophile Association of Toronto
CIA	Central Intelligence Agency
CLGA	Canadian Lesbian and Gay Archives (Toronto)
CNR	Canadian National Railways
CPC	Commission for Public Complaints against the RCMP
CSIS	Canadian Security Intelligence Service
CSP	criminal sexual psychopath
DEA	Department of External Affairs
DL2	Defence Liaison Division 2, Department of External Affairs
DMI	Directorate of Military Intelligence
DND	Department of National Defence
DSI	Directorate of Security and Intelligence
DSO	dangerous sexual offender

FBI	Federal Bureau of Investigation
FLH	Front de libération des homosexuels
FTAA	Free Trade Area of the Americas
GAE	Gay Alliance for Equality
GATE	Gay Alliance towards Equality
GLF	Gay Liberation Front
GLOV	Gay and Lesbian Organization of Veterans
GO	Gays of Ottawa
HALO	Homophile Association of London Ontario
IPC	Intelligence Policy Committee
IPP	internationally protected person
IWD	International Women's Day
KGB	Committee for State Security (USSR)
LAC	Library and Archives Canada
LIP	Local Initiative Program
LJS	Ligue des jeunes socialistes
LMDF	Lesbian Mothers Defence Fund
LOON	Lesbians of Ottawa Now
LOOT	Lesbian Organization of Toronto
LOR	Ligue ouvrière révolutionnaire
LSA	League for Socialist Action
LSO	Ligue socialiste ouvrière
MP	Military Police
NAC	National Action Committee on the Status of Women
NAFTA	North American Free Trade Agreement
NATO	North Atlantic Treaty Organization
NCO	non-commissioned officer
NDP	New Democratic Party
NFB	National Film Board
NGEC	National Gay Election Coalition
NGRC	National Gay Rights Coalition
NMI	New Marxist Institute
OCAP	Ontario Coalition against Poverty
OFY	Opportunities for Youth

PCC	Public Complaints Commission
PCO	Privy Council Office
QR&O	Queen's Regulations and Orders
RAWA	Revolutionary Association of the Women of Afghanistan
RCAF	Royal Canadian Air Force
RCMP	Royal Canadian Mounted Police
RCN	Royal Canadian Navy
RMG	Revolutionary Marxist Group
RWL	Revolutionary Workers' League
SID	Special Investigations Detachment
SIU	Special Investigations Unit
SPP	Security and Prosperity Partnership
SWP	Socialist Workers Party
TGA	Toronto Gay Action
THA	Trent Homophile Association
TWC	Toronto Women's Caucus
TWHC	Toronto Wages for Housework Committee
UTHA	University of Toronto Homophile Association
WAVAW	Women against Violence against Women
WD	Wages Due Lesbians
WTO	World Trade Organization
YS	Young Socialists

THE CANADIAN WAR
ON QUEERS

Queering National Security, the Cold War, and Canadian History
Surveillance and Resistance

> We even knew occasionally that there was somebody in some police force or some investigator who would be sitting in a bar. And you would see someone with a ... newspaper held right up, and if you ... looked real closely you could find him holding behind the newspaper a camera, and these people were photographing everyone in the bar. (May 12, 1994)

This is David speaking about his experiences of police surveillance around 1964 in the basement tavern at the Lord Elgin, which was one of the major gathering places for gay men in Ottawa.[1] Surveillance was one way that the RCMP collected information on homosexuals during the Canadian Cold War against queers. David's story is a remarkable example of how the men in the bar resisted police surveillance strategies.

> We always knew that when you saw someone with a newspaper held up in front of their face ... that somebody would take out something like a wallet and do this sort of thing [like snapping a photo] and then, of course, everyone would then point over to the person you see and, of course, I'm sure, that the person hiding behind the newspaper knew that he had been found out. But that was the thing. You would take out a wallet or a package of matches or something like that ... it was always sort of a joke. You would see somebody ... and you would catch everyone's eye and you would go like this [snapping a photo]. And everyone knew [to] watch out for this guy. (May 12, 1994)

Rather than diving under the tables or running for cover, these men turned the tables on the undercover agents. David's story reveals not only the 1960s national security surveillance regime but also how people resisted it. In *The Canadian War on Queers*, we weave together stories of how people resisted the security regime, and, starting from the social standpoints of those who were watched, interrogated, and purged, we develop an analysis of the social organization of that regime and its war on queers.

David is among the thirty-six gay or bisexual men and ten lesbians we interviewed about their experiences with the anti-homosexual national security campaigns of the 1950s and 1960s. David, who was not a civil servant, was involved in gay networks in Ottawa during the 1960s. His entanglement in the security campaigns began when a friend gave the RCMP his name during a park sweep of one of Ottawa's cruising (or meeting) areas for men interested in sex with men. These sweeps were fairly common, and the RCMP had jurisdiction over the city's parks. According to David, the RCMP was far more interested in getting the names of homosexuals than in arresting people for "criminal" activities. Officers would threaten to lay criminal charges against the men they apprehended unless they gave them the names of other homosexuals.[2] David described how he first came into contact with the RCMP:

> I had a telephone call to say that a mutual friend of my caller and myself had been caught in flagrante delicto [caught performing a sexual act by the police] and had given my name, among others, to the RCMP in order to avert their giving away his identity [and revealing] his situation to his employer and his family ... The mutual friend then phoned me in great consternation to let me know that my name had been given to the RCMP. And sure enough, about ten days later I had my first contact with the RCMP.

David was interrogated and followed; his home was searched by RCMP officers. He reported that, when he went in to talk to the officers, "they asked me to confirm that I was gay. I felt there was no use to ... not admit what they obviously knew or they wouldn't have asked. So I agreed I was gay. They then wanted me to give the names of all the people who I knew who were gay, and I just simply said to this I was not the person who'd been caught in the indecent act" (May 12, 1994). In this account, the police were interested in collecting the names and identities of other gay men. David refused to cooperate. RCMP surveillance work and investigations extended into the lives of those who were not public servants, who, at times, played an important part in providing information for the security regime. As informants, these people were integral to the RCMP's public service surveillance, and they were its weakest link. We return to David's story when we explore the surveillance and interrogations of homosexuals outside the public service and their resistance to these security campaigns.

Thousands of lesbians, gay men, and those suspected of homosexuality were directly affected by these campaigns, especially following the specific targeting of homosexuals in the late 1950s. In 1959, the homosexual screening program was initiated in the federal public service. Total reports of suspected and confirmed homosexuals, including those outside the public service, went up from 1,000 in 1960-61 to 8,200 in 1966-67. By 1967-68, the list had expanded to 9,000 names.[3] David was one of the more than nine thousand "suspected," "alleged," and "confirmed" homosexuals the RCMP investigated in the 1960s.[4] The people who appeared on this list were based in the Ottawa area, and most were neither public servants nor involved in the military.[5] Hundreds (if not thousands) of others were purged, demoted, and forced to inform on friends and acquaintances. Of this number, many were forced to resign or were transferred. At the core of this screening program was the belief that gay men and lesbians suffered from a character weakness that made them vulnerable to blackmail and subversion, thus rendering them susceptible to the machinations of Soviet agents.[6] The RCMP collected the names of thousands of possibly gay men and lesbians, and the government funded and sponsored research into ways of "scientifically" detecting homosexuals – research that came to be known as the "fruit machine" (see Chapter 5).

In 1960, the RCMP reported that, over the previous two years, it had conducted investigations in "high security" areas such as the Department of Agriculture, the Central Mortgage and Housing Corporation, the Department of National Health and Welfare, the Post Office Department, the Public Works Department, the Unemployment Insurance Commission, and the Department of Transport.[7] The National Film Board and the Canadian Broadcasting Corporation were also caught in this investigative net. Indeed, the security campaign extended throughout the public service and beyond. However, investigations did tend to focus, especially in the early years, on the Department of External Affairs (DEA) and the Royal Canadian Navy (RCN). For example, it was reported in 1960 that, in the RCN, 123 members had been confirmed as homosexuals and another 76 were suspected of being homosexual, for a total of 199. Of these, 90 had been released (or discharged). The same 1960 report stated that 59 suspected homosexuals had been identified in the DEA and that, of these, 9 had resigned, 1 had been released, 1 was retired, and 2 were deceased. These numbers were out of a total of 363 people in government work who were classified as "confirmed," "alleged," or "suspected" homosexuals and out of a total of 117 who had died, resigned, retired, transferred, or been released.[8] These security practices and the reactions to them had a major impact within the DEA.

A memo written in 1961 stated: "the RCM Police have identified some 460 public servants as confirmed, alleged, or suspected homosexuals. Of these about one-third have since left the service through resignation or dismissal."[9] In 1961-62, the RCMP reported having identified 850 suspected and confirmed homosexuals in the civil service.[10] Unfortunately, the documents we have been able to acquire do not provide a clear "homosexual count" for later years.

David's account of surveillance and resistance not only gives us a sense of the extent of the national security regime but also demonstrates that the gay networks in which he participated were aware of the security campaigns. These men were not simply victims of the national security war on queers; rather, within the major social constraints of the day, they creatively exerted their own agency and resistance.[11] We explore the social and historical conditions that made such resistance possible. David's story also provides us with the social standpoints taken up in this investigation – namely, those of the men who had sex with men and the women who had sex with women who were directly affected by these security campaigns. This places us outside the confines of national security discourse and ideology.

Viewing national security as an ideological practice is crucial. We use the term "ideological" not to refer to "biased" or "non-objective" knowledge but, rather, to refer to a social practice of knowledge production that comes to rule over people's lives. Ideology is separated from people's lived experiences and from the social practices through which the very concepts used to explain the world are themselves produced. It is thus separated from social relations.[12] It follows that the concept of "national security" is an ideological practice in that it is separated from the social practices through which it is produced and is part of the relations that rule and manage people's lives. Throughout this book, we try to resist ideological practices by grounding knowledge in people's lives, social relations, and practices.

REWRITING HISTORY AND CHALLENGING MASTER NARRATIVES

We disrupt the master narrative of heterosexual hegemonic mainstream Canadian history by placing the social experiences (including the resistance) of queers at the centre of our analysis. To begin, it is necessary to clarify our terms. "Heterosexual hegemonies" are the social practices and ideologies through which lesbian, gay, and queer sexualities are constructed as deviant, abnormal, and unnatural, and through which, simultaneously, a particular male-dominated form of heterosexuality is naturalized and normalized. "Hegemony," as used by Italian Marxist Antonio Gramsci, describes how coercion and the manufacturing of consent are joined in the social organization of ruling.[13] As a major form of sexual regulation, heterosexual hegemony brings together coercive means of enforcing heterosexuality with the manufacturing of consent to the idea that heterosexuality is the only natural sexuality.

Our use of the phrase "war on queers" parallels anti-poverty movements' use of the phrase "war on the poor." Without trivializing the experiences of warfare and colonialism, we wish to point to the serious and systemic character of the national security campaigns against lesbians and gay men and to the devastation these have wrought in thousands of lives. At the same time, notions of "war" – as in the "Cold War," the "war on drugs," and the "war on terror" – have often been colonized by right-wing usage.[14]

We use the word "queer" in order to reclaim a term of abuse and stigmatization. The idea is to ensure that it can no longer be used against us as a form of derision and to turn it back on our oppressors. We also use it to identify with newer forms of queer activism, although it should be noted that we do this in a way that differs from what is done in queer nationalism or queer theory.[15] The term "homosexual" has a clinical connotation, and "gay" and "lesbian" are often defined very narrowly. "Queer," on the other hand, entails a broader scope of practices than do "lesbian," "gay," or "homosexual," including non-normalized, non-heterosexual consensual sexual and gendered practices not easily captured by the latter terms (e.g., bisexual, transgender, two-spirited, and other sexual/gender practices).[16] In other words, "queer" allows us to point towards the diverse social character of sexual and gender practices and identifications that do not fall under the rigid categories of "homosexual," "lesbian," "gay," "bisexual," or "heterosexual" – or even "male" and "female." Many people who identify as heterosexual, for instance, engage in same-gender sex, and the term "queer" can encompass aspects of such experiences. This notion of queer practice also permits us to construct a place from which to challenge heterosexual hegemony and the taken-for-granted two-gender binary (or "opposite") way of doing gender.[17] Used in this broader sense, the word "queer" captures the experiences of people engaged in sexual and gender practices that defy heterosexual hegemony and the restrictions of the male-dominated two-gender system.[18]

Sexuality is a historical and social creation that builds on and transforms our physiological potential; it is not an innate biological essence rooted in our genes or hormones.[19] Many people engage in same-gender sex, but how this is made sense of and lived will vary dramatically in differing social, cultural, and historical contexts. Language becomes a problem when attempting to describe the identifications of people who engage in same-gender sex and sexual practices more generally. While in many ways we prefer the rather cumbersome "same-gender sex" or "same-gender eroticism," for practical reasons (albeit provisionally), we often use "homosexual," "lesbian," "gay," "bisexual," and "heterosexual." In doing so, we do not mean to suggest that any of these terms has an ahistorical biological essence.

In response to our 1998 research report, in some media interviews Gary was accused of producing "revisionist" history.[20] Some journalists posited that the Cold War context justified concerns over blackmail and security risks, and that for us to suggest otherwise was to rewrite history – to be revisionist. Gary submitted that many of the gay men and lesbians we interviewed who were purged from their jobs or interrogated by the RCMP reported that the only people who tried to blackmail them were the RCMP. It was, after all, the RCMP who tried to force them to give the names of other homosexuals. We reject revisionism as a way of framing struggles over history; however, we do intend this to be a work of transformative historical sociology that will change Canadian history. *The Canadian War on Queers* challenges current Canadian historiography: it is based on previously excluded and denied social experiences, making visible what was invisible and giving voice to what was silenced. It therefore points towards a more accurate social and historical account of what transpired in Canada during the second half of the twentieth century.

MAKING US THE PROBLEM: A TASTE OF THE NATIONAL SECURITY DISCOURSE

The national security discourse that constructed queers as a security problem permeated David's experiences with surveillance and his resistance to it. It was this discourse that mandated the RCMP practices of surveillance and interrogation. The term "discourse" refers to a social language that is tied to social power relations – relations that define how we can name and define problems and how we can speak about our lives. In this case, the language of national security is integral to the social power relations of Canadian state formation. National security is a social language, and, when actively mobilized, it carries with it immense social power. Our use of the term "discourse" is informed by the work of Michel Foucault, but it goes beyond his focus on statements to view language as produced and used by people to coordinate and organize social practices and relations.[21]

In the national security discourse, homosexuals were constructed as suffering from an unreliable and unstable character, which made us a threat to national security. The notion of reliability was central to this construction, as is illustrated by the following passage from a 1959 Security Panel memorandum. This memorandum was written by Don Wall, who was secretary of the Security Panel, the interdepartmental committee responsible for coordinating national security:

> Sexual abnormalities appear to be the favourite target of hostile intelligence agencies, and of these homosexuality is most often used ... The nature of homosexuality appears to adapt itself to this kind of exploitation. By exercising fairly simple precautions, homosexuals are usually able to keep their habits hidden from those who are not specifically seeking them out. Further, homosexuals often appear to believe that the accepted ethical code which governs normal human relationships does not apply to them ... From the small amount of information we have been able to obtain about homosexual behaviour generally, certain characteristics appear to stand out – instability, willing self-deceit, defiance towards society, a tendency to surround oneself with persons of similar propensities, regardless of other considerations – none of which inspire the confidence one would hope to have in persons required to fill positions of trust and responsibility.[22]

From the late 1950s, regulations influenced by the ideas outlined in documents such as this 1959 memorandum caused problems for hundreds of lesbians, gay men, and others who lost jobs or who were demoted to less "sensitive" positions in the federal public service. In these security texts, homosexuals are depicted as a security problem because of our "weaknesses," "unreliability," and "immoral" or "unethical" traits, which supposedly make us vulnerable to blackmail and compromise. In this discourse, the essential character of the homosexual is presented as a security problem. In part, Wall drew on earlier constructions of homosexuals as "psychopathic personalities" who were unable to control their sexual impulses and who suffered from an absence of moral regulation.[23] These earlier categorizations, coupled with Cold War security ideology, informed national security concerns regarding character weaknesses.

Wall was also influenced by and drew from US anti-queer national security discourse, particularly that of former CIA director Admiral Roscoe Hillenkoetter, at the height of the early 1950s US anti-sex-pervert campaigns. Hillenkoetter portrayed the homosexual character as dangerous and perverted and, thus, as a security risk:

> The consistent symptoms of weakness and instability which accompany homosexuality almost always represent danger points of susceptibility from the standpoint of security ... The moral pervert is a security risk of so serious a nature that he must be weeded out of government employment ... In addition homosexuality frequently is accompanied by other exploitable weaknesses such as psychopathic tendencies which affect the soundness of their judgement, physical cowardice, susceptibility to pressure, and general instability ... Lastly, perverts in key positions lead to the concept of a government within a government ... One pervert brings other perverts.[24]

Much of the language employed by Hillenkoetter informs the discourse Wall developed for the Security Panel and was given its own "Canadian" character when used in texts produced by that panel, which was the epicentre of national security policy in the Cold War era.

National security discourse regarding homosexuals was also connected to the right-wing anti-queer discourse of the 1950s and earlier. Referring to a 1935 RCMP surveillance report on the Communist Party's activities on university campuses, Hewitt writes, "There is the subtext of the report which equated communism with immorality, specifically illicit sexuality, so that reading communistic literature took on the status of masturbation or homosexuality, acts also deemed reprehensible in Depression-era Canada. Such discourse had American echoes: J. Edgar Hoover described the route to communism as 'perverted' and compared communists to drug addicts, while the rhetoric of the state linked the conversion to communism with sexual weakness or degeneracy."[25]

Initially, queers and communists were seen as fellow travellers in right-wing Cold War discourse because we transgressed sexual, class, social, and political boundaries. This idea built on earlier moral and political constructions of homosexuality and heterosexuality. Heterosexuality was associated with the natural, normal, clean, healthy, and pure; homosexuality was associated with the dangerous, impure, unnatural, sick, and abnormal. R.G. Waldeck's "Homosexual International," published in 1960, is an example of this conservative discourse:

Homosexual officials are a peril for us in the present struggle between West and East: members of one conspiracy are prone to join another ... Many homosexuals from being enemies of society in general become enemies of capitalism in particular. Without being necessarily Marxist they serve the ends of the Communist International in the name of their rebellion against the prejudices, standards, ideals of the "bourgeois" world. Another reason for the homosexual-Communist alliance is the instability and passion for intrigue for intrigue's sake, which is inherent in the homosexual personality. A third reason is the social promiscuity within the homosexual minority and the fusion of its effects between upper-class and proletarian corruption.[26]

In Waldeck's understanding, the problematic "homosexual personality" is associated with Marxism and its challenge to capitalism. By challenging erotic and social boundaries, gays and lesbians are also seen as transgressing class and political boundaries. Crossing class boundaries in the context of erotic liaisons between elite and working-class men is perceived as a particular social danger.

There are important connections between this conservative discourse and that of the Security Panel. While Wall's discourse shifts from this overtly right-wing form and moves away from earlier conceptualizations of homosexuality as psychopathology, it still suggests that homosexuals suffer from instability, tend to defy society, and have a specific homosexual personality. The links between these different texts and discourses demonstrate a dialogical relation within national security texts, whereby later documents are infused with the language of earlier documents. In other words, they are informed by the discourses of other texts even as they shift these discourses in a different direction. All language and discourse – including that of national security – exist in relation to other languages, discourses, and speakers.[27] In the case of the security purges of gay men and lesbians, the 1950s anti-queer right-wing discourse lives on within Canadian national security discourse, even though it has a somewhat different character. At the same time, the discourse as an ideological practice tends to portray itself as having a singular monological voice, thus denying the diversity of the social dialogues that surround and challenge it.

THE SECRETIVE SOCIAL ORGANIZATION OF NATIONAL SECURITY AND THE CAMPAIGNS AGAINST QUEERS

Canadian historians are recording the involvement of Canadian state agencies and national security campaigns in the internment, surveillance, and interrogation of ethnic and racial groups, trade unionists, socialists, communists, and their sympathizers.[28] The recording and understanding of the involvement of Canadian state agencies in attacks on queers, by contrast, is still in its nascent stages.[29] Historical work has revealed that, contrary to popular mythology, Canadians were not spared the traumatic experience that Americans endured under the McCarthy campaigns. Part of this mythology is centred on the fact that, generally, Canadian national security campaigns were much more secretive than were those south of the border. Canadians were not exposed to the same level of publicity and visibility that went along with the McCarthy hearings, the "sex pervert" investigations, and the State Department purges. Canadian state agencies were especially invested in keeping security issues cloaked from public view; however, this supposed veil of secrecy did not in any way reduce the impact these security campaigns had on people's lives.

Interestingly, it was an American who first scrutinized the secretive behaviour of the Canadian state. In a 1956 right-wing publication, Canada's security practices and policies were described as suppressing individual rights in favour of those of the state:

> Canada ... has a stringent program to protect Government secrets against subversives, cocktail party talkers, and people who associate with Communists ... Policies and standards are set by a committee of high officials representing several Canadian agencies [the previously mentioned Security Panel]. The Special Branch of the Royal Canadian Mounted Police ... has a representative on this policy-making body. The identity of individual members of this panel is not disclosed to the public. Only a few in Government know who the members are. The panel meets in secret. The Government refuses to tell who makes the major decisions about security or what those decisions are ... In Canada, the security system is a tough one. There is less concern than in the United States about the rights of individuals involved. To Canadian officials, safety of the state comes first.[30]

The phrase "safety of the state comes first" expresses a key feature of the social organization of national security in Canada. Maintaining a security system while preserving individual rights was considered to be a difficult task. In the context of the postwar era and the insecurity surrounding the implicit loyalty and reliability of citizens, the American and Canadian governments established surveillance and interrogation campaigns to respond to security concerns.

In the early 1960s, Prime Minister Diefenbaker made the following statement regarding the supposed conundrum security officials faced as they grappled with the problem of policing the "other" while preserving individual rights:

How are you going to maintain security while at the same time preserving and maintaining the fundamental rights of the individual? It is a difficult problem. It is so easy to criticize, but it is so much more difficult, having that responsibility, being desirous of maintaining those freedoms, to be able to carry out one's wishes. Loyalty is expected of all Canadians. It is imperative as a quality of public service. There are many cases in which the loyalty of the individual is not a question. But that individual may still not be reliable as a security risk ... because of defects of character which subject him to the danger of blackmail ... It is a fertile field for recruiting by the USSR, where public servants are known to be the companions of homosexuals. Those are the people that are generally chosen by the USSR, in recruiting spies who are otherwise loyal people within their countries.[31]

It was believed that homosexuals, who might otherwise have been considered loyal citizens, were unreliable. Therefore, homosexuals would continue to be viewed as security risks if they were put in compromising positions by Soviet agents interested in blackmailing public servants who had secrets to keep as well as access to Canadian, American, and British security information.

All Canadian national security campaigns were secretive, but those against homosexuals were especially so. This secrecy and its concomitant silence are what is reflected in most research on the national security campaigns, though there have been important breakthroughs. John Sawatsky's pioneering work on the internal workings of the RCMP Security Service provides a starting point for the project of uncovering the security campaigns against gay men and lesbians. Dean Beeby's later work, which involved gaining access to security documents on the anti-homosexual purges, has also been crucial.[32]

The silence surrounding the Canadian war on queers not only distorted history in official Canadian Cold War historiography but also shaped the experiences of gay men, lesbians, and others during these years. Many people who were investigated and purged knew very little about the extensive social organization behind the security campaigns. As has been said, security regime practices that ensnared suspected gay men and lesbians were mediated through the use of classified state texts that defined homosexuals as security risks suffering from a character weakness.[33] The social organization of these practices would have been invisible to most people because it was produced through the conceptual framework of the security regime and the official courses of action that it set in motion. One goal of this book is to make this framework visible and to reveal what would have been only partially perceptible to many people from the vantage point of their daily lives.

During these years, gay activists outside of Ottawa had little or no awareness of the Canadian security campaigns. Throughout the 1950s, Jim Egan, Canada's first gay activist, wrote articles against the American anti-homosexual security campaigns. While he was aware of the McCarthy campaigns, he had little knowledge of what was happening in Canada.[34] He remembered that "whatever investigations were being conducted in Canada did not get the publicity of the McCarthy hearings ... To be perfectly frank with you I was not aware that there was this intensive campaign going on in Canada ... In those days there was nothing in the newspaper about a purge" (January 5, 1998). For Jim Egan (and, in the 1960s, for Doug Sanders, an active member of the Association for Social Knowledge [ASK], Canada's first gay rights group), the US security campaigns were the main reference point. As Egan said: "I guess what I did was spend far more time reading American literature because it was easier to get your hands on. A lot of the articles that I wrote were obviously based upon information coming out of the United States" (January 5, 1998).

Although the magnitude of the state-sanctioned security purges against gay men and lesbians was largely unknown, some sense of its presence was felt, especially in Ottawa. Throughout the public service, the military, and in Ottawa gay networks, there were plenty of rumours regarding the security campaigns. A number of the people interviewed expressed an awareness both of the campaigns and of advice regarding coping strategies in the event that one was caught in the interrogation net. This "queer talk" and network formation was the social basis for non-cooperation with and resistance to these campaigns. With the expansion of gay movements and community formation in the 1970s and 1980s, these capacities for resistance developed further.

GROUNDING THE INVESTIGATION: STORIES OF THE DIRECTLY AFFECTED

The Canadian War on Queers begins not with the official discourse proclaiming gay men and lesbians as national security risks but, rather, with the stories of those who were purged, transferred, interrogated, and spied upon – and of those like David, who resisted these campaigns. This social standpoint informs our investigation of security regime practices and provides the entry point for our exploration of security regime relations. The stories of those people whose everyday lives were affected by security regime practices ground this investigation in *their* social experiences rather than in the ideology of the national security regime. We begin from and constantly return to the experiences of those most directly affected. We begin not in abstractions or in a discourse separated from social practice and relations but, rather, in the social worlds of people's experiences. And we ask how those experiences were socially organized.[35]

Our research reveals a disjuncture between national security discourse and gay/lesbian accounts of the security campaigns.[36] Our major question concerns how these campaigns could create such problems in the daily lives of gay men and lesbians – problems with a continuing legacy today. We want to make visible what these first-hand accounts reveal regarding the social organization of these campaigns.

Since the postmodern turn, "experience" has been seen as "contaminated" by discourse. Our intent is not to reify the experience embodied in these accounts as the "truth."[37] While social experiences are always shaped by social discourse, they are also extremely useful in that they can place us in the midst of the rupture between official accounts and social experiences. They provide a different starting point than do the security texts – one that allows us to see much more and that moves us beyond the confines of the security regime. The light they throw on historical events helps to reveal social organization and relations.[38] Based on the standpoints of oppressed and marginalized people, those whose lives were disrupted by official policies, these narratives enable us to see aspects of the social process that are concealed from the standpoints of those in positions of power (e.g., the RCMP, military police, members of the Security Panel [and later CSIS]).[39]

These narratives constitute a form of resistance that makes visible the social knowledge that national security texts actively suppressed. We collect these stories and let them come to life as you, the reader, enter their worlds and interact with them. Given our commitment to preserving the voices of those most affected by the national security campaigns, we offer quotes that are longer than those typically found in texts, whether academic or non-academic. We do this because we do not want to decontextualize them.[40] These different voices are crucial to this investigation, and, in important ways, *The Canadian War on Queers* is a co-production between the interviewees and the interviewers (although the analysis is, of course, entirely our responsibility). These accounts provide us with access to "the social" from numerous viewpoints, and this, in turn, enables us to critically explore the social organization of Canada's security regime.[41]

The official discourse of the national security regime attempts to create a unitary monologue. First-hand accounts often disrupt this monologue and open up spaces for critical inquiry, allowing us to grasp aspects of the regime's social organization that are hidden within official discourse. These narratives display the multiple and diverse voices that are suppressed within the monologic voice-over of official discourse.[42] These voices include those of our research participants, activists, politicians, the police, security regime texts, and ourselves. Our analysis of the national security regime grows out of the dialogical character of the social world. There is not just one official story: rather, there are multiple stories, and they allow us to expose the partial and ideological character of the official story. It is our hope that the reader will enter into and use these stories to develop her or his own analysis of the national security war on queers. As an active text, this book encourages the reader to consider whether or not the analyses we have developed based on these experiences and stories are accurate.[43] We do not want *The Canadian War on Queers* to become yet another monologue.

The narratives we present are based on discussions with gay men and lesbians who had some direct experience of the security regime during the 1950s and 1960s. We also draw on several first-hand accounts and a number of interviews conducted by others. In this chapter, the participants are David, Sue, Yvette, Harold, Herbert Sutcliffe, Albert, Robert, Hank, and Arlene. We briefly introduce their stories in order to contextualize the postwar period, and we return to their narratives in Chapters 4 and 6. For the 1970s, 1980s, and 1990s, we meet another group of participants, including people active in queer organizing.

The interweaving of these stories with our developing analysis of the social organization of the security regime is key to our method and theory. We integrate experience, analysis, and theory in order to display the relations between the social experiences of lesbians and gay men, which include the problems created in their everyday lives by the security regime, and the wider social relations of the national security state. We move from first-hand accounts to the wider social and political relations that shaped them. This exploration leads to a broader social and historical analysis of the national security campaigns than has thus far been offered.

When we started this research in 1993, we thought that the security campaigns in the public service and those in the military were distinct from each other – and they often are – but we quickly discovered that they were all part of a common campaign. The RCMP participated in military investigations, and national security concerns were used to justify purges in the military. The Department of National Defence (DND) was centrally involved in the Security Panel and in the development of the fruit machine. Until the late 1980s and early 1990s, the military, like the RCMP, was vociferous in its opposition to allowing lesbians and gays to become members. These first-hand accounts suggest both common and diverse queer experiences organized through national security regime practices. We begin with narratives from the military, then move on to those from the public service, and conclude with an account drawn from outside both the military and the public service.

Sue: "So I've lost my career"

The military provided a place where some women could survive outside heterosexual marriage and could seek career advancement and economic independence from husbands, individual men, and their families. The military also provided a place where women interested in sexual relations with other women could meet in a same-gender context; however, as an organization, the military had strict regulations prohibiting sexual and emotional relations between women. In particular, lesbian sexual relations were subjected to severe regulations.[44]

Sue was forced out of the militia in Halifax in the early 1960s for being a lesbian. She described the sequence of events leading to this dismissal:

> I was going to make it [the military] my ongoing career. And I had been out with this woman who had a child [and] who had a husband. He found out that she was a lesbian [and] had a current lesbian lover. And, may I say that the shit hit the fan. He found all these love letters and said, "What is going on here?" ... He says, "I want my daughter, we're going to court." He said, "Will you testify on my behalf?" I said, "No!" He said, "How would you like me to go to your colonel? How would you like me to go to your parents, your place of employment?" I said, "What is it that you would like me to say?" It's called blackmail, and when you are eighteen, you are scared to death. And I had no rights, couldn't go to a lawyer, couldn't talk to anyone else. And we did go to court over custody. Her lawyer was a military colonel in the Canadian Intelligence Corps ... I said to the judge in court, I said, "I don't want to talk about this." And he said, "Well, nothing will happen to you from this." And I said, "You're going to assure me that I won't lose my career, that nothing will happen?" He said, "No problem, you can speak." Well, I want you to know that his honour was a liar. 'Cause here's this military chap writing down my name, anybody else's in the courtroom, trying to figure out what was going on. Within a month and a half, there was this cute little colonel knocking on my door, saying, "Would you like to leave the military?" I said, "No, I really like it." And he said, "Well, I'm telling you, you'll be leaving." So he passes me this letter

and he said, "You got two choices, you can leave or you can be court martialled" ... He said, "Yeah, think of the publicity and embarrassment to your
family." I said, "Well, I think probably by next week I could have things tidied
up and be out of here. No problem, I will leave" ... So I've lost my career, and I
had just gotten a promotion to a lance corporal, the youngest ever. (February
23, 1996)

Sue's account reveals the link between civil legal proceedings (which brought
her lesbianism to the attention of military authorities) and the military's policy
to "dispose" of lesbians. What this meant to Sue was the loss of her career in the
military. The threat of blackmail was used against her, and it was orchestrated
through anti-lesbian policies and the social stigma attached to lesbianism.

Yvette: "So, sexual orientation ... made me a non-person in their eyes"

Yvette, a franco-Ontarian woman from Northern Ontario, was discharged from
the Royal Canadian Air Force (RCAF) in the late 1950s for being a lesbian. She
had joined the RCAF in North Bay with the specific intention of finding other
lesbians (although, at the time, she did not know this word). She developed a
sexual relationship with another woman on the base. This led to a rumour about
her being involved with a woman, which incurred a great deal of stress. She was
eventually taken to a psychiatrist at St. Mary's Veterans' Hospital in Montreal.
Even though she had been valedictorian, had a good service record, and had
been recommended for a commission, there was concern that, being a lesbian,
she would be subject to blackmail. As Yvette put it, "[My] sexual orientation ...
made me a non-person in their eyes." She was given a Five D Discharge (i.e., an
honourable discharge for medical reasons) and was deemed unsuitable for
further service.[45]

Harold: "I have undergone an experience which has destroyed the efforts of my life to date"

Harold's account, written in the early 1960s, tells of his experience of being
purged from the RCN in the late 1950s. He described the impact this had on
his life:

Until recently I was a trusted, respected citizen. I held a position of responsibility and had spent years working hard in what I believed – and still do –
was a worthwhile, if not highly remunerative, organization. Then one day, the
culmination of months of severe mental stress, I was dismissed ... I have

undergone an experience which has destroyed the efforts of my life to date ...
I have been deprived of two basic human needs – a reason for living and a
degree of self-confidence ... At an age when I had commenced to reap the
benefit of years of conscientious and highly commended effort I have been
removed from my position and world because ... my superiors discovered I am
a homosexual.[46]

Harold's words reveal the fault line between his lived experience and the security regime practices that made him a security problem, the "solution" to which was his forced resignation. Harold's experiences were shaped through both security regime practices, which defined homosexuals as threats to national security, and the policies of the Canadian military, which called for the "disposal" of all "sex deviates" – policies that predated and developed in tandem with the security campaigns.[47]

Herbert Sutcliffe: "I'm in a daze. I don't know what's going on"

Herbert Sutcliffe, who died in 2003, was also forced out of his position in the military.[48] He described being in a daze when he was confronted by his superior officer with the following accusation:

The fatal day was the 6th of June 1962. That morning I went into my office, and when I left the apartment the movers were moving my furniture into their van to take it to Washington because I had been posted to the Pentagon, which was one of the choicest postings that the military had. I had hardly reached my desk when the phone rang and I picked it up ... A female voice said, "The director [of military intelligence] would like to see you right away." So I walked down to his office ... and [he] said, "You are not going to Washington, there will be no luncheon for you. The RCMP has advised us that you are a homosexual and you'll be out of the military in three days. Return to your apartment, wait for me to contact you." Period. I'm in a daze. I don't know what's going on. I come out of his office, I go down to the street and I take a bus and I come back to my apartment, and the people are just putting the last of the furniture in the van. And I said, "I can't explain anything, just take everything out of the van and put it back into the apartment. And I'll contact you later." And then I went and hid myself somewhere until I heard the van go. Then I came back out. I went to the bedroom. I had a [type of gun]. So I got the [gun] out and I put the bullets in it. I came back and I looked out the living-room window. I put the [gun] on the TV and I went into the kitchen and poured myself a scotch and soda, and I had a couple of drinks. Then I tried the [gun] against the side of my head, and I'm standing there, and then I say, "Fuck them, they're not going to kill me, the bastards!" So I go and put the [gun] away. (March 1, 1996)

Due to the secret nature of the social organization of the security investigation, Sutcliffe was completely unprepared to face the accusation of homosexuality. He was about to be appointed as an integrated Canadian officer to G-2 Intelligence at the Pentagon. Although he was cleared for counter-intelligence, it is likely that a new security check had been conducted because the new posting required a higher level of clearance (questions regarding military advancement and security checks for high levels of clearance are explored in Chapters 3 and 4). Herbert Sutcliffe's story clearly reveals the connection between the RCMP and military intelligence.

Robert: Tom Was Asked "Very Politely" to Leave the DEA

Robert, a gay man working in the DEA during the late 1960s and early 1970s, described what happened to his gay friend Tom, who had been posted with him to New York City: "It was shortly after I was with the NATO-NORAD division [in Ottawa] that Tom was let go. Actually, he was asked 'very politely.' They knew that he was gay and that [this] was not, for security reasons, conducive to future work. And he was given the 'option' of leaving as opposed to being ... just drummed out. And Tom did leave, and actually, he totally left the country" (October 10, 1996).

According to Robert, "[Tom received an ultimatum] to either leave on his own or else this would all come out ... They would basically tell all his family and it could be published. He was being dismissed because of security reasons because of the fact that he was gay." Officials used outing, or threats of outing, as a main tactic in their attempts to force people to resign from their positions.[49] As Robert remembered, "[Tom] had been called in and asked a great number of questions. He said that it was not pleasant. It was an experience he did not want to remember ... They knew of his sexuality, they knew what he had been doing, they knew where he had been. They knew of people he had been with. And when they were talking to him they had names and addresses and photographs and it was just – 'we know.' And so like – 'You're gone.' You're gone from the Foreign Service and the government" (October 10, 1996). The "option" of resigning quietly was a common form of dismissal. This account of Tom's experience also indicates the detailed surveillance work that would have been required to gather names, addresses, and photographs.

Albert: "I was confronted by my director"

Albert's long career in the civil service came to an abrupt end in the late 1960s, when, thanks to media coverage of a court case in which he was involved, his superior discovered he was a homosexual:

> When I returned to the office I was confronted by my director. He indicated to me that I should no longer be associated with the type of work [that] dealt with personnel matters because of the trial, since it would appear I might be a homosexual and should not be dealing with people that had personnel [sic] problems, such as alcoholism or drug-related difficulties or even collective bargaining ... As a result I was transferred from that work to another area. So this did affect my employment since this was an area I felt I was reasonably skilled in, and it was going to be denied me because of a judgment they had read in the press and which was not even proven. There was no day in court, there was nothing but a statement of fact. I accepted this since there was no point in challenging it since it would only lead to more disaster on my part. (October 19, 1993)

Albert's story highlights how court cases initiated outside the security regime itself could affect security investigations. Cases like this provided valuable information for the RCMP, who did rely on police and court information regarding criminal charges and proceedings involving homosexuality. This story indicates that, within the public service, homosexuality was seen as incompatible with personnel responsibilities and even with collective bargaining. Albert's sense of futility with regard to resistance is indicative of the social power relations that constrained public servants.

Hank: A Very Intimate Surveillance

Hank started work in the public service during the late 1960s. Some time in the late 1960s or early 1970s, a gay RCMP officer was "forced" to investigate two other gay men, including Hank. The officer was, in effect, blackmailed by his superiors, who had discovered his homosexuality. It was only on the condition that the officer investigate Hank and another public servant that he would be eligible to be released from the RCMP with a workable service record. This officer sought Hank out at various parties in Ottawa and eventually developed a personal and sexual relationship with him. One day, when they were in bed together, the officer revealed that Hank was under surveillance. Hank was outraged. The officer also mentioned that he was dating another gay man for similar reasons (February 20, 1995). Even though it is unlikely that the RCMP officially authorized these sexual liaisons, it did force this officer to conduct surveillance work on these two men. Eventually, the officer left the RCMP with a workable service record. Hank's story suggests the extent of some of the RCMP investigations as well as the pressure exerted on individual officers.

Arlene: "I am a national security risk!"

Refused a pardon in the 1970s due to a prior conviction a decade earlier, Arlene was informed that she was a national security risk:

> I went for a pardon, for my criminal record. I can't get a pardon: they classed me as a national security risk. I am a national security risk! And I did a real sneaky thing. Freedom of information came up, and I got my file, which wasn't worth the paper it was written on because three-quarters of it was deleted. And under the deletion it said: "National security list." So I phoned Mark Bonokoski at the *Sun*. And he said, "Okay, I've got a friend, a connection at the RCMP." And I said to my lawyer at the time: "Don't tell Bonokoski I'm gay." And within an hour after I talked to Bonokoski, he got back to me and he said: "Why didn't you tell me you were a lesbian?" I said, "Since when does being a lesbian have to do with B&E [breaking and entering]?" I said, "I didn't think that was a predisposition of gay women. I thought it was more of a criminal disposition." He says, "Well, I'm telling you, the first thing the RCMP handed me was, you're gay." (Lesbians Making History, 1987)

Here we see the interrelation between local police work and RCMP surveillance, the implication being that the Toronto police, who knew Arlene was a lesbian, had forwarded this information to the RCMP.

In all these narratives there is an experiential rupture between the accounts of lesbians and gay men who were directly affected by the national security regime and the official discourse of the Canadian war on queers. It is with this rupture that our inquiry begins. These accounts enable us to undertake a critical analysis of the official national security regime discourse as well as the discussions we had with people who were active in that regime (specifically, in the RCMP and the DEA). The critical interrogation of those who were involved in the regime is informed by our reading and analysis of the first-hand accounts of the gay men and lesbians who were affected by its campaigns.[50]

A PASSION FOR REMEMBERING: THE ANTI-QUEER CHARACTER OF CANADIAN STATE FORMATION

In *The Canadian War on Queers,* we remember the deep roots of heterosexism in Canadian state and social formation and argue that, given this anti-queer history, which continues to shape our present, queers require a much more profound social transformation than that constituted by simply winning the right to marry. We confront current claims that same-sex marriage is the solution to past oppression (and, to some extent, present oppression). We bring together the past and the present of queer oppression and the national security campaigns in the hope of producing creative and productive tensions. As David McNally points out, drawing on the work of cultural critic and theorist Walter Benjamin, "rather than something laid down once and for all the past is a site of struggle *in the present.*"[51]

In part, capitalism and oppression rule through what we call "the social organization of forgetting," which is based on the annihilation of our social and historical memories. This process also leads to the acceptance of social mythologies that assert that the Cold War was "good" and that our notions of the "nation" and "national security" are unproblematic. This social organization of forgetting is crucial to the way in which social power works in our society. We no longer remember the past struggles that won us the social gains, social programs, and human rights that we now often take for granted.[52] This is also how strategies of respectability and responsibility gain hegemony in queer communities, and these strategies are related to class. We have been forced to forget where we have come from; our histories have never been recorded and passed down; and we are denied the social and historical literacy that allows us to remember and relive our past and, therefore, to grasp our present. By telling these stories of resistance – stories that the national security regime did not and does not want told – this book is an act of rebellion.

We try not to forget the development of human and social capacities for agency, creativity, and resistance.[53] If we simply rely on official stories and national security campaign texts, which attempt to subdue other voices, this development can be overlooked. Relying on official texts, even critical readings of them, can trap us in the discursive processes of reification, whereby social practices and relations between people are transformed into relations between things, variables, categories, or concepts. Reifying approaches to social history prevent us from remembering past struggles and compromises. As Theodor Adorno and others have stressed, "all reification is a form of forgetting" – that is, a forgetting of the human social practices involved in creating our past, present, and possible futures.[54] One limitation of Foucauldian and post-structuralist-inspired analysis within queer theory is that it often remains trapped within the confines of official discourse, even though it is based on a critical reading of it. This is why we move beyond reinterpreting and rereading texts and, instead, attempt to rediscover social organization, social relations, and social practice.

QUEERING THE COLD WAR

One of the most insightful parts of queer theory involves the notion of "queer-ing" aspects of social life from the social standpoints of queers. The marginal-ized experiences of queers become central in this process of queering social discourses and relations. An aspect of queering pursued throughout this book is related to the Cold War and national security. We are not simply adding the campaign against queers to the established historiography of Cold War Canada; rather, we are queering and transforming our very analysis of the Cold War. A shortcoming of official, and even of more critical, narratives regarding the Cold War is that they emphasize only the conflict between the American and the Soviet empires.[55] We use the term "Cold War" in two different senses. Although, from the 1940s to the 1980s, the Cold War era was characterized by proxy battles between "West" and "East," it was also, and more broadly, an era that witnessed Western campaigns against political, social, and sexual others.[56] The move beyond a narrow reading of the Cold War was signalled in *Whose National Security,* which indicated the need to rethink the basis of national secur-ity and expand the analysis of the Cold War to include relations of ethnicity, immigration, race, gender, sexuality, and class.[57] The Cold War was not only about defending Western capitalism and the expanding US empire against the bureaucratic class societies that emerged in the USSR and elsewhere.[58] Primar-ily, it was about pushing back and weakening the struggles of working-class and oppressed peoples.

The national security campaigns of the Cold War period, including the war on queers, came out of a particular configuration of social and political forces. The United States, in a leadership role with other Western powers, responded to the growth of the Soviet bloc and Third World national and social liberation movements by attempting to contain the Soviet Union, China, and Cuba through wars (e.g., in Korea, Vietnam, Nicaragua, and El Salvador) and through destabilizing and overthrowing governments seen as opposed to capitalist, Western, and US interests (e.g., Guatemala, Iran, Indonesia, Chile, and Grenada). Key to these cold and hot wars was the defence of capitalism, whiteness, the patriarchal family, "proper" forms of masculinity/femininity, and heterosexuality. These were wars for normality and against political, gender, and sexual deviance. The effects of these wars resonated into the 1990s with the collapse of the Soviet empire and helped to shape the current national security campaigns and the war on terror.

In the early years of the Cold War, the United States positioned itself as the military, political, and economic hegemonic power. For example, the Marshall Plan (1947) was a strategic reconstruction initiative used by the United States to secure its economic and ideological influence in western Europe. The Marshall Plan was also a vital tool to repress the actual and potential uprisings of the working class and poor.[59] New socio-economic approaches, such as Keynesianism, were developed in response to workers and social struggles. These approaches spread to western European countries and Canada, where limited social funding provisions and the "social wage" were used to attenuate the contradictions of capitalism and stifle rioting in the streets by ensuring that the poor could continue to purchase some commodities.[60]

The Cold War was centrally a war *against* Third World liberation movements and *for* neocolonialism. This war for imperialism and empire-building had a racial character and was part of the hegemonic production of a white middle-class way of life on a global scale.[61] This Cold War against the Third World and for white hegemony continues – from the US blockade of Cuba, to Western-imposed "structural adjustment programs," to the global food crisis, to the war on terror, to the wars and occupations in Afghanistan and Iraq, to the more recent threats being made against Venezuela and Iran.[62]

Cold War strategies also focused on gender and sexual "normality" with regard to the remaking of heterosexist and patriarchal relations after the social disruptions of the Second World War, especially in the West but also around the globe. These built on earlier practices of gender and sexual regulation. During the war years in the West, sex and gender relations were transformed as women entered the wage labour force in unprecedented numbers, daycare centres were established, and more queers came out in these altered sex/gender conditions.[63] After the Second World War, others were forced "out" and into emerging queer ghettoes in response to the reconstruction of patriarchal and heterosexist relations that opposed these potential and actual queer and feminist threats.[64] A central aspect of the Cold War was, therefore, gender and sexual regulation, and the war on queers was an integral feature of this. The scrutiny of queers was not simply a mistake; nor was it about individual homophobia. Homophobia, used to refer to the "dread of being in close quarters with homosexuals," focuses on an individual phobia and thus obscures how heterosexist practices are shaped through broader social relations.[65] Anti-queer aspects of the Cold War are central to its deeply rooted and socially mediated character. Consequently, in this period, queers were constructed as a threat not only to heterosexual hegemony but also to national security. By the late 1960s and the 1970s, these continuing anti-queer mobilizations were focused on attempts to contain the re-emergence of gender and sexual political struggles.

A key objective of Cold War mobilizations was the creation of the "normal," as Mary Louise Adams and others have persuasively argued.[66] Moral regulation was always an essential feature of these mobilizations as certain forms of social practice were defined as moral and normal, whereas others were constructed as immoral and deviant.[67] This making of the normal was posited against "others," "dangers," and "risks." A central and continuing aspect of the Cold War was the construction of sexual normality and sexual deviance. Linked to this were the mobilizations against queers and those for heterosexual normality.[68] In effect, we are thrown outside the fabric of the "nation." But this is also a relational social process, with the Cold War being fought *for* heterosexual hegemony – producing heterosexuality as being in the national interest, as loyal, and as safe. Heterosexuality becomes the national sexuality.

The Cold War, in its various phases, was directed against differing forms of political, social, sexual, and cultural subversion. The adaptability of the concept of "subversion" was and is key to the Cold War and the national security discourse. As Grace and Leys argue regarding state definitions of subversion,

> Many writers on subversion have complained that the term refers to a "grey area" and is difficult to define. Our view is that it has always referred to a fairly clear reality: legal activities and ideas directed against the existing social, economic and political [and we add sexual, gender, and racial] order ... Any radical activity or idea with the potential to enlist significant popular support may be labeled "subversive" ... [Subversion] is invoked ... to *create* a "grey area" of activities that *are* lawful, but will be denied protection from state surveillance or harassment by being *declared* illegitimate, on the grounds that they *potentially* have unlawful consequences. In capitalist societies the targets of this delegitimation have been overwhelmingly on the left.[69]

Through the application of the concept of subversion in national security discourse, some groups are excluded from the nation and become targets of surveillance.

The term "subversion" is linked to terms like "national security risk" and even "terrorist." It is an administrative collecting category into which, at various historical moments, assorted social and political practices can be placed and thus be read out of the normal and national social fabric.[70] These conceptualizations can be expanded or contracted depending on social and political contexts. Some groups are denied their rights and become objects of surveillance in a "cutting out operation" that separates them from the nation.[71] Once categorized as subversive or as a national security risk, these groups can then be denied their human and citizenship rights. For example, communists, socialists, peace activists, trade unionists, Red Power and Black Power activists, Quebec sovereigntists, immigrants, feminists, high school students, and queers have all, at one time or another, been designated subversive in Canadian state formation.[72] More recently, the state designation "terrorist" has been applied not only to al Qaeda and violent Islamic fundamentalists in general but also to members of left Palestinian resistance groups such as the Popular Front for the Liberation of Palestine and to global justice and anti-poverty activists who engage in direct action politics.[73]

Cold War mobilizations against queers have had major and lasting consequences for the left. They have affected not only those who supported the USSR (where homosexuality was often seen as "bourgeois decadence" or as linked to fascism) but also those who rejected Stalinism.[74] For instance, in the context of the social mobilization of heterosexism and the US Cold War on queers, the Trotskyist Socialist Workers Party (SWP) viewed lesbians and gays as security risks and prohibited them from party membership.[75] Accepting blackmail as a risk but reversing the focus so that the US government became its source led the SWP leadership to view gay and lesbian members as a risk to the party, as people who could supposedly be blackmailed to reveal party secrets to US security agents. Cold War mobilizations against queers helped produce the heterosexism on the left that the gay and lesbian liberation movements confronted in the late 1960s and the 1970s (see Chapter 8).

MAPPING OUT THE BOOK: WHAT COMES NEXT?

In Chapter 2, we focus on theory and method, providing a historical, sociological, and critical analysis of the ideology and practice of national security.

In Chapter 3, we locate the national security campaigns against queers within their broader social, political, and historical contexts in order to clarify their socially mediated character. In Chapter 4, we return to a detailed analysis of the first-hand accounts of those most directly affected by these campaigns in the 1950s and 1960s. Here we develop an analysis of the social relations of surveillance and interrogation employed in the national security campaigns. In Chapter 5, we investigate the attempt to construct the fruit machine, which involved the development of a battery of psychological tests whose purpose was to scientifically identify homosexuals. In Chapter 6, we examine the possibilities for non-cooperation with and resistance to the security campaigns as developed through the expansion of gay and lesbian networks, community formation, communication, and solidarity. We also explore how the RCMP responded to this non-cooperation through the local policing of gay men and lesbians. In Chapter 7, we unearth the continuing security campaigns of the 1970s. In Chapter 8, we look at the extension of RCMP spying operations to lesbian and gay liberation and rights organizations in the 1970s, including the RCMP's construction of the "gay activist" and the "radical lesbian." Chapter 9 focuses on the relation between sexual policing and national security, with the sex scandal in Ottawa and the Olympic clean-up campaign leading up to the bath raids of the early 1980s. Chapter 10 highlights the continuing national security campaigns in the 1980s in the military, the RCMP, and in the newly created Canadian Security Intelligence Service (CSIS), whereas Chapter 11 covers the use of the equality rights section in the new Charter of Rights and Freedoms and the ending of the most overt forms of the national security campaigns in the public service, the RCMP, and the military. In Chapter 12, we move into our historical present, where some queers are now perceived as being within (as opposed to without) the nation and national security. We draw together insights from this investigation and also point to the new targets of the national security regime in the context of the war on terror. We conclude with a call for continuing queer opposition to the ideologies and practices of national security.

2

Queer History and Sociology from Below
Resisting National Security

This chapter explores the theory and method behind our critical inquiry into the ideology and practice of national security. We do not use the term "theory" in the abstract but, rather, as related to research that clarifies the social practices in which people engage. While distinctions can certainly be made between method and theory, we foreground their interrelationship. Our analysis is committed to active agency and anti-reification (i.e., it is opposed to the transformation of relations between people into relations between things). The social world is produced, and can be known, only through the social practices of people who exist within socio-historical constraints. In adopting this standpoint, we avoid developing an "objective" top-down analysis and, instead, develop a reflexive, dialogical, bottom-up analysis.[1]

INSPIRATIONS

There are a number of theories/methods that inspire this investigation into national security as sexual regulation. The first is a historical sociology from below, which is influenced by the social historical work of E.P. Thompson.[2] Unfortunately, Thompson's work does not adequately address relations of gender, race, or sexuality or how they are mediated through class relations. However, his analysis has been a great inspiration to working-class, women's, black, and lesbian and gay historical work. Our approach rewrites history from below, specifically, from the view of the exploited and oppressed, by releasing knowledge based on their social experiences of exploitation and oppression – knowledge that is suppressed within ruling histories.

Thompson focuses on the social and historical character of experience. Class, for Thompson, is a social relation involving class struggle.[3] There is an important connection between history from below and social transformation from below, and this focuses on how a new society can be built only from the bottom up and must be based on forms of working-class and oppressed people's democratic self-organization.[4] This use and reading of Marx moves far beyond the confines of political economy, or what is often referred to as "orthodox" Marxism, which generally emphasizes the power of capital and portrays workers and the oppressed as passive victims of exploitation and oppression. Instead, drawing on the insights of autonomist Marxism, we focus on the activity and agency of working-class and oppressed people as they resist and force changes within capitalism, seeking to build their own autonomous power.[5]

We combine Thompson's history-from-below approach and the insights of autonomist Marxism with the sociological work of Marxist-feminist Dorothy Smith regarding developing sociologies for women and the oppressed.[6] This approach produces social knowledge for the oppressed and not for those ruling them. Smith's sociological contribution also includes developing a critical analysis of ideological practices and text-mediated social organization as well as an alternative way of doing sociology, which she refers to as "institutional ethnography."[7] This work has been extended into developing sociologies for gay men and lesbians.[8]

We start our inquiry from the social standpoints of those most immediately affected by national security campaigns. Using Smith's critical analysis of text-mediated social organization, we read the national security texts as actively used to organize campaigns against gay men and lesbians. These texts and their conceptual framings of queers as national security risks suffering from a character weakness were employed to mandate the purging of queers and spying upon gay men and lesbians.

In particular, we draw upon Smith's institutional ethnography approach, which we use in a more historical context.[9] Ethnography, as applied in anthropology and sociology, is the study of how cultures work, of how social organization operates; it is based on developing rich descriptions of cultural and social organization.[10] Institutional ethnography turns the illuminating capacities of ethnography, normally used to study "other" cultures, on the ruling institutional relations in our own culture. The focus is on how these institutional relations work to create problems in people's everyday lives. A central feature of institutional ethnography involves mapping out social relations from the standpoints of those experiencing problems within these relations. We use "mapping" here not in the colonial/imperialist sense of mapping out the world for colonization, control, and division from above but, rather, in the sense of mapping out social relations from below.[11] This allows us to use the insights of ethnographic analysis to critically interrogate the relations of national security from the standpoints of queers.

Foucault and Queer Theory

Michel Foucault's work, in particular that on disciplinary power and power/knowledge relations, is also key to this investigation.[12] We explore the social organization of the security regime as a concrete form of power/knowledge relations based on social surveillance, normalization, and disciplinary power. Foucault's focus on power/knowledge relations, on social surveillance and the practices of normalization (the power of social norms to discipline and regulate people's lives), as central parts of new forms of disciplinary authority in Western societies also figures prominently in our analysis.[13]

Disciplinary power is based not on repression, the law, or the state but, rather, on the self-disciplining of our own actions through surveillance and normalization. It operates through power/knowledge relations such as those constructed between the psychiatrist and the person diagnosed as mentally ill or between the doctor and the patient.[14] In Foucault's work, discourse is central, especially ruling forms of discourse associated with power/knowledge relations, such as national security discourse.

There are clear connections between the operations of the national security state and disciplinary power. Foucault's work helps us focus on the technologies of surveillance. Key aspects of disciplinary power involve strategies of surveillance and normalization, both of which are relevant to analyzing the social organization of the national security campaigns. Foucault enables us to examine the forms through which power operates in surveillance and interrogation.[15] In the security campaigns, the technology of surveillance includes photo albums, photographs, interrogations, tape recordings, filing systems, following people, and watching people and places.[16]

Foucault was also a major influence on the development of queer theory in the late 1980s and the 1990s. *The Canadian War on Queers* is both in dialogue with and a critique of queer theory, which is a discourse-based theoretical approach that questions the polarity, or binary opposition, between homo and hetero sexualities.[17] As Eve Kosofsky Sedgwick, a key American architect of queer theory, writes, "an understanding of virtually any aspect of Western culture must be, not merely incomplete, but damaged in its central substance to the degree that it does not incorporate a critical analysis of modern homo/hetero-sexual definitions."[18] This position is extremely refreshing as it places on the agenda the contestation of heterosexual hegemony. However, its challenge is limited to the realm of "culture." The main aim of queer theory is to contest heterosexual hegemony on literary, discursive, and cultural terrains. The social world, however, cannot simply be read as cultural or as based on literary texts.

Queer theory can lead theorists to reduce the complexities of social practices and relations to the discursive domain alone. Its theory of language, which is drawn from postmodernism and poststructuralism, has a non-social character that obscures the way in which language and discourse are embodied social practices that people accomplish daily.[19] Given the claim by postmodernists and poststructuralists that their theory focuses on language and discourse, this is especially troubling.[20] One of our objectives is to give the insights of queer theory a more social, historical, and materialist grounding, to make its insights relevant to critical historical and sociological investigations and activism.

For instance, Sedgwick's influential *Epistemology of the Closet* offers major insights into the centrality of the closet in the construction of Western culture.[21] However, her view of the closet as largely cultural and discursive in character is limited when it comes to attempting to analyze its social relations in the context of national security campaigns. We agree that the closet is cultural and discursive in nature, but it is also social, historical, and material. Further, it was put in place, at least in part, through the national security campaigns.

Historical Materialism for Queers, Queering Historical Materialism

We use the term "materialist" in a broad sense to include human sensuous practices. In doing so, we draw upon Marx's "Theses on Feuerbach," in which a new social and historical notion of materialism can be seen as a synthesis of vulgar materialism and the active side of consciousness developed by philosophical idealism.[22] We do not view Marx as an economic determinist or as a political economist; rather, we see Marx's work as a profound critique of how economics operates as a form of reification – obscuring the importance of social relations and practices.[23] Marx's aim was to constantly disclose the social relations between people, which are hidden behind the power and appearance of things.

Developing historical materialism for queers "queers" historical materialism.[24] This queering shatters the natural and ahistorical appearances of heterosexual hegemony and the present gender system, disclosing the oppressions lying beneath the naturalized appearance of these hegemonic practices, excavating the socially and historically constructed character of sexualities and genders, and putting heterosexuality and the current gender regime in question. This shift points us towards the possibilities of overturning heterosexual hegemony and transforming erotic and gender relations by linking them to the transformation of state, class, gender, and race relations. Marx's work and method continue to demonstrate the dynamics of capitalist social relations and how these shape the lives of queers. Our attention to class relations and struggles, including within queer communities, also informs our approach to Canada's national security regime.

The Mediated Social Character of National Security and Sexual Regulation

Finally, we draw on dialectical theories of mediation, which call for combining the mutually constructed character of social relations while also preserving the moments of autonomy of each specific form of social oppression and exclusion. Dialectics is a way of thinking and theorizing that focuses on process, movement, contradiction, negation, struggle, and transformation.[25] Within dialectical theory, each moment has its own autonomy, but all moments are also constructed in and through each other.[26] In relation to sexuality, this has important consequences. We are never solely queer (or heterosexual, for that matter) as various forms of oppression and exploitation intersect in our lives and histories. In other words, queerness is always mediated by or constructed through other social relations, including class, race, and gender.[27]

The Cold War against queers cannot be grasped by examining only its anti-queer dimensions, cutting these out from the broader relations of national security campaigns and practices of sexual and gender regulation. We also need to see how its class, anti-socialist, racist, anti-immigrant, anti-feminist, and other aspects shape its anti-queer character.[28] At the same time, to deny the autonomy of the anti-queer dimensions of the Cold War is to subordinate them to narrow notions of its class or anti-communist character. This, until recently, has been standard in Cold War history, and it ignores how campaigns against queers, or sexual regulation more generally, were central to organizing the Cold War and national security.[29]

SOURCES AND SOCIAL STANDPOINTS

Texts, Power, and Ideological Codes

The Canadian War on Queers is based on two major sources of data: interviews with those who were interrogated, spied upon, and purged; and critical analyses of the security regime texts.[30] For this work, "texts" generally refers to the documents used by the Security Panel, the RCMP, and the military to conduct campaigns against gay men and lesbians. We read these texts critically and understand them as actively mobilized to produce queers as a national security threat.[31] Using institutional ethnography, we read these texts for the social organization they reveal, but we start from the social standpoints found in the first-hand accounts of queers.

A critical reading of state security documents provides deep insights into the social organization of the major anti-gay/anti-lesbian campaigns that were part of the history of Canadian state formation, but it also raises a crucial problem regarding historical sources.[32] With the release of these documents, even with their many gaps, we now have a broader account of how security campaigns were discussed from "above."[33] Critically analyzing these texts requires us to resist their apparent stability. They cannot be read as a variant of the truth; rather, they must be read as having been written and used by people to carry out national security campaigns.

Our critique of national security denies the neutrality of these texts since they were crucial parts of the practices that generated problems for gay men and lesbians. The texts were used against queers and also attempted to respond to and subdue their strategies of resistance. Even though they were altered in response to social and legal struggles, they continued to be used to create problems for lesbians and gay men in the public service, the military, the RCMP, and CSIS.

Security Regime Documents as Active Texts

We read these security texts "against the grain" for the social organization that they reveal, while remembering that they do not act on their own. They were written, read, and used by people, and they were integral to the social organization of the national security campaigns. Rather than viewing these texts in a purely discursive fashion, we see them as parts of text-mediated social organization. We view them as one of the ways through which social relations are coordinated.[34]

We interpret these texts as part of an ideological code of national security. We find Smith's analysis of an ideological code that "coordinates multiple sites within the intersecting relations of public text-mediated discourses and large-scale organization" to be useful in critically examining the discourses and practices of national security.[35] Those entering into the ideological frameworks of these texts come to reproduce the ideological code of national security. Within the confines of the texts, this code is taken for granted, which necessitates a reading of them that extends beyond it.[36]

We assess texts critically, looking for contradictions, for residues of resistance, for the problems that the security regime was confronting and with which it had to contend. We trace the extra-discursive (or non-discursive) within ruling discourse as it is the extra-discursive that shapes the ground upon which the discursive is constructed. We view the extra-discursive as crucial since social subjects are not simply created by and through discourse. The possibility of conducting this kind of critical, engaged reading increases significantly with access to the accounts of those directly affected.

There are major limitations to historical and social analysis that is generated simply from readings of official discourse.[37] A critical approach in and of itself does not ensure against being trapped inside the relevancies of ruling forms of discourse, especially when one lacks any grounding in a social world beyond it. Relevancies of the security regime can get written into our analysis, trapping us within the ideological code of national security.[38] For instance, a "liberal" reading of these texts may suggest that the anti-homosexual campaigns were simply a mistake or a policy aberration. This supposition results in portraying the campaigns as based on the homophobic attitudes of individuals in power or of particular departments (such as the RCMP), as errors that were made due to a misguided acceptance of stereotypes and/or backward homophobic ideas.

"Homophobia" quite accurately describes the panic some heterosexuals feel when confronted by lesbians and gay men. Homophobia, however, has also been used to account for lesbian/gay oppression in general and, as such, tends to simply reverse existing psychological definitions of homosexuality as a mental illness, turning them back onto heterosexuals who have difficulty dealing with queers. As a concept, homophobia does not seriously dispute these psychological definitions; rather, it detaches the practice of lesbian and gay oppression from its social and historical contexts.[39] We also have difficulties with queer theory's use of the concept of "heteronormativity" in its attempt to theorize queer oppression.[40] Queer oppression and heterosexual hegemony reach beyond the construction of norms and normalization, and continue, always, to be defined by relations of violence and coercion. For this reason, "heterosexism" and "heterosexual hegemony" are more effective tools for analysis than are homophobia or heteronormativity when it comes to grasping the social relations and practices involved in queer oppression and institutionalized heterosexuality.[41]

An uncritical reading of official texts that accepts their boundaries and demarcations fails to see these practices as rooted in the heterosexist character of Canadian state formation and the interrelation of the security campaigns with other regulatory strategies regarding same-gender sex. National security is not recognized as part of a broader network of oppressive sexual and gender regulation. Even the most critical analysis of official texts, however, cannot always move us beyond official discourse. We noticed this in our own work, even as we read these texts with some grounding in the accounts and experiences of those who engaged in same-gender sex in the 1960s. We felt a tendency to become captured inside the relevancies of the security regime, to want to argue that we were not *really* security risks, that a mistake had been made, and to distinguish too much between the campaigns against lesbians and gay men and the interrelated security campaigns against the left, union activists, and others. By implication, this kind of reading suggests that, though lesbians and gay men were not real security risks, these other groups were. Reading the texts can seduce one into the ideological world of national security. It creates the possibility of taking the position of security regime officials who did not want a broader campaign and who wanted to separate the security campaign from the criminalization of homosexuality as well as from the employment prohibition against lesbians and gay men in any capacity. What needs to be explored is the actual social construction of lesbians and gay men as national security threats and the historical and social conditions required for this construction.

Daniel Robinson and David Kimmel's early article on the Canadian security campaigns against homosexuals is an example of what can occur when one depends on the official documents as the sole basis of analysis.[42] A major drawback of their article is its inability to read these texts for the social organization that they helped to coordinate. As a result, Robinson and Kimmel embrace what they describe as the "liberal" position in these documents. This position concerns a debate among security regime officials regarding how far the anti-homosexual campaigns should proceed. Robinson and Kimmel describe military/RCMP officials as "conservative" or "hard line" and many of the other members of the Security Panel as "liberals." In this categorization, liberals are not understood as they would have been in the early 1960s as the supporters of the Wolfenden Report position, which advocated the partial decriminalization of homosexual activity (see Chapter 6). For Robinson and Kimmel, liberals were the officials who focused on demoting or transferring homosexuals to less sensitive positions. They were not in favour of a wholesale purge of homosexuals; nor did they want the security campaigns to spread outside the public service and the military. Hardliners, on the other hand, wanted to extend the campaigns against homosexuals and prohibit them from being employed anywhere in government.

This liberal position falls well within the ideological code of national security. In this context, Robinson and Kimmel make a distinction between a narrow "security rationale" (to which they give legitimacy because it called for the curtailment of the campaigns against homosexuals, especially those outside the public service and in low security areas) and "outright homophobia."[43] We argue that, given the social and historical context, this is an untenable distinction. This security rationale was one of the means through which heterosexism was organized and the security campaigns against queers socially accomplished.

Because nobody within the security regime was putting national security itself in question, Robinson and Kimmel read the security regime texts as a version of the truth, accepting the basic parameters and the ideological code of national security. They do not read the texts from the standpoints of gay men and lesbians who were affected by them. This is most obvious in their failure to mention homosexual non-cooperation with the campaigns in the 1960s, even though there are signs of this in the RCMP texts they studied.

These historians approached the texts in this particular fashion because they believed that the problem lay primarily in *individuals* who had prejudiced ideas about homosexuals, and who were concentrated in the military and RCMP, rather than in the campaigns more generally. This argument ignores the broader social and institutionalized character of the security state. Because Robinson and Kimmel read Diefenbaker's late 1950s attempt to distinguish between "ideological" and "character weakness" threats as a liberal initiative, they argued that the anti-homosexual campaigns were its "unintended consequences" and did not see the danger of identifying homosexuals as a distinct risk to national security.

What is missed is an analysis of power/knowledge relations at work. The identification of homosexuals as a particular kind of threat, separated from ideological disloyalty, leads to a specific focus on homosexuals as a security threat. Robinson and Kimmel suggest that the same 1963 meeting "that approved the Orwellian-like Wake project (also known as the 'fruit machine') also saw a majority of members express support for a flexible and liberal approach to the homosexual question."[44] Meanwhile, the vetting continued and the RCMP was given a wide enough mandate to extend the campaigns. In spite of this so-called liberal stance, Security Panel members still saw homosexuals as a national security risk and argued for their demotion and transfer.

In our research, we develop an approach that does not simply construct those affected by the security campaigns as victims, thus denying their agency in responding to surveillance and interrogation. The evidence we have gathered, along with a critical reading of the RCMP reports, demonstrates individual and group forms of "prepolitical" resistance from some gay men and lesbians who were able to respond actively to the security regime.[45] A very different picture emerges from that found in the conclusions of Robinson and Kimmel: "Of course, for the many homosexuals affected by Ottawa's actions there was only defeat, accompanied, in all probability, by prolonged anguish."[46] This was only partly the case. By starting with first-hand accounts, we locate the agency, negotiation, complicity, and non-cooperation of the men and women who were most directly affected by these campaigns.

SHIFTING STANDPOINTS IN INTERROGATING THE SECURITY REGIME

Starting from the Stories of Those Who Were Affected

Our decision to start with social experience and first-hand accounts also relates to sociological and historical analysis and theorizing.[47] We are not attempting to generalize from the relatively small number of people interviewed but, rather, to reveal the generalized social character of security regime practices across different sites and time periods.[48] We have not objectified the research participants as a representative sample or, indeed, as a sample of any kind. We are interested in learning from their stories in order to identify the social relations of the security regime that orchestrated problems in these men's and women's lives, and how these practices have shifted in different historical periods, partly in relation to social and (later) legal struggles. Such accounts provide entry points into these broader social relations and preserve the subjectivities and agency of those affected most directly. We argue that the generalized character of the national security regime is a feature of the social organization of that regime. The generalized character of these institutional relations may be seen in the questions asked during interrogations and in the emphasis of the interrogations on gathering the names of other gays and lesbians. The military also instituted interrogations in the 1970s and 1980s that examined sexual practices as one way of confirming people as homosexuals.

The interviews were open-ended, semi-structured discussions. They were often focused conversations with an interactive and reflexive character.[49] As interviewers, we needed to be actively engaged with the conversation and to have good listening skills; we had to ensure that transcripts were produced with great sensitivity and care and that they were then read over very carefully. The interviews concentrated on what happened to these men and women, and attempted to ascertain how this security regime was socially organized. We asked about their experiences and memories of surveillance and, where appropriate, interrogations. If they were interrogated, the emphasis was on what took place, a typical query being "What questions were you asked by the RCMP or military intelligence?"

THE SOCIAL ORGANIZATION OF MEMORY AND FORGETTING

Given the different ways in which people's lives were affected by the security campaigns, the interview questions and discussions shifted a great deal from one interview to the next. Sometimes this required us, as interviewers, to fill in historical context (for instance, RCMP activities in 1964), which helped people to remember some of their experiences. Often this meant bringing into view what we had learned from other research participants without breaking confidentiality.

Remembering and memory are produced socially and reflexively. The liberal individualist notion that memory is some sort of asocial and ahistorical essence is not consistent with how memory works as a social practice. Memory always has a social and a historical character. Our experiences are remembered through social language and through how we make sense of them to ourselves and to others.

The interviews we conducted involved a reflexive/dialogical process in which both the participant and the interviewer constructed knowledge together. Typically for oral research, some discussions worked better than others, and a few did not work very well at all. Throughout the research, we accumulated knowledge from those with whom we spoke. We learned about the social settings and practices of their lives and how the security regime affected them. Each interview provided leads for new questions and, at the same time, enabled us to build upon what had been learned in earlier interviews.

There are, of course, important problems with memory, and what we call "the social organization of forgetting," when talking to people about experiences that occurred in the past and that may have had a devastating impact in their lives.[50] Many of us lack a historical sense about our lives because we have been denied access to a language of social and historical literacy that allows us to remember our experiences. The lack of a historical memory makes it hard to remember social aspects of our pasts and their implications for our present.

Particular difficulties arose when we talked to people about events that had irrevocably altered their lives. When we spoke to Harold in 1994, for instance, it became clear that he had not simply forgotten things that had happened long ago but that part of his survival strategy had been to attempt to forget the surveillance, the interrogations, and his forced resignation from the navy. About remembering, Harold said: "One of the problems I have with this [remembering] is that it took a lot of forgetting, and I deliberately tried to forget. And people would say to me, 'Well, why don't you use your rank in civilian life?' My own family would say, 'Why don't you use your rank?' Well, I pulled the curtain down on it and that life was finished completely and I was starting again. So I guess deliberately my mind is blurred about the actual dates and so forth" (February 21, 1994).

The reason for his discharge prohibited Harold from using his rank, so he was quite clear regarding why he could not cite his military career. Still, he vividly remembered the basic features of the interrogations he endured and how he felt when his career was destroyed. For his part, Herbert Sutcliffe was terrified by the security investigation (March 1, 1996); and Marty, in recalling Leo Mantha's 1958 murder of Aaron Jenkins and the ensuing investigation, said, "There are things that I blocked out of my mind" (May 19, 1996). Yet, even with all the limitations of memory and all the attempts to forget, first-hand accounts like Harold's, Herbert Sutcliffe's, and Marty's enable us to start our inquiry from a point outside of that provided by the official discourse.

What we gain access to in the interviews are not the actual events in some unmediated asocial sense but, rather, an account of these events produced after they took place, based on people's reflections and attempts to make sense of their experiences. This is how memory is formed and produced, made sense of, and remembered. For instance, when Gary (Kinsman) talked to Harold, the latter's conversation was very similar to the written account he had produced in the early 1960s. As research on the national security campaigns against gay men, lesbians, and others is publicized, it becomes more possible for memories to be spoken and remembered. In this sense, the production of the accounts of those who were affected, as well as this analysis, becomes part of the historical and social memory of this period. Documenting and analyzing these accounts is very much about producing memory and remembering as a social practice.

The social character of language can begin to make visible the broader social practices and relations that need to be investigated through sociological and historical research.[51] On a few occasions, people with whom we spoke were talking about experiences/memories for which they had never tried to account. These interviews were usually more stumbling and tentative than were those involving people with whom we had spoken previously or who had written accounts of their experiences. The social character of people's accounts provides us with insight into how their social experiences were put together.

Interviewing "the Enemy"

We also talked to those involved in the security regime. We had to resist pressure to shift from the viewpoints of those affected to the relevancies of those involved in the regime.[52] Discussions with security officials were based on what we learned from a critical analysis of the security texts, especially as they related to people's areas of work or documents in which their names appeared. Interviewing these people was at times uncomfortable because, as security officials, they had been directly implicated in the security regime. We attempted to bracket (i.e., set aside) these concerns and feelings for the purpose of the interview.[53]

When interviewing people involved in the administration of national security, we tried to get them to talk about how their work was socially organized. There is a difference between those involved in security work and those in administrative and/or managerial positions. The former often talked about their daily work process, while the latter tended to have institutionally defined memories and were less able to speak about the work they did. Finally, most of the security officials we interviewed were still bound by an oath of secrecy, which, of course, obstructed our ability to extract memories of past experiences.

Retrieving information about their actual work from those with legal training, from people involved in the administration and governance of the DEA and the RCMP, and from government officials such as former justice minister Davie Fulton proved difficult. This was the case even when they were shown documents that indicated their presence at Security Panel meetings. We suspect they were constantly thinking about the legal implications of what they were saying.

We read both the security regime texts and the interview transcripts (whether of those directly affected or of the security operatives) for what they reveal about social organization. This is a different reading strategy than that often used in sociology or history. We do not read for truth, or content analysis, or to place statements and words into classificatory or coding schemes, or to determine attitudes, beliefs, or variables; rather, we read for what these accounts and texts illuminate regarding the social organization of the security campaigns. At several junctures, we bring these first-hand accounts and official texts together in order to see what can be learned from relational social analysis. We use this method particularly regarding the social relations of interrogation and surveillance, the non-cooperation that the RCMP encountered from gay non-civil servants, and when exploring military policies of interrogation, reporting, and discharge in the 1980s.

DOING INSTITUTIONAL ETHNOGRAPHY

One of our main objectives is to make visible and to document how people lived and resisted these security campaigns "from below." We are not interested in interrogating the accounts of those most affected; instead, we approach them as valuable resources for investigating the practices of the security regime. These stories are where our questions for further inquiry arise, and they constitute a crucial building block for developing an institutional ethnography of the regime.[54]

Institutional ethnography has three main features.[55] First, it involves moving beyond the institutional ideology of the security regime and engaging in a critical analysis of its ideological practices. Second, it is based on a broad notion of work and activity derived from the feminist domestic labour debates. These debates were influenced by theoretical insights leading up to the wages for/against housework approach, which attempts to make visible all of the concerted activity that takes place to produce and resist institutional relations.[56] Similarly, institutional ethnography allows us to grasp the work of security operatives that is not recorded in the official texts and to see the possibility of gay and lesbian resistance to these national security campaigns.

Consider the interrelation of RCMP practices and the shaping of the experiences of gay men and lesbians in interrogations. For instance, we reveal the connections between the various interrogatory practices (such as showing cardex files and photo albums, and asking whether "so and so is a homosexual") and how these practices were organized in the RCMP's security work. Formulating a list of individuals was not just the result of a fetish for names but, rather, was mandated by the classifications shaping RCMP work. This, in turn, illuminates the social relations and practices through which security campaigns were organized. Asking questions related to the sexual practices of members of the military suspected of homosexuality was not simply the result of interrogators' "prurient" interests but also of the textually mediated character of military regulations governing the identification and release of homosexuals.

The third and final feature of institutional ethnography is that it allows us to connect local institutional analysis with the broader social relations of which it is a part and which it helps to accomplish. These broader social relations include the character of Canadian state formation, the influence of US national security, the defence and security arrangements of the Canadian state, the criminalization of homosexuality and forms of sexual policing, and prohibitions against the employment of homosexuals in the military and the RCMP.[57]

Whose National Security?

The critical reading we are suggesting brings into view a number of important questions regarding official discourse. Which nation and whose security is being defended through these security practices? It is essential not to take constructions of the nation and national security for granted, seeing them as just plain common sense. The campaigns against gays and lesbians were structured through a number of ideological concepts that are central to how ruling is organized within the security regime. As ideological concepts, "national security" and "character weakness" were crucial to how these campaigns were conducted. These concepts, and the national security discourse of which they were a part, were also used by security forces in the United States, Britain, and Australia.[58]

In standard usage, national security has two aspects. First, it refers to external security, or the military protection of the nation-state's borders and its secret documents. Second, it refers to internal security, or the defence of the nation-state from enemies within. For instance, within the boundaries of the Canadian state, certain groups and individuals have been constructed as "other," as threats to national security. In the Canadian context, this distinction between external/internal is arbitrary as some of the internal security threats are constructed via the external security arrangements organized through alliances with other states.[59]

The concept of national security rests on notions of what constitutes the interests of the nation, which, in Canada, are defined by capitalist, racist, heterosexist, and patriarchal relations. Within national security regime discourse, national security was defined in opposition to various "subversive threats" to a particular image of the Canadian nation.[60] Canadian state formation is historically based on the subordination of indigenous peoples, the Québécois, and Acadians, this being performed in alliance with the British Empire and, later, with US imperialism.[61] A 1994 Treasury Board Report on Information Management and Security defines national interest as "concerns [relating to] the defence and maintenance of the social, political and economic stability of Canada."[62] In typical pro-capitalist fashion, social, political, and economic stability is seen as inherently in the national interest; consequently, any challenge to it is seen as a challenge to the national interest. This broad definition of national interest is mobilized against protesters and subversives of various sorts who disrupt "stability" in Canada. Under this conceptualization, the nation is constructed as monolithic, and its many social differences and inequalities are denied.

Homosexuality, categorized as dangerous, figured prominently in this conceptualization of the nation. As Les Moran suggests, during the post–Second World War period, "homosexuality was put into circulation in such a way that it produced the idea of homosexuality in opposition to the nation."[63] There was a shift in the 1950s from a focus on communists and their sympathizers as a security threat to an emphasis on homosexuals. This shift took place at different times in the United States, Britain, and Canada.

In the early 1960s, Harold was already assessing security as problematic: "'Security' is a sacred cow of a word, in the name of which highly dictatorial and sweeping actions are possible for which no explanation can be forced."[64] In contrast to hegemonic "common sense," this comment is a critical "good sense" observation based on Harold's experiences with the military and the national security regime. Notions of the nation and national security can effectively draw people in, building a seductive social consensus. Who would be opposed to Canada's national security? These constructs can be very useful for making ruling-class hegemonies and, consequently, can obscure who is being excluded. It is also important to ask who is being actively placed at the centre of the social fabric through these constructs.[65]

Ultimately, the standpoint of national security was defined by, on the one hand, the security police, the military, and concerns over national defence, and, on the other hand, by the anti-communist, anti-Soviet, and anti–Third World liberation alliance led by the US government and the Western military network. Canada's alliance with the United States was solidified by its engagement with the international military network of the Cold War era and involved a tacit partnership that upheld security surveillance and global investigations. As the Royal Commission on Security (Mackenzie Commission) put it, "the United States is the leader of the western alliance."[66] Davie Fulton, justice minister from 1957 to 1962, concurred with this, noting that "the United States was the leader and team motivator of security investigations and that would be at all levels of our government" (May 17, 1996). In US right-wing and national security discourse, homosexuality was seen as a major security danger, sometimes portrayed as a virus sweeping across the continent.[67]

Canadian state participation in international security agreements permitted the US national security regime to set standards in Canada. Even for private-sector research clearances, the United States set standards for Canadian researchers and firms involved in defence and security-related research. Canadian public servants often needed access to US information and therefore had to conform to that nation's security regulations. In 1948, the US War

Department was willing to share classified information with the Canadian Department of National Defence and other government agencies providing that "all personnel handling such material had been cleared from a security standpoint." The Security Panel recommended that full security precautions be taken in certain government branches to facilitate this information transfer.[68] Security connections also existed between the RCMP, the Federal Bureau of Investigation (FBI), and the Central Intelligence Agency (CIA).

Notwithstanding significant US influence, it would be a mistake to view hostility to gay men and lesbians in Canada as simply an American import. Heterosexism in Canada has its own history, and the stigmatization and criminalization of homosexuality, which involved prohibiting gay men and lesbians from being employed in the military and the RCMP, established the foundation for the presentation of homosexuality as a national security threat.[69]

National security was the first ideological construct to inform the practices of the security regime and its mandate. According to Moran, the ideological practices of nation and nationalism "provide not only a modern regime through which a person may form subjectivity, but also produces people as objects of a nationalist pedagogy."[70] To demonstrate how this operates, we look briefly at the Mackenzie Report and its conceptualization of security.

The Mackenzie Report was submitted to the Canadian government in October 1968. Its terms of reference mandated a confidential inquiry into the operation of Canadian security methods as used to maintain the security of Canada as a nation, the rights and responsibilities of individuals, and Canada's relations with other governments. These terms of reference comply with a hegemonic ideological code with regard to nation, national interest, and national security. Maintaining secrecy, the commission conducted its work in private/in camera.[71] Material in the published report was omitted or amended "in the interest of national security."[72] If information is successfully submitted as being in the interest of national security, it can be removed from public documents and can become a secret text. The social construction of national security is also, centrally, that of secrecy. For example, with respect to access to information, the report states: "Neither does an individual have a right to confidence; on the contrary, access to classified information is a privilege which the state has a right and duty to restrict."[73]

The way in which the relationship between the interests of the nation and individual rights gets presented is key to how, wherever there is a conflict, the text places national security above individual rights. Individual rights and the rights of groups are superseded if they can be shown to be counterposed to the defence of the nation's security. This is quite standard in national security regime discourse and is still used today to bolster state arguments in favour of national security.

Questions of citizenship and loyalty are discussed in the section of the Mackenzie Report entitled "Security, Privacy and the Individual." This section begins with the admission that the privacy rights of the individual need to be subordinated to the security of the nation.[74] In other words, individuals can be denied social and privacy rights. Citizenship is defined not only by place of birth but also by loyalty to the state. If you are not loyal to the state and are deemed a risk to national security, you lose your citizenship rights, becoming subject to surveillance and interrogation.

This conceptual construction permits the hegemony of national security discourse, with the result that the rights of groups and individuals can be curtailed if they are seen to pose a risk to national security. In effect, the process of constructing these groups as threats legitimized their surveillance and interrogation. Human and civil rights could be sacrificed when it came to dealing with those perceived as national security risks. Thus, the successful claim that an individual or a group is a threat to national security acts as a "cutting out" device that denies people their human, civil, and citizenship rights.[75]

EXCLUSION AND INCLUSION: HETEROSEXUALITY IN THE INTERESTS OF THE NATION

"Nation" and "national security" are collecting categories that bring together a number of different social processes so that they can be dealt with through common administrative classifications.[76] They interweave the interests of the nation with the maintenance of capitalist social relations, participation in US-led security arrangements, and notions of "proper" politics, gender, family, sexuality, ethnicity, and race relations. Similarly, immigration and citizenship policies have been used against immigrants, migrants, and refugees.[77] The popular notion of the nation as "everyone" contrasts with its construction as something that excludes, or differentially includes, many people from its imagined borders. Some people are included, while others, defined as threats to national security, are excluded. During the years under study, queers were constructed as threats to national security and were excluded from the nation, whereas heterosexuals were perceived as safe. "Respectable" and "responsible" queers, usually coded as white, are only now being accepted into the fabric of the nation and can even be mobilized against others designated as national security risks (see Chapter 12).[78]

Consider the following passage from the Mackenzie Report. Under the heading "Immigration and Security," the report states that "Canada's requirement for immigrants must be balanced with the need to protect the safety and health of the state and its people by excluding certain classes of persons who appear to be undesirable."[79] Exclusion is justified on the grounds of health, safety, and undesirability. This builds on earlier constructions and practices of public health, which argue that some groups are "vectors of infection" into the "general population" and that designate some people (in this case immigrants) as undesirable.[80] Exclusion continues in new forms in the current war against terror, leading to the tightening up of borders for migrants, immigrants, and refugees and to clampdowns on "suspected terrorists" coded as Arabs, Muslims, and other people of colour.[81]

National security is viewed not only as the standpoint of state relations but also as that of the nation. As a result, on a popular level, "nation" and "national security" encompass all those who identify with the Canadian nation and, by extension, with Canadian national security. This is the common sense level of the construction of Canadian national identifications. Identifying as Canadian can mean providing an almost automatic support for the defence of Canada's national security, especially if one has no experiential basis from which to criticize it. The morally condensed symbol known as "our country" becomes associated with a particular historical and social formation of nation and state, one that is part of a specific ideological project.[82] As Benedict Anderson has stressed, nations are always "imagined communities" and are active social constructions.[83] It is easy, then, to fall into the trap of naturalizing and normalizing the nation and national security. This can lead to a nationalism, or patriotism, that is adamantly opposed to any critique of Canadian state formation.

At the same time, however, the social differences of class, sexuality, gender, race, language, and nation – and especially of indigenous peoples and the Québécois – are obscured by the image of the Canadian nation. For instance, as a white settler state, Canada is built on land taken from indigenous peoples. Building on the work done by anti-racist feminist Himani Bannerji, Alan Sears suggests that "every time we refer to the continent of North America, and call the northern part of that Canada, we are making certain assumptions about whose land this is and how it got to be this way. The violent subjugation of Aboriginal peoples and their claims to the land simply vanish in the everyday act of referring to the place in terms that are explicitly Europeanized."[84]

The image of the unitary nation of Canada is based on the suppression of the actual history and social differences that constitute Canadian social formation. The Canadian nation-state rests on these social differences, but simultaneously they are separated from the unitary national interest through being defined as outside the "normal," as "different" and "deviant." National security constructs heterosexuality as being in its interests, and it views homosexuality as not being in its interests. The presentation of the "normal" as at the centre is part of "how the centre holds."[85]

THE TEXTUAL CONSTRUCTION OF NATIONAL SECURITY

Nestled within common sense ideological images of the nation and national security are more official textual constructions of national security located in the security policies and courses of action adopted by Canadian state agencies and the agreements that the Canadian state enters into with the United States, Britain, and NATO. In highlighting the importance of security procedures and clearances, the Mackenzie Report argues that the "continued flow of information" from the United States and Britain "is at least partly dependent upon the apparent adequacy of Canadian security measures."[86] The assumption is that the Canadian state depends on this information. In order to continue to have access to this network of international secret information, Canadian security officials needed to adopt the security procedures defined by their US counterparts and those of other countries. Those policies were imposed on Canadian institutions, but they were also actively taken up and fought for by Canadian state agencies, who considered them to be in their own interests.

Operationally, national security involves security screening, clearance procedures, and the construction of national security risks. It is realized through surveillance and information management. It is accomplished when the policies and procedures in a Security Panel document are properly followed, or, in a different sense, when suspected homosexuals can be moved into the confirmed homosexual classification and purged from or demoted within the public service. Clearly, national security is performative in character.[87] It is a language and a set of procedures that not only states but also performs and accomplishes a certain form of social organization.

Struggles over who should have access to security information lead to mobilizing the "interests of the state" against gay men and lesbians holding positions in which they may have access to security information. In 1969, the Mackenzie Commission argued that, "in the interests of the individuals themselves as well as in the interests of the state, homosexuals should not normally be granted clearance to higher levels, should not be recruited if there is a possibility that they may require such clearance in the course of their careers and should certainly not be posted to sensitive positions overseas."[88] The phrase "in the interests of the state" operated not only to define the state as being above the individual but also to construct homosexuals as being in opposition to those interests. We can also see how, within the social security discourse, the social organization of higher and lower levels of security clearances operated to exclude homosexuals from the former. This discourse continued to influence the social organization of security clearances throughout the latter part of the twentieth century.

Character Weakness

In the context of defending national security, homosexuals were placed within the ideological collecting category known as character weakness. Although character weakness included a number of "afflictions" that could supposedly result in a person being blackmailed, in the late 1950s and 1960s, it became increasingly homosexualized.[89] After the general construction of national security, the more specific concept of character weakness was the next moment in the generation of the anti-homosexual security campaign. Within the national security discourse, homosexuality was presumed to be a distinct form of sexual practice, and anyone who engaged in same-gender sex was considered to be a homosexual.

In his interview, Fred, an RCMP officer, confirmed the use of homosexuality as a security threat. He reported that, although the notion of character weakness covered alcoholism, sexual promiscuity, having illegitimate children, and gambling, during the period in which he served as an RCMP character weaknesses officer (1967-69), the focus was "ninety percent homosexual" (October 21, 1994).

As mentioned earlier, the conceptualization of moral failings and character weaknesses as security threats developed unevenly within security regime discourse and, by the mid-1950s in Canada, became more separated from other ideological constructions of security threats.[90] In the mid- to late 1950s, the Security Panel discourse on homosexuality and security asserted that the Soviets "follow a consistent policy of searching out and exploiting character weaknesses" and that "persons with character weaknesses are always afraid of exposure to their families ... and therefore must be regarded as susceptible to blackmail even if their employers were to display a more sympathetic and frank attitude towards such weaknesses."[91] While it is clear that Soviet security services attempted this on a number of occasions, at least in the Canadian context, they were not successful.

Following recommendations regarding security clearances, the Royal Commission on Security included a list of people "that should not have access to classified information" unless a security check showed that the "risk appears to be justified." This list included "a person who is unreliable, not because he is disloyal, but because of features of his character which may lead to indiscretion or dishonesty, or make him vulnerable to blackmail or coercion. Such features may be greed, debt, illicit sexual behaviour, drunkenness, drug addiction, mental imbalance or such other aspect of character as might seriously affect his reliability."[92]

National security discourse built on and transformed earlier conceptualizations of homosexuals as psychopathic personalities unable to control their impulses (as stipulated in psychiatric and psychological discourses as well as in military discourse and procedure).[93] Homosexuals were viewed as unreliable, as having something to hide, or as suffering from a moral failing. This image fed into a newer conceptualization of character weakness, which was deployed in a heterosexist fashion, directly linked to discourses of masculinity and femininity. Previously, the homosexual had been perceived as a sexual and criminal danger but not as a specific risk to national security.

THE SOCIAL RELATIONS OF THE CLOSET

That homosexuals have to hide who they are is not an ahistorical, natural feature; rather, it was produced, in part, through the Cold War and national security campaigns against queers. The reasons for secrecy are rooted in the social relations of heterosexual hegemony, not in some essential feature of the homosexual "personality" (as the security texts claim). The national security campaigns were a central part of organizing the social relations of the closet – the closet itself being a fairly recent historical development. There is considerable evidence that there was far more openness to queer erotic and gender practices earlier in the twentieth century, prior to the fuller emergence of heterosexual hegemony.[94] This position, of course, requires moving beyond the mainstream – and often gay and lesbian – social mythology around past oppression, which is only now being slowly eroded. We have found that, in both Victoria, BC, before the police and military investigations of Aaron Jenkins' murder (see Chapter 3) and in Ottawa before the initiation of the anti-queer security campaign in the late 1950s, there was more openness to queer practices.[95]

The national security regime itself made use of and intensified the social space of the closet in order to organize national security campaigns.[96] As a Foucauldian reading shows, the security regime both helped to produce the social space for the closet and used it for its investigations, which, in turn, produced even more reasons for the existence of the closet. The security regime fed on the terror produced through the threat of discovery, yet the fact that the practices that it mandated actually created some of these secrecy needs is never made visible. The regime could, therefore, define the need for secrecy as what made homosexuals vulnerable to subversion, while not acknowledging how it was mobilizing that very need as part of its security campaign. Rather than removing the social basis for the threat of blackmail through calling for the repeal of anti-homosexual laws and heterosexist social practices, the regime intensified the need for secrecy through the employment of surveillance strategies.

While 1960s gay and homophile organizing was beginning to call for the repeal of anti-gay laws and social stigmas as a way of addressing blackmail concerns, the RCMP and national security discourse viewed the need for secrecy and invisibility as inherent to the homosexual personality.[97] It was not seen as a response to specific social and historical conditions. Members of the Security Panel did not suggest that there was a need to repeal the laws criminalizing homosexuality in order to alleviate blackmail.

Moran's study of the portrayal of homosexuals as a national security threat in Britain during the 1950s is both useful and important because he is one of the few theorists to have addressed these questions critically.[98] He notes that initial reports on the English homosexual spy Guy Burgess made no mention of his homosexuality as being indicative of disloyalty. Burgess occupied a privileged class and social position, and this offered a limited space for the homosexual, provided he lived in the closet.[99]

Moran also raises questions about the dialectics of class, homosexuality, and earlier wartime state and military needs in the British context. As he puts it, "known homosexuals were not necessarily precluded from service in sensitive posts, nor did knowledge of their sexuality lead to their later exclusion during wartime."[100] There is evidence in the Canadian context that, during the mobilization for war, homosexuals were sometimes tolerated in the military despite policies prohibiting them as "psychopathic personalities" with "abnormal sexuality."[101] As the need for recruits and for civil servants increased in the postwar era, the invisibility and silence around homosexuality allowed for a certain inclusion. As Moran suggests, "the homosexuality/danger conjunction is neither necessary nor inevitable" and "homosexuality may be deployed as either irrelevant to national security or, providing it is deployed in accordance with the requirements of invisibility as evidence through the recruitment of known homosexuals, as in the national interest."[102]

Moran shows that, decades earlier, images of homosexual danger were constructed in relation to sodomy and being barred from the armed forces. In the late 1940s and early 1950s, neither Britain nor Canada had adopted the idea of the homosexual as a threat to national security. Homosexuals were constructed as a social, criminal, and sexual peril before they were seen as a danger to national security.

In Canada, social space for homosexual men in high-level positions within the public service may also have existed, at least for those who were invisible about their sexuality. However, given the pervasive American influence on Canadian state formation and the American campaigns against homosexuals, which began in the late 1940s, this space would have been more precarious in the Canadian context than in Britain. And this space provided one source of official resistance to the anti-homosexual campaigns. The presence of some homosexual men in high-level public servant positions indicated that the public service was one available career option for closeted homosexuals. These men would have been seen as loyal servants of the state as long as they did not expose their sexuality.

The minutes of a Security Panel meeting on October 6, 1959, record N.A. Robertson, the undersecretary of state for external affairs around the time that John Holmes was purged from the DEA (see Chapters 3 and 4), stating: "A weakness such as homosexuality might exist in an individual of great discretion and with a brilliant capacity for public service. In many cases ... the security dangers of this particular sexual propensity might well be neutralized by other aspects of the person's character."[103] Here we see the argument that character strength could counter character weakness, with the notion of character becoming a contested terrain between different social forces. Robertson generally bent to the dynamics of the national security campaigns, which always saw homosexuality as a national security risk.

Jeffrey Weeks has argued that, in Britain, the presence of known and well-respected homosexual men in high-level civil service positions throughout this period worked against the kind of full-blown purge that occurred in the United States.[104] In Britain, these security concerns led to "the perceived need to purge a social elite closely associated with the State and thereby to separate out social status and sexuality."[105] In 1950s Britain, connections were made between the vulnerability of youth to homosexual advances, on the one hand, and homosexual "decadence" and "corruption" as a threat to the well-being of the state, on the other. Similar developments, albeit with different features, took place in Canada.[106]

Anti-homosexual national security campaigns were produced for domestic political and social reasons that went beyond anti-communism. For example, in Britain, the Montague (1954) and Wildeblood trials gave homosexuality a new and prominent place on the social agenda, and, in the 1950s, there was a dramatic increase in police activity against sex between men. Consequently, homosexuals became not only the "other" of normalized heterosexual identifications but also the "other" of the nation.[107]

A significant shift occurred in the development of Canadian state formation regarding security and defence questions. This was based on a movement from the procedures followed by Britain towards those pursued by the United States. This occurred as US state formation came increasingly to dominate Canadian state formation.[108] With the enforcement of US hegemony regarding national security questions in the Western alliance, we can see some of the ways in which this change was accomplished. National security is a specific social and historical achievement. It is not fixed but arises out of processes of mobilization, struggle, surveillance, and interactions between the security policies of different states and the forms of resistance they encounter.

According to Moran, the Burgess affair was not the prime factor motivating the emergence in Britain of the homosexual as a national security risk; rather, it was the 1952 leakage of security information regarding atomic energy. He posits that "the official silence relating to homosexuality as danger up to the mid-1950s might suggest that the actual immediate strategic concern of the period remained the threat of communism."[109] The focus on character weaknesses and the need to uncover more homosexuals required the state to develop more extensive police surveillance networks than existed in the 1940s. According to Moran, "it would appear that the idea of homosexuality as security risk gained significance and was used to secure American co-operation, to enable the UK to be a party, not only to important alliances, but also to have access to secret, particularly atomic research."[110]

By the mid-1950s, the earlier framing of security risks, which did not focus on homosexuals, began to change. According to Moran, "the State needed and promoted the idea of homosexuality-as-danger for the purposes of promoting international relations and establishing national security ... Through the production and deployment of the specific regime of representation the homosexual is produced as a threat to the state, the nation, national security."[111] National security required the accomplishment of those procedures that would allow the British or Canadian states to have access to US national security and defence information and to fully participate in national security arrangements. This specific construction of national security was textually accomplished and performed through made-in-Canada perceptions of homosexuals as social, sexual, and criminal dangers.

In Britain, the first brief public declaration of homosexuality as a character defect and, hence, as a security threat occurred in 1956. As Moran says, "the enemy within was officially established as the chief source of danger to national security: the public servant replaced the professional foreign agent as the prime potential threat to the security of the nation."[112] The very invisibility of homosexuality, which, earlier, had provided some protection for homosexual men, was now taken as a danger. Moran points out that the homosexual's "sexuality is produced through its invisibility" and that this "invisibility becomes the sign of sexuality as danger, conspiracy, perversity, weakness, luxury, mystery, ... confusion [and] instability. It is invisibility that comes to symbolize the threat to the established order."[113]

The previous invisibility of homosexual men in the ruling class and in bureaucratic positions came to be identified as an important national security danger. Whereas earlier it was accepted that some men in prominent positions could be queer as long as they remained "invisible," these men now became suspect precisely because of their invisibility. They were now viewed as being vulnerable to blackmail and, therefore, as possible risks to national security. This set the stage for a major purge of the government service.

As we show when we deal with the 1990s and the early twenty-first century (see Chapters 11 and 12), currently only some people who engage in same-gender sex are considered a threat. And this signals yet another change in the relation between homosexuals and national security. The limited presence of so-called responsible and respectable queers can be seen as part of promoting "diversity" and "multiculturalism" in the interests of national security.[114] For now, however, it is time to explore the broader social and historical basis for how Canadian queers were constructed as security risks.

3

The Cold War against Queers
Social and Historical Contexts

GENDER AND THE NATIONAL SECURITY CAMPAIGNS

The national security war on queers is situated within a social and historical context that was shaped by a number of social relations, including gender relations, military policies, the criminalization of same-gender sexual practices, the campaigns against the left, and links to the national security regime in the United States. In this chapter, we examine this context before returning, in Chapter 4, to the accounts of those who were purged and interrogated in the late 1950s and the 1960s. We begin with an exploration of the gendered construction of national security and of the Cold War against queers.

The national security campaigns were gendered: they were initially largely carried out by men and their first targets were often (but not always) men. As Steve Hewitt puts it, "The intelligence business was gendered male. The maleness of those who participated influenced their perceptions of society and the way they performed their work. For a woman to be involved in radical activities, or even to be involved in a non-traditional role, there had to be, in the eyes of the police, something not quite right about her."[1] In the military, suspected lesbians were often targets of the war on queers, but the national security regime was also based on, among other things, women's labouring in the expanding state bureaucracies. In the context of these growing bureaucracies, the Cold War against queers was also a battle for the entrenchment of "proper" codes of masculinity and femininity and for the association of queerness with "deviant" gender practices.

The Invisibility of Lesbians

There are two key historical reasons for lesbians being less visible than gay men in the national security campaigns (aside from those in the military in which they were prominent). First, because men held most security positions in the federal public service, the security regime texts and the practices they helped to organize initially focused on men.[2] Historian Hector Mackenzie described DEA practices in the 1950s and into the 1960s, pointing out that there was "overwhelming male recruitment [and that] women were finally allowed to compete for foreign service jobs. But there was still a strong bias against hiring women, and there was also a tendency for, you know [the attitude that] if women showed any interest in getting married or having a life of their own they were itching to find their way out of the department. So, it was not a hospitable environment for women" (September 26, 1999).

Given the gender division of labour in the waged work force, women in the public service were concentrated at the lower levels. As more women entered secretarial and clerical areas of work, which were coded as "women's work," and sensitive information and texts were typed, processed, coded, and communicated, more security concerns were raised. The development of the national security regime depended, in large part, on the work of women. John Starnes, who was a deputy minister in the DEA (1958-61) and director general of the RCMP Security Service (1970-73), writes:

> From the outset scores of women, serving as secretaries, archivists, under-cover agents, translators, transcribers, librarians, executive assistants, and in many other capacities, have carried out important and highly sensitive tasks in security and intelligence. I have in mind, for example, those who served Bryce, Heeney, Pearson, and Robertson in such capacities and were privy to virtually all the information that these men had, including sensitive details about intelligence and personnel security. They acted as custodians of such information and were indoctrinated and cleared to handle it ... In the RCMP Security Service, women performed such duties as being members of the Watcher Service (physical surveillance), translating and transcribing audio-tapes involving intercepted telephone communications (in many different languages and dialects), and conducting clandestine microphone operations. Much of this sensitive, difficult work was performed by women who were dedicated, trustworthy professionals.[3]

The cheap female labour pool was not only implicated in the formation of the national security state but also came to play key roles in its maintenance. Because of this, women began to fall within security surveillance practices.

The second reason for lesbians being less visible than gay men in the national security regime had to do with the construction of homosexuality as a more pronounced social threat than "lesbianism."[4] During these years, "sex pervert" and "sex deviate" were generally coded as masculine, whereas the construction of women's sexuality in national security discourse focused on mistresses and prostitutes as participants in blackmail efforts. The suggestion was that enemy agents used these women to gain incriminating information about men so that the latter would reveal security information. In Canada, the Munsinger affair is one example of this. A prostitute with some apparent ties to Soviet intelligence, Gerta Munsinger developed a relationship with Conservative minister of national defence Pierre Sevigny in the late 1950s, and a commission of inquiry followed in the 1960s.[5] Like homosexuals, men who used prostitutes or who had mistresses were seen in security discourse as vulnerable to blackmail and, therefore, as possible security risks. However, the security regime's focus on this particular character weakness was much less strong than that on homosexuality.

Although the number of women suspected of lesbianism or of "promiscuity" who were caught in the surveillance net is unknown, we do know that they were perceived as national security threats and that they were targeted by the RCMP. For example, David reported that, in the late 1950s or early 1960s, he was approached by the RCMP about a woman who worked as a secretary in his office (May 12, 1994). He was asked about her "moral weaknesses," and it was not entirely clear whether they were investigating her for lesbianism or for promiscuity. She was, however, a lesbian and may have been perceived as a threat because she was seen as subverting proper femininity and heterosexuality. As producers and reproducers of future citizens, women were considered central to the social organization of the national security state, especially through the institution of the family. The "non-productive" and non-male focus of lesbian sex was constructed as a threat to the maintenance of heterosexual hegemony.

The Cold War attacks on gay men also profoundly shaped the public perception of lesbianism, with serious consequences.[6] Jennifer Terry identifies some of the American psychiatric and psychological discourses during the 1950s that also had an impact in Canada. These discourses viewed lesbians as a social threat related to "momism" – that is, an excessive attachment to one's mother, or, conversely, over-protective mothering. They emphasized the moral strength of the home and held mothers responsible for the psychiatric/psychological problems of children, including the development of character weaknesses. This was apparent in the Canadian psychological discourse regarding sex offenders, with deviations often being blamed on "deficient" mothering practices.[7] In the context of the national security campaigns, deviation from proper gender practices, such as "effeminacy" in men and "masculinity" in women, was constructed as "treasonous." Momism was not only seen to have an effeminizing effect on sons but could also be cited as the reason why daughters turned to lesbianism. It was one way in which "treasonous moms" could push their daughters into the evil vortex of lesbianism and thus endanger the nation: "Lesbianism represented a pathological interruption in the normal development process toward motherhood. Treasonous moms could poison their daughters against heterosexuality by describing it as repulsive. In addition, a mother's lack of affection or her own masculinity could induce lesbianism in a daughter. In fact, many descriptions of demonic moms implied that their bitterness and frustration was a form of latent lesbianism."[8]

American military psychiatrist Edward Strecker wrote two books on these topics, both of which were available in Canada. One of these addresses the way in which "mannish" moms could turn their daughters away from motherhood and heterosexuality. Strecker's work is a diatribe against feminism and women's independence, and he argues that solutions to gender and sexuality "problems" can be found in the advice of experts.[9]

In 1950s psychological discourse, lesbianism was constructed as a social and sexual danger.[10] The correlation between lesbianism and obscenity erupted into a court case involving pulp fiction. In March 1952, National News, an Ottawa periodical distributor, was charged with distributing obscene materials. It was convicted on all counts and an appeal was rejected. One of the obscene items was the novel *Women's Barracks,* which included depictions of sexual relationships between women, and it became the centre of the court case, eclipsing the more heterosexually oriented materials that were also found to be obscene. The representation of sex between women was considered more obscene and shocking than that of sex between women and men. Judge McDougall rejected the defence's arguments that the novel was a cautionary tale against lesbianism and found, instead, that the book "deals almost entirely with the question of sex relationships and also with the question of lesbianism. A great deal of the language, and particularly the description of two incidents of unnatural relationships between women, is exceedingly frank."[11] McDougall's remarks construct lesbianism as a medical and psychological problem that cannot be addressed in a more sexually explicit and popular context. This decision fuelled the legal construction of queer representations as more obscene than similar heterosexual examples – a construction that continues to this day.[12]

The classification of character weakness includes lesbianism, but the latter was rarely openly written about in security regime texts. Usually the references to "homosexuals" discussed gay men or men who engaged in sex with other men. Another reason that the RCMP security campaigns did not focus on lesbians as much as they did on gay men was that it was more difficult for the police to conduct surveillance work on the former. There was a scarcity of lesbian informants and a lack of knowledge about lesbian networks. According to Fred, in late 1960s Ottawa, the subdivision of the RCMP that dealt with character weaknesses had little understanding of or contact with lesbians. He estimated that there was about one woman for every hundred men they investigated for homosexuality. As he put it, "Women can be seen walking around holding hands, lesbians are tougher to identify, they don't stick out, and one woman living with another woman was not seen as necessarily bad or as making one a lesbian" (October 21, 1994). Fred's comments notwithstanding, being a lesbian was not any less oppressive than being a gay man. Their more restricted access to social space and their invisibility was partly due to the general denial of the social and economic autonomy of women and to the specific denial of lesbianism in the construction of heterosexual hegemony. This lack of public visibility was compounded for the RCMP by the difficulties male officers had when attempting to spy upon and learn about lesbian networks. According to John Sawatsky, "Lesbians ... rarely cooperated and virtually never became informers. The Force attributed this to protective motherly instincts and the belief that they just did not like men anyway. Since all RCMP investigators were men, the Force for a time considered hiring women investigators to handle lesbians."[13]

Women in the Public Service

Examining the historical development of the gender division of labour in the public service, which shaped gender relations in this sector during the 1950s, 1960s, and into the 1970s (when the feminist movement and women's union organizing began to more profoundly challenge and transform these relations), is central to our project. By the early twentieth century, women began to enter the lower ranks of the civil service in spite of the fact that the Civil Service Commission placed limitations on the hiring and promotion of women. Kathleen Archibald suggests that the reason for this was that "women were not considered suitable for, or capable of, work at more responsible levels."[14]

The Royal Commission on the Civil Service, 1908, and the Civil Service Act, 1918, officially restricted women to the lowest level of the service. From the beginning, the Civil Service Commission maintained a system of occupational gender segregation that was to determine the character of women's work in the civil service for decades. After 1910, the most important positions were reserved for men. Later restrictions in 1918 and 1921, respectively, virtually excluded women from all permanent positions in the federal public service, leading to a rapid decline in female employment.[15] Restrictions on married women were finally revoked by the commission in 1955. Until then, female civil servants who were engaged were obliged to resign.[16] Significantly, once restrictions on married women were revoked, the number of women working for the government increased from 40 percent of the total government workforce in 1954 to 47 percent in 1956.[17]

Although women became a more common feature in the federal government, some departments continued to practise gender segregation. Robert remembered that, as late as the 1960s, "on the Hill, a lot of the secretaries were male. And even in the Foreign Service the secretaries were men because it was easier for them to travel. And of course, it was more common because of the British influence. It was very common to have male secretaries" (October 10, 1996). Here, Robert is referring to an area of work that, given the prevailing division of labour, some gay men came to occupy. Later, these men would become suspect.

The 1962 *Report of the Royal Commission on Government Organization and Management of the Public Service* (the Glassco Report) signalled some recognition of women's subordinate position in the civil service. Indeed, the report mentioned that, although there was no official policy regarding gender segregation, discrimination against women was rampant. Women often lost out on promotions on the grounds of "suitability" for employment; they were often rejected because of travel requirements; and there were few cases of women being appointed to senior levels of management. This also meant that women were not usually located in positions requiring higher security clearance levels. Only in the Public Service Employment Act, 1967, was sex (gender) added to race, national origin, colour, and religion as a prohibited ground of discrimination.[18] This did not prevent forms of institutionalized discrimination against women from continuing in the public service.

When the federal government began to expand rapidly, the Civil Service Commission and Ottawa were not prepared. The need for a female "army of cheap labour" meant that the commission embarked on a cross-country recruitment strategy.[19] These active recruitment strategies, the acute labour shortages, and the expanding bureaucracy after 1941 meant that the Civil Service Commission downgraded its qualifications, especially in the area of security clearances. Indeed, the RCMP security branches could not keep up with the huge number of applicants who were offered positions. This caused the Civil

Service Commission considerable anxiety, but the physical need for a large number of young women to fill the positions of stenographer, typist, clerk, and secretary sometimes came into conflict with the security discourse of the period.

In 1942, responding to the housing shortages and inadequate lodgings that faced these new federal workers, the government built a residence, called Laurentian Terrace, for Grade 1 female government workers.[20] From the outset, discourse concerning Laurentian Terrace was couched in paternalistic and heterosexist language. The working conditions that these young women faced were becoming an increasing source of concern for Members of Parliament, probably because of complaints from their constituents who received news from their daughters working in Ottawa. In keeping with Second World War rhetoric around women as the foundation of a "strong nation," most Members of Parliament argued that it was the duty of the government to build such residences as Laurentian Terrace in order to ensure the "future welfare of the nation."[21]

The plethora of government policies formed, and women's residences built, in the Cold War era regulated women's labour and sexual activities. An acute anxiety over the labour of and sexual possibilities for women emerged as the moral and patriarchal dictates of an earlier era slowly translated into a renewed interest in maintaining a heterosexual hegemony based on "traditional" feminine and masculine practices. The national security campaigns against queers were part of this larger project to enforce proper gender practices. The following section explores how this gender anxiety manifested itself on the bodies of female civil servants as they participated in the federal government's beauty contests, which were organized at the same time as were the security campaigns against queers. Far from being a mere consequence of the postwar mentality that women should return to their place in the home after serving as war workers from 1940 to 1945, these beauty contests were used to ensure that ideals of heterosexual femininity were not only an entrenched practice but also central to gendered social relations.

Bureaucratic Gender Anxiety

Like much of the waged and salaried work world, the public service had a series of social and occupational regulations governing personal interactions established for men by men. The civil service's organization was derived from the military and paramilitary forms of organization inherent to Canadian state formation. Civil and public servants, especially at the higher levels, were presumed to be men who were capable of following bureaucratic regulations. This regime of bureaucratic formal rationality was coded as male and masculine.[22]

These men were presumed to be heterosexual, but the work environment of the public service was constructed as a non-erotic one, partly because of the small number of women employed there in earlier years.

The notion that bureaucratic forms of organization are also sexual spaces (even if constructed as non-erotic) is useful with regard to exploring gender relations and heterosexual hegemony in bureaucratic organizations. Bureaucratic regimes are based on a formal rationality, whereby civil servants are expected to be devoted to "objective" rational organizing principles and to follow proper rules and procedures. Bureaucratic forms of organization shape what some describe as "the bureaucratic personality," characterized by methodical, rational, disciplined, and unemotional practices and by conformity to bureaucratic rules and regulations. This personality was constructed as masculine and professional in character.

Women and homosexuals were perceived as disruptive of these relations of bureaucratic rationality in that they introduced a "subjective" eroticism and emotionality into these allegedly non-erotic institutional settings, thus subverting hierarchical relations between superiors and subordinates.[23] Before women entered bureaucratic organizations in large numbers, the assumption was that, by virtue of his rational, disciplined, and unemotional practices, the male public servant was asexual in his work world. The entry of women into government work challenged this assumption, and new gender regulations were created. With new definitions of proper masculine and feminine behaviour came new boundaries of gender relations and practices. Rosemary Pringle and others insist that any understanding of gender divisions in bureaucratic forms of organization must be accompanied by an analysis based on gender and sexual power.[24]

Women's access to work outside the home increased with the wartime mobilization efforts, and the postwar reintegration of women into the home was couched in the discourse of loyalty and duty.[25] That duty consisted of women willingly and happily accepting what was seen as their proper place in the home – as wife and mother. Yet, the lives of those women who continued to participate and be drawn into the wage labour force were also highly regulated. Postwar management of women workers was geared towards "feminizing" women's work. Imposing work practices on these women (e.g., dress codes) helped to enforce and produce the discourses and practices of heterosexual femininity.[26] This almost obsessive need to reintroduce femininity into these women's social practices is described by Janice Irvine as "gender insecurity," or gender anxiety. At the core of this anxiety was the idealization of women's position in the family, which permeated cultural consciousness in the postwar era and was a socially organized response to the entry of women into the public realm during the war mobilizations.[27] The intrusion of women into the male-dominated spaces of the public service in the postwar years defied existing social, gender, and sexual boundaries. As a result, new forms of gender regulation were constructed to manage and contain these women.

The notion of gender anxiety is useful for our investigation since it helps to account for how sexist and anti-queer practices became so prevalent within the federal government. In the context of the federal bureaucracy, the influx of women and, through the security campaigns, the developing awareness of the presence of gays and lesbians threatened an idealized version of a heterosexual, male-dominated existence. Women, including lesbians, and gay men destabilized patriarchal work relations in which civil servants were expected to dedicate their lives to the service of state and nation.

The expansion of the public service was tied up with that of documentary forms of record-keeping and communication as well as with the expansion of the production, communication, and classification of documents relating to national security. Documents multiplied and so did the number of people with access to them, which posed a security challenge and led to the elaboration of different levels of security clearance. There was a mobilization of concern regarding who would have access to security texts as well as regarding the design of authorized classifications and procedures relating to security information and clearance levels.

Sports networks, women's residences like Laurentian Terrace, and military residences for women were all potential areas of resistance to the official story told by the security regime texts. These same-gender spaces opened up new opportunities for women to meet other women to form friendships and sexual intimacies. No longer a male bastion, the federal public service culture had to be socially reorganized to deal with and regulate these young women so that they were not a threat to gender and sexual boundaries. Heterosexual femininity as the ideal for women workers was based on the invisibility of lesbians and was accompanied by the construction of the normal male public servant as heterosexual. "Normal" men were not homosexuals.[28] Gays and lesbians in the federal public service negotiated this heterosexual norm by adopting a number of survival strategies. The need for these intensified as gay and lesbian networks, including those in the military, were subjected to security surveillance in the late 1950s and the 1960s.

During this period, an important site for negotiating femininity and gender and sexual boundaries was the Miss Civil Service beauty contests, held from 1950 to 1973.[29] The contests were unique in that they legitimized women's working in a previously masculine domain without compromising strict codes of gender difference. Beauty contests helped to manufacture a gendered workplace culture and discipline, in effect defining the proper gender and sexual practices for those employed in the federal civil service. Miss Civil Service became the symbol of the "typical government girl," an ideal defined by a set of feminine and heterosexual practices.[30] Not surprisingly, clothing played an important role in producing that image and the practices that accompanied it. This was the construction of a particular discourse and practice of femininity – one that excluded lesbianism. The legacy of these practices persists in the gendered dress codes that were established in the public service (to which we return when investigating the security campaigns in the 1970s).

Women's Sexualities and the Military

Women in the military were affected by the campaigns against "sex deviates" in major ways. Given that the military was understood as a masculine institution, the entry of women into its ranks introduced a series of contradictions. According to Allan Bérubé and John D'Emilio, in the United States, "as unmarried female volunteers in an intensely masculine institution women in the military formed a socially deviant group that too easily fit the popular stereotype of lesbians."[31] Military nurses and recruits had to be defended against charges of heterosexual promiscuity and prostitution as well as lesbianism. During the Second World War, this tension was handled by both asserting and bending gender norms. Women in war production and the military were told that they were there only "for the duration" of the war.[32] They were kept firmly out of any "combat" or "offensive" positions and were segregated into women's sections of the military.

The military did not want recruits to violate gender and sexual norms, and it wanted female recruits to be feminine and heterosexual but not promiscuous. Given the patriarchal history of military organization, the notion of a woman member is fraught with contradictions that do not apply to the military man – unless he is identified as queer. The military elite wanted women who performed their gender and sexuality as feminine and heterosexual, but, at the same time, it often attracted women who were not the most "feminine" and/or heterosexually defined.[33]

Lesbians were seen as a threat to proper femininity in military organizations and were purged during the postwar period.[34] The military established a contradictory social space for women in that it provided them with some economic and social independence as well as with the possibility of meeting other women for emotional and erotic relations while, at the same time, prohibiting those relations. Dress codes for women in the military attempted to enforce a feminine presentation of self as a way of moderating the threat posed by independent women.[35] As part of the military's sexist gender organization, anti-lesbian policies have worked to keep all women in line; however, some women worked to resist and subvert these regulations.

Although some women's motivation to join the military may have included a sense of patriotic duty, Gloria Cameron's experience shows us how the military provided women who experienced gender, class, and regional inequalities with another choice. As Gerald Hannon states, Cameron joined the military because she "wanted a job – the army had one that gave her training, more money than she could likely make on the outside, and the promise of regular promotion. And there was the added attraction of being able to work with other women, strong women with minds of their own. The army can be a very important employer, particularly in underprivileged regions of the country. 'In parts of the Maritimes,' said one source, 'a woman either joins the army or the welfare rolls. Or gets married.'"[36] For lesbians from working-class communities, and especially for those who identified as butch, the military was not only a social space in which to meet other women in a potentially friendly environment but also, at times, a welcome reprieve from financial obstacles.

Yet, the military was far from a safe place for lesbians or same-gender sex encounters. In the United States, women recruited into the Women's Army Corps were asked whether they had ever been in love with a woman.[37] While recruits were not asked this question in Canada, the "official line on lesbianism – though not publicized lest people think it widespread – was that 'it must be watched for, always,' and not in the least tolerated."[38] In the United States, an affirmative answer was grounds for rejection; however, during the Second World War, when more bodies were needed, instructions were issued not to engage in any unfounded or unnecessary witch-hunting against lesbians.[39] Indeed, as in the federal government, so in the military: the twin forces of labour shortage and expansion meant that women were actively recruited. As a result, lesbian activity was "tolerated" as long as it remained relatively invisible. In 1943, the US Women's Army Auxiliary Corps prepared a series of sex hygiene lectures aimed at officer candidates. The officers were warned against conducting anti-lesbian hunts except with regard to the most overt, disruptive, and intransigent lesbian "addicts," who were seen to jeopardize the morale and efficiency of the unit.[40] These guidelines were not always followed, and at times there were active searches for and harassment of lesbian personnel. In the postwar period, when these women were no longer needed, thousands of them were purged for engaging in same-gender eroticism.[41] At least during the war years, unlike in the United States, in Canada no women were court-martialled for homosexuality, and there were no specific investigations into lesbianism.[42]

After the war, the US military intensified its efforts to detect and discharge gays and lesbians. At this time, discharges for homosexuality averaged more than one thousand per year; by the early 1950s, this rose to more than two thousand per year.[43] In 1952, in the context of the Cold War campaign against communists and "sex perverts," teams of naval officers were told to indoctrinate naval personnel with the idea that homosexuality was "one of the very bad things in life." These teams were instructed to inform the ranks that "homosexuality is wrong, it is evil, and it is to be banned as such." They explicitly denied the notion that homosexuality was a "mental illness," arguing instead that it was a crime. In a 1952 program of lectures delivered to female navy recruits, it was suggested that there was no distinction between "first timers" engaging in lesbian acts and the "practising homosexual": both should be immediately discharged. A surveillance system that encouraged military personnel to inform on each other was put in place. The content of the lectures on homosexuality was imbued with "traditional" family and feminine ideology and was rife with stereotypes of lesbians as "sexual vampires." As one of the lecture notes read, "A woman is not tried for being a homosexual, she is tried for committing a homosexual act."[44] The focus was not only on the butch, or "gender-inverted," lesbian but also on any woman who engaged in same-gender erotic acts, even if she performed her gender as very "feminine." This is similar to the Canadian military's focus, in the late 1950s, on all men who engaged in same-gender sex rather than solely on those who performed "effeminately." This broader movement away from gender inversion theories of homosexuality and towards theories of sexual orientation and character weakness affected the national security campaigns against queers.

This shift illuminates a number of the debates within Canadian military and national security discourses concerning whether homosexuality was an act or an identity, a crime or a mental illness.[45] Increasingly, there was movement towards focusing on sexual acts, but this also came to be grouped with homosexuality as a character weakness and involved a certain ambivalence as to whether those committing the acts were criminal or mentally ill. The association between homosexuality and mental illness drew psychiatric and psychological discourses into military regulations and national security practices. In the Canadian and the US military, women were often far more profoundly affected by the anti-homosexual policies than were men. At the same time, the boundaries of heterosexual masculinity and definitions of male homosexuality were also being redrawn.

MASCULINITIES AND HOMOSEXUALITIES

The Leo Mantha/Aaron Jenkins case provides insight into the gender assumptions of the anti-queer practices in the military and the national security state more generally. Mantha murdered his estranged lover Jenkins in 1958 and was put to death by the Canadian state in 1959. Both had been investigated by military psychiatrists. Jenkins sought help from naval neuropsychiatrist Dr. Douglas Alcorn after he was stationed at Esquimalt, British Columbia, in 1957. Alan Hustak reports that "Bud [Jenkins] confided his frenzied sexual behaviour, and his revulsion from the compulsion. He was, he admitted, easily aroused in the presence of other men on the base, and told Alcorn he had ample opportunity to perform oral sex on servicemen every other night ... Alcorn diagnoses Jenkins as a 'Homosexual of the feminine type.'" However, the same report concludes that the other sailors with whom Jenkins had been intimate were "simply individuals who have fairly normal tastes, but who wish to experiment in other ways."[46] Alcorn recommended a military discharge on administrative grounds and warned that "Jenkins is almost certain to get into serious difficulties if he continues any longer in the service."[47] Jenkins, however, was not discharged.

The discourse upon which Alcorn drew constructs homosexuality as a particular psychiatric disorder – one that is linked to notions of the "true" homosexual as a gender invert. This also shows how Jenkins had to present his experiences within the power/knowledge relations established by military psychiatry in order to merit its attention. In this period, psychiatric and psychological discourse distinguished between, on the one hand, men who had some of the marks of gender inversion and who engaged in sex with other men and, on the other, men who might occasionally have sex with other men but who performed "normal" masculinity. In this construction, the former were "real homosexuals" and the latter were not.

Historian George Chauncey found similar examples in the US Navy earlier in the twentieth century, when only the effeminate men who engaged in homosexual practices were seen as a problem.[48] Marty reports that Jenkins was referred to "as a fairy" by others in the navy (May 19, 1996). This word was used to refer to effeminate, mainly working-class men who had sex with other men.[49] This parallels the construction of gender inversion in relation to lesbians, which focused on the masculine, or butch, women and not on the more feminine women involved in same-gender sex.[50]

The nation-state was constructed as male and was associated with order, strength, rationality, and stability.[51] In contrast, the homosexual man was perceived as feminized and was portrayed as unnatural, weak, unstable, and prone to conspiracy, decadence, and irrationality. Leslie Moran states that "manliness ... is constructed in relation" to and in opposition "to homosexuality." There is a relational character to the construction of heterosexual masculinity and that of homosexual non-masculinity. As Moran points out, "Manliness as rationality depends upon the displacement of irrationality onto the other that is homosexuality."[52]

With the emergence of homosexuality in the 1950s as a sexual object choice, as a sexual orientation, and as a character weakness, both effeminate and more masculine men became suspect.[53] Even the man who occasionally engaged in sex with other men but who was otherwise masculine could be blackmailed because he was now seen as suffering from a character weakness and therefore had something to hide. The homosexualization of character weakness and the identification of homosexuality as a major national security risk were part of a process of renegotiating the boundaries between homosexuality and heterosexual masculinity. Occasional participation in same-gender sex could now place one beyond the boundaries of heterosexual masculinity. Now, all men who had sex with other men, not just those who were effeminate, could be targeted within the military and through the security campaigns. Thus, the number of men suspected of being homosexual was expanded, and the borders of proper heterosexual masculinity were tightened up. The RCMP used this logic and even consulted a dictionary: "The Oxford Dictionary describes 'homosexual' as: 'having a sexual propensity for persons of one's own sex.' This definition is perhaps too broad for the purposes of security. Our interest is in only those persons who manifest this propensity by engaging in actual sexual acts with persons of the same sex ... It is in the performance of a homosexual act that the persons involved run the risk of being apprehended, watched or photographed, from which a subsequent compromise attempt may be made."[54] This position can be seen as an attempt to counter the Kinsey Report, which expanded the boundaries of heterosexual masculinity to include some homosexual activity during the course of a heterosexual man's life, seeing it as part of a broad continuum of sexual practice.[55] The RCMP's position, in contrast, attempted to make even experimentation with same-gender sex suspect and a possible risk to national security. Professor Frank Wake, who designed the fruit machine (see Chapter 5), also questioned the association of male homosexuality with effeminacy. Contradictorily, however, he felt that psychological masculinity/

femininity tests could be part of a broader array of tests for homosexuality. In Wake's initial suggestions for research, he argued that "it is commonly believed that homosexuals are effeminate; *some* are, but some are accomplished athletes."[56] Here Wake inverts the usual association of sports with heterosexual masculinity to dramatize that fact that even masculine men can be homosexuals.

In suggesting how homosexuals could be identified, a 1961 RCMP paper moved beyond common stereotypes regarding homosexuality as gender inversion:

> There are a number of popular concepts about homosexuality which have been found to be misleading. The first of these is that the homosexual is an effeminate looking person. This is applicable to only a small segment of the homosexual population. From our own experience we have found that the majority of homosexuals cannot be identified from the rest of the community on the basis of appearance ... Nevertheless, the investigator should not overlook the fact that there is a good chance that an effeminate looking male is a homosexual ... The second misconception is that homosexuals gravitate to employment in beauty shops, florist shops, clothing stores and as artists and interior decorators. Here again this belief is valid for only a segment of the homosexual community. Experience has shown that the homosexual may be found in any and all types of employment; his intelligence, education and employment preferences are apparently not controlled exclusively by his sexual aberration ... A third misconception is that homosexuals lack the virility and courage usually associated with the average, normal, male; in effect they are considered "Sissies." This also is only partly correct.[57]

This shift was part of the push against the simple equation of male homosexuals with effeminacy, which came from changing psychological definitions of homosexuality as well as from new national security concerns regarding it. In national security discourse, conceptualizing homosexuality as a sexual practice and orientation instead of as a gender inversion articulated with viewing homosexuality as a character weakness. This occurred unevenly within the military and the RCMP, with many of the assumptions of gender inversion continuing to inform their practices into the 1960s and 1970s. While the concept of gender inversion was not always displaced or superseded, the emerging notions of sexual orientation and character weakness led to a focus on sexual acts. Now anyone who engaged in a homosexual act could be susceptible to blackmail, not just those associated with gender inversion. Within this discursive framework, a homosexual became anyone who engaged in a same-gender sexual act. At the same time, notions of gender inversion continued to be cogent in national security campaigns.[58]

The account of George Marshall, who was discharged from the military, gives us some insight into how constructs of gender inversion intersected with the newer ideas of sexual orientation and character weakness. In 1966, the Toronto gay magazine *Two* printed an interview with Marshall regarding his experiences in the Canadian military. When he was finally processed for promotion, the RCMP investigated him. He was subjected to various tests, which showed him to be "extremely masculine." These tests included a questionnaire consisting of 350 multiple-choice questions (this was probably one of the masculinity/femininity psychological tests, perhaps even one of those used in developing the fruit machine). The RCMP discovered him to be homosexual: "They even claimed I'd been a homosexual prostitute. The bastards even knew I'd been buying pornographic physique photos from a firm in Sweden."[59] Marshall had to fight for an honourable discharge and was successful only because of a conflict between the psychiatrists and the medical doctors due to his "masculine" appearance. Others were not as lucky.

MILITARY ORGANIZATION, THE SECOND WORLD WAR, AND PSYCHOPATHIC PERSONALITIES WITH ABNORMAL SEXUALITY

The military is an important component in the emergence of the patriarchal capitalist nation-state. As an institution, it has a privileged position in state formation and plays a central part in state-building and in defending national security. The military is under the jurisdiction of central state authorities and, as such, develops an intimate relation with state bodies. This was especially the case in the contexts of the Cold War and the expansion of the national security state. This close linkage with core state relations gives the military a special kind of influence and privilege with regard to "defence" and "security."[60] Within patriarchal, capitalist relations, the military develops its own bureaucratic administrative relations, with a sharply defined hierarchy, internal divisions of labour, and specialized tasks. It resembles what sociologist Erving Goffman described as a total institution: "A place of residence and work where a large number of like-situated individuals cut off from the wider society for an appreciable period of time, together lead an enclosed, formally administered round of life."[61] There is a long history of the prohibition of erotic relations between men in the British and Canadian military, particularly against buggery and sodomy.[62]

The Second World War mobilizations expanded possibilities for same-gender eroticism in the military and in the surrounding war industry. People actively seized these new social spaces to create erotic relations, and this produced a regulatory response. While this has been well documented for the United States, the same cannot be said for Canada.[63] One major reason for this is that the anti-homosexual campaign in the Canadian state was neither as public nor as explicit as was the one south of the border.

Major tensions existed between military administrative practices mandating the discharge of homosexuals and military medical service practices that were more informed by psychiatric and psychological perspectives. Whereas the military administration tended to rely on military law and courts martial to make an example of those branded as homosexual, as the war went on, psychiatry was having a growing influence on military administration and policy. Paul Jackson argues that "military law was the central feature in the regulation of homosexuality," but he also describes the growing influence of the medical and psychiatric wings within the military.[64] Jackson's detailed investigation informs us that there was no consistency to the way in which the military addressed sex between men. There were tensions between the medical military policies calling for the discharge of "military misfits" and military laws calling for men to be court martialled and even imprisoned for homosexual "indecency." In part, this reflects a series of turf wars within the military.

In addition, there were conflicts between official military policies and "manpower" needs at the local level. Men identified as homosexual were sometimes able to use these conflicts to their advantage. Some managed to build alliances with local commanders and/or military doctors, using contradictions between the military law and medical policy and the need for personnel, especially in times of shortages. For instance, some commanders and, especially, doctors focused exclusively on the "true homosexual" rather than on the masculine man who might participate in queer sex. It was the person with the homosexual identification who needed to be addressed by military policy, not the masculine recruit who was otherwise able to demonstrate his heterosexual credentials. Most men who engaged in sex with other men were never discovered; however, many of those who were discovered were made an example of, whereas still others were quietly discharged.

During the Second World War, the Canadian military medical services defined people involved in same-gender sex as suffering from "psychiatric disorders" (which included psychoneurosis and psychosis) and, more specifically, as "anti-social psychopaths" and as "psychopathic personalities" with "abnormal sexuality."[65] This built on earlier practices directed against "buggery," "sodomy," and same-gender eroticism between men in the military, all of which were considered a threat to hierarchical and bureaucratic forms of organization.[66]

"Psychopath," a concept that originated within nineteenth-century forensic psychiatry as a collecting category for habitual criminals, became a key concept for psychiatrists in the military. It was used by Heinrich Kaan and Krafft-Ebing with regard to "abnormal" sexual activities.[67] Those categorized as psychopaths were, at first, often "hypersexual" women and unemployed or transient men who lived beyond the boundaries of familial and other forms of social regulation. By the 1930s, psychiatrists and psychologists were investigating gender and sexual "deviance" and, while doing so, were creating a sharper definition of heterosexual masculinity.

Increasingly, those who displayed deviant masculinities became targets for psychiatric and psychological investigation. Two developments unfolded during this period: first, male sex deviants were seen as a danger to children, and second, homosexuals began to emerge as an important part of the category of psychopath.[68] The conceptualizations used in different discourses and institutional sites were uneven. Sexological and psychological discourse preferred "homosexual," whereas psychiatric discourse preferred "sexual psychopath." At this time, the social conceptualization of homosexuality was still in the process of being generalized within official and popular discourses.

Military mobilizations before and during the war created a series of problems that psychiatric personnel, among others, were tasked to manage. As people with abnormal sexuality were identified as a danger, or as a disruptive influence, in the military, an official course of action was implemented to deal with this "problem," the solution to which involved the amalgamation of military classification and discipline with medical and psychiatric discourse and professionals.

Thousands of Canadian women and men were discharged under the psychopathic personality provisions of the medical military service regulations, including for participation in same-gender sex.[69] They were classified as subgroups within these broad psychiatric collecting categories, not as a specifically demarcated homosexual type. Thus, people's experiences were inscribed into a highly psychiatric concept that privileged psychopathic personality over same-gender sexuality. This may account for the fact that the Canadian war mobilization seemed to play less of a role in forming and expanding visible homosexual and lesbian networks than did the American war mobilization. In some US discourses, the terms "psychopath" and, especially, "sexual psychopath" were used almost as code for homosexual.[70]

While in the United States during the war mobilizations, women and men were actually asked whether they were homosexual, in Canada lesbians and homosexual men were categorized under more diffuse and heterogeneous headings, such as "psychiatric disorders" and, more specifically, "anti-social psychopaths" and "psychopathic personalities" with "abnormal sexualities."[71] Throughout the war effort, the Canadian military kept medical records and statistics, a practice that stemmed from a growing reliance upon the psychiatric and, later, the psychological professions.

The 1943 medico-military instructions assisted doctors and psychiatrists in diagnosing psychopathic personalities: "The chief characteristic of this disorder is inability of the individual to profit from experience. Men with this disorder are unable to meet the usual adult social standards of truthfulness, decency, responsibility, and consideration for their fellow associates. They are emotionally not to be depended on. They are impulsive, show poor judgement and in the army they are continually at odds with those who are trying to train and discipline them ... Among this group are many homosexuals, chronic delinquents, chronic alcoholics and drug addicts. All such men should be regarded as medically unfit for service anywhere in any capacity."[72] A year before these instructions were instated, a committee on the nomenclature of mental disorders concluded that such "cases exert a bad influence on their fellow soldiers and are therefore unwanted in any unit."[73] "Psychopathic personality with abnormal sexuality" was the "diagnosis used when abnormal sexuality [was] the basic feature of the case, and [was] not apparently based on mental deficiency, psychosis or psychoneurosis."[74] The job of military psychiatrists was to "facilitate the disposal of [these] cases."[75]

In practice, there was some flexibility in applying these classifications; consequently, these psychiatric policies often had a more limited impact than a literal reading of these texts may suggest.[76] In most of the reported statistics, it seems that "psychopathic personality" was not differentiated from other psychological and nervous disorders. But it is clear that, during the Second World War, thousands of men and women were discharged for having psychopathic personalities, and some of them were so categorized for sexual-related reasons.

In the postwar years, those marked with psychopathic classifications for abnormal sexuality could experience problems seeking employment, and some were labelled queer. Groups of queer people expelled from the military helped form the basis for the postwar growth of gay and lesbian networks in the larger urban centres and the social basis for later forms of gay and lesbian resistance.[77]

In the 1950s and 1960s, there was a shift in military regulations and medical diagnoses from "psychopathic personality with abnormal sexuality" to "sex deviates." The latter category grouped homosexuality with other forms of sex deviation but was less psychiatrically defined than was the former. Military policy explicitly stated that sex deviates would be expunged from the military. Prior to the unification of the armed forces in 1967, the army, navy, and air force each had its own regulations for dealing with sex deviates.

Following unification, an administrative order (Canadian Forces Administrative Order 19-20), issued in 1967, stated that sex deviates (including homosexuals) could not be members of the Canadian Armed Forces. Military exclusion policies helped to create the basis for, and also merged with, the national security campaigns. In the 1950s and 1960s, these campaigns against queers were also shaped by attempts to extend the criminalization of queer sex.

CRIMINAL SEXUAL PSYCHOPATHS AND DANGEROUS SEXUAL OFFENDERS: EXTENDING THE CRIMINALIZATION OF HOMOSEXUALITY

In 1948, a section on "criminal sexual psychopaths" was added to the Canadian Criminal Code. A criminal sexual psychopath was defined as "a person who by a course of misconduct in sexual matters has evidenced a lack of power to control his sexual impulses and who as a result is likely to attack or otherwise inflict injury, loss, pain or other evil on any person."[78] During the 1950s, criminal sexual psychopath legislation became a key component in the criminalization of same-gender sexual activity through constructing such activity as criminal sexual danger. This legislation was rooted in the attempt to create "moral panics" over violent sexual crimes, particularly against young people.[79] It was also grounded in the state's reliance on psychiatric experts to provide the solution to social problems.[80]

This legislation mandated a course of action that linked several state and professional sites, including the Criminal Code, the police, the Office of the Attorney General, psychiatrists, and the prison system. It was initiated following police arrests related to specific "triggering" sex offences. If the individual was convicted of one of these offences, an application was made at sentencing, with the attorney general's approval, for the individual to be designated as a criminal sexual psychopath (CSP). The sentencing procedure required psychiatric testimony to determine whether or not the person fit the definition of a CSP. If sentenced as a CSP, he or she would be incarcerated for an "indefinite period."

In 1953, "buggery" and "gross indecency," two of the primary male homosexual-related sexual offences, were added to the list of offences that could result in the application of the CSP procedure. All homosexual-related offences now became triggering offences. Homosexual sexual activity reported by the police and resulting in a conviction could result in one being subject to the CSP procedure. It did not matter if the acts were consensual, occurred between adults, or took place in private. With all gay sex being defined as illegal, this legislation was used in a more severe fashion against men having sex with men and/or with adolescent boys than it was against people engaging in violent heterosexual acts. As Freedman states with regard to the situation in the United States: "As long as he did not mutilate or murder his victim, the rapist might be considered almost normal and certainly more 'natural' than men who committed less violent, and even consensual, sexual acts such as sodomy and paedophilia. Accordingly, men diagnosed as psychopaths were more likely to be accused of paedophilia and homosexuality than rape or murder."[81]

Psychopaths were visualized as a small group of men who suffered from an inability to control their sexual impulses. The ideological framing of homosexual men as sex crazed fit easily within the sexual psychopath frame. The CSP definition and procedure focused on deviant males – those situated outside local, familial forms of regulation – as the sexual danger. CSPs were not usually familially related to those against whom they committed offences, even though we know that much sexual violence against women and young people is committed by fathers and husbands.[82]

The Royal Commission on the Criminal Law Relating to Criminal Sexual Psychopaths (the McRuer Commission) was established in 1954 and released its report in 1958. This report held in place the basic criminalization of homosexual acts. In 1961, Parliament changed the designation of "criminal sexual psychopath" to "dangerous sexual offender" (DSO), as argued for in this same report.[83] Although the new designation was promoted on the grounds that it was less psychiatrically defined (and the term "psychopath" was being increasingly challenged within the psychiatric profession itself), the court still had to hear testimony from at least two psychiatrists. The legislation drafters at the Department of Justice added a new clause – "or who is likely to commit another sexual offence" – apparently to give an alternative definition so that the sentencing rate would increase.[84] As a result, being convicted of gross indecency could lead to being classified as a DSO since, under the newly added clause, there was a perceived likelihood of continuing to engage in these activities.

The strategy of extending the criminalization of homosexuality, while shifting from CSP to DSO, was fundamentally held in place. This can be seen as a display of the recursive features of social organization, whereby the same basic social form is retained while being partially modified.[85] In the 1960s, the development of this legislation set up a tension between the extended criminalization of homosexuality enacted in Canadian law (influenced by developments in the United States) and the limited "liberalization" advocated by Britain's 1957 Wolfenden Report (see Chapter 6).[86] The Wolfenden Report supported the partial decriminalization of "private" homosexual acts and began to be used to contest the influence of the extended criminalization strategy.[87]

Within Canadian state relations, these emerging strategies led to different responses to the regulation of same-gender sexualities. Heterosexual masculinity was more integral to the ideological organization of some sites within state relations than others. Generally, those sites most tied into defending national security and policing, such as the military and the RCMP, were the most hostile to queers.

An early part of Canadian state participation in the US-inspired national security campaigns against queers was an amendment to the Immigration Act, the purpose of which was to keep homosexuals out of Canada. The Canadian Immigration Act, 1952, treated homosexuals as "subversives." The decision to revise the Immigration Act was made in the fall of 1948, and an interdepartmental committee was struck to draw up the proposals. The first draft called for the exclusion of "prostitutes, homosexuals, lesbians and persons coming to Canada for an immoral purpose." Later, in 1951, the proposal to include lesbians was dropped, and a clause that included "living on the avails of prostitution or homosexualism" was added.[88] For the first time, an act of Parliament explicitly referred to the homosexual as "a status or a type of person." Previously, only specific acts, such as buggery or gross indecency, were of legal concern. While there was some controversy over whether or not homosexuals should be barred from Canada under the Immigration Act, the RCMP was strongly in favour of doing so.[89]

At this time, the anti-homosexual campaigns south of the border were reaching a fever pitch.[90] When the immigration bill was introduced in the House of Commons in June 1952, there was no debate on the section covering homosexuality, and it quickly passed. The status of homosexuals under the Immigration Act did not change until 1977, after a series of commissions had heard protests from lesbian and gay groups.[91]

The Cold War against Queers

The notion of character weakness fit well with the construction of the homosexual as a social and sexual danger, making queers a national security risk. This was accomplished through the mediated social character of military exclusions and Criminal Code procedures, which, themselves, were tied to psychiatric and psychological constructions of homosexuality. However, major omissions occur if we approach national security campaigns against queers as though they could be violently abstracted from other regulatory practices.[92] As we see in the following section, those involved in same-gender sexual practices were affected by various dimensions of the national security campaigns.

CAMPAIGNS AGAINST THE LEFT, LESBIANS, AND GAY MEN

In the 1950s, state agencies made associations between communism and sexual deviance. Homosexuals were constructed not only as violators of sexual and gender boundaries but also as transgressors of class, gender, and political boundaries. Lesbians and gay men were affected by both these campaigns as well as by the security campaigns against leftists and peace, immigrant, student, social justice, and other activists.[93] If there were any hints of homosexuality or sexual deviance, this provided additional evidence for the security police to use against individuals. Many people's lives were affected by these investigations, including lesbians and gay men who were investigated for communist, socialist, or leftist connections.

Jim Egan remembered first encountering the claim that gay men and lesbians were a threat to national security "in the McCarthy era. He [McCarthy] moved from trying to root out communists from the State Department to equating communists with homosexuals. He figured that if he got his hands on a homosexual he had his hands on a communist" (January 5, 1998). The association made between homosexuality and communism was entirely ideological, and many gay men and lesbians were not involved with, and were even at times hostile to, the left. Still, the connection had some currency as many gay men and lesbians were involved in left-wing and social justice movements, and, of course, leftist gays and lesbians worked in early gay organizing efforts.[94] In Britain, through a series of publicized trials and scandals, homosexuality came to be associated with treason and spying for the USSR. By the mid- to late 1950s, this, in turn, affected how homosexuality was portrayed in official circles in Canada.[95]

Lesbians Making History, an oral history group located in Toronto, collected the following story from Lois, who recounted how she got caught up in the campaign against communists and socialists. She described her sexual and personal relationship with an American woman:

> We got together every weekend we could. We used to camp for the summers, and that was great. We had four kids together and everything was fine until this McCarthy thing came up. We both espoused left-wing causes, she more than I. She was left-wing and her husband was a communist ... She and I ran some camps, international, interracial, and left-wing – it was advertised in the left-wing newspapers ... My husband was working for the Department of National Defence at this point, in the early 1950s – it was the wrong time, and we got caught up in the Rosenberg murders – you know they were murdered, of course – and we were really working to try to prevent them from being murdered ... But when all this happened to us, W. [her husband] was told he had to resign. And it was even mentioned, you know, the Rosenberg thing ... So he lost his job and I was told I might lose mine ... Somebody in the department told W. they'd been following us; we'd been under twenty-four-hour surveillance because she had come up to Canada to live with us. And this is what the guy told W.: "The reason that this has happened is that friend of your wife's. Get rid of her." And so he came home and the whole world just collapsed again. They threatened me with losing my kids as well as losing my job. In fact they suggested that I give up teaching. It was "too sensitive a job" to work at.[96]

In a later interview, Lois pointed out that her husband had initiated a request for a security clearance in 1953 "because he had to be cleared for a certain level for his job and he had asked for clearance." He was asked, "Are you sure your wife is not a communist?" This question was asked because of her relationship with her woman lover, who was living with them at the time. Lois felt that, since their house was under surveillance, the state must have been aware of the relationship between her and her lover: "They must have known. They realized we had a close relationship. They were surveilling us, you know. My goodness, if they surveilled the house they had to know, you know, because we were all there living in the house" (February 22, 1995). As there was a close working relation between the FBI and the RCMP, information about Lois' lover and her connection to left-wing groups would have been supplied by the former to the latter.[97] Obviously, the security collaboration between American and Canadian agencies was one institutional network involved in the social organization of the national security regime. The Security Panel was a crucial component of this network.

THE SECURITY PANEL: "SAFETY OF THE STATE COMES FIRST" [98]

The experiences of Harold, Herbert Sutcliffe, Sue, Yvette, Albert, Hank, Robert, David, Arlene, and the others we talked to and learned from were shaped by the policies and practices of the national security regime. This regime was built on the basis of previous practices of security screening and surveillance developed in Canada in the 1920s and 1930s, which included fingerprinting in the civil service, the military, the merchant marine, and factories involved in the war effort. The target of most of this surveillance was the political left, union activists, and, in particular, the Communist Party. [99]

Key to the coordination of this regime from the 1950s through the early 1970s was the interdepartmental Security Panel, which brought together a section of the political and bureaucratic elite, including the Privy Council and members of Cabinet, the military hierarchy, and the RCMP, and extended into the management of the federal public service. Firings and transfers were carried out at the urging of the Security Panel, which existed until 1972 as a small secret committee of top civil servants, RCMP, and DND officials. In that year, the interdepartmental committee system changed. The Security Panel and the Intelligence Policy Committee were combined to form the Interdepartmental Committee on Security and Intelligence.

Established in 1946 by the Cabinet Defence Committee, the Security Panel was influenced by the Royal Commission on Espionage's (Kellock-Taschereau Commission) proposals for the increased coordination of security measures (made as a consequence of the Igor Gouzenko spy affair). [100] It was set up as an interdepartmental, advisory, and policy-making committee under the auspices of the Privy Council Office, which provides secretariat support for Cabinet and for Cabinet committees. The Security Panel formulated security policy for the approval of Cabinet and was primarily concerned with security in government departments. It was also responsible for the interpretation and application of government security policies. [101]

Initially, members of the Security Panel were the directors of intelligence of the three armed services, the director general of defence research, representatives from the Department of External Affairs, and the RCMP. The Cabinet Committee on Emergency Measures as well as the Cabinet approved the reconstitution of the Security Panel in 1953. By this point, it included representation at the level of deputy minister. The Security Panel was chaired by the secretary to the Cabinet, who reported directly to the Cabinet. Permanent representatives on the panel included the Privy Council Office and the departments of national defence and external affairs as well as the RCMP, with others occasionally present, including the deputy minister of justice. The deputy minister for external affairs would represent DL2 (the internal security arm of the DEA) at these meetings, although it depended on the specific agenda items to be discussed. DL2 had continuous contact with the Security Panel. A long-serving deputy secretary to the Cabinet, Don Wall, kept the minutes and acted as the key liaison between the Security Panel and the Cabinet.

In 1957, the membership of the Security Panel increased to include the chair of the Civil Service Commission, which expanded the national security campaigns into the civil service.[102] The 1963 Cabinet Directive on Security Clearance gave the security panel a formal part in the security screening process by requiring that the secretariat of the panel review all cases in which a department was proposing to deny an employee a security clearance. Aside from security screening policies, the Security Panel had relatively little direct impact on the security and intelligence activities of the RCMP.[103]

The organization of security networks included a series of committees and subcommittees. For example, until the formation of the Cabinet Committee on Security and Intelligence in 1963, the Security Panel reported either directly or, at times, indirectly to Cabinet.[104] With the focus on character weaknesses and on homosexuality as a security risk, a "character deviate committee of the Security Panel" was set up in the early 1960s.[105]

The Security Sub-Panel was also created to deal with more detailed problems of security and to advise the members of the Security Panel. The McDonald Commission report described the formation and work of the Security Sub-Panel: "In 1953 ... there was formed a Security Sub-Panel made up of officials from the same departments as were represented on the senior committee, but who were of lower rank. This body was chaired by an official in the Privy Council Office. The Security Sub-Panel carried out much of the preparatory work in formulating policy proposals for the Security Panel."[106] Chaired at the time by the assistant secretary to the Cabinet, the Security Sub-Panel membership included the head of the Defence Liaison Division 2 (DL2) of the DEA, the head of the Special Branch of the RCMP, the chairman of the Joint Security Committee of the Department of National Defence, the director of industrial security of the Department of Defence Production, the director of immigration of the Department of Citizenship and Immigration, and the secretary of the Security Panel. The presence of the Privy Council was felt through the secretary of the Security Sub-Panel, who was a member of its staff.[107]

The RCMP was the investigative agency for the Security Panel and was responsible for conducting security investigations under the mandate of Cabinet directives. The RCMP had the sole authority to make inquiries in all civilian departments. Nathan, a high-ranking RCMP officer in the 1950s and 1960s, described the relation between the RCMP and the Security Panel: "The RCMP was a member of the Security Panel ... Anything that was being done by the RCMP in the way of security was mainly initiated at the Security Panel. And during that time ... they had developed the policy that homosexuals should not be in security positions. Once they established the policy that homosexuals should not be in security positions the RCMP handled it and we didn't report in detail. It was left to the RCMP. And the RCMP was the operative organization because they couldn't do much about security unless it was put in the hands of the RCMP. We were a kind of focal point of most of the discussions on the Security Panel" (July 22, 1999). Each department also had its own departmental security services (e.g., the DEA's DL2), which focused on ensuring that employees of that department followed security procedures.[108]

THE PUBLIC SERVICE AND SECURITY TEXTS

The postwar expansion of bureaucratic state institutions and relations overlapped with the security purges against the left and communist organizations and against subversive "elements" in the United States and Canada. The end of the Second World War witnessed a growth in the bureaucratic state due to the expansion of state intervention in a number of social sites and the increased reliance on the production, classification, and communication of documentary information. Bureaucratic forms of administration are characterized by textual forms of communication, legalistic standards, and specialization.[109] These forms of organization were mediated through the proper interpretation and implementation of rules and regulations, which were often contained in documents. Thus, who had access to these documents became an important security question.

Security practices regarding access to information classified as secret had a particular impact on those working in the public service. A 1952 Cabinet directive declared that "loyalty to our system of government is an essential qualification for employment in the public service of Canada."[110] Homosexuality and lesbianism were constructed as a major form of disloyalty to the state and its system of government. The Canadian government, however, did not place the same emphasis on loyalty oaths as did its American counterpart.[111]

The Social Organization of Security Clearance Levels and Promotion

Terry uses the expression "loyalty-security discourse" to emphasize the interconnection between national security and the construction of loyalty.[112] National security means little without the construction of loyal subjects. Within national security discourse, the notion of security can be quite flexible, depending on the context. In relation to public servants, for example, access to secret texts is granted in a restrictive and selective manner. In the Canadian context, this often meant meeting the requirements established by the US security regime.

One crucial way in which loyalty was secured was through security screening and the organization of a series of different security clearance levels, with more rigorous security checks for higher levels. It was higher-level officials in state departments who determined the security clearance levels required for particular positions. These clearances became integral to the social organization of the public service. As state work began to rely more heavily on documents, and as these texts were classified according to various levels of secrecy, security clearances became crucial to the actual operation of the government. Moreover, Cold War mobilizations increased the need for access to secret documents from the United States, Britain, and the NATO military alliance, which came to play an important part in Canadian state formation. This was especially the case in areas relating to defence and security. Different security clearance levels resulted in the textual construction of security. The level of security clearance granted to an individual regulated her or his level of access to documents and also reflected her or his level of promotion within the public service.

Queers were often discovered in the public service and the military during security investigations relating to applications for a higher level of clearance. There was a clear relation between promotion and clearance level. Security classification levels thereby became one of the major organizing features of the national security campaigns, and this continues to the present. Before examining some of the security regime documents that describe these levels, we turn to some first-hand accounts of those who were directly affected by these security practices.

Albert described some aspects of this security process during his extensive experience as a civil servant: "There were a lot of government jobs where all you needed to do [was] a so-called name check, which for the majority of jobs was all that was required. This had to do with the degree of confidentiality you had. Then, if you were getting into areas of secret and top secret information, a more thorough examination was required, and then there was even one or two higher ratings than that. It was at these one or two higher ratings that I

The Cold War against Queers

found my employment" (October 19, 1993). When, in the late 1960s, it was discovered that Albert was gay, it was also made clear that he should not have had these higher ratings, and thus, his career was over.

Robert started as a civil servant in the Department of Manpower and Immigration and then moved into the DEA in 1968 (October 10, 1996). He had his first security check and clearance when he worked at the former: "When I went into External, they did a heavier one because I was a rotational staff member. 'Rotational staff member' means that you were postable ... so that meant that I could be posted to wherever in the world. So I had to go through the whole security clearance, and it was this long list of sheets of questions, you know, that you had to answer about yourself, your parents, your brother, your mother, your grandparents ... And then the RCMP went off and did their little check and they checked – and they talked to neighbours – [I know this] because some of the neighbours told me that they talked to them" (October 10, 1996). Robert's account gives us a sense of how extensive these security checks could be and of the concerns that arose in the DEA when staff could be posted in other countries.

Security clearance levels also affected gay men and lesbians in the military. As mentioned earlier, *Two* magazine printed an interview with George Marshall, who had been involved in *Gay,* another mid-1960s Toronto publication. Homosexuals were automatically given a special military rating, says Marshall, since, "according to government authorities [all] homosexuals are emotionally unstable – unable to accept authority, unable to tell the difference between right and wrong."[113] According to Marshall, though it was possible for privates or corporals to be closeted homosexuals because they needed only a confidential clearance, officers required a secret clearance, which meant a security check involving an RCMP investigation. Marshall repeatedly got drunk in order to avoid promotion because "promotion would mean exposure."[114] This was the strategy he employed in order to avoid being detected. When Marshall was finally processed for promotion, the RCMP investigated his life, going back a full ten years prior to his joining the army. He described the police as "pretty ruthless." He was discharged from the military.

Andrew's account of the relation between state documents and security clearance levels comes from his experiences of working as a civilian employee for the Department of National Defence in the 1980s. His account also provides a sense of what was happening during earlier years:

> It's the nature of the work that you [do that determines that you] have to have [security clearances]. Like Treasury Board reports or submissions or people's

Performance Evaluation Reports, those things were considered protected and/or confidential. But something more damaging to the security of Canada (was considered secret or even top secret) ... that is how they classify these things. Something that would present a more serious risk, that would require a secret level ... Let's say it had all been confidential classification, well, suddenly there is a document at work that has to do with some sort of missile or something, and they need people to word process that – well, they are going to have to do extra field investigations on those people, clear them for secret, and give them their secret [clearance]. And then let them work on the documents. (December 19, 1994)

When one examines the social organization of security clearance levels, it is useful to look at a 1956 document that was adopted by the Security Panel and that was published as a manual that set out policies regarding the classification of security information.[115] In its preface, Robert Bryce, the chair of the Security Panel, argued as follows: "Security means the taking of measures to prevent, or at least hinder, the collection of classified information by agents of any foreign power. These measures are also designed to prevent or hinder any unauthorized persons from having knowledge of classified information, since through ignorance, carelessness or weakness they may become channels by which classified information may reach agents of a foreign power."[116]

Here, we see that "weakness" had already been mobilized as an important security concern. The text deems security control to be a departmental responsibility, and this would have been the focus of departmental security agencies. Each department was required to appoint a security officer. As the McDonald Commission report put it with regard to the DEA:

All of the departments and agencies of the federal government have Security Officers. These Departmental Security Officers are responsible for the physical security of departmental premises, property and communications. They also have responsibilities with respect to personnel security. Decisions as to whether a person should be granted a security clearance are made by the Deputy Minister of each Department on the basis of information given to the Department by an individual applicant and information supplied by the RCMP Security Service. Departmental Security Officers co-ordinate this security clearance process within each department [DL2] ... The security and intelligence responsibility of the Department of External Affairs is carried out by three components of the Department: (a) the Security Division and (b) the Intelligence Analysis Division

... and (c) the Bureau of Economic Intelligence ... The Security Division of the Department of External Affairs has responsibilities which are closely related to the RCMP Security Service ... The National Security section of the Security Division has the most extensive links with the RCMP Security Service.[117]

At this point there were four classifications for documents: top secret, secret, confidential, and restricted. These classifications were generally recognized by NATO and were used within the Canadian state (again displaying the linkages between Canadian state formation and international security alliances). Texts were to be classified as top secret "when their security aspect [was] paramount and when their unauthorized disclosure would [have] cause[d] exceptionally grave damage to the nation."[118] These included defence documents, texts on munitions of war, and those on defence alliances. Texts were to be classified as secret "when their unauthorized disclosure would endanger national security, cause serious injury to the interests or prestige of the nation, or would be a substantial advantage to a foreign power."[119] These included minutes or records of Cabinet meetings, documents pertaining to negotiations with foreign powers, particulars of the national budget, new scientific and technical developments regarding defence, and/or the identity or composition of scientific or military units. Texts were to be classified as confidential "when their unauthorized disclosure would be prejudicial to the interests or prestige of the nation, would cause damage to an individual, and would be an advantage to a foreign power."[120] These included information of a personal or disciplinary nature and minutes or records of interdepartmental committees that were not sensitive enough to be classified under other categories. Finally, texts were to be classified as restricted when they were "not [to] be published or communicated to anyone except for official purposes, and when they [were] not classified in any of the three previous categories."[121]

On the security of staff, the text stated: "Security in the public service of Canada is essentially a part of good administration, which may be placed in jeopardy either by persons who are disloyal or by persons who are unreliable because of defects in their character ... It is also essential that persons whose defects of character may lead to indiscretion or dishonesty, or may make them likely subjects of blackmail, be denied access to classified information."[122] Character defects or weaknesses were deployed as an important security concern, which, in turn, was integral to "good administration."

These security concerns were cited as the reason why the government performed background checks. Under the Civil Service Act, civil servants had to swear an oath of allegiance and sign the Official Secrets Act, 1939, which covered not only "the period of employment but also [the time] after employment with the department has ceased."[123] The manual stresses that, "when new employees are engaged, security regulations and practices should be thoroughly explained, together with the reasons behind them" and that periodic lectures and courses should be given to all departmental and agency security officers. If a breach of security occurred, it was the departmental security officer's responsibility to ensure "whether or not there [was] any indication of malicious intent." In the event that malicious intent was proven, these officials were instructed to contact the RCMP, Special Branch, and were to "take every possible precaution to ensure that the person or persons suspected [were] not alerted."[124] It was left to the security officer's discretion to decide whether or not the RCMP should be called in.

Initially, a security clearance level request of confidential or restricted led to a simple record check. This entailed a criminal record check and a search of RCMP files to determine whether the person in question had any link to subversive organizations. These procedures could potentially uncover homosexuals if they had been charged for violating legislation regarding sex acts. For secret and top secret clearances, a record check and a field investigation into the employee's past was initiated. Former employees and people closely connected to the person were contacted and interviewed.[125]

A 1964 document on the security screening of public service employees reported that, for access to top secret information, "a fingerprint check, a subversive indices check and a field investigation" were required. For secret information, the investigation included a "fingerprint and subversive indices check"; if "derogatory" information were uncovered during the record check, "a background investigation [would] be conducted."[126] Similar procedures applied to people employed in defence industry and related work. The manual pointed out that, "because of Canada's participation in NATO and close alliance with the United States and the United Kingdom in defence and research, the Force [i.e., the RCMP] has certain commitments in the security screening field that allow more latitude in the scope of our operations." It stressed that "the security status of an individual is determined not only by his political reliability but also by his character" and that RCMP divisions were responsible for "determining if there [was] any indication of general deviation, particularly homosexuality, on the part of the applicant or spouse; sexual deviates are potential targets for blackmail and, as such, poor security risks."[127] These were some of the crucial ways in which security was performed and accomplished in the public service.

An article from a right-wing US publication reprinted in the *Civil Service News* in 1956 provides a useful account of the security screening process.[128] According to this article, the security investigations were carried out by the Special Branch of the RCMP, which became the Directorate of Security and Intelligence in 1956. It offered the following description: "Among those subject to investigation are approximately 140,000 classified civil servants, many thousands of others who work for private industrial firms handling defence contracts and members of the armed forces. Agents of the Special Branch dig into almost every facet of an employee's past and present behaviour. The civil servant's personnel file, listing former jobs and places of residence over a 10 year period, is only a starting point."[129]

The article points to the importance of the documentary files and records integral to the work of the security regime: "Police agents talk with former employers and fellow employees. They interview neighbours, social acquaintances, and old schoolmates. They dig into the employee's political leanings, go back to his school days to find out whether he belonged to left-wing groups and how much leftist beliefs rubbed off on the mature man. Debts and ability to pay them are investigated to determine whether an offer of money might tempt an employee. How much and on what occasions does the employee drink – and does he talk too much when under the influence of two or three cocktails?"[130] Sexuality is brought into focus after the employee's financial situation and drinking habits, which are categorized as moral or character failings, are discussed: "Is there anything unusual in his sex habits? How does he spend his leisure time? What clubs and organizations does he belong to? Any phase of the man's life that might make him subject to pressure is probed. Investigation extends even to the civil servant's relatives and to the relatives of his wife."[131]

Many aspects of a person's life were judged to be important enough to investigate for security reasons: no personal realm was considered off limits. Individuals being promoted were reinvestigated, and according to the article, employees in "sensitive posts [were] re-checked at intervals of not more than five years."[132]

Generally, the security regime in Canada placed more emphasis on secrecy and secret proceedings than did its counterpart in the United States, where, during the McCarthy years, the House Committee on Un-American Activities turned a public spotlight on the state's questions regarding disloyalty. While there were major problems with these witch hunts, the security campaigns in the United States had a more public character than those in Canada, and this allowed for limited possibilities to challenge the proceedings and to appeal decisions. In the more secretive Canadian system, which was based largely on

British procedures, there were no grounds for appeal until the 1960s. This secrecy, produced through different historical strategies of state formation, also meant that there was even less respect for the individual's right to appeal in the Canadian context than there was in the American context.

The same article points out that these security procedures were initially set up under Louis St. Laurent, who was minister of justice during the 1946 royal commission hearings into the Gouzenko affair. St. Laurent, who later became prime minister, explained that the appeal procedure was deliberately rejected because "this matter of confidence in the reliability of others [was] not something that [could] be decided as a result of a trial," which is what would, in effect, result from a hearing on specific charges. When doubts were raised about reliability, the official view was as follows: "It is not possible to give the individual the benefit of the doubt. In the view of Canadian officials, as explained to critics in the House of Commons, the government must feel strongly confident that its secrets are safe – and the Cabinet believes this undercover system best assures safety. The Government operates on the theory that it is impossible to detect and eliminate all foreign spies. Consequently, it feels, it must be sure that spies' sources of information inside the Government are dried up."[133]

THE OFFICIAL STORY OF HOW THE CANADIAN SECURITY REGIME CAME TO FOCUS ON HOMOSEXUALS

Clearly, there were security investigations before the 1950s that touched on same-gender sexuality. For instance, while attending a Canadian religious university during the Second World War, one man commented that he liked men, and this was enough to make him a "suspect," as it called into question his moral character.[134] But, in Canada, the focus on homosexuals as a major national security threat did not really develop until the late 1950s.

How is it that, in Canada, the major campaign against queers took place from 1958-59 on, whereas in the United States it began much earlier, roughly in the late 1940s and early 1950s?[135] In North America, the national security regimes' focus on homosexuality emerges unevenly. According to David K. Johnson, the purges in the US State Department began in the late 1940s and continued at an intense pace until at least 1958.[136] In Britain, they developed in the mid- to late 1950s.[137]

We are not suggesting that anti-gay security investigations did not exist in Canada prior to 1958. Clearly, there were many (e.g., the 1952 prohibition on homosexuals entering the country). Yet, in 1958-59, a more specific focus on

The Cold War against Queers

homosexuality as a national security threat developed, and the concept of character weakness was homosexualized. One reason for this was that the RCMP had developed a separate filing system for suspected homosexuals.[138] And this textual separation of suspected homosexuals from others perceived as security risks was a main feature of the security regime.

Canadian state formation related to national security during these years was affected not only by developments south of the border but also by the continuing influence of Britain. This British influence was one of the reasons that the focus on queers as a national security threat developed later in Canada than it did in the United States. The highly publicized spy scandals involving Guy Burgess and Donald Maclean, not scrutinized as "homosexual" in character until the mid- to late 1950s, also affected Canadian security policies. At the same time, Canadian national security hinged on communication networks and the sharing of security information with Britain and the United States, which, effectively, meant that anti-homosexual national security developments in these countries were embraced by Canadian state officials. This was crucial to maintaining the flow of security information.

In 1952, Cabinet Directive 24 introduced the distinction between loyalty and reliability in the Canadian context. Disloyalty involved membership in the Communist Party or Marxist organizations, whereas unreliability "referred to 'defects' of character that might lead an employee to be indiscreet, dishonest or vulnerable to blackmail." The directive went on to produce the standard line, reported earlier, regarding the Soviet shift towards "the exploitation of the vulnerabilities of individuals rather than their ideological principles."[139]

With regard to who was perceived as a security threat, there was a growing separation between those ideologically committed to the Soviet Union, such as communists and "fellow travellers" (the earlier targets), and those who suffered from character weakness. Concern with the latter had always been present in the security campaigns, but, in the 1950s, these people gradually emerged as a distinct and major security threat.[140] By mid-decade, reports within national security circles claimed that the Soviet Committee for State Security (KGB) had begun to realize that there were not enough ideologically driven people to provide it with information and that, therefore, other avenues of recruitment had to be developed. The KGB, it was argued, was refocusing on the development of entrapment and surveillance schemes, especially with regard to detecting homosexuality and other character weaknesses. In spite of the lack of evidence, this ideological assumption informed security regime discussions.

Building on security approaches from the 1950s, the McDonald Commission report recounted that

With the change in the international climate there were indications that the Soviet bloc intelligence agencies were altering their method of recruiting spies abroad. A 1955 Royal Commission Report in Australia and two US Congressional Committees indicated that the Communist intelligence services were relying upon the exploitation of the vulnerabilities of individuals rather than their ideological principles. Homosexuality was a form of behaviour thought to be particularly vulnerable to blackmail. Compromise techniques followed by blackmail and attempted recruitment had been used by the Soviets against several homosexuals in the Canadian government. As a consequence of this change in tactics by the hostile intelligence agencies, the RCMP's Security and Intelligence Directorate began a Canada-wide programme of collecting information about homosexuals.[141]

In March 1956, a British conference of privy councillors on security highlighted "Soviet attention to the blackmailable practice of homosexuality."[142] With regard to this "Canada-wide programme," the McDonald Commission commented:

> This programme began as a result of reports in the mid-1950s that the Communist bloc Intelligence services were involved in operations to recruit homosexuals with access to classified information. By the late 1950s a seven-man team was established to investigate homosexuals in sensitive government positions. In 1960 a special squad of investigators was established to interview homosexuals in Ottawa not in the government. On the basis of interviews and Morality Squad records, the Security Service had, by the 1960s, a fairly thorough knowledge of the members of the homosexual community. Because of the effectiveness of these investigations the teams of investigators were gradually reduced.[143]

This special squad of investigators was likely the beginning of the character weaknesses subdivision of the Directorate of Security and Intelligence (DSI). The assertion that, by the 1960s, the Security Service had a fairly thorough knowledge of the "homosexual community" is undermined by the non-cooperation and resistance that it also encountered. Although the number of people in the character weaknesses subdivision was reduced, this did not seem to adversely affect the RCMP investigations. It did, however, affect the allocation of resources, and it also meant that officers in other positions became involved in the surveillance of homosexuals.

In an effort to explain how foreign spy agencies began to turn their attention towards government workers who had "deviant characteristics that were regarded as unsociable," Robert Bryce, chair of the Security Panel, offered this recollection:

> There was also the problem of whether there were things in their behaviour or character that made them susceptible to blackmail. This was one of the less understood risks, but we had learned through other security services as well as through some experience that this was an important risk, especially an important risk of people going behind the Iron Curtain because the Russian and Allied government were very skilful in exploiting these people. They would get them in compromising situations, take pictures of them and then bring pressure to bear on them. Well, as a result of this, people who had any deviant characteristics that were regarded as unsociable, you know, that they would not want to have made known, were regarded as risks themselves.[144]

Bryce argued that homosexuals were considered the most serious of these blackmailable cases, although he never offered any evidence that they were caught in compromising situations. Instead, he cited an example of one gay man who revealed himself to authorities:

> The largest of those groups and the most serious problems were the homosexuals because in those days, it is hard to realize it now in the era of gay rights and gay militancy, but in those days it was a very serious thing for many men – found out to be practising homosexuals. Well, we tried to find ... answers to these problems [that] would be consistent with the kind of life these people were leading and that would not expose them to blackmail. In a number of cases, I can well remember one in a unit for which I was responsible where we decided to continue employing a homosexual, who was openly a homosexual, or at least open to us. He informed us of the nature of his living arrangements ... [and] we said you can continue working where you are but on the condition that you don't go abroad because there are places where there are traps made for people like you, and if you are caught in one of those traps you don't know what sort of pressure will be brought to bear by other countries.[145]

Bryce makes reference to a later sorting out of this problem, adding that state agencies solicited the assistance of medical professionals: "Well, gradually these things sorted themselves out, but these cases of homosexuals were very difficult cases to handle because ... there were enough of them to be a problem not in terms of aggregate numbers but in terms of important jobs they occupied, some of them in, say, senior positions ... And we tried to get the help of psychiatrists and psychologists and all that sort of thing; this was only to understand it rather than to try to cure it."[146] Bryce put a rather liberal spin on his recounting of the national security campaigns against queers (which, of course, were never intended to help homosexuals). Don Wall, who, for much of the late 1950s and 1960s, was secretary to the Security Panel, also offered a liberal retrospective:

> The government was becoming ... increasingly concerned with the problem with homosexuals in the public service and in sensitive positions. The old procedure tended to be if a guy was found to be a homosexual in a sensitive position he was fired. That's that. He was simply told, "We have found out about the nature of your private life and it does not rack up with your job so out you go." We lost some very good people as a result of this, some very talented people indeed. I remember people being increasingly concerned about this, including the then prime minister Mr. Diefenbaker – who ask[ed] the Security Panel to see if it were not possible to devise a means of dealing with this problem that was fair and more humane ... and at the same time preserve some of the talent that was going down the drain simply because one guy was found out to be slightly different in his sexual habits than most people.[147]

Nathan, reiterating this institutional language, commented:

> We were interested in homosexuals in security positions and the reason was because we had learned from experience, mostly experiences of other security services, that they would become or were targets of the KGB. And if they were not in security positions they were in a position where they were likely to be promoted into security positions. So if they were close to those security positions they were of interest to us. We were not concerned about the morals of homosexuality, we were concerned about the possibilities of them being compromised, blackmailed, and becoming agents of the KGB. That was basically the interest of the RCMP ... I am glad of the opportunity to say so because everyone thought we were on a wild chase and it was great sport for us to do this, whereas there was something very serious and proper about it. (July 22, 1999)

Nathan also described the connections between the Security Panel and the RCMP when it came to homosexuals: "I think that the interest in the Security Panel was brought about by the interest of the RCMP in reporting to the Security Panel. I went into the Security Service ... in the late 1950s, and we were fairly aware at that time of the danger of homosexuals in security positions within the government ... We were conscious of KGB activities and the danger of homosexuals in security positions. And I don't know the numbers involved, but there were quite a few" (July 22, 1999).

Following up these general concerns regarding the danger presented by queers, we now look at two incidents: the first is an RCMP account of a DEA investigation involving the Canadian embassy in Moscow that resulted in the discovery of homosexuals in the civil service in Canada and abroad; the second is a murder investigation on Canada's west coast that resulted in both the RCMP and the military recognizing the scope of the homosexual "problem." These two incidents – one external, the other internal – became interwoven as the security regime's focus shifted to the danger of homosexuality.

FOCUSING ON CHARACTER WEAKNESSES

In 1949, the RCMP reported that, in its first batch of security investigations after the Gouzenko affair, of 213 adverse reports only 27 involved "political subversion." The remaining 87 percent of these cases involved character weakness or moral flaws.[148] Shortly after the passage of the 1952 Canadian immigration law prohibiting the immigration of homosexuals, a new Cabinet directive (number 24) was issued.[149] This was reiterated three years later in Cabinet Directive 29, which argued that "such defects of character may also make them unsuitable for employment on grounds other than security."[150]

In a general sense, "defects of character" made homosexuals unsuitable employees on grounds other than those directly mandated by national security concerns. Deputy Minister of Justice Wilbur R. Jacket expressed this position at a 1959 Security Panel meeting during a discussion on homosexuals as security risks. According to the minutes, Jacket "considered character weaknesses to be of concern in the public service from the general point of view of good administration and not exclusively from the security point of view."[151] This argument continued to be reasserted throughout the national security campaigns against queers.

According to John Sawatsky, in Canada, one of the earliest dismissals of homosexuals on national security grounds occurred in 1952 in the Communications Branch:

A homosexual was discovered working in a middle-management position at Canada's most secret institution, the Communications Branch, which intercepted radio signals ... The individual's loyalty or honesty were never in doubt, but the authorities feared more than anything that the Americans would find out, thus jeopardizing the arrangements for shared intelligence, which would be a severe blow since Canada received more than it gave. The case was investigated personally by George McClellan, then head of Special Branch, and the man, who admitted his homosexuality, was asked to resign. There was no attempt to transfer him into a nonsensitive position elsewhere in the civil service.[152]

That this individual was discovered in the Communications Branch was significant, given how central this branch was to maintaining security information links with the United States and Britain.

In 1956, discussion at a Security Sub-Panel meeting centred on how to proceed regarding an employee who was working on a classified contract for the construction of the mid-Canada radar warning line. In his personal history, this person had not revealed that he had recently been released from a penitentiary, where he had served time for having committed a homosexual offence. Again, we see a connection between policing and the courts, which reveals how the national security campaigns were tied into broader aspects of sexual regulation and policing. The Security Sub-Panel decided to recommend that the director of industrial security assess the security risk involved in the man's continued employment on the radar project, in the event that the firm in question agreed to keep him.[153] In the late 1950s, the DEA received a copy of a Soviet intelligence training manual that described techniques for blackmailing people who had character weaknesses.[154] At the same time, a 1958 Security Panel memo mentioned that there were no cases of a homosexual having committed an act of treason under the threat of blackmail.[155]

By the late 1950s, the Canadian government claimed to have its own example of apparent Soviet-bloc attempts to capitalize on same-gender sex. In security circles, a story began to circulate that, in the Soviet Union, for the purposes of blackmail, Soviet intelligence had set up and photographed a Canadian official in the course of a homosexual encounter. The Canadian official involved did not capitulate but, instead, reported the incident to his superiors. Yet, this story was used to emphasize the danger of homosexuality as a security risk and to raise the question that similar operations might exist to compromise Canadian representatives.

The RCMP responded to the threat by forming a special squad of investigators in A Division and a separate filing system at headquarters to identify homosexuals in the government service and to inform appropriate department heads of those posing a security risk.

The Cold War against Queers

At the same time, Prime Minister Diefenbaker directed the government's Security Panel to consider whether and in what way it might be possible to treat cases of character weakness differently from those involving ideological beliefs, without weakening security safeguards. In light of the efforts of Soviet-bloc espionage apparently shifting from relying on ideological sympathies to exploiting human frailties, this proposition was rejected, though not without reservations on the part of some deputy ministers. One official thought it possible that excluding homosexuals from posts involving the handling of classified information might deprive the government service of brilliant individuals whose homosexuality would be more than adequately neutralized by their proven discretion.[156] As the number of apparent and suspected homosexual public servants threatened to be in the thousands, in 1960 the RCMP asked the Security Panel to provide explicit and effective guidelines on investigating and reporting procedures.[157]

The only case cited in the official history of the RCMP regarding a homosexual being caught in a surveillance scheme occurred in 1962 in Moscow; this involved British Admiralty clerk W.J.C. Vassall. Vassall maintained that "his actions were caused by blackmail procedures used by Soviet agents to take advantage of his homosexuality."[158] This report expresses frustration with the Security Panel and government policy, which prevented the RCMP from going further in its campaign against gays and lesbians: "The RCMP holding to a similar attitude on the importance of screening for exploitable character weaknesses, nevertheless, could not get from the Security Panel any further rigorous guidelines such as they had requested in 1960 to assist them in devising adequate screening measures. Character weaknesses and homosexuality in particular, remained obvious matters of security risk which however evidently suggested enough uncomfortable questions about civil liberties to impede the imposition of the full extent of procedure necessary to maximize security."[159]

DAVID JOHNSON AND THE CIPHER CLERK

An attempted blackmail case at the Canadian embassy in Moscow mentioned in the official history of the RCMP is also discussed by John Sawatsky and Dean Beeby.[160] Sawatsky reports that, in the early 1960s, the RCMP was given evidence of KGB operations against the Canadian embassy in Moscow, including a blackmail operation against a homosexual Canadian ambassador.[161] This ignited an important security investigation.

Originally, the RCMP thought this was a reference to David Johnson, who was ambassador to the USSR from 1956 to 1960, since he had been identified as a homosexual two years earlier. Johnson was recalled from Moscow and was summarily dismissed in 1960 as part of a broader purging of the Canadian embassy in Moscow. He helped to precipitate his own exposure by the open manner in which he handled the case of one of his embassy clerks, who had fallen into a KGB homosexual surveillance trap. Johnson followed procedure and returned the clerk to Canada to be investigated. The DEA fired the cipher clerk, who apparently revealed that the ambassador was also a homosexual. He talked to the RCMP about his past, produced an address book, and divulged information about his relationships stretching back to his years in Ottawa. Many of his partners were apparently civil servants, some of whom had been in sensitive positions and who had access to secret information. His contacts likely included the DEA's John Holmes. This suggests that part of the problem for the national security regime was that this clerk had had relationships with civil servants who had received high-level security clearances.

Sam, a DEA official who left the department in 1958, described this situation:

> We have to turn to the story of the embassy clerk. He had been picked up or picked up a Soviet citizen at the ballet ... and they had had sex together and then the clerk had been passed on to another Soviet citizen, who was in contact with the Soviet Security system. This was a piece of entrapment, and there are a number of links ... The first contact was someone who was not in the security services for the Soviet Union. Now, after the clerk had been passed on a couple of times, the Soviet security circles took photographs of him with a sexual partner in bed in a hotel in Moscow. And then when they tried to put the screws on, the clerk was at the home ... outside Moscow of one of the gay Soviet citizens, and while there a Soviet commissar came with the photographs and he then made it plain that they wanted something, they ... were after information ... There is no doubt that the Soviet Secret Services at this point in time were attempting to use blackmail against gay men in the foreign services of NATO countries. However, there is one thing that I don't think ever came out. In spite of that entrapment and that effort at blackmail, there was no case where a Canadian diplomat, either an officer or member of his staff, buckled under. There is no evidence for the transfer of secret information. (October 9, 1998)

Sam emphasized that, despite all the official concerns over blackmail, there was no case of a homosexual diplomat or a member of the diplomatic corps ever having been successfully blackmailed. He continued, "Now, the clerk went to the ambassador, who was David Johnson. David Johnson, who was himself gay, sent the clerk back to Ottawa. Now, I knew at the time that John Holmes had a sexual affair with this member of the staff at the Canadian Embassy, and I can only surmise that, although the clerk didn't succumb to Soviet pressure, he did give the RCMP quite a few names of gay members of the Department of External Affairs, either in embassies abroad or in Canada" (October 9, 1998).

This is the case referred to in the RCMP's official history. What is particularly striking is the importance of lists of names and address books to its surveillance work. Soon after the RCMP interrogations of this clerk, the Security Service investigation swept through the public service, especially the DEA.

JOHN WATKINS: DYING DURING INTERROGATION

The RCMP eventually discovered that its clues did not lead to Johnson since new Soviet defectors identified the source as predating him. The RCMP then went after John Watkins, who was ambassador to Moscow from 1954 to 1956.

In 1948, Watkins was posted to Moscow as chargé d'affaires. In 1951, he came back to Canada due to illness but returned to Moscow during 1954-56 as ambassador. According to John Starnes, "during this period, Soviet Intelligence tried unsuccessfully to entrap Watkins because of his homosexual leanings ... I was as surprised and shocked at the unwelcome news as any of John's friends."[162] Sawatsky tells us that, shortly after his posting to Moscow, the Soviet security service became aware of his homosexuality and that he had had an affair with a Russian. Soviet agents then arranged to photograph an encounter between Watkins and this Russian and to use the photos to pressure him into revealing information. Watkins neither gave in to this pressure nor informed the DEA about it. He admitted having a homosexual liaison but denied that the blackmail had succeeded.[163]

Still, Watkins was caught in the RCMP's surveillance net. The series of RCMP interrogations, nearly a month long, focused on Watkins' sexual activities and the contacts he made while working as a civil servant. On October 12, 1964, he died of a sudden heart attack in the midst of one of these RCMP interrogations in a Montreal Holiday Inn.[164] Since the coroner did not know that Watkins had been in police custody at the time of his death, no autopsy or inquest was performed.[165] Accounts of what happened to Watkins, written by Ian Adams and later by David Martin, John Sawatsky, and Chapman Pincher, led to calls in the House of Commons for an inquest. Such an inquest was called by the Quebec government in 1980.[166] The RCMP refused to release a full report of the interrogation that led to Watkins' death. Leslie James Bennett, who directed the interrogation, was unwilling to come to Canada from Australia, where he had retired, to testify. Coroner Stanislas Dery ruled that the diplomat's death was due to "natural causes." And, because he permitted no inquiries regarding why the RCMP was questioning Watkins, he thereby limited the scope of the inquest.[167]

Watkins never succumbed to Soviet blackmail, but the pressure exerted by RCMP interrogators was more than he could bear. John Starnes remembers that "both of the experienced RCMP investigators, Harry Brandes and Jim Bennett, reported that there was no evidence to suggest Watkins had been a traitor."[168] Nathan offered the following:

> I liked Watkins but we had certain information that bothered us ... I don't know what it was that triggered it ... but we decided that Watkins should be interviewed. Watkins had heart trouble and had retired ... He came back to Canada and it was understood that we would interview him. Jim Bennett was a civilian employee of the Force. Jim was very knowledgeable [about] counter-espionage ... Anyway, he was being interviewed, and as far as we were concerned the interview was progressing very nicely ... He was giving us perhaps not the specific knowledge, but he was giving something on which we could base a conclusion with some certainty. And of course we were conscious of the fact that he had a heart condition, and we were just interviewing him in relays of short periods – then he would go and rest, then he would come back. And of course we wanted to keep him alive as long as possible and we didn't want to do anything to create a heart attack ... We were proceeding with this interrogation, and then of course he had a heart attack [from] which he died. When it was reported that he had died, my first suggestion to them was this: "Get in touch with a coroner immediately." In other words, under those circumstances it would be easy to accuse us of a cover-up and so on ... because we had killed the guy or we had done something. Get in touch with, and cooperate with, the coroner as fully as you can. We concluded that Watkins was not a formal KBG agent. He didn't have to be. He was manipulated sufficiently by the KGB [so that] they didn't have to recruit him. They didn't have to go that far because they could manipulate him in any way they wanted. (July 22, 1999)

In this account, the RCMP's responsibility for creating the context in which Watkins died is obscured.

Throughout the 1950s and early 1960s, as its capacities for social surveillance and policing increased, the RCMP learned more about homosexual individuals and networks. The new national security focus on homosexuality was not based solely on information from the homosexual cipher clerk sent back

The Cold War against Queers

from Moscow; it was also grounded in military and RCMP investigations in Canada. In part, the anti-homosexual security campaign was a response to the emergence of more visible gay and lesbian networks not only in larger Canadian urban centres but also within the public service and the military. Many in state, defence, and policing circles viewed this as a threat.

With the expansion of gay networks, the security campaign, especially as carried out through the activities of the RCMP, began discovering far more homosexuals than it could handle. In 1961, in a paper by William H. Kelly, then assistant director of security and intelligence, we find this comment: "Our limited investigations to date have shown that the homosexual community is much larger than had been anticipated."[169]

THE LEO MANTHA–AARON JENKINS CONNECTION: STARTING A PURGE CAMPAIGN ON THE WEST COAST

In light of the security regime's emerging focus on character weaknesses and homosexuality, we asked whether, in the late 1950s, there might have been some particular event or series of events that prompted the RCMP and the Security Panel to pay more attention to "the homosexual" as a security threat. We argue that there is a link between the investigations following the murder of Aaron (Bud) Jenkins by his estranged boyfriend Leo Mantha on September 6, 1958, in the Nelles block of the HMCS *Naden* naval base in Esquimalt, British Columbia, and the sharper focus on homosexuals as a security threat. Mantha was the last person to be hanged in British Columba, and this occurred on April 28, 1959. While discussions to clarify the Security Panel's policies regarding character weaknesses were initiated prior to the Jenkins murder, Wall's report, presented on May 12, 1959, indicated a specific mobilization against homosexuals.[170]

Mantha was born in 1926 in a working-class suburb in Montreal.[171] After completing Grade 8 at the age of fifteen, he left school and began to work in a munitions plant. He worked in the plant for one year and then moved on to work for the Canadian National Railways (CNR), first in the office and then at the shops located in Pointe St. Charles, a west-end suburb on the island of Montreal. It was while working at the CNR at the age of sixteen that he had his first sexual encounter. During an interview with a psychologist while in prison, Mantha was asked about his relationship with women. In a frank admission of his sexuality, he explained that he had never experienced any serious feelings or relationships with women, with the exception of a Montreal woman whom he said he liked more as a "kid sister." His feelings towards men were an entirely different story: "Yes, I tried lots of women but attempts at intercourse were never satisfactory and I gave it up. Yes, had erections but wouldn't last – yes, get erections easily in homosex, too easily – even talking about it with a fellow."[172]

Mantha's sexual adventures became more pronounced once he joined the RCN. He would often seek out gay bars and clubs, especially in San Francisco and other foreign ports, where he would get drunk and have sex. He regularly frequented a bar in the Empress Hotel in Victoria. Mantha had been discharged from the navy in 1956, partly for his homosexuality.[173] In a report written by a medical officer, we learn about Mantha's violent encounter with another man, which is what led to the military's discovery of his homosexuality: "In 1955, during a twenty-four hour binge in San Francisco, Leo made a pass at a man who did not appreciate the gesture. He was beaten up and woke up with a massive scalp wound. After the injury he began to experience chills, fevers and headaches. He checked himself into the military hospital at Esquimalt, and during neurological tests doctors discovered his homosexual depression and his deep-seated feelings of 'inferiority and inadequacy.'" As his doctors informed the naval brass, "Obviously the service is the last place in the world for a man with this sort of conflict."[174]

However, the incident that would dramatically change Mantha's life had yet to occur. Donald Perry, a gay bartender at the Empress Hotel and cousin to Aaron Jenkins, introduced Mantha to Jenkins in the summer of 1958. At this point, Mantha was working on a tugboat. In his final interview with Dr. J.P.S. Cathcart, Mantha recalled that he had never before been "involved so deeply (affectionately) with anyone as with Jenkins and it had been going on that way for a month, from day to day, we were going steady for 3 or 4 months, yes, having relations regularly. I was getting pretty mixed up at the time – yes, drink and sex and very little sleep."[175]

The military psychiatric evaluation of Mantha centred on his homosexuality, which it defined as a sickness that he could not control: "His troubles are entirely psychiatric and revolve principally around a mental conflict due to homosexual tendencies. The homosexual tendency is present continually but he finds that he can keep it under control in normal circumstances, however, if he gets drunk he feels he may give way to his suppressed desires."[176]

This military medical and psychiatric discourse gives us some indication of how homosexuals were diagnosed during this period. During the murder trial, navy psychiatrist Douglas Alcorn was called in to diagnose Mantha, whom he testified was suffering from Kempf's disease (otherwise known as "homosexual panic"):

The Cold War against Queers

He has shown the features that I encounter frequently in homosexuals. These are that the individual only with the greatest degree of mental effort secures control. Society expects from the homosexual a degree of chastity and a total deprivation of any expression of their emotional drives that would under other circumstances only be expected from a person who had taken a vow of celibacy. This results in time in gross mental disturbances. In some instances these amount to such disturbance that a name, Kemp's [sic] disease, has actually been given to it ... [This manifests itself in] an acute state of panic, fear or rage that occurs in homosexuals. During this period the patient is capable of violence directed both towards himself and to other people; other times, Kemps [sic] disease is characterized by ungovernable rage, mainly fear or panic.[177]

Alcorn drew on current psychological and psychiatric knowledge and its use in the United States.

Jenkins was born in 1935 in Coles Valley, Nova Scotia. He completed Grade 11 at age eighteen and aspired to be a teacher; however, he was unable to enter teachers' college.[178] Before he joined the RCN in June 1956, he worked as a clerk for the Royal Bank but quit because of long hours and low pay. According to a June 1956 document entitled "Personnel Selection Board," Jenkins joined the navy because he could not find a job and he needed money. He thought that if he did not like the navy he could simply leave, but he soon discovered that this was not the case. This same document describes Jenkins as "immature, highly effeminate and emotionally unstable." It continues, "He is quite unsuitable for Service. He is quite intelligent and likely able, but wonder if men would like to have him around. He is very unhappy at present. He understands grounds are missing for his release but is going to apply for it. Assessment – very poor recruit."[179]

By October 1956, Jenkins had been transferred from HMCS *Brunswicker* to HMCS *Cornwallis*. One of his superiors on the *Cornwallis* recorded a change in Jenkins' attitude towards the navy: "[He began to] like the Service and to look forward to his work in the Supply Branch. I feel that he is very well suited to be a PW."[180] His second assessment was conducted while on the HMCS *Hochelaga* in April 1957 and again on the HMCS *Naden* in March 1958. His assessments describe a person who was "well-mannered," a "steady-type," and good at his job as a pay writer.

However, documents generated between these dates show a different story. On July 18, 1957, Jenkins was referred to Alcorn after complaining of "personal problems." In his consultant's report and under "COMPLAINT," Alcorn typed, "he is a homosexual and cannot get along in the Navy."[181] Alcorn's commentary, based on a medicalized model of homosexuality as abnormal, emphasizes language associated with gender inversion. After providing a brief history of Jenkins' childhood experiences of being called a "sissy," getting along with girls, and not having the same interest as boys his own age, Alcorn labelled him as a "homosexual of the feminine type." He also reported that Jenkins "dressed in" and "prefers" women's clothing and that he would "rather have liked to have been a woman."

Another important aspect of Jenkins' psychiatric assessment involves the details that Alcorn compiled as part of his patient's "history." For example, his notes reveal the gay network that Jenkins belonged to while living in New Brunswick, duly noting Jenkins' encounters in Sussex and then again in Saint John. A second consultant's report dated November 1, 1957, continues to outline Jenkins' sexual activities and encounters, this time under the heading "PROGRESS REPORT." Alcorn reported that, while on a trip back from a stay in New Brunswick, Jenkins made stops in Boston, Buffalo, and Chicago, where "he found that all he had to do was wear his sailor's uniform on the street to make contacts with homosexuals and generally had an exciting time."[182] Alcorn's concluding remarks warned that Jenkins' life might be in danger if he continued to serve, and he held that "grave consideration should be given to his discharge on executive grounds, as he will almost certainly not be able to complete his term of Service under the circumstances."[183]

The incidents that led to Jenkins' murder are obscured by the various legal and medical discourses that are used to describe Mantha and what happened on the night he stabbed Jenkins at the Esquimalt base. In the interview with Cathcart, Mantha blamed Wagner, also a sailor, for the breakup with Jenkins. Mantha recounted how, a week before the stabbing, he and Jenkins were having many arguments due to a sexual encounter between Jenkins and Wagner during a party Jenkins had organized. It was on the following Friday that Jenkins tried to break off his relationship with Mantha. According to Mantha: "[He told me that I] was just a sucker, that he was just taking me for everything I had. We use to go out a lot and I would usually foot the bill, well, he was trying to tell me that he was no longer interested in me. He was telling me that he was 'commercial' a term we use (a professional homosex whore). Yes, it hurt my feelings – yes, I was hurt to the core."

During his trial, Mantha's defence lawyer, George F. Gregory, relied heavily on an understanding of homosexuality as a mental illness. Nancy Renwick argues that, although the prosecution led by Lloyd McKenzie tried to paint Mantha as a cold-blooded killer intent on inflicting a fatal blow, Mantha's lawyer portrayed the homosexual relationship between the two men as the true culprit behind the killing.[184] Gregory used the existing social and psychiatric theories about homosexuals as emotionally disturbed to show that Mantha's behaviour was the result of rage over Jenkins' rejection. Gregory argued that, due to his alcohol consumption and "homosexual tendencies," Mantha was incapable of the premeditation that was necessary to argue for the death penalty. According to Renwick, although homosexuality did not figure prominently in newspaper accounts of the trial, when it was mentioned it was constantly linked to mental illness.[185]

Gregory used testimonies and reports from Alcorn and psychologist W.H. Gaddes to substantiate his defence. Alcorn testified that, because of the immense stresses that homosexuals felt in a society that was hostile towards them, they were more prone than were heterosexuals to "outbursts of rage, panic and fear."[186] In his report, Gaddes described Mantha as an "inadequate neurotic rather than [an] inadequate psychopath." In his remarks to the jury, Justice J.G. Ruttan reminded them that they were not dealing with an "ordinary human being, but with an 'abnormal' one."[187]

Mantha and Robert Chapman, another man convicted of murder, were scheduled to be executed together. Chapman's death penalty, however, was commuted by John Diefenbaker's Cabinet four days before he was to die. In an article written forty years after Mantha's execution, Pat Johnson interviewed prosecutor McKenzie, who believed that Mantha's homosexuality "was a very strong factor militating against him" and that it "was a strong motivator as far as Ottawa was concerned in refusing to commute [his death sentence]."[188]

We argue that this case, together with the 1958 Moscow case, associated national security threats with homosexuality. What is most significant for us, though, is not the murder, or even the legal case itself, but the police, military, and RCMP investigation of gay networks that it provoked. An examination of the broader social/sexual context of the Mantha case gives us a glimpse into the military and medical construction of knowledge about homosexuals during this period. And this, in turn, provides us with an understanding of how the military and RCMP gained insights into the extent of the queer threat, especially when we examine the impact of the Jenkins investigation on local homosexual networks.

The Investigation
Following the murder of Jenkins, RCMP officers were sent to Victoria from Ottawa in order to assist in the investigation. An address book belonging to Jenkins was found by the investigating officers, and it included the names of a

number of men in the military, merchant marine, and civilian gay networks on the west coast. Indeed, these security investigations may have initiated the RCMP collection of lists of suspected men (in this case with the assistance of Naval Intelligence). This became the basis for a much more extensive process of surveillance and interrogation. Naval security and the RCMP tried to trace these names. A number of military men and civilians were interrogated as part of this investigation, and some who were presumed to be gay were either purged or transferred.

Bruce Somers, a gay activist, commented that, prior to the murder, gay networks that linked men in the navy with civilians in bars and with men who used washrooms, house parties in Victoria and in the country, and even beach parties and picnics were relatively open and not highly policed: "We used to drink at that time at the King's Hotel. And that was a very heavily-loaded-with-armed-forces-personnel drinking spot and was pretty well known to be very gay ... So there was enough openness that, prior to the murder, ... sailors certainly cruised quite openly downtown ... or at the King's Hotel ... and sometimes in the Churchill Hotel ... The bus depot was another major cruising area which was very flagrant" (June 10, 1994).

Marty, who lived in Victoria in the late 1950s and worked at the naval base, described how military men were involved in cruising: "At night time the cruising grounds were down by the Parliament buildings, and I would say half of the contacts that I made at that time were military." Marty also reported on house parties, a hotel that had a gay section, and cruising in front of the Empress Hotel (May 19, 1996).

Merv, who was in the navy in the late 1950s, worked with Jenkins as a pay writer and was a friend of both Jenkins and Mantha. He reported that, before the murder, "we had lots of fun, lots of parties ... we had good times" (January 12, 1998). At first, the only gay bars were in the Esquimalt area. Later, some, like the King's Hotel, opened up downtown. For men wanting to meet other men, Merv mentioned the bus depot and parks. In the navy, Merv remembered: "They used to carry on in the navy barracks, like nobody would try to hide ... You could carry on and no one would think anything of it." One man was really flamboyant and eventually "did get out" of the navy; however, Merv noted that few men were involved in these gay networks.

Merv's friends organized gay parties outside Victoria, and these included men from the navy as well as civilians. According to Merv, the different ranks went to different parties, and they "didn't have too many ranking officers [at their parties]." In these networks, "we had our own little code or secret language so we could talk freely to each other, but straight people wouldn't have a clue what you were talking about" (January 12, 1998).

Following the murder and the subsequent investigation, much of this social activity stopped as many feared they would be called in for questioning. According to Bruce Somers, "Things changed drastically. And, of course, the entire gay subculture was terrified ... because people were hauled in for questioning and were taken for hours by the ... city police, initially. They [the city police] obviously cooperated with the military because it should have fallen under the jurisdiction of the military. It was a civilian who committed it, but it was a joint operation." Somers also remembered the interrogations:

> Well, there were questions about who they knew ... obviously the police were looking for lists of names, they wanted names so they could interrogate ... But everybody was afraid, of course, that they were on the list and that they were going to be brought in for questioning because, as flagrant as it [the cruising] was, still we were all living in the closet other than maybe a very small handful ... And people were afraid ... first that their family would find out and then [that] their employer would find out. That the police might come to visit them to question them at work. I mean, it was, as it always has been, a police state in that sense ... You could be as flagrant as you wanted in certain areas and with certain people, but there was always the fear of police discovery, police interrogation and exposure.

Somers reported that concerns regarding cruising practices shifted after the investigation began: "You were always somewhat afraid the police were going to come along, you knew they might ... But you didn't have nearly the amount of apprehension that you did after the murder ... It wasn't a long time after that that the bus terminal got knocked out of the picture" (June 10, 1994).

Simon, a gay man then living in Victoria, also told us that people tended to go underground after the murder and the interrogations: "One friend of mine who was working for the local transit ... was so terrified he just really went underground ... Some people were very terrified and, in a sense, justly so ... And, boy, did they ever scatter! The people that were questioned just left Victoria ... Some went back to their hometowns, some of them went to Vancouver or escaped elsewhere" (May 16, 1996).

For men in the navy, the intensified surveillance meant that the military no longer offered the same kind of possibilities for same-gender erotic activity. According to Somers, "They shipped off to other areas in many cases. And some of them, not too long after that, did apply to get out [of the navy] because things obviously did begin to clamp down. It became a lot more uncomfortable ... Just that sense of repression ... It became magnified, at least for a time ... The fear of somebody saying, 'Oh, I think so-and-so has a set of photographs.' I didn't know whether I should keep the photographs or destroy them. So, obviously, the fear of discovery was quite strong" (June 10, 1994).

Marty reported that, following the murder, things changed: "People were in more jeopardy. We noticed people that we'd associated with in the gay circles, disappearing. They'd be gone ... I would hear from co-workers that so-and-so left, and so-and-so left, and they left the services. We knew that they were gone. And they had been involved in the investigation ... Now it was very tight, and for the longest time you were almost afraid to go cruising in case you got picked up by the plainclothes person or decoy."[189] According to Marty, these rumours started "immediately after the murder." Marty was aware that Naval Intelligence was interviewing people, and he knew some of them. He told us of one person who was interviewed: "[He] went to sea just after that and ... was brought back as a psychiatric [case]. They flew him back to Vancouver under psychiatric care. He was diagnosed as having latent homosexual tendencies." He said that this was one of the classifications the military used to diagnose homosexuals and to initiate actions that would lead to their dismissal from the armed forces. Marty also mentioned police raids in the Victoria area: "There were also the gay raids they used to have occasionally, there would be a gay raid and they'd [the local police] take everybody's name ... These raids would take place at the bar or sometimes they'd crash into the private homes and do it" (May 19, 1996).

Merv was interviewed by Naval Intelligence shortly after the Jenkins murder. They asked him "to reveal the names of anyone [he] knew in the armed forces who was gay" (January 12, 1998). He remembered that they were "interviewing all kinds of people, including civilians" and that "they railroaded some completely innocent people" who were in the armed forces. Merv's request to be transferred to the east coast was refused, and he was discharged in early 1959. He reported that, when he was discharged, "[it] just came to me where I spent my last day in the navy. Shore patrol came and got me and threw me in a cell." He did not know why this happened, and he did not remember being asked any questions. He was just "whisked out" of the navy. After he was discharged, Merv remembered that he was at his parents' home about the time that Mantha was hanged in April 1959: "A sergeant from the RCMP came over to where I was staying and asked me to come down to the RCMP barracks with him and he interviewed me. He asked me questions ... like, can you give me

The Cold War against Queers

some information on who might be security risks and names and things like that ... I think he came from Ottawa." He remembered that the officer said: "Give us names and we can get rid of them. It was homosexuals he was after" (January 12, 1998). John Grube, who lived in Victoria during these years, commented: "After Bud's [i.e., Jenkins'] death and the witch hunt everyone ran for cover ... I arranged to leave actually ... I [thought that I'd] better get the hell out of here. I'm close to those people [being investigated]" (March 1, 1996).[190]

Morgan, a naval seaman at the time of the murder, was questioned by Naval Intelligence: "Anyone who knew [Jenkins] was subjected to very intense investigation ... including RCMP visits to their families, to their neighbours, to see who they brought home ... They did extensive interviews with others who were taken away or called for interviews many, many times. And anyone who was in the address book was particularly harassed." Morgan stated: "My sense was that there were at least a dozen sailors who were suspected of being homosexual." He remembered that a petty officer gave lectures to the assembled navy members on the base following the murder, saying that homosexuality "was considered to be mentally ill behaviour, but the most important thing ... was that it was against the Queen's [military] regulations." Morgan continued, "A dressing down was given to the division about appropriate behaviour or the way that 'men' behaved. What was expected of men as opposed to pansies, faggots, and degenerates ... It was always the most degrading tone of voice and vindictive spirit heaped upon the person who was perceived as being not a 'man' or 'effeminate'" (October 22, 1994). Morgan's comments offer a glimpse into the military language that was mobilized against homosexuality.

Simon remembered that friends who organized gay house parties outside Victoria called him after the murder: "They phoned up in a panic to warn me that the RCMP were questioning people. They said, 'They're starting to check on other people, people who have been here. They're starting to check on people who were military out here.' But I said, 'Well, what could they possibly do?' Until I [saw] a boy who said, 'This is what they do. They sit you in the back seat of a car and, with a very heavy index finger, they emphasize points on your shoulder, and the next morning it's black and blue.' They're literally intimidating you. So I did see evidence of this questioning. They wanted names of people ... 'Do you know any military people?'" (May 19, 1996). While the RCMP usually questioned people in an interrogation room, there were also stories, like Simon's, that involved them taking someone for a ride in a car. Sandwiched between two RCMP officers in the back seat of a car, individuals were asked the same type of questions used in the interrogation room. These interrogations had a very similar social form: their focus was on the collection of names and people's identities. Clearly, intimidation was a standard feature of both types of interrogations, but those that occurred in cars had rather different features.

Simon recalled a difference between being questioned by "the local boys" (the Victoria police) and being questioned by the RCMP: "[The RCMP's] method of questioning was different than the local boys. The local boys were not as harsh on the people they were questioning as [the RCMP] ... When they [the RCMP] question you, and corner you, and seat you between two stalwart bodies in the back seat of a car ... and take you to some isolated spot and question you, you don't know whether you are going to come out alive or not." From the accounts we heard, RCMP officers were centrally involved in interrogations in Victoria, especially focusing on obtaining the names of other homosexuals. In other words, they not only collected information but also played the part of "heavies."

Marty was aware of Jenkins' diary and "was petrified that [his] name might be in it." Marty, who was never interrogated, remembered from discussions that people were asked questions such as, "Is so-and-so a homosexual?" As he put it, "It was scary because you never knew who was going to be questioned." One of his friends was involved in Mantha and Jenkins' circle: "And I was petrified that he might use my name. But my name was never mentioned." Marty estimated that he was aware of ten to fifteen people who were interrogated, and some of them "were forced to leave" the military. Any person who did give names to the RCMP investigators was called "a traitor." According to Marty, "They called him everything. He was seen as a turncoat against his fellow gays. There was a fear in the gay community in Victoria ... of exposure." Marty reported that, in the gay networks with which he was involved, there was a general sense that people should not give names. He also recalled that a man being pressured by investigators wanted to get out of the military and so went to a company dance in drag "and was immediately let go [from] the navy" (May 19, 1996).

Marty, who later worked in Halifax in a military psychiatric ward, said that homosexuals were "let go under medical reasons" and eventually discharged. He also noted: "I do know of patients in the psychiatric unit that were up for discharge, and they would keep them for evaluation and then they would discharge them. I don't think they got a dishonourable discharge, but they were discharged as unfit for service ... They were brought into the military hospital in Stadacona for evaluation. In the psychiatric unit there they used to evaluate them, and if they were gay, they were discharged" (May 19, 1996). They were evaluated by being subjected to "various tests ... and probably self-confession" (May 19, 1996). This suggests the interrelation between psychiatric/

psychological testing and security campaigns. The US employment tests developed in the 1940s and 1950s, which contained specific loyalty questions and psychological tests, were used in Canada in the 1950s and 1960s to try to determine homosexuality.[191]

As we can see, the Jenkins murder investigation alerted the RCMP and the Security Panel to the possible extent of the homosexual threat and provided a subtext that sharpened the focus on homosexuality. The RCMP officers sent from Ottawa returned with stories about the wide scope of the homosexual problem.

DISCUSSIONS AND DEBATES IN THE SECURITY PANEL

Possible limitations in existing security procedures regarding homosexual character weaknesses were raised in May 1959 in a memo from Don Wall to other members of the Security Panel.[192] This was based on the separation in security discourse between political disloyalty and character weakness. For example, "communists" and "homosexuals," who were often conflated in right-wing and security discourse, began to be separated. But the 1955 Cabinet directive made no such clear distinction.

Wall's memo asserted that homosexuality was the character weakness that was most frequently exploited by Soviet intelligence.[193] Bryce pointed out, referring to the situation in Moscow, that "in only one of the cases investigated ha[d] there been evidence that an attempt ha[d] been made to blackmail any of these persons for intelligence purposes."[194] Wall mentioned that the DND believed that homosexuality made a person unsuitable for employment whether or not he or she had access to classified information.[195] The DND was a major force in pushing the anti-homosexual campaign further.

Wall's memo allows us to discern the contours of some of the debates and struggles occurring in and around the Security Panel. It contains discussion regarding the separation between security threats related to ideology and those related to character weakness, the homosexualization of character weakness, and how widespread the surveillance and investigation of character weakness should be. While there was agreement that homosexuals were security risks, the RCMP, often with the support of the DND, struggled to defend and expand this campaign and did, in fact, extend its security investigations outside the public service to procure the necessary informants for its surveillance work. The active debate concerning the scope of the security campaigns included procedural matters and struggles over the wording and interpretation of different texts.

Debate took place in October 1959, when the Security Panel finally discussed Wall's memo.[196] Chair Robert Bryce argued for a relatively wide-ranging approach but did not think that homosexuals should be automatically dismissed from the public service; rather, he thought that they should be transferred to less sensitive positions. The RCMP and the deputy ministers of justice and national defence argued for a wider interpretation, with the deputy minister of defence questioning "whether persons suspected of homosexuality should be permitted to enter the public service in any capacity."[197] As a result of these disagreements, the Security Panel could not recommend any change to existing security policy. A belief common to all members of the panel was that homosexuals were vulnerable to being compromised by Soviet agents. This was constructed as "common sense." Security Panel documents show a clear belief that all homosexuals stationed outside Canada were vulnerable to "blackmail."[198]

For the next three years, these were crucial terrains of debate in the Security Panel. In 1959, the homosexual screening program was initiated in the federal civil service. The RCMP struggled to defend and expand this campaign, extending it to investigations outside the public service and collecting thousands of names. RCMP tactics were shaped by the criminalization of homosexuality since all homosexual acts were against the law and tended to overlay security discourse with the criminalization of homosexuality discourse to create a wider basis for the anti-homosexual campaigns. As a police force mandated to criminalize homosexual activity, the RCMP enjoyed relative autonomy from direct security concerns and from the Security Panel itself.

Others on the Security Panel, including representatives of the DEA and the Civil Service Commission, articulated a narrower approach to the security campaign than did the RCMP, suggesting that it should not be extended beyond the civil service and the military. They also argued that homosexuals should be transferred or purged from the civil service only if they held security positions. However, we do not mean to suggest that this stance was either liberal or supportive of homosexuals.[199] Both positions shared the same general heterosexist assumptions, and neither ever raised the possibility of partially decriminalizing homosexual acts.[200]

The RCMP: Extending the Campaign

In May 1960, the RCMP submitted its contribution to the Security Panel discussion, a document entitled "Homosexuality within the Federal Government Service." It requested clearer terms of reference and argued that existing policy restrictions "which prohibit our interviewing homosexuals should be set aside from this type of investigation." It also insisted that "necessary provision be made for us to interview at our discretion any person who we may consider to

The Cold War against Queers

be of assistance to our enquiry."[201] In a slightly earlier text, the RCMP stated: "During the period under review an extensive investigation was started into the identification of known and suspected homosexuals employed in federal government departments and agencies. The investigation was precipitated by the knowledge that persons with this particular character weakness are highly susceptible to compromise and blackmail."[202]

The RCMP had investigated 393 suspected homosexuals, confirming 159 as homosexual and saying: "New names continue to come to light and it is felt that only a fraction of the total number of homosexuals in the federal government service has been identified to date. One self-admitted homosexual estimated there are three thousand homosexuals in the Ottawa area."[203] Despite the ebb and flow of security scares during this period, the RCMP, along with the military hierarchy, was consistent in its insistence that homosexuals should not be in government service.

The RCMP argued that, in order to obtain a more complete picture of the problem, the surveillance campaign needed to be extended beyond the public service itself and to investigate homosexuals outside government employment. It wanted to watch homosexuals outside government employment for two reasons: first, these individuals might later seek government employment; second, they were necessary sources of information on public servants. As Nathan pointed out: "The danger for us was that the KGB would recruit homosexuals in government at whatever level through the homosexuals outside, so that is why there were so many involved. We had to know the whole picture ... If there is a homosexual in government they have contacts outside probably. So you would interview homosexuals outside" (July 22, 1999). Record checks rarely uncovered direct evidence of homosexuality, so the RCMP depended on the friends and acquaintances of homosexuals for information. Interviewing homosexual government workers was difficult because official policy prohibited the disclosure of any employee investigation and, in general, prohibited direct interviews of alleged homosexuals presently in the public service. The RCMP was also concerned about the discharging of "cooperative" homosexuals, who would then cease to be sources of information. The manner in which RCMP surveillance work came to be organized was dependent upon the knowledge provided by, and the cooperation of, gay informants who were located largely outside the public service and the military.

It is also important to remember that the RCMP was not acting on its own. Its work was mandated by Cabinet directives and Security Panel policies. As Starnes puts it:

Since vetting of public servants is such an arcane matter, long shrouded in secrecy, a number of observers tend to blame the RCMP for the government's regulations dealing with security clearances, particularly for the denial of access to classified information for those deemed to have a "character weakness." Some commentators have criticized the RCMP for its "Cold War security mania about homosexuals as security risks." The force may have displayed unnecessary zeal in pursuing homosexuals in the public service who posed potential security risks, but it was doing no more than following the explicit directives laid down by the cabinet, revised from time to time during the 1950s and 1960s, and practised throughout the public service.[204]

For the RCMP, criminal constructions of homosexuality were often conflated with national security constructions, and local policing of gay men's sexual practices provided one of the ways through which security information on homosexuals was obtained.[205]

Military and RCMP positions on homosexuality were mandated not only by security concerns but also by their own internal practices, which prohibited sex deviates from membership and organized the exclusion and dismissal of gay men and lesbians.[206] This was premised on the association of proper masculinity with heterosexuality. Homosexuality (especially between men but also between women) was officially seen as threatening to both workplace discipline and bureaucratic hierarchy.

In June 1960, the Security Panel discussed an RCMP memo on homosexuality in the federal service.[207] Only a quorum was in attendance since, as R.B. Bryce reported, they tried to keep the discussion "limited to the smallest circle possible." In the discussion, the commissioner of the RCMP reiterated the request for more explicit guidance, especially given that "recent investigations indicated that the problem [of homosexuality] was becoming increasingly widespread, and the accumulation of the names of persons against whom allegations had been made was growing with each new enquiry."[208]

In response to the RCMP proposal for extending the campaign against queers, E.W.T. Gill, undersecretary of state for external affairs, pointed to "the danger of this kind of investigation developing into a sociological survey in which the security aspects were lost sight of." He "suggested that it did not serve [the Security Panel's] present purpose to make a determination of the probable proportion of homosexuals in the population."[209] Gill stressed that the RCMP should be concerned with investigating homosexuals only if it were a security matter.

Although all participants in the discussion saw homosexuality as a security problem, they also felt "that the question of prosecutions for homosexual offences would probably not arise through present investigations." In the clash between the broad and the narrow security frames, the majority of the Security Panel members at this meeting sided with the latter. The minutes stated that, "where security was not a factor, there did not appear to be any reason for the RCMP to report allegations of homosexuality to the employing department."[210]

However, at the same time, the minutes recorded that "there appeared to be some reduction in the risk to security if the RCMP and the employing department were aware that an employee had homosexual tendencies."[211] This provided an opening for the RCMP to extend the campaign as it suggested certain struggles and compromises among panel members. The minutes concluded with a call for the secretary of the panel to prepare a report setting out its proposals and that it consider a meeting with the prime minister and the minister of justice on these matters.

This led to Bryce's memo to the prime minister and the minister of justice. The December 1960 version of this memo contains a fairly strong defence of expanding RCMP security investigations, including moving beyond the civil service.[212] However, this did not seem to be enough for the RCMP. In a second version of the document, written in early 1961, a long section was added. It reads:

> The Commissioner of the RCMP has explained that for a number of reasons the scope of these investigations was further expanded to include the investigation of homosexuals who were not employed in the government service on classified work or were employed outside the government service entirely. In the early stages it became evident that the homosexual, irrespective of employment, was the most productive source in identifying and providing factual information on other homosexuals employed in or by the government. Employees not having access to classified information were included in the expanded investigation on the assumption that they obtain access at some future date through promotion or change of employment. Homosexuals outside the government service were investigated and interviewed because existing security screening policies were interpreted as precluding any extensive interviewing of homosexual government employees on the grounds that as the subject of a security investigation they, as individuals should not be made aware of the reason for any subsequent action taken against them. Another reason for investigating homosexuals outside the government service was based on the possibility that they could be used by a

foreign intelligence service to identify and perhaps otherwise assist in the compromising of homosexuals employed in the government on classified work.[213]

Here the RCMP attempted to provide a broader reading of security concerns – one that extended far beyond sensitive positions in the public service and, indeed, far beyond the public service itself. In this addition to the original memo, we see the strength of the RCMP's influence in the Security Panel as well as the relative autonomy of the RCMP, which was not under direct political/governmental control.

Bryce's memo also stated that investigations "should not be widespread, but limited to those persons who were vulnerable to effective exploitation by foreign intelligence services, except in cases where further investigation was necessary to establish the validity of information concerning employees in vulnerable positions." The government was asked to give the RCMP a clear directive to the effect that, "where security was not a factor, the R.C.M. Police were not required to report allegations of homosexuality to the employing department."[214]

The Security Panel asked for ministerial approval for "the following proposed courses of action." The first priority was "that the Security Panel ask those departments with missions abroad to classify according to risk those positions whose nature and location is such that their incumbents might be subjected to pressure for intelligence purposes" and "that these departments, with whatever assistance the RCMP are able to provide, make a careful study of the incumbents of these positions to ensure, in so far as possible, that they are not susceptible to blackmail, either through homosexual activity or other indiscreet behaviour" and "that in cases where the incumbent of a vulnerable position is found to be a homosexual, departments be asked to consult the Secretary of the Security Panel before any action is taken concerning the employee."[215] The second priority involved considering whether positions other than those abroad were vulnerable as well as providing support for research on homosexual detection. The RCMP wanted this investigation and research to include the identification and exclusion of homosexuals since they were "usually practising homosexuals who engage[d] in criminal sexual activity."[216] Bryce's revised memo was discussed by the Cabinet on 26 January, 1961.

A New Cabinet Directive

These meetings, memos, and Cabinet discussions led to a new Cabinet directive in December 1963.[217] Public announcements regarding this document were

The Cold War against Queers

made by Lester Pearson, the new prime minister, and Minister of Justice Lionel Chenier. It referred to good personnel administration and distinguished between those who were politically disloyal and those who were unreliable. For the first time, a Cabinet directive mentioned specific character weaknesses that could lead to unreliability. At the same time, the language used in this document differs somewhat from that in the Security Panel and RCMP documents. Rather than using the term "homosexual," for example, it refers to "illicit sexual behaviour."[218] In a covering memo for this directive, the secretary to the Cabinet stated: "The most important modifications in the new Directive involve an attitude of much greater frankness with employees whose reliability or loyalty is in doubt, and provide related procedures for reviewing such cases both within the responsible department or agency and if necessary by a Board of Review composed of members of the Security Panel."[219]

It was never easy to get a review. In a number of areas, as a partial outcome of Wall's 1962 report, the directive attempted to bring Canadian procedures more into line with American equivalents. Indeed, it laid out a course of action that would coordinate national security practices for decades. This course of action was as follows: If a person applied for or was promoted to a position in the civil service that would give him/her access to what was designated as classified information, either the Civil Service Commission or the department/agency concerned would initiate security investigations. The RCMP would be called in, with the possible involvement of a deputy minister or head of the agency concerned. If the person were discovered to be a homosexual or to be otherwise unreliable, he/she would either be transferred to a less sensitive position or be dismissed. There was now the possibility for review within the department/agency, including review by the deputy minister or head of the agency or by a review board made up of members of the Security Panel.[220]

MAPPING THE RELATIONS OF NATIONAL SECURITY FOR THE 1950s, '60s, AND '70s

The set of relations described here, and the terrain on which the national security campaigns against gay men and lesbians was organized in the 1950s, 1960s, and into the 1970s, have a distinct historical and social character and may be seen in Figure 1.

With these broader contexts in mind, we now turn to investigating the social relations of surveillance, interrogation, and detection, starting with the narratives of those who were most directly affected.

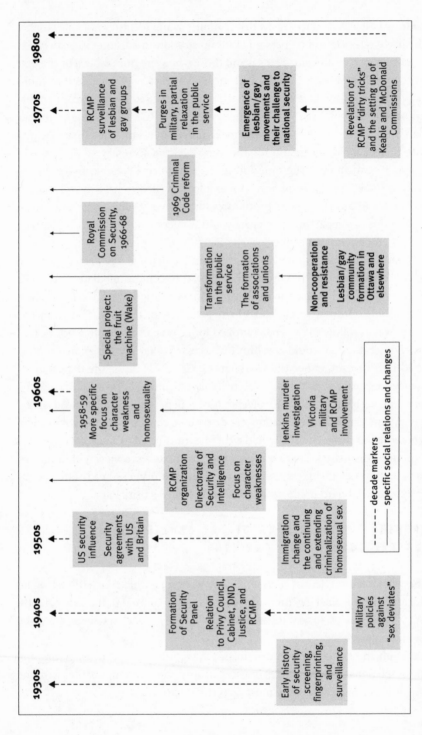

Figure 1 Mapping of social relations of the Canadian war on queers up to 1980

Spying and Interrogation
The Social Relations of National Security

In order to learn more about the social relations of surveillance and interrogation, we return to the first-hand accounts of those who were spied on, interrogated, and purged. We begin with the narratives of gay men and lesbians in the military, and then turn to the stories of those in the public service (starting with the Department of External Affairs [DEA], where security policies had a devastating impact). The national security campaigns encompassed the defence industry as well as the appointment of non-governmental personnel beyond the borders of the Canadian state. We analyze the social relations of spying and interrogation by bringing together first-hand accounts and presenting them along with a critical analysis of the official security texts. We also examine the social organization of the RCMP, which was central to these national security investigations.

THE MILITARY SECURITY REGIME

In the military, women and men were subject not only to military regulations prohibiting the employment of "sex deviates" but also to the national security campaigns. As stated earlier, the RCMP was often involved in military investigations, was consulted for security clearances in the military, and, at times, conducted extensive investigations for military advancement. While military policies prohibited membership of sex deviates, the RCMP focused on questions regarding security and the criminalization of homosexual sex. The military was a central part of the national security regime in both defending Canadian "state sovereignty" and carrying out important intelligence and internal national security work. Cabinet Directive 35 mandated the military to carry out its own internal security program, and this linked it with RCMP security work.[1]

The impact on the lives of people purged from the military is difficult to document. In the 1980s, Blair Johnston, a gay activist, talked to men and women who had been purged from, or who had had difficulties with, the military. He remembered: "[I received] a call from Vancouver one night [from] this hotel manager ... and [he] was reminiscing about an event in the 1950s when he was in the military and he and his lover were caught in the bath together on a military base in Toronto by the security police. They were torn apart, and he said, 'I ratted on him, and he probably ratted on me, and we never saw each other again ...' This man was tossed in jail for awhile and held there and was eventually released with a dishonourable discharge. He drifted west to BC to try to make a new life for himself. He was just recalling his regrets over the fact that he'd never been able to see his lover since; he had no idea whatever happened to him" (February 1, 2001).

Harold's Story: The Destruction of a Career

Harold's narrative demonstrates the social relations of military surveillance and interrogation.[2] We devote considerable space to Harold's story both for the richness of the narrative and because it displays features of the relations of surveillance and interrogation that are present in many of the other accounts in this chapter. We also bring in other people's narratives to assist in analyzing the social experiences made visible by Harold.

"I have received allegations that you are a homosexual"

Harold had a long naval career and was assistant director of a naval department stationed in Ottawa when his problems began in the late 1950s. He was most likely entangled in the investigations radiating out from the Jenkins murder investigation and the implication that various people in the navy on the west coast (where Harold had been stationed) were queer.[3] In his text he writes:

> One day, chillingly, I realized I was undergoing somewhat heavy-handed investigation. My telephone behaved oddly ... could it be tapped? Surely not, this is the vaunted home of personal freedom. Of what am I guilty? Homosexuality ... but "they" must know that. Then, four months after my first awareness of something unusual in the air, I was called to the office of ... Security Agency A [Naval Intelligence]. On arrival I sat down for awhile 'til the official concerned leafed through some papers. The silence didn't bother

me – I'd sat through similar scenes before. Then, he turned in my direction and said, "I have received allegations that you are a homosexual. What do you have to say?" To have admitted homosexuality would have caused my immediate dismissal and the destruction of the basis on which I had built my life. I answered to the effect that such charges are easy to make but how does the accused prove they are untrue?

Harold was aware of the military policies that prohibited homosexuals from membership in the armed forces but assumed that either the navy already knew he was a homosexual or that his rigid separation of his professional career from his homosexual life protected him. He continued,

There followed some three hours of polite, restrained, remorseless interrogation. I take some pride in the fact that I told no lies. Admittedly, I withheld the entire truth, but I was fighting for my right to be considered a worthy citizen. Eventually, I was allowed to leave ... I was badly shaken by this event but, by the time six months had passed, I had recovered some aplomb and no longer picked up my telephone in dread of a further summons ... Until, one day, my office phone rang and a speaker, identifying himself as a member of Security Agency B [the RCMP] announced his desire to have a talk with me. Any doubts I may have had concerning the subject were quickly dispelled when I suggested my home at a certain hour. He did not need to be told where I lived – he knew. That evening, two security agents [RCMP] appeared at my door, presented their credentials, and, without further ado, stated they knew what I was and that they had come for information – which meant names. I was not prepared for this. The philosophy I had established to help me surmount my downfall, should that occur, had not taken into account the possibility of being pressured into the role of an informer.

Harold's experience of this attempt to force him into becoming an informer offers a glimpse of how the RCMP organized its interrogations.

"Which is the greater treason: treason to your country or treason to your friends?"

In a 1994 interview, Harold described how the RCMP was much more heavy-handed during interrogations than was Naval Intelligence. According to Harold, the RCMP repeatedly asked for the names of homosexuals and taped its interrogations. He also said the two officers interviewing him would make statements such as: "'Look, you've got to know something, for God's sake. Tell us,

, tell us! We won't hurt anybody, but tell us! Come on, tell us!' [Bangs on table] Boy. You have no idea ... how I hated them" (February 21, 1994). The following is Harold's written description of the interrogation:

> This particular agency [the RCMP] does not operate with kid gloves ... It is true that ... the terms used by these agents were, mildly expressed, forceful, but the method of attack was decidedly clever ... I was told that persons of my calibre are so much easier to handle than "drugstore cowboys." To my enquiry why, the answer was that I was an individual of responsibility, integrity, and background [and] could readily understand the terrible import of the question, "Which is the greater treason: treason to your country or treason to your friends?" Or, "A person like yourself must realize what a serious disservice you may do your country by withholding the names of people we must ensure are never exposed to treasonous blackmail" ... All they wanted was that I should talk, give names and suspicions.

Loyalty to his gay friends was counterpoised to loyalty to the nation. With homosexuality having been constructed as a treasonous act, loyalty to his homosexual friends became disloyalty to Canada. Other narrators encountered this type of accusation. Peaches Latour, a French Canadian drag performer and hair stylist, was exposed to a similar line of questioning in the late 1960s: "[The RCMP officer] said it was my civic duty to tell on them [other gays] – and I mean, being French-Canadian and not [well] educated, I didn't have a clue what he meant. I said, 'Well, explain it to me' ... 'Well,' he said, 'it would be on your shoulders that [some gay acquaintance] would be a traitor to Canada.' I said, 'A traitor? All I do is shows!'" (August 31, 1994).

Inverting the Problem of Blackmail
RCMP interrogations were oriented around security and blackmail concerns. According to Harold,

> They were, of course, applying a form of blackmail very difficult to resist. It contained an appeal to patriotism and reason, the pseudo-flattery of apparent recognition of integrity and a thinly veiled threat. "We are not concerning ourselves, right now, with the criminal aspects of the situation." To my sickened dismay, even the success I had achieved in keeping my professional and personal lives strictly separated was turned against me. I was told I must know quite a "ring" of homosexuals in professional circles, and my statement that I did not was immediately and emphatically rejected as a lie.

Here, Harold points out that, in his case, rather than being vulnerable to blackmail from Soviet agents, he was vulnerable to blackmail from the RCMP (who also threatened him with charges under the Criminal Code).

This notion of the RCMP or military authorities as blackmailers resonates with other accounts we received. Hank stated that he was "only ever blackmailed by the RCMP" (February 20, 1995). Similarly, according to Sue, "My homosexuality really had nothing to do with my ability to be a military person. But they made it become one because they permitted me to be blackmailed. *They* did that, not me. And that's what's wrong with it. I mean, like, I've shot their silly gun, and I've driven their tank and read their map and done all the rest of that crap just as well as the next woman. But they had something on me, and they created it and perpetuated it, for sure." Referring to the colonel who approached her, Sue commented: "I certainly recognized it as intimidation [when he said], 'Here's your choice, we'll court martial you.' ... So then I ha[d] been blackmailed by the colonel, been blackmailed by the husband of this woman because he want[ed] me to stand up in court and say, 'Yes, his wife [is] a lesbian, I was with her.'" When Sue did agree to resign, she responded to the colonel in the following fashion:

I said, "Will you give me an honourable discharge?" He said, "Yeah, but I don't want to." I said, "I want an honourable discharge or we will have the court martial." So I get an honourable [discharge]. I says, "How will I know I get one?" I says, "I want to type up the orders that say it." He said, "Don't you trust me?" I said, "No Sir." So I had the gall to look at him and say, "Would it be OK for me to go ahead and go to camp with the girls?" He says, "Not on your life, you're not ever going to sleep with any of my girls." Yeah, his girls. Even if they were heterosexual, I hope they were not his girls.

Sue continued, "[He then] passed me a type of document stating that I would [be] court martialled if I didn't voluntarily leave. I was at work, and here's this guy showing up out of the blue. All of a sudden saying this to me, when I thought the judge had said no repercussions would take place. And, in fact, there were. They had a written document in the court of law that said I was [a lesbian] ... They had all the letters I had written" (February 23, 1996).

Lesbians and gay men in the military (and elsewhere) faced blackmail from the RCMP, other police, and military authorities. Moreover, given the criminalization and social stigmatization of queer sexualities, they had no recourse under the law. These stigmatizing social practices produced many of the social pressures that forced many gay men and lesbians to live a double life.

National security campaigns created the space for these blackmail experiences. Security regime texts took for granted homosexual vulnerability to compromise and blackmail, even though little evidence of this was ever provided. Here, it is worth noting that even the US Navy's internal Crittenden Board report, completed in 1957 and long suppressed, found that the "concept that homosexuals pose a security risk is unsupported by any factual data" and that "the number of cases of blackmail as a result of past investigations of homosexuals is negligible."[4]

For gay men and lesbians, blackmail was often linked to fears of police harassment or official sanction. Morgan, who was not in the military and who lived in Toronto in the 1960s, commented: "We heard stories about people who had sexual relationships and then had been photographed and were being blackmailed by individuals. We'd hear about so-and-so being a blackmailer, to avoid that person, not to have anything to do with them because they were blackmailers. Typically, what they would do is threaten to find out the real identity of the person and they would threaten to tell their family or their employer if they didn't receive payment" (October 22, 1994).

This account echoes Axel Otto Olson's 1956 private session testimony, as a gay man, to the Royal Commission on the Criminal Law Relating to Criminal Sexual Psychopaths, in which he argued that "certain police officers" carried out blackmail efforts and that the government was investigating and blackmailing men in the civil service. He forcefully stated: "I don't believe the sex deviate, so to speak, is the main problem. I think the most serious problem is the problem of the blackmailers."[5]

The social space of the closet and the practice of living a double life were constructed, in part, through the national security campaigns.[6] Living in the closet refers to performing oneself as a heterosexual to most people and living a relatively isolated, invisible life in relation to same-gender desires; living a double life refers to producing oneself as heterosexual in the workplace while participating in underground gay networks. The social relations of both have an important social and material basis.[7]

Homophile activists, from the early German homosexual rights movements to homophile organizing in North America in the 1950s and 1960s, raised blackmail as a concern.[8] They argued that blackmail was possible only because of laws criminalizing homosexual sex. Early gay activist Jim Egan noted that the security campaigns

> ignored the fact that the only reason they [homosexuals] were possibly subject
> to blackmail was because of the laws that made the whole thing illegal. And if

Spying and Interrogation

they had issued a directive to every commanding officer [or person in charge of a government department] that he was to inform his men that, if they were approached by a foreign agent, that they could report the matter to their commanding officer, who would guarantee them absolute immunity, ... they could have cooperated in trapping foreign agents. Instead of that they thought the solution was the wholesale firing of anyone who was or was suspected of being gay. (January 5, 1998)

As Yvette explained: "They say that being a lesbian or a homosexual puts you as a target for blackmail. Well, if it were legitimized ... there would be no blackmail."[9]

The perspective that vulnerability to blackmail was the result of the criminalization of homosexuality led to an argument for law reforms that would help to dismantle the social basis for blackmail. Harold had read about the 1957 British Wolfenden Report, which recommended the partial decriminalization of some homosexual acts performed in private between two consenting adults aged twenty-one or over. The Wolfenden Report's liberal regulatory strategy towards sexual activity focused on public/private and adult/youth distinctions; however, at the same time it left unchallenged major features of the oppression and criminalization of same-gender eroticism.[10] By the early 1960s, gay and other activists contested the expansion of the criminalization frame with regard to regulating homosexuality. They did this primarily by using arguments drawn from the Wolfenden Report. Meanwhile, until the late 1960s, the hegemonic regulatory strategy defined homosexuality as a social, sexual, criminal, and national danger.

Gays and lesbians found that the Wolfenden Report provided a limited (and limiting) basis for resistance, especially when arguing for legal reform.[11] "Rationally enough," Harold argued, "if the law would permit a homosexual to live under the same terms as anyone else, at a stroke, treasonous blackmail could no longer loom so large in the minds of the watchdogs of democracy." Changes in the law could then address some of the social bases for blackmail and the construction of the relations of the closet. The Security Panel did not pursue this option. At the same time, the stigmatizing social practices facing gay men and lesbians went far beyond specific laws criminalizing sexual acts.

Aware of the existence of the closet and of people who were living a double life, the security regime used this knowledge to its advantage. We see this in a 1996 comment from former justice minister Davie Fulton:

My acceptance of a security policy which classified a homosexual as a security risk was not on the basis that it was character weakness but, rather, blackmail vulnerability. Because, at that time, sexual aberrations or sexual abnormalities were taken as being quite wrong. And so a person who was guilty of homosexuality was not necessarily mentally, if you like, weaker than anybody else and therefore guilty of character weakness. But he had a physical characteristic which renders him very subject to blackmail ... At that time, as I say, there was no doubt that if a person was a homosexual and performed a homosexual act then he was subject to blackmail because generally it was thought of as a social sin or fault. It was not acceptable. And so he would feel compelled to attempt to conceal it and stop it by doing whatever his blackmailer asked him. (May 17, 1996)

What exactly Fulton meant when he described homosexuality as a physical characteristic remains unclear. What is more important, the security regime defined the need for secrecy as a threat without ever acknowledging how it mobilized this very need as part of its security campaign. Rather than removing the social basis for the threat of blackmail by calling for the repeal of anti-homosexual laws and heterosexist social practices, the security regime intensified the construction of the need for secrecy through the mobilization of surveillance and detection strategies. This, in turn, shaped the social boundaries of living a double life.

Living a Double Life as a Survival Strategy

We now return to Harold's story to illustrate how gays and lesbians used the strategy of living a double life to negotiate the obstacles created for them through the national security campaigns and the social relations of the closet. Harold developed a double life as a response to military and social practices. He noted: "I formed what became a life-long policy of completely divorcing my professional and private lives." The double life strategy was common among those with whom we talked in the military and public service. Harold continued,

> [I] lived for awhile with a great friend of mine – a lover. I was in downtown
> Vancouver, and we would leave in the morning and I would be in uniform. He
> would not, of course. And one day he said to me, "You know, Harold, when
> we leave the house, you're Harold, but we get into the car and drive a couple
> of blocks and you're a lieutenant commander and no goddamn horseshit." I
> remarked to the director of Naval Intelligence that, whatever my private life
> was, I had never in any way endangered the navy nor was I susceptible to

blackmail. The director replied, "Yes, we heard all about [how] when you left the house you were Harold but very shortly after that you were a lieutenant commander." (February 21, 1994)

Herbert Sutcliffe went further than Harold with regard to his strategy of concealment: "I was usually very careful and nobody in DMI [Directorate of Military Intelligence] or the military ever had a suspicion I was gay. Whenever there was any function on, I always had a very attractive female on my arm." With regard to gay hangouts, he said: "In most cases, of course, when I'm doing this I'm out of uniform and no one has any idea I'm military. And I would never indicate to any extent that I was. And there would be no indication in my apartment either" (March 1, 1996).

Harold: "I was caught"

Sometimes, however, even the most carefully constructed precautions crumbled under the investigations of the RCMP and Naval Intelligence. Harold wrote about the site of surveillance and interrogation: "I had to realize that I was caught. It could only be a matter of time before Agency 'B' [the RCMP] conferred with Agency 'A' [Naval Intelligence], resulting in my summary dismissal." Later in the same text, he wrote: "Two independent security agencies, each working without knowledge – until the final stage – of the other's activities, spent more than a year and a very large sum of money to 'get' me."

Naval Intelligence and the RCMP, however, did not work entirely separately but, rather, coordinated their investigations. They were linked together through a mandated course of action, which brought the RCMP into military investigations. Naval Intelligence most likely contacted the RCMP when it began to suspect Harold might be a homosexual. These two agencies and their interrogations appeared quite separate in Harold's local experience because their respective social organizations were not fully visible to him.

Regarding his final interrogation with Naval Intelligence, Harold wrote that the "protracted investigation had proved [his] 'guilt'" and that he was offered this ultimatum: "Resign or be fired. If you resign, nobody will hear anything of the events of the last few months. If you don't – well, we have to give reasons and they must go through the 'usual channels.' So, I resigned ... When I finally received my marching orders I was mentally and physically exhausted. The strain of the previous ten months had been heavy ... It was the immediate and devastating collapse of not only my career but a philosophy and way of life which had taken most of a lifetime to build."

As Harold commented: "All I can say is, the bottom just drops out of everything. My professional career was impeccable. What was heart-breaking was that all of that counted for nothing." In order to avoid facing a court martial, Harold resigned under the military regulations that prohibited homosexuals from membership in the military. He was also denied the military pension to which he was entitled. He remarked: "It seemed so goddamn cheap that I was not entitled to those allowances. It sort of was a disastrous end to what had been a good career. A life I loved."[12]

Harold spoke about the many problems that the security campaigns created, including employment difficulties. These stemmed from being denied security clearances on the basis of his homosexuality. This excluded him from state and military employment as well as from any job requiring a security clearance. Any security check would quickly discover his military discharge: "One of the final twists of the knife was [that] when I left the service, there were various organizations that wanted to employ me, mostly selling life insurance. But one outfit approached me. They said, 'Look, we are looking for a security person and it seems like you are just the person we need.' It was a big salary ... So my heart sunk knowing perfectly well that they would apply for a security check. If they did they would discover the reason for my discharge" (February 21, 1994). Harold told us that he could not cite his extensive military record because of the potential questions this would elicit.

As Harold noted, "Rebuilding a life is not easy." He felt he had to warn other gays to stay away from him since he was probably under surveillance. He also knew about an officer in the navy who had been "dragged from his overseas post and set in this god-awful hot motel for days and days [and interrogated before he was eventually released]" (February 21, 1994).

Herbert Sutcliffe's Story

When Herbert Sutcliffe was about to be promoted to a position in G-2 Intelligence in Washington, he was identified as a homosexual and discharged from the military. In Sutcliffe's case, his homosexuality was discovered through a series of surveillance leads.[13] As he recalled: "I guess six months after I was thrown out, I'd gone to Montreal. And I was down on St. Catherine Street, and this short chap came up to me and he said, 'I'm awfully sorry, I didn't want to do it but they made me.' And then he walked away. And I never thought anything about it for months, then I finally identified him as a French-speaking civil servant in Ottawa who I had taken home one night. And the RCMP had pressured him, and he was the one who gave them the evidence" (March 1, 1996).

Its investigations of civil servants provided the RCMP with Sutcliffe's name. Sutcliffe also mentioned being entrapped by police while in Washington:

> About a month before this happened [i.e., the discharge], I went to Washington. I worked with the people I was going to work with in the Pentagon. The night before I came away, I went out to the gay bars. I was picked up by a rather attractive male, who said, "Would you like to come back to my place for a drink." And I said, "I'd love to." So we go back to his place for a drink and we're having a few drinks. So then I obviously make the wrong move, and he said, "I am a member of the FBI. You are under arrest. Come with me." And they put me in a car and drove me to a police station on the outskirts of Washington. They stripped me ... [and] put me in a cell. Later on they called me out and they sat down and started taking notes [regarding] what I was doing and who I was. And of course again, I'm in limbo. [They ended up not charging him with anything.] I eventually get back to my hotel at four in the morning, and that afternoon I'm flying back to Ottawa. I have to check through the personnel section of the Canadian mission in Washington, and I said, "Incidentally, I got into a little bit of trouble last night. I was in a ... [urinal] and somebody came along and said I was playing with myself and they took me to a police station and charged me with being a homosexual." I said, "There's no truth in this whatsoever." But from that moment I figured, by the time I come back to Ottawa, they'd say, "You!" And it was another four, five, six weeks before anything happened, and then, after this young French-Canadian saying that they had made him talk, this probably was confirmation of what Washington suspected. (March 1, 1996)

There was a clear FBI-RCMP-Military Security connection in Sutcliffe's security investigation. Confirmation from a civil servant in Ottawa, from the Washington police, or from the FBI would have clinched Herbert's shift from a suspected to a confirmed homosexual.

Sutcliffe reported to the RCMP: "And then three days later, I went through the personnel section of army headquarters and then I got in my car and I drove to Toronto. And within a week I was sent to the personnel depot in Toronto and I had a medical. By the time I'd been there an hour I was a civilian" (March 1, 1996).[14] Sutcliffe did get an honourable discharge but, like others, was faced with how to tell people that his military career was over: "When this breaks open I'm panic stricken. What am I going to tell my family? And I finally came up with something. I said that when I had found out that they had given my posting to the Pentagon to someone else I decided I would get out. Normal people, who were not particularly familiar with how the military works and wouldn't have the slightest idea I was gay, would accept this" (March 1, 1996).

Sutcliffe reported that none of his military friends got in touch with "[him] after [he] was identified as a homosexual. None of all [his] close friends, officer friends, NCO [non-commissioned officer] friends and the intelligence corps made any attempt to contact [him]. They were obviously told not to. With the exception of one person" (March 1, 1996). This suggests that, at least in parts of the military, it was known that one did not associate with people who had been discharged, especially if they were homosexual. Sutcliffe survived, briefly selling insurance and then managing to get a teaching job.

Sue reported that accounting for the end of a military career was also a problem for women who had been discharged. Those women who had fathers or other family members in the military, or who had expressed a passionate commitment to the military, encountered particular difficulties once caught in the security net. In these situations, how to explain one's sudden departure from the military became a major concern. Sue had to deal with this very problem:

> My father was in the army; it was an honour to serve. And they screwed it up. So I had to go home with some kind of crazy story about why I didn't want to do this anymore. So here we were – forced to lie to our families and to other people after having said how it is getting a promotion, being bright, all of these things, and then all of a sudden you don't want to do it. [This] happened to a lot of young women: their families had been in the military, it was expected that they would probably go. They had to go home and say, "I'm out of here." A lot of women had full-time jobs with the army, navy, or air force. They lost their jobs, they lost their homes. They had given, what – ten, twelve, fifteen years of service – with no other problems other than the fact they were gay. (February 23, 1996)

Marty, stationed in Victoria during the late 1950s, described the climate for gay men who cruised and picked up other men as follows: "In all respects your job was at stake if you were caught in the services, particularly, but ... the civilian gays also had problems with their jobs if they were caught. You always felt uncomfortable because you were not able to be free ... We were not in a closet, we were in a vault" (May 19, 1996). In Marty's story, we see that family members who were in the military could sometimes be allies in desperate circumstances:

Spying and Interrogation

I was picked up once for cruising in an inappropriate area, and I didn't use the tearooms [i.e., washrooms]. I was frightened of those for some reason, I guess it was the traffic. But I was cruising and I was picked up by the police and turned over to the ... navy shore patrol. Well, the military asked if I was navy and I was put there. And it just so happened that the duty officer happened to be my brother, and he knew I was gay ... Everything was squashed right there by my brother. (May 19, 1996)

Marty's story reveals the connection between the local police and the military police (MP), indicating that all military personnel picked up in the course of a local police raid were turned over to the military police.

There may have been extensively organized surveillance networks in the navy. Morgan reported that he learned from a petty officer in the navy that, in the late 1950s and early 1960s, this officer had been involved in a campaign "to seek out, discover, and trap men in the navy who were suspected of being homosexual." Morgan continued,

And he told me about his involvement and his activities at that time and how they entrapped people [who] were then psychologically grilled over a period of months to determine who all their contacts were. And they would be prom-ised that they would be discharged on medical grounds if they cooperated. Otherwise they could be facing a prison term and dishonourable discharge and so on. He was involved in that program for several years ... with the approval of the Admiralty. (October 22, 1994)

During these years, people in the navy faced a broad security web that in-cluded Naval Intelligence and the RCMP, and even more specific surveillance and entrapment within the navy itself.

Sue's Story: "We were just dyking it up"

Although the military ensured that femininity and lesbianism were highly regulated, it also provided many women with a space in which they had some autonomy from men, thus allowing the exploration of same-gender desires. Sue's account gives us a sense of these possibilities and the dangers associated with them. She got involved in the militia while living in Halifax:

I moved to a new neighbourhood, two doors over there's another girl who's thirteen. Up the street is another who's twelve. The three of us were lesbians, [although] we didn't know what a lesbian was. But we started hanging out together, then the older one joined the Canadian militia, with her husband. She gets in there – she's a dyke, right, but she is married to this guy – and she says, "There [are] all kinds of lesbians in here, you should join." So by the time we get to be teenagers and we're old enough to join, we join. She went out and found them for us. (February 23, 1996)

Younger women learned the ropes from older women, and Sue gave us a sense of lesbian cultural formation in the military: "The older women were meeting us, actually. Yeah. They were just delighted to have a new crew. And we were such enthusiastic little darlings. And we wanted to meet older women, we wanted to meet lesbians. And we were just dyking it up. I used to walk down the street in Halifax and we used to holler, 'Hey, you bull dyke!'" (February 23, 1996). Sue recounted a conversation she had with her father after she had joined the militia and he had warned her of the dangers that lurked in certain barracks:

My father, who had been in the military himself, was a sergeant, and he said to me, "Now listen, when you go away to summer camp," he said, "I want you to know that there are lesbians up there." I said, "Really, Dad!" He said, "Yes, and I want you to be careful, they're in huts H and J." I said, "H and J, Dad?" He said, "Yes." I said, "OK, I'll be careful." I go in to check in [and], of course, one of my lesbian buddies is on the desk. She says, "What huts do you want?" I said, "Either H or J would be just fine." (February 23, 1996)

The intensity of regulation and surveillance in the militia was considerably less than that in the regular military, but problems persisted. According to Sue, if you got caught, you "were sent home." She remembered hearing stories of what had taken place earlier in the Canadian Women's Army Corps: "The chauvinist darlings had found a use for [women] during the war, and [for] some of our other military women that served during that war, who were lesbians. They were allowed to be as gay as they wanted to be, so long as there were hostilities. What happened after the war was that they were punished. They were not going to get any pension and they were literally shit upon" (February 23, 1996).

Yvette's Story: "Somehow I knew that I'd find other lesbians there"

Yvette was discharged from the Royal Canadian Air Force (RCAF) in the late 1950s for being a lesbian.[15] She joined the RCAF in the mid-1950s with the intention of finding other women like her:

Spying and Interrogation

While I was in North Bay, I saw recruiting posters. The RCAF were doing a whole recruiting campaign. They needed fighter cops for the Dew Lines and the Pine Line for defence, and so they were recruiting women and they were really romanticizing the adventure and all of this. And there were some great-looking women in uniform and I would see these huge billboards and, "Come and join us," and somehow I knew that I'd find other lesbians there. I still hadn't named it. I still didn't know the word, but I knew that there were others like me.

While serving, Yvette met a woman in whom she was very interested:

One of the fighter cops came in to visit her friend who was [my] roommate ... They had these regulation blue cotton pyjamas and I was in that. And of course we had to keep our hair off our collar, and I was all done up in pin curls and in came the future love of my life ... Anyway, I think her friend had to leave and I thought, well, "How do we get close?" She came to visit again ... And so I got all my pictures out, and this was a perfect way of getting close to someone that you were interested in without having to say anything and without being too blatant about this. So we sat on the cot and, of course, there's closeness there. And, oh, the thrills! I was just, my knee, my thigh was just electrified [laughter], and I would suspect strongly that hers was too. And so we became lovers.

However, it was difficult to have a secret relationship on a military base:

It's tricky business. And particularly if you're the kind of person I am, where I'm very emotional and it's very difficult for me to play at something I'm not. I tried, but I guess it was evident, and one of the women that I worked with – I was a medical assistant – and one of these women I worked with suspected it very strongly, and it was a complex kind of thing ... She started going around and telling men mostly that I was a lesbian. And I was asked by one of the gang ... He said, "I really have to talk to you. Meet me at the canteen." So we did. We talked. And he said, "You know what's happening ... [this woman] is going around saying that you're fooling around with women and you're like that." And the word "lesbian" wasn't mentioned ... I was very angry. I didn't know how to really deal with it. I just felt pressured. I felt paranoid. I felt it was in everybody's mind.

This proved to be too much for Yvette. As she recalled,

I went into work, into the infirmary one morning, and the staff was gathering around. We had our coffee break before the shift started, and somehow, I knew ... I'd have to speak it. And I took my coffee cup and hurled it, and I ran to the back of the infirmary and one of the civilian nurses came. She was a great support, actually. And, anyway, I ended up having sodium pentothal and I was in an ambulance and I was brought to St. Mary's Veterans' Military Hospital in Montreal ... Well, they wanted me to cooperate with the psychiatrist, this was a psychiatric problem. I wasn't very cooperative. Finally, there was one doctor – and I respect this person a lot today – he named it. He talked [to me] about being a lesbian and he legitimized it for me ... And so within a few sessions after meeting this particular doctor, I felt strong enough to face what I knew would be the end of my career. And even though I'd been a valedictorian in my class and I'd been recommended for commission, from the moment it was spoken that I was a female homosexual ... my career was over and, as far as I was concerned, any contribution that I could make was reversed instantly ... I was unsuitable for further service.

While Yvette was being discharged, mention was made of the danger of blackmail. And so ended Yvette's military career.

THE PUBLIC SERVICE

Given the general awareness of security policies and investigations in Ottawa's lesbian and gay circles, most gay and lesbian public servants were reticent about doing anything to identify themselves openly. According to Peaches Latour, who was involved in the Hull/Ottawa gay scene in the late 1950s, "the mood in the fifties was that anybody who had a prominent job was not out at the time ... So anybody who had a good civil servant job [was not out]. I had a friend who was on the Parole Board and he was petrified all the time of being identified" (August 31, 1994).

Class Tensions: Overts, Coverts, and a Government City
Tensions were generated between, on the one hand, public servants who did not wish to be identified as queer and who were living in the closet or living a double life and, on the other, those who were out. This meant that gay public servants tried not to associate with anyone who identified as, or who was identified as, gay, homosexual, or queer. Peaches Latour found that those in important positions would not associate with him. As he remarked: "All those

who had important positions didn't want their security clearance to be tarnished [by associating too closely with] the regular gays who were hairdressers and orderlies or all the jobs that were at the time known as homosexual professions ... I always say that it was the hairdressers who paved the way for the gays ... It was the gay hairdressers that had more courage, and we had to be very strong to be openly gay in the fifties" (August 31, 1994). In his study of gay networks in early 1950s Montreal, Maurice Leznoff made a similar distinction between the "overts" (working-class or self-employed men who were relatively out) and the "coverts" (middle-class or professional men who lived a double life and who minimized their contact with the overts).[16] This distinction relates to the construction of class relations, but it also relates to national security campaigns in the Ottawa region. For men in the public service or the military, the need to deflect suspicion of homosexuality would have meant staying as far away as possible from networks of overt gays. The RCMP, of course, would have generally drawn its network of gay informants from these more overt networks.

Bruce Somers reported that the handful of public servants who became involved in the Canadian Council on Religion and the Homosexual (CCRH) were all afraid for their jobs: "They were very concerned about press releases and had concerns over secrecy," and "you know they wanted to make very sure that they didn't get anything in the mail" (June 10, 1994).[17] Given this situation, as Barry Deeprose suggested, many in the public service would have resigned once confronted with a security investigation rather than have people find out they were gay (February 21, 1995). Security officials often gave people the option to resign, and contract workers were easily dismissed without being given any reason.

THE PURGING OF EXTERNAL AFFAIRS

In the early years of the Canadian war on queers, the DEA was hit particularly hard by RCMP surveillance practices. This focus on the DEA paralleled the early security campaigns against sex perverts in the US State Department.[18] RCMP investigations in the DEA began at a high level of intensity in late 1959, after which many of the department's homosexual employees were fired or forced to resign, including David Johnson, Canada's ambassador to Moscow (1956-60), and John Holmes (see below). From his reading of the RCMP documents, Hector Mackenzie, a DEA historian, suggests that, in 1960, within the DEA they had identified nine confirmed, seventeen alleged, and thirty-three suspected homosexuals, for a total of fifty-nine.[19]

The DEA expanded in the early postwar years but, according to Mackenzie, was still not a "huge department" by the late 1950s/early 1960s (September 26, 1999). The security campaigns hit the DEA especially hard after a period of growth and development. At the higher levels, the DEA remained a male bastion, and even though "women were finally allowed to compete for foreign service jobs there was still a strong bias against hiring women" (September 26, 1999). As a result of the purges, many people with valuable knowledge and skills were lost. As Mackenzie stated, this had an impact "on policy and policy formation, the key one being relations with the Soviet Union." He further noted that "the impact of the purges on the Department of External Affairs was significant and exceptional, with the senior ranks of the institution seriously depleted and the advisory capacity in certain areas devastated" (September 26, 1999). This had a major impact on the DEA as a workplace and, of course, had serious administrative consequences.

Officials within the DEA, under pressure from the RCMP and the Security Panel, were forced to interrogate and purge people they knew, people who were sometimes their friends. For instance, many of those purged were acquaintances of Deputy Minister Norman Robertson. As Mackenzie pointed out, "Robertson knew many of these people personally, they were friends. They shared many of the same interests" (September 26, 1999). A climate of mistrust, betrayal, fear, and suspicion permeated the DEA during these years, adversely affecting morale and recruitment.

Some of the problems for the DEA were created by earlier departmental policies. Mackenzie reported that, in the late 1940s and the 1950s, the DEA policy was to post bachelors to the Soviet bloc because these postings were thought to be especially difficult for men with families and familial responsibilities (September 26, 1999). Some of these men, however, engaged in same-gender sex, and so this policy created a certain social space for the closeted homosexual. These "bachelors," because they could not produce the proper heterosexual credentials, all became suspect when homosexuals became national security threats. According to Mackenzie, "the category of males (unmarried) most likely in the social context of the time to include homosexuals was that most likely to be sent to missions later seen as venues for blackmail or entrapment. In that way, the 'security risk' as defined by the Security Panel was unwittingly increased."[20]

Sam, who held an administrative position in the DEA in the 1950s, confirmed this. He had this to say about the DEA policy of placing single men overseas: "I remember [name] who I served with in Washington (I believe he was the ambassador), saying, with mock seriousness – but he wasn't entirely

Spying and Interrogation

mocking – saying, 'Wouldn't it be wonderful if we could have a foreign service made up of single men entirely?' External affairs was responsible for bringing on itself these problems" (October 9, 1998).

In July 1958, the DEA reported that it "was keenly interested in the matter [of homosexuals] because it had to consider character weaknesses not only as a security problem, but also from the point of view of Canadian representation abroad."[21] This heterosexist merging of security and representational concerns shaped the security regime in the DEA. Not only did a gay man raise national security concerns, but he was also not a "proper" representative of the Canadian state. The anti-gay laws that existed in most of the countries with which Canada had diplomatic relations at this time, and the defence of these laws by the Canadian state, also raised difficulties.

The DEA was often linked to the policies of other governments, especially to the security policies of the United States and Britain. This is one of the reasons why, as suggested in the security regime texts, there was particular care to avoid having suspected homosexuals stationed abroad. The perception was that no department, with the possible exception of the navy, harboured more queers than the DEA. According to Sawatsky, in 1960 all known homosexuals were arbitrarily fired from the DEA.[22] The DEA set up its own security division, known as Defence Liaison Division 2 (DL2).

DL2: Organizing Internal Security

DL2 dealt with both security and intelligence matters, including communications intelligence, foreign intelligence, security agencies, and personnel security questions. An internal division of labour within DL2 was established to address these concerns. DL2 reported directly to the deputy minister (Norman Robertson, for many of these years). While the department had the responsibility of deciding whether or not an employee would get a security clearance, it also relied on information from the RCMP. The RCMP was obliged to give data on DEA employees to DL2, and, in turn, DL2 was obliged to give information to the RCMP. At times, this was a source of friction.

In the DEA, those who were not in DL2 had little awareness of this internal security work. Without much understanding of how or why, employees were moved around or were dismissed. John Starnes was the head of DL2 from the middle of 1958 to 1961, the key early years of the purge campaign.[23] He reported on the expansion of security matters, which was necessary since "we were now dealing, not merely with a dozen or so cases but with scores, from security guards to ambassadors."[24]

Sam left his position in the DEA during the late 1950s, in part because he felt that his sexual relations with men could lead to his being identified as a threat to national security. In his work, he had contact with DL2. According to him, "the security services in Canada and elsewhere at that time were very hard to control," and the working relationship between DL2 and the RCMP was not only "very close," it was "too close." As he described it,

> [It was a] rather incestuous relation, and that was one of the reasons why it was so difficult to really get control of what was going on. By and large, I think that the anti-homosexual campaigns were home grown, but I have continued to understand that it's always a difficult thing to exercise control over the security services. And one reason it's difficult to control is that there is so much contact between the security services here and in Great Britain and in the US and ... you often get the feeling that the head of DL2 is much closer to someone in the FBI or CIA than he is to you. (October 9, 1998)

According to Sam, there was a long-standing "umbrella agreement for intelligence cooperation between external affairs and the CIA." Starnes added, regarding security information and documents, that "we discussed ways in which such material might be made available to Canada and how to protect it in order to meet US security standards."[25]

Robert also described how DL2 operated by stating that:

> [DL2 was] responsible for internal security. Within external, there were post-able and non-postable positions. And they were the ones that would, if you got security infractions ... they would call you in and they would say, "Too many security infractions. What's going on? You're not paying attention." You would get your little slap on the wrist, get a lecture. "You're not to do this" and this sort of thing ... But internal security was responsible for internal security, for monitoring people and security infractions, and ensuring that they were maintaining that level of security within the area you were working. (October 10, 1996)

There was a division of labour, with DL2 focusing on ensuring that departmental security policies were followed and the RCMP investigating those perceived to be national security threats. Yet, there was also an interactive relation between DL2 and the RCMP.

There was some resistance within the DEA to the security campaign targeting of its members. This resistance was based on the belief that those targeted were valuable members of the department, with important skills and knowledge. In Chapter 2, we discussed comments made by Undersecretary of State for External Affairs Norman Robertson in 1959, around the time that John Holmes was purged from the DEA, to the effect that a homosexual who was discreet and devoted to public service might be able to avoid the security dangers of his "sexual propensity."[26] In part, this was an attempt to defend valued members of the social and class elite from the full onslaught of the anti-queer national security campaigns.

In a pro-Robertson account, John Starnes reported that, at this time,

> the department was experiencing personal security problems, some of them complex and worrying, and all of them involving personal tragedies in varying degrees. Invariably Robertson had to make difficult decisions, some of which affected life-long friends and close colleagues. He carried out this most unpleasant aspect of the job promptly and with scrupulous fairness. He never complained, though clearly he hated the task. Deputy Ministers personally decided whether to grant or withhold security clearance for personnel in their department. In a department such as External Affairs, where so much material was classified, without a top-secret or higher security clearance ... it was impossible to work, especially on top-secret intelligence reports from our allies, which entailed rigid restrictions on handling and dissemination.[27]

Nathan, an ex-RCMP officer, provided a rather different account, referring to several instances in which the RCMP reported to Robertson that a person in the DEA was a homosexual:

> It is important to remember that the RCMP itself did not fire anybody since that was the responsibility of the department involved after receiving security information. It was simply our duty to say to Mr. Robertson, "You have got a homosexual who is in a security position." In two or three cases Robertson said, "Oh, he can't be a homosexual." We would respond, "Mr. Robertson, our information is that he is a homosexual," and we would leave it with him. I remember one case. It was a particularly bad case ... I told Robertson to check on this and it is fairly substantial. He wouldn't believe me. So I said, "That's fine – it's your problem." He knew, of course, that we would have to raise that matter at the Security Panel. Here we had someone who we thought was in a security position, and later the same complainant called up and said, "My God, you have got to get rid of him." ... I got back to Norman Robertson and I said, "Look, do you want this to become public? This man is kind enough to

tell us about it to get this man out of there, and if you get him out of there he has got to leave his job." Reluctantly, and after some time, External Affairs took him off External Affairs ... and gave him another job in the government. And that is the way things were. (July 22, 1999)

Whatever Happened to John Holmes?

One of the more significant people purged from the DEA during these years was John Holmes, a senior and well-respected official in the DEA in the late 1950s. Like Norman Robertson, he was also close to and worked with Lester B. Pearson. He joined the DEA in 1943, served as chargé d'affaires in Moscow during the 1940s, and was assistant undersecretary of state for external affairs from 1953 to 1960.[28] Holmes, from all accounts, was shattered by the ending of his promising career in the DEA. He continued with an impressive scholarly career and died in 1988.

In 1992, in response to media focus on the anti-homosexual campaigns following the release of Security Panel documents, former RCMP inspector William Kelly reported that one of the homosexuals who had been forced out of government service was Holmes.[29] While this was only now confirmed by Kelly, it had long been rumoured. Officially, it had been a secret; only a small group of officials in the DEA and in the RCMP knew for sure.

Sam knew Holmes in the 1950s, when he was in the DEA. It was in this capacity that he "came inside the loop" regarding what happened to Holmes. Sam said: "What I'm going to tell you includes things that John Holmes told me after I had left the government service. John Holmes asked to see me. What John told me was that he had had a homosexual affair when he had been the chargé d'affaires in the Canadian Embassy in Moscow. He had had this affair with an embassy clerk ... and he left me to surmise that that had led to the RCMP getting in touch with him" (October 9, 1998). Holmes' name was most likely brought to the attention of security officials by the same clerk whose interrogation, conducted after he had been sent back from Moscow, also led to the purging of David Johnson. According to Sam,

[As a result of] the revelation of this sexual contact with Holmes by the embassy clerk to the RCMP, a number of officers in DEA were informed of this homosexual liaison. I was out of the department by then, and there's several things that I think I must tell you. The whole thing was kept very, very secret. This is important because that is how John Holmes wanted it to be kept ... I knew the department wanted that too. The department went to considerable trouble to find a position for John ... arrang[ing] for him to go almost at once

Spying and Interrogation

as a visiting professor to Duke University. Norman Robertson was then the undersecretary, and when I went to see him, for entirely different matters, he did say something like this: "Had John Holmes asked to get in touch with you?" And I said, "Yes." And that was about all that was said. (October 9, 1998)

Sam stated: "John told me that, on behalf of the government, he was requested to go and tell the story to Pearson, the leader of the opposition." This may, in part, have been because of Holmes' previous working relationships with Pearson. Sam went on: "There's no doubt he was interrogated, and I think both inside external affairs and by the RCMP, but I say that only because of the general sense I had from having some knowledge of security intelligence work ... Almost certainly both the RCMP and external affairs conducted interrogations." Sam talked to Holmes in the fall of 1959, and the latter's response, once confronted with evidence of his homosexuality, was to resign as soon as he could and to take up a teaching position at Duke University. According to Sam, "[Holmes] made an extraordinary recovery and went on to another and different and more successful career, I would say. And this is the central issue and success of his whole life" (October 9, 1998).

Starnes also knew Holmes and described what happened to him in the following way:

> I was completely surprised to learn of Holmes's sexual orientation and very upset to discover that because of this he had attracted the Soviets' attention. Norman Robertson delegated me to take Holmes to RCMP headquarters for questioning, but I was not present during the interview. Exhaustive inquiries found absolutely nothing to suggest that Soviet Intelligence had succeeded in recruiting John or that he had been disloyal in any way. Under the provisions of cabinet documents, Robertson, as Holmes's deputy minister, had to decide his future. With Holmes's concurrence he decided to look for employment for him outside External Affairs. Robertson quickly found him a post in academic life, where he soon became a respected commentator on many aspects of foreign affairs and a distinguished author.[30]

It was not usual practice for the head of DL2 to accompany someone to RCMP headquarters. According to Starnes, "Holmes was a great Canadian. In my opinion, he was one of two members of Canada's fledgling Foreign Service during the formative post-war years whose ideas and initiatives had valuable and lasting effects."[31]

Nathan, in a somewhat conflicting account, stated:

[Holmes] never really to my knowledge came within our purview. We knew
that Holmes was a homosexual, at least we concluded that he was a homosexual, and he realized, we thought, what was going on within his department
because it was – I won't say rife with homosexuality but there were some real
dandies in there ... Anyway, I am sure that John Holmes felt that it would only
be a matter of time before he would be pointed out ... He knew that he would
be a target, and he decided that he would leave the department and go into
other intellectual work on the basis of the knowledge he had gained over his
years as a member of external affairs. So I have always felt that John Holmes
was a decent fellow who realized the providence and thought he had better
get out and leave. And there is not any doubt in my mind that, had he remained in the DEA, he would have become the subject of some considerable
investigation on our part ... The only thing I know is that the Holmes case did
not create any concern of ours because it was brought up and disposed of.
(July 22, 1999)

Robert's Story: Avoid "Come Ons" and "Queers"

After Robert was granted his security clearance, he was sent to a security briefing given by two RCMP officers:

[It was held in] this room in the East Block of the Parliament Buildings.
And they talked about bugs and the KGB ... and INTERPOL, the British secret
service and the ones around the world ... They showed us this room and they
showed us where bugs could be hidden in the room ... And they would say,
"Here is a room. Where do you think a bug could be hidden?" And then they
would go around and show us where the bugs were in the room ... So when
we got to New York we were taking the phone apart and we were looking
where we thought the bugs could be! (October 10, 1996)

This appears to be the same room to which Starnes referred:

In 1946, while working closely with George Glazebrook, [Bill] Crean established
a professional capability for dealing with hidden electronic listening devices. In
the labyrinths of the basement in the East Block, Room 77, he set up a sophisti-
cated, top-secret training facility for "sweep teams" and for personnel posted
abroad. It contained all the latest in audio-surveillance equipment used by Soviet

Intelligence and other, now-hostile intelligence services (lent to us by the British and the Americans). Apart from its general educational role, Room 77 offered professional training for "sweepers" employed to ensure that diplomatic missions abroad remained free of such devices.[32]

They were still using this room in the 1960s. During this training, Robert was also warned about "come ons":

> Come ons, like when people would start chatting you up and then conversations would start to [become] work related ... And this is where we started hearing about gays and lesbians. This was mentioned with security. That they were a "high security risk" and that, in a lot of the countries where they might have been, the KGB would find out about them and put them in a compromising position. But that is how these people got compromised, because they were not up front with their security. And some of their families might not know, so they would just put them in a position of blackmail ... They said that, "Well, gays and lesbians are usually compromised because they are hiding this deep, evil thing." (October 10, 1996)

As Robert recalled,

> [They said that] gays and lesbians were a security risk, a threat to the country, a threat to the nation ... The language would go, "lesbians and gays," "queers," "faggots," "perverts" – you know, "deviant." Those words would be peppered in there, and you would be sitting there and you would go [rolls eyes], "All right, we're just going to be very butch right now!" [Laughs] If I remember correctly, it was mentioned at the security briefing that they had a means of determining whether or not a person was gay or lesbian. They had a means, they could prove it. (October 10, 1996)

This may have been a reference to the fruit machine research. In any case, Robert's comments illustrate how some public servants would have become aware of the anti-homosexual national security campaigns through these briefings, which also targeted communists and socialists.

Steve, another DEA employee, stated that in 1964 he and his fellow Class 1 Foreign Service officers took "sort of a course about the dangers of being blackmailed or spied upon by the Soviet Bloc." He went on: "It gave technical information; it gave examples of people who had put themselves in compromising positions. They did specifically mention the dangers of being blackmailed for gay activities. That, as I recall, was pretty well the last we heard of it" (June 27, 1998). Responding to a question about what they were told regarding blackmail and homosexuality, Steve said: "The only thing I can remember is an officer used an example of an officer who was posted to Moscow and was picked up by a young good-looking man ... I can't honestly say that they put a great deal of emphasis on it. It was something that was made very clear but not at great length" (June 27, 1998). This may be a reference to the same clerk who was "compromised" in Moscow and whose information under interrogation compromised Holmes and Johnson.

While at the DEA, Robert had a tour of duty at the United Nations General Assembly in New York City. He remembered that a number of people from his circle in Ottawa moved to New York. As he reported: "We knew each other. We had met because prior to being posted one of them had a party at his place and when I got there I realized that there were other gay people." When in New York, Robert recounted: "We knew we ... had to be very careful ... Because most of us ... had direct contact with the ambassador to the United Nations and with anything that was being presented to the United Nations by the Canadian government. So, you know, I got my knuckles rapped a few times for security reasons ... Once, I left the blinds open in front of me and someone photographed the office from across the street and the people could tell what was on my desk." DL2 undertook this surveillance work.

Robert also described how he lived his gay life in New York City. "I was sexually active when I was in New York," he said, joining a health spa that was also a gay spot: "And it was risky. I took a chance." Robert remembered that Tom, one of the men posted in New York, "was very flamboyant." As he put it, "Tom was very homo. He was tall and very lanky and he wore this cape. I mean this black cape with flaming red silk lining and he would throw it over his shoulders and rave through the hotel!" Tom had been through a security clearance in which his homosexuality was either "not an issue or it was never brought up." As Robert said: "[Tom] was very flamboyant but not to the point where he said, 'I'm gay and I like it.' That was never said. But he was very ... you know, off to the opera, off to the ballet ... Anyways, we just had a wonderful tour of duty in New York, we just had a riot." Robert, who was "basically still coming out," would often "chum around" with Tom, who was already out, and they would talk about their experiences (October 10, 1996).

After their tour of duty, Robert and Tom returned to Ottawa, where Robert was posted "to work in the section that handles NATO and NORAD documents." He went on:

Spying and Interrogation

This is where I got what they called my "cosmic top secret" clearance. So then I had to go back through and revamp my last security clearance, which wasn't that long ago, and it was an even more intense search ... There were forms everywhere. But they went in and did a more intensive background search on me. And I got the clearance! So I was stunned because I got cleared for the highest clearance. And it was people who only handled NATO-NORAD documents. (October 10, 1996)

Tom, on the other hand, as mentioned earlier, was forced out of the DEA at this point. Robert described a bit of his own survival strategy during these years: "Most of the time I hung around with mostly straight people. Things that I did in the gay world were separate. I was extremely discreet." Robert was living a double life.

Robert also commented on different strata in the civil service, which relates to overt and covert queer networks: "As you got higher up, of course, it sort of got more and more closed. Then there was the diplomatic level." He said that it was hard to touch those who were in the diplomatic core without very obvious evidence of homosexuality and that these men were generally very "discreet." He recalled, "You would never see these men at the bars." They did not want to be seen with the out gays – "the overts." Among this elite, there were homosexual/gay card-playing parties at people's houses. Some of these card parties would include people "from the Rockcliffe crowd," a reference to an affluent area of Ottawa (October 10, 1996). These men were well connected in business and other professional fields. In other words, they had important middle-class connections and were both more difficult to accuse of homosexuality and less likely to participate in the emerging urban gay networks. Men at lower levels would not have this protection and were, therefore, more vulnerable to accusation and more likely to have participated in the urban gay networks.

Richard Goreham's 1995 research report details conversations with some DEA employees.[33] One of them found that his career was totally blocked when he came back from an assignment in Europe. Subjected to an interrogation about his sexuality, he was asked if he was aware of other homosexuals in the DEA. He refused to cooperate or to admit the charges and received no promotions, no pay increases, and was given no opportunities to go on assignment abroad. In 1969-70, this man's position was eliminated. Reportedly, this was the case for a number of other "undesirables" who were grouped together and given less and less work. There was also mention that those entering the department in the 1960s would be interviewed by a psychiatrist. Reputedly, this psychiatrist had the capacity to identify possible homosexuals and also worked closely with DL2. This may indicate a connection with the fruit machine research.

Steve's Story: Do You Have "Tendencies"?

Steve was employed by the DEA from 1964 to 1970 and was posted abroad after working one year in Ottawa. In the first half of 1964, he reported "a lengthy wait" while he was processed for his security clearance. As he put it, "[This caused] some concern because, had they been particularly effective at their job, they could certainly have uncovered things which I think would have led to the clearance being refused. I can only assume it was not a particularly thorough investigation, and I had no trouble" (June 27, 1998). Posted in a South American country from 1965 to 1968, Steve said: "I was quite conscious of the dangers of being overtly gay. Though I did meet gay people ... I was very conscious of that. I was very conscious also that the Americans had an eye on us; this was the peak of the American influence in [this South American country]. Their embassy literally had more staff than all the other embassies put together ... I knew that they exchanged security information with us and that was disturbing. You know, it was always there in the background."

Steve reported that all seemed fine until the fall of 1969. He had taken a holiday in Europe after his posting and then returned to Ottawa, where, after a year and a half, he was interviewed by DL2. A promotion may have prompted a new investigation of his security status (June 27, 1998). Or new information on him may have become available to DL2. Steve shared the details of his interview:

> The chap was the deputy head of DL2. He asked me a series of questions
> whose purpose became evident almost at once – particularly about what I
> had done and whom I had known in [a country in South America]. He asked
> me specifically if I had what you called "tendencies." He asked me about a
> diplomat in one of the neutral countries and he raised something, which had
> happened more than two years before, in 1967. I came back from [this South
> American country] on a holiday to see my family and to go to Expo. While
> I was there, my family had not yet arrived and I met a friend who had also
> been posted in [the same South American country]. And he was a young
> man [a Canadian diplomat], he was married – still is – but we had too much
> to drink and various intimacies took place, nothing terribly heavy. It took
> place in the hotel, and the man interviewing me in October 1969 knew about
> this, which certainly gave one a lot of food for thought because the only way

they could have found out was by interviewing the other party or because the room was bugged and the other party knew about that ... I can't believe they bugged every room at the hotel ... There must have been some form of set-up. To this day I don't know why. I do think, and I can't prove and will never be able to prove, that the other person was in some way pressured, [but] I think that must be true. What pressure they had on him I have no idea. (June 27, 1998)

The DEA told Steve that it had information about his being a homosexual; in particular, it had the tape recording of a late night conversation he had had with the Foreign Service officer mentioned above. This also showed the extent to which DL2 (and perhaps the RCMP) would go in its investigations:

I can't recall now that he raised anything else specific. That may be due to shock; it was of course a great shock. My recollection is that it wasn't a very long interview because I realized right away that there was no point in denying all this. That they clearly had the evidence or they wouldn't have done this. He said, which I think was the standard thing to say at that time, that I would not progress further in my career, which was a major piece of news. I'd done quite well; I had just been promoted to a first secretary, which was good going for five years. So I said immediately that, in that case, I would leave as soon as I could make other arrangements. And the other arrangements were to go back to university. (June 27, 1998)

Steve stated: "He [the interrogator] knew there were others in the service. He did not name any names ... He asked me whether I knew of any others and I can't remember exactly what I said, but I didn't give them any names. And, of course, I had, and still have, several friends in the public service who are gay ... He tried to pump more information out of me. I don't believe he got any. He certainly didn't get any names." Steve's promising career in the DEA ended, and he returned to university and completed his doctorate. Because going back to university was a standard course of action for people leaving the public service, he was able to avoid having to explain what happened with his career in the DEA.

Steve also mentioned a friend who was a Swedish diplomat. He was a bit surprised that DL2 knew about the sexuality of a person working for the foreign service of another country: "I was struck by the fact that (a) they knew about him and (b) that they cared. The country was Sweden and it was not an ally."

He also recalled a story about a friend and colleague's experience with the security regime:

> Some years later the same thing happened to another friend who is bisexual. He was told the same thing, that his career would not progress, and he is still in the service as of this moment ... And his career has not been meteoric. I don't think he will ever be an ambassador, but he has been promoted ... So it's hard to know. But I think, what I felt immediately, I didn't even think, I just knew it was not for me, to spend the rest of my life stuck at one level while all your friends, people ... who are not more able than I was, moved upwards. That would not have been any fun at all. It was a very competitive organization, it was full of highly educated people and I think after awhile it would have become painfully obvious that something was wrong in my case. So, as I said, I didn't even have to think about it. Yes, it's true that it ruined my career. (June 27, 1998)

Given the role promotions played in careers for the public service, freezing someone's career could have the same impact as outright purging.

Steve described the experience of another man who was living in fear of discovery during these years: "Somebody I know very well and ... actually he's about to retire, I think that has shaped his whole life. He's had at least a reasonable career; I think it's prevented his ever having a relationship of any significance. I think that is the sad thing about those people who are still in [the DEA] and the way they lived into the present era of tolerance, but it's too late [for them] in some ways" (June 27, 1998). The organization of these security campaigns within the DEA requires more detailed investigation. We now turn to look at the impact of these campaigns in other parts of the public service.

THE WAR ON QUEERS IN OTHER PARTS OF THE PUBLIC SERVICE

Albert's Story: "This did affect my employment since this was an area I was skilled in and it was going to be denied me"

Albert's career in the federal bureaucracy was interrupted in the late 1960s when he was shifted out of his position. This transfer took place around the time of the 1968 Royal Commission on Security and at the onset of the official discussions of homosexual law reform.[34] As Albert stated: "This did affect my employment since this was an area I was skilled in and it was going to be denied me."

Spying and Interrogation

Albert's career in the civil service was frozen when, through local Ottawa media coverage of a non-work-related court case in the late 1960s, his superior discovered he was a homosexual. Albert was to be a witness in a legal case regarding a man who had stayed at his place. The use of the courts as sources of intelligence information is important to the organization of RCMP security work, linking it to the criminalization of homosexual acts. Cases initiated outside the security regime, and media coverage of them, affected security investigations. These cases provided valuable information for RCMP investigations, and the RCMP did rely on police and court information regarding criminal charges and proceedings involving homosexuality.

Albert's account also points out how the investigation of one individual could set off investigations of that person's associates. According to Albert,

> [I had known another man] for a number of years, and I had worked with
> him, and it was apparent in the organization where he worked that he might
> be a homosexual. But once my trial had hit the press, within a matter of days,
> perhaps weeks, he was no longer employed. I can only assume that he was
> called on the carpet and was asked directly if he was a homosexual or not ...
> I think it was a situation where they were putting two and two together, and
> if my court case had not come along then I think he would not have been
> dismissed or forced to resign. (October 19, 1993)

Later, in 1969, Albert applied for a policy analyst position with a government department: "I won the job hands down but I was denied the job because a person on the board suspected I was a homosexual, although he didn't know me personally and had no knowledge of my capabilities at work. I suspect that his decision was based on my allegedly being a homosexual. As a result, the competition was cancelled and the position was never filled" (October 19, 1993). This was not just a personal suspicion. Security operatives (probably DL2) provided this information to the board member or to some other official because of a security check (although this would not have been obvious to Albert). Once discovered, Albert understood that his homosexuality meant that he would never be able to progress in his career, and he eventually resigned.

Hank's Story: Sleeping with the RCMP

Hank took a position in the civil service in 1967-68. He waited six months to get his security clearance. Like that of others, his survival strategy was to separate his gay and work worlds. His experience with the security regime reveals yet another RCMP tactic for securing information about homosexuals.

The RCMP was interested in investigating Hank because of the gay social networks and parties in which he participated. To help it infiltrate these circles, the RCMP asked a gay officer whom it was going to purge to investigate Hank. Hank was shocked when he realized he was sleeping with an RCMP officer who was, in fact, spying on him. RCMP officers once came to his home, where they banged on the door, wanted to search his place, and threatened him as follows: "If you don't let us in now we will turn up at your office tomorrow" (February 20, 1995). They asked him personal questions about his friends and told him that he would suffer the consequences if he didn't cooperate. It is possible that he was under surveillance for much of the 1970s, although he said the situation eased after 1976-77. In the end, he suffered no negative long-term repercussions from these investigations.

Shawn's Story: "I'm not an acceptable person anymore"

Canadians posted overseas in non-governmental positions were not immune from the state's security campaigns. Posted in Rangoon, Burma, for a development agency, Shawn told us his contract was abruptly terminated in the early 1960s. Before he was to be posted to Rangoon for the second time, he had been sent to join the Canadian delegation at the United Nations in New York City:

> Among the people that I met was a secretary who was also a gay man, and I took no notice of it other than the fact that we were there. Well, about a year later, when my contract was coming up for renewal in Rangoon, I was informed that it was not going to be renewed and that I would be coming back to Canada. So, no reason [was given]. No reason whatsoever. So, I had no choice but to come back. After I came back, my friend the MP made a special trip to explain to me personally what had happened. And it was this secretary who had been indiscreet and got himself exposed somehow or other, and he blew the whistle during interrogation, I assume on anybody that he knew [who was] associated with the UN or in the government. He just listed down all the names. The paranoid people in the government decided I'm not an acceptable person anymore. (July 20, 1995)

Because this secretary gave his name, the MP mentioned above also lost his position on a government committee that, in the early 1960s, addressed international affairs. As a member of this committee, he potentially had access to security information. Shawn's story suggests clear connections between the RCMP, the security regime more generally, and the DEA regarding approval for Canadians stationed overseas on non-governmental organization contracts. In this case, it appears that the list of names the secretary gave was forwarded to the RCMP in Ottawa and then on to DL2 and the DEA. It was relatively easy to stop the renewal of contract workers since the reason for termination need not be revealed. Shawn would not have known the reason for the termination of his contract if he had not been told by this MP.

Military-Related Industry and Research

Security screenings also affected civilian employees of firms producing materials for the US military or for any of the NATO military forces. These civilian employees underwent security checks, which included being investigated for communist or socialist connections and for possible homosexuality. This built on earlier practices, including fingerprinting. In an early 1950s article, Blair Fraser describes this process:

> Any company undertaking a contract for secret work must send to Ottawa a list of all employees who will have access to "classified" information. The list is checked by the RCMP. If RCMP files contain any information about any person named on that list that information (but not the source) is sent back to the Defence Production Department. The department then has to make up its mind whether or not each individual is to be trusted with military secrets. Naturally they try to be very careful. An unfavourable report wouldn't necessarily mean a man is a Communist: it might be only that he talks too much, or drinks too much, or has a military record showing instability.[35]

Fraser wrote this article prior to the time in which sexual "indiscretions" became a major security focus. As John Sawatsky pointed out, "Canada did a lot of contract work for the US defence industry and a lot of it was secret or top secret ... Anyone who worked on these projects had to be cleared. And of course the Americans insisted, 'If we're paying – if this is for our defence or for the US Defence Department – then it has to live up to our security standards or we won't let you have the contract'" (January 4, 1996). The intermeshing of Canadian and American state formation meant that US security policies were able to directly affect Canadian employment practices.

The work of L.C. Cragg of the Department of Defence Production was referred to in a 1958 Security Sub-Panel discussion: "His role in handling security cases involving character weaknesses was complicated by the fact that his relationship with industrial employees was necessarily indirect. His function was to advise individual companies on all security matters, and he was unable to exercise the close supervision in the handling of security cases which was possible for government security officials in their own departments."[36] In 1964, the Security Panel discussed a memorandum that focused on the Department of Defence Production's responsibility for the security of classified information entrusted by the Government of Canada to Canadian industrial firms and other non-governmental organizations. The objective was to defend secret and confidential information from "persons who may be disloyal to Canada and her system of government or ... persons who are unreliable because of defects in their character." This latter group was made up of people who were considered to be unreliable "because of features of ... character which may lead to indiscretion or dishonesty, or make [them] vulnerable to blackmail or coercion." One of these character defects involved, in the words of Cabinet Directive 35, "illicit sexual behaviour."[37]

Peter, a security officer who was secretly gay, worked for a firm in Montreal that, in the late 1960s, was involved in military production for NATO countries. Although he reports never having had a security check, he did mention that "anyone employed in the production of military equipment would be security checked. A form would be filled out and it would be processed, in Ottawa, by the security officers up there" (July 20, 1995). According to Peter, one person was released for attending communist-linked events while at university; however, for security reasons, this man was not informed that he was being released for security reasons. This sort of screening would have enabled the RCMP to compile the names and identities of possible "subversives."

Through the granting of research contracts, government work was extended to the university. Bruce Somers and Doug Sanders mentioned the experience of Herman, a university professor who was involved with the Association for Social Knowledge (ASK) but who did not want to be identified as a member.[38] The research that he conducted at the University of British Columbia was funded by the DND and required a security clearance. Sanders described the circumstances of the professor's compromise:

> Herman was very concerned about his security clearance because of the federal government funding issue. There was, in his view, clearly the potential of his whole research career being undercut by a security clearance problem. And therefore [there was the need for] a decision on his part that he could not participate in any of the public meetings of ASK or come to any of the meetings at all. So he, "yes" supported [us] but "no" he couldn't be involved at all. There were contracts of money coming to UBC, from the defence department. The people involved had to have security clearances. (June 10, 1994)

Spying and Interrogation

This suggests that Herman was clearly aware of the consequences for his security clearance level and future funding possibilities if he were identified as a homosexual.

SURVEILLANCE AND INTERROGATION OUTSIDE THE PUBLIC SERVICE

The surveillance work that the RCMP conducted outside the public service was central to its work. It was often from this group of gay men (and, to a much lesser extent, lesbians) that the RCMP learned of homosexuals in government employ. This was also a weak link in RCMP surveillance as, by the early 1960s, the police started encountering forms of non-cooperation and resistance. We examine two narratives in order to get a sense of how this important part of the security campaign against queers was organized. There are common features as well as major differences in the experiences of David and Marvin.

David's Story: "I was treated like the enemy"
David came to the attention of the RCMP when a friend of his, who was caught in a park sweep, gave his name. A gay friend of David's who was in the RCMP (and was later purged) told him not to cooperate with the security investigations. The RCMP interviewed David on a number of occasions. However, as he commented:

> Since they had no evidence against me, I refused to give them information on the basis that, in the first place, I knew nobody of any importance and, in the second place, I felt that it was not in my position to give that sort of information because if I knew somebody I would consider the person to be a friend and I would never be able to face them again. If I had ratted on them, so to speak. There were a number of interviews in which they had me in various locations, anywhere from sitting having a beer in a bar to being brought into their office to being put into what amounted to almost an unpadded cell ... I think they tried various situations because they thought maybe they could do it. But of course the way to get information from a person is not ... to interview [them] in the way I was interviewed. They just got my back up because it was so unpleasant you didn't feel like cooperating under any circumstances. I was treated like the enemy. (May 12, 1994)

During the interrogations, one officer would act more sympathetic and the other more hard-line:

[In] many of the interviews there would be only one person there. But, especially in the time in the cell, you definitely had a big, dark, hairy-chested guy who ... He looked as though he hadn't shaved for days. Along with him was a smaller, very pleasant, blue-eyed, blonde guy who ... almost seemed to be flirting with me ... as he would seem to ... be sympathetic to me. He was always apologizing for the heavy-handed actions and speech of the other guy, but I'm sure this was well rehearsed. (May 12, 1994)

This was common for RCMP interrogations in the 1960s. According to David, these were conducted over a three-year period in the mid-1960s: "It was not every day; it would be from time to time. I would have no knowledge of when these interviews were going to happen again and it was always sort of a surprise; an unhappy surprise." David suspected that the police bugged his telephone:

The first indication was, one of my friends telephoned me and said, "That was a funny ring." So I asked him what he meant. He said, "It started to ring and then the ringing sound stopped." As far as he was concerned, it was a warning sign you hear on the telephone. My phone didn't stop ringing, but the sound that he got was cut off ... I didn't think too much about it at first. But then, when several people had reported this thing to me, I tried telephoning myself ... and I found the same thing happening. Then I started listening carefully as I telephoned out from my apartment, and I found that there were a series of one or two clicks which would take place just a few seconds after the telephone started ringing at the other end. And then finally, a person who is in the middle executive level of Bell Telephone Canada [and] who was an acquaintance ... of mine, I asked if he would listen in ... I said, "Would you please dial my home and listen and see what happens?" And he in fact did, and as soon as he heard this he hung up. He said, "Yes, your line is definitely bugged." (May 12, 1994)

This phone tapping was a standard part of the RCMP surveillance repertoire. David's mail was also slow in arriving and, according to him, it was "being opened and very carefully resealed." He was also followed:

I started noticing I was being followed; always by the same car no matter where I went. Whether I walked or took my car this same black Ford sedan, about a five-year-old at that time. It was always just about a block behind me. If I looked around it would just be parking; if I was driving my car, it would be far enough behind that it would seem to be part of the traffic unless I went down a deserted street, in which case it was always there. And it would be there if I left to go curling on Sunday evening. I would leave to go over to the curling club and this black sedan would follow me ... And when I was finished curling I'd go out and there it was, always about a block or so away, and as I drove back to my place it just followed me like a shadow. And I didn't try to hide the fact that I knew that he was there, I didn't try to shake him loose. My only feeling at that time was, "What a waste of the taxpayers' money." I'm a person that has no "state secrets." I know nobody who has "state secrets," and here they were wasting all their time putting people following me. (May 12, 1994)

Being followed was a standard feature of RCMP surveillance. Further to this, David's apartment was searched:

On one occasion I sensed that my apartment had been searched. Incidentally, I had that corroborated by a very frightened ... lady who had more or less told me she must let them in and she must not tell me that she had given them the keys to go through my apartment. But she did tell me. Of course this ... invasion of my apartment when I wasn't there probably would be considered by today's standard to have been illegal. They took nothing, but they looked in my apartment to see what was there. I could tell that somebody had been there ... Things weren't quite where I'd left them. Everything had been looked at and put down, and I'm sure they went through drawers and everything else. (May 12, 1994)

These were standard features of surveillance of gay individuals whom the RCMP wanted to convert into informants. At the conclusion of this period of overt surveillance and harassment, a different RCMP officer approached David and apologized for the earlier harassment:

The first thing he did was to apologize. He said that they should never have done that, that they realize that they were in error, and he was apologetic and very pleasant. He acted more like the "nice guy." But he came on that occasion asking the same general questions: "Would I be still interested in giving information on anybody who I felt might be putting themselves in jeopardy." [This] was what he went after. His approach to the whole thing was that, first, you can protect civil servants who might put themselves in "jeopardy" from situations where they might be subject to blackmail ... So they wanted to get a listing of all these people so that they could be assured that they had the backing of the police and that they needn't stay hidden. But if they had any problem they ... were going to tell these people get to the police, and the police would be behind them and back them up and help them out of their problems, you see. And he was very nice about it. First, he explained the switch in ... attitude was not to get people in trouble but to try and help people out, and, of course, they had the usual thing, asking me if I can give information. I went through my same statement. In this case it was much more relaxed, I was able to say exactly what I had said before but in a much nicer tone because he had approached me in a nicer way. And on subsequent occasions he came, and he would occasionally come in armed with photographs and names and ask me for information. I said the same thing to him I had said to the others, that it would be unfair for me to give any information. I didn't give information wholesale the way some people did. I think that the ... vast majority of people who went in for questioning did not have the previous counselling that I got from this member of the RCMP. And so they didn't know how to comport themselves ... Many of them broke down and gave information they later very much regretted having [given]. Some tried to do it by telling untruths. And I think, under the circumstances, I was very fortunate in having been told just how to respond to these questions. (May 12, 1994)

Here, we get a sense of the shift in RCMP tactics in the later 1960s. Clearly, the RCMP would still use any information it collected to identify homosexuals and raise security concerns about them. After this last officer left his post, David did not remember being interviewed again. He speculated: "He may have left some sort of a note saying, 'This is a dead end, don't bother.' But nobody ever approached me after that."

David remembered the interviews as being "scarier" than being followed: "Because the part of being followed was almost ludicrous. At that point I felt some uneasiness because you feel as though your privacy is being invaded. And I also warned all my friends, 'Don't be seen in my presence while this thing is going on unless it's OK.'" David felt enough solidarity with his gay friends to warn them against being seen with him since the consequences meant the possibility of being investigated by the RCMP. He also told us that, by the mid-1960s, anyone coming out into the Ottawa gay scene would learn about the RCMP investigations and strategies of non-cooperation.

David commented on police entrapment practices in the 1960s:

At that time they would have people posing as homosexuals in the park. And what they would do is, they would dress in jeans and a T-shirt and be very husky, good-looking guys, and they would just sort of lounge around and they would give the eye to people walking by and if the person in any way

Spying and Interrogation

responded, they often [would] just make themselves very, very available until the person approached them. And they didn't just stop at that, often they made the first move. And furthermore, they – friends of mine who got caught, and I don't see any reason to not believe them – [said] that in many cases these people went into a full homosexual act, including their own orgasm. And then, having had their fun, would then nab this person and say, "This person put a hand on me." And this happened often enough that people told me about this [so frequently] that I can't imagine all of these people coming up with the same story if [it] weren't true. (May 12, 1994)

The threat to lay charges was an attempt to get the names of other gays: "I think, in most cases, these people were put into a compromising situation so that they would have to give names. I think the RCMP were mostly interested in gathering information rather than arresting people. City of Ottawa police would be more interested in arresting people, but they would mostly put the people in a very, very uncomfortable situation, and the only way to extricate themselves was to hand over all the information they had on their acquaintances." This suggests a division of labour, organized through the Criminal Code sections dealing with queer sex, between the RCMP (which had jurisdiction over the federal parks) and the Ottawa police. David also reminded us that, in the 1960s Ottawa area, men having sex with men faced not only the RCMP and the Ottawa police but also the Ontario Provincial Police. And those going into Quebec faced the Hull police:

They were all doing some form of harassment or investigation. But they looked at it from different points of view. The OPP [Ontario Provincial Police], the City of Ottawa, and City of Hull police were more interested in arresting people. Whereas the RCMP, I'm sure their main interest was getting information about who was gay. I don't recall too many times hearing of a person being thrown in jail by the RCMP. More likely they would be interviewed and scared to death. The arrest would be just used as a sort of a threat to try to get people to divulge information. And of course, as a result, people lost jobs [when arrested by] the RCMP, a lot more than they did with the arrests from the others ... But in every case there was an awful lot of entrapment going on. (May 12, 1994)

David remembered people being arrested in bars, at gay parties, and even at cottages. At the same time, the local police fed information to the RCMP. Even acts of violence against men who had sex with men in parks could be an opportunity for an RCMP investigation and park sweep (May 12, 1994). David's capacity to resist these forms of harassment was rooted in the gay networks of which he was a part and in the advice he received from his gay RCMP friend.

Marvin's Story: The "investigation would be going on for another ten years"
Like David, Marvin encountered national security campaigns in the early 1960s while working outside the public service. He worked for two airlines, and it was through this work that he first became aware of RCMP operations in Ottawa. He informed us that an RCMP officer used to come out to visit their planes and look at the luggage if the planes were carrying Russians (May 1998). One of Marvin's friends who worked at the airline became friends with this RCMP officer and later became an RCMP officer himself:

> A friend I'd worked with for a couple of years came in one day. Nice fellow, terrific guy, I always liked him. He asked, "You want to have a coffee?" and I said, "Sure." So we went to this restaurant and sat down. There were two men in this one booth, then I noticed near the back of the restaurant one man sitting by himself, and he was in a dark suit, plainclothes. Well, he stuck out like a sore thumb. I know for sure that he was with the RCMP because my friend ... [who had] worked at the airline, had joined the RCMP as an undercover agent ... And that's the first time I'd seen him in about five years. So we had coffee. I thought it was rather odd, and I noticed this man, and he'd glance our way quite often. So for some reason, my friend might have been identifying me to this man that I was gay. (May 1998)

Marvin himself came under investigation in the early 1960s. His phone was tapped and his place was broken into:

> I know my apartment had been broken into sometime after that. It wasn't an obvious break-in. Nothing had been done about the lock on the door, and there was no disturbance inside the building. Except when I opened a drawer in the dresser, I noticed some things had been shifted around, just slightly. I think somehow they must have got in and possibly were looking for pornography or something that would show me in a bad position, where they could possibly arrest me for pornography, performing a "lewd act" or whatever you want to call it. (May 1998)

The RCMP also undertook surveillance of him and his associates:

I was going downtown for lunch one day, and I just had turned the corner around Bank heading towards the Parliament Hill area. I saw a friend, so we stopped and both walked to the side ... to get out of the pedestrian area. And we were standing there on the sidewalk talking. Now, I can't remember if he was straight or gay because I had a lot of straight friends, but I just glanced around to my left and there were two plainclothes RCMP standing against the building right beside us. They just stood there looking at us all the time we're having this conversation. (May 1998)

The RCMP visited Marvin at work with books of mug shots of people they wanted him to identify. They later contacted him about coming in for an interview:

I didn't want to go. What they did tell me was that, unless I cooperated with them, that they would get me in a compromising position, and I'd spend fifteen years in jail. That's why I went there. They said I had to make this interview. And I knew if they would go as far as to take these mug files into my office they could do a lot of other things in the office as well. And my ass could be out on the streets ... Anyway, I did go down to the office ... So I went to the offices on the second floor. Of course, the chaps were there. They took me in a room, and it looks as if it had been at one time a large office, it was divided down the middle, split into maybe two interview rooms, because there was a partition down the middle. There was one large window at one end of the room; the room would be at least twelve feet long and maybe, at the most, six feet wide. And there was a plain wooden table, like your ordinary government-issue tables, and two chairs beside this one table against one wall. And just to the right, up over my shoulder, ... was a small glass in the wall, but you couldn't see through it. It was only about maybe six by eight inches, and I thought right away there might be a camera in there. I never thought of two-way glass at the time. (May 1998)

The RCMP began to question Marvin:

They said I had to answer the questions. They knew I was gay, and they knew where I drank, and they knew where I lived: they knew everything about me. They knew most of my friends. There was nothing about me that they didn't know ... But I also understood that they [knew] because we knew they'd be following us in the clubs and maybe even in the YMCA steam bath. I sat down in the chair, and this little peep hole was behind my head, maybe a couple feet above me behind my head ... Anyway, one guy sits down and he starts to ask me questions. Well, "Who do you know in Ottawa?" I thought, in fact I think I thought about this before I went down there, the night before I did a lot of thinking about how I was going to get around it, and I knew I'd have to give them something but I didn't know how or what. So I thought the only thing I can do is give them the names of people that they saw me drinking in the hotels with. And these were names that I knew they already had; I knew for sure because there was a loose group of about eight people that used to hang around with friends. I don't know if I mentioned more than two or three names or not, but they did ask me who I was sleeping with at the time. And they asked me about other people I'd been in bed with. But there were times between affairs when I would have one-night stands. And half the time I never knew their name. Anyway, there were dentists, doctors, or lawyers; there was everything in the circle, at that time, of the gay community. But not all of them were out. (May 1998)

They also asked him about people in Montreal, which suggests that the RCMP surveillance of gay public servants was already extending, based on the knowledge that covert homosexuals in the Ottawa area felt they could be more out in Montreal:

They asked me about names of people in Montreal. Well, I did Montreal for two years before I came to Ottawa and I remembered a few names, but I told them I couldn't remember any names at all. So they didn't seem to push that issue at all. But one thing they did ask me, and this bothers me even to this day as to why, ... they did ask me who I'd been to bed with. They wanted to know what we did: was it mutual masturbation, was it fellatio or anal intercourse? I thought, "Why would they want to know that?" I think they were enjoying it. I said, "Mostly mutual masturbation" ... I thought the other guy might come in; this guy had been very pleasant, and I thought the other guy might come in and start getting rough. I didn't know exactly how it worked. But it didn't end up that way. That was about the end of the interview, and I think I might have been there twenty minutes to half an hour at the most. And they didn't ask me for any more names. (May 1998)

Asking such detailed questions about sexual practice was another way of trying to confirm Marvin's homosexuality and, perhaps, to learn more about queer erotic practices. But it also prefigured the types of sex practice questions that military intelligence (Special Investigations Unit [SIU]) would ask in the 1970s and 1980s. At the end of the interview, the RCMP tried to further intimidate Marvin:

[They told me that the] investigation would be going on for another ten years and, again, [they] can get you in a position with an undercover agent, who happens to be gay, as quite an easy thing to do, get you into a hotel room with some good-looking fellow, take pictures of you and put you in jail for, like, he said, fifteen years. And so they said, when I went to the door ... "We'll be talking to you later." So that, to me, was the end. I couldn't have stayed there, waiting for them to knock on the door or to call on the phone or to walk in my office. I couldn't take another ten years of that. (May 1998)

In response to this intimidation, Marvin left the country in 1960, at which point the RCMP investigation had lasted about six months. Some of his friends had supportive families, which helped out in such situations, but Marvin was not out to his family: "I never once admitted to my parents that I was gay, from the time I left home. I know they knew that I was, but they would never mention it to me. In the late forties or early fifties, you didn't talk about those things. So I didn't want them to know. So I thought, I can't do anything that's going to hurt my family, nothing at all" (May 1998).

Marvin remembered that the RCMP investigations had a major impact on others as well: "In those days a lot of people were leaving town, and one of my ex-lovers left town. A lot of people left town because they knew of this investigation and they were afraid of being interviewed." There was a mini queer exodus from Ottawa at this point, with some similarities to what took place in Victoria after the Jenkins murder. According to Marvin, some men moved to other parts of Canada – specifically, Toronto, Montreal, and Vancouver – with some going to the United States and a few to Europe. Marvin's links to the local gay scene were not as solid as David's, and his experience with the purge occurred before gay networks had developed strategies for resisting it.

This surveillance and pressure disrupted Marvin's ability to develop relationships and to have sex: "I haven't slept with anybody in Canada; I haven't spent a night in Canada with anybody since 1964. Count the years" (May 1998). Clearly, the security campaigns significantly curtailed people's relationships and sex lives. And this is an aspect of the national security campaigns that is usually neglected.

These stories show us how, from the late 1950s through the early 1970s, the lives of gay men and lesbians were affected in a variety of overlapping and different ways by the security policies of Canadian state agencies. In the next section, we turn our attention to an analysis of the social relations of surveillance and interrogation within which people were caught. Key to the organization of this was the RCMP.

THE SOCIAL ORGANIZATION OF RCMP SURVEILLANCE WORK

The RCMP was pivotal in establishing the social relations of national security surveillance and interrogation. It and other police forces were exceedingly masculinist and anti-homosexual institutions. Don Wall confirms this: "I think most police forces have found homosexuals within their own ranks. And it has been a source of acute embarrassment to the force as a whole to find rotten apples in their barrel so to speak. And I think there is in police training a continuous thread of manliness as it's generally understood. That you know, you ride a lot of horses and shoot a lot of guns ... So there are some built-in prejudices against something like homosexuality."[39]

The Directorate of Security and Intelligence
The work of the RCMP's Directorate of Security and Intelligence (DSI), which was central to organizing its national security work, was shrouded in secrecy.[40] In 1963, journalist Sidney Katz wrote an article in which he reported that the Security and Intelligence (S&I) branch of the RCMP employed an estimated five hundred of the RCMP's eighty-five hundred men and that its office "occupie[d] the entire top two floors of the RCMP's five-story headquarters building in Ottawa."[41] The S&I offices were sealed off from other RCMP offices, and agents from this branch "ha[d] their own special training courses, never [wore] uniforms, never associate[d] publicly with" other RCMP officers; nor did their names appear "on the published nominal role of RCMP strength." Katz reported that, at this time, communists were still the number one enemy according to the RCMP.[42]

There are only two references in Katz's article to homosexuality. Calvin MacDonald, a former infiltrator in the Canadian Communist Party, went public with his claims that communists had penetrated many organizations. According to Katz, "[MacDonald] said he knew of a number of homosexuals in the civil service and was preparing a manual about them." Commissioner Harvison of the RCMP reported to Katz that "the S&I agents are not only looking for subversives – they're also seeking to identify the alcoholic, the homosexual and the weak character."[43]

Spying and Interrogation

According to Fred, in the 1960s RCMP headquarters was divided into five directorates, including S&I. Within S&I, A Branch was responsible for the security screening of all government employees, including cases regarding character weakness. Generally, the RCMP was "divided into geographic divisions across the country (for example 'K' Division covered Alberta, 'O' southern Ontario, 'C' Montreal, and 'J' New Brunswick."[44] Hewitt's research shows that, "by the end of the 1940s the intelligence wing had splintered into 'B' Branch (counter-espionage) and 'D' Branch (counter subversion)."[45] Reports from across the country "proceeded slowly upward through the hierarchy of the RCMP establishment. Once they reached headquarters in Ottawa, 'reader analysts' usually known simply as 'readers,' pored over all the pages to determine what was of significance and therefore eligible for parcelling out to various other file categories, branches, or desks devoted to specific areas."[46]

According to Fred, the character weaknesses subdivision had contacts with military intelligence, but this liaison was organized through contacts at a higher level. Fred confirmed that the RCMP had important working links with the FBI and the CIA and that these groups held common conferences on security questions. When a known homosexual from Canada went to the United States, security forces there were informed. The RCMP worked with a liaison officer from the US embassy as part of this communication network (October 21, 1994).

According to Sawatsky, the RCMP set up an investigative unit known as A-3, so called because it was the third subsection of A Branch. It is likely that A-3 became the character weaknesses subdivision within which Fred worked. Its purpose was to hunt down, identify, locate, and purge homosexuals from RCMP ranks and from the government.[47] Agents and informants would watch bars and parks frequented by gays and attempt to get homosexual men to inform on others. This apparently met with some initial success.[48]

In 1963, the A-3 unit produced a map of Ottawa, using red dots to designate sites where homosexual activity took place. The map was soon so covered with dots that it became practically useless: "A second larger map was purchased, this time from the City of Ottawa – the largest one available. It too, was overcome by red ink. A third and final effort was made. A Mountie approached the Department of National Defence with a request to fly over the city with high-resolution cameras for the purpose of producing an extraordinarily large map. The department was experiencing an austerity program at the time and refused. The map exercise died."[49] Sawatsky also points out that, in their coding system, the RCMP designated homosexuals by adding an extra digit to the code number on the individual's file: "The normal file number D939 followed by five digits indicates that the person has been subjected to a field investigation. Suspected homosexuals had their index read D939-7 followed by five digits. The extra digit, always a seven, identified the subject as a homosexual."[50] D-939 were files on people applying for government employment and were known as "character files"; D-939-7 were files on public servants who were suspected homosexuals.[51] Suspected homosexuals were thereby classified differently from others whom the RCMP investigated. Files and file numbers were crucial to the organization of the national security campaigns and were never simply "neutral"; rather, they carried with them the power/knowledge relations of those campaigns.[52] This was an important aspect of the textual construction of the homosexual in the documentary practices of the RCMP.

The "Enemy" Within: Queers in the RCMP

The RCMP investigations were also turned against queers who were members of the security police. Kelly reports that "about six gay members of the RCMP were ferreted out and fired."[53] David also reported that he knew of "quite a few" gays in the RCMP. One of them became his mentor, but this person was also put under surveillance, interrogated, and purged from the RCMP:

> The sergeant in the [RCMP] who basically speaking ... took me by the hand
> and led me into the gay world, he himself was investigated. And they wanted
> to finally get the goods on him and cashier him ... I think he thought he was
> untouchable. He was very, very popular in the gay scene. He would walk into
> the bars, and wherever he sat people pulled their tables up to him because
> he was so popular ... Everybody loved him. He was a nice guy, a very good-
> looking guy ... But the thing is he used to have parties at his place and didn't
> try to hide them. People were told not to pass on the information, but he
> didn't try to hide the fact that the party was on.

However, the RCMP eventually found out about this gay party:

> So on one particular night there happened to be a building under construc-
> tion directly behind that building ... and the RCMP positioned themselves on
> an upper floor right opposite his bedroom. And they had a camera and they
> took pictures of anybody who went out on the balcony, whether for a smoke
> or to fondle one another. And then later that night, using an infrared or some
> other camera, they took pictures of him in bed with his selected person that
> night. And he was obviously very recognizable in the prints, and so he was

picked up by the RCMP. But he knew he was being followed and watched for awhile before this, and he was the one who gave me the advice, thank goodness, [on] how to comport myself when I got caught. He had a really rough time; they grilled him for about four months before he was actually kicked out. And it was almost every day ... He told me quietly that he had a really rough time before he was actually kicked out of the RCMP. (May 12, 1994)

Again, we see the significance of photo surveillance to the work of the RCMP.

Stories of RCMP Interrogation

Over the course of conducting interviews with the gay men and lesbians who had been interrogated, certain common features became visible. Consistently, they reported that they were repeatedly asked questions such as: "Is so-and-so a homosexual?" and "Do you know of any other homosexuals who work in external affairs [or some other department]?" They were shown photographs of particular individuals and were asked whether they were homosexuals or not.[54] Some were shown photo albums or mug shot files, whereas others were shown cardex files. The technology of RCMP surveillance revolved around the collection of photographs, identities, and names and was coordinated through broader social relations. We begin to explore the social organization of RCMP interrogation and surveillance by looking at what can be learned from those who were its targets.

Herbert Sutcliffe reported that, following his identification as a homosexual,

I was finally told to report to the RCMP, which I did. I could scream nowadays, because instead of going in when they said, "OK, will you point out anybody who you know is a homosexual," instead of ... saying, "Fuckin' bastards, you've killed me. Do you think I'm going to help you kill other people?" But I was terrified that if I said anything to them that they might be able to hold me in Ottawa and I [wouldn't be able to] get back to Toronto. So all I did was to go through all the pictures, "No, no, no, no." (March 1, 1996)

Sutcliffe, describing the RCMP interrogation, made this observation: "There were a series of photo albums with pictures of people who the RCMP believed were homosexuals." When asked how many pictures there were to a page in these books, he replied: "Five, six [pictures] and probably forty pages in one book. And I went through about four books. So I was there for a long time. And I must say, I didn't really know if I did recognize anybody, really, but I knew some of the people in the Ottawa-Hull area, civilians. I never had anything at all to do with the military ... since at some future date they might be under my command." In response to a question about what they asked him, Sutcliffe said: "They might have asked for names, I don't remember. I was so petrified at the time I didn't know what I was doing. But I just made sure that I never [made] any indication that ... I knew any of these people ... I was so terrified at the time that all I could remember is being in this office with this one RCMP officer bringing out these albums, and we sit down [and] turn page after page after page. And I would just say, 'No, no, no'" (March 1, 1996).

When questioned about whether she was asked to identify other lesbians, Sue replied: "No, he didn't [ask] that day. He didn't ask. But one of the things that they certainly [asked] was who was I hanging out with. Who were my pals? And systematically every one of the pals were asked to leave [the militia]. They did a cleanup like you wouldn't believe. You were my friend and you were gone." She believed that about six women were discharged because they had associated with her. In Sue's words, "I mean, we were petrified of military police" (February 23, 1996).

After Albert was identified as a homosexual, a member of the RCMP approached him and asked him to go to the RCMP office in Ottawa:

[The officer] wanted me to cooperate with the RCMP as much as possible in helping to identify people who they already had in a file to try to determine whether or not these people were homosexuals. His terms of reference [were] that he didn't want any information from me unless I was absolutely certain that this person had committed a homosexual act. I think that their criteria was that they would not act on any particular file unless they had more than two or three direct indications that this person was homosexual. Of course, a lot of these people were in security positions, particularly in external affairs but not exclusively in external affairs. It was just a cardex, and I was requested to go through it ... My understanding was that once they had two to three concrete identifications, then this particular file was brought to whatever committee or agent ... was dealing with this subject. (October 19, 1993)

The RCMP officer informed him that they needed to get a number of positive identifications in order to shift someone into the confirmed homosexual category. A central focus of RCMP surveillance and interrogation work involved attempting to get this confirmation.

In the late 1950s, Bob, who was living in Ottawa, was shown a photo album and asked to identify homosexuals. At the RCMP headquarters, Bob was told that half a dozen identifications would get these men called in for interviews.

Spying and Interrogation

The RCMP was particularly interested in Bob's friend, who was stationed with the diplomatic corps in Moscow, regarding letters and possible pressure from the KGB. Bob remembered that two RCMP officers interrogated him, one of whom was quite intimidating, and that he was visited at home as well (October 14, 1994).

Peaches Latour remembered two encounters with the RCMP at its Ottawa headquarters in the 1960s and being shown "tons and tons of pictures." According to Latour, "They would show the pictures and I would have to put a name to them and who they were and he [the RCMP officer] said, 'When you come to somebody you know please identify them.' I looked at all of them and I didn't identify anybody" (August 31, 1994). However, he remembered recognizing 50 percent to 75 percent of the people in the pictures, which was not surprising because Ottawa was "a small town and the gay community was so small." From the numbers of photographs and names, Latour suspected that, given how poor many gay men were at the time, the RCMP had received its information "with money." This raises the important question of how many of the homosexual informants were paid for their information.

Marvin remembered RCMP visits at work:

They came into my office and this was the icing on the cake. We had a fairly large office ... And so the desks were basically in one large room and they were not that far apart, maybe six feet apart at the most. And these two guys – I saw them from the door and of course I knew right away who they were. And they had something under their arms; I couldn't see what it was at the time. But one sat in front of my desk, the other one just stood there, and they plunked [down] these huge big brown leather loose-leaf type books. I thought they were my files, of course, and they started to open them up. And the other girls in the office could see very well what was going on. I said, "I can't have that here." And he said, "Do you know anybody in this book?" I said, "I can't look at these here." I said, "I'm busy, I have clients coming" and so on. So they packed up their books and left. I think he said he'd call me later. I did see one photograph, on the page they did open, of a fellow I knew of ... I didn't know him but a friend of mine ... had gone out with him ... It freaked me out. (May 1998)

David had a similar recollection:

At first they just ask[ed] me to list everybody; they didn't have a list of their own. Later, they came out with ... photo albums with people's pictures and names and asked me to run through and identify the people who I knew who were in their albums. I just felt the best thing to do was to say nothing because if I said these people "are definitely not," and then another person I refused to give information about ... they'd surmise that that person was [homosexual]. And so I felt the best thing to stay with was a blanket statement: "I will not give any information whatsoever." However, they kept after me. Every so many months they would be after me again and always led by one person ... And none of these were pleasant interviews whatsoever. They were, frankly, scary. But the whole idea was not to let them know you were scared, and I just tried to remain as calm as I could under the circumstances.

David was not shown cardex files:

What I saw were flat albums. But they had the same things on it. The albums were probably easier to transport and these were shown to me ... I guess the first time was in my own apartment. See, these interviews took place in various places – in an office and in this ... I have to call it a cell. It was not with bars and it was not padded but it was a room, which had no windows, with what appeared to be a very heavy wooden door and a desk with three, four chairs around it and nothing ... no pictures on the wall. It was a very, very stark room. That was where the most unpleasant interviews took place.

David also remembered that the interviews lasted no longer than three-quarters of an hour because, "[When] they found that they were getting nowhere they just let me go. I think that they were probably very frustrated. I was commended later by a member of the RCMP that I was the only person who did not either tell a whole bunch of lies or tell all" (May 12, 1994).

These investigations and surveillance procedures extended to Montreal, where at least some members of the Ottawa public service frequented gay bars in an effort to avoid detection. As Steve put it, from the mid- to later 1960s, "We went to places in Montreal. I recall going once to one in Ottawa, but really, it just didn't seem worth it, they weren't the most exciting places to be in and, you know, Ottawa is still small, it was even smaller then. And Montreal, you got on the train at 5:15 you were there at 7:15. And yes, we went to Montreal fairly regularly" (June 27, 1998). In the early 1960s, Jake, then a graduate student who would later become an employee of the National Film Board, told us that a gay man who worked for the RCMP in Ottawa went to a gay bar in Montreal on the weekend. He was apparently photographed there and lost his job the following Monday. As Jake explained: "One weekend he went to Montreal [and] went to a bar. On Monday he was fired, and he had been photographed going into a gay bar. So he called me and said they have also made copies of all [the names in] his address book and my name was in the address book. So he said, 'I just want to alert you'" (May 21, 1995). Surveillance of known gay spots and the collection of diaries and address books containing names were crucial to the RCMP's work of identifying homosexuals.

The Work of an RCMP Officer: Fred's Story

According to Fred, close to 90 percent of his work involved dealing with homosexuals, almost all of whom were gay men. He said that it was difficult to identify lesbians and that they were more suspicious of male RCMP officers than were male homosexuals. Fred described much of his work as making contact with gay men, cultivating friendships, and then converting them into informants (October 21, 1994). We use the term "informant" rather than "source" to describe the people who supplied information to the RCMP because we think that it more clearly describes the social relations of surveillance than does "source," which is most often used by the RCMP.[55] Fred reported that it was relatively easy to get informants, especially when the RCMP officers assured them that information acquired would not lead to the actual prosecution of individuals. Fred's work entailed meeting with gay men five nights a week. He asked informants about gay house parties and who was present, taking particular interest in learning if anyone new attended these events. If the informants answered in the affirmative, Fred made a point of asking whether these people were public servants and where they worked. If a gay man was or appeared to be a public servant, the officers in the character weaknesses subdivision would photograph him, using a camera with a telephoto lens. To confirm identification, the informant was shown the photograph. Fred went to some of these parties with some of these informants and even accompanied them to gay dinner parties.

In order to eliminate potential errors, Fred spent considerable time rating the reliability of the informants. The RCMP had to try to ensure that those who were identified by informants would be unable to determine who they were. Central to this was the RCMP-informant relation, a critical aspect of Fred's work.

When the character weaknesses subdivision identified a homosexual government employee, it would report this information to the public servant's departmental security officer. Fred stated that interviews with public servants would often occur in the offices of these security officers and that an RCMP officer might or might not be present. These interviews started with statements such as, "Information has come to our attention that you are a homosexual." Fred reported that public servants identified as homosexuals by the RCMP would be asked to quietly resign.

Fred stated that the photograph books of suspected homosexuals that were used to verify identifications were becoming less relevant by the late 1960s. With regard to the cardex file, he said that names of suspected homosexuals were added as they became available. This file was used for identification purposes and to shift individuals from "suspected" to "confirmed" homosexuals. Asked how many identifications were required to accomplish this, Fred stated that it depended on the reliability of the sources and that it had to involve more than just "mannerisms." According to Fred, people had to be "seen with a sexual partner" or in the context of "a homosexual relationship." He said that, with reliable sources and his own investigations, he "was never wrong." He tried to follow the rules of evidence to produce a case that, if necessary, could stand up in court (October 21, 1994).

The Textual Construction of the "Confirmed" Homosexual

This work that Fred described of identifying and confirming suspected homosexuals through the use of informants was an essential part of the RCMP's interrogation work; it also contributed to the building of an RCMP-informant relation. The social organization of surveillance and interrogation included important technological dimensions, including the use of cameras, telephoto lenses, photographs, photo albums, files, interrogation rooms, and tape recorders. Related to this is the coding and the use of the extra digit to textually classify the suspected homosexuals, who were thus separated from other names and files the RCMP were collecting. RCMP work revolved around locating suspected homosexuals and shifting them to the confirmed category. Indeed, this was the basis for evaluating the effectiveness of the work.

The RCMP classified those investigated into three categories: "Confirmed, alleged, suspected. The 'confirmed' are those who have been interviewed and admitted being homosexuals or who have been convicted in court on a charge of sexual deviation with another male. The 'alleged' are those who have been named as homosexuals by a source or sources whose information is considered to be reliable. The 'suspected' are those who are believed to be homosexuals by a source or sources whose information is considered to be reliable."[56] Of these three categories, "confirmed" was the most important. We learn from those who were interrogated and, in a different way, from Fred, that information from gay and sometimes lesbian informants could be used to produce the confirmed homosexual through a series of identifications.

This was a textual construction that built upon a number of different identifications given by informants with various levels of reliability and/or through RCMP field investigations. Only when placed in the confirmed category was an individual, textually speaking, a real homosexual. Once people were moved into the confirmed category, they could be purged from their position or transferred to a lower-level position. Some other form of action could also be taken against them. These classifications came to mediate and organize the work of the RCMP and its relation to various government departments.

This required that the surveillance campaigns be extended far beyond the confines of the public service. The RCMP had to find informants who could provide it with information, and, in Ottawa, it developed informant networks outside the public service. The RCMP could often exert persuasive social power over these informants. This also meant, however, that the RCMP was to some extent dependent upon the information it acquired from these people. This RCMP-informant relation was the weak link in the social organization of the security campaigns because it was easily disrupted by non-cooperation.

There is no doubt that creating networks of informants and engaging in field investigations in the late 1950s and the 1960s was expensive and time-consuming. This created pressures that led to the fruit machine research, which was supposed to provide a scientific basis for determining sexual orientation. This, in turn, would avoid costly fieldwork and the problems encountered with relying on informants. We now turn to an investigation of the development of detection technology as part of the Canadian war on queers.

5

The Fruit Machine
Attempting to Detect Queers

PROFESSOR WAKE, PSYCHOLOGY, AND THE FRUIT MACHINE

The attempt to devise a machine or a battery of psychological tests that could scientifically detect homosexuals was part of the growing obsession with identifying queers as a national security threat. The Security Panel mandated research on the detection of homosexuals, hoping to find a mechanism for both uncovering and disposing of queers. In the words of Frank Robert Wake, the Carleton University psychologist who was commissioned to create such a test, homosexuals were dangerous because "heterosexuals have some sort of negative emotional feelings when homosexuality seeps into the atmosphere around them."[1]

In this attempt to detect homosexuals, the security regime continued to rely on scientific knowledge (especially psychological knowledge) and technological solutions. Previously, it had relied on fingerprinting.[2] According to Hannant, security screening of civil servants in Canada started as early as 1931 and increased during the Second World War. The RCMP was especially fond of technologies created in the interests of furthering security work as it attempted to deal with the growing number of national security directives and the increasing fear of the "other."[3]

According to John Sawatsky, who provided the first public account of the fruit machine, Wake's "Special Project" was given its name by members of the RCMP who did not want to participate in the "normal" control group.[4] As he remarked, they did not want to risk being determined to be "fruits" (January 4, 1996).[5]

Wake's research was a way of addressing a number of obstacles encountered by the security regime. First, the RCMP was facing increasing difficulty getting information from homosexual informants as queer solidarity and networking grew in the early 1960s. The hope was that a successful detection device could provide reliable scientific information. Second, the RCMP found that it was putting a great deal of energy into costly field investigations, and it felt that a scientific means of detection would resolve these financial and personnel problems. Third, there was a presumption that, being "scientific," the device would remove any risks of subjectivity. It was expected to eliminate the possibility of errors in the high stakes of security spying.

Detecting homosexuals was thought to be a difficult task because, most of the time, they could not be easily distinguished from heterosexuals. But this was not always the case. According to Wake, some homosexuals "do not care that their proclivities are known – rather they appear to insist that they be noticed. 'Visibility' is high because of mannerisms, dress and places frequented."[6]

Overt homosexuals, with their "mannerisms" (read "effeminate" gestures), were considered the most unsuitable for work in the civil service. Because they subverted gender-appropriate practices, highly visible homosexuals directly challenged the notion of masculine men. Such queers were believed to be unsuitable for work in the upper echelons of management for the same reasons as were women: effeminate men, like women, were thought weak and soft, both physically and intellectually.

The homosexuals who successfully concealed their secret, on the other hand, were just as dangerous as those who did not, but for different reasons. Men and women who could pass as heterosexual were considered subversive and vulnerable. Their vulnerability stemmed from their secret, which, although it did not necessarily make them disloyal, rendered them unreliable. Heterosexual men were normal and devoid of character weaknesses because they performed socially acceptable gender practices. The assumption was that all heterosexual men were emotionally stable, physically strong, and virile. Like earlier notions of gender inversion, character weakness was associated with gender deviancy.

The work on the fruit machine was initiated at the Security Panel. An RCMP document reports that one of the proposals discussed was

the establishment of a research program in search of clinical tests which could discover homosexual tendencies in applicants for government positions ... A small team of Ottawa psychology and psychiatry research experts was engaged in 1961 by the Security Panel. Its director ... by late 1962 [blacked out] ... was prepared to undertake clinical testing of some possibly useful techniques. The RCMP Directorate of Security and Intelligence was called upon to assist to some degree in providing general information and recruiting some test candidates, but the project dragged on through the 1960s with little positive result, practically for lack of sufficient individuals to test.[7]

In a January 1961 Security Panel document, the potential for a detection device that would not only purge homosexuals from the civil service but also prevent their actual hiring was offered as a possibility. It was argued that

> consideration be given to setting up a program of research ... with a view to devising tests to identify persons with homosexual tendencies. It is hoped that such tests might aid in the identification of homosexuals already employed in the government service, and eventually might assist in the selection of persons who are not homosexuals for service in positions considered vulnerable to blackmail for intelligence purposes. (The Commissioner of the RCM Police feels that these tests should be extended to prevent, where possible, the initial engagement of homosexuals in the government service on the grounds that they are usually practising criminals under Sections 147 and 149 of the Criminal Code of Canada.)[8]

This proposal led to research on the fruit machine.

As secretary to the Security Panel, Don Wall was sent to Washington, DC, in 1961 and 1962. His report, based on these visits, not only covered the various security and screening practices in use but also pointed out that security screening in the State Department involved psychiatric examinations, psychological tests, and the possible use of the polygraph (lie-detector). Wall also fully supported Wake's Special Project proposal.[9] This reflected the security regime's orientation towards studying and using US security procedures, and his visits south of the border made Wall aware of homosexual detection research. In a 1960 memo, RCMP inspector William Kelly reported that Wall advised the commissioner of the RCMP "that next year [was] a sabbatical year for Dr. Wake ... and [that he] propose[d] to spend the year in the United States on a study of sex deviates." Kelly also reported that Wall had spoken to John Starnes, of the Department of External Affairs, and was going to speak to Dr. Cameron, of the Department of National Health and Welfare, to secure the estimated $5,000 "that it [would] cost to have Dr. Wake undertake the work proposed."[10]

In a 1980 interview, Wall talked about some of the initial work leading up to the fruit machine research. He tended both to appropriate Wake's work as his own and to provide too much of a liberal spin to his own approach:

One of the things that I was asked to do was to talk to several of the American organizations (the Federal Bureau of Investigation, CIA, National Security Agency and Security Service Commission in the State Department) as to what their approach was to this problem. Again I found in all of those organizations in various visits I made to Washington a number of highly able, intelligent, perceptive, sensitive people and some real hard rocks. Their approach ... tended to be mechanistic. They wanted a gimmick. An easy way of determining whether a guy was a homosexual or not. And their prime tool was the polygraph machine which was used in most of these agencies as part of the selection procedure or if a doubt was raised about a guy's behaviour after he had been in the service for awhile he would be brought back and was subjected to what to my mind was a pretty horrendous series of tests that were stacked up next to a polygraph and asked a series of very pointed questions the purpose of which was essentially to arise anxiety to the point where he would confess ... I found it to be an intrusive and essentially unfair process. In the report that I made to the government of Canada when I got back I strongly recommended against the use of that approach. I thought there must be a better way of determining this ... We had known that the Soviets and others had used this one proclivity as a point of leverage for blackmail and used it quite successfully ... We got some outside help. Psychologists, psychiatrists and some others. And there was a project set up to see if there were not some acceptable and humane means of first of all, identifying people with this propensity and then determining whether if they had it or not they would pose a danger in terms of their vulnerability. The project in itself didn't come to much. We never found a gimmick that would work.[11]

Following up on the approval for this study in 1961, Wake, who was central to providing the outside help to which Wall referred, was funded by the Department of National Health and Welfare to go to the United States to research detection technologies regarding homosexuality.

Wake was born in Knoxville, Tennessee, in 1914 and died in 1993 in Ottawa.[12] His family moved to Quebec during his adolescence. Wake began his bachelor of arts degree at McGill University in 1947, finishing with a doctorate from the same institution. His dissertation was on fear and aging, a research

1　Dr. Frank R. Wake, professor of psychology, Carleton University, c. 1960s | *Credit:* Archives and Research Collections, MacOdrum Library, Carleton University

interest that continued in various forms throughout his career. He began his academic career as an assistant professor of psychology at the University of Kansas in 1950 but made the move to Carleton in 1952, where he worked until he retired in the mid-1980s. Wake figured prominently in the founding and history of the psychology department at Carleton (see Photo 1). When he was hired in 1952 (the year that Carleton College was endowed with university powers), he was the psychology department's first chair and full-time faculty member. He was responsible for establishing the graduate program and recruiting new faculty to bolster the department. Finally, Wake was an active member of the Canadian Psychological Association, the Ontario Psychological Association, and the Ontario Board of Examiners in Psychology.

From 1954 to 1958, Wake was a medical researcher for the Royal Commission on the Criminal Law Relating to Criminal Sexual Psychopaths.[13] Dr. G.W. Cameron, deputy minister of national health and welfare, knew Wake through his work for this commission. Wake was also employed as a consulting psychologist by the Mental Health Division of the Department of National Health and Welfare and engaged in work on Ontario mental health questions.[14] Cameron was the government official who recommended Wake and other "advisory personnel ... who might assist [the Security Panel] in research and the development of testing techniques [regarding homosexuality]."[15] There was already an interaction between psychiatric knowledge and the criminal justice system regarding the criminalization of homosexual activity (see Chapter 3 regarding the addition of "criminal sexual psychopath" and "dangerous sexual offender" to the Criminal Code). This integration was now expanded with the security regime privileging of psychological knowledge regarding homosexuality. Indeed, psychological work played an active part in constructing the security campaigns.[16]

The connection between Carleton University's psychology department and the federal government and military, however, was much broader than Wake's foray into the Royal Commission on the Criminal Law Relating to Criminal Sexual Psychopaths and is one Canadian example of how psychology as a discipline was applied in the context of the Cold War. In a brief institutional history of the psychology department, this relationship is evidenced by the number of faculty and lecturers who, in the 1950s and 1960s, were drawn from the civil service and military or who had some sort of formal link to these state institutions. From roughly 1950 to 1964, a total of seventeen department members worked for the following government agencies: the Defence Research Board, the Department of National Defence, the Canadian Army (Regular) Personnel Selection Service, the Royal Canadian Navy, the Royal Canadian Air Force, and the Canadian Broadcasting Corporation. Staff from the psychology department also gave lectures to the RCMP on various topics.[17]

Ellen Herman has documented the ties between psychology and the military machine. She argues that the Cold War "advanced psychological knowledge production on all the various fronts that constituted the psychological enterprise."[18] This included the development of psychology as an "administrative discipline specializing in testing and classification; as a 'helping profession' advancing psychotherapeutic techniques; and as a behavioural science devoted to investigating human motivation and action for the purposes of understanding, prediction, and control."[19] It was this dedication to using scientific method and expert knowledge that justified the funding of such projects as the fruit machine. The profession's claim to be able to predict personality and behaviour was considered increasingly paramount in the context of the Cold War, where the "enemy" was not always obvious.

Wake's writing and research focused on questions of personal stability and loyalty, aggression, juvenile delinquency, and physical cruelty.[20] Various directories of psychologists show adolescence and youth, aging, and health psychology as his areas of expertise.[21] In the psychology department, graduate students and colleagues were aware of his interest regarding eye movement and the pupillary response test. His major areas of study were considered to be juvenile delinquency, smoking, and eye movement in the context of learning. It was also generally known that he was interested in and had some involvement in sex-related research.[22]

In the 1960s, Wake gave presentations on sex education and young people in Ottawa. In February 1965, in a program initiated by a young minister apparently motivated by the increasing number of young unwed mothers using the Children's Aid Society, he talked to a group of teenagers about sex education. At this session, Wake responded to questions on sexual intercourse, homosexuality, and masturbation, but he placed the most emphasis on sex in the context of marriage. A newspaper article reporting on Wake's talk quoted this statement: "There has been a sad lack of research into the broad sweep of questions concerning teenage sexual behaviour. He [Wake] has done some probing but there has been little work actually studying youth."[23]

In his 1961 memo to the Security Panel, Wake called for more research and insisted that a "fully considered research program be instituted in order to develop suitable methods of selecting personnel for sensitive positions."[24] It was on this basis that Wake produced the 1962 report that got the fruit machine research going.[25]

Wake had some contact with a network of sex researchers in the United States, including Wardell B. Pomeroy of the Kinsey Institute, John Money, William H. Masters (of Masters and Johnson), and Evelyn Hooker. Most of the sex researchers at the Kinsey Institute opposed these security detection procedures.[26] Evelyn Hooker's liberal psychological approach, and that of others whose basic objective was to disprove the then widespread psychological theory that gay men were mentally ill, does not seem to have influenced Wake, except in so far as he described his wish to remain in contact with them: "It might be well for a member of the Department of National Health and Welfare to assume a liaison role with these people, for they know of new developments in the field.

However, anyone effecting this liaison probably will have to have a front to cover his interest in 'suitability.'"[27] One gets the sense that "suitability".was a crossover term that could be coded with both national security concerns and more liberal research concerns.

In North America, there existed a link between the psychological profession, security technologies, and psychological tests being set up to establish loyalty and suitability. The expansion of personnel management during these years involved the adoption of psychological knowledge in social administration, including the widespread use of psychological tests, which were informed by particular constructions of masculinity/femininity and heterosexuality.[28] Employees found to be "unstable" or "unreliable" – sometimes because they did not display proper masculine or feminine practices – were deemed unsuitable. By the mid-1960s, however, there was growing resistance to the use of psychological tests in the US government. This resistance was heard not only in Senate hearings but also in the pages of *American Psychologist.*[29]

The fruit machine research was more psychologically oriented than were earlier studies of homosexuality, which sometimes focused on biological anomalies (such as marks of gender inversion on the body).[30] It was directed at finding a scientific way of testing involuntary responses that "demonstrated" sexual orientation. This research arose both from Wake's interest in conducting studies on homosexuality (disguised as a desire to research employment suitability) and from a need to improve upon the surveillance used in RCMP field investigations. It was the promise of precision and efficiency that piqued the interest of both the Security Panel and the RCMP. The latter, however, was at times rather ambivalent about the research as it actually developed (see below).

Homosexual detection research both continued and shifted earlier practices for revealing homosexuals. Now that homosexuality was distinguished from broader collecting categories, tests for detection were developed much more extensively. No longer was this research based simply on the imagery of gender inversion; now the focus turned towards sexual object choice and sexual orientation. As a result of his investigations, Wake argued that there was no distinct homosexual personality type. This signalled a move away from notions of homosexuals as gender inverts and as psychopathic personalities. A parallel situation was occurring in psychological and sexological circles, with the articulation of homosexuality as a "sexual orientation" based on a deviant sexual object choice. Less focus was placed on homosexual personality traits and more on homosexual activity. There was a heavy reliance on psychiatric and psychological knowledge in this research, which viewed gay men and lesbians as psychologically abnormal, as suffering from a disorder. As in most other research, the normality of heterosexuality was simply assumed, and homosexuality was defined as the problem.[31]

The fruit machine project, which involved psychiatrists, psychologists, the RCMP, the DND, and the Department of National Health and Welfare for a period of four years, never did work, and the Defence Research Board eventually cut its funding in 1967. It received support from the National Research Council, health and welfare, and the Privy Council. The project suffered from major technical problems as well as from difficulties in getting an adequate number of research subjects, which included "normal" as well as homosexual men and women.

The difficulties encountered in recruiting homosexuals may have prompted Wake to approach the Canadian Council on Religion and the Homosexual (CCRH) in Ottawa to request that its homosexual members fill out a questionnaire in the mid-1960s.[32] Bruce Somers got involved with the CCRH when he moved to Ottawa in late 1964. According to him,

> [Wake] gave us a pile of these questionnaires to be anonymously handed out to various members of CCRH to fill out and to get back to him as anonymous. But it was a pretty hefty questionnaire ... The intent was for all of them to be homosexual ... He was a professor doing psychological research, you know, at that point anything we could do that would help to provide any kind of liaison we were happy to do ... He only had limited contact with us, it wasn't as if he spent a lot of time with us ... He gave us a whole series of brown manila envelopes ... to hand out. There was quite a pile for us to give out. I would estimate it was six to twelve pages. (June 10, 1994)

Wake was attempting to compile a set of homosexual responses that could be compared to their heterosexual equivalents in the process of constructing a homosexual profile.

THE FRUIT MACHINE TECHNOLOGY AND ITS CONTRADICTIONS

Since Wake argued that there was no single, distinct homosexual personality type, there could be no single test for homosexuality. Under the heading "Methods of Detecting Homosexuality," he surveyed the various detection tests and technologies that had been used to try to identify homosexuals. These ranged from psychiatric interviews to medical examinations to various tests for changes in emotional conditions. Some of these tests included the plethysmograph, which measures blood volume in the finger by electronic or pneumatic means; the Palmer sweat test, which measures perspiration; word association tests; the pupillary response test; the span of attention test, which measures the time spent in attending to various images; and masculinity/femininity (M/F) tests, with all their gender and sexuality assumptions.[33]

The use of M/F tests was one major way in which gender assumptions entered into this research. The tests were based on the coding of male homosexuality with effeminacy and lesbianism with masculinity. Subjects taking the tests were asked to answer "true" or "false" to statements grounded in gender stereotypes emphasizing heterosexual performances of masculinity and femininity. The tests worked from the assumption that, depending on whether a subject was male or female, there was a correct answer to each statement; thus, it was believed that one could determine the possibility of gender inversion or, at the very least, character weakness according to adherence to cultural formulations of gender codes. Underlying this main assumption was the notion that gender exists as a binary: one is either male or female. The idea was that male subjects should respond with "true" to statements that were coded masculine (such as leadership in politics or confidence in solving particularly difficult problems). Some of the statements in the M/F test in Wake's "Special Report" include the following:

I want to be an important person in the community.
I'm not the type to be a political leader.
When someone talks against certain groups or nationalities, I always speak up against such talk even though it makes me unpopular.
I like mechanics magazines.
I think I would like the work of a librarian.
I'm pretty sure I know how we can settle the international problems we face today.
I like to go to parties and other affairs where there is lots of loud fun.
If I were a reporter I would like very much to report news of the theatre.
I would like to be a nurse.
I very much like hunting.
I would like to be a soldier.
It is hard for me to start a conversation with strangers.
I think I would like the work of a building contractor.
I think I would like the work of a dress designer.[34]

Describing the various levels of usefulness of each test, Wake generally dismissed the overall perspective of the M/F test, indicating its limitations while maintaining that it was a useful tool in identifying homosexuals. He reported that, "although conventional use of M/F scales has not proved fruitful, intensive research might be more successful."[35]

In his commentary, Wake suggested that the Palmer sweat test was best used in conjunction with a word association list that would test for anxious responses to "homosexual" words. Words with definite homosexual meaning, according to the appended list, include queen, circus, gay, bell, whole, blind, bull, camp, coo, cruise, drag, dike (dyke), fish, flute, fruit, mother, punk, queer, rim, sew, swing, trade, velvet, wolf, blackmail, prowl, bar, house, club, restaurant, tea room, and top men.[36] Clearly, some of these words were taken from the gay language of the day. This suggests some knowledge of gay culture on the part of the researchers, who may have drawn upon research under way in the United States. Many of these words had double meanings and gay cultural associations.[37]

It is important to analyze these homosexually coded words not only for their association with gay talk but also for their meaning in the minds of the medical experts. Analyzing the so-called neutral words can also be a critical exercise in decoding what Wake and his band of experts believed to be normal words.[38] Words such as breast, farm, hammer, blonde, stiff, radiator, erect, politician, stroke, cigar, child, newspaper, fight, and asphalt were all considered neutral. In themselves they were held to have very little meaning but were significant next to the words designated as homosexual. When these neutrally coded words were used, they were thought to heighten the distinction between neutral words and homosexual words. Wake's assumption was that the latter were part of a lexicon that would generate some reaction on the part of people who were familiar with their hidden meanings.

While being asked word association and M/F questions, individuals would be connected to both a Palmer sweat test and a plethysmographic device to test their reactions. A greater level of anxiety in response to homosexual-related questions was supposed to indicate the possible homosexuality of the research subject.

Wake found the pupillary response test to be quite "productive" with regard to detecting homosexuals. It measured different interest patterns by means of a machine that simultaneously projected a visual stimulus and photographed the pupil of the eye. In the test, research subjects peered through an opening in a box to look at the projected images. This procedure was supposed to produce an involuntary "response that [could not] be controlled by the subject."[39]

The Fruit Machine

Wake encountered this procedure and technology through his research in the United States, where Eckhard H. Hess and his assistant J.M. Polt, researchers at the University of Chicago, had developed them.[40] Hess started his career as an associate professor at the University of Chicago and became head of the psychology department in 1963. One of his major interests was pupillometrics, which measures pupillary response to viewing emotionally charged stimuli.[41] In conversation with Dean Beeby, Wake suggested that his research relationship with the University of Chicago was at arm's length; however, professional and academic links were important in his security regime research.[42]

Wake's report refers to a study conducted by A.L. Seltzer, a graduate student who was studying with Hess, using the Hess-Polt apparatus. In Seltzer's study the "stimuli were slides made of pictures from physical culture magazines (some of which were near pornographic) plus neutral pictures of good paintings and at least one modified picture of Christ on the cross."[43] Physique magazines, which often had a large gay male readership, seem to have been commonly used by American psychologists in this period.[44] They were also used in aversion therapy, a form of "therapy" based on giving aversive substances or shocks to an individual in the hope that this would prevent her/him from engaging in queer activities. This use of physique photos suggests an awareness of the formation of gay men's cultures. Wake argued that the "results clearly permitted Seltzer to distinguish the homosexual subject when the results of *all* pictures were compared." Wake reported that "not only was the change in size of pupil indicative of the direction of sex interest but the pattern followed by the eyes (and recorded on film) was very important (eg. the homosexual who could not take his eyes away from the genital area of the vaguely-seen Christ on the Cross)."[45]

In emphasizing that the tests were viable, Wake offered the following statement: "Perhaps the most important incidental finding in this experiment was the confession of a homosexual subject who reported that he had done his best to defeat the machine but knew he had failed." In conclusion, Wake remarked: "Here, then, is a most promising instrument for detection, not only of homosexuals but of homosexual potentiality."[46]

Wake must also have been aware of the early 1960s research conducted by Hess, Seltzer, and John M. Shlien on the pupillary response of heterosexual and homosexual men to pictures of men and women (based on Seltzer's earlier work).[47] This US research was conducted around the same time as the fruit machine research, and the findings and assumptions of the former shed light on the latter. In a paper based on their research, Hess, Seltzer, and Shlien commented: "Change in the size of the pupil of the human eye has been reported to vary with the subject's interest in various pictorial stimuli."[48] They added that "male subjects had a larger pupil while looking at pictures of women than when looking at pictures of men. The reverse was true for female subjects: they had larger pupils looking at men." They hypothesized that, if this was the case, "then a homosexual would be expected to show a larger pupil response to pictures of their own sex." They reported that, in the course of their work, "a few subjects ha[d] given a larger response to pictures of their own sex; as measured by pupil size, same-sex pictures seemed more interesting to them. Review of these anomalous cases increased the plausibility of the idea that this same-sex response might be typical of homosexuals."[49]

The pilot study described in their report consisted "of a small group of overt male homosexuals," which, they argued, "strongly support[ed] that hypothesis."[50] They tested ten adult male subjects. In five of them, "their sexual outlet was judged to be exclusively heterosexual." The authors added that the remaining five subjects admitted "to have overt homosexuality as their sole or primary sexual outlet."[51] The description of the apparatus used in this research is remarkably similar to descriptions of that used in Wake's fruit machine study:

> In a dimly-lit room, a subject was seated before a viewing aperture, fitted with a head-rest, which was inserted in a large plywood panel. The panel concealed the working of the apparatus from the subject. Resting his head against the aperture, the subject faced a rear-projection screen, set in an otherwise black box, at a distance of two and one-half feet from his eyes. A 35 mm. slide projector behind this screen projected a nine- by twelve-inch picture onto it. Changing of slides was controlled by the experimenter from his position behind the panel where he also operated a concealed 16 mm. camera fitted with a frame counter. As the slides were being viewed a half-silvered mirror placed at a forty-five degree angle across the subject's line of sight permitted unobtrusive filming of the eye, at the rate of two frames per second.[52]

Central to this apparatus were the images that were shown. The strategy was to maximize responses based on visual sexual interest. In the logic of these researchers, the responses could be secured only by showing a series of pictures that were "representations of the human figure," predominately nude. Hess, Seltzer, and Shlien reported that the "'male' pictures ... considered to be the homosexual equivalent of pin-ups, were culled from physique magazines." They also included five art slides. Why? Because, among other reasons, "homosexuals are often thought to have artistic interests, and, indeed, most of the homosexuals in this study did verbally indicate such interests. It was useful, therefore, to include a group of slides which would permit appraisal of response to the artistic quality of pictures separate from their representation of sexual objects."[53]

Drawing on a common stereotype, the researchers constructed male homosexuals as having particular artistic sensibilities. In attempting to justify their choices, they offered the following rationale: "Such a separation of pictorial content from its artistic mode of expression appears feasible since 1) the homosexuals, as a group, showed a high response to the artistically good but sexually ambiguous art slides but 2) they also showed a high response to the artistically crude male pictures yet 3) they showed a low response to the artistically good female pictures."[54]

Interestingly, Hess, Seltzer, and Shlien also reported on the complications they encountered in the calculation of pupil size, which suggests that they experienced some of the same technical problems that occurred in the fruit machine research. In their results, they noted that "all heterosexual males show a larger response to pictures of women than to pictures of men ... Four of the homosexuals show a larger response to pictures of men." In their discussion section, they wrote that "some of the 'female' pictures drew a high positive response from some of the homosexuals and some of the 'male' pictures drew a high positive response from some of the heterosexuals. Therefore, response to any single stimulus did not serve to categorize individuals." As it suggested a diversity of interests in and reactions to images across the heterosexual/homosexual binary, this interesting finding could have led to the deconstruction of the central assumption upon which the study was based. Instead, the researchers quickly moved past this possibility to argue that "the total response of a group of subjects to any single stimulus, however, usually served to categorize that stimulus. Total heterosexual response to three of the five 'female' pictures was positive. Total homosexual response to each of the five 'male' pictures was positive ... The information they have given us and more recent advances in our technique – especially in the matter of brightness matching of pictures – now permit the formulation of a test battery of pictorial stimuli designed to give a more absolute reflection of a single subject's sex-object interest."[55]

We get a clear sense that the researchers had to constantly tinker with the technology and tests in an attempt to get the results they hoped for. They refer to the remarkable "cooperation" of their "homosexual subjects," whom, they point out, were all used to a "customary defence against identification as homosexuals," further noting that they were all "operating in a normal" (read "heterosexual") environment. Although the subjects lived in the closet or led double lives, "the pupil technique, using a response that is non-verbal and beyond voluntary control, was able to differentiate [the homosexual subjects] from the heterosexual subjects." This is not to say that the pupil response "as an index of preference is a predictive substitute for the ultimate criterion of the behaviour itself. It does mean that where both preference and behaviour are homosexual, even though socially concealed, the pupil response has been shown in this sample to have discriminating power."[56] These conclusions were similar to those of Wake, and they bolstered the approach adopted in the fruit machine research and the centrality of the pupillary response test.

In the conclusion to his "Special Project" report, Wake argued that more research was needed. He proposed the following experiment, which would combine "the Hess-Polt pupillary test with suitable visual stimuli; a measure of skin perspiration ... ; the plethysmograph with a modification to measure pulse rate. Subjects: Fifteen normal males; fifteen normal females; fifteen homosexual males; fifteen homosexual females. As the experiment progresses, additional normal and homosexual subjects in unspecified numbers. All subjects to be supplied by the RCMP."[57] There are several important features to highlight in this proposal. First, we see another side of the construction of power/knowledge relations in the research context and its direct linkage to national security through the RCMP. Second, heterosexuality, in contrast to homosexuality, is normalized. Wake uses language that does not specifically name heterosexuality, as such, in this report (which was written prior to the emergence of "heterosexuality" as a popular term following the rise of gay liberation and lesbian feminism in the 1970s).[58] Third, the research design places equal emphasis on homosexual females and homosexual males.

In his report, Wake outlined the procedure to be used: "The experimental stimuli will be pictures designed to elicit the subject's interest in males and females ... The first sixty subjects will be processed to determine the reaction patterns of normals and homosexuals. Then, using these patterns as criteria, the experimenter will attempt to distinguish homosexuals presented by the RCMP, where nothing of the subject is known to the research team. Those methods proving successful will be retained for continuing research."[59] The fruit machine research required a part-time senior social scientist and a full-time master's-level clinical psychologist as well as between $5,000 to $10,000 annually. A board of federal officials, including the RCMP, was to oversee the project. In early 1963, with Minister of Justice Fleming present, the Security Panel approved the project.[60]

The RCMP was to procure the homosexual test subjects for the research. Later in its development, Fred delivered men to the National Defence Medical Centre for the project (October 21, 1994). He never met Wake but said that his partner in the character weaknesses subdivision did. He reported that, by this point, the senior levels of the DND seemed most interested in this study, and he believed that the military was in charge of getting the "normal" control group for the experiments. He identified a lieutenant at the National Defence Medical Centre as crucial to the research. This was after its organization and funding had shifted towards national defence. Whereas the RCMP was still responsible for getting the homosexual subjects, the "normals" were now provided from the much larger pool of the military. Fred's job was to provide "confirmed, active" homosexuals for the research (October 21, 1994).

He reported that, for a brief period, he took a gay man to the third floor of the National Defence Medical Centre on Smythe Avenue every night. He remembered taking a total of ten to fifteen gay men to the centre for these tests. These men were promised total anonymity. According to Fred, an overhead machine projected images of women undressing, but he never saw images of naked men's bodies. He found recruiting lesbians for this research to be particularly difficult, but he did manage to talk to a few (October 21, 1994).

Our interview with Fred is substantiated by a brief 1969 article co-authored by Wake and James Lawless, which was published in *Psychophysiology*.[61] The shift to the DND as the department responsible for the fruit machine research meant that Wake was put in contact with Lawless, who worked for the National Defence Medical Centre. This article made no specific references to homosexuals or to military or security issues, but the tests Wake and Lawless described for their investigation of pupillary response to visual stimuli regarding "nude and partially-nude pictures" were virtually identical to the "apparatus" described in the "Special Report." The pupillary response test spoken of in their article worked as follows: "A visual stimuli consisting of 20 colour slides of varying subject content were presented to subjects in a supine position while pupillary diameter, heart rate, and respiration were continuously recorded using a modified Hess-Polt apparatus. Pupillary records were scored for diameter, latency, reaction times, and response-to-recovery times."[62]

Wake and Lawless reported that "preliminary investigations" were performed on "14 male and 7 female subjects," some of whom may well have been the same men that Fred delivered to the National Defence Medical Centre. This, of course, was a much smaller group than was suggested for the fruit machine research. Although the article did not mention the fruit machine, it is clearly based on the research Wake and Lawless conducted on that project.

The article focused on the contradictory results they encountered in using and adapting the Hess-Polt technology in direct response to Hess' 1960 article on visual stimuli in *Science* and Hess, Seltzer, and Shlien's 1965 article in the *Journal of Abnormal Psychology*. Wake and Lawless seem dedicated to confirming

Hess' results, perhaps as a way to lend more credence to the tests that, as early as 1962, Wake initiated using the Hess-Polt pupillary response test. The 1965 article was more directly concerned with homosexuality and sexual identification, and, in it, Wake and Lawless made the following comment:

> Pupillary diameters were subjected to four methods of statistical treatment including a replication of Hess' (1965) method. Two of these methods were ultimately rejected as being too gross, but all four methods produced similar results, which were contrary to those obtained by Hess. It was found that on the parameter of pupillary diameter alone, both male and female subjects ranked the visual stimuli in essentially the same fashion, and that the relative M/F score (Hess 1965) did not produce significantly different results for male or female subjects. In other words, males and females showed no interest difference in slides depicting males and females.[63]

Rather than using this finding to challenge the central assumptions of Hess' and their own research, Wake and Lawless viewed their contradictory results as indicating difficulties inherent in Hess' methods rather than with the overall premise upon which both studies were based. Their refusal to see the study and apparatus itself as flawed resulted in their further pursuing this research.

Wake and Lawless found one exception in the battery of tests that they scrutinized. They discovered that Hess' findings on pupillary dilation responses to nude or partially nude photos may not have been based on sexual interest but on interest in nudity itself. Thus, Wake and Lawless concluded that the male subjects' greater response to the pictures as opposed to the female subjects' "smaller dilation" was consistent with the concept that males were more responsive to visual erotic stimuli than were females.[64] This has since become a central assumption of psychological work in this area.

THE FRUIT MACHINE AND QUEER NETWORKS

There was some knowledge of this research program in Ottawa's gay networks and even among public servants in the city. As Robert reported,

> I knew of a machine ... It was almost like word association, a pictorial, like pictures and stuff like that. And they could register – basically they could tell if somebody was gay by this machine because it would register if you saw a picture of a man, if you would be really aroused, or if you saw a picture of a woman, there was no reaction type of thing. And they could tell if you were

gay or lesbian ... Now, I don't think Tom or anyone I knew had ever been tested on this machine. There were many times that a lot of us would feel like this was just a hoax. You know, like this is just some sort of gizmo, like almost a scientology type of thing. I heard about it but I never heard of anyone that actually had been tested. (October 10, 1996)

Rumours regarding the special project filtered into gay networks and parts of the public service. Steve did not remember anything specific about a detection machine, but he did recall rumours of "a series of tests": "Yes, I certainly never had them ... I remember thinking what an unpleasant idea it was that they had some way of recognizing people's sexual orientation without their knowledge" (June 27, 1998).

Brian Drader's play *The Fruit Machine,* which dramatizes aspects of the fruit machine research and the security campaigns, including quotes from Wake's "Special Project" report, triggered significant memories for some audience members.[65] Drader reported that he was approached by a man who had been purged from the military and who told him that he "was given the choice of either honourable or dishonourable discharge." According to Drader, this man "believed that he was tailed and was photographed ... The whole nine yards." Prior to this, "he was taken through a series of tests that were identified as stress tests and he, to this day, does not really know what they were because most of what happened to him ... was through other circumstances – they had photographic evidence that he was at least keeping time with known homosexuals" (January 16, 1998).[66] We know that members of the military were tested with regard to aspects of the fruit machine research. This man may have been subjected to the test to measure his response as a confirmed homosexual or as part of a normal control group comprised of military personnel.

Men in the public service also received the questionnaires used in the research. Drader reported that he received a phone call from a heterosexual man who wanted to share his experiences. This man had

worked in external affairs in the mid-1960s and his brother was gay and he did associate a lot with his brother and his friends. He knew nothing about the fruit machine at all, he had missed the whole thing in the press when it came out. Near the top of the play he started to recognize some of these questions; there was an air of familiarity about them. About half way through the play, like a lightning bolt, he realized that he had actually partaken in some of this ... It was short lived and there were never any repercussions from it. It was not until he saw the play that he realized that (a) this whole thing had happened

– the context of it and (b) that he had been slightly involved in it. His brother who was also working for the government was also never dismissed ... and was never disclosed as a homosexual for whatever reason. It really impacted on him ... because it would impact on anyone that you had been involved in something that big and that huge and to not realize until some thirty years later that that is what had happened. (January 16, 1998)

The memories triggered by the play's re-enactments included the questions that formed part of the tests. Drader recalled that this particular man was able to reconstitute some of the questions that were contained in the M/F scales: "The true or false [questions] were the ones that started to twig him in and actually 'the agree, strongly agree,' those ones, that's when it hit him because those ones he thinks ... that he actually recognized specific questions. Which is very interesting because all of those questions were all taken from the documentation ... [from Wake's "Special Project" report]. It was the 'strongly agree, agree, unsure, disagree' ones – there were several of them he said that just hit him like a lightning bolt but, 'Yes, I remember that question specifically.' Which I find very interesting because it speaks to the nature of the questions too since they are so odd, some of them."[67]

In discussing this man's specific recollections about the M/F scales, Drader added that he was quite specific about the context in which he had been asked these questions:

He and a number of his fellow employees were asked to partake in these tests. Among the people who were asked to take the test there was no sense of any importance [being] put on it. At the time he hardly remembers taking them because ... most of them were questionnaires they were asked to fill out. In one case he was talking to a fellow who came to the offices and they were just kind of pulled into a little office and they were asked mostly background information. He can't remember what the ... context was because it was all very casually done. There was no hoopla. He remembers mostly himself and a couple of friends getting together for drinks afterwards and talking about how strange the questions were and how odd they were and what the hell was that all about. (January 16, 1998)

In retrospect, this man felt he might have been recruited for these tests because of his association with his gay brother and, through him, with other gay men. But it is also possible that he was selected as part of a normal control group of government workers for this research.

CONTRADICTIONS AND LIMITATIONS: IT NEVER DID WORK

Predictably, the attempt to operationalize Wake's research encountered many problems. From the beginning, a major difficulty involved getting enough subjects for the research protocol. In a 1963 memo, issued shortly after the project was approved by the secretary of the Security Panel, RCMP Assistant Commissioner and Director of Security and Intelligence J.R.M. Bordeleau wrote:

> While we are most anxious to assist Dr. Wake in his research programme we feel that we cannot meet his request in its entirety. We are in the process of contacting known male homosexuals in this area [Ottawa] and soliciting their co-operation in the proposed tests, however we are not yet in a position to determine how many will volunteer for the project ... We have no contacts within the female homosexual community in this area and no safe ground upon which an approach might be made to these persons. In this respect, we would suggest that other government departments, who will benefit directly from the results of the tests, might be requested through your office, to solicit the co-operation of female homosexuals known to them ... We have some doubts also as to the propriety of our soliciting normal females to participate in the tests. We believe that this should be undertaken by some government department or departments which have a large pool of female employees under their control ... Similarly we believe that the required number of normal males should be drawn from the government service at large.[68]

If one reads between the lines, this account suggests that RCMP members themselves resisted participating in this research. As Sawatsky suggests, RCMP members feared being identified as "fruits" should they participate as normals in the experiment.[69] Possible or perceived interest in naked men would compromise their performances of heterosexual masculinity. The RCMP response was to try to get other government departments involved in enrolling subjects. This helped to produce the situation whereby the research program came to be sponsored by and to rely more on the DND than on the RCMP. The obstacles encountered by the RCMP led to this shift towards the military, which had a larger number of potential subjects for the normal control group. The military also assumed major financial support for the research.

It is possible that some RCMP officers may have felt that the project was nonsensical and that the people directing it were "quacks." For example, Nathan remarked: "I felt that it was something that somebody had cooked up and really wasn't going to get anywhere. Now we were forced to cooperate with them because it came as a directive of the Security Panel and ... to me it was a complete waste of time." He remembered that "it sort of faded into other spheres" (July 22, 1999).

In April 1992, Wake told Beeby that thirty to thirty-five people were actually tested. This was not enough to meet the research design, which called for an initial sixty subjects.[70] In Beeby's interview conducted the very next day, Wake suggested that the fruit machine was never used "in a practical sense" to identify homosexuals in the civil service. In 1992, Wake continued to maintain that, due to the national security character of his research, he was "restricted in what [he could] say."[71]

Elsewhere, Beeby pointed out that, by 1964-65, "51 individuals had been tested with inconclusive results."[72] The 1965-66 *Directorate of Security and Intelligence (DSI) Annual Report* stated: "To date the tests have been inconclusive, the main obstacle to the Program being a lack of suitable subjects for testing purposes."[73] In the DSI's 1966-67 report, it is stated that, "although the research group has made some progress, the objective has not, as yet been achieved."[74]

Perfecting the technology, which failed to account for different heights, different-sized pupils, and variations between eyeball distances, was a major problem in operationalizing the experiment.[75] The technology and research were based on a series of flawed assumptions about the relation between stimulus and response, the power of visual images as simulators, the common responses of homosexuals as viewers, and the notion that there were two, and only two, essential sexualities. Men or women who were sexually interested in both men and women undermined the basic research assumptions.

The main assumption behind the fruit machine was that some sort of discernable difference distinguished the responses of homosexuals from those of "normals." This was never demonstrated, and the underlying assumption about differences in homosexual/heterosexual responses to images was destabilized. Predictably, the fruit machine never worked; it was abandoned in 1967.

THE FRUIT MACHINE LIVES ON

The image of the fruit machine continues to appear in the cultural imagination of the early twenty-first century. Alex Brett's mystery novel *Cold Dark Matter* delves into the national security campaigns against lesbians and gay men and, specifically, into the fruit machine.[76] While this is a fictional account containing some departures from what we know about the special project, it draws attention to the political uses of science in Canadian history and raises crucial questions about national security and surveillance.

The publication of this book was followed by the spring 2005 unveiling of an exhibit at the Canadian War Museum that claimed to be about the fruit machine. Following are Gary Kinsman's comments regarding the show:

I went on a field trip to the War Museum in late August 2005, finding the exhibit in a section called "A Violent Peace, the Cold War, Peacekeeping and Recent Conflicts, 1945 to the Present." Included in this Cold War section was a display on the Igor Gouzenko affair as well as the Greta Munsinger affair. Under the heading "Home Front Paranoia" was an apparatus on display labelled the Mathison Electropsychometer, accompanied by the following text: "Security Officials used this device, the electropsychometer (or E-meter), in the 1950s and 1960s to help ascertain people's sexual orientation, assuming that homosexuality made individuals more susceptible to blackmail by enemy agents.[77] Data from the so-called 'fruit machine' cost more than 100 Civil Servants their jobs. The church of scientology still uses such machines to assess the mental state of its parishioners."

There are a number of problems with this exhibit. First, the fruit machine displayed bears no resemblance to the research and experimentation involved with Wake's special project. The pupillary response test was at the core of his research, and it involved a larger and more complex technology and battery of texts than did the machine in the exhibit. While the E-meter was used in the United States and may have been used in the Canadian military as detection technology, it was not what the Canadian state tried to develop in the 1960s. It is a battery-powered electronic instrument that was invented in the 1940s by Volney Mathison to aid psychiatrists and psychotherapists in measuring nervous reactions.[78] Although similar in some respects to the fruit machine, the E-meter was not part of Wake's proposal.

Second, the E-meter was not mentioned in the "Special Project" report. Richard Burnett commented that the War Museum's Dean Oliver said that the E-meter on display "came to [the museum] from a private source and was in the collection before [he] arrived."[79] Putting this technology on display and referring to it as the fruit machine is both misleading and inaccurate. The technology involved in the E-meter is much less imposing than that of the fruit machine and its series of tests. Further, the museum cites no sources to back up its claim that the use of the machine on display led to the firing of more than one hundred civil servants. The comment regarding the Church of Scientology's use of this technology (although accurate) adds to the sense of bizarreness surrounding this technology, but it does not encourage people to reflect on how and why Canadian state agencies tried to develop it in the 1960s. Coupled with the heading "Home Front Paranoia," and with no broader social and historical context, the display suggests that the development and use of the fruit machine was simply a paranoid response to a Cold War atmosphere rather than part of a state-sanctioned war on Canadian queers.

It is significant that someone at the museum felt that the anti-homosexual aspects of the national security campaigns needed to be mentioned and the fruit machine story exposed. This is admirable, especially given official state denials of responsibility for the anti-queer campaigns. This makes it all the more unfortunate that the display was not properly contextualized and that the technology presented was not actually that associated with the fruit machine.

One of the major reasons for the development of the fruit machine was the emergence of queer non-cooperation and resistance. It is to the social organization of this resistance and the security regime's response to it that we now turn.

Queer Resistance and the Security Response
Solidarity versus the RCMP

The national security campaigns against queers encountered major obstacles, including queer non-cooperation and resistance. Lesbians and gay men were never just passive victims; they were active agents who negotiated and resisted the campaigns. We begin with narratives of and experiences in the military. We then briefly investigate the public service before focusing on those outside it.

IN THE MILITARY: "WINE, WOMEN, AND SONG"

Sue's account indicates that, among some women in the military, heterosexist practices and policing regulations encountered non-cooperation. In the militia, Sue faced less severe constraints than she would have had she been in the regular military. She was able to defy base regulations in the militia and, later in the 1950s, at military camp:

> The deal was you were supposed to go out with men. So what we did was, at military camp, we went out with the men in the early part of the evening, and then, because we were very virtuous young women, we said, "Oh, we have to go home early." And the military being very accommodating said, "This is where the women sleep; this is where the men sleep." We said, "Fine, that's cool, we'll go back with the women." Back we go with the women, [and] who's sleeping next to me but somebody in the Intelligence corps, who is supposed to be watching me ... But let me tell ya, I ditched her. What we used to do, we dykes, we would want to go out and party. And we would take our bunk beds

and we would fill them with pillows. And then we would say to the heterosexual women, "We really want to meet Charlie." We would lie to them and
they would cover 'cause they thought we were goin' out to meet men. We were
goin' out to meet women. But we had it set up at the back of the barracks and
took over this room. We barricaded it from one side, and then we had women
on the other side guarding it 'cause that's where we were with Charlie. But
they never saw Charlie! So here we had all these straight women guarding us
and guarding our beds and making sure that the authorities never knew we
were out. And we weren't supposed to be. (February 23, 1996)

Here we see creative resistance to military policies, which included using heterosexual women to provide protection for lesbian activities. Sue continued,

So, we would be out with sergeants, staff sergeants, corporals, privates, lieu-
tenants. No rank was untouched. So we would be running all over camp. And
the deal was you weren't allowed to leave the premises, so of course, we wanted
wine, women, and song. So in order to get wine, women, and song you had to
leave the base. So you had to go out, but you weren't allowed to wear butchy
clothing, you had to wear a dress. So what we used to do was pull our pant legs
up and hide them with our skirt. And you'd go out and through the gates in
your skirt, right, lookin' all femmy and lovely. Well, this one night we came
home and we got a little too drunk. Well, trust me [when I say] that the pants
were down. And we were up on charges the next day for being in some place
we weren't supposed to be, improper attire, all kinds of things. So we learned
that we shouldn't drink too much.

Military regulations regarding dress codes and the construction of proper gender
codes for women were significant for lesbians and their experiences. Wearing
clothing considered to be outside of these codes, such as "butchy" attire, was
penalized.

Sue also recounted that lesbians both inside and outside the military met
other lesbians through women's sports teams and events: "Sports were always
a great way to meet women. So we had a tri-service, army, navy, and air force.
And the joke was 'try-the-service,' and we tried everybody. We tried the army,
we tried the navy, and, I mean, it was just like a free-for-all. I mean, we·had a
camp set up in the woods where you had wine. You could make out in the
woods, behind the baseball field." After Sue was forced out of the militia, she
reported:

We started hanging out with some navy folks. And what used to happen in Halifax, because it was a military place, every two years they rotated the people who worked there. So every two years you got a new crop of lesbians, in the army, in the navy, and in the air force. So for a young dyke it was just like you had died and gone to heaven. So when they kicked me out, they had given me an ID card, right? And I thought, "They're not getting that back" 'cause I wanted to go on bases to meet more women. Can you imagine the nerve? Nothing would stop me! We go to Prince Edward Island to the air force base and I flash the card, they let me right through ... The air force women were just as smart. They had taken over the barracks, they barricaded the back part of their mess so that they had it sealed off from the heterosexuals, just like we did. Then they went upstairs in this barracks, and they said to the other women, "Will you bunk in with the other women, so that we can have a guest room so that if we get anybody we want to sleep with, we can have this room?" They did.

Following the declaration of the War Measures Act, 1970, Sue remembered being with lesbians in Halifax:

We're out drinking with the navy women, and they said, "Do you want to come back to the barracks?" I said, "Ah, we can't get on the base." "Ya, no problem, get in the trunk of the car" ... We went up to their place, had some more drinks, made out, [and then I] said I had to go home. They said, "No problem, we'll drive you off." And we're going out of the Stadacona main gate with these guys with rifles with real ammo. I lift up the trunk and go, "Yaa-na-yaa-na-yaaaa-na!" [giggles] ... We were down the street before they even had a chance.

Sue also reported that gay women in the military had "different ways ... to figure out who was a lesbian." She went on: "And one of the ways is to say, 'Do you have a number, are you one?' And if you said, 'Are you one?' you were one 'cause you knew the code. One of the other things was a tradition, in the army anyway, [and it] was that if you got to sleep with somebody, if they had a rank, you got to have one of their badges. It was like an honour [to have] somebody else's military insignia." When Sue was purged, she did not suffer any devastating consequences as one of her lovers changed her birthdate: "And somebody said to me, 'Well, how did you do that?' I said, 'Well, I slept with the captain.' She changed it ... So we had a network, whereby we were changing military records.

And we just said, 'Piss on ya. If you want to do this to us, we will do this to you.' Because later on in life I had to have a security clearance done through the RCMP [when she worked as a consulate officer] ... a security check and a police check, he couldn't find anything" (February 23, 1996). Through these strategies, Sue was able to foil security information-gathering practices. Consequently, she was promoted and experienced no further work-related difficulties as a result of her discharge.

Within the regular military, possibilities for non-cooperation were more restricted; however, it was still feasible for people being purged from the military, such as Herbert Sutcliffe or Harold, to refuse to give the RCMP any names.

NON-COOPERATION IN THE PUBLIC SECTOR AND BEYOND

Narratives from Steve, Hank, and others in the public service demonstrate that, in the 1960s, it was possible to refuse to inform on others. However, given departmental security and, especially, the security activities of the RCMP, resistance was difficult. Possibilities for non-cooperation were much greater for those located outside the public service because they faced fewer institutional constraints and had a more direct connection to queer community formation. In turn, this allowed them to be privy to discussions about resistance strategies against the RCMP, even though the Criminal Code continued to limit the space for non-cooperation (e.g., the RCMP often threatened people with arrest if they did not supply names). It was in trying to get information from gays outside the public service that the RCMP encountered its most challenging obstacles.

The RCMP Recognition of Non-Cooperation
From a critical reading of the official discourse of the security regime texts, we get a sense of the obstacles the regime confronted. A crucial aspect of the relations of surveillance was the RCMP-informant relation. RCMP officers would watch places frequented by queers (such as the Lord Elgin in Ottawa, the Chez Henri in Hull, or various parks) and attempt to get men to inform on others.

The RCMP faced problems with non-cooperation from homosexual informants. In 1962-63 it reported: "During the past fiscal year the homosexual screening program ... was hindered by the lack of cooperation on the part of homosexuals approached as sources. Persons of this type, who had hitherto been our most consistent and productive informers, have exhibited an increasing reluctance to identify their homosexual friends and associates."[1] These people placed loyalty to their friends above those of Canadian security interests and the RCMP. In 1962-63, the RCMP wrote, "During the year the investigation to

Queer Resistance and the Security Response

identify homosexuals employed in or by the Federal Government resulted in initial interviews with twenty-one homosexuals, four of whom proved to be uncooperative, and re-interviews with twenty-two previously cooperative homosexuals, seven of whom declined to extend further cooperation."[2]

The construction of a distinction between cooperative and uncooperative homosexuals was crucial as it played a role in shaping the RCMP-informant relation and rating its usefulness. Here, we may recall Fred's comments regarding the important role of informants in his work for the RCMP. With the growth of resistance and non-cooperation, previously amenable homosexuals became uncooperative.

In the next section, we examine the interaction of official discourse and first-hand accounts. What created the social basis for this lack of queer cooperation? What can we learn from these accounts of resistance? To help answer these questions, we explore non-cooperation in interview/interrogation situations and then in more explicit forms of resistance.

REFUSING TO GIVE THE RCMP NAMES: RESISTING SURVEILLANCE AND INTERROGATION

The other side of this lack of cooperation is described by David, whose gay RCMP officer friend gave him some advice on what to do if he were to be interrogated:

> I was under no obligation to give any information at all. These were voluntary questionings and, no matter how much they would try to ... bully me, ... I was not obligated in any way to give any information at all. Except, if I had been actually caught myself and then in a court of law I would have to tell the truth. And in the other situation, if ever I were subject to blackmail, then it would be to my advantage to let the police know what the situation was ... So, they got nothing from me, and I'm very proud to say I did not give any information. (May 12, 1994)

This was also part of broader advice being circulated in gay networks in Ottawa by the early 1960s.

"Is it true that you ride sidesaddle?"

Michael, who had been a civilian employee of the military and became a non-civil servant who was interrogated by the RCMP in the 1960s, stated that the advice in the gay networks was to say nothing to the RCMP about people's identities. He also said that "if anybody did give anything they were ostracized." There seemed to be a clear ethical position regarding not giving names. Michael reported that, when he was left alone in the interrogation room with one RCMP officer, the following dialogue took place: "[The officer said,] 'Is it true that you are a homosexual?' and I said, 'Yes!' And he looked at me, and I said, 'Is it true that you ride sidesaddle?' And he laughed, and that almost ended the interview. I mean, my intent was there – don't bother me any more – because I had begun to get the impression that it was a witch hunt" (July 15, 1994). We have already encountered a number of other accounts by people who were not public servants, including that of Peaches Latour, who refused to give names to the RCMP, and Marvin, who remembered hearing from gay friends about the RCMP interrogations:

> I don't remember when we heard. But I remember I talked for a long time with my friends ... They were either interviewing or had been interviewing gays in Ottawa. I don't think anybody mentioned it was the civil service generally ... They were all worried. I remember one time, I thought, why don't we get together and hire a lawyer. I wouldn't have gone to a lawyer on my own because I was too afraid, because it was illegal to be gay and I could have gone to jail quite easily if I was caught. So you're afraid to do those things on your own. But if about four or five of us got together and went to a lawyer, maybe he could give us some advice. In fact a friend of mine did this, a doctor friend of mine, he went to his own lawyer at the time, and he was maybe ten years older than I was at the time. When the RCMP did contact him ... he said he went to a lawyer and the lawyer said, "You don't have to talk to them at all." And he said, "If you want, if they force you to go, I'll go with you." So when the RCMP did contact him, he said, "Fine, but I'll be taking my lawyer with me." And they decided not to interview him. They said, "We'll call you back." He never heard from them again. (May 1998)

For those with the connections and finances to do so, attaining legal assistance was one possible strategy of non-cooperation; however, this option was not available to most queers who were caught in the security campaign. Before the emergence of gay/lesbian networks and spaces, any form of non-cooperation was extremely difficult.

Individuals engaged in various forms of partial non-cooperation. For example, Marvin was brought into the interrogation room where, according to Dean Beeby, "They put the pressure on to name friends and everything. And after that experience he quit his job or he stopped working. He left town and he's never been the same since" (interview by Beeby, February 26, 1995). Beeby suggests that, even within these constraints, the man was able to resist giving the RCMP names they did not already have. This is how Marvin put it: "I tried to figure out how I could [submit to an RCMP interrogation] without giving the names of people ... So I thought the only thing I can do is mention the names of a few people that I used to drink with publicly in the [Ottawa] bars. The people who I also knew because they were public with their gayness would also be interrogated or investigated" (interview by Beeby, February 26, 1995). This strategy could be effective and was used by others in order to side-track the RCMP.

Exposing and Turning the Tables on the Security Investigators
But sometimes these forms of non-cooperation moved beyond the individual. David's story, which is related in Chapter 1, reveals that his networks were aware of the security campaign as well as a collective sense of resistance to it. Queers turned the tables on an undercover RCMP officer who was taking pictures of the men gathered in the basement of the Lord Elgin Hotel in Ottawa, thus exposing the police agent and making it clear that he was not welcome in their social space. They obstructed the security campaign by making it visible and declaring it unwelcome. David's account gives us a glimpse into the beginnings of collective resistance and speaks to disruption and mockery as a survival strategy.

David also recounted an episode concerning a group of young gay men who had been detained by the RCMP: "One group of about seven friends all got pulled in. All were asked to give names. They all said, 'I know the following people' and gave the names of the other six. And the next person would give the names of the other six. All they [the RCMP] did was get that one circle of names." While he was under heightened surveillance, David told a heterosexual friend about his predicament, and they decided to resist:

I'd mentioned to a friend of mine who was in a diplomatic corps with
another country that he should be careful about anything he said. And he
brought that to a rapid end by one night arriving [at my] home from a party
and then, in a somewhat drunken situation, actually playing the part of a very
heavy-handed spy. And then, at the end of the conversation, he, his girlfriend,
and I all had a big laugh, and now this will give the RCMP really something to
listen to. And then, in the end, he said, "I thought that all the police states were

in Europe and on the other side of the Iron Curtain; I had not realized until this point that Canada was a police state." This may have caused the RCMP to decide that perhaps the word was getting out about their operation because it wasn't very long after that [that] all of the overt ... spying on me came to an end. I think it was a matter of two weeks after [that] I was no longer aware that anything was going on. (May 12, 1994)

This tactic shows the potential for heterosexual-identified people to provide meaningful solidarity in the context of these anti-queer campaigns.

Camp, Humour, and Queer Solidarity

These stories of non-cooperation and resistance flesh out the social organization of the non-cooperation mentioned in the RCMP texts. David's story of the response to the undercover RCMP officer in the Lord Elgin, in particular, suggests that people were able to move beyond simply exposing the officer or informant; they could also make fun of him as well as the security and police campaigns, using humour and camp as a way to survive. Camp sensibility and humour is a cultural form that was produced by gay men during these years to manage and negotiate the contradictions between their particular experiences of the world as gays and the institutionalized heterosexuality they encountered. A crucial part of this cultural production involved denaturalizing normality and heterosexuality by making fun of it.[3]

As David noted, "I think that the way people coped with the whole situation of surveillance and harassment was basically to make the best of it, and turn it as much as possible into a humorous situation. So when we talk about the oppressive times, I think the people sometimes had more fun" (May 12, 1994). The social basis for this non-cooperation and resistance was the overt gay networks in 1960s Ottawa. This resistance was rooted in a sense of group solidarity in response to the attacks of the national security campaigns and the developing awareness that the RCMP was not invincible, that, indeed, some of its surveillance strategies could be disrupted.

One must also consider the limited resistance provided by the relations of the closet and living a double life, and how gays came to defend this in the face of the fear of blackmail and exposure. John Grube refers more to the code of secrecy among gays than to the closet itself when he says: "The closet can be regarded as a positive feature in the assertion of this community resistance, in the sense that you would never tell a cop somebody else's name, or another person." If you did reveal someone's identity to a heterosexual person "and it ever got back to anyone, [you'd] be mud" (March 1, 1996). This was a limited form of resistance, and individual gay men had little social power in relation to the RCMP; however, for many who were caught in the web of the security campaigns, there were few options.

The RCMP was able to exert different forms of pressure on different groups of potential homosexual informants. Those potential informants outside the public service who were part of gay networks had more possibilities for non-cooperation than did those in the public service. It was in these emerging networks that the social basis for solidarity and the formation of a community ethics developed.

Of course, there were many moments when people caught in the surveillance nets felt compelled to cooperate. Some collaborated with the RCMP because they feared the consequences of not doing so. It is also possible that a few may have agreed with the national security campaigns, although this was true of only one gay man with whom we talked, and then only retrospectively. Many others survived in this period by living double lives or remaining in the closet. We need to explore the social basis both for resistance and for collaboration.

Ethics and Resistance

In contrast to attempts to construct homosexuality as a moral problem and a national security risk, moral regulation became a contested terrain. Some gay men and lesbians challenged the basis of the security campaigns by refusing to give names and by placing their erotic, emotional, and social ties to their friends and other queers above the interests of Canadian security. In contrast to state agency attempts to morally problematize queers, expanding gay and lesbian networks in the 1960s provided the basis for an ethics of resistance. The development of this ethics within gay networks had a very different character than did that of the moral regulation that drove the national security campaigns.[4]

Ruling forms of moral regulation, or "morality from above," rely on rules that are ideologically portrayed as absolute, law-like, and ahistorical. Contrary to this, the ethics of resistance was developed "from below" and had an affective, erotic, contextual, social, and historical character. In addition, it was established by the oppressed themselves in resistance to ruling forms of regulation.[5] In the 1960s, in overt gay and lesbian networks, queer people articulated a collective ethics of non-cooperation with (and, at times, resistance to) the security campaigns. Because they placed their ties to other queer people ahead of national security, this posed significant problems for the RCMP and the national campaigns.

This non-cooperation was based in queer network and community formation, including the establishment of certain limited queer social spaces, such as the basement tavern at the Lord Elgin or the gay section of the Chez Henri in Hull, which Peaches Latour described as "the original gay bar" (see Photo 2). As a partly queer space, the Chez Henri helped to solidify identification and solidarity outside the confines of official discourse.[6] Other queer spaces identified by Latour for the late 1950s include the Honeydew on Rideau Street, which was the "original meeting place where we were all accepted" (see Photo 3). Parks played a critical role in the social-sexual space for queers. Two parks discussed

2   The Chez Henri, located in Hull, was a popular gay and lesbian hangout in the 1950s and 1960s |
Credit: City of Ottawa Archives, CA 4618

3 Rideau Street, c. 1962, included two major gay and lesbian spots – the Byward Market and the Honeydew Restaurant | *Credit:* City of Ottawa Archives, CA 2405

by Latour are Major Hill's Park, located behind the Chateau Laurier and adjacent to Parliament Hill, and Nepean Point, where "homosexuals congregated" (see Photo 4). He also reported that there were house parties every weekend, that people in the 1950s were very poor, and that most gay people lived in rooming houses. Latour informed us that there was cruising along the Rideau Canal and that the Coral Reef was one of "the founding bars in Ottawa" (August

Queer spaces in Ottawa, c. 1962

This legend corresponds with the adjacent map. Information pertaining to this Ottawa queer geography is based on the interviews we conducted (combined with a search through city directories and maps created from the 1950s onwards). Not included are the locations of house parties. Also, some locations mentioned by interviewees that could not be confirmed were excluded (e.g., the Orleans Hotel on Montreal Road, in Vanier, which was a lesbian hangout in the 1970s and 1980s; and Mother Goose on Somerset Street, which was popular with gay men living in Ottawa in the 1950s and 1960s).

1 TERRACE DE LA CHAUDIÈRE: This government building located in Hull, Quebec, at the corner of Alexandre-Taché Street and Eddy Street (facing the Chaudière Bridge), housed a restaurant/bar, whose name is unknown. Throughout the 1970s and 1980s, in the evenings this restaurant/bar became a mixed gay bar.

2 LE PUB: Located on Wellington Street in Hull directly behind the Terrace de la Chaudière, this two-storey dance club was a very popular queer hangout in the 1980s and 1990s. It closed after an explosion in 1995.

3 HOTEL CHEZ HENRI: Located in Hull at 179 rue Principale (now Promenade du Portage), it stands as a historic monument. In the 1950s and 1960s, queers and heterosexuals visited the upper-level cocktail lounge to enjoy performances by female impersonators such as Peaches Latour.

4 CHATEAU LAURIER: On the lower level of this Ottawa institution, visitors and gay men enjoyed the steam room, a sauna, and an exercise room, using the facilities as a bathhouse. The hotel still stands between MacKenzie Street and Sussex Drive on Wellington Street (also known as Confederation Drive). In the 1960s, it faced the Union Station (Ottawa's train station).

5 UNION STATION: Ottawa's train station until the early 1970s. The massive columns on its facade make Union Station an imposing structure. The station and the bushes along the train tracks were cruising areas for gay men (the tracks were removed in the 1970s). These train tracks ran along the Rideau Canal, which runs through the city and was also known for its cruising activity.

6 THE HONEYDEW: A restaurant/diner on 34 Rideau Street next to the Chateau Laurier in the old Daly Building (no longer standing), where gay men congregated in the late 1950s and 1960s.

7 BYWARD MARKET: Known as a fresh produce market by day, by evening the market was a notorious cruising ground for gay men. Throughout the 1960s and 1970s, the boundaries of this gay male cruising area extended from Rideau Street to Murray Street and from Sussex Drive to King Edward Avenue.

8 THE CORAL REEF: The Coral Reef opened its doors in 1968 and closed in 2000. Primarily a mixed queer bar, on Friday nights it catered exclusively to lesbians. The Coral Reef (affectionately known as the Oral Grief) was also famous for its drag shows. The Reef was in the basement of the Rideau Centre's parking garage at 30 Nicholas Street.

9 CHAMPAGNE BATHS: On King Edward Avenue, the Champagne Baths housed a public swimming pool and other recreational facilities. It was also used as a cruising area in the 1950s and 1960s. It still stands today.

10 THE TOWN HOUSE MOTEL: Located at 319 Rideau, next to the Bytowne Theatre and between King Edward Avenue and Nelson Street. In the 1970s, it was the site of weekly lesbian dances organized by LOON.

11 THE LORD ELGIN HOTEL: The Lord Elgin, on Elgin Street (on the corner of Laurier Street, facing Confederation Park), was a two-minute walk from the YMCA and a popular "watering stop" for gay men in the 1960s. Unfortunately, it was also a favourite surveillance spot for the police. Gay men socialized in the tavern downstairs.

12 YMCA: The Y, a historical gay cruising ground, was known for its informal "no-bathing-suits-required" rule. It was on the corner of Laurier Street and Metcalfe Street. The YMCA/YWCA is now at the corner of Argyle Street and O'Conner Street, facing the Museum of Nature (which, in the 1960s, was known as the National Museum).

13 RIALTO THEATRE: At 413 Bank Street between Gladstone Street and McLeod Street, the Rialto was known as a busy hangout for queers in the 1950s and 1960s. It has since been taken over by the Metropolitan Bible Church(!).

14 BUS TERMINAL: Located on Albert Street between Bank Street and Kent Street, near the YMCA. The bus depot was yet another cruising area. Not far from the bus terminal, on Slater Street, there was a bar that turned into a bathhouse at midnight (name and exact location unknown).

Parks

A REMIC RAPIDS LOOKOUT: Built along the Ottawa River Parkway, between the Prince of Wales Bridge and the Champlain Bridge, this park served as a cruising area for gay men in the mid-1960s and continues to do so today. The National Capital Commission maintains Remic Rapids. As a federal initiative, this park falls under RCMP jurisdiction. It remains a heavily patrolled park.

B NEPEAN POINT: A bronze monument of Samuel de Champlain presides over this cruising area adjacent to Major's Hill Park and behind the National Gallery (the site of the Laurentian Terrace, a women's residence established by the government to house civil servants from the 1940s to the 1960s). It is also within walking distance of the Byward Market.

C MAJOR'S HILL PARK (also known as MacKenzie Park): Located behind the Chateau Laurier Hotel and at the right of the Parliament Buildings, this park is perhaps one of the most popular cruising areas in Ottawa. It is flanked by MacKenzie Street, which was a main drag for male prostitution. Male prostitutes often took their clients to Major's Hill Park.

D STRATHCONA PARK: Another gay male cruising area in Sandy Hill on the edge of the Rideau River, within walking distance of the University of Ottawa.

Other locations

a BIKE/WALK PATHS: These run throughout the city, but there were several areas that were known as cruising sites. Of particular interest are the bike/walk paths directly beneath the Peace Tower in a dark, wooded, and secluded area bordered by water and accessible from the Ottawa Locks, which are nestled between the East Block and the Chateau Laurier (a1); along Queen Elizabeth Drive (a2); and along Colonel By Drive near the University of Ottawa (a3).

b ELGIN STREET: A busy Ottawa street in the centre of town lined with restaurants, coffee shops, and some small businesses. One of our interviewees mentioned that the Snow Goose, an upper-level bar frequented by queers, was on this thoroughfare in the late 1950s and 1960 (exact location unknown).

c BANK STREET: This critical centre-of-town artery is three blocks west of Elgin Street. The Rialto Theatre was on Bank Street. According to Peaches Latour, one of the people whom we interviewed, Bank Street was frequented by queers throughout the 1950s and 1960s and, thus, was patrolled by the Ottawa police and the RCMP.

4 View from Nepean Point of Major's Hill Park, with the Parliament Buildings in the background |
Credit: City of Ottawa Archives, CA 6307

31, 1994). Union Station was also a gathering place, as was the swimming pool and health spa in the Chateau Laurier's lower level (see map on p. 202). Queer hangouts and cruising spots expanded during these years, ranging from house parties to the bars and parks to women's sports teams.

Patrick, a gay man who lived in Ottawa in the 1950s, recalled several cruising areas for gay men, such as the old railyards near the University of Ottawa, the parks and train station near the Chateau Laurier, the Honeydew near the Chateau Laurier, and parts of Elgin Street (July 1994). Marvin remembered a more open atmosphere for gays, which was curtailed by the security campaigns:

> Well, there was a lot of gays ... and there were also gays that were basically open and went to the gay bars, the Chez Henri of course ... and the Lord Elgin. But they were very discreet ... And then you had another group who didn't go to

the bars at all, who we'd never see anywhere in the pick-up spots around town, bars, or even in parks that were cruising at that time ... Mainly the one along the Rideau Canal, that was the main one, that's the only one I'd ever gone to. Except once I went to the one behind the Chateau Laurier, Major's Hill ... But it was a pretty comfortable town to be gay in because there were nice people in Ottawa, it was a beautiful place to live, and it was a very comfortable place to be gay. All the people I worked with at the airlines, they knew I was gay, yet nobody would ever say anything to embarrass me in any way shape or form. It just didn't happen. And on payday we would all go out for Chinese food after work, and [I] even met some of them when I was on holidays [in] various places [when] I might be with another gay person. One time I was with a hairdresser, and he was my lover at the time, and I met one of the girls I worked with and [he] happened to be her hairdresser. But Judy wouldn't have said anything in a million years, she would have [just] said, "How are you?" ... So it was that kind of town, where you could be openly gay and yet weren't condemned for it ... I did have gay lovers but we'd never be seen together in public, in restaurants or bars or any place like that. So it was a good place to be gay in the 1950s. It wasn't as wild as Montreal and Toronto, but it was a comfortable place. (May 1998)

While the Ottawa gay scene was "comfortable" before the onset of the main national security campaigns, Marvin's comments illustrate that queers also experienced the city differently based on whether they were "overt" or "covert" and on their level of participation within gay networks. The security campaigns led to a small-scale gay exodus from Ottawa in 1959-60.

Marvin remembered that, in the later 1950s, a section of the basement tavern of the Lord Elgin became a meeting place for gay men and gay public servants:

On the right side section of wall was where most of the gay people sort of went. There might be five to eight or nine there at any one time. I don't remember ever seeing a gang in there. And there might be a couple scattered around the rest of the bar, but you'd never see more than ten or twelve in there at any one time. But a lot of the civil servants used to go in there because they loved to see that the old World War II buildings were still being used then ... And a lot of guys would go in there in the afternoon and have a few drinks.

Marvin also described the Chez Henri:

Just to the left of the bar, where a few people sat at tables, but mainly at the bar itself, was all gay, and [at] the farthest section of the bar it would be basically straight. But they had a great way of cleaning people out at night, because often you drink in Ottawa maybe first for a couple hours and then you go to Chez Henri to close off. And of course everybody wants the last drink and then another last drink and then they cut off, so you order two at the last drink. What they used to do – and I'm talking men in their twenties, thirties, and forties – you go out Saturday night, you're looking and smelling your best. So what they used to do to clear the bar, they had these huge flood lights in the ceiling, they'd turn on all these flood lights about 1:15 AM, and you'd see people running for that door to try to get out of the bright lights. (May 1998)

Bruce Somers talked about the Lord Elgin in the 1960s and being aware of police activities:

The watering stop in Ottawa itself, of course, was the Lord Elgin. Then, one certainly became aware because people talked about whether or not there were police watching here. And you mentioned a story about a police informant, a policeman, sitting in the Lord Elgin with a hole cut in that paper. That was not a new story to me when you told me that. That was something I was aware of then ... There was this feeling of potential entrapment ... We were constantly on guard against strangers or against people we suspected of being snoops because they weren't gay, they weren't there to cruise, nobody knew them from sexual contact. (June 10, 1994)

Robert reported that, in the late 1960s, there were a number of gathering areas. He mentioned the Coral Reef, which became a major lesbian bar, "and there was another bar above the Snow Goose on Elgin Street." Robert also talked about the Lord Elgin: "There was the tavern downstairs ... A lot of gays were there. One of these washrooms was active. They had a security guard on it all the time. There were glory holes [i.e., holes in stalls through which penises could be inserted to facilitate sexual contact]. There was more stuff going on in that washroom than you can shake a stick at! There was the piano bar upstairs, and that's where a lot of people would go to meet" (October 10, 1996). Robert noted that other piano bars attracted people: "And then there was another [bar] on Slater Street. Well, on the second or third floor there was a club, and then at midnight, when drinking hours stopped in Ontario, it turned into a bathhouse. It drew the drapes, these canvas drapes, and it became a bathhouse."

Regarding parks, Robert mentioned Major's Hill Park, Strathcona Park, the canal, and Rockcliffe Park. He also mentioned the lower level of the Chateau Laurier, describing it as having some of the aspects of a gay bathhouse with cubicles:

> There was a door and a room. It was about the size of a phone booth with a
> little bench. That was it. You dressed in there and left your clothes and you
> locked it. But, of course, you could also sit there and cool off, and people
> would walk by and people would walk in. Just like a bathhouse. And it had
> a steam room. You couldn't see the back wall, but as you started walking
> through there were benches and there was stuff going on in the back room
> and in the showers. No crew would raid the Chateau Laurier. You could keep
> your door open, and [if people were interested they could] just go into that
> little cubicle.

Robert also recalled the YMCA: "[It] is a hotel now. The main pool in there you did not wear bathing suits. Even the lifeguards did not wear bathing suits. They also had those little change rooms ... There was no door. There was just this canvas screen that you could pull across and you had privacy." Robert mentioned that, in the 1970s, health spas, especially Vick Tanny's, were "just notorious." He added that "the universities were always very cruisy," as was the bus depot, the train station, and "the department stores downtown like Ogilvy's ... And then of course, the Market in those days was far more notorious than it is today" (October 10, 1996).

Fred recalled that, during his period with the RCMP in Ottawa, homosexuals could be found at the Chez Henri, at Mother Goose on Somerset, and at Major's Hill Park. He reported on a gay party in Wakefield in the Gatineaus, referring to it as "swish city" (October 21, 1994). Wealthier gay couples would have their summer residences in the Gatineaus.[7] Steve, a DEA employee, also participated in a gay dinner party network and spent his summers in the late 1960s living with other men in cottages in the Gatineaus (June 27, 1998).

Lesbian Networks and Social Space

As with more recent gay and lesbian community formation, in the 1950s and 1960s, lesbians had access to less social space then did gay men. But lesbian spaces did emerge, including, by the later 1960s, the Coral Reef bar. Sue reported that, when she was in Ottawa in 1967, she easily found lesbian networks and lesbians:

There were lots of them, and they worked for the civil service, and they were in the military, and they played baseball. And they used to go drinking at a place ... up in the Gatineaus. And when you got drunk, you called it the Cash and Bagged. And they used to hang out at the Orleans Hotel at that time. That's on Montreal Road, in the older part of the town, on your way out to Montreal. And they used to drink and hang out there, and another one over in Hull called the Chez Henri ... But they were there, they were working in the civil service. They weren't out at work. They lived primarily in apartment buildings. They would go to baseball games, they'd go to the Grads Hotel. (February 23, 1996)

The government character of Ottawa led to a particular disciplining of women's bodies and social space. Particular constraints facing lesbians in Ottawa included employment (government service was generally low paid) and limited housing for single women. There were clusters of lesbians in a few government departments.

Our interviews began to make visible women's social-sexual geography in Cold War Ottawa. For lesbians, women's sports networks were often key to their ability to find each other. Indeed, female civil servants engaged in sports leagues offered by the Recreational Association throughout the 1950s and 1960s. Here, the obligatory skirts, blouses, and pumps were discarded for jeans, baseball caps, and baseball jerseys.

Women lived in women's residences and in apartments around the city, and these constituted one possible site for the formation of lesbian networks. Lesbian networks in Ottawa were not as visible as were gay men's networks. While gay men had some bars and cruising areas where they could congregate, lesbian socializing usually took place through a network of house parties. This "invisibility" made it more difficult to prove that a particular woman was a lesbian, and it operated as a survival strategy.

What we call "queer talk" developed in these social spaces. It had an important social character in that it enabled the communication of vital information, including methods of interaction with other gays, lesbians, and heterosexuals and what to do if approached by the RCMP or other police. One key aspect of this queer talk involved advice and discussion of how to deal with and to survive the security campaigns within the emerging queer networks. We need to continue to explore this development of gay/lesbian space and network formation and to uncover more of its social conditions of existence.[8]

Constraints on the development of queer social spaces included not only the policing of gay sex in the city and the national security campaigns but also the lack of social, economic, and sexual autonomy for women, the social organization of housing, the regulation of bars and other establishments, and the fact that Ottawa was a government town. All this shaped the character of the city and lesbian and gay community formation.

ASSOCIATIONS, UNIONS, AND EMPLOYEE RIGHTS

In the late 1960s and early 1970s, another, more limited, basis for possible non-cooperation involved the development of associations and unions in the public service. As employment expanded in the early and mid-1960s, there was increasing discontent in the public service. Public employees clashed with the hierarchical form of organization they faced in the public service, which employed disciplinary measures that had been derived from the quasi-military forms of organization that it had developed prior to and after the Second World War. Public-sector workers wanted less arbitrary authority and discipline, higher wages, and more job security. This led to the formation of associations and unions, including the Public Service Alliance of Canada in 1967. There was also a wave of strikes in the public sector, including a series of crucial union struggles in the post office. These developments created a social and work context in which it became more possible for some public servants to resist security campaigns.

At the same time, any official association or union support for gay and lesbian workers during these years was extremely limited, and there is considerable evidence of association/union collaboration with the security police against "communists" and other "security risks" in the 1960s.[9] While this was most clearly apparent in security surveillance of communists and socialists, it included queers as well. Prejudice against queers in these early public-sector unions was common. Until the later 1970s and the 1980s, unions encountered considerable difficulty dealing with homosexual security investigations. It was only then that they began supporting lesbian and gay rights, especially in relation to human rights.[10] Not surprisingly, union support for gay and lesbian rights was pushed forward by lesbian and gay union activists.

There was official concern about how unions might interfere with the operation of security procedures. A 1964 Security Panel discussion raised the following problem: "It had been agreed that the draft [in a directive concerning security policy in the defence industry] should also take into consideration the possible complications which might be posed by the involvement of trade unions in the process of the dismissal of an employee of an industrial firm as a result of a denial of a security clearance by the Department of Defence Production." And, in relation to the directive to the Cabinet Committee on Security and

Intelligence, it added that "problems related to trade unions dominated by Communists should be set out for the consideration of the Cabinet Committee."[11]

In 1967, the Security Panel discussed the dilemma it faced in allowing individuals who were about to be dismissed to cross-examine the commissioner conducting the inquiry. This could lead to the employee being able to "ask the reason for which dismissal was being considered." It was suggested that the Department of Justice draw up guidelines to minimize potential security problems created through these hearings. It was also pointed out that "the inauguration of collective bargaining was likely to have an effect on the processing of security cases" and that the provision of the Cabinet directive should be applied to "cases involving doubtful loyalty" as well as to those "involving unreliability on other grounds (sexual problems, drinking problems etc.)."[12]

The Security Panel also discussed the handling of this potential problem: "it might be necessary to make a clear distinction between disciplinary and security procedures."[13] It wished to interpret unions and associations as being allowed to raise concerns regarding "disciplinary" but not "security" procedures; however, in practice, it was very difficult to separate these two. By making this administrative distinction between discipline and security, the Security Panel was attempting to have security questions addressed separately and secretly.

THE RCMP RESPONDS: EXTENDING THE RELATIONS OF HETEROSEXIST SURVEILLANCE

During 1963 and 1964, the RCMP reported that, "given a growing reluctance on the part of homosexuals to identify their associates, additional emphasis is being placed on establishing close liaison with the morality branches of police forces, particularly in the larger centres."[14] The non-cooperation and resistance of homosexuals forced the RCMP to devise new strategies to secure the cooperation of homosexual informants. One response was the RCMP interest in and participation in the fruit machine research; another was developing clearer working relationships with the morality branches of various police forces and enlisting local police support to procure homosexual informants. This extension of the security net was not entirely new as there had been previous relations constructed with local morality squads, but it represented a new stage in this relationship. The RCMP, as the "national" police force, "had special relationships with police forces across the country."[15] In 1958, the Security Sub-Panel had asked the RCMP to obtain from the Morality Squad of the Ottawa City Police any relevant information concerning its experiences with cases involving "character weaknesses."[16] This was, at the very start of the Canadian national security war on queers, an attempt to collect more information on homosexuals. As David pointed out, in the Ottawa region the RCMP developed connections with the Ottawa and Hull police as well as with the Ontario Provincial Police (May 12, 1994).

Given the criminalization of all homosexual activity, local police could "lean on" those who had committed offences and on street informants to get them to provide information to the RCMP. This information gathering was based on power relations growing out of the criminalization of queer sex, which extended the social relations of surveillance to include local police morality squads. It also reconstructed the police-informant relation, building on the existing criminalization of same-gender erotic practices. This brought the relations of local policing and the criminalization of the sexual practices of gay men more directly into the relations of national security spying. The RCMP was able to extend its powers of surveillance through local police forces, thus demonstrating the power/knowledge relations actively constructed through this security campaign.

Another effect of this extension of the security net was to expand the pool of possible RCMP informants. This likely led to park sweeps, which is how David got caught in the net. RCMP reports indicate that it was now easier to get homosexual informants to provide information. Morgan, who lived in Toronto in the 1960s, gave us a sense of how the police-informant relation worked: "You know, [the police] would start with the bargaining stance of, 'Well, we know you were just caught up in this but we want to really find out who the real people are.' And then they would attempt to get the names of every contact that you ever had, you see, ... in return for not having charges laid against you or [having] lesser charges or not being beaten" (October 22, 1994). Thus, the more general police-gay relation was transformed into a police-informant relation.

Local Policing
The extension of these relations of surveillance rested on the forms of sexual policing of gay men and lesbians already in place, and it had an important impact on emerging gay and lesbian networks. Robert reported that, in Ottawa, "there had been raids on parks. Periodically ... they would go into the Lord Elgin and arrest people" (October 10, 1996). Barbara told us that, for the 1970s, Major's Hill and Remic Rapids were raided frequently, as were the bars (July 14, 1997). These raids led to important information being fed into the RCMP national security campaigns.

Marvin mentioned on a case of police entrapment that involved bringing together local policing and military security practices. He had a friend who was in the navy:

[This person] had this apartment and, with a friend, went to a bar, picked up two young fellows, nineteen, twenty. At that time twenty-one was the drinking age. They were only in the apartment half an hour or so, sitting drinking beer, and I guess the police came to the door. Anyway, to make a long story short, they were arrested for giving beer to minors. These kids were old enough to get married, they were old enough to serve overseas, but you couldn't give them a glass of beer. Something ridiculous. Anyway, that was the law at the time. So my friend was arrested and [given a] dishonourable discharge and five years in Kingston Penitentiary, which literally destroyed his life. (May 1998)

In this instance, the police used drinking laws and age of consent for the purposes of laying criminal charges and bringing about military discharges. This was accomplished through networks linking local policing, the RCMP, and military security.

In an informative study on Ottawa police practices, Alex Fadel showed that, between 1910 and 1967, over two hundred criminal cases involving homosexual activities were brought before the police magistrate in Ottawa, most involving gross indecency charges.[17] According to this study, fifteen men were charged in the 1950s, and sixteen suffered the same fate between 1960 and 1967. Fadel highlights a 1956 case in which two constables dressed in civilian clothes concealed themselves "in bushes bordering the lower pathway by the canal." The officers were on "special duty" for a period of seven weeks, and their job was to keep an eye on a problem area where several crimes had occurred. They saw two men come down the pathway and reportedly drop their pants. The two undercover officers charged the men with buggery and gross indecency, claiming they had witnessed anal intercourse. In 1959, two men were charged with gross indecency after being caught in a park.[18]

In 1965, two men were caught at Nepean Point and charged with gross indecency after being spotted in a car by two morality officers. One of these men was reportedly quite talkative about other men with whom he had had sexual relations. He was employed as an advisory counsel in the criminal law section at the Department of Justice.[19] In Ottawa, local sexual policing resulted in the apprehension of public servants who provided information that was fed into the RCMP surveillance web. One man was charged with buggery and twelve counts of gross indecency. There was an attempt to have him sentenced as a dangerous sexual offender (DSO), even though all the sexual activity in which he engaged was apparently consensual. There was conflicting psychiatric testimony in this case, and, as a result, the application for DSO was abandoned.[20] Clearly, RCMP surveillance came to rely upon these local police practices.

The police were a pervasive problem for gay men and lesbians during these years. Grube reported that many of the out gay men whom he interviewed "did have trouble with the police" in 1950s and 1960s Toronto (March 1, 1996).[21] Elise Chenier says that, of the sixteen women interviewed in connection with the Continental (a lesbian bar in Toronto that was popular in the 1950s and 1960s), only two were directly affected by security campaigns but that many had problems with the local police. Women were taken by local police to Cherry Beach in the Toronto harbour area and often beaten.[22] Morgan talked about how police raids on gay bars sometimes resulted in gay men being taken to Cherry Beach, where, in the fall and winter, they were forced into the water and then left to walk home (October 22, 1994).

Arlene: Sexual Policing, Violence against Lesbians, and Becoming a National Security Risk

Lesbians and gay men were entangled in this extension of police security surveillance. Arlene, whom we met earlier, was one of the women who frequented the Continental and was arrested and convicted for a break-and-entry in the 1960s by local Toronto police. Her probation worker and the local police knew she was a lesbian. Her police charge and conviction ended up on the RCMP national security list, which clearly suggests that the local police and the RCMP were working together. A documentary record of Arlene's confirmed lesbianism was discovered when her request for a pardon was being processed. This shows that, in the early 1970s, lesbianism was still considered a risk to national security.

Arlene identified as a butch lesbian. The butch's social performance of masculinity was not a mimicking of heterosexuality; rather, it involved shifting the practice of masculinity from its heterosexual contexts and, in so doing, transforming it into something appropriate to a specifically erotic butch-femme lesbian culture. Butches played an important part in fighting for distinctly lesbian social space in the 1950s and 1960s.[23] Arlene told the Lesbians Making History oral history group about being taken to Cherry Beach by the police:

> They'd just pick you up, take you to the car. And you were lucky if they said
> two words to you. And these were big cops – like they were good-sized cops.

And they take you down to Cherry Beach and handcuff your hands behind your back and beat the shit out of you. And leave you there ... If you were lucky they left your clothes. That was another dirty trick: take your clothes and make you walk home stark [naked] ... You couldn't do a thing. You couldn't go and charge them. And you were even afraid [to] go to the hospital because what would you say? If you opened your mouth and said it was the cops, they would just pick you up and do it all over again for opening your mouth. So you just sort of "rode with it." You just tried not to get arrested. (May 6, and June 3, 1987)

A gendered dress code was enforced on butch lesbians and transgendered people: "One thing that was really stupid: you had to at all times have three articles of women's clothing on you. There was some law – I don't know exactly what the law was – but there was some law that you could be picked up for cross-dressing." This policed the gender performances of lesbians and trans people and enforced practices of "femininity" on lesbians. On the policing of butch lesbians, Arlene recalled, "They picked me up – I was on my way home, we didn't see them. And it was the morality detectives that are quite well known. When they were on the street you had enough sense not to go on the street. Only nobody had spotted them, so nobody had warned anybody ... I ended up on Cherry Beach. They stripped me. Raped me. Left me there. Took my clothes and hauled off." Arlene had just turned seventeen at the time. She remembered that other women were raped as well, "quite a few of them." But "there was nothing you could do; you couldn't lay complaints ... They handcuff[ed] your hands behind your back; we didn't have any protection ... You couldn't walk up and say, 'This ... cop did this'; you'd land in jail on something. But this kind of brutality was normal" (May 6, and June 3, 1987). Clearly, physical and sexual violence was an integral part of the sexual policing of lesbians.

THE ROYAL COMMISSION ON SECURITY AND LAW REFORM

By the later 1960s, there was significant support for reform of the law under which male same-gender sex (especially buggery and gross indecency) was criminalized. Pressure was organized by early homophile groups, liberal churches, psychological and medical circles, and the legal profession. The push towards law reform occurred in the context of broad social transformations in capitalist and patriarchal relations in the postwar years, which led to less reliance on the centrality of the heterosexual family to social life and administration.

The distinction between acts that occurred in public (which remained criminalized) and those that took place between two adults in private (which were decriminalized), which was put forward in the Wolfenden Report and enacted in English and Welsh law in 1967, served to organize these Canadian law reform efforts on the official level.

The 1967 Supreme Court of Canada decision in the Everett George Klippert case pushed forward law reform efforts and led to Justice Minister Pierre Elliott Trudeau's remark that "the state has no place in the bedrooms of the nation." In *Klippert,* the Supreme Court majority decided, in a literal reading of the DSO section, that Klippert was a DSO and should therefore remain under indefinite detention. The timing of this decision, following the law reform in England and Wales, provoked widespread opposition. This helped set the stage for the reform of the Criminal Code in 1969, when homosexual acts performed in private between two consenting adults (aged twenty-one and over) were decriminalized.[24] Although homosexual law reform had no direct impact on national security practices or on the definition of homosexuality as a character weakness, by the mid- to late 1970s it did have a general impact on national security practices in the public service.

The Wolfenden Report argued that the military and other disciplinary institutions should not be affected by its proposed reforms. The 1969 Canadian law reform, therefore, had little direct influence within the military and the RCMP. With regard to the armed forces, the Wolfenden Report states:

We recognize that within services and establishments whose members are subject to a disciplinary regime it may be necessary, for the sake of good management and the preservation of discipline and for the protection of those of subordinate rank or position, to regard homosexual behaviour, even by consenting adults in private, as an offence. For instance, if our recommendations are accepted, a serving soldier over twenty-one who commits a homosexual act with a consenting adult partner in private will cease to be guilty of a civil offence or of an offence against Section 70 (1) of the Army Act, 1955 (which provides that any person subject to military law who commits a civil offence shall be guilty of an offence under that section, and hence liable to be dealt with by Court Martial). The service authorities may nevertheless consider it necessary to retain Section 66 of the Act (which provides for the punishment of ... disgraceful conduct of an indecent or unnatural kind) on the ground that it is essential, in the services, to treat as offences certain types of conduct which may not amount to offences under the civil code.[25]

This passage articulates central arguments that the military used for over three decades to resist the inclusion of lesbian and gay members.

In formulating its position, the Wolfenden Committee heard deputations from the Admiralty, the Air Ministry, and the War Office, all of which were determined that law reform should not endanger the maintenance of a disciplined hierarchy in the military. When, in Britain, the Wolfenden recommendations regarding homosexuality were implemented in the Sexual Offences Act, 1967, the act's provisions did not apply to the military or the merchant navy. Any male member could still be charged under military provisions against "disgraceful conduct of an indecent or unnatural kind."[26] A similar situation existed in Canada. The extension of the Wolfenden reform to the military, which meant the creation of a realm of privacy for homosexual acts in the military, clashed with military hierarchy and discipline. Private space occupies a precarious place in the armed forces. The military, being under direct state jurisdiction, is defined as part of the public realm. Under military codes of discipline, "sexual deviance" is defined as being a public act, no matter whether or not it occurs behind locked doors. In a total institution such as the military, there is no privacy left for queer activity. As a state-run disciplinary regime, the military can use the public/private strategy to maintain and continue practices of exclusion with regard to lesbians and gay men.

The British Ministry of Defence justified its position through three main arguments: the potentially disruptive influence of homosexuality in a closed community, the need to ensure no abuse of authority in regard to younger or junior personnel, and the conviction that homosexuals and lesbians may be subject to blackmail and to becoming security risks.[27] These were also central arguments in the Canadian military.

It is in this context that the 1966 Mackenzie Commission responded to criticisms regarding the adequacy of review procedures for security screening and to the controversy surrounding the dismissal of postal employee George Victor Spencer.[28] The Royal Commission on Security published sections of its report not deemed to be matters of national security in 1969, a year after its completion. The report included a review of security policies and argued that security screening should be extended to all employees of the civil service, not just to those who had access to classified material.[29] The commission came to the following conclusions regarding homosexuality:

> The question of homosexuality is a contentious area as social mores change. It is a fact demonstrated by a large number of case histories, that homosexuals are special targets for attention from foreign intelligence services. What is more,

Queer Resistance and the Security Response

there seems to us clear evidence that certain types of homosexuals are more readily compromised than non-deviate persons. However, we feel that each case must be judged in the light of all its circumstances, including such factors as the stability of the relationships, the decency of the incidents, the public or private character of the acts, the incidence of arrests or convictions, and the effects of any rehabilitative efforts.[30]

The assertion that homosexuals are special targets who are more easily compromised than "non-deviate persons" is reiterated. In this somewhat more liberal national security discourse, it is still assumed that all homosexuals are security risks but that certain types of them are greater risks than others. This is especially true if they do not have stable relationships, have recently engaged in homosexual activities, participate in more public-related activities, have been arrested or convicted of homosexual offences, or have not been "rehabilitated." This shows the very interesting entry of a series of distinctions, including public/private and the stability/instability of relationships, into this national security discourse. The Mackenzie Commission issued its report at the same time as reforms to partially decriminalize homosexual sexual activities, modelled on the Wolfenden Report, were being discussed by the federal government. The discourse in the Mackenzie Report embodied a series of moral evaluations of homosexuality and a seeming acceptance of it as a sickness or mental illness in need of rehabilitation. The report states that "past homosexual or even current stable homosexual relationships should" not always prevent employment in public service at low levels of security clearance. At the same time, it argues that, "in the interests of the individuals themselves as well as in the interests of the state, homosexuals should not normally be granted clearances to higher levels, should not be recruited if there is a possibility that they may require such clearance in the course of their careers and should certainly not be posted to sensitive positions overseas."[31]

Past participation in homosexual practices and in monogamous homosexual relationships was not considered a security risk per se. At the same time, we also see the interesting formulation "in the interests of the state" being used as well as "sensitive positions overseas." The report also introduces an important distinction between low levels and high levels of clearance, thus precluding homosexuals from being recruited into positions where they might *ever* require higher clearances. Clearly, homosexuality is still very much problematized, but some new lines of administrative distinction were being developed. The basic assumption of the security regime regarding the association of gay men and lesbians with risks to national security is held in place, with a slight administrative shift. The identification of gay men and lesbians as security risks continued through to the 1990s.

The Mackenzie Commission's recommendations were only partly implemented. The Security Review Board, which would have considered protests from public servants regarding security decisions, was never created. Individuals who were transferred, who failed to obtain a promotion or position, or who had a contract terminated were not provided with a right of appeal.

The Association for Social Knowledge and the Royal Commission on Security
A gay group known as the Association for Social Knowledge (ASK) made a submission to the Mackenzie Commission that apparently had little impact on its findings. This was one of the first submissions by a gay individual or group to a government body since Axel Otto Olson's 1956 private session submission to the Royal Commission on the Criminal Law Regarding Criminal Sexual Psychopaths and Jim Egan's letters to several government bodies. Doug Sanders, on behalf of the Vancouver-based ASK, made this submission in 1968. He described the context in which it was written:

> I don't have any sense of a big reason for doing the submission other than the sense that the security issue was an issue embedded in the discourse of that time in terms of homosexuality ... I had no sense that it was a real issue in terms of ASK ... that it was a real issue in Canada. That this was a kind of formal occasion on which something was said in the name of an organization like ASK ... So I do a very formalistic thing. I write to the Civil Service Commissions as opposed to actually having any kind of discussions ... among people who are members of ASK ... I didn't have any notion of the purges, so in that sense the [gay] constituency was not a data source because of my preconceptions ... So I wasn't driven by local concerns or perceptions of local reality and therefore it had a very kind of abstract character to it in the way it's argued. (June 10, 1994)

In this brief, Sanders critiqued the two main arguments used to deny homosexuals security clearances: that they suffered from a character weakness and were not emotionally stable, and that they were more subject to blackmail.[32] He used and relied on Hooker's work and the Kinsey Report, which undercut the psychological construct of homosexuals as mentally disturbed.[33] Sanders argued that "the idea that homosexuals as a group are less stable than heterosexuals is not supportable." Moreover, he posited that "there have been no homosexual 'witch-hunts' in Canada," adding that "the potential for blackmail is greatly over-estimated in Canada." Again, this points out how invisible the security campaigns could be outside Ottawa in the 1960s, even to someone involved in homophile organizing. Sanders also highlighted how many homosexuals experienced insecurity in employment, arguing "that insecurity can only be eliminated by clear statements from the governments involved that a homosexual who is competent and stable will not be fired or denied a security clearance. Simply clearly expressing these policies will reduce greatly the potential for blackmail." To clarify this situation, he called for the passage of the Wolfenden-type reform proposed by Trudeau in 1967.

In the process of collecting information for this submission, Sanders wrote letters to provincial civil service commissions, the Public Service Commission of Canada, and to the minister of national defence, asking whether they had policies that excluded homosexuals from employment. None of them reported having such policies. Sanders wrote: "Appendix C contains a statement from the Minister of National Defence that homosexuals can enter the armed forces and can obtain security clearances."[34] Clearly, this was not the case at the time, especially in the military.

Sanders recalled that, at an ASK meeting following submission of the brief, one member challenged what the minister of national defence stated in his letter to ASK:

It was before I left Vancouver. It was after the brief had gone in. The brief
was really my work; it really wasn't vetted in any real way. It may have gone
to some meeting, but there were no comments or revisions of it so the text is
mine unaltered. But I recall that, ... it would have to be later in '68, that someone
said, "Oh, there have been purges in the military, and the letter from Cadieux
[the minister of national defence] was nonsense." As I recall it, it was not someone saying he had been purged but [someone] saying that he knew this story
about purges that occurred in the military earlier. And that therefore this letter
from Cadieux was not to be believed ... I believe it was purges that had occurred
in British Columbia [to which he was referring]. (June 10, 1994)

This submission was made in the context of a movement towards homosexual law reform, something that ASK had long advocated. However, these reforms were not enacted according to ASK's perspective. Instead of the popular education and acceptance of homosexuality for which it had hoped, there was now a new form of public/private, adult/youth sexual regulation. Sanders' comments on the 1969 reform are most helpful here. According to him, Trudeau's infamous remark about getting the state out of the bedrooms of the nation takes the gay issue and describes it in non-homosexual terms ... Unfortunately, legalization [i.e., what we would call "decriminalization"] occurs in a way in which the issue is never joined. The debate never occurs. And so homosexuals are no more real after the reform than before ... I felt an issue had been stolen from us. That we had forgotten that the reform issue was an issue that could have been used for public debate and it had been handled in such a way that there had been none. The only thing that had a promise of helping people was a public debate. It didn't happen.[35]

Gay and lesbian non-cooperation and resistance was a major obstacle confronting the RCMP in the 1960s. The push towards homosexual law reform was limited and had little effect on national security practices or in the military. In the 1970s, the possibilities for queer resistance expanded, and lesbian and gay organizing itself became a target of RCMP surveillance.

The Campaign Continues in the 1970s
Security Risks and Lesbian Purges in the Military

THE 1969 CRIMINAL CODE REFORM: NATIONAL SECURITY TRUMPS PRIVACY RIGHTS

The 1969 Criminal Code reform led to the partial decriminalization of certain homosexual acts in private between two consenting adults (defined as age twenty-one and over). This maintained the criminalization of queer sexual practices that involved younger people or that were defined as public in character. The distinctions drawn between adult/youth and public/private shaped the sexual policing of gay men and, in a different way, of lesbians.[1]

This reform had little immediate impact on national security practices, given that there was no direct connection between the criminalization of homosexuality and the national security practices against queers. The RCMP's campaign against queers in the 1950s and 1960s had been informed by the criminalization of queer sexual activities but was not dependent upon it. Regardless of the 1969 reform, state bodies and the RCMP continued to view gay men and lesbians as security risks who were suffering from a character weakness. The criminalization of same-gender sexual acts in public (including acts between more than two adults) or involving young people persisted. The policing of sex between men actually intensified in the 1970s and early 1980s.

National security concerns overrode the public/private regulatory distinction embodied in the Criminal Code reform. Whether homosexual acts took place in public or in private, and even if these acts no longer contravened the Criminal Code, blackmail was still possible as long as there was something to hide – or so went the security argument. In the eyes of Canadian state agencies, homosexuals continued to pose considerable risk to national security, thereby justifying pervasive anti-queer social practices. In the military and the RCMP, exclusion of lesbians and gay men continued.[2]

Notwithstanding its limitations, the 1969 reform and the profound social transformations of the 1960s created the social conditions for the expansion and visibility of gay and lesbian networks.[3] Gay liberation and lesbian feminist networks emerged in the context of the anti-war, student, youth, feminist, Québécois independence, anti-racist, Red Power, and Black Power movements.[4] The 1969 New York City Stonewall riots against police repression led to the formation of gay liberation fronts across the United States, Canada, and around the world.[5] These movements also occurred within the broader context of transformations in postwar Canadian social relations. The impact of these changes led capitalist and state relations to become (albeit unevenly) less dependent on the heterosexual family form as well as to a certain moral deregulation of "deviant" sexual practices.[6] In turn, possibilities for resistance to and non-cooperation with the national security campaigns expanded.

Trudeau: Homosexuals Remain a Security Problem

Despite his liberal stance on homosexual law reform, or, more accurately, because of it, Prime Minister Trudeau rose in the House of Commons in 1973 to speak to homosexuality and security clearances. In his statement, suspected homosexuality continued to be one of the reasons considered by the government when granting security clearance to federal employees.[7] Trudeau put forward a similar view in a 1978 letter to David Garmaise of the National Gay Rights Coalition (NGRC), a cross-country coalition of lesbian and gay groups, in response to the NGRC's argument for eliminating these security practices. Blair Johnston, who was involved in Gays of Ottawa in the early 1980s, remembers that Garmaise wrote to Trudeau many times before he finally received this response (February 1, 2001):

> The most difficult problem the government faces in this area concerns security. In particular, problems are likely to be encountered in relation to sensitive positions in the public service, and related services, where security clearances to a high level are required. The RCM Police, the Department of National Defence, and the Department of External Affairs have found that homosexuals are targeted for blackmail to a greater extent than heterosexuals. They are particularly vulnerable in postings abroad, and I should add that in some countries the legal provisions relating to homosexuals could cause serious problems for federal

employees ... With respect to the employment of homosexuals by the Department of National Defence, there is no policy to bar homosexuals from civilian positions. The Armed Forces however, have found due to the special character of the Force, individuals who are found to be homosexual are given discharges which do not cite specific reasons for release, in order to avoid harassment and for their own benefit. There is no government policy, either overt or covert, to discriminate against homosexuals. There is, however, a security problem which the government, in carrying out its responsibilities must take into consideration.[8]

While this letter claims that, in general, there is no discrimination against homosexuals, the concept of "security" is deployed to introduce that very discrimination. Trudeau raises the problem of the anti-homosexual laws of other countries and the difficulties these supposedly present to posting homosexuals there, and he also cites military arguments for the exclusion and disposal of sex deviates. In an interesting example of doublespeak, Trudeau portrays this not as discrimination but as a security problem, and he even suggests that military policies of exclusion are for the benefit of homosexuals. Again, we see how the conceptualization of security mandates social practices of discrimination.

Johnston recalled that this official admission of discrimination in some areas of state employment enabled gay organizations to approach various government departments to inquire into whether or not they discriminated against gays and lesbians (February 1, 2001). Although discrimination in some areas of the public service began to taper off towards the end of the 1970s, it was still pervasive and continued to have important gendered dimensions.

Queers in the 1970s Public Service

Negotiating the federal bureaucracy in the 1970s continued to pose serious personal and employment problems for queers. Barbara, a public servant in Ottawa in the 1970s, remembered, "We were so well hidden in those days" (July 14, 1997). A female director general approached her: "I was offered a promotion if I'd sleep with her." This woman was one of the few women in the late 1970s who was in upper management: "I mean, you always presumed when you were working with the government, 'Yes, OK, you're a lesbian.' You just don't let anyone else know because of job security. And, I mean, it really blew me away that she would do something like that. It was almost like breaking a silent contract that we all had. You know, fine, meet them out in the bar if you want, but don't pull them into your office" (July 14, 1997).

Barbara described how lesbians and gay men survived in the public service in the 1970s:

A lot were extremely well hidden. A lot married just to hide the fact. Because it was a scary time for anyone who was gay. I honestly don't think that I could say that I knew a gay man while I worked [in a government department]. They were so well hidden. The whole acting straight, the way they dressed. In those days there was a dress code for the government. Lesbians and gay men would be keeping to themselves ... socializing with people in the office but not really socializing. Like sort of sitting on the outskirts but having lunch with the guys, you know, teasing and all that stuff. You know, it was a fact of life back then ... if you wanted to stay in the government. And unfortunately, at that point in time, the majority of us worked on terms [i.e., term contracts] so twenty-four-hour notification [and] you're out. (July 14, 1997)

A key survival strategy involved performing oneself as heterosexual in order to remain employed. This strategy was even more crucial considering that union protection from discrimination and firings did not yet exist. Part of maintaining the heterosexual appearance involved perpetuating a gender-specific and conservative dress code, which Barbara described as follows:

For women, no jeans, no tank tops, no tube tops. Actually, you weren't allowed to expose the shoulders. Women are not supposed to be wearing sleeveless shirts at the office. You couldn't show your belly. The pants couldn't be skin tight. They preferred skirts to the knee. They didn't like mini-skirts and cleavage. Women in Ottawa have no cleavage. [Laughter] You could get away with jeans if you worked in stock or supply ... But for the guys, no shorts. Or, if they did wear shorts they had to be Bermuda with knee-high socks. Women could wear dress shorts that looked more like skirts with nylons in the dead of summer. The guys, you know, shirt and tie. But again, if you worked in stock or records, an open neck but no T-shirts, nothing like that. Men couldn't wear earrings, and if they had long hair it had to be tied back. (July 14, 1997)

Regarding housing, Barbara said that gay men faced more problems than did lesbians:

You always hear the rumours that someone had lost their apartment, especially the guys ... Like, you couldn't rent an apartment in Ottawa if you were two guys living together. It was virtually impossible. Two women, that was OK. As I say, we're hidden ... But yeah, I heard of people losing their places. A couple lost jobs thinking that it could be because they were gay. Of course, we've got no proof whether that was the reason or not. Not receiving promotions, I mean, that's a big one. I'm quite sure that's where I'm sitting right now. I will never get promoted ... A lot of it has to do with the fact that I'm a lesbian and the fact that I'm a woman ... I do the same job as the guys who are two levels higher than me with the same amount of experience. (July 14, 1997)

Although Barbara did not personally know of any women who were purged or demoted because of their lesbianism, she did know of women "that [would] never move." In her words, "They stay stagnant. They will be transferred to other departments but they will never get a higher [security] classification. Yeah, there were people that their terms were not extended. Now, I mean, it's always hard to tell if it's because they're lesbian or because they're lousy workers ... They never really overtly got rid of anyone that was gay. They always found another reason because I think that was to protect management."

Barbara described working in pay and benefits from the late 1970s to about 1986: "[Out of seven pay clerks] five of us were gay. I mean, we dragged the other two out to drag shows! It was a very open department, which was nice, I mean, it was such a change. I mean, no one actually said, 'Hey, I'm gay.' I mean, you just looked around and said: 'Whoa, I'm home!' ... It was common knowledge that the majority of [us], at least in Personnel, ... were, well, lesbians. There was, you know, maybe one gay guy. But, I mean, there are hardly any men in Personnel anyway" (July 14, 1997).

By the 1970s, lesbian networks had developed in some workplaces. Barbara noted that women went to the Coral Reef: "It was women's-only night at the Coral Thursday nights. So we'd all be dragging our butts into work Friday morning. Then it moved to Friday nights. So basically every Friday everyone would hit the Reef because it was the only women's-only place." She also noted that the network from work went to "straight bars a lot of times. Because, I mean, we would do it Friday afternoon after work, so we just looked like a group of people coming over for a drink before going home. We never got hassled ... In the evenings if we went out there would be a smaller more select group of us that would go out and over to Hull because there were a couple of bars over there." Barbara recalled the Ottawa lesbian scene of the 1970s:

A lot of it was private parties. You know, you sort of hooked up [with] a little group and that's who you hung out with. There were a couple of ball teams [laughter]. But a lot of it was private parties, but you had to know someone to be invited somewhere. So, I mean, if you were a stranger, you couldn't go anywhere until someone got to know you. Sort of our own little security system because we wanted to make sure [everything] was on the up and up. But, as I said, the Coral was really the only place in the '70s that women went. (July 14, 1997)

This also reflects the smaller amount of social space available to lesbians in the 1970s in comparison to what was available to gay men, given the lower wages women earned and the general denial of social, economic, and sexual independence for them. As a result, fewer commercial establishments existed where lesbians could congregate. Finally, lesbians were less likely to participate in the public forms of cruising in parks or washrooms.[9]

CONTINUING PURGES IN THE MILITARY: HOMOSEXUALS BECOME AN ADMINISTRATIVE PROBLEM

Blair Johnston was in the military in the 1970s and living in the closet. He encountered many men in the military who were having sex with other men. The assumption that most people were heterosexual and that all gay men were "fairies" or "gender inverts" provided cover for those in the military who performed their gender as masculine:

I met a number of gay people in the military, but in the ... mental space I was in at the time, I did not consider myself to be gay or a homosexual because I didn't wear dresses. And many of the people in the armed forces had that same image of themselves, that they couldn't be homosexual, this ... had nothing to do with being a fairy ... I met people who were lovers, who lived together and they were just considered to be best friends. There was a certain blindness in the military to that sort of stuff. (February 1, 2001)

Johnston was later involved in security work:

One of my responsibilities was finding homosexuals, under Canadian Forces Order 19-20. It was a strange position to be in because I was starting to analyze what the hell was a homosexual. It seemed to deal more with sexual impropriety, but it was never very, very specific. It was very difficult to say what is homosexual and what isn't. I mean, I've been on board ships where guys are goosing each other all the time, but that was considered normal good fun. There's a line that almost cannot be drawn between what we would call homoerotic heterosexualism and homoerotic homosexualism. But it was at that time I realized I just could not stay in the military, I was going to be found out eventually. So about 1974 I left the military. The people I did know in the military that were gay were very closeted. (February 1, 2001)

Johnston had a top secret security clearance during the early 1970s. No questions were ever asked of him, and he was never identified as gay. After leaving the military he worked with the Atomic Energy Control Board and then with the DEA. His security clearances in the military helped him in his new positions:

I should mention that the whole issue of being a gay person never came up for quite some time simply because I'd gone through all the hoops coming from military college and the air force. It's like getting your pass: once you're into the fairgrounds you get to use all the rides. That's part of the status and class structures that we have in Canada. Once you have your university degree, for example, you are not just considered to be a secretary; but if you are a secretary, forget it, because you can't be what we call officer class or management, or at least it's very difficult. (February 1, 2001)

Johnston's account gives us a sense of the relation between security clearances and other forms of gaining credentials in the construction of class relations, both in government work in general and in the military in particular. Meanwhile, purges continued in the military in the 1970s.

"Pictures of my car in known cruisy areas"
Frank Letourneau's story starts in the mid-1960s and culminates in 1970. Letourneau had a successful naval career based in Halifax, where, in 1965, he was promoted to lieutenant at age twenty-three. According to Letourneau, by that time he had come to "realize that being gay was not something [he] was going to grow out of and [he] was actively pursuing gay encounters in Halifax's various cruising areas" (December 7, 2008). He described how, in late 1968, a "flamer" who was a leading seaman "had been posted to the Chaplain's Office in the shore base, a well-known procedure utilized to handle personnel suspected of being gay." Letourneau was the ship's duty officer when this man "came aboard and asked to see [him]." According to Letourneau, "He told me that letters had been found in the possession of another CF member which incriminated him and that he would likely be forced to leave the navy. With some trepidation, I asked him if my name had come up. He reassured me that

it hadn't and that he was not going to mention it." Letourneau went on to say that "things, however, did come to a head" a few years later. He explained:

The ship's second in command (my executive officer, or XO) asked me to come to his cabin and informed me that the military police wanted to see me the next day. When I asked why, he told me that I was suspected of being homosexual and that he and the ship's captain had been made aware of this. He added that he was not expecting me to comment, that he would accompany me and assist me any way that I would need. The next day, we drove up together to the Military Police Office at Stadacona, and I was interviewed by relatively junior non-commissioned personnel. My XO offered to stay but I told him I'd be all right. Actually, I was anything but all right as my interrogators began to flip through a thick binder containing pictures of my car in known cruisy areas, details of my comings and goings, people I had befriended onboard ship, et cetera. The main focus of the questions seemed to be to incite me to give them other names of serving gay personnel I had associated with. The only name I offered them was of someone I had met one or two years earlier who had presented himself as a naval photographer (he had the uniform and he sure had pictures!) but who turned out to be a civilian cleaner employed at the naval base. They weren't at all interested in this person, for reasons which became obvious. As it turned out, the military police had caught him many months earlier as he was engaged in a homosexual "activity" with a sailor in the enlisted men's barracks. The level of details the MPs had on me could have only come from him, and I learned later that he had indeed provided them with the names of a number of individuals who were then placed under surveillance. I know of one other officer, a helicopter pilot, who was caught up in this witch hunt and subsequently released. I agreed to write out a statement, the contents of which, after all these years, are very fuzzy, but which did not dispute the main conclusion. (December 7, 2008)

Letourneau then went on to say:

[I was] driven back to my ship by an MP corporal who, as we drove under the Angus L. Macdonald Bridge, said, as he looked up: "I hope you won't be doing anything foolish." I curtly told him to get me back to my ship, where I met with the captain and the executive officer. Both offered their support and sympathy, with the captain saying how appalled he was at the way a fine naval officer was being treated. He also mentioned that many heterosexual service

personnel had their own skeletons in their closets but were not being persecuted because those were hetero skeletons. As my only option was a clean break
from the navy, I wrote out my resignation, which, needless to say, was promptly
accepted, and I was honourably released in 1970. (December 7, 2008)

It is interesting that Letourneau's captain was able to discern the heterosexist
double standard whereby heterosexual skeletons could be ignored but homosexual ones could not.

My Brother: "His life was destroyed" and Other Military Stories
In 1973, John Robert MacPherson, who was then eighteen, was discovered in a
homosexual act by military authorities on the west coast. According to his
sister, Ellen Skinner, he was interrogated and "asked to inform on others" who
were involved "in the circle" of homosexuals in the military. He apparently did
inform on others, and he later "felt lots of guilt over informing on people" (June
16, 1999). According to Skinner, when MacPherson was arrested by military
police, his family in Edmonton "was not informed he was being held, we did
not know where he was." He was given the standard choice of either resigning
or facing a court martial: "Either an honourable or a dishonourable discharge.
And if it is dishonourable it will be on your record." Given this choice, he resigned and received an honourable discharge.

At first MacPherson told his family he had been discharged because of
drugs since he had been a medic in the military. But soon it became clear he
had been purged because he was a homosexual. The military "forced him out
of the closet," and the response he received from most members of his family
and the local community was hostile. By outing him, the military set in motion
a social course of action leading to his being ostracized and stigmatized. Mac-
Pherson's younger brother and his father, also members of the military, hardly
spoke to him, and his mother never admitted he was gay. As Skinner put it, John
(her brother) "was not ready to come out." Nor was he prepared for the social
and familial rejection he encountered. As Skinner said, "He tried very hard to
live a straight life for mother after he came back."

According to Skinner, MacPherson felt that "his life [had been] destroyed":
"He felt they had forced him out. He loved his job, he loved the military. He
was devastated since he wanted to stay in the military. He felt like his life was
over at this point ... He was also afraid because he told on others, including
those of high rank, including officers. He lived in fear of retribution and did
get threats." Eventually, Skinner moved away: "So he lost me as well." In 1974,

MacPherson took his own life, although his mother "never admitted that he killed himself." Skinner wants her brother to be "honoured and remembered" (June 16, 1999).

In 1974, Martin Hogarth of Ottawa was expelled from the armed forces after admitting, under interrogation, that he was gay. His twelve-year career in the army was ended abruptly by the application of Canadian Forces Administrative Order 19-20 (CFAO 19-20), which prohibited lesbians and gay men from belonging to the military. His case was publicized by the NGRC in briefs presented to Members of Parliament regarding the Federal Human Rights Act.[10] The NGRC was aware of many other cases of homosexuals who were expelled but who were unable to go public with their cases.[11]

The first person to take the armed forces to court over its discrimination against gays and lesbians was Jacques Gallant. He joined the forces in 1969 in Trois-Rivières, Quebec. Seven years later, in 1976, in Lahr, West Germany, he was called before his commanding officer and told he was under investigation as a "sex deviate." Gallant appealed his discharge to the Federal Court of Canada, asserting that his actions had in no way scandalized the forces or impaired his ability to perform his duties. He noted that, had he been allowed to present a defence in French, he could have put forward arguments to support his case, thus suggesting that he was being discriminated against on the basis of language. The Department of Defence simply countered that the court had no jurisdiction in this matter since military law and regulations were not subject to civil law. It won.[12]

In 1976, Darryl Kippen of Winnipeg was told during basic training at the Cornwallis base in Nova Scotia that the "Armed Forces is no place for queers and that if anyone was approached by a queer they should get a bunch of the guys, take him into the barracks and beat the shit out of him." The instructor stated that, in order to protect the attackers, his report would indicate that the assaulted victim had fallen down the stairs. Clearly, the military hierarchy tolerated, and sometimes incited, violence towards queers. In response to this, Kippen decided that he would not have sex with military men. Discovered three years later, he was purged from the armed forces.[13]

Herself purged from the military, Gloria Cameron reported: "I spoke recently to a man who had been drummed out of the Forces some years ago under CFAO 19-20. He said most people knew he was gay, and it didn't seem to make much difference. Until the day a superior officer asked for a blow-job, and this man said no. Within a week he had been given his release papers to sign, and his career in the army was over."[14]

Military policies excluding queers from membership continued in the 1970s. According to a 1993 letter from Minister of National Defence Tom Siddon to the Gay and Lesbian Organization of Veterans (GLOV), "Prior to 1970 homosexuality was a criminal offence under the Criminal Code and the SIU conducted their investigations as criminal investigations. After 1970 when homosexual activity between consenting adults was no longer considered a criminal offence, homosexuality was considered as an administrative matter by the Canadian Forces and SIU investigations were then conducted as administrative investigations."[15] Siddon cites the wrong year for the partial decriminalization of buggery and gross indecency, although military practices may not have changed until 1970. He suggests, however, a shift in military investigation policies following partial decriminalization, with more emphasis being placed on administrative procedures. This meant that military investigations were less focused on actual or potential Criminal Code offences and more on violations of military administrative policies.[16]

The administrative order prohibiting lesbians and gay men from belonging to the military was modified slightly in 1976. This modification allowed for an alignment with contemporary discourse and finally took into account the 1969 Criminal Code reform. The new title was "Homosexuality, Sexual Abnormality, Investigation, Medical Examination and Disposal." Key to this change was the use and definition of the term "homosexual." Prior to 1976, service policy did "not allow the retention of sex deviates in the Forces." In 1976, this was changed to "service policy does not allow homosexual members or members with sexual abnormality to be retained in the Canadian Forces."[17]

NGRC spokesperson David Garmaise commented: "They probably foresaw that they would some day have trouble proving that homosexuality was a sexual deviance, so they decided it had better specifically include gays in the regulation" (May 13, 2000). This also instigated a more specific focus against homosexuals and homosexual sexual activity. A homosexual was defined as "one who has a sexual propensity for persons of one's own sex." "Sexual abnormality" was defined as "any form of sexual behaviour not conforming to accepted moral standards or constituting an offence under the Criminal Code of Canada, e.g., voyeurism, exhibitionism, gross indecency, bestiality." In effect, the military attempted to establish a category that covered homosexuals who had not engaged in any criminal sexual offences. This allowed for queers to be expelled from the armed forces for engaging in acts not defined as "crimes." The 1969 Criminal Code reform did not extend to the armed forces, and those who engaged in "criminal acts" could be purged under "sexual abnormality." At the same time, references to moral standards left the definition of sexual abnormality ambiguous and, thus, operational as a means of moral regulation.

The stages outlined for dealing with homosexuals in the military were investigation, discipline, disposal, and release. People released under this provision were considered "not advantageously employable" as opposed to "voluntarily released," which was the earlier formulation.[18] Cases of suspected homosexuality were now under the jurisdiction of the Special Investigations Unit, a corps of military police that replaced the earlier Special Investigations Detachment.[19] These regulations also called for the mandatory reporting of homosexuality: "If a person subject to the Code of Service Discipline [in the armed forces] becomes aware or suspects that a member of the Canadian Forces is homosexual ... he shall report the matter to the commanding officer."[20]

PURGING LESBIANS: GLORIA CAMERON AND BARBARA THORNBORROW

The Canadian focus on purging lesbians from the military was similar to that in Britain. Between 1978 and 1982, over one-third of all 3,160 soldiers dismissed from the British Armed Forces for homosexuality were women. Women in the British military were ten times more likely than were men to have their lives officially investigated.[21] In Canada, a few lesbians began to come forward in the 1970s to publicly challenge their expulsions. This was possible due to the development of activist movements and more visible community formation as well as the extension of lesbian and gay networks within the military.

After working for eight years for the Canadian Armed Forces and having reached the highest level within the ranks without being made an officer, Gloria Cameron was purged from the military under CFAO 19-20. There were thirty-three Canadian Armed Forces women working at the US naval base in Argentia, Newfoundland, a number of whom were part of a lesbian network. On April 2, 1977, Cameron and eight other women signed their final papers formalizing their release from the Canadian forces.[22] Cameron described what happened: "Though I'd known a lot of gay kids since I arrived at the base – there were at least a dozen gay women that I knew quite well: maybe half that number of gay men. Anyway, two of the women decided to marry, that was last December. And they did. And there was a little ceremony in one of the cabins we had access to off base. I wasn't there myself, but I heard about it."

But less sympathetic members of the military also heard about it. At the end of February, Major Bernie Hogan, following the regulations regarding mandatory reporting of homosexual activities, contacted Maritime Command Headquarters in Halifax to request a special investigation, as required by military policy. Two men from the SIU arrived and, separately, called in the women involved. Cameron was called in early March:

> I was one of the last to be called in ... I was really nervous and afraid. I wanted to stay in the Forces, but I guess I'd known from the beginning what their position was on gay people. I'd just always lived with the fear of being found out ... I always felt eventually I would get caught. It's not a nice way to live ... They asked me if I was a homosexual. I said I wasn't. I denied everything. Maybe that was an awful thing to do but I wanted to stay in the Forces so bad.

She was allowed to leave the interview, but two days later she was called back:

> It was the same except this time there was a polygraph, a lie detector, in the room. They asked me if I knew what it was. I said I did. They asked me if I would take the test. I said I wouldn't. So they began to question me but it wasn't just about the services, or who I knew, but they asked about my family and my background and probed away about my grandparents and all kinds of personal things ... It went on 'till eight o'clock that night and I just broke down ... Mostly because I knew I was going to be kicked out. But I admitted it. I told them that I was gay. But I didn't implicate anyone else.

Cameron eventually submitted to the lie-detector test, which, in the 1970s, became common practice in the military. Barbara Thornborrow shared this experience. Gerald Hannon described what happened to Cameron: "They told her they wanted to 'test her loyalty to Canada' and for about a half an hour she answered questions about official secrets and what she knew and who she told. When it was over they told her she was 'clean.' Then they asked her to sign a statement of confession, and she did, exhausted and broken by nine hours of grilling."

Cameron was found to be "loyal," but they also proved her lesbianism. What is visible here is the social organization of an SIU investigation. Evidence of lesbianism was reported to the military authorities and an SIU investigation was initiated. Cameron's preliminary interview was followed by a series of interviews that brought together the information gathered and extorted from others. Her second interview was set in a more intimidating context, with the presence of the lie detector. The image and mythology surrounding the lie detector, and its ability to reveal the "truth," carries a particular social power.[23]

The SIU was also interested in interrogating Cameron about her knowledge of secret information. The assumption of homosexual blackmail figured quite prominently in its approach. Part of its tactics involved making the interviews exhausting. Hannon continues,

> Two days later the special investigation team returned to Halifax. They left behind a shattered and terrified gay community. Because there was some small sense of community among the gay people on the base – they knew each other, and from time to time they were able to arrange clandestine little parties somewhere off base ... But all that was gone now. The gay people stayed away from each other. They were afraid – companionship, community was compromising. And for three agonizing weeks nothing happened, no word from Halifax ... On March 28th it happened. They were informed that they had "finished work." That was five women from Argentia, three women in Halifax who had been in Argentia before that. Shortly thereafter, one more [woman] turned herself in. She said that she was "tired of living like a rat in a hole."

Cameron went public with her case in late May. She filed a redress of grievance to the chief of defence in Ottawa, and the media covered her story.[24] She told Hannon, "I felt it was important to do it that way. I wanted as many people as possible to know what happened, and I thought other gay people would feel better knowing that some of us are fighting back ... Maybe they would think of doing the same thing."[25] In Cameron's language, we see the unmistakable influence of the gay and lesbian movements. In response to her action, Cameron received letters from a number of women who encouraged her – women who, as Hannon puts it, "did feel better knowing 'that some of us are fighting back.'"[26]

On July 2, General J.A. Dextraze, chief of defence in Ottawa, sent a letter to Cameron. He informed her that her appeal had failed and that she was not "suitable" for the Canadian Armed Forces. It went on: "It is deemed necessary to discriminate against those who, having admitted or demonstrated behavioural traits such as homosexuality, might attempt to impose them on others, particularly youthful members ... Despite the admissions you have made openly and notwithstanding that your loyalty to Canada has not been questioned, a potential hazard to security remains."[27] Thus, though she had not been disloyal, she needed to be discriminated against because of her behavioural traits.

As Hannon points out: "No further appeal is possible. And part of Gloria's life has come to an end. The same is true for the other eight women. She's still in touch with most of them, and they're still looking for jobs. They think that what she is doing is great, but none of them feel they can follow her example. You can understand why. It's hard enough to get a job as it is; harder yet when your last reference claims you're not 'advantageously employable.' You are not going to kill what small chances you do have by dancing out into the spotlight as an upfront dyke." The practices of heterosexist employment discrimination continued to keep these women caught within the social relations of the closet and living a double life.

Cameron also told Hannon about previous anti-lesbian purges of which she had heard, including a "similar investigation which occurred in Halifax-Shearwater back in 1970/71 which resulted in about 15 women being dropped from the Forces."[28] This resonates with the account provided by Sue and her friend Joan, who lived together in Halifax in the late 1960s and early 1970s. Sue and Joan explained how this purge began and some of the techniques that were used. Sue remembered: "One of the women tried to commit suicide, didn't succeed, and blabbed her guts about everybody. She was a young woman who was looking at her sexuality, was having trouble with it, all she really needed was some counselling. And they took advantage of her. They truly did, they tortured her" (February 23, 1996). Held for more than twenty-four hours, this woman was prohibited from leaving or talking with anyone. Two men interrogated her at the Stadacona naval base. Sue told us that "you'd tell them anything after 24 hours especially if you were already in a very upset emotional situation. And they did, they got her, which I think is despicable" (February 23, 1996). It was very difficult for individual women to deal with the security campaigns in the military. Sue noted: "We were not about to turn on our sisters, if you will, unless we got interrogated, we got blackmailed, or our lives were threatened." Joan remarked: "I don't even blame those women [who did give names] anymore. I was angry in the beginning ... and then when I found out what they went through, I don't blame them." The disciplinary power that could be mobilized against these women severely limited possibilities for non-cooperation.

Sue and Joan also told us about the surveillance of house parties in the Halifax-Dartmouth area in the early 1970s (across the country, the networks of lesbian house parties provided important gathering places). Sue reported: "We used to have parties with civilian women and navy women and we would come out of the apartment and there would be some Gomer [i.e., term referring to a man] standing out there with a camera or in a coat doing surveillance." Joan added, "And a tape recorder. Caught one guy with his foot up against the door. Some of the young women coming along had decided that they still wanted to be in the military. And they were hanging out with some of us and they had applied. Samantha was one of them. They said, 'I don't think we want you.' They wouldn't even let her in. They hadn't proven who she was, they just said, 'You're not coming.' They did the security check. They said, 'NO way!'" Joan became aware that security forces had her name: "They were [doing] more than compiling [names]. I had nothing to do with the forces, but my name was there, hers was [a friend's], my son['s] was. Yes, they were more than compiling: they were investigating all of us ... And that's how they worked their games, one person says one name and the next person, they'd use that name to get the next person to tell them another one." A network of surveillance covered lesbian networks in Halifax-Dartmouth, especially focusing on interactions between civilian and military women. According to Sue and Joan, this collecting of names netted the name of a heterosexual woman who was part of their social circle. Basically, Sue and Joan lost their housing because of the house parties they held (February 23, 1996).

Gloria Cameron was inspired by Barbara Thornborrow, who went public with her struggle against discrimination in the military. Thornborrow's case started later than the Argentia investigations but culminated earlier, with Thornborrow going public in mid-May. On May 9, 1977, Thornborrow was called into the office of Sergeant Cochrane of the Canadian forces SIU. She had served for sixteen months and had applied for a voluntary release from the forces. A sergeant and a military policewoman questioned her about alleged homosexual activities, informing her that she was being questioned for reasons of national security because she was "susceptible to blackmail."[29] They searched her room after this interrogation, and some personal belongings were seized. In another account of this search, Thornborrow reports that the police seized some gay pamphlets and old love letters, but they missed the photographic box on her desk, which contained letters from her lover.[30]

Thornborrow's experiences with the Hamilton-McMaster gay liberation movement enabled her to come out publicly and fight against her expulsion.[31] Despite this earlier activist involvement, she had no problem joining the military. As she put it, "I discovered that even the RCMP had nothing on file about me being gay."[32] Thornborrow is not sure how they found out about her sexuality: "I really don't know. They might have been routinely checking on me and discovered this while they were at it. They must have had some direction though, because they told me my lover's name and asked if I was having an affair with her. Perhaps one of the women in the barracks here mentioned our relationship to the wrong person."[33] When they searched her room, Thornborrow said that she "was upset, but tried not to show it." She continued, "Finally the officer came right out and said, 'We've got all the stuff, and it's quite obvious that you are, so why don't you admit it?' So I said, 'Alright, I am.' He gave me two choices:

either sign the documents admitting I was gay and expect my release in less than a month or see a psychiatrist. The whole thing took place in a single day."

In response to the two choices, Thornborrow declared: "I don't need psychiatric help."[34] She went on: "[I spent a few days] just walking around Ottawa looking nervously over my shoulder. I called up my girlfriend and told her to clear out everything from her room that could possibly connect her with me. Eventually I called Marie Robertson [spokesperson for Lesbians of Ottawa Now (LOON)]. I'd known her previously from Hamilton. She got hold of David Garmaise [from Gays of Ottawa (GO)], and we decided to get together and discuss it, and perhaps write up a news release." At first she was hesitant about going to the national media with her case. As she recalled, "I guess I was concerned about my parents. They knew I was gay but it is a different thing to tell friends and relatives ... But it's my life, not theirs, and I have to live with it too." She was very glad that she went public: "I'm really glad I did, 'cause so many good things have happened. People I work with have been forced into the situation of what to do with a lesbian woman, and they've all been great."[35]

In an interview, Thornborrow was asked why, at that point, she didn't have a roommate. She responded: "Well, at first they questioned her about me, and even asked her to spy on me. Then they asked her to move out, which she didn't want to do. But it was either that, or spy, so she moved out." In response to the threat of blackmail she said: "Well, you go ahead and try to blackmail me! They also used the argument that living in close quarters with a homosexual is bad for morale, but 90% of the women living with me in this building would say 'bullshit' to that. Nothing they've given as a reason applies to me."[36]

At a May 16 joint meeting of LOON and GO, Thornborrow was told that there was little chance she would keep her job in the service but that she could help other gays and lesbians by going public with her case. By the next evening, the NGRC had issued a press release and arranged for Thornborrow to accompany its members to Parliament Hill, where the Standing Committee on Justice and Legal Affairs was then discussing the Canadian Human Rights Act. The media were out in full force to interview Thornborrow. Prompted by her case, Justice Minister Ron Basford stated that national security justified the exclusion of sexual orientation from the act.[37] By the next day, her picture was on the front page of the papers, and her story was being told across the country through major media interviews. This became one of the most publicized cases of anti-homosexual discrimination in the 1970s, along with the employment discrimination experienced by John Damien and Doug Wilson.[38]

The Canadian Armed Forces finally responded to Thornborrow's concerns by arguing that homosexuals were discharged because their presence in such confined quarters as barracks and ships could lead to conflicts in inter-personal relationships, which, in turn, could affect morale and efficiency. It also claimed that homosexuals, being subject to blackmail, were asked to leave for their own safety. Thornborrow responded: "That's ridiculous. If I am open about it, how can I be blackmailed?" Then, on June 20, 1977, the Canadian Armed Forces discharged Private Thornborrow under release order item 5(d) as "not advantageously employable." She was informed by her commanding officer that she was to be dismissed. Thornborrow revealed publicly that she was being harassed for alleged lesbian activities and threatened with expulsion from the forces. The military tried to argue that she had already applied for permission to leave voluntarily and that this permission had been granted before the lesbian issue came up. She had never been informed of any response to her application. She suggested that the media coverage was the reason for the military's statement regarding the rapid granting of her voluntary release.[39] Her June 20 dismissal demonstrated that this release had never actually been granted.

In Thornborrow's words, "[The dismissal came as] a surprise. I was prob-ably far too optimistic. I was surprised and shook up. I have no idea why they waited so long after the story broke. Maybe they wanted to wait until the news died down and [people] forget." She was told on June 20 that she had until the end of the week to be off the base. She said: "My biggest concern now is that I have four days to pack and leave."[40] Thornborrow has never received any apol-ogy or compensation for what was done to her.

DARL WOOD: "I'M FUCKING DANGEROUS TO NATIONAL SECURITY BECAUSE I ... ENJOY HAVING SEX WITH THE WOMAN I LOVE"

Darl Wood was discharged from Canadian Forces Base (CFB) Halifax in the late 1970s, when word leaked to the SIU that she was a lesbian. Wood does not know how the military learned she was a lesbian, but she was dismissed after an investigation conducted by two male SIU officers. She and her partner "were told their actions posed a security risk, and set the military up for blackmail."[41] She later wrote about her interrogation, mostly in the third person. First, she says: "One of the men asks if she wants a woman present while being questioned. 'It is your right to have someone with you – a woman' ... 'Eh ... no ... no, thank you, I don't think so.'" She described their questions about lesbianism and lesbian sex practices:

"When did you first know you were a lesbian?" They want to know, two men interrogating her about her sex life. What are they saying; can they ask questions like that? They do, over and over; she desperately needs to challenge their right to do this, but doesn't, intimidated. "Look, what do you want from me, I've already told you that I'm gay." It's not enough, they want details: when, where, even how; tribadism, digital manipulation, on and on repeating the same questions over and over until she wants to scream. "Are you sure Sergeant Adams is the first woman you've made love to?" "Yes." "Is she the only woman in the Service you've been involved with?" "Yes the only one, I've already told you that a dozen times." They change the direction of their questioning abruptly, "Do you know what cunnilingus is?" "Yes" she says, "I know what it means." "Did you perform it on her?" "Yes ... no ... I don't know." "Did she do it to you?" This is degrading, she refuses to answer ... Make them just leave me alone ... She contemplates asking them if they are enjoying their sport, do they get their rocks off on it. Why are they harassing me and why am I complying? Group sex, lesbian circles, whips and chains – what are they saying now? What do they think I am? She raises her eyes to them slowly. Are they serious? They are. She can't help herself; she burst into a tense laugh, not into tears. She's gradually becoming aware of the insanity of the situation. Shocked into regaining a sense of perspective she tells them point blank, "I'm not going to answer any more personal questions."[42]

In the later 1970s and 1980s, an important strategy used by military interrogators to identify homosexuals involved asking questions regarding sex practices and collecting evidence of participation in queer sex. Wood reported that, after having exhausted these questions, her interrogators turned their attention to the identification of other homosexuals:

They warn her that if she knows of any other persons in the Forces that are homosexual it would be better if she told them now, they would hate for it to come out later. They tell her that it is necessary for her to sign a statement admitting to her deviation. No longer a person, labeled now, a sexual deviate. She glowers at them, her eyes narrow trying to identify with the concept. Deviant, a quote from the Queen's Regulations and Orders. She also has to promise that she will not tell anyone anything she has learned since joining the Forces ... Shit, me a security risk, all of a sudden I'm fucking dangerous to national security because I happen to enjoy having sex with the woman I love.[43]

Wood lost her job and had to leave her lover behind. When she went to the Canadian Human Rights Commission in 1980, it could do nothing for her since sexual orientation was not included in federal human rights legislation. Moreover, she was told that what the military was doing was entirely legal. However, Wood did testify, quite effectively, about her experiences during the Special Parliamentary Committee on Equality Rights hearings in 1985 (Svend Robinson, July 30, 2002).

"Not advantageously employable"
Tim Reid, involved in the Gay and Lesbian Organization of Veterans (GLOV) in the 1990s, was purged from the military in 1978. He was discharged with the designation "not advantageously employable," which, as he put it, was "the term used to shred the careers of many individuals, their only crime was to Love and Serve their Country." He argued that he was one of the only people to "break the code of silence that surrounds this whole issue."[44] Both the SIU and the RCMP investigated Reid. He remembers:

> After struggling with my sexuality and coming to the conclusion I was gay, I
> was duty bound to report myself to the base CO. After doing so I was asked to
> wait outside his door. Ten minutes later I was *arrested* and taken to the base
> hospital. I was *ordered*, not asked, to take *tranquilizers* for my nerves, *which
> were quite fine before this.* What comes after this was best described as *mental
> torture.* For five days I was grilled by the SIU. Considering the fact I had told
> them point blank I was gay, [this] seemed secondary to the real investigation
> [emphasis in original].

We did not hear of the use of tranquilizers in any other interrogation or purge situation, but this appears to have been an instance of the use of medical treatment to make military confinement more tolerable. Like Wood, Reid was asked a series of sex practice questions designed not only to prove participation in homosexual activities but also to get him to implicate others in same-gender sex:

> Who did I sleep with? What did I do? Hundreds of photos followed by, did you
> have sex with him? Was it oral or anal? Did you enjoy it? I refused to give them
> what they wanted most, names of military personnel. Most of all names of
> officers and senior ranks. All the while I was ordered, under supervision, to
> take my tranquilizers, polygraphs did not work. Signed statements by others

in the military saying that I had allegedly slept with them were waved in front of me. So and so said you slept with him and did this or that, do you deny it? Here is his picture. "So and so should be so lucky" was my response.

Here we see the interrogation focused not only on Reid being identified as a homosexual but also on attempts to get him to name others as participants in homosexual activities. As in other military investigations during this period, the use of a polygraph was standard. They also searched his apartment and confiscated his diary. He was stripped of his security clearance (a crucial feature of these investigations) and was discharged from the military: "I was stripped of my uniform, of my top secret security clearance and told to read the Official Secrets Act twice. I was told if I violated it *ever*, I would be tracked down and imprisoned in a military prison! I was told at this point I was a security risk and shown the front gate." In this account, the code of silence to which Reid referred earlier was enforced. Under the Official Secrets Act, a security clearance meant that revealing any information was a crime; consequently, anyone who talked about her/his experiences in the military and of the reasons for her/his expulsion could be apprehended and imprisoned.

By the end of the 1970s, military policies excluding homosexuals were starting to come under increasing attack, and this continued into the 1980s. In a 1979 letter from Admiral R.H. Falls to R.G.L. Fairweather, chief commissioner of the Canadian Human Rights Commission, we read the comment "unless and until social attitudes change considerably it is impossible to place homosexuals in positions where a security clearance is required. Such persons are still, in our society, subject to blackmail either directly or indirectly because of the involvement of a partner."[45] In the 1980s, the military continued to rely on these arguments to justify its exclusionary policies.

"The SIU is watching you now"

Military surveillance of gay and lesbian spaces came under the scrutiny of gay and lesbian rights groups as they emerged in the 1970s. In 1977, the Gay Alliance for Equality (GAE) set up a community centre and dance club called the Turret at 1588 Barrington Street (where it remained until 1982) in downtown Halifax.[46] GAE quickly became aware that it was being watched by the SIU. Across the street from the Turret was the Green Lantern Building, where it was believed that the SIU surveillance team was located. People would often wave to the SIU from the front steps of the Turret (Robin Metcalfe, August 10, 2006). Two GAE activists, Anne Fulton and Robin Metcalfe, wrote a song that they performed at the national gay conference held in Halifax in 1978. It was sung to the tune of "Santa Claus Is Coming to Town," and its purpose was to alert people to the SIU surveillance and to make fun of it:

> You'd better watch out,
> You'd better be sly,
> You'd better keep out,
> I'm telling you why.
> The SIU is watching you now.

> They're making a list,
> They're checking it twice,
> They're gonna find out who's naughty or nice.
> The SIU is watching you now.

> They know who you've been sleeping with;
> They know if you're of age.
> They know if you've been gay or straight,
> So be straight, for goodness sake.

> You'd better watch out,
> You'd better be sly,
> You'd better keep out,
> I'm telling you why.
> The SIU is watching you now.[47]

This song had a dual character. On the one hand, it warned people that the military was watching queer spaces. On the other, it also demonstrated a form of campy resistance to national security surveillance.

While purges continued in the public service, and especially in the military, the RCMP began more specific surveillance of lesbian and gay groups that were emerging across the country and challenging the national security war on queers. This is what we investigate in the next chapter.

"Gay Political Activists" and "Radical Lesbians"
Organizing against the National Security State

INVESTIGATING THE SOCIAL ORGANIZATION OF SPYING ON QUEER ACTIVISM

Lesbians and gay activists in the 1970s often felt they were being spied upon by the RCMP and other police forces. Frequently, this was only a vague sense and remained unproven.[1] But they were right. Widespread RCMP surveillance of gay and lesbian groups in Canada did take place, and it focused especially on queer leftists who were active in these organizations.

The RCMP encountered something new and different in the gay and lesbian activists it confronted in the 1970s. These younger people affirmed that "gay is just as good as straight" and were willing to publicly come out and proclaim their queer pride. Their politics focused on developing lesbian and gay pride, public visibility, and fighting for human rights and liberation for lesbians and gay men.[2] Early liberationist slogans, such as "out of the closets and into the streets," captured this new direction. While this chapter highlights histories of gay/lesbian organizing in relation to the national security campaigns, it does not offer a comprehensive history of queer movements across the Canadian state in the 1970s.[3]

These activists challenged the basis of the national security campaigns against queers, which lay in the secrecy surrounding homosexuality. Their public visibility began to unravel national security regime discourse and practice. These were no longer isolated gays and lesbians living a double life or in the closet. The people involved in this new movement directly challenged the practices of the security regime itself as well as broader discrimination in employment, not to mention the social organization of the relations of the closet. What, in one document, the RCMP refers to as a change in "attitude" points to how many gay men and lesbians were not as afraid of public exposure as were those whom the RCMP had encountered in the 1960s.[4]

This wave of activism created a new social struggle, which undermined the basic features of national security regulations. By developing a more public movement and community that was increasingly unfettered by fear of exposure and blackmail, and by challenging heterosexist discourses and practices, the new movement undermined the social conditions in which the concept of "character weakness" could have any relevance. This queer activism and the growing number of out queers destabilized the social relations of the closet and created possibilities for more lesbians and gay men to organize their lives outside these relations. Discrediting the justifications for the security war on queers through increased visibility and activism, these lesbians and gay men set the stage for the uneven and long-term collapse of the security campaigns against queers, which persisted into the late twentieth century.

The RCMP also investigated gay and lesbian movements because members of left organizations were involved in them, especially people from the League for Socialist Action (LSA), its youth group the Young Socialists (YS), and, later, the Revolutionary Marxist Group (RMG). Indeed, the RCMP was already investigating these organizations as "subversive." Officially, the RCMP was not as concerned with individual Marxists and socialists as it was with "unaligned Marxists and pressure groups," the heading under which gay/lesbian activism was investigated in the mid-1970s. The RCMP discovered that the "New Left" it had been tracking in the late 1960s and early 1970s had exploded into a series of movements, ranging from feminist to gay and lesbian to anti-racist to environmental and others. The surveillance of gay men and lesbians was inspired by concern over the subversive character of this new gay movement as well as over its involvement with subversive left groups. Lesbian and gay liberation movements were part of a broader left composition of struggle.

Hewitt demonstrates that, in the 1960s, the RCMP had a number of difficulties in conducting its surveillance of the student movement and the New Left. In its encounters with activists and their organizations, the RCMP learned that it could not use the strategies developed to address the "old left," especially the Communist Party.[5] Similarly, the RCMP in the 1970s had difficulty understanding and regulating the new gay and lesbian activists it encountered.

In this chapter, we continue to critically interrogate the national security ideology of subversion. Unlike national security discourse, we do not use the

"Gay Political Activists" and "Radical Lesbians"

term "radical" in a negative fashion; rather, we reclaim it, as Judy Rebick urges us to do. After all, it means "to get to the root" and, quite properly, is used by people who want to get to the root of the problem.[6]

Given their direct incorporation into major aspects of Canadian state formation and exclusionary policies in the military and RCMP, national security policies, though contested, had significant staying power. Throughout the 1970s, the Canadian political and bureaucratic elite reasserted, and tried to defend, major features of the security campaigns forged in the previous period.

As requests continue to be submitted under the Access to Information Program (ATIP), the pages of partially released security documents on gay and lesbian groups are growing, and more details of RCMP surveillance can be pieced together.[7] One helpful feature of our making multiple requests and acquiring different documents involving the work of different ATIP officers is concisely expressed by Hewitt: "Mistakes ... are sometimes made, and information is released that would normally be cut. I also sometimes encountered multiple copies of the same document but with different bits excised, which enabled me to reconstruct by mixing and matching."[8]

The documents cover the period from 1971 to 1984. They begin with the first major stirrings of Canadian and Québécois(e) gay liberation activism in the summer of 1971, lead up to the August 1971 demonstration on Parliament Hill, and continue through gay and lesbian activism in early 1978 Toronto. The last two entries are from the 1980s and come from the generic Canadian Gay Liberation Movement file (e.g., there is a clipping from 1983 on the continuing response of the movement in Toronto to the bath raids).[9]

From our engaged, situated, and critical reading of these documents, a number of things are clear. First, official security regime discourse continued to construct gay men and lesbians as suffering from a character weakness and as risks to national security. Second, the gay movement, especially "gay political activists" and "radical lesbians," represented potential social threats. Third, the surveillance of gays and lesbians in the form of monitoring queer organizations continued until at least the late 1970s.

There was an evident cross-country pattern to this surveillance work, and the RCMP security services in different parts of the nation-state requested information on groups in other areas and exchanged data. For instance, a number of the reports on gay groups were generated in response to a 1976 request from the Montreal Security Service in relation to the Olympics, the associated campaign to "clean up" gay bars and bathhouses, and the resistance the Montreal police were encountering to this.[10] This suggests an important tie-in between police actions against emerging gay community institutions and the national security campaigns. This exchange of information was based on the criminalization of gay sexual practices and the RCMP's requests for more data about gay activists to assist police in handling the protests they had produced in Montreal.

A number of documents are attached to transit slips, which are issued when information is requested by one section of the RCMP and is in transit to another. There are a number of requests for information coming from D Branch Operations (Ops), which handled the surveillance of the LSA, regarding its involvement in various gay/lesbian organizations, thereby alerting other sections of the RCMP to actions of the gay movement. Many of the RCMP reports are divided between a section entitled "Information," in which they report their observations, and a section entitled "Investigator's Comments," in which more evaluative remarks are made by the investigating officer or team. These often include noting whether the organization requires continuing investigation and in what form. Suggestions on a course of action in response to the threat represented by the group may also be outlined.

Tensions within the RCMP over how far to go in its investigation of gay/lesbian groups are also visible. A 1974 transit slip request regarding the Gay Liberation Movement – University of Waterloo file reported that "the attached Gay files are of little or no subversive interest and in view of your area of operations you may wish us to card the names." To "card" means to record the names and perhaps to open files on these individuals. It is interesting that, even though the group was thought to be of little or no subversive interest, the RCMP still suggested recording the names of the people involved it. The reply stated: "Names should be carded on selective basis – for us to get involved much beyond this would be beyond our capabilities and direct interests, bearing in mind that our primary function ... is security/homosexuality as it relates to Govt. service."[11] The implication is that the central concern was surveillance of homosexuality as it related to government employment. There may have been tensions within the RCMP between its earlier mandate of investigating homosexuals in and around state service and its newer practice of investigating gay and lesbian organizations.

The RCMP organized the majority of its surveillance work through the development of files on organizations and individuals. As Hewitt points out, "Regardless of its content, a file is by its very nature neither a neutral document nor isolated from other elements of intelligence operations."[12] This new surveillance developed in relation to the emergence of queer activism. RCMP investigations of queer groups were motivated both by the public activities of this new liberation movement and the surveillance of left groups such as the LSA

"Gay Political Activists" and "Radical Lesbians"

and the YS.[13] According to Hewitt, in response to new threats like the gay and lesbian movements, "what did not change was the idea held by the police that no matter what the form of radicalism practised by individuals or groups, the tactic and goal remained the same: infiltration and subversion."[14]

RCMP activity involved the surveillance of these groups, with undercover officers or informants being present at and writing reports on meetings and demonstrations and, in some cases, undertaking photographic surveillance. There were two tiers to this work – active surveillance and monitoring – each of which had a rather different character. The former involved more direct intrusion into the activities of gay/lesbian activists, through spying, following people, photographing activists and demonstrations, and questioning or interrogating activists. Monitoring entailed a more removed but continuous collection of information on groups and activists (this could include clippings from the mainstream print media, news stories, and announcements of community events by the left and gay media as well as leaflets and other materials produced by gay and lesbian activists).

A substantial number of the documents to which we gained access were clippings from the mainstream media that had been placed into the files of particular groups. Clearly, the RCMP relied on media coverage to learn about and monitor activities. Given that, generally, there was minimal coverage of lesbian and gay experiences in the early and mid-1970s, this also meant that the RCMP's monitoring work relied on the mainstream media framing of gay topics regarding what was considered newsworthy.[15] In many of these clippings, the names of individual activists and the groups that they belonged to were underlined. If the monitoring work led the RCMP to seek additional information on a person or group, it would then pursue other forms of surveillance.

In the documents we have examined, this monitoring includes clippings from the mainstream print media, the alternative media (*Guerilla* [Toronto] and *Georgia Straight* [Vancouver], which sometimes had articles on and columns by gay groups or activists), the left media (*Labour Challenge* [the publication of the LSA] and the *Old Mole* [published by the RMG]), and the emerging gay media (including the *Body Politic*). Although we did not receive a surveillance report on the important January 1975 founding conference of the Coalition for Gay Rights in Ontario (CGRO), a provincial coalition of gay and lesbian groups, clippings from *Labour Challenge* and the *Old Mole* found in the RCMP files dealing with the conference were included.[16]

The information compiled through the surveillance and monitoring of queer groups was brought together in RCMP investigations. Central to this was the creation and maintenance of files on these groups – files to which we have only now managed to gain partial access. We have not been able to gain access to the files on individuals, and many of these may have been destroyed or re-organized following revelations of "dirty tricks" committed by the RCMP against the Quebec nationalist movement. The Keable Commission (Commission d'enquête sur des opérations policières en territoire québécois) and the Mc-Donald Commission also curtailed the ability of the RCMP to undertake this type of information collection on individuals (see Chapter 10).

This RCMP security work was organized somewhat differently in various places across the country and at different times in the 1970s. Much of this early work was done through D Ops.[17] The surveillance of sections of the left and social movements was also undertaken under the heading "Unaligned Marxist and Pressure Groups" in Toronto and in Ottawa. According to an RCMP report, this "desk [was] established just over a year ago [1975] in Toronto," and there was "a corresponding section in Headquarters." Gay and lesbian groups came under this heading. One of the RCMP reports mentions that, "formerly, this area was called the New Left, which was later renamed Anti-Establishment Activities and Community Groups. Thus it is now an appropriate time to pre-pare a paper whose task is to analyze the trends in the Unaligned Marxists and Pressure Groups in Toronto. This assessment will include an analysis of the characteristics of the Unaligned Marxists and a profile of their organizations as well as an analysis of the type of Pressure Groups, which are, for various reasons, of Security Service interest."[18] Hewitt's comments on the 1960s as a "decade that had started as a battle against a major enemy, communism, and a lesser one, Trotskyism, ended with the RCMP facing a fractured array of adver-saries, ranging from the polymorphous New Left, to Red Power, Maoists, and Québec separatists, along with Communists and Trotskyists as before" help to contextualize the RCMP view of the left.[19]

This 1975 report is divided into two parts: one on unaligned Marxists and the other on pressure groups. However, the document reminds the reader that "in certain cases this is an artificial division as there is an extensive amount of interaction between the two areas, both on an informal and formal level, through individual contacts."[20] In conceptualizing the gay/lesbian movements and other social movements as pressure groups, the RCMP constructed them as being of possible security service interest. Social movements, at least those influenced by the left, were viewed as potential risks to national security. The RCMP also continued to associate these pressure groups with Marxism, even if in an un-aligned way.

The anti–Vietnam War movement in Canada provides us with one example of RCMP surveillance of social movements. The purpose of the Canadian anti-war movement was not only to get the US troops out of Vietnam but also to end Canadian state and corporate complicity with the US war effort. The surveillance of this movement led the RCMP into the gay movement since the early gay/lesbian liberation groups organized lesbian/gay contingents in anti-war demonstrations. RCMP documents reported the following: that surveillance of the Comité Québécois contre la guerre en Indochine revealed Mouvement de la libération des homosexuels involvement, that a pamphlet entitled *Gay Rights Now!* was distributed at a 1972 event organized by the Vietnam Action Committee in Vancouver, and that Toronto Gay Action (TGA) participated in a Vietnam Mobilization Committee demonstration against the Vietnam War and the US Amchitka nuclear bomb blast in the Alaskan Aleutian Islands, which took place on November 6, 1971.[21]

> I was at and helped to organize high school students for this action. Thousands of high school students joined the protest because of the upcoming Amchitka underwater bomb test off the Alaska coast close to BC. I remember it raining and we chanted, "End Nixon's rain!" Paul MacDonald spoke for Toronto Gay Action from a flat-bed truck. I also remember going to Ottawa for the April 15, 1972, demonstration against the war in Ottawa, when Richard Nixon was there, and seeing and talking to people from the gay contingent organized by Toronto Gay Action.

Vancouver Gay Liberation Front: A "militant revolutionary group"

In the first mention of a gay organization in relation to security surveillance, the Vancouver Gay Liberation Front (V-GLF) was caught up in the general surveillance of radical activism. The V-GLF, formed in November 1970, was the first gay liberation (as distinct from homophile) organization in the country. Gay liberation fronts appeared across the United States and in many other countries following the establishment of the New York City GLF after the Stonewall riots in 1969.[22] The various GLFs took their name to identify with the National Liberation Front in Vietnam, which was fighting against the US military and state occupation of its country.

In the year following the October Crisis and the imposition of the War Measures Act against not only the Front de libération du Québec but also Quebec popular and independence movements more generally, an RCMP report detailed a supposed assassination plot, concocted by one of more than forty radical groups in Vancouver, against BC premier W.A.C. Bennett and Vancouver mayor Tom Campbell. The documents suggest that Campbell planned to ask the federal government to impose the War Measures Act to deal with dissent in Vancouver. Groups mentioned include the Yippies (the Youth International Party, which, in the United States, was associated with Jerry Rubin and Abbie Hoffman), the Vancouver Liberation Front, the Gay Liberation Front, and the Maoist Communist Party of Canada (Marxist-Leninist).[23] The RCMP report comments: "The Vancouver area continues to encompass the most inflammatory assortment of revolutionary activists in Canada beyond the boundaries of Québec, comprised of at least 40 structured organizations which in turn can rely on a further number of less radical groups and the dissident hippie movement for support." It further states that there was "evidence of a far greater degree of prior coordination and planning by different revolutionary groups."

The report remarked that a "militant revolutionary group" called the GLF "was organized to attract homosexuals and claim[ed] a membership of 150."[24] As former V-GLF member Tom Sandborn writes, the RCMP report exaggerated the influence, organization, and coordination of radical groups in Vancouver at the time, including that of the GLF. However, he also states that "many of our most paranoid imaginings – when we suspected the cops of bugging our phones and sending spies to our meetings in the old days – were absolutely accurate."[25]

The emerging gay/lesbian liberation organizations encountered other aspects of the national security surveillance against the left and progressive social movements. RCMP surveillance reports on demonstrations against the prime minister in the 1970s often revealed gay activist participation. A report on the LSA's participation in a demonstration against Trudeau in Vancouver in 1972, where the prime minister grabbed one of the demonstrators, also tells us that some members (about twelve) of Gay Alliance towards Equality (GATE) were there but that "they received little support or attention."[26]

A 1973 composite report on potential security problems at the University of Toronto, which included mention of gay groups, gives us a sense of the broad-ranging surveillance work undertaken on university campuses. The report referred to the University of Toronto Homophile Association, the RMG, the Communist Party, Students for a Democratic Society, the Canadian Liberation Movement, the Communist Party of Canada (Marxist-Leninist), the Young Socialists, the Movement for an Independent Socialist Canada (which developed when the Ontario Waffle was expelled from the NDP), the Faculty Reform Caucus, the Campus Co-operative Day Care Centre, the University of Toronto Faculty to End the War, and the Black Student Union.[27] Hewitt reports that, from 1971 to 1973, the RCMP targeted gay and lesbian groups in Calgary

"Gay Political Activists" and "Radical Lesbians"

(where they were designated a "limited threat"), Saskatchewan (a "limited threat"), and in Waterloo (a "significant threat").[28] The RCMP spied on various campus groups, from the University of Guelph Homophile Association to the University of Saskatchewan Gay Student Alliance to the Gay Liberation Group at McMaster University. The RCMP spied on this last group "even though the force admitted, in an internal communication, that it was not being used as a 'front by any subversive organization.'"[29]

Often the surveillance of queer activists was not only directed against lesbians and gays but, given the intersections between differing forms of oppression and movement organizing, had a mediated social character as well. The surveillance of gay and lesbian groups overlapped with RCMP surveillance of other social movements. For example, during this period, on campuses across the country alleged connections to the US-based American Indian Movement (AIM) (which was viewed as advocating "Native extremism") were seen as making the Native movement and Native studies itself into a threat to national security.[30]

Other anti-racist activism also came under RCMP surveillance, including a Vancouver rally to prevent black activist Rosie Douglas from being deported to Dominica. GATE-V was cited as one of the organizations that sponsored this rally. The RCMP report argued that the chair of this meeting was "very pro-RMG."[31] The RMG, in which Gary Kinsman was involved, was quite active in the unsuccessful campaign against this deportation. It also participated in the campaign to stop the deportation of AIM activist Leonard Peltier to the United States, where he remains in jail for a murder he did not commit. During this period, the RMG was devoted to anti-racist organizing. It provided support for the Black Workers' Congress in Toronto, which Rosie Douglas helped establish in the mid-1970s after his 1974 release from jail. Douglas had been serving time for his part as a leading activist in the 1969 protest against racism at Sir George Williams University in Montreal.[32] The white character of the RCMP led the "Security Service to borrow an informer, Warren Hart, an African American, from the FBI. Until his arrival at Sir George Williams University, the RCMP had had to rely on information from only one source."[33]

As a member of the RMG I remember seeing Warren Hart as Rose Douglas's bodyguard at meetings in the lead up to his deportation and around the Black Workers' Congress in the mid-1970s. We only learned much later that Hart was an RCMP agent. There were important security concerns in the RMG – so much so that we used pseudonyms to refer to each other – and there were various rumours about who the RCMP infiltrator might be, but nothing came of this.

Barbara, whom we have already met, was an early activist in the Trent Homophile Association (THA) at Trent University in Peterborough. She got caught up in the security campaigns, in part because she was a Native studies student in the mid-1970s:

> What happened when I was in university is I majored in anthropology and I minored in Native studies, which is automatically a politically militant group ... Plus I was one of the founders of the Trent Homophile Association.[34] So the RCMP didn't like me very much! And they put me under surveillance at the university. They got my fingerprints off a beer mug from a bar ... So, I mean, I heard rumours about this. You know, you never think that the RCMP is going to do this ... I went into the bathroom, my beer was gone. They said a guy had come to the table, taken my glass [and] no one else's, and it wasn't our barkeep. So you say, "Hmmm." And plus in Native studies they had warned us. They said anyone who took Native studies is automatically on file with the RCMP. (July 14, 1997)

According to Barbara, "[A] number of us in the THA missed glasses periodically. A couple of people lost articles of clothing from their apartments or their residence rooms." Later, she had this confirmed when, during a security clearance procedure, she was asked whether she would go through fingerprinting: "[Barbara said,] 'You already have them on file' ... What the constable did was he got on the telephone and he came back and said, 'Thank you, we do not need your fingerprints.' So I knew they were on file." A friend who worked for the RCMP at the time told her that she was "on file for [being] 'Native militant' and 'gay.'" With regard to the core group of the THA, Barbara said: "[We] all knew we were under surveillance but sort of generally. Yeah, I think the ones of us that were picked out for surveillance were the four of us who were actually running the organization" (July 14, 1997).

In 1974 and 1975, in both Ottawa and Waterloo, RCMP files included reports on rallies and demonstrations against the racist and heterosexist Green Paper on immigration. The gay and lesbian movement mobilized across the country to insist that the immigration legislation drop its prohibition on homosexuals entering Canada. In 1977, this became one of the first victories won through cross-country gay/lesbian organizing, when the explicit formal prohibitions on homosexual entry were removed.[35]

We critically read and interrogate these RCMP documents as active pieces of the social organization of the national security campaigns. As mentioned

"Gay Political Activists" and "Radical Lesbians"

earlier, we read them for what they reveal when considered from the social standpoints of queer activists. This is one of the reasons why, as much as possible, we begin our interrogation of the RCMP documents with the accounts of queer activists themselves.

We critically analyze the language used in these RCMP texts. For instance, many of them assume that lesbians and gay men are marginal and lack popular support. In RCMP discourse, this is not only a description but also a construction of reality. The ideologies and practices of heterosexual hegemony are simply taken for granted. It is also suggested that this marginality is what made these groups vulnerable to leftist infiltration.

The New Conceptualization: "Gay political activists"
In trying to comprehend the new form of activism, a 1976 RCMP report talks about "gay political activists" who are "predominantly young, ranging in age from 20-25 years old, and unlike the older homosexuals they are eager to display their homosexuality through such acts as demonstrating."[36] Highlighting the youth of these activists coded this new activism along generational lines. The politics of coming out and this novel way of organizing created obstacles for the RCMP. The report goes on: "Interestingly, these individuals have been joined in loose alliance with certain lesbian communes in the city as both groups see they have common cause. It must be noted that the gay political activists are non-violent and their tactics have always followed those of pressure groups who are without political power and view themselves as a minority." This report suggests some understanding of the tensions, differences, and commonalities between gay male activists and lesbian feminists; however, we see no real sign of "radical lesbians" here, aside from what might be hinted at by "lesbian communes."

The same report notes: "Our interest has been in those gay groups controlled and directed by Gay Political Activists." This conceptualization of gay political activists allows the RCMP to differentiate between gay groups in terms of their potential security threat. More moderate or liberal groups (e.g., the Community Homophile Association of Toronto [CHAT]), which were closely monitored in the early 1970s, were no longer felt to be much of a threat, because gay political activists did not usually control them. On the other hand, groups identified with gay political activists came under more intense surveillance. These included the TGA, GATE-V, GATE-T, and, to some extent, Gays of Ottawa. Thought to be controlled by gay political activists, the CGRO and the National Gay Rights Coalition (NGRC) also came under security surveillance.

One RCMP assessment report on GATE-V, which we examine later, argues that the creation of a new "liberal" gay group could diminish the latter's influence.[37]

Groups run by gay political activists were seen as being more open to infiltration from left groups such as the LSA, the YS, and the RMG than were groups run by more liberal queers. In its report on gay groups, the RCMP produced the following analysis: "The Gays have received little public support as the public still views homosexuals in a negative light. However, certain of the ultraleft groups, mainly Trotskyists, have been involved in gay groups in an attempt to radicalize them. (It has been found that those ultra left members involved in gay groups were also homosexuals)." Trotskyists are supporters of Leon Trotsky, who was a leading figure in the 1917 Russian Revolution. Later, he became a major opponent of the rise of the Stalinist bureaucracy.[38] "Ultraleft," as it is used here, implies that Trotskyists are on the extreme left, almost beyond the pale. In left discourse, the term "ultraleft" describes groups who are *too* leftist. For instance, the Communist Party might critique Trotskyists for being ultraleft, and some Trotskyists might critique some anarchists for being ultraleft. The RCMP report lifts the term from left discourse and places it into the national security discourse.

According to this report, because gays and lesbians are opposed by mainstream society, gay political activists are more open to offering a critique of capitalist social relations. Although the investigator writing the report concludes that there was no popular support for lesbian and gay liberation, he or she fails to recognize the important part that state policies play in organizing heterosexual hegemony. It is these policies, and the ways in which they shaped social relations, that led to this lack of popular support. It is interesting too that the writer points out that the ultraleft activists are also homosexuals. The investigator almost seems surprised that the outside infiltrators were also gay. Here we encounter both a heterosexual assumption and a certain difficulty in seeing Trotskyists as queers.

The report goes on to describe how this lack of popular support opened up a space for Marxist influence: "This in part explains why some of the gay political activists have been increasingly taking on a Marxist analysis of their position, equating homosexuals as an oppressed minority in a capitalist system. (They fail to bring up the point that in the Soviet Union and Cuba homosexuals are imprisoned)." What is not recognized is that a critical Marxist analysis of our social position might actually be a useful strategic way of grasping the social relations at the root of lesbian and gay oppression. This reference to the continuing oppression of gays and lesbians in the USSR shows that the RCMP

"Gay Political Activists" and "Radical Lesbians"

officers involved had little understanding of Trotskyism. Trotskyists were critical of the undemocratic bureaucratic and family policies in the USSR.[39] Although the Cuban example is more complex and has a different history, many Trotskyists were also critical of the Cuban regime.[40] According to this report, Marxist influence generated political divisions within the movement: "This has lead [sic] to the major ongoing debate within gay groups between those who seek only to increase the civil rights for gays and those who seek gays to become involved in larger political issues believing that only a radical social change can bring about gay liberation."[41]

There is a certain awareness in the text of some of the internal debates within and between GLF- and GATE-type groups. Although there were tensions and debates between more radical and more moderate currents within the movements, these were not the result of some external ultraleft or Trotskyist influence, as suggested here. In fact, they emerge internally in all social movements.[42] When it constructs divisions as being the result of external communist or Trotskyist input, the RCMP profoundly misunderstands the dynamics of social movements and the varying composition of their respective struggles. From the standpoint of national security, the actual dynamics of social movements – and how they grow out of internal contradictions within capitalist, patriarchal, racist, and heterosexist social relations – cannot be grasped.

Gay political activists are defined by three major characteristics: youth, being out and committed to public visibility and pressure tactics, and an openness to leftist ideas. What is new is the change of attitude among gays. They now use pressure group tactics and, thus, are more visible in their demands for gay rights.[43] These activists could be a security problem. In contrast, it often seemed that, by the mid-1970s, the more moderate and liberal gays – those who stayed in the closet and did not publicly demand their rights – were no longer considered to be a major security threat. At the same time, if they were working in the public service, especially in the RCMP or military, the discovery of their same-gender erotic practices could still be grounds for transfer, purgation, or denial of promotion or security clearance.

"IT HAD A SENSE OF HISTORY ABOUT IT": THE FIRST CROSS-COUNTRY DEMONSTRATIONS IN 1971

Ottawa 1971: "Smash Heterosexual Imperialism"
When activists gathered for the first cross-country gay rights demonstration on August 28, 1971, in Ottawa, RCMP observers were there, including RCMP

5   First gay rights demonstration on Parliament Hill, August 28, 1971 | *Credit:* CLGA 1982-001_01P (02) 01

photographers (see Photos 5 and 6). The protest was initiated by Toronto Gay Action, with support from many groups across the country. Initially the action caucus of CHAT, the TGA split from CHAT when members voted against its continued inclusion by two votes. Because CHAT supposedly represented all homosexuals, some of its members argued that it could not support such a demonstration.[44] According to Brian Waite, an organizer for the TGA demonstration and a member of the LSA, CHAT finally supported the protest, and George Hislop (of CHAT) was one of the main speakers at the event (July 27, 2000).

> I remember being aware of this event since I had joined the Young Socialists the previous spring, and I even thought about attending it, even though I had not yet really begun to identify as gay.

"Gay Political Activists" and "Radical Lesbians"

6 Charlie Hill speaking at the first Ottawa demonstration, August 28, 1971 |
Credit: CLGA 1986-032_01P (19) 09

John Wilson, an early gay activist, was also a member of the LSA in the early 1970s. He was involved in organizing for the Ottawa protest (see Photo 7), and he offered some general impressions about the demonstration and the presence of police:

> For most people it had a sense of history about it. We were quite aware that it was the first time that we had held a demonstration like that ... It was relatively short ... and it started to pour. And there was nobody there except for the CBC reporters and the RCMP. Everybody was quite amazed by the RCMP because it was almost like they were afraid to come too close to us, as if they would catch something. People were joking about this ... These guys were in uniform, I am sure there was undercover too. Spirits were pretty good. It was pretty successful. It wasn't a huge number of people, but I think it was a lot more

7   John Wilson, front centre, holding "End Job Discrimination" placard at the August 28, 1971, demonstration | *Credit:* CLGA 1986-032_01P (19) 03

than a lot of people thought we would get out ... I think people felt we had really accomplished something ... I remember the person who spoke for the Front de libération des homosexuels from Quebec. This was quite exciting for people, and it was not expected that anyone from Quebec was going to speak. (May 25, 2000)

When asked about any awareness of undercover cops or informants at the protest, Wilson said, "I don't recall anybody talking about it. I sort of assumed that at anything around the LSA/YS or to which it was connected that there would probably be RCMP around at some point or other. But I don't think anyone suspected particular individuals that might be informants." Brian Waite added that, at the time, "we were neither aware of nor particularly concerned with RCMP surveillance" (July 27, 2000).

"Gay Political Activists" and "Radical Lesbians"

Wilson also wrote an article on the demonstration, entitled "Marchers Demand Full Rights for Gays," for *Labour Challenge*, and this was included in the RCMP files.[45] The RCMP, which collected this as part of its overall monitoring of the LSA, transferred it into its developing files on the gay organizations mentioned in the article. In contrast to the RCMP national security reading of this article, our reading reclaims it for gay/lesbian activism, to give us a sense of what the event was like for those who participated in it. This requires looking beyond the objectifying practices that intrude even into left journalism. As Wilson wrote,

> Despite drenching rain, 125 men and women converged on Parliament Hill today to hold a militant demonstration for full legal and social equality for homosexuals ... The rally chairman started off by reading a telegram from the Vancouver Gay Alliance towards Equality (GATE), which was holding a rally in Vancouver at the same time as the Ottawa action. "Two million Canadian homosexual men and women are watching us" stated Charles Hill, speaking for Toronto Gay Action (TGA) which spearheaded the organization of the march. "We are here to demand equal rights." Hill said that amendments made to the Criminal Code two years ago have "done nothing for us as gays. There's not a homosexual problem in Canada, there's a heterosexual problem!" The rally roared approval, chanting slogans, many giving the clenched-fist salute. The marchers were also addressed by Pierre Masson of the Front de libération des homosexuels (Montréal) and George Hislop and Pat Murphy of the Community Homophile Association of Toronto (CHAT).[46]

The statement read by George Hislop for CHAT included the following:

> There is no law against *being* a homosexual and *there never has been*. Homosexuals are oppressed simply because they are not Heterosexuals. No person should be ashamed of their sexuality. Because people have lived in fear it has become necessary to join together in organizations to fight the ignorance that creates this fear. We call upon our Heterosexual Brothers and Sisters to no longer stand silent in the face of our oppression. Let them speak forth and join with us to bring about the changes that will benefit all Canadians. If one Canadian is oppressed surely we are all oppressed.[47]

Echoing Hislop's link between oppression and hegemonic heterosexuality, signs with slogans such as "Smash Heterosexual Imperialism" were carried that day.[48] According to John Wilson, "The demonstrators sought to present their brief demanding civil rights for gay people to a government representative, but no one could be found to receive it, despite the fact that the government had been advised of the demonstration and the brief well in advance."[49]

The demonstration presented an impressive series of demands to the federal government, including a number that focused on the national security campaigns against queers. The way these demands were raised and argued shows the influence of the black civil rights and Black Power movements on these early gay/lesbian liberation activists. Brian Waite and Cheri DiNovo wrote the cover letter to the brief on behalf of the August 28th Gay Day Committee. According to Waite, one of the reasons they signed the letter was that they were two of the very few people who were involved in the TGA and in organizing the protest who were willing and able to be out at the time (July 27, 2000). They wrote,

> In 1969 the Criminal Code was amended so as to make certain sexual acts between two consenting adults, in private, not illegal. This was widely misunderstood as "legalizing" homosexuality and thus putting homosexuals on an equal basis with other Canadians. In fact, this amendment was merely recognition of the non-enforceable nature of the Criminal Code as it existed. Consequently, its effects have done but little to alleviate the oppression of homosexual men and women in Canada. In our daily lives we are still confronted with discrimination, police harassment, exploitation, and pressures to conform which deny our sexuality. That prejudice against homosexual people pervades society is, in no small way, attributable to practices of the Federal government. Therefore, we, as homosexual citizens of Canada, present the following brief to our government as a means of redressing our grievances.[50]

Attached to this letter was a document entitled "We Demand," whose points included the repeal of the existing gross indecency and indecent act sections of the Criminal Code, the removal of gross indecency and buggery as grounds for sentencing as a dangerous sexual offender and for vagrancy, a uniform age of consent for all female and male homosexual and heterosexual acts, that the Immigration Act be amended so as to omit all references to homosexuals and "homosexualism," that homosexuals be granted all the same legal rights that currently existed for heterosexuals, and that all public officials and law enforcement agents employ the full force of their office to bring about changes in the negative attitudes and expressions of discrimination against homosexuals. Finally, they included the need to address the police harassment of homosexuals.[51] Several demands directly related to the national security campaigns against gay men and lesbians, and the exclusionary practices in the military and the RCMP figured prominently.

What was the knowledge base from which these early activists drew regarding these issues? According to Waite, "We Demand" was put together by a TGA working group. One activist who had some academic background wrote the first draft (July 27, 2000). An earlier June 16, 1971, draft exists, less elaborate, but similar in content to the final version.[52] Waite was involved as an outside visitor to the University of Toronto Homophile Association (UTHA), which was formed in October 1969. When UTHA began to attract large numbers of gay men and lesbians not affiliated with the university, CHAT was formed. Later, Waite was involved in the action caucus of CHAT and then in the TGA (July 27, 2000). During 1970-71, members of UTHA investigated state policies regarding homosexuality. This included a June 1970 investigation into whether the recommendations of Paragraph 100 of the *Report of the Royal Commission on Security* had been applied in the public service. Charles Hill, a founder of UTHA, wrote to Minister of Manpower and Immigration Otto Lang in January 1971, protesting the anti-gay clauses in the Immigration Act.[53] These inquiries provided some of the knowledge upon which "We Demand" was grounded.

Another knowledge base included stories gay and lesbian activists were told regarding people being purged from the public service and military as well as about past and present police surveillance. At the same time, it must be remembered that no one had access to a documented or official record of the national security campaigns against queers in the 1950s and 1960s. As Waite put it, "we had a general notion of gays being defined as a security risk but were totally unaware of the massive purge campaign in the 1960s" (July 27, 2000). A generational rupture between homophile activists and the new gay and lesbian liberation activists (even though, for a period, some adopted the term "homophile" in the Canadian context) also prevented the later activists from enhancing their knowledge through the wisdom of their earlier counterparts. A few individuals, like Hislop of CHAT, did bridge this divide; however, early activists such as Jim Egan and Doug Sanders had little knowledge of the Canadian security campaigns against queers.

"We Demand" put the early gay/lesbian movement in direct conflict with state national security policies and practices. These demands included "the right of equal employment and promotion at all government levels for homosexuals." The rationale for this demand included the following argument: "While the intent of the [1969] Criminal Code amendment ... was to make private homosexual acts a non-issue in Canada, the proposed implementation of Paragraph 100 of the Royal Commission on Security, does, *in fact,* make one's homosexuality an issue in the promotion of incumbent and the recruitment of prospective civil servants" (emphasis in original). The public version of the Royal Commission on Security text, and especially its Paragraph 100, was one of the few official state texts available to early queer activists. Later in this section of "We Demand," the authors quoted Paragraph 100 in its entirety. The significance of the 1969 reform, however, was not that it made private adult homosexual acts a non-issue but, rather, that it transferred them from Criminal Code and police jurisdiction to the terrain of counsellors, therapists, and the medical profession. According to the authors of "We Demand," "this practice subverts the intent of the law." Perhaps for tactical and rhetorical reasons, they exaggerated the impact of the 1969 reform by suggesting that the intent of the law was to eliminate practices of employment discrimination in the public service. This conflicts with the cover letter's claim that "this amendment was merely recognition of the non-enforceable nature of the Criminal Code as it existed."[54]

Highlighting the flawed logic of Paragraph 100, "We Demand" makes the following argument:

> The "reasoning" of Paragraph 100 evidently relates to the homosexual's supposed susceptibility to coercion or blackmail arising from his or her wish to prevent disclosure of his or her homosexuality (past or present) to family, spouse, friends, employers, constituents, etc. The individual might suffer from such revelation due to the prejudice against homosexuals in most areas of our society. However, with the great changes taking place in our social mores, individuals are less and less afraid to admit their homosexuality unless a specific negative factor will result from such admission, e.g., dismissal or denial of promotion. Thus the recommendation of Paragraph 100 comes full circle, reinforcing the situation the Report is trying to prevent.[55]

In looking at other sections of the *Report of the Royal Commission on Security,* the authors of "We Demand" deconstruct the contradictory situation created through state and social policies. On the one hand, homosexuals are deemed a security risk for being susceptible to blackmail, while, on the other, it is state policy that forces homosexuals to hide who they are and therefore become susceptible to blackmail. The reference to changes in social mores is part of the argument that it was now easier for lesbians and gay men to come out:

> It is evident that if an individual freely admits his or her homosexuality and is not afraid of disclosure and engages solely in legal acts, that person is hardly

susceptible to blackmail. One cannot profitably threaten to others what is already known. The effect of Paragraph 100 is to *force* homosexuals into a furtive situation in which they *might become* susceptible to coercion. Thus Paragraph 100 again becomes self-defeating. If "homosexuals are special targets for attention from foreign intelligence services" this is evidently due to the threat of dismissal from employment, a situation which could be greatly improved by a more open policy on the part of the government.[56]

The liberationist argument, like earlier homophile arguments, makes the case that security rationales would implode if individuals could be open about their sexuality; thus, it calls for gays and lesbians to come out publicly. Smashing the relations of the closet would begin to explode the need for secrecy for growing numbers of lesbians and gay men. The homosexual threat, as defined in national security regime discourse, begins to disappear as more queer social space is established.

The authors of "We Demand" proposed a theory as to why the Royal Commission on Security took a position against homosexuals in its report: "We suspect that in this report, despite the supposed magnitude of case histories, homosexuals were specifically noted simply because they represent a distinguishable minority divorced from the social existence of the writers of the Report." Here they make an important critique, locating the heterosexual (and heterosexist) social standpoint of the Royal Commission on Security, suggesting that an account from the standpoints of gays and lesbians would look very different. They also begin to critique the crucial homosexualization of the concept of character weakness: "While the authors were aware of the majority's potential for adultery, homosexuality appeared to them to be a lesser potential and therefore one that could be mentioned without indicting too large a portion of the population. The result is that homosexuals have been used as scapegoats, while the issue of each individual's ethical conduct has been ignored." They implicitly show how the homosexualization of character weakness leads to a focus on the homosexual as the problem rather than on any heterosexual activities that might also make people "vulnerable to compromise." The authors also attempt to turn their reading of Paragraph 100 against the antihomosexual security campaigns: "As stated in Paragraph 100, 'each case must be judged in the light of all its circumstances' for all levels of government employment, regardless of sexuality, individuals should be accepted or rejected based on their own merits, their personal integrity, their stability and their professional capabilities, and not barred from promotion solely on the ground of a minority status be it colour, race, creed, sex or sexuality." Of course, Paragraph

100 continued to justify and mandate the exclusion of homosexuals from higher-level security clearances and from positions in which promotion might eventually lead to higher-level security clearances.

The authors of "We Demand" criticize the military's exclusionary practices, calling for "the right of homosexuals to serve in the Armed Forces, and therefore the removal of provisions for convicting service personnel of conduct and/or acts legal under the Criminal Code; further the rescinding of policy statements reflecting on the homosexual." They suggest that the 1969 reform is contradicted by military policies and procedures that continue to exclude homosexuals: "Given the fact that [the 1969 Criminal Code reform] ... makes homosexual acts between consenting adults in private, legal, it seems anomalous that [military regulations] ... suggest that these above sexual acts may be considered punishable offences in the military. Thus, this effectively contravenes Section 149 ... of the Criminal Code, and, thereby, the principle that the military law should be subordinate to civil law."

Unfortunately, here the authors again exaggerate the impact of the 1969 reform. That reform simply decriminalized homosexual acts between two adults in private and, as a Criminal Code reform, had little direct impact on military policy. Military regulations would not even officially recognize the 1969 reform until the 1976 amendment.

"We Demand" continues its critique of military policy prohibiting homosexual members:

> Paragraph 6 of Canadian Forces Administrative Order 19-20 ("Sexual Deviation-Investigation, Medical Examination, and Disposal") reads: "Service policy does not allow retention of sex deviates in the Forces." This is conjoined with [other military regulations] ... so as to specify the manner of discharging persons convicted of homosexual acts while in military service. Again, the mere fact of one's sexuality should be no more a basis for determining the suitability of military personnel than it should for civilian employees. We do not accept that the military is exempt from Section 149 ... of the Criminal Code due to the supposed susceptibility of homosexuals to breaches of security through blackmail anymore than we accepted the reasoning of the Royal Commission on Security, Paragraph 100.[57]

The activist coalition also directly criticizes the surveillance and interrogation policies of the RCMP and asks "to know if it is a policy of the Royal Canadian Mounted Police to identify homosexuals within any area of government service

"Gay Political Activists" and "Radical Lesbians"

and then question them concerning their sexuality and the sexuality of others; and if this is the policy we demand its immediate cessation and destruction of all records so obtained."[58]

In hindsight, we know that the RCMP was engaging in a wide-ranging campaign of identification and interrogation; however, given the secretive social organization of these campaigns, at the time this would have been hard to ascertain from state documents and released policies. There was a definite lack of awareness on the part of activists regarding the extent of the national security campaigns. Activists were just starting to organize against the campaigns and were still learning about them. No one who had been directly affected by them had yet come out publicly to fight against them or to seek the assistance of gay/lesbian activists. This section of "We Demand" concludes, "Identifying and/or questioning individuals on the basis of their sexuality is both irrelevant and inconsistent with the spirit of [the 1969 reform] ... Moreover, we view such a practice as an inherent breach of the CANADIAN BILL OF RIGHTS, Part 1, Section 1 (b): 'The right of the individual to equality before the law and the protection of the law.'"

Suggesting that the 1969 reform renders these discriminatory and exclusionary policies irrelevant again exaggerates the impact of this legislation. As we have learned, the Criminal Code reform in and of itself challenged neither practices of employment discrimination (it did not provide lesbians and gay men with human rights protection) nor national security practices. We also see how the rhetoric of civil rights is invoked to argue for an end to these security practices. Indeed, "We Demand" posed major challenges to the national security war on lesbians and gay men.

THE RCMP ACCOUNT: AN EXTERNAL ORGANIZATIONAL STANDPOINT

The social character and spirit of the August 1971 demonstration in Ottawa, and the demands it raised differ greatly from that found in the official discourse of the RCMP surveillance reports. In the RCMP accounts, these events are decontextualized – that is, they are removed from the experiences of lesbian and gay activists and from queer experiences more generally – and formulated as possible "security threats" while being inscribed into policing and national security discourse.

The files to which we gained access indicate that existing surveillance and monitoring of the LSA informed the RCMP of the Ottawa demonstration.

On August 13, 1971, as part of the general surveillance of LSA forums, an RCMP undercover officer/informant took notes at a public meeting organized by the LSA in Toronto and entitled "Gay Liberation, the Movement for Homosexual Rights in Canada." At this meeting, the upcoming Ottawa demonstration was a major focus.[59] We examine this surveillance report when we discuss the connection between the surveillance of the early gay movement and the LSA.

The above report, along with monitored articles from *Labour Challenge*, led to requests and reports being sent to the security services in Ottawa. On August 24, 1971, Superintendent S.V.M Chisholm sent a message from D Branch to the VIP Security Section, which covered security on Parliament Hill. The course of action set out moves from D Branch's surveillance of LSA activities to reporting what was learned about gay activism to the relevant security divisions. This led to the more specific surveillance of gay groups. Chisholm writes: "According to a recent article in the 'Labour Challenge' (Trotskyist publication), a newly formed organization known as the Toronto Gay Group (TGA) (a Homosexual group which is believed to have Trotskyists within its membership), is planning a demonstration at the Parliament Buildings in Ottawa on August 28, 1971." Here the name of Toronto Gay Action is given incorrectly (but the acronym is right). The major focus is not so much on the gay activists themselves as on that fact that the TGA has Trotskyists among its members. Members of the LSA were actually playing an important part in the TGA and in organizing for the August 28 action, but the RCMP read this as an instance of Trotskyist infiltration, which raised security concerns. Indeed, Chisholm uses "Trotskyist infiltrated" in direct reference to this demonstration.[60]

There is also an action request to the Government of Canada's Security Service regarding this demonstration. On the 1971 transit slip, an attachment read, "Looks like we may have a 'GAY' time in Ottawa on Aug. 28/71. Necessary liaison with VIP will be conducted as plans materialize."[61] This use of the word "gay" mocks the gay liberation movement and provides us with a clearer sense of the view taken up by at least one RCMP officer in relation to these protests.

We also gained access to part of the report by A Division (Ottawa) on the demonstration itself.[62] The report begins, "Observation was conducted of a demonstration held by the Toronto Gay Action [blanked out] on Parliament Hill, Ottawa. A group of 75-80 people gathered near the East Block and at approximately 3:00 pm they marched to the front steps of the Centre Block, Parliament Hill." The standpoint of external observation constructed here is crucial to the social organization of the RCMP report. The first part of the report describes the event from the standpoint of police surveillance:

The demonstrators marched in front of the Peace Tower carrying signs and chanting slogans. The banners and signs displayed by the demonstrators carried various messages and slogans such as "Canada – The True North Strong and Gay," "Equal Rights for Gay People," and "Smash Heterosexual Imperialism" ... After marching ... the group gathered in front of the Peace Tower and were addressed by several speakers. The first speaker was [blanked out] from Ottawa, [blanked out] claimed the protestors represented groups from Toronto, Waterloo, Guelph, London, Montreal, and New York State.[63]

This reads like a neutral description of "what actually happened"; however, as John Wilson remembers, the demonstration involved more people and lasted longer than the RCMP suggests (May 25, 2000). After reading this document, Wilson remarked: "Some of the observations [the RCMP made] are quite obvious. Some are the same observations that are made in newspaper reports. Some of the observations were blindingly obvious [Laughs]" (May 25, 2000).

Hindered by the removal of information by ATIP officers, we were nevertheless able to reconstruct the identity of some of the speakers blanked out in the original document (our additional information appears in [ ]):

[blanked out – George Hislop], Chairman of the Community Homophile Association of Toronto (CHAT) [blanked out] from New York [blanked out] from Toronto. [blanked out – Charlie Hill] called for amendments to the Criminal Code and read a list of demands his organization (CHAT) intends to present to the Federal Government ... [this is from the "We Demand" text]. One of the speakers (name unknown [Pierre Mason]) represented the Front de Libération des Homosexuels [blanked out].[64]

The A Division report lists the demands made at the demonstration, including those that challenged employment discrimination and RCMP practices. Gay activists were a threat not only because of Trotskyist infiltration but also because they were challenging the national security policies of the Canadian state and the RCMP.

The RCMP presence (perhaps two undercover officers or informants) was sufficient for it to obtain the basic meaning of what people were saying at the rally. This was not just surveillance undertaken by an observer at a distance writing down notes on what was displayed on placards and banners. The RCMP heard the sounds of people's chants and could record what speakers said. At the same time, the people writing the report did not seem to be very familiar with gay organizing.

The A Division report includes specific mention of people who were present at the demonstration, but these names were removed before it was released. The names are one of the crucial pieces of information contained in this report as they were used for surveillance purposes against groups and individuals and to establish files on them. In other words, the gathering of the names was a key part of the organization of national security surveillance.

The report also notes that members of the Ottawa LSA attended the demonstration: "The following members of the Ottawa League for Socialist Action [blanked out] were recognized as having participated in the demonstration: [blanked out]." Cars parked near Parliament Hill and near the LSA Ottawa office on Seneca Street were mentioned in the report, including a partial listing of licence plates and types of car. The surveillance of cars was part of the repertoire of RCMP tactics and reveals the character of RCMP surveillance. Of course, previous surveillance of the LSA was probably used in identifying these cars as well. Later, the report states: "Photographic coverage was afforded this demonstration and the results are being processed."[65]

We assume that, as the report refers to an Observation Team whose names are entirely blanked out, this surveillance operation involved the work of a number of undercover (and perhaps some uniformed) RCMP officers.[66] Under "Investigator's Comments," there is a discussion of where copies of the report should be forwarded. This report included information from D Ops and K Branch, a research body of the Security Service staffed by civilians and used for follow-up on investigations of gay/lesbian organizing in their areas.[67]

The A Division report is based on a series of more limited reports prepared by the various officers (and perhaps informants) involved in this operation. It is not written from the stance of an individual directly involved in the demonstration; rather, it is an organizational account reflecting the standpoint of RCMP surveillance. Dorothy Smith describes some of the features of organizational accounts based on police work:

> The knowledge therefore does not arise as a continuity of observation by one individual and is not situated in relation to his context of observation. It arises ... from a number of individuals, namely the police, who were present themselves, on the occasion ... The basis of the account is itself organizational. The account appears to us a report without a reporter, hence having the character of a presentation of the events without an intermediary. This gives us that effect of objectivity, which results from the structural erasure of the witnesses to the original events as tellers of the tale.[68]

"Gay Political Activists" and "Radical Lesbians"

This is a standard feature of the social organization of the RCMP reports, which produce external organizational accounts that focus on surveying and managing local forms of protest. The standpoint of external organizational observation is central to the social character of these reports and to their construction as "objective."

The Vancouver Connection: A Cross-Country Movement Emerges

As has been mentioned, the Vancouver and Ottawa demonstrations took place simultaneously, and this may have contributed to the RCMP's belief that the new gay movement constituted a cross-country security threat requiring further surveillance. In the RCMP surveillance reports on the Vancouver demonstration, we find many of the same features that appear in its reports on the Ottawa demonstration.

In *Labour Challenge,* John Wilson writes, "In Vancouver, 20 gay militants and a sympathetic crowd of 150 to 200 listened to GATE [Gay Alliance towards Equality] chairman Roedy Green read out the list of demands in the TGA-brief [the same as were read out in Ottawa]. Another GATE speaker stressed the historic significance of the first cross-country rally of homosexuals demanding an end to second-class citizenship. The rally was addressed also by a spokeswoman from Vancouver Gay Sisters and Gay Liberation Front."[69] The RCMP conducted surveillance at this demonstration, reporting that fifty people gathered to watch the event "out of curiosity, but did not show any degree of sincere interest."[70] This remark dismisses the significance of this action and the response to it, and conflicts with Wilson's account of the event.

"Investigator's Comments" reveals that the RCMP was conducting surveillance on a group with which it was not familiar. According to the report, "GATE had not come to our attention prior to this demonstration. Most of the people involved have shown an interest in either the Gay Liberation Front (GLF) – Vancouver, BC [blanked out] or the Canadian Gay Activists Alliance (CGAA) – Vancouver, BC [blanked out] in the past." This indicates that surveillance of the GLF and the CGAA was being carried out prior to the formation of GATE. As we have already seen, the GLF had come to the attention of the RCMP when it was probing for "radicals" in Vancouver earlier in 1971.

There is another RCMP report from Division E. This makes no mention of GATE except as a name on a placard; however, it refers to the "Gay Alliance," "GLF" and two members of the "Women's Liberation Front" "Gay Faction."[71] Perhaps members of the RCMP were confused because some of the members of GATE used to be members of other gay groups, and GLF members spoke in support at the demonstration. According to the Division E report, "The demonstration on the whole did not seem to be too successful although some press coverage was given. At no time did there appear to be more than 100 onlookers." This suggests that the protest was not very "successful," even though it was the first of its kind in the city, and indicates the RCMP's view as dismissive of early gay organizing. Continuing the focus on the LSA and its youth group the Young Socialists, the report mentions that the paper "'The Young Socialist' was being sold." It concludes as follows: "It was stated by members of the 'GLF' that further demonstrations are planned for the future, some of which will be attended by members of this section and reported on accordingly." This, of course, justified further RCMP surveillance. The RCMP also took photographs at the Vancouver demonstration, later stating that these activities would be closely watched and that any further demonstrations would be attended by members of the special "L Section."[72] The Division E report argued that demonstrations of this sort warranted continuing surveillance.

The RCMP was particularly concerned with the cross-country character of these protests and actions. The 1971 launch of the *Body Politic,* a cross-country gay liberation magazine, was seen as so significant that the entire first issue was included in RCMP files.[73] This new publication was considered a central means of communication and organization for the new gay liberation movement across the Canadian state. A collective of activists (initially including Brian Waite) who emerged from Toronto Gay Action produced the *Body Politic.* The magazine was a crucial source of information for the RCMP with regard to its attempts to monitor different parts of the gay/lesbian movement. The RCMP was developing an interest in the media used by subversive groups and in how those media could be used to expand their influence. For example, it included clippings in the files of various gay groups indicating where the *Body Politic* could be bought.[74]

Front de libération des homosexuels: Linking Gay and Quebec National Liberation Struggles

The War Measures Act, declared in October 1970 following kidnappings by the Front de libération du Québec, was not only used against the left wing of the independence movement in Quebec but was also invoked to justify raids on and closures of some of Montreal's gay bars. One of the first gay-liberation-type organizations in the Canadian state, along with the GLF in Vancouver, was the Front de libération homosexuel (FLH), which was formed in March 1971.[75] This group quickly came under RCMP surveillance, apparently due to the RCMP's

"Gay Political Activists" and "Radical Lesbians"

established procedures for spying on the left and the Trotskyist movement as well as on the Quebec independence movement. Many francophone Québécois gays and lesbians encounter oppression based on language and nationality as well as on sexuality (and often on class). Their experience of sexual oppression is mediated through that of linguistic and national oppression.

The February 1971 issue of *Mainmise* ran an article entitled "Pour un front gai à Montréal," and this initiated the genesis of the FLH.[76] Ross Higgins explains that the use of "front" was deliberate. Gay liberationists wanted to be associated with the radical nationalist movements, including the earlier Front de libération nationale in Algeria, which waged a war of national liberation against the French occupation, and the feminist movement in Montreal, the Front de libération des femmes.

A contingent was organized to participate in the anti-Confederation demonstration held on July 1, 1971, which came under RCMP surveillance. The demonstration ended up at Parc Lafontaine, and Denis Côté, the first president of the FLH, addressed the crowd. In *Labour Challenge*, L. Paquette writes, "This was the first time in Canada that a gay group has participated in a public demonstration under its own banner ... A representative of the Homosexuels pour un Québec Libre spoke from the platform during the rally held at the end of the march, pointing out that the same society that oppresses the Québécois, oppresses gay people."[77] Here we get a sense of the overlapping of the surveillance of the Quebec independence movement, the left, and the emerging gay movement. It was the surveillance of the Quebec independence movement, which became a major focus in the late 1960s and 1970s, that led the RCMP to stumble across the gay activist movement in Montreal.

The FLH opened the doors of its headquarters on St. Denis Street in October 1971. Hundreds of gays visited this office. Like many other gay groups in the 1970s, the FLH contained members who were inclined to radical political action and to making alliances with other oppressed groups as well as to conducting social and cultural activities. In November 1971, many of the founding members left when the membership decided to incorporate and to become more service and socially oriented. The first headquarters was closed down by the city in May 1972. In June 1972, the FLH held a party at its new headquarters on Sainte-Catherine Street, and this was raided by the police. Forty people were charged with drinking in an establishment that did not have a liquor licence. The charges were later dropped on a technicality, but attendance at the centre declined as many members had been scared away, and the executive resigned. The FLH folded in the fall of 1972. Ross Higgins suggests that police repression

was a major reason for the dissolution of the FLH. The first Quebec gay liberation organization that articulated its politics in a Quebec nationalist context
was extinguished by police action.

Surveillance of the independence movement in Quebec was central to the
RCMP national security campaigns in the 1970s. These campaigns were motivated in part by fear that the struggle for Quebec independence would come
together with other social struggles. Hewitt writes that fear of the connections
between the Black Power movement, the Black Panther Party, and the Quebec
independence movement led the RCMP to engage in the notorious barn-
burning incident. This incident, which "was an attempt to prevent a meeting
between members of the Front de Libération du Québec and the Black Panther
Party," soon "became a source of embarrassment for the force."[78]

"TROTSKYIST INFILTRATION": LSA/YS CONNECTIONS, THE RMG, AND UNAFFILIATED MARXISTS

As aforementioned, a principal route for early RCMP surveillance on the gay/
lesbian movement was through the pre-existing surveillance and infiltration
of the LSA. As Hewitt points out, the RCMP infiltrated both the LSA and the
Young Socialist Alliance (later the Young Socialists), which the LSA launched
as its youth group in 1964. The RCMP did this "with numerous sources, who
offered intimate details on the activities of the two organizations, including
their members and plans. A long-term RCMP source, who was code named
A358 because 'A' Division in Ottawa recruited him, infiltrated the Trotskyist
movement at Trent University in the early 1970s."[79]

Members of the LSA were involved in early gay movement activities. Brian
Waite was aware that the LSA was under RCMP surveillance, and he told us
that a woman with whom he lived while he was still in the closet and who was
also a member of the LSA was being interviewed by government officials. In
these interviews, speeches she had given at internal LSA meetings were quoted
back to her (July 27, 2000). In RCMP national security discourse "Trotskyist"
was coded in a similar fashion to "Communist," carrying subversive connota-
tions and mandating investigations.

In the early 1970s, the LSA was the Canadian section of the Fourth International, which was founded in 1938 by supporters of Leon Trotsky and the
remnants of the left opposition. Since Trotskyists were critical of the undemocratic character of Stalinism, of bureaucratic rule in the Soviet Union, and of
bureaucratic policies in defence of the "proletarian" (heterosexual) family, they

"Gay Political Activists" and "Radical Lesbians"

were often (but not always) more receptive to the emergence of gay liberation than were others in the organized far left. Waite told us that in the 1960s in the LSA, unlike in the US Socialist Workers Party (SWP) to which the LSA was tied, homosexuals were never prohibited from membership on the basis that they were "security risks" who could be victimized by the state. In the SWP, homosexual members were defined as a security risk to the party – an interesting inversion of state national security discourse.[80]

John Wilson, who was involved in the leading bodies of the LSA in the later 1960s, was widely known in the group to be gay. According to Waite, "When the gay movement emerged [many gay members of the LSA] got involved in it without the approval of the organization." A number of gay and lesbian members of the LSA and the YS became important activists while building these early gay groups. Within the LSA and the YS, lesbian and gay members "would also 'zap' the activities of the organization [by doing things] like dancing together at LSA social events" (July 27, 2000).

Initially, pushed on by this activist involvement, the LSA and the YS responded positively to the gay/lesbian movements. In August 1971, for the first time a Central Committee meeting of the League for Socialist Action/Ligue socialiste ouvrière (LSA/LSO) formally discussed gay liberation. It called for opening up a dialogue with gay liberationists, offering educational and propagandistic support to the gay movement.[81] This was similar to a slightly earlier "probe" of the gay liberation movement on the part of the SWP.[82]

In contrast to the RCMP framing of Trotskyist infiltration, a number of queer LSA members played formative roles in early gay activism, including at the August 28 demonstration in Ottawa, in the TGA, and in GATE-V. Counter to the image of infiltrators entering groups with which they did not really agree and using them for their own ends, these leftists played key parts in initiating and building various activist groups. As John Wilson, who was involved in the TGA and later in GATE-T, said when referring to the RCMP documents that deal with Trotskyist infiltration, "[This] just actually shows that they didn't understand very much since people who were Trotskyists at that time were actually quite pivotal in a number of the early gay groups. They obviously didn't know or have much insight into what was going on. Their kind of mind-set was always that the far left was out to use other people and other movements and manipulate them. Of course everyone was trying to manipulate them except the RCMP [laughs]" (May 25, 2000). Waite pointed out that gay members of the LSA played an important part in developing the human rights strategy in the gay movement "by extrapolating the broader political notions of the LSA and applying them to the lesbian and gay struggle" (July 27, 2000). Centring on single-issue movements and mass action led to a focus on the struggle for human rights protection.[83]

In contrast to this, according to the RCMP, LSA involvement in the gay movement made the latter a terrain for "subversion" and mandated security investigations. The same has been demonstrated for the RCMP surveillance of high school students in Toronto in the late 1960s and early 1970s. The involvement of YS members in high school student activism, including that regarding the availability of birth control information in schools and for women's liberation, led the RCMP to conduct surveillance on high school student activists and to define their activism as "subversive."[84]

The major left group upon whom the RCMP had conducted surveillance was the Communist Party of Canada, and this surveillance continued into the 1970s. Since the Communist Party was hostile towards lesbian and gay movements during these years, with few exceptions it does not turn up in the RCMP files in relation to these movements. A few composite reports on activism on university campuses and on the *Body Politic* in the RCMP files for GATE-T and the NGRC make passing reference to Brian Mossop's 1976 expulsion from the Communist Party for being too involved in the gay movement and for "advocating homosexuality."[85]

Later in the 1970s, the LSA moved away from its support for gay liberation, especially in its refusal to adopt the gay/lesbian liberation perspective that "gay/lesbian is just as good as straight." Consequently, many gay/lesbian activists left the LSA and the YS.[86] A similar situation occurred in the Socialist Workers Party in the United States.[87] John Wilson described what happened in the LSA:

> Initially, we had a reasonably good reaction to gay liberation, and beginning around '73 we went into a stall. They [i.e., the LSA leadership] were waiting to see what the Socialist Workers Party [in the United States] was going to do. I left in September 1973. I had concluded at that point that they were not serious about a discussion and they were not going anywhere with that and so I quit. I think probably underneath it all I had some doubts about the continued viability of the organization in some ways too. I just thought there was no point in talking to these people, you're just wasting your opinion – they are not going to move. (May 25, 2000)

Brian Waite had left the LSA a bit earlier. As he put it, "they didn't criticize us, they just left us out on a limb." And he was critical of the lack of support lesbian and gay members were given for the work they were doing in the gay movement.

"Gay Political Activists" and "Radical Lesbians"

Maurice Flood, a central activist in GATE-V, left the LSA in 1974. In his resignation letter, he wrote,

> The zest of gay revolutionaries found no reflection inside the Trotskyist movement. Their efforts met with cold indifference and outright hostility. The leadership at no point launched a thorough-going scientific inquiry into the nature of human sexuality and its objective role in the revolutionary process. They failed to develop a programme of internal education of their members. The effect and purpose of their thinking was to hold back and artificially downplay the importance of the gay movement.[88]

Later in 1977, gay activist Stuart Russell resigned from the LSA because of its "inadequate and Un-Marxist" position on gay liberation. In 1976, the LSA Central Committee finally adopted a position on gay liberation, rejecting all the amendments put forward by members active in the gay and lesbian movements. In his resignation letter, Russell wrote, "ever since the gay question was first formally raised for discussion in 1971, the LSA/LSO leadership has attempted to brush the issue under the rug."[89] Throughout much of the 1970s, however, some LSA members remained active in gay/lesbian struggles.

Even with all these difficulties, Trotskyist groups continued to be the far left current from which the gay/lesbian movement was able to draw some support in the 1970s.[90] Other currents in the radical left, including the New Tendency (a loose collaboration of independent leftists based in Toronto, Windsor, Winnipeg, and Kitchener-Waterloo that was inspired by political developments in the Italian revolutionary left) and some anarchist collectives, also offered some support to queer struggles. Activists in the Windsor Labour Centre, which was connected to the New Tendency, helped establish Windsor Gay Unity.[91]

We encounter the LSA, the YS, and the RMG in a number of the RCMP documents analyzed below. The RCMP was clearly collecting clippings from the LSA's paper *Labour Challenge,* including articles on the gay movement. The first clipping in the files to which we gained access is on the gay contingent at the July 1, 1971, demonstration for Quebec independence.[92]

RCMP Surveillance of the LSA

The RCMP had an informant or officer taking notes at the forum on gay liberation in Ottawa in August 1971.[93] The O Division report noted that there were about seventy people in attendance and that the first speaker, whose name was blanked out,

[d]escribed the make-up of the Community Homophile Association of Toronto (C.H.A.T.). He stated that CHAT has been in existence for six months and that in effect it was made up of two groups, one a militant group and the other pacifist in nature. About one month ago the militant group broke away from CHAT and formed their own splinter group called Toronto Gay Action (TGA). [Blanked out] stated that CHAT donated $80.00 towards building the TGA rally in Ottawa.[94]

This description suggests that the relationship and differences between CHAT and the TGA were an important concern for the RCMP. There was an awareness that groups like CHAT did not, per se, require surveillance but that their links to more clearly "militant" groups (like the TGA) were major concerns. These more militant groups were believed to require consistent attention. We do know that the speakers at the forum were George Hislop and Pat Murphy (representing CHAT), Cheri DiNovo of the TGA, CHAT, and the Toronto Women's Caucus (TWC), and Brian Waite (representing the TGA and the LSA).[95] Under "Investigator's Comments," it is pointed out that two of the people named in the first paragraph of the report (both names are blanked out) "are members of CHAT, [blanked out] being an executive member."

Surveillance of the left and the LSA prompted the RCMP to conduct surveillance on the early gay movement in other ways as well. For instance, the RCMP Security Service in Vancouver was monitoring a series of protests organized against a 1972 visit of Prime Minister Trudeau and focused largely on the presence of the LSA. Clearly, an undercover officer or informant was present. This person or persons reported that a number of activists from the Canadian Gay Activists Alliance joined the demonstration and distributed leaflets.[96]

The RCMP had at least one agent/informant inside the LSA who acquired copies of the LSA *Internal Discussion Bulletin*, which was available to LSA members only. As a result of this, the RCMP had access to LSA documents relating to gay and lesbian issues.[97] A six-page excerpt from an internal LSA *Discussion Bulletin* from June 1972 was included in the files. This excerpt focused on the relationship between CHAT and the TGA and the Canadian gay liberation movement.[98] This was part of the RCMP's attempt to establish a better understanding of the distinction between militant groups and their more moderate counterparts. John Wilson pointed out that there "certainly would have been lots of other documents" (May 25, 2000) on the gay discussion that were written during this period and that were not given to us as part of our request.[99]

In a 1971 RCMP report on the University of Waterloo Gay Liberation Movement, possible linkages between the LSA, the YS, and the Fourth International are suggested.[100] It also comments on the cross-country YS educational conference held at the University of Waterloo in 1971, which was attended by about four hundred people. The file includes an article from the *Kitchener/Waterloo Record* entitled "Gay Liberationists Seek Rights, Plan Ottawa March August 28th," about a panel held at the Cross Canada Socialist Educational Conference.

> I was at this conference – I joined the YS in the spring of 1971. I remember hundreds of people being there, including openly gay people. There was a certain presence of the gay liberation movement at the conference. I was very intrigued by this but had yet to really begin to come out.

In at least one case, the RCMP used blackmail against a gay man to help it in its spying on the LSA and its Quebec wing, the Ligue socialiste ouvrière (LSO). On April 9, 1979, Harry Kopyto appeared before Keable Commission officials in Montreal, who were investigating RCMP dirty tricks against the sovereignty and left movements in Quebec.[101] He urged them to investigate letters in French that had been circulated in Montreal and Toronto and that were of the same general character as were the English letters that the RCMP had circulated, which identified one of the leaders of the LSA as suffering from a mental disorder (see below). Kopyto also insisted that an investigation be conducted into the admission by a Montreal homosexual that the RCMP blackmailed him into infiltrating the LSA/LSO.

This spying occurred in the early 1970s. The RCMP had taken photos of the gay man in question in "compromising" situations and had used them to blackmail him into spying on the LSO for a period of nine months. After this period of time, he apparently told the RCMP that there was nothing wrong with this group and that he could no longer spy on it (Kopyto, July 7, 2000). The RCMP officers themselves were the "blackmailers," using this man's queer sexual activities to force him to spy on a left organization. Here, we see a reversal of the RCMP's mythical Trotskyist infiltration of the gay movement, with the RCMP blackmailing a gay man into infiltrating the Trotskyist movement.

This climate of surveillance made the YS and LSA leaderships worry about members using drugs such as marijuana. They feared RCMP harassment of the organizations and their members for "non-political" reasons, and this led to their prohibiting recreational drug use.[102] As Hewitt points out, there was some justification for this fear since one tactic used by the RCMP "and used with frequency by the FBI against the New Left, was to report infractions like drug use to colleagues on the criminal side as a means of eliminating an opponent."[103]

> I had never smoked marijuana until doing it with other members of the Young Socialists in downtown Toronto. I also experienced the use of this policy prohibiting drug use against left political dissidents within the YS in particular. Two left oppositional members in the Toronto YS were expelled on this basis in the summer of 1971.

At the same time, in the 1970s the RCMP was involved in a broader surveillance of the LSA/LSO and many other parts of the left. During the Quebec October Crisis and under the War Measures Act, many leftists were among the close to five hundred people taken into custody with no charges having been laid against them.[104] These included two leading members of the LSA/LSO. The LSA/LSO supported Quebec self-determination, independence, and socialism for Quebec, and was involved in the defence of Quebec political prisoners, making this organization a target for the RCMP.

Ross Dowson, a leading figure in the LSA/LSO for much of its history, compiled a book on his struggles with the RCMP.[105] In it he reveals that "the LSA ... was targeted by the RCMP in its Operation Checkmate, [which was] designed to harass and if possible destroy organizations of completely legitimate dissent."[106] Operation Checkmate officially spanned the period from September 1972 to December 1973, and it was an RCMP campaign against the left. "While the LSA and the CP are named" in the documents that were released, "it would appear obvious from the available evidence that Checkmate was directed against many prominent individuals and took into its target-area the NDP, its left wing Waffle, Maoist organizations and other organizations, including cultural and religious organizations that are sometimes designated by witch hunters as peripheral to the Left and 'fronts.'"[107] The RCMP's Operation Checkmate involved the forging of letters and an income tax return, the intimidation of custodians of a meeting room in order to deter them from renting it to a study group, the interception of mail, and the "pollution of the gas tank and demobilization of a car owned by a targeted person so that he and an important visitor would be forced to use the car of an informant that has been already bugged."[108]

In one case directed against the LSA/YS, the RCMP forged and circulated letters at a convention of the Young Socialists in 1972 and throughout the LSA/LSO more generally.

"Gay Political Activists" and "Radical Lesbians"

In December 1972, when I was at a Young Socialists convention in Toronto, I remember coming back after lunch and finding a letter placed on every chair stating that one of the leaders of the LSA (the parent group of the YS) was mentally unstable. It was an attempt to disrupt the group, given the organization was then going through major political discussions and tensions. A joint statement by the YS leadership (the majority) and the left opposition (the Internationalist Communist Tendency, which I supported and which would become part of the Revolutionary Marxist Group) was made opposing this letter.

In 1979, in response to legal and political challenges, RCMP officials finally admitted before the Royal Commission of Inquiry into the Confidentiality of Health Records in Ontario (Krever Commission) "that they forged, altered and circulated false documents at an LSA-Young Socialist convention held in Toronto in 1972 and circulated similar letters to members of the LSA." RCMP superintendent Taylor admitted that the RCMP wrote and circulated the letters, falsely claiming that John Riddel, then a leading member of the LSA and later of the Revolutionary Workers' League (RWL), was forced to get psychiatric help in order to "sow dissension in the socialist community."[109]

The RCMP claimed the LSA and its successor organization, the RWL, was "violence-prone" and in fact "subversive" as defined in the Criminal Code – that is, "advocating social change by violent and undemocratic means."[110] The RCMP claimed it was implementing the secret Order-in-Council "'mandate of the security service' formalized on March 27, 1975." Although excluded by law from using Ontario Health Insurance Plan data, unemployment insurance, and social insurance numbers, "[the latter's officials] not only gave the RCMP unlimited access from the start but in 1969 a special Telex number."[111]

RCMP testimony at the 1977 McDonald Commission into RCMP wrongdoing confirmed this. A memo written by an unnamed member of the triumvirate headed by Superintendent S. Chisholm, who was in charge of Operation Checkmate, was revealed in reference to a discussion that he had had with RCMP director general John Starnes. Its opening words read, "With the DG's wish in mind that this organization should be destroyed." In testimony from Starnes, the word "destroyed" referred to a note he had sent earlier to another officer, which read "with a view to neutralizing and isolating them and where appropriate destroying them."[112]

In 1977, Ontario attorney general Roy McMurtry affirmed that the RCMP did have a presence in the Ontario NDP. His media release quoted RCMP officials, who justified their interference in the NDP "because of alleged infiltration by 'ex-communists' and the League for Socialist Action and its 'subversive' leadership, upon the invitation of that party's left-wing, the Waffle."[113] The Waffle was the left-wing Canadian nationalist opposition that, in the early 1970s, emerged in the NDP across English Canada. Largely made up of young people and student activists, the Waffle soon gained a following among some trade union activists as it engaged in important strike support activities. This was seen as a threat to the existing trade union leaderships, and, in 1973, they pressured the leadership of the NDP to expel the Waffle from the Ontario NDP. The RCMP was especially concerned that the existence of the Waffle allowed left groups to "penetrate" the NDP.[114]

Revolutionary Marxist Group

Another major Trotskyist organization in Canada was the RMG, which was formed in 1973 by activists involved in the student movement (the Old Mole), the Red Circle in the NDP's left-wing Waffle group, and former members of the LSA/YS.[115]

I found that much of the politics of the Young Socialists and the LSA were simplistic and rather on the moderate side. I came to no longer believe that mass actions were spontaneously revolutionary and felt that a more radical approach was called for. I came to support the International Communist Tendency and the Revolutionary Communist Tendency, who supported the more left-wing position of the majority of the Fourth International based in Europe. In 1973, members of the International Communist Tendency left the Young Socialists, and I became a member of the RMG. This group generally had a more left position than the LSA but was slower in coming out in active support for lesbian and gay liberation than the LSA. But a number of members in the RMG were involved in gay and lesbian activism and also came under RCMP surveillance.[116]

In the RMG a small number of gay and lesbian members began to elaborate a position in support of gay/lesbian liberation and to argue for this in the group as a whole. An early statement we produced was called "Workers of the World Caress, Sexual Liberation through Revolution, Not Reform!"[117] We participated as an autonomous group of the RMG in the gay and lesbian movements and attempted to radicalize the gay/lesbian movement and to get it to support other liberation struggles. Along with feminists in the RMG we were making some important headway in the group by 1976-77.[118]

One gay RMG member, Josh, who was a non-citizen and was involved in gay activism, reported that, in 1973, while working for a federal government agency, he had been a marshal at a gay rights march on Queen's Park on a Saturday. The following Monday, he was called into his coordinator's office. Luckily, his coordinator was also a leftist, although heterosexual. He told Josh that the Ontario regional coordinator for this government branch had received photographs of the demonstration:

[In particular, he told me] that the RCMP had identified me as a federal employee. So if one hand of the bureaucracy was spying on me, the other could deport me. The regional coordinator told the director that it was okay because he had no problems with gays. But if it had been another province, he said, I probably would have been fired. The main point was of course to tell me that they were watching and they could get me. (December 12, 2000)[119]

Josh's anecdote brings together surveillance of gay activism and of federal state personnel, thus showing how surveillance of the gay movement could also lead to RCMP reports on state employees. This account demonstrates the speed with which surveillance and reporting could operate, the centrality of photographic surveillance for identification purposes, and the particular problems facing non-citizens in relation to security policing (this deserves emphasis, especially in our current context). There was a clear division of labour, with the RCMP quickly reporting its findings to this government department. We also get a sense that, by the early 1970s, being identified as gay did not always lead to losing one's position or to demotion and that administrators had a certain amount of discretion in these cases.

In 1977, the LSA/LSO, the RMG, and the Groupe marxiste révolutionnaire (which was linked with the RMG in Quebec) merged under pressure from the leadership of the Fourth International to attempt to reunite some of the different currents of Trotskyism and to create a stronger organization. The newly formed Revolutionary Workers' League/Ligue ouvrière révolutionnaire (RWL/LOR), which, for a brief period, was a rather substantial far left organization with hundreds of members across the Canadian state, was also active in the gay/lesbian movement for a few years.[120]

When the RMG and LSA were discussing fusion, a number of gay and lesbian members of the RMG tried unsuccessfully to point out that a major difference between the two groups was that, while the RMG fully supported gay/lesbian liberation, the LSA no longer did. We tried to get this clarified and addressed in the fusion discussions but to no avail. As a result, the newly formed RWL had an unclear and ambiguous position on gay/lesbian liberation.

By 1976-77, the SWP leadership moved into open opposition to the gay movement. It argued that the gay and lesbian movements were "peripheral," lacking the "social weight" of industrial workers and other movements, and that they were defined by "lifestyle" politics. This position was then forced onto the Canadian RWL through the Canadian supporters of the SWP (the ex-LSA) and others who were able to gain a majority, thus obliging the lesbian/gay liberation tendency within the RWL to leave. Ironically, even though the SWP leadership and the ex-LSA bloc within the RWL claimed that lesbian and gay liberation was peripheral to the struggle for socialism, this became a central issue around which they were able to undermine and divide the ex-RMG (and ex–Groupe marxiste révolutionnaire in Quebec) leaderships. They did this by attacking the gay/lesbian liberation tendency within the RWL and, by the early 1980s, establishing their hegemony. Rather than being peripheral, the attack on lesbian and gay liberation became central to the political project of the SWP and the ex-LSA leadership in the RWL between 1978 and 1980.[121]

We formed Tendency Z (with the last letter in the alphabet) in the RWL to fight for integrating the acquisitions of gay/lesbian liberation into the theory and practice of the organization, arguing for the centrality of lesbian/gay liberation to broader class struggle politics. We made important theoretical advances but were constantly under attack by the leadership of the ex-LSA, and, unfortunately, some of the former leaders of the RMG, as we were denounced as "petite-bourgeois lifestylists" and "anti-Leninists." It became clear to us that the leadership and much of the organization were not willing to deal with our political perspectives, and many of us began to leave the organization since it counter-posed our involvement in the revolutionary organization to our activism in the gay/lesbian movements. One of the conclusions I drew from this experience was that what is called "Leninism" as a theory of organization and consciousness is an obstacle in not being able to transform itself in relation to new social contradictions and social struggles. We have to develop forms of anti-capitalist and radical organizing that can learn from new forms of struggle like feminism and lesbian/gay liberation while at the same time transforming what revolutionary politics is all about.[122]

In my view, there is much to be learned from Trotskyism, including from its critique of Stalinism, the theory of permanent revolution, and the theory of uneven and combined development it is bound up with, as well as from the notion of transitional demands, which begins to challenge the social relations of capitalism.[123] But it also has profound limitations. Its critique of the bureaucracy in the

"Gay Political Activists" and "Radical Lesbians"

USSR was inadequate since it still saw the USSR as a "degenerated workers' state" requiring only a political revolution rather than as a bureaucratic class society of a new kind. Its critique of bureaucratic and state relations never went far enough, and it remains ensnared within statist notions of revolution – with a focus on taking power and seizing control of "the state."[124] Trotskyism does not adequately grasp new social contradictions and struggles and leads to a top-down vertical approach to establishing socialism. The basic postulate of Trotskyism from the later 1930s on has been that the central problem is the crisis of leadership of the working class rather than a crisis of self-organization and mobilization. This focus on the crisis of leadership has often led Trotskyists to see the revolutionary vanguard party as external to class and social struggles rather than as inside these struggles and movements.[125]

Surveillance of the RMG

The RMG appears less often than the LSA in the released RCMP documents; however, there are two substantial references in the released files on GATE-T.[126] The first reference appears in conjunction with a demonstration at the *Toronto Sun* office in October 1974. This protest, organized by GATE-T, responded to an editorial in the *Sun* that referred to homosexuality as "unnatural and abnormal" and as an "aberration."[127] Reporting that there were about forty people in attendance, the investigator wrote that "other organizations which were observed participating at this demonstration were: Revolutionary Marxist Group (RMG) [blanked out] League for Socialist Action (LSA) [blanked out]."[128] The document noted that "surveillance [was] conducted by [blanked out]." Once again, we encounter the external gaze of state surveillance. The standpoint of the individual who wrote this is from outside the demonstration, even though it is likely that he or she was an undercover informant who participated in the demonstration. Moreover, the "Investigator's Comments" reveal observations on differences between the LSA and the RMG: "It is felt that the LSA were present at this demonstration in order to publicize their mayoralty candidate [blanked out] ... The RMG on the other hand, were there to show physical support of an issue which they feel discriminates against minority groups, and also to take the opportunity to expose their political line."[129] Here we get a sense that the reporter may have a bit more knowledge about the differences between the LSA and the RMG than what would have been generated simply through surveillance.

A report on GATE-T also stated that the RMG participated in a demonstration organized by the Coalition for Gay Rights in Ontario. This demonstration focused on the John Damien struggle and employment rights as well as human

MARCH FOR GAY LIBERATION

REINSTATE JOHN DAMIEN!

AGAINST THE OPPRESSION OF
GAY WORKERS

gays, women & all workers unite

AGAINST DAVIS' PHONY 'WAR' ON 'SIN'--NO TO CAPITALIST POLITICIANS

ALL OUT SEPT. 13   1=30 p.m.   QUEEN'S PARK
behind LEGISLATURE

JOIN THE PROVINCE-WIDE COALITION FOR GAY RIGHTS IN ONTARIO (CGRO) DEMONSTRATION.

RE-INSTATE JOHN DAMIEN!   ADD SEXUAL ORIENTATION TO THE HUMAN RIGHTS CODE!
JOIN THE LEFT CONTINGENT
OPEN IMMIGRATION TO GAY PEOPLE.   EQUAL CUSTODY RIGHTS FOR GAY PARENTS.

NO FIRINGS ON THE BASIS OF SEXUAL ORIENTATION.   SEXUAL RIGHTS FOR YOUTH.

ABOLISH THE AGE OF CONSENT LAWS.   NO ANTI-GAY CLAUSES IN UNIONS.

FIGHT POLICE HARASSMENT

*SEXUAL LIBERATION THROUGH SOCIALIST REVOLUTION. NO REAL SOCIALISM WITHOUT SEXUAL
LIBERATION.*

REVOLUTIONARY MARXIST GROUP   *368-7313*

8   RMG poster for the Coalition for Gay Rights in Ontario (CGRO) demonstration, September 13, 1975 | *Credit:* Gary Kinsman, personal archives

"Gay Political Activists" and "Radical Lesbians"

rights protection for gay men and lesbians (see Photo 8). Damien was a racing steward who was fired in 1975 for being gay, and his case was the first in Canada that involved major public organizing against anti-gay discrimination.[130] The RCMP reported that the demonstration was "supported by the Revolutionary Marxist Group (RMG)."[131] On September 13, 1975, it stated that there were "approximately 250 persons in attendance, [and] approximately twenty were members of the RMG. Because of the number involved the local police permitted the demonstrators to walk on the street." This was a large demonstration for this time, and clearly the surveillance officer found the presence of the RMG to be significant.[132]

> The RMG supported this demonstration and we distributed our own poster for it calling for rights for gay and lesbian workers. I remember the poster had a bunch of miners hugging each other on it. We organized a feeder march that joined with the CGRO protest at Queen's Park. We invited members of the Groupe homosexuel d'action politique, a group with an anti-capitalist perspective, to join this contingent, and about six of them came down from Montreal to support this demonstration.

In the late 1970s, RMG members and other gay and lesbian leftists made attempts to get the gay/lesbian movements to support the struggles of other oppressed groups, including the feminist movement and the right of the people of Quebec to self-determination. These attempts generated some opposition from others in the gay movement, including a sharply critical editorial in the *Body Politic*.[133]

> At the 1976 gay/lesbian conference in Toronto [the RMG gay/lesbian caucus] brought forward motions of support for lesbians and gays organizing in the union movement, the feminist movement, and for Quebec's right to self-determination. The motions of support for the feminist movement and for Quebec's right to decide its own future were defeated. When a number of lesbians heard about the defeat of the motion of support for the feminist movement, they came back to the plenary session and took over the front to protest the defeat of this motion. It was in response to this that the TBP [*Body Politic*] editorial criticized the RMG. At this conference Gillian Chase, of the Other Woman collective, also criticized the way in which the John Damien defence campaign was focusing on Damien as an individual and not linking his struggle to broader questions of lesbian/gay liberation.

Trotskyist activists of various persuasions were not infiltrators of the movement, as the RCMP classified them, but often important initiators and builders of it. This significant connection became a central focus for RCMP investigation of gay and lesbian activism.

Unaligned Marxists and the Gay Marxist Study Group

Other sections of the left connected to the gay movement also came under surveillance. A 1976 report on the "unaligned [M]arxist and pressure groups" section in Toronto included monitoring of the New Marxist Institute (NMI), an educational association offering classes and sponsoring public talks on a range of topics relating to Marxism and socialism that existed until at least 2004.[134] Mentioned are a series of public lectures and discussions in March 1975 titled "Sexism and Capitalism" that was co-sponsored by the Canadian Women's Educational Press and GATE-T.[135] This series, subtitled "Perspectives from the Left on Sexist Oppression of Women and Gays," included Walter Bruno, a gay shop steward with the Canadian Union of Postal Workers, Barry Adam of the Gay Academic Union, Chris Bearchell of the John Damien Defence Committee, and Eli Zaretsky, an American author who spoke on the family.[136] In April 1976, the RCMP stated: "It has been learned [blanked out] that GATE is one of 7 gay groups in Toronto and one of these is the Gay Marxist Study Group [blanked out] which originated from the NMI."[137]

In the summer of 1975 "Marxism from a Gay Perspective" was offered in the NMI course series (instructors included Walter Bruno and Tim McCaskell). The course was offered again in the fall of 1975, and it was from this course that the study group mentioned in the RCMP report emerged.[138] The RCMP was interested in possible connections between GATE and the NMI around the speakers series as well as the fact that the Gay Marxist Study Group emerged out of this institute.[139]

> The Gay Marxist Study Group emerged out of a course offered at the NMI. After it was over, we decided to continue to meet as a study and sometimes action group. I was a member of this group, which was mostly a discussion group, but we also engaged in strike support activity. For instance, I remember walking the picket lines with others from the group when library workers at the University of Toronto library in the Canadian Union of Public Employees Local 1230 were on strike in 1975 and were fighting for sexual orientation protection in their contract. This local also had a number of out gay and lesbian workers. Many of those who were involved in the Gay Marxist Study Group went on to participate

"Gay Political Activists" and "Radical Lesbians"

in the gay movement in a number of different areas in Toronto, Montreal, and elsewhere.

In the connections between the NMI and GATE, and between the NMI and the Gay Marxist Study Group, the RCMP believed it had found a direct tie-in between Marxist groups and pressure groups (the category in which the gay movement was located in this discourse). "Unaligned Marxists" seemed almost to be of as much concern to them here as "Trotskyists."

SPYING ON FEMINISTS AND LESBIANS: "RADICAL LESBIANS" TAKING A "PERVERSE PRIDE IN DE-FEMINIZING THEMSELVES"

In the 1950s and 1960s, in its national security campaigns against the left and the union movement, the RCMP spied on women's groups ranging from the Housewives Consumers' Association to the women's auxiliaries of the Mine Mill union.[140] As the feminist movement re-emerged in the 1960s, it came under RCMP surveillance, partly because it developed from the New Left and other protest movements. The RCMP conducted surveillance of the Royal Commission on the Status of Women, which was formed in 1967 and reported in 1970. This focus was partly due to the involvement of the Voice of Women and the Congress of Canadian Women, two groups the RCMP believed were infiltrated by the Communist Party. However, the association of feminism with subversion also motivated the surveillance of feminist organizations.[141]

The RCMP spied on the first cross-Canada action of the feminist movement, which was the 1970 Abortion Caravan. The Abortion Caravan's mandate included protesting the major limitations of the 1969 reform relating to abortions (part of the same omnibus bill that led to the partial decriminalization of some homosexual acts). This reform established a very limited right of access to legal abortions on "health" grounds but only when these were approved by doctors and therapeutic abortion committees. The caravan started in Vancouver and arrived in Ottawa on May 8, 1970. The protesters managed to "breach security" at the prime minister's residence, and about thirty women chained themselves to their chairs in the House of Commons visitors' gallery, causing the suspension of Parliament. The RCMP surveillance documents focus on the "unfeminine clothing" and "slovenly attire" that some of the women supposedly wore.[142]

In the summer of 2008, there was a brief media focus on the RCMP's spying on singer Rita MacNeil in the early 1970s. MacNeil was involved in the early feminist movement and in the Toronto Women's Caucus (TWC), which is where her singing career started. This was part of a much more widespread surveillance of feminist organizing across the country.[143]

I remember hearing Rita MacNeil sing at feminist events in the early 1970s in Toronto. She was involved in the TWC, which also had a number of members of the Young Socialists and the LSA involved in it. This may have been one of the reasons why it came under RCMP surveillance.

One of the problems encountered by RCMP surveillance teams regarding the feminist movement was that, until 1974, the RCMP, with the exception of female clerical workers, was entirely comprised of men. Consequently, infiltrating the feminist movement proved to be a difficult task for the RCMP, who had to rely largely on developing women informants in the feminist movement.[144] RCMP surveillance of feminist activism also led to surveillance against lesbians who participated in feminist activism. Lesbians experience oppression based on their gender and their sexuality (and, for many, race, class, and ability). As a result, many lesbians were and are very involved in feminist organizing. Building a social and organizing network for analysis and action was central to lesbian involvement in feminist activism.

We gained access to a 1971 surveillance report on a meeting of the TWC, at which an informant was present. This report was included in the GATE-T file because the TGA was then using the TWC office for its meetings.[145] There is also a 1975 RCMP surveillance report of a feminist demonstration supported by Gays of Ottawa as well as by the Ottawa Women's Centre and the Canadian Women's Coalition to Repeal the Abortion Law. The demonstration protested state inaction during International Women's Year and had considerable lesbian and gay participation. Marie Robertson of GO and LOON was one of the speakers (see Photo 9).[146] The support of gay and lesbian movements for feminist activities could also bring queer organizations under RCMP surveillance.[147]

Lesbians were uncovered as part of the surveillance of the feminist movement. For instance, RCMP surveillance of the Toronto Wages for Housework Campaign (TWHC) quickly led to the discovery that (surprise, surprise!) there were many lesbians among the supporters of Wages for Housework. The involvement of lesbian activists in the TWHC may also have attracted RCMP attention. Wages for Housework was a campaign based on an analysis of how domestic labour performed by women was key to producing capitalist social and economic relations. It called for women to be compensated for this labour, including for housework, as part of what it called the social wage. Demanding a wage

"Gay Political Activists" and "Radical Lesbians"

9 Marie Robertson of GO and LOON speaking at the 1975 International Women's Day rally in Ottawa on the steps of Parliament | *Credit:* CLGA 1986-032_08P (10) 01P

was meant to provide more social and economic power for women and to lay bare the basis of capitalist relations. It was an attempt to create more equality between women and men within the working class. Ultimately, the goal was to build autonomy and social power for working-class women. Initially, this campaign emphasized wages for housework as framed within an autonomist Marxist notion of how capital becomes a social factory – that is, how it becomes a network of social relations that extends far beyond actual factory walls and that depends on paid and unpaid labour. This theory is developed in the works of autonomist Marxist feminists such as Mariarosa Dalla Costa, Selma James, and Silvia Federici, whose analyses show how women's unpaid domestic labour benefits *both* individual men and capital.[148]

In Toronto, although there was an earlier wages for housework group, the TWHC emerged from women associated with the New Tendency and developed into a feminist campaign involving other left feminists. As Dorothy Kidd, who was involved in the New Tendency and then in the TWHC, tells us, the group arose out of tensions within the New Tendency between workplace organizing (the main focus) and community organizing:

I think there was a certain amount of lip service to community organizing [within the New Tendency]. There was a sense that the work going on in the auto plants or the post office was more exciting and it certainly took more energy of the group ... I do think that it was one of the reasons why the women split with the men when we started working with the Mother Led Union and other welfare rights groups ... Inspired by Selma James and thinking that the men in the New Tendency were primarily preoccupied with the workplace struggles, and wanting to have our own leadership ... working with working-class women's struggles, we decided to work on our own. (July 5, 2008)

Unfortunately, the TWHC in Toronto became a more isolated group as its form of organization became more developed and hardened. This created disconnections with other feminist and movement organizing of the time, and some groups were forced out of the network.[149] As Dorothy Kidd described it, "I think in the seventies, given the sort of libertarian tendencies of the movements, it was a pretty foreign idea to be as tightly organized as we were ... Now, I think it was also an organizational form that didn't quite work, but it needs to be said that the larger environment was really resistant to that organizational form" (July 5, 2008). There was a tendency for TWHC to focus on wages for domestic labour almost as a single issue rather than as a broader left-feminist organizing perspective. The committee focused on money issues, such as the family allowance, welfare rights, and grants/supports for women students, but also took up reproductive rights and support for lesbian mothers.

A 1976 RCMP report on the TWHC was organized under the "Unaligned Marxist and Pressure Groups" section of the Toronto RCMP. The police seemed particularly interested in the TWHC because it was part of an "international network" and because its "leadership cadre ... [was] composed of radical Marxist feminists."[150] The RCMP was especially concerned with "international networks" as threats to national security as well as with Marxists (and, in this case, "radical Marxist feminists").

The 1976 RCMP report continued, "There is also a high concentration of radical lesbians in the T.W.H.C. who have their own sub-group called Wages Due (WD)."[151] Wages Due (WD) was an autonomous lesbian group within the international Wages for Housework campaign.[152] Dorothy Kidd described the formation of the WD as follows: "It certainly wasn't a separation, it was more in the sense ... of how Selma [James] understood autonomy. It was not something that, for example, the straight women in Wages for Housework disagreed with in any way. It was the sense that lesbians have something very specific to say and needed to spend some time figuring out how to articulate it politically and what the demands would be" (July 5, 2008). The involvement of these "radical lesbians" is one reason cited by the RCMP for establishing this investigation.

"Gay Political Activists" and "Radical Lesbians"

In 1976, Ellen Agger of the WD argued that "lesbians want wages for housework so [that] we are no longer forced to hide our lesbianism," the point being that, in a capitalist society, money is crucial to women's independence from men.[153] Dorothy Kidd described one of the early activities of the WD in Toronto – a petition campaign in response to government cuts to the family allowance: "I can remember going door to door in Regent Park [a public housing development in downtown Toronto] and other places arguing for this petition as a lesbian, and saying, 'Just because we're lesbians doesn't mean we don't also do housework and we're not also involved in mothering.' So, that was sort of my coming out experience in many ways ... going as a lesbian into Regent Park and talking about mother's work. I have to say that was probably one of the most profound organizing experiences I've ever had" (July 5, 2008).

In Canada, the WD did much of the critical early work in supporting lesbian mothers and their struggles for custody of their children. During these years, it was routine for mothers who came out as lesbians, or who were discovered to be lesbians, to lose custody of their children. In March 1978, the WD launched the Lesbian Mothers Defence Fund (LMDF), which provided lesbian mothers in Canada with important legal, financial, and emotional support until 1987.[154]

A sexist and heterosexist social standpoint informed the RCMP account of Wages for Housework and the WD. For example, the 1976 report states: "T.W.H.C.'s membership has been described by [blanked out] as being 'Born Losers' who in appearance and attitude are both lower working class and welfare cases and involved in living alternative life-styles [blanked out]." Stigmatizing expressions such as "lower working class and welfare cases" emphasize the RCMP's elitist and class nature. By reducing the women referred to in the report to "living alternative life-styles," the RCMP attempted to dismiss those who tried to transform the social character of everyday life. Other comments emphasize the physical appearance and employment status of the women: "This is especially true of the radical lesbians in W.D., who take a perverse pride in de-feminizing themselves by cultivating the dirty and unkempt appearance. The general employment level of the membership is either menial office work [blanked out] the social service field i.e. social workers or unemployed. Also most seem to be single and just about everyone is under 30 years of age."[155]

Here the anti-working-class and anti-poor perspective combines with a particular gendered view to defend the hegemonic practices of the discourse of femininity.[156] Because the lesbians in the WD constructed and performed femininity differently and engaged in lesbian cultural practices of gender performance, they are defined as taking a perverse pride in defeminizing themselves.[157]

Clearly, an anti-lesbian perspective is combined with the defence of hegemonic heterosexual practices of femininity.

This formulation of "radical lesbians" is a key conceptualization in this RCMP report. The RCMP use the term "radical" to mean *politically* radical, as in left-wing activism. It is similar to the use of "radical" that we find in other RCMP reports on gay political activists. It is also possible, although highly unlikely, that the RCMP used "radical" as it was employed within the feminist movement with reference to radical feminism. A current within feminism that prioritizes the struggle against patriarchy and gender oppression, radical feminism often defines men as, on some level, the enemy. However, it is much more likely that the RCMP use of the term "radical lesbians" derived from mainstream media framing of radical feminists as bra-burners, man-haters, and, often, as lesbians. Notions of proper femininity and gender certainly enter into the formulation of this report.

The report goes on to describe the TWHC's political isolation: "Another significant characteristic of the membership is their sense of isolation. They are isolated and alienated from society as a whole and are unable to work with, or relate to, other groups or organizations. They have tried to co-operate with the Gay Alliance towards Equality [blanked out]. However, they feel they are being ignored and created as inferiors by them."[158] Always interested in identifying possible tensions, the RCMP comments on some of the political differences existing within and between the feminist, lesbian, and gay movements. Although members of GATE-T worked with members of the WD, there were some important differences between them as the former did not subscribe to the view that getting paid for housework would lead to the disappearance of lesbian oppression. Indeed, this was a common misunderstanding of the WD position.[159]

I was a member of GATE during these years. It was largely a men's organization and, in my view, most often tended to be male-dominated. The GATE Lesbian Caucus did exist, and its most dynamic member was Chris Bearchell. It was small, and while it undertook some important initiatives, it was rather distant from the feminist movement most of the time.

The RCMP report also mentions the tensions experienced with the Other Woman feminist collective, which published a feminist magazine by the same name.[160] However, despite its "isolation," the RCMP felt that the TWHC required surveillance and monitoring.

The report refers to two conferences, one of which was organized by the WD in July 1976, concerned strategy for the lesbian movement, and involved

"Gay Political Activists" and "Radical Lesbians"

about fifty women. According to the RCMP, "Interestingly [blanked out] the RMG was present and attempted to bring the discussion around to what they intended to do about the army stationed in Montreal for the Olympics."[161] This was a reference to the anti-gay/anti-lesbian "clean-up" campaign then going on in Montreal. In its conclusions on the TWHC, the report argues: "They do represent an excellent example of Unaligned Marxist group operating in the extremes of the Feminist Movement. Thus, our present low level of coverage is going to be maintained on this organization."[162] Due not only to its radical feminism and Marxism but also to the presence of "radical lesbians," the RCMP justified its continuing surveillance of this group. Dorothy Kidd attended these events and offered the following comments regarding the RCMP documents: "It was creepy reading that stuff because now I know that somebody was there watching and we always thought there was somebody there. We were cautious at the time ... but it's just creepy to see that was the case. On the other hand, reading the report, I don't have a sense that it was an internal person, it sounded like it was somebody who wasn't around that much" (July 5, 2008).

Barbara, whom we met earlier, told us that, among Ottawa lesbian and gay networks in the late 1970s, it was common knowledge that the offices and members of LOON and GO were watched by the RCMP. GO was formed in the fall of 1971, following the August demonstration on Parliament Hill. LOON was established in Ottawa in 1976 by lesbians who felt that GO was not meeting all their needs.[163] Marie Robertson, one of GO's founders, remembered that, outside one of the main gay activist households in Ottawa, there were often undercover cops in unmarked cars conducting surveillance work on people in the house. She reported that, on at least one occasion, a person coming out of the house went over, knocked on the car window, and told the officer to "fuck off" (July 15, 1999). This is similar to the story that Denis LeBlanc and John Duggan, who were involved in GO in its early years, told of RCMP officers in a black car conducting surveillance on a gay activist house in which signs were being made for the 1975 National Gay Rights Coalition conference demonstration. Eventually, one of the house residents took two cups of coffee out to the car and asked the officers if they would like to come up and join them.[164]

Robertson also remembered being told stories by people "who knew they had been under RCMP surveillance," including civil servants and former civil servants (July 15, 1999). She received a phone call in the mid- to late 1970s from a high-ranking secretary of state employee who was closeted at work. She refused to talk over the phone for security reasons and insisted on a personal meeting. This woman recounted that, at a meeting, views were expressed indicating that the Canadian government felt very threatened by, and fearful of, the emergence of the lesbian and gay movement.[165] She indicated that both LOON and GO were being watched. Although Robertson reported that this woman's story "got me scared" in general, she said that, during these years, activists in LOON and GO never took the threat of police surveillance "too seriously" (July 15, 1999).

RCMP documents include a surveillance report on a woman's dance held in 1977 in London, Ontario. This dance was put on by the Working Women's Alliance and was held at the Homophile Association of London Ontario (HALO) Centre. The RCMP learned of this dance because it was mentioned in the monthly calendar of events published by the Women's Resource Centre. This monitoring of feminist publications led the RCMP to conduct surveillance on lesbian-related activities. The report notes: "Discreet surveillance on 30 June 1977, revealed a sizeable turnout of women for this event. It is estimated that approximately 100 persons, mostly women were in attendance." "Discreet surveillance" probably refers to surveillance from a car parked nearby. The report mentions that some women arrived on foot and some by taxi; others could be traced to vehicles in the area. Although much of the document is blanked out, the fact that people were traced back to cars in the area could mean that a number of officers were involved in this operation. The report concludes "that the Women's Working Alliance and this Lesbian activity is related. The numbers of people involved indicate that this organization is becoming a political and social force for London women."[166] Basically, the RCMP determined that the Working Women's Alliance was an organization for lesbians (making it sound as though it were a lesbian "front"). And the statement that it was becoming a political and social force implies that it warranted continuing investigation.

RCMP surveillance of lesbian and gay dances also occurred at the University of Western Ontario and many other locations. Clippings of announcements of lesbian and gay dances were found in most of the files on the gay groups.[167] The RCMP considered lesbian and gay dances to be one source of knowledge on lesbian and gay organizations. "Subversion," for the RCMP, encompassed dances and social events as well as meetings, rallies, and demonstrations.

Whereas lesbian activists often came under the RCMP gaze, lesbian organizations, lesbians involved in the feminist movement, and lesbian social events all came under specific investigation. What is of particular interest is that, unlike gay male activists or members of the Trotskyist movement, the lesbians in the WD were conceptualized in an overtly heterosexist and patriarchal fashion. Although notions of gay men as gender inverts did not appear in these RCMP reports, such notions were present in their portrayal of "radical lesbians." Because

"Gay Political Activists" and "Radical Lesbians"

of their association with feminism and their subversion of heterosexual femininity, these radical lesbians were seen as a type of threat differing from that posed by "gay political activists."

GOVERNMENT GRANTS AND RCMP SURVEILLANCE

As part of mandatory security checks, the RCMP conducted surveillance work on gay groups who were applying for state funding. During the early 1970s, government grants were made available for various initiatives across the country, especially for employment projects oriented towards young people.[168] The period was dominated by the ideology of Keynesianism and the "welfare state"; thus, social spending was seen as a means of containing and managing social troubles.[169] This translated into an important source of funding for fledgling gay groups.

Applying for state funding was one more avenue through which gay groups came under RCMP surveillance. We do know that, in 1972-73, following an RCMP request, all applications for federal Local Initiatives Program (LIP) funding were reviewed by security services. According to Jennifer Keck, "There is little evidence that this provision was designed to hold back approval of individual projects. The review was intended to keep members of the RCMP 'abreast' of the activities of particular project sponsors."[170] A major objective of this security review was to collect more information on the groups that applied. Particular security concerns were raised when CHAT received Opportunities for Youth (OFY) (an employment program initiated by the Trudeau government and aimed at young people) funding in 1971 and then LIP funding in the early 1970s.

George Hislop, who died in October 2005, reported that he "had no direct contact with the RCMP until 1971 when the Community Homophile Association of Toronto (CHAT) had spun out of the University of Toronto Homophile Association." CHAT was fundamentally oriented towards establishing a community centre and social service support for gays and lesbians, and it grew to about four hundred members in the early 1970s. The group also warned gay men about police entrapment and initiated early legal support work for gay men charged with "sexual offences." CHAT applied for and received an OFY grant to work with street kids.[171] This may have been the first time that a gay organization received financial assistance from the Canadian government.

CHAT was awarded the grant, but Hislop was asked to stop by the house of one of the men who was influential in the disbursal of these grants:

So I got there and there were two guys there, and he introduced me to them and then he said they were from the RCMP and they were doing some sort of routine check on the backgrounds of people that were getting grants. Well, all right. And they asked me questions about who was involved in CHAT, and they were particularly interested in Brian Waite and [a lesbian who was a left-wing activist in CHAT] ... They were interested in anyone who was left wing. (August 1996)

These interviews with the RCMP were part of a security check regarding CHAT and its OFY application. Brian Waite was then heavily involved in organizing for the August 28 action on Parliament Hill.

Hislop also remembered plainclothes RCMP officers and other police coming to CHAT meetings in the early 1970s. The RCMP, and much of the media, continued to be concerned about further government grants that CHAT received in 1972 and 1973.[172] CHAT was relatively successful in getting these grants, and, in 1972, the internal LSA bulletin (included in the RCMP files) reported that, through OFY and LIP grants, "CHAT [was] financing a full-time staff of eight."[173]

In 1973, the opposition Tories criticized LIP for giving grants to "far out and leftist groups" and "Satanists."[174] The funding that CHAT had received in 1971-72 had been the subject of some debate in the mainstream media. CHAT's 1973 application to finance telephone information, counselling, and court work "was supported by the program staff and Executive Board because it satisfied the aims and criteria of LIP." As Keck points out, however, in the context of trying to keep the projects "low-key" despite "a strongly supportive review from the Executive Board, this project was rejected by the Minister [of manpower and immigration]."[175] The RCMP file suggests that CHAT's activities were consistently monitored throughout the early 1970s. It seems that the RCMP was gathering as much information as it could on CHAT and on Hislop.[176]

CHAT was not the only group affected by this form of surveillance. When Vancouver's Canadian Gay Activists Alliance (CGAA) applied for LIP funding in 1971 to provide employment prospects for homosexuals through the establishment of a community centre called the Open Doors, it also faced a security check.[177] Written at the top of the RCMP document is "No Objection." The RCMP reported that it engaged in a careful examination of Department of Manpower and Immigration grants and LIP grants before they received final approval. In April 1972, the CGAA discovered that some of its outgoing mail had been opened by the Department of National Revenue. Earlier, the CGAA discovered that its telephone had been tapped. The phone taps and mail opening

"Gay Political Activists" and "Radical Lesbians"

may be related to investigations flowing from the CGAA's funding application. In May 1972, the CGAA received an OFY grant for $9,329 for its Project Open Doors.[178]

Also in its reports on Gay Liberation Movement – University of Waterloo, the RCMP seemed particularly interested in the fact that funding for the Operation Socrates Handbook, which it used to identify what it called "active Canadian gay groups," came from an OFY project.[179] Clearly, surveillance relating to state funding applications provided yet another means for spying on gay and lesbian groups.

GATE VANCOUVER: THE RCMP SEES DANGER IN ITS INFLUENCE

Given that it had connections to the LSA and the YS, and given that it was one of the more militant gay rights groups in the country, GATE-V was the object of considerable RCMP surveillance in the early 1970s. According to an article in the *Body Politic*, GATE-V, founded in June 1971, evolved out of the GLF, which viewed gay liberation as "part of a wider revolutionary movement" and did not concern "itself with the problems of the gay community only." GATE opened it doors just as the GLF folded. GATE founders stated that it was "founded by gays who had been in the GLF until they felt it could not provide the means for organizing gays. They criticized the undemocratic and unstructured forms of GLF pointing out that it allowed a small group of leaders to speak and act in the name of the group without being responsible to the membership for their words and actions. They felt that a gay liberation organization would encourage all gays to join and fight for liberation, not just those who considered themselves 'revolutionaries.'"[180]

In a very different kind of text, the RCMP reported on a 1972 sociology lecture given at Vancouver City College by members of GATE-V. Its title was "Homosexuality in Today's Society." Clearly, an informant was present in the lecture hall (and may even have been an RCMP member who was enrolled in the class). The investigator reported learning that GATE was an offshoot of the now defunct Canadian Gay Liberation Movement (probably the Gay Liberation Front) and that its main objectives were guaranteed freedom for homosexuals, restructuring the Criminal Code, and gaining more recognition of the legal rights of homosexuals. Under "Investigator's Comments," it is noted that "all the subjects" had a good background knowledge of homosexuality and spoke about "the alleged" wrongs against it. An interesting comment indicates that

10 Maurice Flood, of GATE-V, in a media scrum regarding the *Gay Tide* case at the Supreme Court in Ottawa (May 22, 1979) | *Credit:* CGLA 1986-032_10P (55) 06P

the speakers were articulate and that they "put forward a convincing argument in favour of the homosexuals' cause." We get a sense that this RCMP investigator is learning about something new. At this time, GATE-V was seen as of such significance that a talk given by its members at a community college warranted RCMP surveillance.[181]

The RCMP also used clippings from the *Province*, the *Vancouver Sun*, the *Grape*, and the *Georgia Straight* to monitor GATE-V's activities in the early 1970s. The *Georgia Straight* ran a GATE column called "Gateway" and sometimes "Gateline."[182] The RCMP was also aware of GATE's publication, *Gay Tide*, which was the focus of a long legal battle between GATE and the *Sun* after the latter refused to print an ad for the gay liberation paper. This case eventually went to the Supreme Court, where it was lost (see Photo 10).[183]

An RCMP assessment of GATE-V was completed in 1973. This was in response to a request from D Branch, which dealt with the LSA and the YS. Once again we see how notions of Trotskyist infiltration organized the surveillance of gay groups. The RCMP reported that GATE had about sixteen members and

"Gay Political Activists" and "Radical Lesbians"

that it wanted to change the Human Rights Act to include sexual orientation protection in the Human Rights Code. In assessing GATE, the report argues that "[blanked out] if all factors remain constant GATE grouping would remain much as it is, about the same size, and with the same effect – none." This is an extremely dismissive evaluation, given the important gay rights activities in which the group was engaged. At the same time, the report argues that, "due to the fact that bigotry and discrimination does to a degree exist against a minority of at least 5 percent of the population in British Columbia, there exists the danger of GATE exposing themselves to a large number of the public through media of GATE and drawing cadre of a liberal and left nature to make themselves a real force."[184] The figure of 5 percent is half the number usually cited by gay activists, who drew on the Kinsey Report.[185] While the report recognizes that "bigotry and discrimination does to a degree exist," it also sees the possibility of danger, especially if GATE's influence were to grow. "Danger" is another loose and fluid term in national security discourse; like "subversive" and "national security risk," it can be expanded and contracted within different historical contexts. In any case, the growth of gay political activism introduced a new "danger."

According to this 1973 report, GATE had difficulties distributing its materials. Apparently, some of the gay clubs were refusing materials due to "hostility" from club owners and even some patrons. Also mentioned is the weak distribution of the *Body Politic* in Vancouver. Still, it points out that an "increase in available gay publications should increase awareness and radicalization of the gay populace in BC. Unless another stronger group takes the initiative – a liberal grouping – leadership and direction of what could be a real force in the gay community and in the community as a whole could fall into the hands of GATE."[186]

The report's core argument is contradictory. On the one hand, it concludes that GATE, continuing at its present level of organization, would have no effect; on the other hand, it suggests, that with the support of a left organization (the LSA), GATE could become a "real force." Liberalism is projected as the alternative to gay political activism. Positioned as a more moderate perspective, liberalism is seen as supporting the existing social order and is counterposed to more radical gay political activism: "GATE therefore is a very possible force unless a large community based 'liberal' force is established which ... would work politically on a low level as well as having a social purpose." The gay liberal approach is given some content here as the report differentiates between gay political activist groups and those groups who may engage in political action on some level but whose main focus is on social activities. These RCMP documents suggest that, unlike less militant groups, groups such as GATE-V are a danger requiring surveillance.

The report also mentions links between GATE-V, the LSA, and the YS. In assessing GATE, it argues: "The League for Socialist Action (LSA) [blanked out] will also be an important factor in GATE. If the Trot paper carried regular 'gay' columns or news and if the party decides to support gay liberation there might be additional forces thrown into GATE, which would make growth easier. Decisions made by the Trotskyist executive would be of a higher calling than those made by [blanked out]." This seems to be a reference to the internal discussions within the LSA regarding support for gay/lesbian liberation, which stalled in 1972 and then went into reverse in the later 1970s. It suggests an awareness of the debates occurring inside the LSA on the gay question as well as the tensions between the LSA leadership and lesbian and gay activists in the LSA (which led some GATE-V members to leave the latter). Under "Investigator's Comments" are remarks on the LSA's relationship with GATE: "it would seem that GATE is not likely to make much headway unless the LSA recognizes and supports their cause; which to date they have not done."[187] The RCMP feared that, with LSA support, GATE would become a more formidable organization.

A second organizational assessment of GATE was conducted in 1975 in response to a request from A Ops, the Ottawa Security and Intelligence Branch, and it used an official "Organizational Assessment Form," which was designed to cover unions or left political organizations. Under "Affiliations and or Links" is listed the "League for Socialist Action/Young Socialists, Vancouver"; under "Membership" is listed "Approximately 16 (5-3-73)." In response to the request for information, the local RCMP consulted its files and looked at earlier reports. Under "Current Executive," the year given is "1973." This suggests that, after 1973, surveillance of GATE-V diminished and that information is drawn from the earlier period. The RCMP also commented: "In 1973-1974 the GATE executive was comprised of members and former members of the League for Socialist Action and of the Young Socialists in Vancouver. These members subsequently quit the Trotskyist movement to pursue their social interests in the homosexual GATE and there are no known Trotskyist members presently within this 'gay' group."[188] As far as the RCMP was concerned, in order to be a Trotskyist, one had to be a member of an organization; one could not be an independent Trotskyist.

A number of these GATE activists left the LSA because of a lack of support for and recognition of the gay struggle. This coincided with the period during which Brian Waite, John Wilson, Maurice Flood, and others left the LSA. The report concludes: "membership or participation in the activities of this group

"Gay Political Activists" and "Radical Lesbians"

in the absence of involvement in a Communist or Trotskyist organization is not indicative of Communist or Trotskyist sympathies or affiliation."[189] The central focus of this organizational review is concern over the involvement of the LSA and the YS. It implies that, with the passing danger of "Trotskyist infiltration," there was less reason for active surveillance of GATE-V.

Surveillance of left groups and movements in the 1970s led the RCMP to perceive the connections between these groups and gay and lesbian liberation movements. Prompted by these new queer activists and their ties to Trotskyists and feminists, the RCMP generated new categories of "gay political activists" and "radical lesbians" as threats to the national security state. In attempting to handle this new public and visible movement, the RCMP was forced to modify its surveillance practices. As gay and lesbian movements and community formation became more visible, sexual policing was escalated against their public character by the mid-1970s with the Ottawa "sex scandal" and the Olympic "clean-up" campaign. The next chapter deals with the mobilization efforts against this intensified policing and the generation of cross-country gay/lesbian rights organizing that challenged the Canadian war on queers.

Sexual Policing and National Security
Sex Scandals, Olympic Clean-Ups, and Cross-Country Organizing

ESCALATING POLICE REPRESSION: THE OTTAWA SEX SCANDAL AND THE OLYMPIC CLEAN-UP CAMPAIGN

The reassertion of sexual policing in the mid- to late 1970s coincided with the growing visibility of the gay and lesbian movements and gay community formation. The provisions of the 1969 Criminal Code reform mandated a clampdown on the public visibility of gays and, to a lesser extent, on that of lesbians, especially on any visibility of queer sexualities. The gay movement's response to this escalated sexual policing in the Montreal clean-up campaign prior to the Olympics led to it being perceived as a security issue requiring more RCMP and police surveillance. Since this section addresses the situation in Ottawa, with regard to both the emergence of a gay movement and the intensification of sexual policing directed against it, we start with narratives about police surveillance and the genesis of a gay movement in Ottawa.

Surveillance and Ottawa Community and Movement Formation: "We knew the RCMP was watching"
As the capital and the epicentre of the national security campaigns, Ottawa was hit especially hard by RCMP surveillance. This affected gay and lesbian community formation and the emergence of gay and lesbian movements. Charles Hill, a gay activist who moved to Ottawa in the 1970s, remembered stories about people being photographed in the Lord Elgin and hustlers being taken outside

and asked for the names of gay men. He had a sense that the RCMP was watching GO, but he had no proof (February 20, 1995).

David Garmaise was involved in GO and became central to the operations of the NGRC.[1] He described the impact of the security campaigns on gay community formation in Ottawa:

> We knew that they had files on us. Without having proof of it we knew. One of the first memories I have in coming out ... is going to the Lord Elgin and somebody saying, "See that car down the street, that's the RCMP. They take pictures of people going into this bar." We just lived under that and we didn't care. We knew that they were doing that ... Ottawa, being a civil service town, was very closety and remained closety throughout the seventies and maybe into the eighties because we knew the RCMP was watching. Some of us were out and it didn't matter, but a lot of people were nervous about that and were afraid to go out to the bars. Or were afraid to do more than go out to the bars. After awhile I think people knew that they stopped taking pictures and people were a little more okay with going out. But they were afraid to be really public and to have their name known. Many, many people – it was not just in Ottawa, but it was particularly acute in Ottawa – lived a double life. They were one person in the bars and another person by day. (May 13, 2000)

Security surveillance and the fear of it was a major presence. It entered into people's work, social, and sexual lives. At the same time, prohibitions against homosexuals in state employment were being relaxed in some areas. Garmaise described his experiences with security checks in his work at the post office:

> By '74/'75 I was already fairly openly out at work. I was visited once by the RCMP at work when they were doing a security clearance on someone I knew that had given my name as a reference. It was a straight woman; she wasn't gay. They were checking her background. And they came and asked me questions about her. And they asked me questions something along the lines of, "Does she go to that club that you go to?" Or they might have mentioned the name, which was the Club Private, which was a gay bar in Ottawa that was sort of a private club ... And I said, "No. As far as I know she is not a member and she does not go." But it is obvious to me that they were not checking about her background, they were checking to see if I was open. At least that is the inference. And I was perfectly open about it and there was nothing further. But I think they were checking up on me and not her with that particular question.

They threw it in the middle of a bunch of innocuous questions. I think that my name turned up on her list of references, and they cross-checked it and, "Oh, let's go see this guy." I think it is indicative of the fact [that] by that time things had changed quite significantly from a decade earlier.

While the RCMP clearly had Garmaise's name on its list of suspected or even confirmed homosexuals, by the mid-1970s his being out at work led to no negative consequences; however, for gays and lesbians in the public service who were not out, major problems continued, as they did for all queers in the military and the RCMP.

Garmaise joined Gays of Ottawa in the early 1970s. He remembered that GO undertook many actions for gay and lesbian rights: "We did a lot of demonstrating over the years, spurred on by the big one on the Hill [in 1971]. There was nothing that big until '75 when we had the conference here. But there were a lot of pickets" (May 13, 2000). A 1976 Ottawa Security Service report notes that GO demonstrated peacefully.[2] GO also supported feminist activities and the October 14, 1976, general strike organized by the Canadian Labour Congress against wage controls.

The 1975 Ottawa "Homosexual Vice-Ring" Investigation

In March 1975, eighteen men, who were customers, as well as the owner of a male modelling and dating agency, were arrested and charged with sexual offences in what the media dubbed the "Ottawa sex scandal." Organized by the Ottawa police and mainstream media coverage, the intended moral panic produced by this "sex scandal" included a social reaction against gay men.[3] The police released information to the media as charges were laid, and the media published the names, ages, marital status, complete addresses, and occupations (a number were public servants) of all those charged. These men were charged with "contributing to juvenile delinquency," "gross indecency," or "buggery." The charges related to activities involving men between the ages of sixteen and twenty-one. Thirteen of the men were charged with gross indecency or buggery, which, given that these acts were then entirely criminalized, meant they were accused of having consensual sex with males between the ages of sixteen and twenty-one.[4] The clients of the male prostitutes involved were the only people charged. It was implied that this prostitution network involved civil servants at the highest levels. This initiated panic in the public service regarding possibilities for exposure, firing, or demotion. Among those charged were the parliamentary reporter of a television network, an RCMP corporal, a university professor, and several highly placed civil servants.

The context for the social organization of this scandal was a moral campaign to "clean up" the city. It focused initially on body rub parlours but shifted to include the clients and the owner of the male modelling agency.[5] On March 3, 1975, the Ottawa police held a media conference at which police superintendent Thomas Flanagan stated: "This is the most sordid crime we've investigated for some time."[6] The police accused the men of being clients of a "male prostitution ring," and much of the Ottawa media amplified this with headlines such as "Male Prostitution Ring Broken," "Boys in Slavery Ring," and "White Slavery Ring."[7] The police alleged a "homosexual vice-ring."[8] The *Ottawa Citizen* and the *Ottawa Journal* consistently employed the term "vice ring," implying that the clients had something to do with the organization of a prostitution service. As the *Body Politic* put it, "They exploited the widely held hostility to gay people by conjuring up the existence (still unproven) of a 'homosexual male prostitute ring' that reputedly involved eleven-year-old boys hired out for rates of $30 to $60 per hour. No pre-teenagers were ever shown to have been involved."[9]

Many of these men were outed, setting in motion the stigmatizing practices of heterosexism.[10] In this case, a social course of action initiated by police activity that made use of the Criminal Code and that also involved media coverage led to the public labelling and stigmatization of these men as homosexuals and, in a number of cases, to their loss of employment. Outing has a long history when it comes to arrests for male homosexual sex (whether or not these men identify as homosexuals) as the identities of those arrested have often been released to the media and printed in the newspapers. It was quite common for men (and sometimes women) accused of same-gender sexual acts to be punished by having their names (and sometimes addresses) published in the media prior to any conviction for these offences.

This amounts to a special form of punishment, and it is a practice of discrimination based on sexuality. The release of information about these sex charges is used to homosexualize these men and to organize discrimination against them. This police-media relation mobilized heterosexist social reactions against homosexuality as well as against being involved in prostitution. This includes the social reaction of employers as well as friends and family members to the news that an individual had been labelled a homosexual. As a result, individuals caught in this mobilization could experience discrimination at work, including termination of their employment.

There is a critical distinction between coming out (a decision made by the individual) to others and naming oneself as a gay man, lesbian, bisexual, or queer, and being outed by others (not based on a decision to identify oneself as queer to others), especially by the police and mass media. Outing is done without an individual's consent. Outing individuals through police and media action leads to special punishment of them, setting them up for harassment and discrimination. In some cases, these individuals may not be gay or bisexual or identify themselves as such.

In his investigation, George Smith describes how the "ideology of fag" operates in the lives of young men in high school. According to Smith, the stigmatizing label of "fag" works to cut these students out of regular social interaction. Labelling someone a fag does not involve simply employing a word; rather, it involves using a word, in the context of heterosexist social relations, as a weapon. To label and stigmatize someone as a fag is to set him up as a target for gossip, verbal abuse, harassment, and even violence. The term is part of a broader ideological practice that mobilizes social practices stigmatizing homosexuality.[11]

Labelling these men as homosexual works in the same way as labelling students as fags: it mobilizes a social course of action that takes a number of forms, ranging from the loss of friends or the disruptions of friendships, to the disruption or ripping apart of family relationships, to the disruption of relations with workmates, to the loss of employment or social status, to various forms of harassment, and, in the most extreme cases, to acts of violence against those identified as queer. It can also create a situation in which the men charged and outed as gay can see no way out and so take their own lives.

This Ottawa experience was not an isolated one; rather, it was part of a course of social action mobilized through the Criminal Code and police practices that criminalized sex between men. In turn, these actions led, through the media, to the public identification of these men as homosexuals and fed this information into the national security campaigns against gays. The police had the social power to criminalize these men's lives and to drag them into court. The media, through publishing personal information provided by the police, produced a social reaction, informed by heterosexism, against these individuals. This reaction was often extended to include the response of employers to the news that one of their employees was homosexual and had been arrested for alleged sex "crimes." This was also tied into the national security campaigns against homosexuals in the public service, which designated an identified homosexual as a person suffering from a character weakness and as a possible security risk, thus mandating his/her demotion or firing.

One of the men charged, Warren Zufelt, a thirty-four-year-old civil servant, returned to his apartment in March after his first court appearance on a charge of gross indecency. He wrote a short note – "Forgive me, I have no other choice" – climbed to the thirteenth floor and jumped to his death. The context within which he made his decision to commit suicide was created through this combined police/media social practice of discrimination. As the *Body Politic* editorialized, "Did he perhaps believe that he had no other choice because despite the outcome of a court trial, he was already destroyed? Destroyed by police politicking and media sensationalism: by having his name publicly 'stigmatized' with those twin labels abhorred by our social morality; Homosexuality and Prostitution."[12] The consequences of this police-media relation did not end with Zufelt's death. Eight of the accused required psychiatric care thanks to the legal ordeal, hate letters, and phone calls they received. Nine of the men charged were fired, suspended, or changed jobs. Two Ottawa policemen were charged with assault for roughing up one of the alleged clients.[13]

On March 20, 1975, GO picketed the police station and the *Ottawa Journal* to protest Zufelt's death, police persecution of gays, and biased reporting in the media as well as to call for a uniform age of consent for all sexual acts. The age of consent for homosexual acts in private was still set at twenty-one. GO representatives argued that anti-gay discrimination, the police, and the media had killed Zufelt.[14] GO also registered a complaint to the Ontario Press Council against the *Ottawa Citizen* for its sensationalist and biased coverage of the "Ottawa Sex Scandal." Its complaint cited the use of terms such as "vice ring" as inflammatory. GO also registered a complaint with the attorney general of Ontario regarding police practices in the arrests of the men charged, especially the ways in which the Ottawa Morality Squad handled the laying of charges and the releasing of the names of the accused. Both complaints were rejected.[15] In recognition of this tragedy, GO established the Warren Zufelt Memorial Defence Fund to help pay the legal expenses of those charged.

The protests against this police operation and its media coverage had an important impact. As David Garmaise recalled,

> My main memory of the vice-ring ... was that it turned the media around. Because this guy jumped off the roof and killed himself there was this horror at what the media had done. And the media was feeling a little guilty [for publishing names] and that brought about a sea change in media attitudes towards our organization. The coverage became much more favourable after that, as if they were making amends or as if this had woken them up in some way. I think most of the cases were thrown out of court. I imagine the effect would have been mostly negative in the short term, in terms of people being scared to do anything because this might happen to them. Maybe in the longer term it was a bit more positive since it turned the media around and advanced our cause. (May 13, 2000)

The outcome of this operation included one suicide and the guilty plea of Michel Gavel, the owner of the modelling agency, to operating a common bawdy house and to gross indecency. After the other trials were completed, not one of the other sixteen received either a jail term or a fine; the charges were dismissed or the men were given absolute discharges or suspended sentences.[16]

Paul-François Sylvestre, who worked for the federal government, was caught up in this vice investigation. He worked for the secretary of state in the summer of 1970 and was then hired in a permanent position in March 1971. He had no problems with his first security check, which occurred around 1974. In late 1975, he began to get involved with GO and started to come out:

> When I had my trial on the vice investigation it came out in the *Citizen* on the first page that I was one of the people charged ... I never read the *Citizen* so I was not even aware that this was being printed. I had received a visit of two police officers and they had questioned me. They said, "Look, we're not interested in arresting you, we want to nail down the pimps, the ones that run this ring. We just want a statement." And I was foolish enough to give them a statement and sign it and I thought it was over ... And they came back ... a week or two later saying that I was charged. (January 2, 1996)

The police visit was part of an information-gathering operation, and Sylvestre was charged with gross indecency.

After the *Citizen*'s publication of the article that included this charge, Sylvestre told us, he was approached by the minister's executive assistant: "[The assistant said,] 'The minister is very pleased with your work, he's not interested in your private life. You're innocent until proven guilty so we're continuing as before.' I think he might have mentioned that there would not ... necessarily [be] many public engagements; like, he wouldn't go out of his way to have me appear in public with the minister. But I would still do the same work in the office and all that." Due to a miscalculation on the part of the police and the Crown, Sylvestre's trial ended with an interesting twist:

> My case was brought to court ... They brought in – what they call the vice-ring, they had a number of the young men. I know I asked the guy who came to my place if he was eighteen and he said, "Yes." I don't think he was, but I really didn't know it was twenty-one anyway. So when my case was brought to court the policemen came in and there were these young men in the court house. My lawyer told me that the policeman had brought in these kids to identify me. And what they found was that the kids they had brought in that day had

never come to my place. So, as soon as the trial started, the policeman asked that the case be remanded because they knew it wouldn't lead to anything. But my lawyer immediately rose and said, "Look, this is an abuse of my client's rights" – they didn't have any proof, they didn't have anyone that had come to my place, and [were] they going to bring me again to court and find out again that it wasn't this person? And [he pointed out] that they were putting me through a lot of stress. And the judge said my lawyer was right. That the policeman didn't do his job properly, so the case was dismissed.

The effect that the "scandal" had on the other men brought to trial was more severe. Sylvestre was visited by another man who worked for the government who had been charged. In his account of their conversation, we begin to see the devastating consequences of these charges:

He said, "Oh, can I have a chat with you?" And he closed the door and he said that he had also been charged and [that] he was really having a hard time ... deal[ing] with this and [that] he couldn't work and he couldn't understand how I was being so calm and not asking for a leave of absence and [that] he was going to leave for at least a few months. I imagine that I told him that I was gay and openly gay with my friends and family. And I think he was probably married and a closet case ... I never saw him after that. (January 2, 1996)

Suffering from fear and anxiety, this man could have lost his government job or been demoted or transferred. The Ottawa sex scandal had an important impact on public servants in the city, reinforcing for many the relations of the closet and living a double life. GO's partially successful resistance to this attempted moral panic forced a certain opening up of the mass media to gay and lesbian concerns.

Due to departmental reorganization, Sylvestre received a new security clearance in 1976. He received his secret clearance but not his top secret clearance. This may also have been related to the charge and the court case, even though the charge had been dismissed:

So I had to fill out a form at one point, and I had to give some references or people that they could call upon to have more information on my character ... They probably had my name because of the vice-ring thing, in some file ... I know that they met [a woman in the same branch with whom he had become quite friendly] – and we were having lunch almost on a daily basis, and she said, "Oh, this RCMP guy came and asked me if you smoked marijuana, if you drank, if you were gay." And she said that when they asked [her] that question she told them, ... "If you asked the question you already know the answer." She said the RCMP officer didn't insist. I don't know if they were looking for a confirmation, but by that time my book had been published so it wasn't something secret.[17] I wasn't in the closet, so no one could tell me, "If you don't give me this cultural policy on film production we'll let the minister know that you are a risk to national security." ... So there was no possibility of me or Charlie Hill ... who ... had security clearances to be in a position to be blackmailed. So that's the only time that I heard that the RCMP had asked about the fact that I was gay. (January 2, 1996)

Sylvestre was able to keep his job because he had the support of those higher up in his division and was seen as a valuable member of his department.

The 1975-76 Olympic Clean-Up

As mentioned previously, many of the reports on gay groups to which we have gained access were written in response to a request for information from the Montreal Security Service. For instance, a report on gay groups in Toronto states: "This is in reply to Montreal Security Service Request of 14-6-76 on File IP215-11, requiring information on gay activities and organizational assessments for SPCUM." The RCMP in Montreal was requesting information from other RCMP divisions both for itself and for the Montreal city police.[18] The Montreal police were encountering a new problem in gay activist organizing – a problem that they had not encountered since the Front de libération des homosexuels in the early 1970s. We also see important connections here between national security, social and moral cleansing (i.e., the cleaning-up of "undesirable" groups), and sexual policing.[19]

This request was made in response to the 1975-76 Olympic clean-up campaign and, especially, the June 19, 1976, demonstration that was being organized by gay and lesbian activists in order to protest it (see Photo 11). It is standard for clean-up campaigns against "vice," including against the gay scene, to be organized prior to major public events. According to Sylvestre, "An employee of the organizing Committee of the Olympic Games has said that a directive was circulated giving specific instructions that all 'non-conforming elements' of which homosexuals are included, must be confined and made hidden."[20] In this case, the police used legislation that allowed them to criminalize consensual homosexual sex.

The growing police action also responded to the public visibility of gay establishments, gay community formation, and gay sexualities. In particular,

11 Demonstration against police repression in the lead-up to the 1976 Olympics, Montreal, June 19, 1976 | *Credit:* CLGA 1986-032_08P (28) 01P

the police began to use bawdy-house legislation against gay bars and bathhouses. Bawdy-house legislation was originally designed to deal with female prostitution; however, in 1917, in an attempt to have it cover massage parlours, it was broadened to include places habitually resorted to for "acts of indecency."[21] Under the Criminal Code, gay sexual activity could be constructed as acts of indecency, with the result that the bawdy-house legislation could still be used against consensual gay sex. Charging an individual as a "found-in" at a common bawdy house required periodic surveillance by undercover police, who could claim that the place was habitually resorted to for acts of indecency.[22] Considered public in character, these sexual acts fell under the jurisdiction of the police and the Criminal Code.

In February 1975, the relative quiet between police and gay establishments was brutally ended by a raid on Sauna Aquarius when thirty-five men were charged as found-ins. This was the first time the bawdy-house legislation was used against a gay establishment; raids and arrests made in baths, bars, and washrooms continued through the spring of 1975. In October 1975, seven gay and lesbian bars were raided by police as part of an attempt to "clean" gays out of downtown bars and public places. This included a raid on Baby Face, a popular lesbian bar. At Baby Face, anyone who did not have a piece of identification was taken to the station and released only if a parent or close friend could provide proof of her age. In November, police arrested about eighty men in the downtown core, including at the Limelight bar.[23]

In 1976, police repression intensified. In January, following two nights of surveillance by undercover officers, the Club Baths of Montreal was raided, and thirty-four men were arrested as found-ins. Given a master key to open all the doors, the police preferred an axe, causing over $500 in damage.[24] In May the raids took on a more "ferocious" character, according to gay historian Ross Higgins.[25] The police raided the Neptune Sauna, forcing their way into cubicles, using flash cameras to take pictures, and arresting eighty-nine men. Some of the men arrested during the raid reported that the police told them that they "were cleaning things up."[26] The notion of maintaining cleanliness, associating gay sex with dirt, has often been invoked to justify the moral regulation central to sexual policing.

The police also seized the membership list for both the Neptune Sauna and the Club Baths. This was a clear attempt to intimidate thousands of men in Montreal. In a press release, the police claimed they were interested in dismantling a major venue for prostitution. The argument that gay baths were fronts for prostitution was also advanced as justification for the raids on Toronto gay baths in 1981. No evidence was provided to further this theory. In May 1976, continuing their campaign, the police again raided the Club Baths, this time charging twenty-six men as found-ins. That same month, they also raided the Sauna Cristal, three gay bars, and Jilly's (a lesbian bar). At Jilly's, patrons were lined up against the wall and searched, and police came in armed with submachine guns. At the Stork Club, patrons were photographed by the police.[27] As the *Body Politic* reported: "For a short period in late May and early June, all the baths in Montreal were closed ... For a lot of men in Montreal, their first experience of the great Olympic 'clean-up' was the sight of a police-man's axe crashing through the door of their room at the baths."[28]

These raids created major upheaval in gay and lesbian networks and in the emerging gay and lesbian communities in Montreal. As Paul-François Sylvestre argues: "Although the police launched a clean-up campaign in order to rid Montreal of its homosexual elements, the exact opposite was reached."[29] An organization called the Comité homosexuel anti-répression/Gay Coalition against Repression (CHAR) was set up with representatives from various Montreal gay groups. It brought together French- and English-speaking activists despite previous linguistic and political tensions. On June 19, more than three hundred gays, lesbians, and supporters joined in one of the largest gay rights demonstration up to that point. It was organized by CHAR and protested pre-Olympic clean-up raids. Demonstrators marched through downtown Montreal chanting: "À bas la repression policière!" (Down with police repression!). The marchers demanded an end to the raids and the dropping of all charges. The protest passed the offices of Premier Bourassa, the Olympic Organizing Committee, and City Hall, and the rally was addressed by the NGRC, GO, GATE-T, the women's contingent of the demonstration, and the LSA/LSO.[30]

This organizing and the plans for the demonstration led the RCMP to appeal for more information on gay activism across the Canadian state. It was trying to secure intelligence information for the Montreal police, thus demonstrating the continuing connection of RCMP surveillance and monitoring of gay/lesbian organizing to the criminalization of queer sexual activities. On June 24, 1976, gay activist Stuart Russell, along with four others, was fired from the Olympic Organizing Committee for political activity. Russell was fired two days after a picture showing him at the June 19 demonstration appeared in Montreal's *La Presse*.[31] The activism of CHAR led to the creation of L'association pour les droits des gai(e)s du Québec, which became the main organization fighting for human rights for gays and lesbians in Quebec. Resistance to the Olympic repression helped to set the stage for the rebellious response to the raid on the Truxx bar. In this raid, which took place in October 1977, 146 men were arrested and charged as found-ins in a common bawdy house. In response, more than two thousand gay men, lesbians, and supporters took to the streets, closing down a major downtown artery. Along with lobbying by L'association pour les droits des gai(e)s du Québec, this produced the context within which sexual orientation protection was quietly added to provincial human rights legislation in 1977.[32]

Because Toronto and Ottawa also held Olympic events, the RCMP investigated gay groups in southern Ontario. In Toronto, this took the form of a meeting with a gay activist. Tom Warner, president of GATE-T at the time, told us that, in the 1970s, "we just took for granted" that the group was under police surveillance. In early March 1976, Warner received a call at home from an RCMP officer in charge of security for the Olympics (July 15, 1999). This "unnerved" him since the RCMP clearly knew how to contact him. This was an attempt to intimidate him. The RCMP's ability to contact Warner rested on prior monitoring and surveillance work. The police wanted to come by his home to ask him some questions, but he asked them to meet him at the GATE office on Carlton Street (July 15, 1999). Two plainclothes RCMP officers visited the GATE office on March 10, 1976, and questioned Warner. John Tyler and Lawrence Lafond, of the RCMP Security Service, asked what plans GATE and the gay movement were making in connection with the July Olympics. Warner told them that the gay movement "was non-violent and peaceful" and that he knew of no such plans at present but that they could materialize if police harassment of the Montreal gay community continued (July 15, 1999). The two officers indicated that other gay organizations could expect similar visits in the near future. That same month, three police officers stationed in the Toronto area visited the apartment of a contributor to the *Body Politic*.[33] Warner also remembered that the Ontario Provincial Police (OPP) and the Toronto police undertook surveillance on the gay movement in Toronto and that there was a report of a possible undercover cop taking photographs of the collective house where he lived with other gay activists (July 15, 1999).

In the lead-up to the Olympics, the Club Baths in Ottawa was raided on May 22, 1978. This was the first raid of its kind in Ottawa and was likely coordinated with the Montreal police. It led to the arrest of twenty-seven men: twenty-two as found-ins, three as "keepers" (staff and sometimes owners), and two for gross indecency. As in Montreal, the police refused the master key and entered rooms by smashing in doors. They also seized the club membership list, securing more than three thousand names.[34] David Garmaise of GO and the NGRC remembered: "Our feeling was that it wasn't so much for surveillance – it was to clean up the gay scene so that tourists wouldn't see it. In other words, if they could [have] close[d] the baths for the period of the Olympics they would have. They were raiding the baths as a way of attempting to do that ... We were all in Kingston that weekend [when the raid took place] at a meeting of the Ontario gay coalition [Coalition for Gay Rights in Ontario].[35] We rushed back to Ottawa to deal with it. We stated that it was connected to the Olympics ... We did a press conference and a media release and got a lot of coverage" (May 13, 2000). The Kingston conference, which consisted of fifteen Ontario groups and was attended by eighty people, voiced its opposition to these arrests. At the conference, Russell, who was still an employee of the Olympic Organizing Committee, informed participants that a directive was circulating to the effect that "nonconforming elements," including gays, were to be "driven underground" from Quebec City to Toronto for the period of the Olympics.[36]

The three members of the GO executive who returned to Ottawa sent out a media release and leafleted the bars to announce a special meeting of GO regarding the raid. On May 24, GO held a media conference, which received significant coverage, linking the arrests to the Olympic clean-up campaign. GO stated that it would not tolerate police harassment in the context of the

Olympics or at any other time.[37] In a May 27 NGRC news release, Denis Le Blanc, then president of GO, stated:

> We know from the chain of events themselves, from remarks made by policemen during their raid of the Neptune Baths [in Montreal], and from inside information which we have obtained from people with confidential information on Olympic security, that this is part of a concerted, national effort aimed at "cleaning up" Canada for the Olympic Games. This effort is not directed solely at gay people. It is common knowledge that police forces have been visiting leftist groups and other organizations which might want to demonstrate during the Games. You are also aware of the stories from Montreal about drunks and winos being given sentences six to eight times their normal lengths in order to keep them off the streets. We have just returned from Kingston where the local prisons are full of drunks who have been given six month sentences instead of the usual couple of days. Our information is that this clean-up extends from Québec City through to Toronto.[38]

GO also heard that, given its previous experience with the "vice scandal," the death of Zufelt, and the actions of GO, the *Ottawa Citizen* had decided against publishing the names of those charged as found-ins. Gay activism in the city had opened up some space for the city's public servants, suggesting they were not now as likely as they were before to get their names printed in the paper if they were charged for homosexual offences. GO's earlier activism in response to the vice scandal produced more favourable media coverage in Ottawa than was the case in Montreal, where the gay/lesbian movements had put much less pressure on the mainstream media. On May 28, fifty people gathered to picket at police headquarters in the largest protest of this kind in Ottawa up to that point. GO also referred the men who had been charged to sympathetic lawyers and offered counselling to those shattered by the raids.[39]

David remembered aspects of the bawdy-house raid on the Club Baths. He pointed out that the police

> wanted to make it seem that they were saving the city from all the gay people ... And what they did, they sent one man in just dressed in casual clothes. I knew several people who were in attendance, the owner and so on. They were all friends of mine at the time. And this one policeman went in, a very husky good-looking guy ... He went and checked in as though he were a person wanting just to partake in the pleasures of the bathhouse. A friend of mine ... was an attendant in those days. He had been sharing the duties at the front

desk and handing out towels and so on. So he got the manager to allow him to go in and see whether he can check out this gentleman. And so shortly after he got in there [the cubicle this man had chosen], the person who I knew performed oral sex on the policeman right to the point of the policeman having orgasm. As soon as this happened, the policeman then identified himself as police, blew a whistle, and they broke down the back door, went in and arrested everybody there. [They] stole or took the ... whole roster of men from Club Baths. The policeman then said that my friend had made a pass at him. Well, the "pass" was far more than a "pass." Now it could be that my friend had made the first move ... but the policeman did not turn him down. The policeman enjoyed himself immensely and waited for the business to be over before he called in the rest. (May 12, 1994)

This officer who had been sent in earlier helped to determine whether "indecent acts" were being performed – acts that would justify classifying the Club Baths as a bawdy house under the Criminal Code. David pointed out that the police also seized the membership lists, which included the names of many public servants and members of the military, thus causing a great deal of fear and anxiety in Ottawa gay and bisexual networks:

They took all of the membership lists. These people were all members of the letter club that I belonged to. So they got the lists of the letter club too. Of course, when they started going over the list, the thing got a lot of publicity. And the first paper announced they would be giving away the names of not only the people who had been found [there] but also listing all the people on the [lists]. But then they started finding very influential names. Senior officers in all branches of the armed forces, senior officers in the RCMP, Ottawa police, politicians and so on. And so, the whole thing was dropped as far as passing out names. (May 12, 1994)

In January 1977, charges were dismissed against sixteen of the twenty-two men arrested as found-ins in the Club Baths. In pre-sentencing remarks to several employees of the Club Baths Ottawa, who pled guilty to common bawdy-house charges, Judge Thomas R. Swabey of the Ontario Provincial Court (Criminal Division) stated that the protections granted to gay people through the 1969 Criminal Code reform "might not extend to people performing sexual acts in a place such as a gay steam bath." These were considered public acts, not private acts. Initially, Judge Swabey assessed a fine of $1,000. When it was pointed out that this was twice the maximum amount permitted by the Criminal Code, he reduced it. In the fall of 1976, Peter Maloney, former manager of Club Baths Ottawa, pled guilty and was fined $500; three others pled guilty to being "inmates" and were fined $100 each.[40]

The escalation of sexual policing, especially in the context of the clean-up campaign prior to the Olympics, led to a major activist response. In reaction to this, the RCMP extended its surveillance of gay activism, demonstrating that national security and sexual policing were linked. The emergence of the gay and lesbian movement and the visibility of gay community formation set the stage for an intensification of sexual policing. At the same time, the visible and militant response in Montreal and Ottawa to the clean-up campaign undermined these police actions. After the raid on the Club Baths in Ottawa, the raids stopped. As the *Body Politic* somewhat over-optimistically put it: "We may have pulled it off. Gay people, drawn to the movement in numbers as never before, may have aborted this country's most organized and vicious attack on gay people."[41] In fact, this situation led up to the massive bath raids in Toronto in the late 1970s and early 1980s and to a further intensification of sexual policing.

NGRC AND THE RCMP RESPONSE: "BECAUSE THIS CAMPAIGN IS LIKELY TO INTENSIFY"[42]

The first cross-country gay and lesbian organizing effort involved the National Gay Election Coalition (NGEC), which was initially formed in 1972 at the suggestion of Maurice Flood of GATE-V and then relaunched at a gay conference in Ottawa in May 1973.[43] A 1972 RCMP report described the earlier NGEC as having sixteen member organizations. An article by Joe Young from *Labour Challenge* reports that the conference held on May 19-20, 1973, had sixty people in attendance. These included representatives from GATE-V, the *Body Politic,* CHAT, and the newly formed GATE-T. *Labour Challenge* reported on provincial initiatives for "sexual orientation" protection in human rights legislation as well as on a proposal to relaunch the NGEC, which had intervened in the previous federal election. According to Young, "NGEC will call for amendments to the Canadian Bill of Rights, for the striking down of discriminatory legislation for gays such as the immigration and security acts, and the implementation of protective legislation for gays [i.e., anti-discrimination]." It was critical to include security policies in this list of concerns.[44]

The NGEC was monitored by the RCMP, but little active surveillance was undertaken. According to an RCMP report, the number of people who attended a meeting of the NGEC could not be determined as the event had not been under surveillance.[45] Gay groups continued to raise concerns over national security policies in ways that challenged the security campaigns against gay men and lesbians. The legal fact sheet that GO prepared for its document "Homosexuals – An Oppressed Minority" mentions the Royal Commission on Security and its reference to the prohibition on allowing gays to get higher levels of security clearance. In the section on the RCMP, GO reiterated earlier calls "to know if it is a policy of the Royal Canadian Mounted Police to identify homosexuals within any area of government service and then question them concerning their sexuality and the sexuality of others; and if this is the policy we demand its immediate cessation and destruction of all records so obtained."[46]

In 1975, a new national coalition of lesbian and gay rights groups was formed. This was the first general cross-country rights coalition of its kind and was broader than previous electoral coalition efforts. David Garmaise told us how the NGRC was formed and how it operated: "We formed the National Gay Rights Coalition at the conference in Ottawa in 1975. It was run as a project of Gays of Ottawa. It never really had a separate office or staff. I guess I was the first coordinator. I was involved with the NGRC, and then it became the Canadian Lesbian and Gay Rights Coalition. Then the coalition continued for awhile and then eventually disbanded in the early eighties" (May 13, 2000).[47] The work of the NGRC in Ottawa was Garmaise's effort, with the assistance of other GO members. As he put it, regarding the number of people who worked

12   NGRC conference at the University of Ottawa, June 28-July 1, 1975 |
Credit: CLGA 1986-032_02P (40) 06

Sexual Policing and National Security

on NGRC projects, "Certainly not more than a couple. I think [I worked] mostly on my own. I pretty well had that dossier. And I would report back at our [GO] meetings." Blair Johnston remembered that there was a small overlapping network of activists in GO and the NGRC who had ties with activists

13 Marie Robertson, third from the left, at the June 30, 1975, conference demonstration in Ottawa | *Credit:* CLGA 1986-032_02P (40) 07

14 Ottawa conference demonstration, June 30, 1975 | *Credit:* CLGA 1986-032_02P (40) 01

in the CGRO and other groups. It was these people who did most of this work (February 1, 2001).

The RCMP conducted detailed surveillance and monitoring of the NGRC, including its founding meeting in Ottawa in late June/early July 1975 (see Photos 12-16). Suspicions that the RCMP was spying on these events were well founded. The RCMP collected media coverage of the conference, including a clipping in the GO file from the *Ottawa Citizen* on the establishment of the NGRC, which

15 Having fun at the 1975 conference demonstration in Ottawa |
Credit: CLGA 1986-032_02P (40) 11

Sexual Policing and National Security

16 RCMP officers watching the June 30, 1975, conference demonstration |
Credit: CLGA 1986-032_02P (40) 05

mentioned that twenty-seven different organizations attended the conference. As part of its system for collecting names and initiating personal files, the RCMP underlined the names of some speakers.[48]

There was also at least one undercover officer or informant present at the conference. In an RCMP report on the activities of GATE-T during the national conference, it is noted that the demonstration was attended by about 150 people. According to the author, "The demonstration was orderly, and entailed the singing of Gay slogans and speeches by representatives from different Gay groups from across Canada."[49] The following commentary was found under the "Investigator's Comments" in the released report: "Approximately 150 representatives ... from across Canada were in attendance ... to try to establish a national coalition of gay right's groups. The coalition would be part of an effort by homosexuals to change legislation affecting them, [blanked out] said in an interview." The keynote address was delivered by John Damien, and the RCMP also blanked out his name; however, the report makes it clear that, "should we come into possession of any photographs, attempts will be made to identify key individuals."[50]

David Garmaise remembers the conference demonstration and the media coverage of it: "We made the 11 o'clock news and we were so excited. I think we just assumed that [the RCMP] would be filming that or taking pictures of it" (May 13, 2000). The inclusion of media articles in the RCMP files suggests a level of monitoring that demonstrates definite RCMP interest in the NGRC.

In the 1976 document prepared in response to the Montreal Security Service requests for information on gay groups (see below), the NGRC was featured as being "of security service interest": "Founded several years ago, this group acts as the national spokesman and umbrella organization for 27 gays groups. Each year it holds a national convention at which time the gays traditionally hold a demonstration in the city hosting the conference. The demonstration is normally to publicize gay rights and to protest police harassment and has always been peaceful and orderly. Last year the conference was in Ottawa and there was a march on Parliament Hill."[51] We asked Garmaise to comment on RCMP reports on the NGRC. In the following section, we interweave our explication and analysis of the security texts with his remarks.

The catalyst for the first RCMP document on the NGRC was *Globe and Mail* coverage of the RCMP on October 7, 1976. An October 5 article in the same newspaper explained that the RCMP wanted to be exempted from proposed Canadian human rights legislation, which, it feared, created the possibility of allowing Canadians employed by the federal government to have access to their federal files. The RCMP was opposed to the opening of files "to those under investigation but also to its own employees." An RCMP spokesman stated that this would "impede normal investigations carried out on prospective officers. Such investigations are done through friends and neighbors and focus on 'character weaknesses' – alcoholism, homosexuality, and traits such as extreme dependence on one's mother ... If friends and neighbors know that the subject will eventually see their comments in his file, they will be less willing to talk."[52] The RCMP was concerned that, if public servants, especially RCMP applicants, could see their files and find the names of the people who gave information, its informants would be compromised. The RCMP wished to continue its control over the intricate surveillance networks and informant pools. In order for policing and regulation to be effective, the identities of informants and individuals who succumbed to interrogations needed to be protected. Indeed, informants were the most effective means of maintaining surveillance of homosexuals.

After the publication of the article, Garmaise, on behalf of the NGRC, embarked on a letter-writing campaign to force key government and RCMP officials to reveal their policy regarding homosexuality and security clearances in the public service. He wrote letters to Solicitor General Francis Fox, asking for a meeting to clarify government policy, to Justice Minister Ron Basford, asking that sexual orientation protection be included in the proposed Human

Rights Act, and to RCMP commissioner M.J. Nadon, criticizing the RCMP statement and calling for human rights legislation that would prevent such discrimination. In the letter to Nadon, Garmaise made comments regarding blackmail, homosexuality, and RCMP tactics. He argued that homosexuality should not be the basis for being refused work in the public service. He pointed to the surveillance tactics of the RCMP as the real problem as it forced some gay men and lesbians to hide their sexuality: "If you say to me that gay people who do hide their homosexuality are open to blackmail, I say to you that they hide their homosexuality because of the attitudes and policies of agencies like the RCMP."[53]

Garmaise described the need to break the silence about homosexuality and national security issues through this letter-writing strategy:

> We launched some things proactively but a lot of what we did was in response to something. And we were pretty good at making a big deal out of whatever we came across in the paper or in somebody's public statement on the airwaves. We just used that to write letters, fire letters off to, in this case, the RCMP and the public service commissioner. We wrote to somebody about public service policy. And we would fire off copies to the media and that would generate more articles and they would respond to that. We operated like that a lot. And we would also generate an article for the *Body Politic*. (May 13, 2000)

Writing letters to government officials and sending copies to the media made visible the national security campaigns against gay men and lesbians in the 1970s. As strategy, letter writing was part of the NGRC's mandate, but it was often generated

> by reacting to what was read in the newspaper. It wasn't so much that NGRC or even the PAC [Political Action Committee] of GO had decided that this was a really important issue that we should try to do whatever we can about it; but it was much more that it came up and then you were able to respond to it and write letters and get media. And bear in mind that this was one person in the PAC covering this whole dossier. We just created the letterhead, gave ourselves a name, and did what we could ... We were mandated to do this when the groups did get together once a year starting in '75.

The letter written to Fox and Basford generated a *Globe and Mail* article entitled "RCMP Bias: Homosexuals Asking for Equal Job Treatment."[54] This gave the

NGRC mainstream coverage for its demands to end security policies against gay men and lesbians. The NGRC had entered into an interactive relation with the RCMP mediated through media coverage.

During this period, the NGRC was engaged in a campaign to try to get sexual orientation protection added to the Canadian Human Rights Act. The act was being discussed in 1975-76 and was passed in 1977. It led to the establishment of the Canadian Human Rights Commission. A 1976 NGRC brief responding to blackmail fears states: "Discriminatory policies create the environment in which blackmail can occur."[55] As part of this campaign, on November 7, 1975, twenty-five members of GO picketed the national convention of the Liberal Party at the Chateau Laurier (see Photo 17). One of the issues raised concerned discrimination against gays in the civil service. According to Don McLeod, the demonstrators demanded the "inclusion of a sexual orientation clause in the federal government's proposed Human Rights Act. The demonstration was held to coincide with Prime Minister Pierre Trudeau's arrival at the convention. When confronted by the picketers, Trudeau just waved and smiled. The protestors also distributed copies of the NGRC/CNDH's pamphlet 'The Homosexual Minority and the Canadian Human Rights Act' to convention delegates."[56] The RCMP probably thought that the NGRC was rather more substantial than it actually was. It viewed the NGRC as an active coalition with groups across the country and dozens of committed activists. The RCMP felt that a potential country-wide coalition of all gay groups would pose a real problem for the government and for security policing. It is for this reason that it gave briefing information to security officers in different departments. This also suggests that the RCMP's level of intelligence regarding the NGRC may not have been very accurate.

In October 1976, an RCMP transit slip requesting information comments on the formation of the NGRC in July 1975. It focuses on the methods the NGRC used to attempt to obtain civil rights for gays and lesbians, and it reports that the coalition had a woman's caucus. Moreover, it indicates that the NGRC was "going after" the solicitor general. As evidence of this, the RCMP appended the October 7 *Globe and Mail* article.[57] Perhaps foreshadowing a more open-minded approach among some RCMP operatives, this document suggests that, in the future, there might be a shift in policy towards no longer excluding homosexuals and other minority groups. We return to this suggestive document later.

During 1976, it appears that the RCMP did a series of security or record checks in relation to individuals associated with the NGRC.[58] In response, David

17 Protesters confront Prime Minister Trudeau (right) at a Liberal Party convention in Ottawa, November 7, 1975 | *Credit:* Paul-François Sylvestre, *Propos pour une libération (homo)sexuelle* (Montreal: Les Éditions de L'Aurore, 1976), 135.

Garmaise pointed out that "the RCMP were responsible for doing all the checks for security clearances for all departments" (May 13, 2000). These record checks may have been sparked by requests from the Montreal Security Service for more information in response to gay resistance to the Olympic clean-up.

On November 2, 1976, an RCMP document written by M.S. Sexsmith (assistant commander and deputy director general Security Service), classified as confidential, and pertaining to "security-screening character weakness (homosexuals)" was produced in response to the NGRC's lobbying and media work. This document reads like a briefing report on the RCMP's position regarding gays being employed in the public service, and it was circulated throughout the RCMP security network. It was drafted in response to what was perceived as the NGRC "campaign to pressure the government into making a statement relative to the rights of homosexuals, particularly in relation to obtaining employment in the public service." According to the RCMP, "Because this campaign is likely to intensify, we thought it might be timely and useful to provide you with copies of the attached material."[59] This document is the clearest indication that the RCMP viewed the NGRC as a threat.

The material stipulating the RCMP's position on national security and homosexuality included the response drafted to a letter received from NDP MPP Michael Cassidy and a copy of Paragraph 100 of the *Report of the Royal Commission on Security*. Cassidy's 1973 letter was in support of the NGEC's and GO's gay organizing efforts. The letter to Cassidy quotes the royal commission report's Paragraph 100. Sexsmith believed that the documents summarized "very well" the current attitude of the Security Service and most government departments. The RCMP reaction to the NGRC's efforts was to go through its files and to locate earlier official state responses to these questions. According to Sexsmith, the Privy Council Office was to formulate a position paper on the issue, which would then be distributed to various state agencies. However, we have yet to uncover such a paper.[60]

Another article appeared in the *Globe and Mail* in August 1977, this one titled "Gay Group Claims RCMP Is Unfair to Homosexuals." This article was also generated by a letter from David Garmaise to the RCMP and to Solicitor General Fox. The NGRC was responding to a letter it received from Fox, which claimed that "there is no Government policy to discriminate overtly or covertly against homosexuals."[61] In response to Fox's letter, Garmaise referred to media statements that revealed that the RCMP kept files on homosexuals, and he called for the RCMP to stop labelling homosexuality as a character weakness. In the article, Superintendent John Bentham, an RCMP spokesperson, stated:

"We consider homosexuality a character weakness for an applicant to the RCMP." According to reporter Lawrence Martin, RCMP documents showed that, for purposes of security screening for job applicants, "there is an 080 interest code classification which pertains to 'character weakness'" and that "character weakness relates solely to D 939-7 files which are files on homosexuals."[62] Thus, it is apparent that, in RCMP files, the homosexualization of character weakness continued into the late 1970s.

Garmaise also remembered the NGRC campaign against the RCMP and national security policies: "I recall asking the RCMP several times for meetings and they kept putting us off, and I don't think we ever met them. I don't remember meeting with [Minister of Justice] Basford or [Solicitor General] Francis Fox. We weren't quite organized enough and pushy enough and visible enough to get meetings with ministers at that point in time. It was all sort of new territory for us" (May 13, 2000).

State agencies and the RCMP were opposed to the NGRC efforts to make the national security campaigns against gay men and lesbians publicly visible. As Garmaise recalled,

We took a very conscious decision to do things very publicly. We thought it was more important to be public and to be seen doing what we were doing than to actually get a change in legislation or a change in policy. We knew that we might be more effective in getting a change in policy working behind the scenes: it was possible using traditional lobbying methods. But we felt that we had to do everything in the open because we needed the visibility and for people to see a face and a name to the cause. (May 13, 2000)

The RCMP did not respond publicly to this campaign as it wished to keep its security surveillance a secret. As Garmaise recalled, "They skated a lot and they procrastinated a lot and we would have to write them again. They seem to have put us off repeatedly. My recollection is that we – whenever we got any results from all this it was because of the media. We would write to the minister and send a copy to the media. The media would call the minister and get more than we could ever get" (May 13, 2000). Garmaise remembered that the campaign against the RCMP and national security policies was integrally connected to the campaign for sexual orientation protection in the proposed Canadian Human Rights Act. At around the same time, in 1977, Barbara Thornborrow was dismissed from the armed forces for being a lesbian. Thornborrow, along with Gloria Cameron, John Damien, and Doug Wilson, were the first public cases of heterosexist discrimination in Canadian society.[63] And in Thornborrow's case, her expulsion from the armed forces was directly related to the exclusionary policies of the military and to national security policies against queers. According to Garmaise:

> There was the Barbara Thornborrow case, which happened right around the time that the Human Rights Act was adopted. She happened to come to our office about two days before the meeting of the Justice Committee that was considering this legislation and we brought her to that committee and she talked to the media there. She then went on to the [NGRC] conference in Saskatoon ... We thought we had a chance to get sexual orientation put into the act. We were wrong. We were a little naive. But we thought that the arguments were so solid ... Actually, it took a long time before they put it in ... But they weren't ready to do it in '77 when the act was adopted. (May 13, 2000)

After this campaign, Garmaise said: "I don't remember any major thrust [of NGRC campaigning] after that. I spent a lot of time organizing the national conference in '79 which was in Ottawa and then I was burnt out and I didn't stick around very much after that. Around 1980, I retired from the gay movement for awhile. So I don't remember anything particularly significant after '77."[64]

In the 1970s, Garmaise and the small network of activists in GO and the NGRC rendered the national security policies directed against gay men and lesbians visible so that they could be contested. Although the RCMP may have felt more threatened by these activists than was actually warranted, and interpreted them as presenting a more radical challenge to security policies than they did, the NGRC played a crucial role in challenging and eroding support for these policies.

RCMP surveillance of NGRC-related activities continued at the Fifth National Gay Conference, which was held in Saskatoon from June 29 to July 3, 1977, and at which Barbara Thornborrow was a keynote speaker. Prior to the conference, there were various requests from RCMP Security Services in different cities for information regarding it, but this was not always forthcoming. There was one RCMP monitoring report on the *Body Politic*'s coverage of the upcoming conference, and there were also reports of posters announcing the conference at the University of Saskatchewan.[65]

The Saskatchewan Security Service conducted surveillance of the conference march, which consisted of 200 to 250 people, for D Ops. This surveillance involved at least one informant/operative, whose report reads, "On 1 July 77, local surveillance by the writer monitored the assembly in front of the Saskatoon Indian-Metis Friendship Centre and march of the Gays. One banner indicated its bearers as representing the Young Socialist League from Winnipeg [blanked out]."[66]

Again, the RCMP seemed especially interested in the presence of left organizations at the conference. It reported that there were people from the RMG and the LSA at the trade union workshop and that "approximately eight LSA members from Edmonton" were in attendance, along with "several RMG and LSA members from Toronto and Vancouver."[67] Gary Kinsman was one of the RMG members present. An informant or agent must have attended at least some of the conference meetings as well. Although RCMP surveillance and monitoring of lesbian and gay groups was still going strong in 1977, by 1978 there seemed to be some change.

A Possible Policy Shift, but Surveillance Continues
By 1978, the situation began to change for the RCMP and its surveillance of gay and lesbian groups. The possibilities for this surveillance were challenged due to growing queer resistance coupled with more general social and political struggles. The human rights cases of John Damien, Doug Wilson, and Barbara Thornborrow highlighted the pervasive social discrimination against lesbians and gay men, as did the passage of the Canadian Human Rights Act, which, even though it did not include sexual orientation, did raise the profile of human rights more generally. The investigation of the Keable Commission and the McDonald Commission into RCMP "wrongdoing" also created a number of obstacles for RCMP surveillance. The public revelations of RCMP dirty tricks, which become a major focus of media attention, challenged the legitimacy of police surveillance, whereas the growth and expansion of gay and lesbian movements and community formation led to the undermining of arguments linking homosexuality, character weakness, and susceptibility to blackmail.

Some of the documents to which we gained access indicate a debate pointing towards a possible shift in RCMP policy. For example, "We are not actively investigating gay groups – only monitoring them" was written across the top of a 1976 transit slip but was dated 1978.[68] This suggests a move away from the active surveillance of gay groups that was occurring in 1976-77 towards a less intrusive monitoring. On a 1976 RCMP report on gay organizations, following "[this] is a brief outline of gay organizations of security service interest," someone has written "Says who 78, 10, 06."[69] Unfortunately, we could not make out the signature.

Part of this change may be foreshadowed in an October 7, 1976 transit slip regarding the NGRC: "Over the last year or two, the liberal thinkers have been thinking it's only a matter of time before all Police departments will have to accept all races of people, all religions, homosexuals, and that height and weight cannot continue to exclude membership in the Police. In the USA some Police departments have already hired homosexuals, because, no doubt of political pressure applied on them."[70] In 1976, this officer reported on a rather "liberal" position for this period. At the same time, "political pressure" could be read as suggesting illegitimate forms of social movement impetus. It is on this document that the above mentioned "we are not actively investigating gay groups – only monitoring them" is scrawled.

Although there are indications of a shift towards monitoring, surveillance of lesbian and gay activism continued in 1978 and, indeed, extended into the 1980s.

ACTIVE SURVEILLANCE CONTINUES: ANITA BRYANT, INTERNATIONAL WOMEN'S DAY, AND THE *BODY POLITIC* RAID

In 1978, the RCMP reported on its surveillance of anti–Anita Bryant demonstrations and on International Women's Day (IWD) organizing in Toronto, which involved many lesbian activists (see Photo 18). In the later 1970s, the moral conservative right wing in the United States began to target lesbian and gay rights and attempted to get local human rights protection for lesbians and gay men repealed where it had been established.[71] On June 7, 1977, Anita Bryant, her husband, Bob Green, and their Save Our Children organization succeeded in repealing the Dade County (Miami) ordinance prohibiting discrimination on the basis of sexual orientation. In response, a series of coalitions and actions against this right-wing crusade was organized across Canada.[72] In particular, these focused on trips by Bryant to a number of places across Canada to spread her message. It was in this context that, on December 30, 1977, the office shared by the *Body Politic* and the Canadian Gay Archives was raided by the police, and charges were laid against three officers of Pink Triangle Press, the publisher of the *Body Politic*, regarding an article on intergenerational sex.[73]

The RCMP conducted surveillance on the January 1978 demonstrations against Anita Bryant when she came to Toronto. This was Toronto's most significant queer mobilization up to that point. The RCMP reported the involvement of the Lesbian Organization of Toronto (LOOT), GATE, BEAVER, "Wages to Lesbians," Gay Youth, the *Body Politic*, and the Gay Teachers Union. And there

18 Lesbian contingent at the demonstration against Anita Bryant in Toronto, January 14, 1978 |
Credit: CLGA 1986-032_10P (56) 01P

was a continuing interest in left involvement, especially with regard to the RWL. According to the RCMP, "the RWL was extensively involved in the preparations around the Anita Bryant [blanked out] actions."[74] The RCMP was conducting surveillance work on the planning for these protests.

The January 1978 demonstrations came shortly after the police raid on and charges against The Body Politic in December '77 for using the mail to transmit "immoral, indecent and scurrilous material" and after months of Toronto organizing, which I was involved in, against Anita Bryant's right-wing campaign against lesbian and gay rights. I was then a member of GATE-Toronto and the RWL. In 1977 the largest demo we had had against Bryant's campaign was about six hundred people. In early '78 more than one thousand people came together downtown for the Saturday night rally and demonstration led by lesbians from LOOT and Women against Violence against Women (WAVAW). This was the largest gay and lesbian liberation action yet in the city. Long-time activists were joined by gays and lesbians from the bars who had not been on demonstrations before. I was one of the marshals for the demonstration, and I remember queer bashers trying to attack us as we moved up Yonge Street, with the police looking the other way. The next night six hundred people demonstrated outside People's Church in North York, where Bryant was appearing. I was interviewed on TV about the action, and my parents saw me on the news. On the way back to Yonge Street, along with another demonstrator, I was set upon by a gang of queer bashers. Luckily, because we were wearing bulky winter coats, neither of us got hurt.

Also in 1978, on the initiative of women in the RWL and other socialist feminists, International Women's Day was again celebrated in the streets of Toronto. These IWD marches and celebrations were to become one of the major annual progressive political events in Toronto, involving thousands of women and supportive men.[75] A report on the feminist organizing meeting for IWD appeared on the same page as the RCMP report on the demonstration against Anita Bryant. This combined coverage of the two events reveals several surveillance practices: first, the RCMP, whether it fully understood the connections or not, actively reported on events that unfolded at the same time; second, RCMP reports reveal the overlapping character of a number of groups and individuals under surveillance in the gay and feminist movements; third, the same officers/informants engaged in the surveillance of both events.

This informant/agent reported on tensions over men's participation in the event. These tensions were between WAVAW members, largely consisting of women identifying as radical feminists (including many lesbians) who focused on opposing men's violence against women, and heterosexual and lesbian socialist feminists.[76] The RCMP reported that there were "about 120 women attending. A lot of radical feminists and Wages to Lesbians [sic] attended with these radical feminists fighting over the question of men taking part in the demonstration."[77] This was a major and defining debate in the Toronto feminist movement for a number of years, with those (largely socialist feminists) arguing for men's participating in a supportive position generally winning out.[78] While active surveillance of lesbian and gay activists may have been lessening in 1978, it was still going on and involved the surveillance of both left organizations and the feminist movement.

CONCLUSION: THE POLICING OF QUEER MOVEMENTS

From our explorations, we see that the national security war on gays and lesbians continued in new forms in the 1970s, with relatively extensive surveillance of gay and lesbian activism. Our critical interrogation of the released documents merely begins to tell the story of the RCMP surveillance of lesbian and gay groups in the 1970s. There were major connections between this surveillance and a broader campaign of surveillance against the left, especially some of the Trotskyist groups. The emergence of gay liberation and lesbian feminism presented a series of new difficulties for the national security campaigns. Activists publicly challenged the campaigns, whether in the "We Demand" document of 1971 or in the organizing of the NGRC. Activists also began to respond to escalated forms of sexual policing, such as the Olympic clean-up campaign, which became intertwined with national security campaigns. Activists in this period could not be dealt with in the same fashion as had the more isolated queers of the past, and the expansion of communities and movements undermined the relations of the closet that the national security campaigns had helped to construct. There are indications that active surveillance of lesbian/gay activism began to taper off at the end of the 1970s but that monitoring continued.

A series of constraints was imposed that hindered RCMP surveillance of queer activists, and, in some parts of the public service, the security focus shifted to closeted queers. Although there was developing opposition to these practices, the national security campaigns within the military and the RCMP continued to escalate.

In the 1980s, expansion of gay/lesbian movements and community formation continued. In part, this was in resistance to the intensification of sexual policing in the form of bathhouse and bar raids in many major centres. Even though RCMP surveillance of gay and lesbian activists diminished by the late 1970s, other forms of police surveillance, harassment, and repression did not. Given the limitations of the 1969 Criminal Code reform, gay sex acts in public or involving someone under the age of twenty-one remained criminal offences. Sexual policing organized through the categories of the Criminal Code intensified, with bawdy-house legislation being used in Montreal, Ottawa, and Toronto.

Gay sex was portrayed as dirty and in need of being cleaned up: the bath raids in Toronto in the early 1980s were conducted under the code name Operation Soap.[79] The massive raids of 1981 were the most serious assault on gay community institutions yet. On February 5, 1981, police raided four bathhouses, arresting 286 men as found-ins and 20 as keepers of a common bawdy house. The next night, three thousand gay men, lesbians, and supporters took over downtown streets in an angry protest against the raids. On February 20, over four thousand gays, lesbians, and supporters rallied at Queen's Park and marched

19 Right to Privacy Committee demonstration against the bath raids, February 20, 1981 |
Credit: CLGA 1983-018_04P (02) 11P, Canadian Council on Religion and the Homosexual

to Metro Toronto's Police Forces 52 Division to protest the charges and to call for an independent inquiry into the police raids (see Photo 19).[80]

I was one of the marshals for the lead group of the demonstration as we headed from Queen's Park towards Yonge Street. At this point demonstrators were not legally allowed to march on Yonge Street, so having the lead contingent well organized was crucial to securing our ability to go on Yonge. If we were organized and together we knew the police would have no real alternative but to let us go down the street. As the march formed up, two men who we as marshals at the front did not know, took hold of carrying part of the middle of the front banner. At first we thought they were drunk so we decided to keep an eye on them. We were suspicious but at first did not do anything. Who they were became clear as we approached Yonge Street and they began to cut the front banner with knives. They were undercover cops who were trying to provoke an incident before we got to Yonge Street so we would be prevented from being able to go on the city's most important street. We quickly exposed them, including to the lead police

Sexual Policing and National Security

officers for the demonstration. As a result, we were able to go on Yonge Street with little opposition. A photographer from the *Clarion* (an alternative newspaper) took pictures of what the police were doing, and the Right to Privacy Committee, the defence organization for those arrested in the bath raids, organized a media conference to challenge the police practices at the demonstration.

Police repression continued to spark powerful waves of gay and lesbian resistance, which acted to undermine the social basis of the national security campaigns against queers in the 1980s. However, though RCMP surveillance was decreasing, its local police equivalent was not. In Toronto, this led to police surveillance of gay community organizations and individuals. In May 2007, the media revealed that Toronto detective Garry Carter had been sent undercover by the Intelligence Squad into the gay community in the 1980s to spy on bathhouse operators, to attend meetings in Alberta, to track gay candidates running for city council, and even to report on how gay activists questioned police budgets.[81] This police infiltration and surveillance was in response to the resistance, organized through the Right to Privacy Committee, to the bath raids and other forms of police repression. Clearly, the police were trying to smear gay activists and bath owners.[82] This spying was conducted on, among others, gay activists George Hislop and Peter Maloney. At that time, Maloney was a gay lawyer involved in ownership of some of the bathhouses that had been raided. His phones were tapped and he was followed. When, in 1991, his friend Susan Eng became chair of the Toronto Police Service Board (a civilian agency assigned the task of overseeing the force), the Toronto police had her under surveillance. The justification for this included unfounded police accusations that Maloney and his friends were involved in drug transactions.[83] The extent of Toronto police surveillance of gay community organizations in the 1980s and 1990s remains to be determined. The concrete connections between this local surveillance of gay groups and activists, mandated through sections of the Criminal Code, and the possible communication of this information to the RCMP and CSIS also remains to be explored.

In the late 1970s and early 1980s, the expansion of gay and lesbian community formation clashed with sexual policing as raids and attacks replaced RCMP surveillance. In the 1980s and 1990s, this expansion of community and movement formation challenged and undermined the anti-queer national security campaigns.

Continuing Exclusion
The Formation of CSIS and "Hard-Core Lesbians"

The national security campaigns against queers continued, at a lower level of intensity, in the 1980s and 1990s, except in the military and the RCMP, where major campaigns against queers persevered into the early 1990s. Problems also persisted in much of the public service. This chapter provides documentation and analysis of the ongoing national security campaigns against queers, and the resiliency of national security discourse and practice, especially in relation to the military and the RCMP.[1]

The expansion of queer community formation and the development of lesbian and gay movements challenged, undermined, and altered the national security campaigns against queers. Lesbian and gay movements fought for and won basic human rights protection, and the increasing visibility of queers undermined the blackmail rationale of the national security state. The revelations of RCMP wrongdoing against the Quebec independence movement and the left in the 1970s led to the genesis of the McDonald Commission in 1977 and to the eventual establishment of the Canadian Security Intelligence Service (CSIS) in 1984, which removed national security work from the RCMP until the response to 9/11 in 2001.[2] In this chapter, we examine the McDonald Commission report and what it had to say about the campaigns against homosexuals, the creation of CSIS, and the continuing purges in the military and the RCMP. Combined with the Canadian Charter of Rights and Freedoms, which we address in the next chapter, this created a new context for struggles for equality rights, which made it more difficult to implement security policies against gay men and lesbians.

THE MCDONALD COMMISSION REPORT: TOWARDS THE "RULE OF LAW" AND A NEW CIVILIAN SECURITY SERVICE

The growing revelations of RCMP dirty tricks led to the formation of the Mc-Donald Commission. It was established as a federalist initiative after the government was unsuccessful in blocking the Quebec government-appointed Keable Commission's investigation of RCMP crimes in Quebec, which included, among other things, withholding key documents in the name of "executive privilege." Ottawa did, however, demobilize the Keable Commission through a Supreme Court ruling that limited provincial constitutional rights. While the McDonald Commission revealed more RCMP wrongdoing, it also "served essentially as a cabinet into which embarrassing matters [were] continually being filled away."[3] One of these matters was the surveillance campaign against gay men and lesbians.

A major state response to such a crisis of legitimacy is to establish a commission of inquiry to investigate and to develop recommendations for change that allow hegemonic social relations to be held in place. This produces official state knowledge, which defines both the "problem" and the "solutions."[4] The focus and mandate of the McDonald Commission was RCMP wrongdoing, and in its public report its primary recommendation centred on the establishment of a new, separate, civilian-based security agency.[5] Conceptually, the commission was oriented towards the improvement of the "overall effectiveness" of the Security Service. This was "to help the Service provide more timely information of higher quality to government about the security threats facing Canada" while, at the same time, reducing "the risks of Security Service members committing illegalities and improprieties in the performance of their duties."[6] It therefore fit within the ideological code of national security, even though it argued for a new institutional basis for the national security force.

The McDonald Commission was committed to the fight against "subversion," but its report made a number of contradictory statements regarding this matter. On the one hand, it suggested that even radical groups, as long as they did not challenge authorities or use violence, should be left alone or only surveyed using non-obtrusive means; on the other hand, it associated subversion per se with terrorism.[7]

The McDonald Commission was committed to the ideology of the rule of law, arguing: "The rule of law must be observed in all security operations ... This means that policemen and members of the security service, as well as the government officials and ministers who authorize their activities, are not above the law. Members of the security organization must not be permitted to break the law in the name of national security."[8] The notion that no fundamental problems would exist if everyone obeyed the law and that all are equal under the law are two main assumptions at the base of this legal concept. The rule of law can restrain arbitrary and illegal state and police action, and it can defend aspects of people's civil liberties from repressive power. The ideology of the rule of law, however, also leads people to view the law as a neutral "truth" or instrument rather than to examine the historical and social character of law as it is constructed through social and class struggles. This view fails to see how the routine social organization and practice of law itself organizes inequality and discrimination. The idea that law is somehow separate from state and class power operates to obscure our ability to see and organize against these social relations of power. The current rule of law leads to the production and reproduction of forms of social oppression and exploitation, whether it secures the legal conditions for the exploitation of labour power or helps to organize heterosexual hegemony. Law can operate to restrict the use of arbitrary forms of police power, but it is also central to the organization of state policing and regulatory powers and, of course, national security. The ideology of the rule of law can and has been used to enable some of the most repressive features of national security campaigns.[9]

The McDonald Report argued for following the rule of law and for a new civilian-based security agency. It mobilized the rule of law argument to push for a new institutional form for national security policing in Canada. The McDonald Commission worked from 1977 to 1981 and delivered its final report in January 1981, which was published in censored form. While similar proposals had been made earlier (e.g., in the 1968 Mackenzie Report on security), they had been blocked by the RCMP and by compromises between the RCMP and political and bureaucratic elites.

The McDonald Commission was working to restore the justification for the security police following a crisis of legitimacy.[10] This crisis erupted due to resistance to the RCMP denial of democratic rights to certain people and to the resulting media coverage of RCMP crimes against the Quebec sovereignty movement and the left. The commission's main argument for restoring the legitimacy of the national security police involved transferring this work from the discredited RCMP to a new service. This was an attempt to resolve the problem without putting the ideology and practices of national security in question. Indeed, the fundamental features of these were maintained in the recommendations of the McDonald Commission.[11]

The investigations conducted by the McDonald Commission were used in state responses to our 1998 research report on the national security campaigns against queers, which, for the pre-1970s period, foreshadows parts of *The Canadian War on Queers*. Our report was dismissed with statements that the matter had been investigated and dealt with by the McDonald Commission.[12] For instance, a January 1999 letter from Solicitor General Lawrence MacCauley to Gary Kinsman states: "After a review of the report, I believe that most of the report's recommendations have been addressed directly by the Commission of Inquiry Concerning Certain Activities of the Royal Canadian Mounted Police (1981), otherwise known as the McDonald Commission."[13] The Privy Council Office's briefing notes for the solicitor general repeated that these "allegations" had been reviewed by the McDonald Commission, adding, "The Commission's recommendation led to the destruction of all security service files opened solely on the basis of an individual's sexual orientation."[14]

This is rather different from the initial 1992 state response to Beeby's articles and to questions from NDP Member of Parliament Svend Robinson. At that time, Prime Minister Mulroney condemned the anti-homosexual purge, stating that it would "appear to be one of the great outrages and violations of fundamental human liberty that one would have seen for an extended period of time." He went on: "[I do not] know much beyond what I have read ... but I have instructed the Clerk of the Privy Council to bring forward for considera- tion ways that we might examine this more carefully because on its face it would appear to be a fundamental violation of the rights of Canadians and, if it is as it has been reported, a most regrettable incident." He refused to call for a full public inquiry, and nothing ever came of this.[15]

We get an initial sense of some of the problems with the responses to our research report. These comments suggest that, though files should not be kept solely on the basis of sexual orientation, they could be kept on people (includ- ing regarding their sexual orientation) if there were security concerns. In the next section, we investigate whether or not the McDonald Commission did, as state bodies claimed, adequately address the national security campaigns against gay men and lesbians.

The McDonald Commission's Inadequate and Limited Investigation of the War on Queers

The McDonald Commission did not focus primarily on the national security campaigns against queers and raised this aspect of RCMP activity in only a few areas, particularly in relation to security screening. While its report recognized some of the problems with the wide scope of the surveillance of homosexuals, no concrete action was taken. For example, there was no official apology to those who were targeted. An inquiry into the organization of these campaigns was not undertaken; nor was any compensation offered to those whose careers and lives had been destroyed by them.[16] There is no information in the published reports on the forms of surveillance used by the RCMP, the careers and lives destroyed, the non-cooperation encountered, the continuing discriminatory practices in the RCMP and the military, or the fruit machine technology.[17] Although the McDonald Report does mention that homosexuals were targeted because of a "character trait," nowhere does it clearly state that homosexuals are not a security risk.[18] Since the purges against queers included several branches of the security state, this omission may be seen to be at least partly due to the McDonald Commission's mandate, which covered only the RCMP. It does not examine the broader socially mediated character of the national security campaigns against queers. These campaigns continued during the time of the commission's work and after the release of the report, including within the RCMP, CSIS, and the military.

From Character Weakness to Character Trait

In the McDonald Report, homosexuals have a "character trait." "Character trait" has a much more neutral and scientific tone than does "character weakness," thus disguising the continuation of heterosexual hegemony. Whereas homosexual relationships are seen as character traits, heterosexual relationships are not. The McDonald Report argues that, in order to "calculate the possibility of a candidate being ... vulnerable to blackmail or coercion, it is not sufficient merely to provide information about certain character traits such as indebtedness, drinking habits or sexual proclivities. Rather, there must be evidence of a connection or a potential connection between these character traits and a threat to Canada's security."[19] Rather than labelling all homosexuals as "suspect," the report insists that, "for a homosexual relationship ... to be of relevance to a security clearance decision, there must be evidence that the candidate is having this relationship or affair with a person who is known or suspected to be a threat to Canada's security or who is somehow connected with such a threat, or alternatively, that the conduct of the candidate is such that it will make him vulnerable to blackmail."[20] Thus, though the report moves away from categorizing all homosexuals as security risks, some homosexuals could still be so categorized and thus denied security clearance. The social relations of the closet and the strategy of living a double life are actively used to construct some homosexuals as security risks.

The McDonald Report recommends the denial of a security clearance when there are "reasonable grounds to believe that he is likely to become, a) vulnerable to blackmail or coercion, or b) indiscreet or dishonest, in such a way as to endanger the security of Canada."[21] Security files are also highlighted in the report, which concludes that "the existing Security Service files on homosexuals [should] be reviewed and those which do not fall within the guidelines for opening and maintaining files on individuals [should] be destroyed."[22] Recommending a *review* of files enabled the security state to argue for the maintenance of some files, especially if a homosexual presented some sort of security risk due to her/his "vulnerability." This formulation is crucial because, even though the report denies discrimination based on sexual orientation, it details how it is actually accomplished for those deemed vulnerable to compromise. This allowed the surveillance of lesbians and gays to continue, especially if they were deemed to have something to hide.

The McDonald Report argues that homosexual "character traits must be related, or potentially related to a security threat [and this] has important implications for the type of information that a security intelligence agency should collect about individuals."[23] The clause "or potentially related" allows for a broadening of the focus on homosexuals:

We are very concerned about the systematic collection of information on individuals solely because such individuals exhibit a certain character trait. As we noted earlier, there has been a concerted effort on the part of the Security Service for over two decades to collect information on homosexuals ... Although in 1969 an amendment to the Criminal Code made a homosexual act in private between two consenting adults no longer an offence, the Security Service continued to collect intelligence on the homosexual community. The security screening branch of the Security Service became responsible for homosexual investigations. There is now one member of that branch responsible for writing security reports on homosexuals and for directing the occasional field investigation.[24]

We can compare this to Fred's account of how, in the late 1960s, there were only two officers centrally assigned to the character weaknesses subdivision of the DSI in Ottawa (October 21, 1994). At the same time, there were many others involved in the surveillance and monitoring of queers in the public service and the military. The McDonald Report concludes,

The collection programme we have described is inconsistent with the proper role of a security intelligence agency. That such a programme has not been halted years ago is a striking illustration of insensitivity about what the Security Service ought to be securing. Moreover, it is illustrative of a poor analytical capability within the Security Service. We believe that the security intelligence agency should no longer systematically collect information on homosexuals or for that matter on any group of people solely because they exhibit a certain character trait ... The existing files on homosexuals that are not relevant to security ought to be destroyed.[25]

While these comments signal a major shift from previous security policies, they also indicate crucial limitations. First, these campaigns represented far more than insensitivity. The war on queers was a key part of the organization of national security from the late 1950s through the 1970s. When the McDonald Report asserts that the Security Service should "no longer *systematically* collect information on homosexuals [our emphasis]," this clearly still allows for the collection of information on homosexuals that is not systematic. Second, it is apparent that files on homosexuals who are deemed relevant to security did not need to be destroyed. The statement that the RCMP had a poor analytical capability came back to haunt it later in the 1980s.

Most of the material referring specifically to homosexuality is in the second volume of the report, specifically, in the chapter entitled "Security Screening for Public Service Employment." This was the main, but not the sole, area of focus for the national security campaigns with regard to the lives of gay men and lesbians. This section covers the emergence of a specific focus on questions of reliability, which include character defects, as distinct from questions of loyalty. The report refers to Cabinet Directive 35 from 1963, which it claims "was aimed at reconciling the needs of security and the rights of the individual," apparently not noticing that, in practice, security needs supersede the rights of individuals and groups designated as security risks. Interestingly, it suggests that, "with a few modifications, this document still forms the basis for the government's personnel security clearance procedures."[26]

The McDonald Report notes that many of the recommendations in the Mackenzie Report were only partially implemented. For instance, there was still no right to appeal for individuals "who were transferred, or failed to obtain a promotion or position, or who had a contract terminated on security grounds," despite the Mackenzie Commission's recommendations. The McDonald Report reminds its readers that, in 1975, new regulations were adopted, "according to ... [which], if the Deputy Minister has proposed that a person be dismissed from the Public Service for reasons of security, a Commissioner may be appointed." However,

no Commissioner has ever been appointed. Since the enactment of the Public Service Inquiry Regulations, no one has been dismissed from the Public Service

Continuing Exclusion

for security reasons, although some have resigned and others have been transferred or have had their careers adversely affected. Many have been denied employment or contract work. The last years for which figures are available, 1972 and 1973, indicate that for these two years 103 were denied employment for various reasons related but not necessarily confirmed as security factors, 6 resigned, and 160 were denied access, of whom 66 were transferred.[27]

While the report states that no one has been specifically dismissed for security reasons, the security campaigns led not only to the denial of employment but also to resignations and to transfers. The impact of the campaigns was much broader than the dismissal of individuals for security reasons. In fact, it was common practice to find a basis for dismissing an employee other than one that would require the use of official security rationales.

The McDonald Report also refers to the major increase in the number of security clearance checks: "In the years 1972-77 the average annual number was 67,602," whereas in the ten years prior to the Royal Commission on Security the average annual number was 43,700.[28] The growing number of people employed in the public service and the connection between security clearances and promotion accounted for this increase in security checks. The report remarks on another possibility for this: "We have noted a tendency in the security community to over classify documents. This tendency to over classify has contributed to overloading the security screening programme since the number of cases requiring screening is related to the quantity of material classified."[29] Regarding this concern, the authors comment: "it is the Top Secret level clearance that is of greatest concern, since it calls for an automatic investigation into the private life of an individual."[30] The McDonald Commission cited that, in 1978, 67,668 requests for screening resulted in 2,405 for top secret clearances, thus requiring a field investigation. The report points to the broadness of the designation "Top Secret" and comments: "Whole areas of employment have been deemed to require Top Secret level clearance regardless of whether each and every individual has direct access to information classified Top Secret. For example, all employees of External Affairs who are eligible for postings abroad must have Top Secret clearances."[31]

Given social and historical changes, the McDonald Commission "propose[d] changes in how field investigations [were] conducted," suggesting interviews and a reference system. Referring to interviews for secret and confidential clearance levels, it states: "In the case of both these lower level clearances, because there has been no field investigation there has essentially been no check on the 'reliability' of candidates, with the one exception of the homosexual records checks."[32] Clearly, there was still a separate filing system on suspected and confirmed homosexuals at the time of the McDonald Commission.

THE CREATION OF CSIS

Government responses to the McDonald Report, which was released in 1981, set the stage for the proposals that led to the establishment of CSIS in June 1984. In 1981, Solicitor General Robert Kaplan, armed with the McDonald Commission's report, said that the RCMP had gone too far in compiling files on 800,000 Canadians, among whom were a considerable number of lesbians and gay men. The government promised swift action, but delays occurred when it stated that action with regard to these files would not be taken until it had generated a policy. This policy took a year and a half to formulate. The procedure involved a review committee consisting of officials from the Security Service, the Department of Justice, and the Department of the Solicitor General. As Bill Loos perceptively notes: "The criteria for retaining files (information collecting will continue on people who require a security clearance for employment, are considered a threat to national security, or those with access to classified information who might be subject to blackmail or bribery) are extremely vague. In fact, they sound remarkably like the justification used for opening the files in the first place."[33] Under these policies, it was still quite possible for files to be kept on suspected homosexuals who required security clearances or who had any access to classified information.

After its publication, two legal opinions commissioned by the minister of justice were released on the McDonald Commission's report. These opinions questioned the commission's central legal standpoint, suggesting that the police could do whatever the law did not expressly forbid them to do.[34] As Michael Mandel points out, however, "In fact we have always had the Criminal Code and the Post Office Act and all the other legislation that made it criminal to do what the RCMP were doing. The [1984 CSIS] Act legalizes these crimes."[35] The McDonald Report itself was never tabled for parliamentary debate. Instead, the federal government created a new security agency, which would transfer security intelligence from the Security Service of the RCMP to a new civilian agency, separating security intelligence from police and law enforcement activities. This move gave a specific legislative mandate to the new Security Service that was quite unlike the rather vague and undefined powers that had rested with the RCMP.[36] In 1983, Bill C-157, which outlined a proposed Canadian security intelligence service, died on the order paper. This bill attracted widespread opposition from gay groups, peace activists, feminist organizations, First Nations associations, and civil liberties bodies.

Gays of Ottawa played a part in founding the Ottawa-Hull Coalition against Bill C-157. Denis LeBlanc and Barbara McIntosh of GO, speaking for the CGRO, addressed a Senate committee in 1983, insisting that the RCMP's "uncontrolled institutional gay-bashing" not be carried over into the new Security Service.[37] In response to a question about whether RCMP practices had changed, LeBlanc told the committee about Stephen's experience. He recounted how Stephen was "hired on a temporary basis by the government and assigned to work as a file clerk for the Security Service. He was given a security clearance of 'secret,' and was awaiting a 'top secret' clearance when the Mounties discovered his homosexuality. He then had his clearance downgraded and was quickly transferred to another job ... Stephen eventually did get his 'secret' clearance re-instated, about 10 days later, although the 'top secret' level he was being investigated for did not ... come through."[38]

Bill C-157 granted enormous powers to CSIS, enabling its members to carry out a wide variety of previously illegal activities in response to "threats to the security of Canada." CSIS would have had the power to tap phones; open mail; gain access to income tax, census, and medical records; arbitrarily enter residences without any proof that a law had been broken; and to conduct surveillance of groups engaged in political dissent. The broad definition of subversion in Bill C-157 allowed CSIS to target groups engaging in lawful activism seeking constitutional changes, such as a restructuring of the federal system.[39] It expanded the powers of the Security Service while, at the same time, minimizing any accountability to political bodies.[40] While aligned with the basic premise articulated in the McDonald Report, CSIS was granted broad extra-legal powers not in keeping with either the rule of law approach or the controls on police operations outlined in that report.

When the bill encountered widespread opposition, it was referred to a special committee of the Senate, which proposed some changes. Following the defeat of Bill C-157, Solicitor General Robert Kaplan introduced a revised version, Bill C-9, which continued the basic features of the previous legislation while incorporating some largely cosmetic revisions proposed by the Senate Committee on National Security. As Grace and Leys state, this bill "was intended to give CSIS a loose mandate and very wide powers," and it was "railroaded through all the stages of the debate."[41] Given the crisis of legitimacy that had emerged for security policing, the government clearly felt the need to get CSIS established as soon as possible.

Three major areas of concern were identified by activists in their critiques of Bill C-157 and Bill C-9: the very broad definition of "subversive activity," the sweeping surveillance powers given to the security police over movements for social transformation, and the lack of parliamentary and democratic accountability. The bill allowed CSIS to commit what it calls "incidental breaches of the law" when this was deemed "reasonably necessary to enable them to perform their duties."[42] Kaplan insisted that these breaches were not to be considered contraventions of the law. He stated that CSIS would be "built on the foundations of the current Security Service of the RCMP" and that all members of the RCMP Security Service would be offered positions as civilians in CSIS. CSIS would encounter minimal parliamentary accountability, and the new inspector general reviewing its operations would be bound by a government oath of secrecy. The new Security Intelligence Review Committee (SIRC), an external review agency, would be similarly restricted. SIRC was to be authorized to review CSIS operations and policies, to investigate complaints against CSIS, and to submit an annual report to Parliament (with all "national security secrets" removed).[43] SIRC was also responsible for the review and appeal process pertaining to security screening decisions affecting public service employment. The legislation indicated that CSIS needed accurate information in order to assess the "reliability and loyalty of employees," a proviso rooted in the old Cabinet Directive 35 approach. Consequently, this could still be used to deny gay men and lesbians security clearances.

For the first time, however, individuals who were denied a security clearance because of their homosexuality could appeal the decision to SIRC. And this became important in some of the legal challenges against the national security regime. However, an individual was not usually informed of the specific reasons for the refusal of a security clearance, and the bill did not stipulate that SIRC would be under any obligation to divulge them, before or after the appeal. In response to protests from civil liberties supporters, the wording allowing agents to break the law with apparent impunity and the wide definition of "subversives" who might become targets of surveillance were tightened up, and more accountability to Parliament on the part of the minister responsible for SIRC was established. The amendments, however, still granted CSIS agents wide-ranging powers of search, examination, and surveillance, and they invalidated laws regarding confidentiality and privacy in a number of areas.[44] Despite opposition and protests, the government pushed this legislation through in June 1984.

The underlying assumption behind "subversive" in the CSIS Act had to do with the extension of this concept as it was used in national security work. The

Continuing Exclusion

term "subversion," used in the 1975 Cabinet directive to the RCMP (which provided the only official basis for the RCMP's anti-subversive activities), was formally dropped from the CSIS Act. Grace and Leys point out that CSIS routinely used the word "subversion" and that, until 1987, it had a counter-subversion branch. The concept "remains clearly formulated in Section 2 of the Act which defines as one of the four 'threats to the security of Canada' ... activities directed towards undermining by covert unlawful acts, or directed towards or intended ultimately to lead to the destruction or overthrow by violence of, the constitutionally established system of government in Canada; but which excludes 'lawful advocacy, protest or dissent,' unless carried on in conjunction with such activities."[45] The use of the words "overthrow" and "destruction" in relation to governments "conflates the means with the end. The effect is to divert attention from the fact that it is really particular political aims, rather than particular means, that are being outlawed here."[46] A group that calls for the overthrow of "the system," even though it engages in lawful actions, becomes a security target. Groups engaging in civil disobedience or direct action who defy what they consider to be unjust laws could easily be targeted as well. Within these boundaries, the vagueness and elasticity of the term "subversive" allows CSIS to target many groups. It is mandated to conduct surveillance on activities that could become potential threats, often throwing its surveillance nets quite broadly. The phrases "directed towards" or "intended ultimately to" can be widely mobilized. For instance, CSIS was mandated to conduct surveillance on groups that might support armed struggles in other countries, where a war of national liberation or a civil war might be taking place. In SIRC's 1986-87 report, it was pointed out that "one internal CSIS report saw opposition to the government of El Salvador, and to US policy there as *prima facie* evidence of a security threat." As Grace and Leys argue: "Ostensibly, all these definitions are supposed to exclude 'lawful advocacy, protest and dissent' from surveillance. But in practice they subject a very wide range of lawful advocacy, protest, and dissent to state surveillance, because all that is required is that such lawful activities be seen as entailing one of the vague 'threats' described in the CSIS Act. (This is, after all, the point of the vagueness)."[47]

The CSIS Act was also cited in response to our research report. In the previously mentioned 1999 letter from Solicitor General Lawrence MacCauley to Gary Kinsman, MacCauley remarked that, in the CSIS Act, "formal guidelines for security clearances have also been established. The Government Security Policy is Treasury Board policy which establishes operational standards and certain technical-level procedures for personnel security in government."[48] And, according to a briefing note from the Privy Council Office,

[T]he CSIS Act is explicit on what constitutes threats to the national security of Canada and on what types of activities can be investigated. When providing advice to concerned government departments who are seeking a security clearance for an employee, or prospective employee, CSIS must provide an assessment of the loyalty to Canada, so far as it relates to the reliability of an individual. CSIS does not discriminate on the basis of sexual orientation. The behaviour of prospective employees is only of concern if they are vulnerable to blackmail or coercion.[49]

This is the same argument developed in response to national security policy challenges throughout the later 1980s and early 1990s. There is no "discrimination" based on sexual orientation, but homosexuals can still be seen as a security threat if they are disloyal or if they are vulnerable to blackmail or coercion. In the CSIS Act, a "security assessment" entails "an appraisal of the loyalty to Canada, and so far as it relates thereto, the reliability of an individual."[50] This constructs a loyalty to Canada that presumes a unitary Canadian national interest and notions of individual reliability that link back to earlier concepts of character weakness. The language of the briefing note is drawn directly from the CSIS Act. Thus, the McDonald Commission did not adequately address the problems of national security policing in relation to queers since that policing simply continued in the work of CSIS in modified form.

THE MILITARY PURGES CONTINUE

Meanwhile, the military engaged in purge policies until the early 1990s, and major problems continued to be organized in the lives of queers in the military. There are conflicting statistics on how many queers were purged from the military in the 1980s. One source suggests that, in 1982 alone, the SIU dismissed over one hundred women and men from the military on the grounds of homosexuality.[51] Others suggest that fewer were purged. Defence Minister Tom Siddon reported the numbers released under CFAO 19-20 as 45 in 1982, 44 in 1983, and 38 in 1984. Reports for non-commissioned officers who were released were 18 in 1985, 13 in 1986, 6 in 1987, 7 in 1988, 10 in 1989, 4 in 1990, and 2 in 1991-92.[52] This would have covered only those suspected queers officially purged for homosexuality under military regulations. Whatever the exact figures, clearly a significant number of people were being discharged for their sexuality. Military members could still be followed on or off base, subjected to arbitrary search and seizures, and humiliated by such questions as "Do you swallow cum when you suck cocks?" and "Did you perform cunnilingus on her?"[53] Asking specific questions regarding sexual practices was an important part of military investigations as the point was to prove actual participation in same-gender sexual acts.

In 1982, a clarification of military policy towards homosexuals was issued in response to a series of questions and challenges, including those from Gays of Ottawa. The following was the first clarification of policy since 1976:

> Current policy does not allow the enrolment or retention of homosexuals in the Canadian Forces. It is considered that because of the unique demands of service life, which includes forced proximity of persons on ships, isolated units and barracks, that condoning homosexual behaviour could create conflicts in inter-personal relationships which would affect morale and have a detrimental effect on operational efficiency of Canadian Forces ... Although not as much a factor as in the past with more admitted homosexuals in society, security could be a factor with "closet" homosexuals who could be susceptible to blackmail ... The safety of a homosexual could also be jeopardized because of non-acceptance by his peers ... Homosexuals in the Canadian Forces receive an honourable discharge under a release item for persons considered no longer advantageous-ly employable.[54]

In this text, homosexuality is still officially viewed as "sexual abnormality" – indeed, no other sexual abnormality is mentioned. Sexual abnormality is equated with homosexuality just as, earlier, character weakness was equated with homosexuality. Concerns are raised over people working in close prox-imity with no private realm. And the key concept of "operational efficiency" is invoked to justify the exclusion of lesbians and gay men, thus becoming the new vehicle through which military national security can be accomplished.

In the above clarification, blackmail remains highlighted but the focus shifts to closeted homosexuals. This registers the effect of gay and lesbian liberation movements and the emergence of more out queer people on military policy. This policy does not argue that out homosexuals would be acceptable in the military but, rather, that excluding them would protect them from the non-acceptance of other members of the military. In other words, heterosexist non-acceptance justifies discrimination and exclusion. In the mid-1980s, these arguments continued to be used against the impact of the equality rights section of the Charter of Rights and Freedoms.

This clarification continues the military policies found in CFAO 19-20 (issued in July 1976) and the Code of Service Discipline. Although federal practice moved towards retaining queer public servants who were open about their sexuality at lower levels of security clearance, this shift did not apply in the military.

On June 5, 1982, John Duggan wrote on GO's behalf to Minister of National Defence J. Gilles Lamontagne in response to Lamontagne's clarification regarding media information on being gay in the armed forces:

> From May 25 to May 27, 1982 Canadian Gays thought that the Prime Minister's commitment to eliminate prejudice towards homosexuals was being honoured by the Minister of National Defence. Then, in a policy reversal which offends every principle of human rights and justice, you confirmed that the Federal Government would continue to discriminate against Gays. Once again, tired mythology is slanderously invoked against Gays. "National Security" is manipulated to cloak the bigotry of the homophobe. According to news reports, you charge that somehow, Gays, even those "out of the closet," are found to be wanting when it is a question of security.[55]

In a "patriotic" inversion of the security arguments that partially trapped him within national security discourse, Duggan commented: "We agree that security is a problem in the Armed Forces, but certainly not in the way that you and your Chief of Defence Staff might imagine." Unfortunately, in admitting that security was a problem, Duggan was constructing his response within the frame of national security ideology. However, drawing an interesting parallel between homosexuals and Japanese Canadians, Duggan added that the vulnerability of homosexuals depended on how governments had discriminated against them. He wondered whether the government "still subscribes to the discredited 'character defect' theory of homosexuality, a concept akin to the inferiority theory of orientals used by Prime Minister Mackenzie King to persecute Canadians of Japanese descent after WWII." According to Duggan,

> Any competent counter-intelligence analysis would quickly identify the nature of the weakness, homophobia, and would formulate an effective policy to, at least, neutralize the problem. Instead, the Federal Government, particularly DND and the RCMP, have continued to unwittingly cooperate with hostile agents by nurturing and maintaining the conditions suitable for blackmail within their respective services. In an ultimate act of irony, the Government furthers that cooperation with the foreign blackmailer by firing the individual, when by reason of personal integrity and loyalty, he or she has exposed the blackmail attempt. In other words, the Government encourages the blackmailing of Gays and then punishes the loyal target. Catch-22![56]

Duggan concluded on a patriotic note: "Mr. Minister, your policies pose a threat to the security of all Canadians, not only that of Gays. How can you justify a policy which would aid the enemy more than benefit a loyal Canadian? When will you have the courage to act with a clear conscience and eliminate your unjust and illogical discrimination against Gays?"[57] Although there are major dangers to this invocation of queer patriotism, which relies on the ideological code of national security, Duggan also pinpointed important contradictions in military security discourse.

In response, Executive Assistant R.L. Lacroix wrote to Duggan on behalf of Lamontagne. Rather than responding to or defending the security policies of the armed forces, Lacroix quickly moved to outline the "bona fide operational impediment" argument that the military hierarchy was now using:

> I wish to inform you that security is not the only concern of the Canadian Forces when it comes to personnel. Homosexuality presents a bona fide operational impediment, in that it is not possible to fully utilize these people to meet the exigencies of the Service, i.e., in some overseas United Nations (UN) or North Atlantic Treaty Organization (NATO) postings where homosexuality is an offence, at isolated postings, in communal life in barracks, on board ship or in the field. As well, experience has shown that the presence of homosexuals can be most disruptive in a military force.[58]

These comments demonstrate the shift from narrow security concerns towards concerns about operational impediment, which, in turn, is linked to the efficiency argument. This conceptualization is developed on the new terrain created by queer activism and queer communities as well as by the legal implications opened up by the Charter of Rights and Freedoms. Increasingly, the military was finding that expressing concerns about operational efficiency was the most useful way of responding to criticism.

Organized Queer Bashing in the Military

The tolerated and organized practices of violence against queers in the military embody the pervasiveness of heterosexism and homophobia. "J," an eighteen-year-old woman from Antigonish, Nova Scotia, who was stationed in Ottawa in 1981, was wakened by a woman who had earlier accused her of making a pass at her boyfriend. She asked J to step outside. Once outside, this woman and another straight woman "started pushing and punching [her] while everyone else stood by and watched. No one tried to stop it." J limped back to her bunk, with bruises and blood on her lips. The two straight women then went to the military police and explained that they had beaten J up because she was a lesbian. No action was taken against these two women, but J was discharged.[59]

The military's anti-queer policies facilitated and encouraged violence against queers. One former infantryman remembered that, in 1986, "there was a guy who had gone out drinking with his buddies and ended up ... telling his buddy that he was gay. The next morning they found him near the latrines. He'd had the shit kicked out of him. He had broken bones, missing teeth, a fractured cheek. He was a mess. And he'd had a broomstick shoved up his ass."[60]

The notorious Canadian Airborne Regiment, which engaged in racist abuse and torture during its "peacekeeping" mission in Somalia in 1992-93, also encouraged organized violence against men identified as gay.[61] Dany Pelletier, a former sergeant in the Canadian Airborne, reported that, in the 1980s, members of the regiment would routinely beat up gay members. Pelletier described the standard response: "They get the keys to [the guy's] room and go in at night with a blanket and throw the blanket over them and beat the shit out of them. The next morning, the big excuse was he slipped on a bar of soap and no one complained because the penalty of breaking the code of silence was also retaliation." Pelletier said this happened often while he was stationed at the Airborne's base in Petawawa between 1980 and 1985. He remembered: "One [soldier] went to a bar in Pembroke and I guess picked up this guy and they were in the car in the parking lot having sex and someone saw him." The soldiers got to him the next night. Pelletier felt there were a number of gay men in the Airborne at the time: "At one point I was commanding a section of 16 [men] and there were probably nine in there." According to Pelletier, "It was okay if you jerked off together, but if you were a confirmed gay man, that was the line."[62] These practices continued into the 1990s.

The Canadian Airborne is an important exemplar of the mediated character of racism, sexism, and heterosexism in the social organization of the military. In her critical examination of the Somalia affair, Sherene Razack discusses a study conducted for the Somalia Inquiry by Donna Winslow in which members of the Airborne were interviewed. They "were mostly convinced that human rights legislation, requiring the Armed Forces to stop discriminating against women and against racial and sexual minorities, weakened the military and contributed to its acceptance of unqualified soldiers. They vehemently opposed homosexuality and saw efforts to discipline soldiers who harassed women and minorities as limiting the military's capacity to produce effective soldiers."[63] This mirrored the military's position on equality rights. Razack's work reveals that men, in an effort to prove their heterosexual masculinity, often objectified women: "As one solider explained, men who spend a great deal of time togeth-er feel a need to prove that they are not homosexual by going out and 'getting themselves a woman': 'When we go out the woman becomes a machine, an object that we'd use as much as possible, and talk about as much as possible because afterwards there won't be any women around.'" According to Razack's study, "men learn to be men through the practices of Othering women, homo-sexuals, and racial minorities." And it points out that what "Winslow fails to see [is] that they learn to be white men, a gendered and raced identity enacted in Africa within an official mission to save Somalia from the excesses of their own culture and society."[64]

Razack also demonstrates that these practices were not exclusive to the Airborne, as was suggested by the inquiry, but, rather, that they were and con-tinue to be widespread throughout the military. The significance of symbolic anal rape, in both the hazing rituals among Airborne members and their torture of Somalians, is highlighted in Razack's work. She draws on Theweleit's analy-sis of the German Freikorps to make this critical point: "The anus is a site of aggression because it represents forbidden territory to a heterosexual man and the ever present possibility that men engaged in homosocial bonding can too easily cross the line into homosexuality."[65] The use of anal rape or sexual assault, usually with a stick, a pipe, or a bottle, was a way of rendering other men pas-sive, penetrated, and dependent. In the brutality enacted against Shidane Arone and other young Somali men, this sexual violence was racialized.

Threats of violence also occurred in other parts of the military. Purged from the navy in the early 1980s, Bernie was threatened when he was stationed on a ship:

The last six months, there were about eight guys who were suspecting me [of being gay]. I was finding letters ... stating that they knew about me, they saw me frequenting the gay bars. And [they] threatened me with revealing that I was gay or hurting me somehow. One guy said to me, "You know, there's a position on board the ship. It's called life buoy sentry. They sit right at the back of the ship for an approximate twelve-hour period and what they are is the last person who will see or hear anything if someone has fallen overboard." Well, I was told that that person could be paid off, and if someone is suspected of being gay, [he] could be thrown into the ocean and nothing would be seen or heard of that person again. (June 27, 2001)

Bernie also remembered,

In my basic training ... one of the master corporals was calling me faggot: "You're a faggot." I was cornered by an army officer when I was stationed in BC, he lived right next door to me and suspected also. He cornered me in the boardroom, because I was a steward in there and he was an officer coming in for a function, and he said, "I know about you, I know all about you and your time will come." I thought, "Just stay away from me and let me do my job." Every time I bumped into this particular officer he was very nasty ... I [also] remember once when we were going into San Francisco. The captain always comes on to the PA system and gives a little speech as to what is going on. His last comment was, "Watch your bums." It was funny, but pretty homophobic. (June 27, 2001)

Purging Lesbians

These policies and practices had a major impact on women in the military, ranging from anti-lesbian violence (which was tolerated by military authorities) to being purged from the armed forces. In the early 1980s, SIU surveillance often focused on women's sport activities in the military. Women's sports teams were one avenue through which lesbians met and maintained networks within the military. In the context of the surveillance of women's broom ball, one woman said: "[My partner] got called in about three or four times and [the SIU] really grilled her. I mean four hours later, they would be still in there grilling her. Finally she broke: she said 'Okay, I am gay.' It took them a month to get her out of the military."[66] Another woman reported that, in 1983, she was interrogated by the SIU: "I was called in a couple times a week before they made their big bust. The MPs (military police) even broke into one girl's room. Two women were kicked out and two others walked out of the military. It was really scary. You are just coming out to yourself after years of denial and it feels great, and then all of a sudden, you are called in and grilled. It was really scary."[67] This frightening climate had devastating consequences for lesbians in the military.

Marielle enrolled in the army in 1976. She successfully completed a number of training programs and courses to become a technician. In the spring of 1980, she was promoted to corporal, but in 1981, when she was stationed on the west coast,

Troubles started when a roommate, also a member of the forces, attempted suicide by taking an overdose of prescription pills. The Special Investigation Unit questioned me a whole afternoon on various subjects, first about her,

Continuing Exclusion

then myself. By the time I got home that night, I knew they were suspicious about my lifestyle. I had heard some stories, then, how you could be watched or tricked by someone posing as gay. Shortly after, I made the decision to tell them and see what happened. I went to my commanding officer and told him: "I'm asking for my release because I'm a lesbian and I did not want any harassment." I explained that I would prefer to continue my career in the forces if I was given the OK, with the army knowing. Well, I was naive in a way. The first thing that happened to me the next day was to lose my security clearance. This meant that I could no longer walk inside my bunker without a guard, everybody looking and asking what was going on ... It was very embarrassing. (March 11, 1998)

The loss of security clearance was a key part of the authorized response to suspected lesbians in military ranks. Prior to being purged, such women would lose their security clearances and be thrown into limbo. Often, they were transferred to a lower-level position that did not require security clearance. In many cases, this effectively outed them since members of the military could, with relative ease, surmise that the person was under investigation and have a good idea as to why. Even if it was never explicitly stated, being queer was one of the major available means of making sense of these demotions and transfers in the military. Thus, we see how transfer and loss of security clearance fed the social organization of talk and rumours.

Marielle's experiences leading up to her dismissal were exacerbated by many months of waiting:

So for a quick solution, they decided to send me with the lineman crew who were going to [another base] every week. We stayed in a motel and I was away from people's questioning eyes. It was a blessing ... because my release did not come from Ottawa for six months ... The work was physically hard but I challenged myself not to let my humiliation get the better of me and [to] do a good job to the end. I was still so sure that they could not let me go just for that reason, not with all my credentials. After all, I had not been accused of any wrongdoing: it was only an admission of something I was all along ... When my release date finally came, my commanding officer wrote me a nice letter of reference and told me I should never have said anything, that they would have spoken for me and nothing would have come of any investigation. Perhaps his words were sincere, but I doubt if my career was not already doomed by then. I was due for a posting and God knows where I would have been sent, and without friends around, it would have been easy to send me into a trap or watch my whereabouts. No thank you. (March 11, 1998)

Being sent away meant that Marielle was no longer the target of gossip and speculation. Despite what her commanding officer told her, it is very likely that, following the initial investigation, the SIU had already classified her as a homosexual.

The Shelburne Purge of "Hard-Core Lesbians"

On February 28, 1985, the *Globe & Mail* revealed the largest single and most publicized lesbian purge – between August and October 1984, five women had been dismissed from the Canadian Armed Forces station in Shelburne, Nova Scotia, for being members of a "homosexual clique" of "hard-core lesbians."[68] Other media referred to a "ring" of lesbians at the base. According to Lieutenant Commander Elliot Smith of Canadian Armed Forces Station Shelburne, their "abnormal sexual activity" threatened "national security." He stated that, "because of the sensitive nature of the work" at the submarine tracking station, "it was determined that they were a security risk."[69] In the media, the military suggested that the women brought the official attention down on themselves through their "flagrant behaviour," even though military policy called for the purging of individuals who engaged in any lesbian acts in the forces.[70]

Later, Smith said that the women were purged not because they were lesbians but because they were "security risks" according to the new standard military discourse, to which he turned to organize his interaction with the media. Military spokesmen distanced themselves from earlier language, stating that, while homosexuality was not a crime, it nonetheless "lower[ed] morale and reduce[d] operating efficiency."[71]

The women's expulsion followed months of SIU investigation, which began in April 1984. As a result of these dismissals, the women lost not only their jobs but also any possibility of career advancement. They faced the full weight of the military and, later, the mass media, which stigmatized them as "social deviants." They were informed that, in the event that they tried to appeal their honourable discharges, no tribunal existed to hear their cases.[72]

Following their dismissal, one of the women stated: "We hoped that it was over with, and that we could now go on with our lives." On the morning of February 28, 1985, they were confronted with the reality that their dismissals had become public information, with several newspapers and radio stations carrying the story. According to Anne Fulton, "They were shocked ... Some were devastated."[73]

This media coverage had a major impact across the country, but especially in nearby Halifax. In response to the purge, lesbian and gay activists in Halifax mobilized against military policy. Darl Wood, now a spokesperson for the Gay Alliance for Equality, stated that the Halifax gay and lesbian communities "were outraged but not surprised that five lesbians were fired." Jim McSwain, a member of the GAE civil rights committee, believed that the military placed homosexuals in a Catch-22 situation: "If you come out and say you're a homosexual, the armed forces fires you and the human rights code can't protect you." According to McSwain, the military argument that homosexuals were a "security threat" was a "red herring used to actively discriminate against" gays and lesbians.[74]

The International Women's Day celebrations on March 9, 1985, in Halifax included a response to the purge at Shelburne. Fulton recalled: "The march ... abounded with posters such as 'There's No Life Like It' [the military recruitment slogan] with two woman symbols intersecting, 'CFS Shelburne is harmful to lesbians and other living things' and 'Hard Core.' These were swept along with innumerable posters reflecting sentiments of anti-militarism and of peace, these being the main themes of the day."[75]

In a letter to Minister of Defence Erik Nielsen, Ken Belanger wrote,

> Gay and lesbian Canadians ... have grown only too familiar with the deplorable tactics employed by the SIU in its increasing "witch hunts" against us: the tapping of telephones, the employment of informers to infiltrate our duly constituted public organizations, the use of stake-outs to clandestinely photograph Forces personnel entering gay-owned premises, and the conducting of humiliating interrogations, such as those of the women in question ... The official reason we are told is that gays and lesbians are viewed, in so many words, as potential criminals, if you will: as men and women who are in danger of "breaching national security, by being blackmailed."[76]

Belanger's comments reveal a significant understanding of military surveillance and its impact on queer space in Halifax. After problematizing the blackmail argument, Belanger continued his critique of the military's logic:

> The real reason for this ongoing campaign to remove us from the military service, and indeed many other forms of employment in our society, is blatant, systematic discrimination against gay and lesbian Canadians because of our sexual orientation ... The "national security" argument is wearing thin, Mr. Minister, especially in the face of the reportedly "spotless" service record of the

women dismissed from Shelburne. It is time to admit that the surveillance, harassment and dismissal of gay and lesbian military personnel is a violation of our human rights, a blatant and systematic form of discrimination based on sexual orientation.[77]

By 1985, lesbian and gay resistance to military policies had become more public and assertive.

Lesbians and gay men in the military reported being followed and spied upon at least into the early 1990s. As a result, during these years they adopted a series of strategies to avoid detection. Crucial to this was living a double life. One lesbian described how, if she was talking on the phone, rather than using people's actual names she would alter the gender of the names to protect both herself and those to whom she was referring. Another woman, who was interrogated about the woman with whom she was living (and who was also her girlfriend), coped as follows: "I hid myself. Like, I wouldn't go to parties because I had no boyfriend, or I would invite my neighbour just so they would think I was with the guy."[78]

Military Reserves: "There was always an element of fear"

Problems continued for lesbians in the military throughout the 1980s, including in the military reserves. Brenda Barnes, who was in the naval reserve and officer training program from 1983 to 1989 at reserve units in Regina, Toronto, Victoria, Montreal, Halifax, and Hamilton, remembered her experience as a lesbian in the reserves in her first summer on the west coast: "I was in training at a facility called Albert Head when I first learned of the policy forbidding the presence of homosexuals in the military ... Because some women I was living in dorms with knew that I was originally from Regina, they asked me if I knew a certain woman who had been there the summer before ... She has been kicked out of the service on the accusation that she was a lesbian. I had not known her" (May 15, 2005). Later that same summer, a training officer wanted to speak to Barnes regarding her "behaviour":

We were about forty-five minutes into the interview and had discussed all my [training] options ... when I asked if I was free to go. After an uncomfortable silence, I was asked whether I had been told the real reason why I had been summoned to the meeting ... I was then told by the training officer I was there because some other women in my dorm had made some accusations about my behaviour, all of which were easy to refute, but all of which suggested I was a lesbian. The accusations, such as that I looked oddly at other women in the communal showers or in dorms when we were dressing, were nonsense and untrue, but the insinuation was not. The truth was that I was in love with a woman, my first lover; however, she was not on the west coast. I was not about to tell the truth about that. The official questioning lasted maybe ten minutes. I don't recall the exact questions as the training officer was more embarrassed than I was. I managed to talk my way out of the interview and nothing further came of it that summer and I was not interrogated nor investigated for the rest of the time I was in the service. (May 15, 2005)

Accusations from women sharing showers and dorms were taken seriously enough to be investigated. It also seems that, in reserve officer training programs, training officers performed initial security questioning without the assistance of the SIU. Barnes recalled that, during her second summer on the west coast,

My sexual orientation became an open secret especially among my officer training peers, some of whom became life-long friends. They protected me while encouraging me to keep a low profile. However, I always felt the sword above my head as other women I knew, women in the lower ranks, became subject to interrogation, entrapment, and dishonourable discharge. In the entire six years I was in the navy, I never knew another woman officer who was a lesbian, so I often "fraternized with the lower ranks" ... in order to avoid being socially isolated. (May 15, 2005)

By this time, as a result of the emergence of lesbian and gay movements and the securing of equality rights, younger women were more likely to choose to come out to their friends; older women, however, tended to be more fearful. Knowledge of and experience with an era during which lesbianism was grounds for automatic expulsion from the military made this fear more palpable for earlier rather than later recruits.

Over these years, Barnes developed significant knowledge about military purge regulations:

What I heard about the military intelligence interrogation sessions was that the Special Investigations Unit (SIU) would show up unannounced at a person's home or their office. The person would be taken to an undisclosed location without benefit of food, water or professional counsel and they would be harassed, intimidated, and questioned until such time as a confession was obtained. Once the confession was obtained they would then be pushed to name other names. The named people would in turn be subjected to the same treatment. The whole system of ferreting out queers worked on the basis of entrapment. After confessions were obtained, persons were processed for dishonourable release, and in keeping with the official policy of the day, their work record forever read "not advantageously employable." I knew several women to whom that happened. They were all part of the same social circle. I heard about a young man in the regular force navy who hanged himself on one of the destroyers rather than have a dishonourable release on his record. I had another man friend who was released voluntarily before being ambushed. (May 15, 2005)

According to Barnes, the length of the interrogations and the conditions under which they were held were instrumental in producing confessions. Pressure to give the names of other lesbians or gays was a standard feature of these interrogations. Once identified as lesbian or gay, people were "not advantageously employable," a life-long designation that permanently limited employment possibilities. However, by the mid- to late 1980s, being purged was not the only option. As Barnes pointed out, "Other people in the ranks I knew who were well known to be gay were not released or questioned, but mysteriously would not get their promotions or training courses they needed to advance in their careers. This was even after the official policy was changed in 1992." In the military, erecting obstacles to promotions or training courses (which may have required higher security clearance levels and more investigations) was similar to freezing people's careers in the public service.

Barnes offered this explanation as to why the investigations of her stopped:

I fully expected to get that SIU knock on my door at any time. To this day I am not sure why it never came. I was well known to other lesbians in the naval reserve, which was a very closed circle and quite separate formally, socially and culturally from the regular force navy ... I suspect I was protected unofficially either because I was an officer or because I knew too many other officers and other ranks who knew about me throughout the whole naval reserve, who would be in trouble for keeping a secret. The domino effect of my prosecution might have been too large to withstand. This rationale occurred to other women in the ranks who had been persecuted and, among them, I falsely obtained a reputation as a snitch. Because of this reputation I was openly

threatened at a bar one evening in Victoria by a woman with brass knuckles ...
Years after I was out of the navy, a former senior officer told me that she
had been questioned by higher authorities about her sexual orientation and
had presumed that insinuation came from me. (May 15, 2005)

Because she was never purged, others who were investigated began to suspect
that Barnes was a snitch. In these situations and through underground lesbian
networks in the military, such rumours were a way of accounting for what was
going on and for identifying whom to avoid.

Barnes was lucky to have supportive friends in the military. And, despite
the anti-lesbian campaigns,

> Overall I found people's sentiments in the navy towards me as a lesbian to
> be quite liberal; though they would only express such sentiments privately.
> I once went out with the daughter of a high-ranking person in the submarine
> squadron on the east coast. When he asked his daughter about me he told her
> to tell me to be careful as I could get into a lot of trouble if the wrong person
> found out ... Most people made it clear that I should be careful, but they were
> not going to be the person who told anyone else about me. However, we all
> heard stories by word of mouth, through friends and lovers, about what hap-
> pened to other people. So, there was always an element of fear that determined
> your actions, what you said and shared and your choice of pronouns. I took
> judicious risks in terms of selecting my intimates and in terms of [with] whom
> I shared the truth about my sexual identity. Among other dykes there was an
> unspoken code of mutual secrecy and protection. We all understood the risks
> we were taking being queer in the environment in which we lived and worked.
> (May 15, 2005)

Barnes described a number of the survival strategies that she and other lesbians
employed, including a code of secrecy (something we encountered in earlier
queer networks). In this context, Barnes told us about her greatest personal
regret from these years: "The policy prevented me from responding to a
woman whom I truly adored. At the time she did not self-identify as a lesbian
and was not fully aware of the risks she was taking in making overtures towards
me, overtures which I declined, though I was in love. I had to choose to give
her up in order to protect her. It was one of the hardest things I have ever had
to do in my life." Barnes left the service because of an impending security
investigation:

I was released from the service voluntarily in 1989 within months of getting my promotion to naval lieutenant and my bridge watch keeping ticket. At the time I was working at Maritime Command in Halifax as an assistant editor of a naval internal publication. I was due for reinvestigation by CSIS for my security clearance and decided it was time to leave before anything turned up in that investigation. By then I had established a social network of gays and lesbians in Halifax and was eager to work in media outside the navy. Most of all ... I was exhausted from always having to keep my guard up, always choosing very carefully what I said and to whom. I was tired of pretending and had become politicized by a system that treated gay and lesbian persons worse that they would treat animals and insisted we had no value to the Canadian workforce. My subsequent activism was largely fuelled by my experience in the Canadian military. (May 15, 2005)

Like others in her situation, Barnes found that her experiences of military regulations and surveillance helped to radicalize her and to propel her into activism.

SVEND ROBINSON JOINS THE STRUGGLE

In the 1980s and 1990s, from the inside of the official political system, New Democratic Party Member of Parliament Svend Robinson played a central and sustained part in the struggle against national security policies. In particular, at the time of the Shelburne purge, he called for changes in the military policy barring lesbians and gay men from the Canadian Armed Forces. However, his concerns were brushed aside by Defence Minister Erik Nielsen. Robinson called the policy discriminatory, and Nielsen responded by stating that the purges were based on existing legislation. He refused to comment on individual cases.[79] Robinson challenged Nielsen's assertion that there was an adequate grievance procedure in place for these women, stating: "They've lost their jobs. They've lost their livelihoods. It was a shattering experience for them."[80] Robinson remembered "[a] sense of outrage that I was raising these issues. Somehow it should be self-evident that we have to rid the military of these 'hardcore lesbians,' I mean they were a 'ring,' right? And they were a grave threat to national security ... The idea that these people be allowed to remain and serve as members of the armed forces was again heretical. And people like Nielsen would be really quite contemptuous ... of any suggestion to the contrary" (July 30, 2002).

We asked when this issue of discrimination in the military arose, and Robinson replied: "Soon after I was elected in 1979 because [it] had been drawn to my attention early on. This was blatant discrimination ... The policies were unambiguous: if you were openly gay or lesbian you were thrown out. We won't allow you to join and the investigative policies were also particularly offensive and repugnant. I don't know when I first raised the issues, but certainly it was in the early eighties" (July 30, 2002).

Prior to the equality rights section of the Charter of Rights and Freedoms,

> the whole notion that gay and lesbian people might be treated as equals par-
> ticularly in the military was regarded as heresy ... certainly by other members
> of Parliament and by military staff ... For example, in the Defence Committee
> there would be just a flood of officers sitting around the room. That is how it
> always happens, all these officers in uniforms. And then the minister would be
> there flanked by an amount of other officers ... and I would raise these issues
> and you could just feel the tension in the room and the hostility in the room
> coming from the officers and certainly from the other members on the com-
> mittee. (July 30, 2002)

Robinson remembered an interaction with an under-briefed minister, whose lack of knowledge clashed with official military policy, thus causing some embarrassment:

> Actually one glorious moment [was] when Gilles Lamontagne was the ...
> Liberal minister of national defence ... and there was a meeting of the Defence
> Committee ... I put to Lamontagne ... the arguments [about] how offensive
> and outrageous these policies were and said surely it was time for the minister
> to change these policies and to recognize that people who want to serve should
> be able to serve without any discrimination on the basis of sexual orientation.
> The minister kind of didn't consult, and he said, "You know, you're right. This
> is something we should be reexamining and ... I am prepared to reexamine it."
> Well, you could hear this collective intake of air, gasps of generals, and I then
> immediately just moved right on to get an answer so he didn't have an oppor-
> tunity to reflect or be briefed ... And then the next morning if not that same
> day the minister's office issued a release saying that, in fact, the minister
> wished to clarify that he did not in any way wish to change the policies of the
> Canadian Armed Forces and once again that was the news story ... Of course,
> during this time – I was not [publicly] "out" 'til 1988 ... – so you can imagine
> the attacks I would get, and some of them [were] quite vicious personal attacks
> ... from members. But most of them were not reported because the media
> would not report them because in a sense just reporting them fed that kind

of thing. All during that period of time, anytime I raised these issues I would get these smirks and comments and the attacks. (July 30, 2002)

THE SOCIAL ORGANIZATION OF MILITARY SURVEILLANCE, INTERROGATION, REPORTING, AND DISCHARGE

Stephane Sirard's and Bernie's stories about their experiences with the military national security campaigns offer an important glimpse into the social organization of military practices against men who had sex with men. In this section, these two narratives illustrate features of the military social organization of surveillance, interrogation, reporting, and discharge. Although both Sirard and Bernie were discharged in the 1980s, their different locations within military relations led to both common and distinct experiences. Their accounts are also tied to the military regulations used to organize these purges, especially CFAO 19-20 (1976) (see Figure 2).

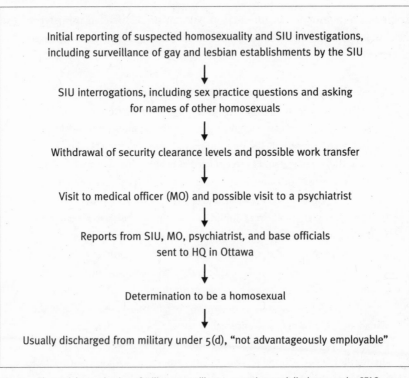

Initial reporting of suspected homosexuality and SIU investigations, including surveillance of gay and lesbian establishments by the SIU

↓

SIU interrogations, including sex practice questions and asking for names of other homosexuals

↓

Withdrawal of security clearance levels and possible work transfer

↓

Visit to medical officer (MO) and possible visit to a psychiatrist

↓

Reports from SIU, MO, psychiatrist, and base officials sent to HQ in Ottawa

↓

Determination to be a homosexual

↓

Usually discharged from military under 5(d), "not advantageously employable"

Figure 2 The social organization of military surveillance, reporting, and discharge under CFAO 19-20

Sirard's Story: Purged for Being "Seen in a Gay Club"

Stephane Sirard, from New Liskeard, Ontario, joined the military in 1979. On March 14, 1982, he was purged from the Cornwallis military base in Nova Scotia. Blair Johnston met him in Ottawa when he (Johnston) was providing advice to people purged from the military and RCMP. Stephane went public and talked to the media about what had happened to him. Here is Johnston's description of Stephane:

> In the 1980s I met a man who was a military police man and he'd just been booted out ... In his mind it was, "Yes, I have sex with other men, but I'm not gay." He didn't know any other gay people in the military. It was only later he found out that they thought because he was in the military police that he couldn't have been gay, so they had the same stereotypes about him. And he found out there's a whole network of sisters [i.e., gay men] on the base he was at, and he just had no idea about these people beforehand. (February 1, 2001)

Many men who have sex with other men do not identify as gay or bisexual. The fluidity of sexual identifications and practices is not captured in the binary opposition of heterosexual and homosexual. Men who identify as heterosexual do engage in sex with other men. Regardless of how these men "make sense" of their sexualities, military and national security policies focused primarily on sexual activity and not on sexual identification. The military campaign against homosexuals could out all these men as homosexuals, fags, or queers.

Sirard documented his experiences by taping an account of them that was partly based on notes and letters he had written to prepare for a possible legal challenge.[81] This account provides useful insights into the military relations within which Sirard was entangled. He was discharged from the Canadian Armed Forces in March 1982, but his investigation began in late October 1981. The evidence used to initiate this investigation involved his having been "seen in a gay club" – the Turret in downtown Halifax.[82]

Sirard's identification as a possible homosexual and his consequent investigation were dependent upon the surveillance practices already in place in Halifax regarding gay and lesbian gathering spots. Some of this has already been seen in Sue's and Joan's accounts of the surveillance of lesbian networks in the Halifax area, in Frank Letourneau's anecdote of the surveillance of his car in cruising places, in Robin Metcalfe's narrative of the surveillance of the Turret, and in the letter Ken Belanger wrote at the time of the Shelburne purge. This surveillance was orchestrated by the SIU.

In 1979, Sirard joined the forces and began training to become a military policeman. In 1980, he was posted to Cornwallis, where he worked as a private in the military police and maintained a solid record. In August 1981, he was informed of an impending promotion to corporal in January 1982 based on his excellent work. He was granted a break and given four days vacation. Sirard decided to go into Halifax, and he and a friend "went to a gay disco." In Sirard's words, during the two years he had been posted at Cornwallis, "I must have went three to five times to that gay disco, the only one in Nova Scotia. Nobody from the base knew about my going to this club." Upon his return to the base, on October 21, 1981, Sirard was called to the office by his superior officer:

> He told me that two men wanted to speak to me at the barrack block. I noticed two men one which I knew was a SIU officer from Halifax and the other I had no idea who he was. They both introduced themselves to me as SIU, detachment Halifax. They told me to relax, sit and talk about myself. I had a funny feeling and I was wondering what they wanted to know. I told them that I had "no time to lose and they had no time to lose either so why don't they ask me what they want to know about." They told me, "We had a confidential source saying to us that you were in a gay club in Halifax during the weekend. What do you have to say about it?" I told them the following: "I have been in there with men and I have been there with women. What I am doing in my own bedroom is not your business."

While making visible the surveillance of this gay spot in Halifax, Sirard also defied the SIU officers by invoking Trudeau's comment about the state having no place in the bedrooms of the nation and extending it to the military. However, Sirard's attempt to construct himself as a bisexual backfired. Claiming bisexuality, which may not seem as "deviant" as homosexuality, was unsuccessful as an avoidance strategy because, in the military, any participation in same-gender sex made one subject to dismissal. Under military regulations, bisexuality did not enjoy a distinct classification.

Bernie's Story: The Confiscation of Gay-Oriented Birthday Cards
Before joining the navy, Bernie was in the militia and the army, where he had no problems with the security state. His difficulties started in the navy while he was stationed on the west coast in the early 1980s. Unlike Sirard, Bernie participated in the navy's gay network:

With our squadron, which was four ships, out of those four ships there were about twenty of us who knew about each other. When we would go to foreign ports, half of us were still on duty, and the other half were free to go and do their thing. That half that were free to go and do their thing would scout the area for gay bars and then come back to the ship and report to us where it was ... Eventually all of us could get together and go out and party. Now, not everybody was gay; some were bisexual. So there was quite a few of us in a squadron of four ships. There were even some officers. (June 27, 2001)

Like Sirard, Bernie had a good record, but he was terminated because he engaged in same-gender sex:

[My troubles started] with being called into the military police because someone had been busted for drugs. In order to lessen his consequences of breaking military laws, he gave names. One of the names was mine and other people that I also knew. At the same time, one of the names that had been mentioned was pulled into the military police, and they asked if they knew me and they stated that they knew me and had smoked a joint with me. Which I denied because I didn't do drugs. (June 27, 2001)

This reveals how investigations into other matters, such as drug use, could lead to investigations into one's sexual practices. The attempt to retrieve the names of other military members involved in "illegal" or "deviant" practices was a standard part of military interrogations. Bernie went on to say:

When they [military police] approached me, they suggested that they do a search of my apartment ... I agreed because I had nothing to hide and when they came in, there was only one military police officer who came in ... He searched drawers in my bedroom, in my closet and just before he was to leave he noticed my birthday cards sitting on my dining room table. He picked them up and noticed that they were gay-oriented. He said, "I'm going to confiscate these cards." At the same time, he said, "You know, it's not against the law in here, not against the law." And he said, "It's not wrong and you won't get in trouble for it." He took the cards and then he went back to the military police station ... and sent me back to base accommodations, at which I worked because I was no longer on the ship at this time. (June 27, 2001)

Even though the search of his apartment was motivated by drug concerns, once the cards were spotted, they were confiscated. Despite what the MP officer said, these became the focus of an investigation into whether Bernie was a homo-sexual. According to Bernie, "Not long after that they called me in to the military police station and started asking me some questions. I had been seen coming in and out of a gay bar, [they said] that I was named on a list of people who were given from someone that had been charged for drugs."

As it shifted from drugs to homosexuality, the investigation moved from the military police to the SIU. According to Bernie, "Sometimes [the SIU] were not in uniform, so they were sneaking around playing civilian." Bernie's and Sirard's stories are similar: in both cases the investigation was based on surveil-lance of gay establishments. Following the confiscation of the birthday cards, the military police and the SIU attempted to conduct more surveillance on Bernie. The potential drug connection was still being raised, perhaps to apply pressure on him to reveal his sexual activities: "I denied the drug part, but it was somewhat impossible to deny the gay part because they already had those cards. At the same time, one of the cards had another military person's name signed on it and he was eventually investigated. I don't know what has become of him."

Bernie reported that a number of other naval members on the west coast were purged at around this time. This was all related to the sailor who was ar-rested for drugs. To "lessen his jail time" he gave the military names, and "then he got a dishonourable release." According to Bernie,

> He brought down approximately two hundred people. They weren't all gay, [they were] people who he'd partied with, who he knew that [used] drugs ... But each person was being investigated individually, and yes, there was another person who I knew. We knew the investigation was going on. He was asked about me and I was asked about him. So it kind of confirmed that this person was going to be thrown out also. When he [i.e., military police or SIU] asked about another person who I knew was [gay], I denied that he was. And I knew he was gay. But he got out before he was found out, before they could continue an investigation of him. Another person was thrown out ... He was also released for being gay. (June 27, 2001)

The Social Relations of Military Interrogation: The Sex Practice Questions
In that Sirard and Bernie were both asked a series of sex-related questions to establish whether they had engaged in homosexual sexual practices, their in-terrogations were similar to those of Darl Wood and Barbara Thornborrow. Sirard was asked, "'Have you ever had anal sex with a man? Have you ever had anal sex with a woman? Have you had sex with a man in a car? Did you ever have an orgy? Have you ever had a threesome?' and on and on. And I told them,

Continuing Exclusion

... 'You are [being] personal and I got nothing else to say. The only thing I have to say is I have been to bed with men and I have been in bed with women, and yes I was in that gay club during the weekend.'" Bernie continued,

> They started off with a lot of questions that dealt with homosexuality, asked me questions such as, "What do you do when you meet another gay person?" ... They would continuously ask questions. It was usually short answers that I would give him, but he would keep drilling me. Eventually, he got a bigger picture of what was going on in my life. Going into full detail such as, "What do you do?" "You hug and kiss someone," I said that. After just meeting and going out and meeting other people, they would ask more personal, sexual questions, "What do you do in bed with somebody?" I tried to explain that. They would ask, "Mutual masturbation? Kissing? Anal sex?" and so on. And the frequenting of gay bars. (June 27, 2001)

In the 1980s, questions about sexual practice were standard parts of military interrogations and were critical for establishing verbal confirmation regarding actual same-gender sexual activity. Sirard, Bernie, Wood, Thornborrow, Michelle Douglas, and others reported the systematic character of the questions relating to sexual practice. While this may have been related to the voyeuristic interests of the interrogators, it was also a basic feature of SIU investigations. Confirming that homosexual sexual practices had taken place established that these individuals had contravened the military regulations laid out in CFAO 19-20.

In 1993, these interrogation practices were clarified by Minister of National Defence Tom Siddon's responses to questions raised by the Gay and Lesbian Organization of Veterans (GLOV):

> Investigations into homosexuality had to establish that a homosexual act had occurred. At what point is an individual deemed to be a homosexual? Before career decisions could be made, decision-makers required some specifics with which to resolve this question. It was also not unusual for individuals to seek to escape from career contracts by falsely claiming to be homosexual. Precise details of sex acts were not required but many homosexuals, once they had conceded that they were gay, furnished more detail than the investigators wished to hear. A complete investigative report would have included this additional detail whether it was desired or not.[83]

These sex practice questions were designed to demonstrate that the individual had enough knowledge of homosexual sex to confirm that he or she had actually engaged in it. These comments also perpetuated the myth that queers are always willing to talk about sex, even under interrogation, and helped to produce the "sexualization" of the homosexual.

Identifying Other Homosexuals: Bernie's Strategies of Refusal and Resistance

Another major aspect of the interrogations involved collecting the names of other homosexuals. As Bernie recalled,

> They were searching, trying to find any possible way to get me out. After all this drilling I even asked the sergeant, "You seem to be a little uncomfortable with sitting here with me." And he says, "Well, I have a son who is gay." I said, "Really. You have a son who's gay, yet you're sitting here drilling me. So don't you feel a bit awkward about that? It sounds like maybe you haven't really accepted it." But he says, "That is neither here nor there." He says, "I'm doing my job." (June 27, 2001)

Bernie's questioning of his interrogator's personal family situation initiated an interesting resistance strategy within a setting in which the suspected homosexual usually has little power. This transgression is then deflected by the sergeant's reinsertion of the standard professional bureaucratic "I'm doing my job," which works to deny all personal responsibility for his actions.

When we asked Bernie if they ever asked him whether specific individuals were homosexual, he replied:

> Yes. They wanted a list of names. First, they asked me, "Do you know anybody else who's gay in the Canadian Armed Forces?" And I said, "Yes I do." And they said, "Well, can we have these names?" And I said, "No, you can't, I'm not giving them to you. I don't care what you do to me, you will not get those names." Then, because I was getting a bit angry with them, I said, "Well, why don't you investigate some of my officers like Major so-and-so, and this person and that person." And they said, "Okay, so there's no officers who are gay." Well, I know for a fact there were. My ship was a training ship, and there were always "baby officers." They were young officers who were lower in rank, who were on their training for navigation and other types of jobs aboard a destroyer or anti-submarine vessel.

When questioned as to whether they asked specifically whether a certain person was a homosexual, Bernie said: "I was not at liberty to give them that information. I just felt, no, you're investigating me, you want me out so bad, and I'm not going to contribute to getting other people thrown out. No way ... They wanted to get rid of everybody. They asked me if I knew certain people. They did ask me, and I said, 'Yes [I know them] and [then] played dumb, 'No, I don't know [if they are homosexuals], you're going to have to ask them'" (June 27, 2001). One of the common SIU and RCMP interrogation strategies was to try to get identified homosexuals to implicate other homosexuals, hence the energy expended on this in interrogations. Bernie briefly described the interview context, revealing a clear sense of the power/knowledge relations: "They had me in there alone, in the police station to question me. They would ask the same questions to see if they were going to get the same answer, I suppose. That's what they did." He also pointed out that only one officer would actually interrogate him.

Part of Bernie's ability to resist was related to the gay network he participated in, which produced a certain social basis for non-cooperation and clearly opposed naming other gay members in the armed forces:

> There's one guy who got out finally without being found out. He said, "Please don't mention my name." So we knew, we weren't mentioning anybody's names. When you were being drilled constantly: Do you know this person? "Yes." Do you know this person? "Yes." "What do you know about this person?" "Well, you're going to have to ask that person." Because I wasn't willing to give out any information, and that's how my other buddies were too ... But I am not sure about one. He may have given some information.

Security Clearance Withdrawal: The Social Organization of Being in Limbo and Outing Fags

These investigations followed the course of action set out in CFAO 19-20, which states: "If a person subject to the Code of Discipline [a member of the military] becomes aware, or suspects that a member of the Canadian Forces (CF) is a homosexual, or has a sexual abnormality, he shall report the matter to the commanding officer (CO)."[84] In Sirard's case, the report to his CO came from the SIU, which had conducted surveillance of the Turret in Halifax; in Bernie's case, the report came from the military police, whose drug investigation had turned up evidence of homosexuality.

After Sirard was identified as a possible homosexual, his superior officer was informed and an SIU investigation was initiated. This initial investigation, which included an SIU interview with Sirard, found that he had admitted to having had sex with other men. This information was then communicated to his superior officer, and it had major consequences regarding the type of work he was allowed to do as well as regarding his security clearance level:

I got called by my superior ... And he told me that I was suspended from duties till further notice. He then requested my badge, credentials and weapon from me. He told me, "It is abnormal to be gay" and that "I destroyed by being gay the name of the Canadian Armed Forces." He told me that he will not have any abnormal person working for him and that I was suspended until further notice, till the report is submitted. He then told me to take a vacation and to go away from the base.

Here we get a clear sense of the military brass' hostility towards homosexuality. Sirard, being a member of the military police, required a high level of security clearance. The initial investigation led to the withdrawal of that clearance, which meant he could no longer be a military police officer. He was then assigned a number of tasks that required lower levels of security clearance. This completely cut him out of his regular work, denied him his badge and gun, and removed him from many military practices in which he had previously been engaged.

Sirard was told he would be working "at a low profile" in the base's gym, issuing sports equipment. Since he had worked as a military policeman, some particular problems emerged at the gym:

When I arrived at the base gym five other persons was working down there, which all were personnel I laid drug charges against or investigated ... They were all suspended from their own duties and their security clearance were withdrawn from them. And they asked me, "What are you doing here ... Are you undercover ...?" I feel like a criminal. There I was working with five guys suspended from their duties because of criminal offences, drugs ... And there I was brooming, washing the floor, and picking up garbage.

While the investigations continued and a series of reports on Sirard was being sent to Ottawa for a final determination, he was shifted around in a number of lower-level positions, one of which involved conducting a traffic survey. This led to questions from his co-workers: "People start to wonder how come the Frenchman is not working anymore on the beat. Some people say he is undercover, others say he is with the SIU, oh no it is because ... he kept some drugs for himself. Or no it is because he is gay that he has been caught seen in a gay club. He is a homosexual." Given that Sirard was no longer working as an MP, one of the interpretations available to military members was that he must be a homosexual. It is in this way that individuals can be outed among other military members.

Sirard went back to his superior officer and was told to take some time off for Christmas:

> In January '82 I came back to the base and I went to the office again to see my captain. He told me, "You are not working for me anymore and I don't want to see you around the military police section or around my guys. You are working for Captain ..." And then I was just frustrated and fed up and I told him, "Sir, I have been working for you for 15 months. You have given me acts of promotion, you give me compliments about my work and then from the day after you found out I was seen in the gay club then you treat me like a piece of trash." He said, "I don't want to talk about it. Just get out from here and keep away from this police section and the other guys." I said, "They are my friends." He said, "It doesn't matter. See them off duty."

There is an important clash between the policies of military management and the language of resistance Sirard was able to mobilize. His superior officer was angry that he kept coming to the police section office and causing trouble from his vantage point:

> I then went to see Major ... He then told me that he didn't hear anything from Ottawa and that I would be working under a Lt ... in the base language school for the first two weeks probably moving furniture as they move the school into a new building ... Then people started to talk. Now everybody was wondering why I was not an MP anymore and then the rumours. Coming back to the same one. It's because he is gay. He is homosexual, he is a fag, and he is a queer. And it went on like that. And then I started to get humiliated, laughed at, pointed at. One night I went to the mess hall on the base and someone walked up to me and said, "Listen Sirard, you are not an MP anymore, you don't have a badge. So you better keep quiet and keep your mouth shut or we will get back at you for the almost 2 years you were an MP."

The humiliation and threats continued:

> I was wondering are they guessing or did they know the real reason why I am suspended ... The only people who knew about my case were my superiors. And then one day ... one friend of mine came to see me and said, "You are my best buddy. I don't mind if it is true or not but people are talking about you ... They are wondering why you are not working as an MP anymore. You don't have to tell me the reason ... And it doesn't matter if it is true or not but what

I heard is that it is because you were seen at a gay club and that you are gay. That is why they suspended you. Is it true?" So then I told him, "Listen, they saw me in a gay club. I told them that I was bisexual. I told them that what I do in my own bedroom, if I sleep with men or with women it is my own business." But they suspended me. He said, "Well, you still remain a friend. It doesn't matter what you are or what have you. You are still a good buddy. But people are going around base and saying you are a fag, that you are a queer, etc. and I wonder where they find out."

Here we see how the "ideology of fag" works as a mobilizing practice within the military context. Prior to the official discharge of the individual as a homosexual, and during the supposedly secret investigation, the social practices within the military help to label the suspended individual as a fag. Interestingly, for Sirard's friend, the military's official anti-homosexual policy had little impact. Sirard went on to say:

I was really upset and I went to see my Major and told him about it. I said, "Get me out of this base now ... you have been playing with me like a ping pong ball ... Get me posted somewhere else until we get this resolved. Now I am getting threatened. I am getting laughed at ... I am getting humiliated ... Everybody is going around the base and saying that they know the real reason because I am gay, or queer, a fag ... Where did they find out?" So then the Major said, "I don't know, the only people who know are myself, Captain ... Captain ... the two doctors and this is it." I said, "You better find out how they found out." He asked, "Who's going around and saying that?" And I said, "It's private [name], private [name], and private [name]." He then gave the three names to a sergeant from the Special Investigations Section. And he investigated where did they find out. Well, it ended up that when I went to the base hospital to talk to the MO [Medical Officer] he filled out my personnel report as Private Sirard under ... CFAO 19-20. And one male by the name of Private ... went to my file [and] opened my personal medical file and saw Private Sirard under investigation for CFAO 19-20 – homosexual case – and then he went around to the other privates telling them, "Sirard is getting investigated because he is gay."

Sirard's visit to the base MO was mandated under military rules and regulations, yet it was that visit, and the documents associated with it, that enabled the leak.

Although military regulations set the stage for the outing of military members who were under investigation and thus denied security clearances, CFAO

19-20 stated: "Any investigation made pursuant to this order must be carefully managed so that innocent persons are not made to suffer, especially since the member under investigation may sometimes be the object of malice. The investigation and all subsequent action shall be conducted so that the subject will be caused minimal embarrassment."[85] It was, however, these investigations themselves that created the basis for rumours and threats.

Eventually, Sirard was again sent on leave without receiving any news about his case from National Defence Headquarters. One of his officers said to him: "I don't know what happened but I have to tell you something. I recommended personally that you remain in the Armed Forces. Because you are a hell of a good worker and personally I don't want to lose you. But if you would be willing to take another trade like cook or mechanic instead of military policeman." In other words, Sirard was offered a demotion:

> I said, "Sir, I did two years of law enforcement course ... to become a police officer. You then trained me as a military policeman. I do not wish to change my trade because military police work or police work in the army that is what I am." He then told me that, "Well, I have a good idea that they are probably going to discharge you but I will try everything in my power to keep you in the Armed Forces and I will be phoning personally this afternoon to find out what happened or what is holding up the investigation. Until we get an answer you are going to be working in an office at the same place ... filing paper like clerk work."

And the humiliation continued:

> He said, "Could you move out from your barracks block?" I said, "Well, where to?" He said, "Do you know anyone living off-base? Then move in with him if it is possible ..." "But what about hockey, going to the gym?" He said, "No more. Keep away from the gym, keep away from the arena and keep away from your other friends." I said, "You are asking me a lot." He said, "It is for your own good ... You said you are getting humiliated, so just keep away from that." I said, "Sir, it isn't my fault. If I wouldn't have been suspended for being seen in a gay club I could have been still working as an MP and nothing would have happened."

Rather than directly addressing the problem of anti-gay harassment on the base, the military authorities attempted to resolve the problem by getting Sirard to move and to limit his use of base facilities. Sirard was constructed as the problem, and thus it was he who needed to restrict his activities. Given that the commanding officer suggested that taking these actions would be for Sirard's "own good," we begin to see how military regulations organized situations in which "the safety of the homosexual could ... be jeopardized because of non-acceptance of his peers."[86] Sirard undermined these regulations by insisting that the problem lay with the military investigation and not with his sexual interests. Sirard continued,

When I was at the police station I went to talk to my [former] Master Corporal ... I said, "I have been working with you for months and you have been happy about my work." He said, "Yeah." [I said,] "What did captain [name] give you for the reason I am no longer working at the police station?" "He said that you were being transferred because your grandfather was real sick." Well, I told him, " ... My grandfather has been sick for the last five months but the real reason is that I was seen in a gay club and I was interviewed by two SIU officers and then they suspended me." He then told me ... , "Steven, you didn't tell them that you are gay?" I said, "I told them I was bisexual." He said, "You shouldn't have but first of all don't let them throw you out or anything. Fight it. I will help you. I will do everything. As far as I am concerned you are the best man I got here and I don't want to lose you."

Sirard also commented on the personal impact of his suspension: "During that period of time I was suspended it was real hard for me to handle the situation. First of all, I was losing a lot of friends and I was getting threatened and humiliated, pointed at, laughed at etc. And now I couldn't enjoy the life anymore. I couldn't go play hockey ... I couldn't go at the gym. I couldn't do anything. Just go to work, finish work, go back to home and that was it." Although Sirard was still in the military, the rumours and the fact that he was no longer able to work as an MP meant that he was in a state of limbo. This experience of being in limbo was created through the military regulations governing the investigation of, the reporting on, and the disposal of homosexuals. The actual investigation, the number of reports government officials in Ottawa required, and the fact that the final decision was made by the Ottawa military bureaucracy meant that being investigated and purged took a considerable period of time.

Given his location in the military, the consequences for Bernie were less severe than those for Sirard. Bernie's investigation occurred over a six-month period, and, unlike Sirard, he was not transferred out of his position (probably because he worked in base accommodations, which did not have the same security focus as did positions in the military police). Yet, Bernie's investigation

Continuing Exclusion

and his identification as a homosexual put an end to his promised promotion: "Near the end, before I was tossed out, my sergeant and my warrant officer presented me with plaques for my time there, my good standing and being a good worker and getting along with others. But the worst thing they did to me was to rip up my promotion in front of me and say, 'You won't be needing this.' It's bad enough when they talk to you, but then they have to dig the knife in a little deeper" (June 27, 2001). The destruction of his promotion papers undercut all the achievements of his military career.

The Text-Mediated Social Relations of Military Reporting

Sirard's story gives us a glimpse into the social relations of military reporting and its textually mediated character. After his first leave, Sirard went to see his captain: "He then told me that they had not heard anything from Ottawa ... but I have to go under a complete investigation which is under five parts. First of all, the SIU report. Then I have to see the MO ... from the base and then I have to have an appointment with a psychiatric doctor in Halifax and then he has to make a recommendation. And all of these reports are sent in one parcel to Ottawa." Such was the mandated military course of action under CFAO 19-20. Here we see the military reliance on medical and psychiatric forms of knowledge to determine whether or not an individual had committed homosexual acts. For example, for Sirard, there was an SIU report, a medical officer's report, and a psychiatrist's report. These reports and others from base officials were added to his file as part of the investigation and sent to the Department of National Defence, where a final determination was made (see Figure 2).[87]

This course of action shaped both Sirard's and Bernie's experiences. For instance, in both cases the MO recommended they see a psychiatrist. In November, Sirard said, "I got my appointment with the MO. He told me after ten or fifteen minutes that he didn't see anything abnormal with me but he has no other choice but to recommend me to see a psychiatric doctor in Halifax. He said he had to go under the order of CFAO 19-20." The work of the medical officer and the psychiatrist was shaped by military regulations, including the definition of homosexuality in CFAO 19-20. Later that same month, Sirard went for his psychiatric appointment:

> I spoke for two hours with the psychiatrist. After two hours he told me ... "I don't see anything abnormal with you. As far as I am concerned you are real sane but I have to tell you that prior to sending in the report that 99.9 of all homosexual cases, or sexual orientation or disorientation are discharged from the Canadian Armed Forces." He said, "I will be honest with you. From talking

with you it seems that you like what you are doing ... I will make a recommendation that you remain in the Canadian Armed Forces but it is not up to me, it is up to National Defence to make the final decision."

Interestingly, the psychiatrist did not diagnose Sirard as suffering from a sexual abnormality but did read him as a homosexual. As the psychiatric report confirmed Sirard's homosexual activity, it helped construct him as a homosexual and, consequently, as someone who should be discharged from the military.

Bernie received a similar series of mandated reports and interviews:

> The psychiatrist, who asked me tons of questions, and he was the one who also asked me about if I was "homosexual, bisexual or heterosexual." I thought maybe they'll lighten up on me and I'll answer bisexual. Well, obviously that wasn't a good enough answer because it was good enough to toss me out ... I guess at that time I was still having problems dealing with it myself. I mean, I was comfortable with going to the gay bar and comfortable with my own peers, but when it came to anyone asking me, I outright denied it. (June 27, 2001)

Bernie later gained access to his military file. His dossier included not only his awards and reports but also the various documents associated with his military discharge. These documents textually constructed him as a homosexual and as someone who should be discharged from the military. In our discussion, Bernie read from a number of these texts, a key one of which was the psychiatric report that confirmed him as a homosexual: "Please be advised that this individual is a self-described bisexual [and] admits to frequent homosexual activity. Number two, the member indicates that he is quite comfortable with his lifestyle and has freely chosen it and does not desire any counsel or rehabilitation." Bernie further described his session with the psychiatrist:

> You know, it was odd how [the psychiatrist] handled it because he knew that I was perturbed, that I'm not happy with what was going on. All I wanted at that time was to get it over with and get out, because I couldn't handle it anymore and I knew that this stuff was being splashed around and that I wasn't going to be able to go back on a navy ship ... So, he asked me if I was "willing to go through rehabilitation" and I thought, "I'm not sick" ... You know, I said, "I'm not willing to go through rehabilitation because I don't know what you are going to do to me." And at that moment he was not at liberty to tell me

what it involved. So I said, "No, I'm not willing to go through rehabilitation." (June 27, 2001)

CFAO 19-20 states: "Before a release is effected under this order, the member may exercise the right to be interviewed by a psychiatrist and to receive counselling and rehabilitation."[88] The questions asked of Bernie were mandated under military regulations. It seemed as though, within the dismissal process, there was room for consideration to be given to an individual who expressed a desire to be rehabilitated. Bernie, however, quite clearly discerned the anti-gay character of notions of rehabilitation, which link it to theories of homosexuality as a sickness. Bernie pointed out that, even though the psychiatric form mentioned the possibility of counselling, the psychiatrist did not: "Right, he didn't mention counselling to me at all. But on that form it states that I refused counselling and rehabilitation. While he had only mentioned rehabilitation." When asked whether the psychiatrist told him what rehabilitation entailed, Bernie said: "No, he did not. He was taking notes and asking me questions and I guess his response was that one notice that he sent to the investigating officer."

Bernie also told us about other documents that were submitted to the Department of National Defence in Ottawa. He described some of the other texts in his file, including a document on the investigation, which stated: "The evidence presented ... is conclusive in establishing this private's sexual deviation ... This private has been advised that the recommendation for compulsory release on his behalf was reported to Maritime command. At the time of interview the private stated that he would not object to a compulsory release and it is recommended that this private be released under item 5D as soon as possible." A number of military officials submitted reports ensuring that all the documentation was in order prior to the final determination that Bernie was to be discharged on the grounds of homosexuality. The above report used the formulation "sexual deviation," hearkening back to the period when military regulations classified homosexuals as sexual deviates. The two central texts cited in these reports are CFAO 19-20 and the release instructions 5(d) of the Queen's Regulations and Orders (QR&O) 15.01, and they bring us to the social relations of discharge and release.

The Social Relations of Discharge and Release

CFAO 19-20 states: "Normally, the member should be released under item 5(d) of ... QR&O 15.01." In other words, the individual was "not advantageously employable," although later this was sometimes expressed as "service is no longer required."[89] Other release orders were to be used if the member had been convicted by a civil court or service tribunal or if he/she had been convicted under the Criminal Code. Both Sirard and Bernie were released under 5(d). According to Bernie, "I didn't get a dishonourable discharge but a code called 5(d); service is no longer required" (June 27, 2001).[90] Although the documents stated that "Terminal Leave Shall Commence [in early] August," they also stated "or sooner if administratively possible." Bernie was released in mid-July. Clearly, despite the slowness of the investigation, once officials in Ottawa gave the word, he was swiftly discharged.

According to Bernie, "One last thing that they did to me before they sent me on my way was to sign this form that said I would not go after the military for this release. I was [later] told by a lawyer that that's just a piece of paper, it would not stand up." In urging Bernie to sign this form, the military wanted him to think he could do nothing about his release. He considered reapplying to the military, but he realized, "Because of my records there, and it actually stating in my records that I was bisexual, that that would be grounds enough right there to toss me."

The men with whom he worked were so comfortable with Bernie and his sexuality that they thought, "Well, we will have to have a going-away party. So they all said, 'Why don't we all meet at the gay bar?' So we all went together to the gay bar ... They were in close proximity with me, but they did come to the gay bar and had a great time. After that I went on my merry way."

There is a major disjuncture between the official military regulations and the response of friends and workmates. Bernie remembered the final stages of his release: "They made me sign the last two pieces of paper in the military, bringing back the uniforms, and certain items that I wasn't allowed to keep; seeing the psychiatrist and seeing the major and seeing the commanding officer of the base. And once I finished off with the last person they said, 'You are now released. See ya.' ... I was done" (June 27, 2001).

Sirard received notification of his release on March 14, 1982:

> Prior to leaving I was called to [the] station by one of my ex-sergeants and
> he told me ..., "We want you here Tuesday night. But not at the police station.
> I want to meet you at ..." I went there and when I walked in I had one of the
> shocks of my life because they were giving me a party because I was leaving.
> Twenty-four of the twenty-five military policemen were there except the
> captain ... They give me a plate, souvenir, a few presents and they were all
> saying they were going to miss me and stuff like that. I felt like crying and
> didn't know what to say. Some knew or suspected and others didn't. But

inside they didn't give a damn if I was [gay/bisexual] or if I was not ... But it doesn't matter what their feelings were. I was discharged from the Canadian Armed Forces.

While we get a clear sense here that the power was still with the military policies, we also get a sense of the kind of informal opposition these policies were generating within the military as they disrupted work and friendships.

Just as in earlier periods, members discharged for homosexuality in the 1980s worried about what to tell their families and friends regarding why they had left the military. Sirard had to deal with his parents: "I moved home and I was unemployed for almost two months. My parents were wondering how come [I] left the armed forces. I had to lie to them and tell them that I disobeyed an order. And then what to do, where to go. I won't let the Canadian Armed Forces destroy my future and my life. There is no way." Although he managed to find employment, he was denied the right to work in his chosen field: "I loved what I was doing and I miss it a lot. Police work is what I always wanted to do. The years I was employed by [the armed forces] were one of the two best years of my life. I regret the whole thing and I would do everything to go back."

A few months after his discharge, Sirard came across two newspaper articles.[91] He was particularly shocked by a May 26, 1982, *Toronto Sun* headline – "Gay OK in Our Armed Forces, Ottawa" – because it contradicted his recent experiences. The headline referred to National Defence Minister Gilles Lamontagne's statement on homosexuality that questioned established military policy (see above). In response to this media coverage, Sirard wrote a letter to Lamontagne, who replied to him. Sirard stated:

> The letter [Lamontagne's] was saying it [homosexuality] was a danger to the Canadian Armed Forces and [that] they cannot be employed fully because in some other countries it is an offence and homosexual people cause a lot of problems, especially in ships or isolated bases. I feel like I wanted to tell them, "Who are you to destroy the life of someone?" I was doing a good job and then bang, they discharged me. I was fulfilling their requirements. They had no right to discharge me. Some would say it [homosexuality] is a danger to the Canadian Armed Forces; homosexuality is a real danger because of blackmail. Well, let me tell you something. Anyone is subject to blackmail ... It does not matter if you are gay or not ... I have seen some officers sleeping with the wives of privates and vice versa. I could have approached and said, "I will tell your wife that you're sleeping with his wife or what have you." That is blackmail and they are not homosexual. So for the blackmail reason this is just untrue.

Here Sirard provides a powerful critique of the military's homosexualization of concerns over blackmail. For Sirard, his experience of the purges had personal and emotional ramifications.

CIVILIAN EMPLOYEES OF THE MILITARY: ANDREW'S STORY

Canada's military policies affected the military's civilian employees as well as members of the armed forces. In 1981, Andrew started work in Ottawa as a civilian employee of the military with a confidential security clearance. In 1984, this was upgraded to secret, which meant that he then had more responsibility for and access to classified documents. During this period, as part of a program on lesbian and gay rights, he was approached to participate on a local TV station as an openly gay man. His troubles with the security state occurred after this exposure in the media.

Shortly after this program aired, an SIU officer visited his place of work and spoke to Andrew's supervisor. The supervisor then summoned one of Andrew's female co-workers, who was interviewed by the SIU agent. Eventually, Andrew learned that this agent was asking about him. The SIU also talked to another gay man who worked in the same building – a man with whom Andrew had just started a relationship. According to Andrew, they grilled this man for names of other gay people (December 19, 1994).

A few days later, Andrew's supervisor asked him to go to military headquarters to meet with this SIU agent. Later, Andrew learned that his supervisor's boss (who was the manager of the office and a military officer) had seen him on TV and felt that, under CFAO 19-20, he had to report him to the SIU. Once the SIU's investigation confirmed that Andrew was a homosexual, they interviewed him. Although a civilian employee of the DND, Andrew was governed by military regulations regarding hiring and retaining personnel. This is how he described his interrogation:

> He was dressed in plainclothes and he escorted me to a little room. And it was
> very small and there was nothing in there but a table, two chairs – one for him,
> one for myself – very plain, and a light ... And he had some sort of file folder,
> some sort of pad ... And he had a tape recorder. So he sat down and he asked
> me if I minded that he tape-recorded our session. And I said, "No." I said, "I
> don't have anything to hide so ... go ahead." He got right to the point ... and he
> said that their field investigations, as they called it, ha[d] revealed evidence that
> I'm homosexual and [did] I deny this. So I said, "Well, no." ... So this interview
> went on for two hours, and basically he asked me everything personal that you

can imagine. And I did not give him any false information at all. I was very honest. I was very explicit. I mean, they even asked questions about sexual practices and preferences, whether I liked certain things more than other things ... And I was also asked who else I knew that was gay. They didn't indicate to me that anything would happen. When he summed it up at the end, he said, "Well, that's it." He said, "I'm very pleased with your responses and your forthrightness and that you are very frank and candid about these things, and I can appreciate that it wasn't very easy." But I was very upset and it angered me. I just kept it to myself. (December 19, 1994)

Concerned with gay liberation organizing, the SIU interrogator asked direct questions about Gays of Ottawa:

The one thing they did ask though because I said I was getting involved with Gays of Ottawa. They did ask me a question, which was that if I ever had to choose ... if there was ever a time when Gays of Ottawa would develop some sort of policy or some sort of protest or strategy against National Defence ... you know, if it went on a rampage against them sort of thing, what would I do? Would I choose my gay politics or would I choose my allegiance to national defence, basically is what they were asking.

This fabrication of a conflict between Andrew's loyalty to a gay rights organization and his loyalty to the DND is reminiscent of the RCMP's earlier construction of a conflict between Harold's loyalty to gay friends and his loyalty to the Canadian state (see Chapter 4). Security regime discourse counterpoises loyalty to gay friends or groups and loyalty to state national security interests. While there are some similarities in the social form of Andrew's and Harold's interrogations and in the types of questions asked, there are major differences in outcome (i.e., Harold lost his job in the navy; Andrew did not). The questioning regarding GO suggests that, in the 1980s, the SIU and the RCMP still viewed homosexuality, and especially participation in gay organizations, as a potential risk to national security. Andrew responded to their questioning as follows:

I very honestly said to them ..., "I don't know." I said, "I would have to weigh it at the time. Because I might lose my job over it." And I said, "But I can't imagine that there would ever be something that would force me to choose between [the] two things like that." Because there are a lot of gay people working in these departments, and Gays of Ottawa strives to be inclusive. Just because Gays of Ottawa had disagreements with [the DND] over hiring policies did not mean that they would single out the DND as a target which they would want to overthrow. Gays of Ottawa would not likely become a fierce threat to DND, and I didn't see how a situation could arise where I would be forced to choose loyalty to either one or the other. He was pleased with that answer.

In the end, Andrew and his friend suffered no direct consequences: "Now, we both had no further repercussions but neither of us have ever progressed from there. We've stayed at the same job level, you know, so that's kind of interesting. Because I get excellent performance evaluation reports ... And I have always had among the best in the office." A promotion would require the next highest level of security – top secret – although in Andrew's case, this would not be relevant since he would never process top secret documents in his particular work setting. He tried to imagine what it would have been like for an individual who was in the same situation and who did not have gay activist friends and support: "It must have been horrific for them. They must have felt, 'Oh, my God, my job!' I was scared, and I had the best support in the world, you know, Gays of Ottawa was behind me" (December 19, 1994).

CONTINUING PROBLEMS IN THE RCMP AND CSIS IN THE EARLY 1980s: "PEOPLE OF THAT PERSUASION"

During a 1982 meeting of the Justice and Legal Affairs Committee, Svend Robinson asked why homosexuals and lesbians were not permitted to join the RCMP. He also asked why they were discharged if they were discovered. RCMP commissioner Simmonds stated: "We feel it is not in the interest of law enforcement or the image of law enforcement, the work of the force that has to be done in the communities and so on, and for a variety of reasons that we think we have a pretty firm backing from the public of Canada on, to not accept people like that knowingly into the police organization." In response to Robinson's question about whether such people would pose a security risk, Simmonds replied: "Possibly ... [t]hrough a variety of well-known techniques that history has disclosed possibly." When asked by Robinson if open homosexuals or lesbians would not be considered security risks, Simmonds remarked: "Not necessarily. Because there are established cases where clearly being quite open about it has not protected people from other people trying to put pressures on them."[92]

Robinson then asked the minister responsible for the RCMP, Solicitor General Robert Kaplan, if he agreed with this policy: "I think that an open homosexual is not, as such, a risk to the national security and that was not the basis on which the commissioner indicated the hiring policy was based. He indicated that it was based on considerations of the image of the Force and its acceptability to the Canadian people."[93] There is a shift in emphasis here, as being out in the RCMP was less of a problem for Kaplan than it was for Simmonds.

During the period leading up to the formation of CSIS, Robinson again questioned Simmonds at a Justice and Legal Affairs Committee meeting:

> The commissioner indicated ... that individuals who are homosexual or lesbian would not be automatically barred from service with the new civilian security service. At least the commissioner said it is not a bar in itself ... The question was how it was handled. If it was hidden and a person was more vulnerable to exploitation or blackmail that was one thing, but if the person was open about it obviously there was not any possibility of blackmail. He [Simmonds] also said that there are a number of other matters people might want to hide, whether it is an ongoing affair or other matters of a personal nature, which would similarly make them vulnerable to blackmail.[94]

These comments suggest that CSIS was developing a more relaxed policy on this question than the RCMP, even though this was not the case. However, the focus did shift towards those who were not out or those who were living with people who were not out, while those who were openly gay were considered to be less of a risk.

Robinson also asked whether there were any changes to the exclusion policy regarding open homosexuals in the RCMP. Simmonds responded by saying that "sexual persuasion [was] not always a bar to a security clearance." But he went on to state: "We do not at this moment knowingly recruit people of that persuasion. If one surfaced that had been in the Force and was otherwise giving good service we would look at the merits of the case, but we do not knowingly recruit." Simmonds differentiated between new recruits and members of the RCMP who were discovered to be homosexual. Later, he stated: "There are few members of any police organization that are comfortable at this moment in our history with people of that persuasion in their midst. I am just saying the way it is. And the perception our organization has of itself and what we believe the public perception of the organization needs to be."[95]

In 1984, Solicitor General Robert Kaplan wrote to Robinson and stated: "The personnel of the Security Service are subject to the same security clearance policy as all other members of the Public Service. This policy was expressed in Cabinet Directive 35." He added that security clearance policy was then under review. In what follows, note that what was once described as "character weaknesses" is now referred to as "features of character":

> On the issue of features of character, I would like to confirm that by themselves they are not automatic bars to a security clearance. There are however, a number of features of character which, if revealed during the security clearance process, are considered in the decision to grant or deny the clearance ... and only influence the decision if a reasonable judgment can be made that they may affect the individual's loyalty or reliability through indiscretion, dishonesty, or vulnerability to blackmail or coercion.[96]

In this perspective, the blackmailable homosexual continues to occupy a central role. Later that year, Kaplan wrote to Robinson:

> An individual's homosexuality per se is not grounds in itself for denial of a security clearance. The relevance of homosexuality to security can only be judged in its full contextual circumstances. With regard to your second question [concerning the employment practices of the RCMP], you were informed by the Commissioner of the RCMP ... that the RCMP does not knowingly recruit homosexuals as regular members of the Force. Homosexuality is not, however, an automatic barrier to employment of individuals other than regular members [i.e., of civilian members as opposed to regular members]. As with the security clearance, an individual's suitability for employment must be judged in the full context of that fact and other circumstances.[97]

Using the smokescreen of "full contextual circumstances," Kaplan argues that people are excluded from the RCMP not because of "homosexuality per se" but, rather, for "security" reasons. It was through the notion of security that heterosexist exclusion was accomplished. At the same time, it began to look as though it was finally possible for civilian members of the RCMP to be openly homosexual/lesbian.

Until 1988, the RCMP Security Service maintained a strict anti-gay and anti-lesbian hiring policy, strongly opposing human rights protection for lesbians and gay men. As late as 1983, a staff sergeant in internal security could still have the following written to him about the unsuitability of homosexual employees:

> Your employment with the R.C.M.P. Security Service requires a "TOP SECRET" security clearance and the process, including full field investigation, was explained

to you during the security interview. You were, in fact, issued a "SECRET" security clearance and hired on the strength of this pending the results of the field security investigation ... The field investigation, confirmed by your behaviour while on the job, has identified you as a homosexual and the Force's position, in line with Cabinet Directive # 35, precludes the issuance of a security clearance to such a level to persons of this sexual persuasion. Homosexuality is an identified reliability weakness identified in the aforementioned government guideline ...

I must inform you that your security clearance is immediately reduced to the level of "CONFIDENTIAL," which, of course, precludes your employment in any area of the RCMP Security Service.[98]

In this excerpt, we see how, on administrative grounds, the security regime discourse accomplished the purging of confirmed homosexuals from the RCMP. The individual's employment was not terminated on the basis of homosexuality but because he/she no longer had the proper level of security clearance. The purge was accomplished administratively, through the denial of security clearance. On the one hand, this obscures the heterosexist character of RCMP practices; on the other, it shows us how heterosexism was socially organized and mandated administratively.

James Stiles' Struggle against RCMP Policy

In 1984, Ottawa resident James Stiles, who joined the RCMP in 1969 and was a member of the RCMP Security Service from 1973 to 1984, was forced to resign after fifteen years of service. Although he denied he was a homosexual, he told Superintendent F.E. Saunders that he had had "homosexual experiences." A few days later, Inspector Ralph Thoreau asked him to name other homosexual Mounties. Stiles said that he did this on the condition that the information be held in confidence.[99] This was clearly not possible, given the RCMP's mandate.

In his statement of claim, Stiles said that his troubles started in 1983, when Assistant Commissioner J.F. Duthie confronted him with the allegation that he was gay. The RCMP stated that it began to investigate Stiles after it received information that he had been seen "in a public establishment frequented by homosexuals." In the summer of 1984, Assistant Commissioner Norman Inkster told Stiles that he met with Commissioner Simmonds and Solicitor General Kaplan and received the latter's agreement to change RCMP policy against employing homosexuals. Stiles claimed that Inkster told him he had to resign at once and become a civilian employee or risk having his employment terminated before the new policy came into effect. This may have been because he no longer had the security clearance to function as an RCMP officer. In any case, no new policy came into effect.

Stiles wrote that one of his superiors assured him that the information he provided would not be used against him or others in the RCMP. Within a month, he was asked by a deputy commissioner of the RCMP to resign or accept a civilian RCMP job. When he refused, he was threatened with dismissal. In August 1984, he finally resigned under "duress and coercion and under threat of the loss of his livelihood and the humiliation and embarrassment of discharge" from the regular RCMP.[100] He became a computer systems analyst and was later transferred to a lower-level civilian position, where he earned less money.

His transfer aroused comment and suspicion from co-workers, and though he was assured that information about his homosexuality would be kept confidential, clearly it was not. Here, as in many other situations, we learn that the leaking of confidential information was an important feature of security investigations. As a result of this leak, Stiles' friends and co-workers avoided him for fear of also facing investigation. Again, we see how transfer and investigation led to the outing of individuals. Stiles tried to re-enter the regular RCMP and CSIS, which replaced the RCMP Security Service, but was turned down because he had been identified as a homosexual.

Stiles fought back. Using Section 15 of the Canadian Charter of Rights and Freedoms, and funded by the Court Challenges Program, he was able to gain an out-of-court settlement despite two attempts by the government to halt the lawsuit. He was reinstated as a regular member of the RCMP and awarded more than $100,000 in damages by the government; he also received payment for legal, medical, dental, and drug expenses incurred while he was a civilian member of the RCMP. At the same time, RCMP commissioner Inkster stated, in contrast to its actual practice, that the RCMP had no policy against employing homosexuals.[101] In 1988, under this legal pressure, discrimination in hiring and promotion in the RCMP ended. But, of course, informal discrimination continued. While out individuals might maintain their positions and clearances, it was clear that closeted individuals could still be excluded from RCMP ranks.

CONTINUING PROBLEMS IN THE PUBLIC SERVICE

By the 1980s, Blair Johnston, an employee of the Department of External Affairs, was a gay activist and the vice-president of Gays of Ottawa: "I had to watch the profile because there was a prohibition against involvement in political activities and political parties ... in the [civil] service. So, I tended to write a lot of the articles for GO Info that would appear under another name because they were in a position where they could sign this and I wasn't at that point. So, I'd do the investigation, edit the articles, and do things like that" (February 1, 2001). For many members of the public service, restrictions on gay political activism continued in the 1980s. Johnston felt repercussions at work for his involvement in activism: "I was reprimanded for using government services like paper and photocopy machines ... And I said I wouldn't do it anymore, and from that point on I paid for a lot of my own stuff ... We were more careful about the fact that living in a government town gives you access to a lot of services that you aren't able to get anywhere else."

Johnston remembered he had another security check in the early 1980s, a practice apparently undertaken every ten years. He spoke to the people with whom he expected the RCMP to talk as part of this security check: "They reported back to me. I just said I'm going up for security clearance ... If they ask you about the fact that I'm gay, please don't try to conceal it. I just want you to be open and honest about it. I never told them to say anything or do anything, I said just be honest, that's all I'm asking ... Out of the three people, two were contacted." Later, when a report on Johnston had been prepared and assessed,

> It was sent to my president and they called me in and said, "We've had reports that you have been involved in homosexual activity" ... And I said, "I happen to be gay, that's what they are trying to say, but I think you really shouldn't use this report. [The RCMP] have such poor analytical capacity ... " They at first asked me to sign a statement saying that if I ever got into a blackmail situation, I would report to them. I said, "Do you require this of all persons?" And they said, "No." I said, "I'll sign it if you require it from everybody." (February 1, 2001)

This bold statement of resistance was enough to cause his superiors to retreat and even to go so far as to say: "We won't tell anybody." Johnston kept his security clearance and reported no problems after CSIS took over security screening.

Pierre: "This episode ruined my entire life"
Pierre got involved in gay organizations in Ottawa in the early 1980s. During this time, his job in the government was declared redundant due to the reorganization of his department. This reorganization also involved a set of new security clearance checks. Pierre wasn't initially worried as he believed the government was aware of his homosexuality from previous security investigations and personnel files. He knew that promotion to a higher level was not possible. After not being selected for a job, Pierre suspected that the new security check must

have discovered his involvement in gay organizations (May 31, 1998). In this particular case, his union did nothing to protect him. Its policy at the time may have been not to defend or support anyone who was gay, given the security clearance restrictions. Because Pierre could not find another position at the same level, this was the end of his career in the public service. He experienced major depression and financial insecurity, which forced him to sell his house. He put it simply: "This episode ruined my entire life" (May 31, 1998).

The McDonald Commission and the formation of CSIS in the early 1980s introduced a new shift in how national security ideology and practice addressed queers. In these pre-Charter years, queer activists continued to critique the national security practices sustained through the McDonald Commission and CSIS. They also mobilized against the continuing purging of queers from the military. The equality rights section of the Charter instituted in 1985 would create new legal possibilities to fight national security practices even as the RCMP and the military defended their exclusion of queers. The next chapter focuses on the openings and the dangers that evolved as the security campaigns and resistance to them entered the post-Charter era.

From Exclusion to Assimilation
National Security, the Charter, and Limited Inclusion

THE CHARTER AND EQUALITY RIGHTS: A MORE FAVOURABLE TERRAIN FOR LEGAL STRUGGLE

The enactment of the Charter in 1982, especially its equality rights section (in 1985), partially altered the character of Canadian state legal formation, making it easier to push for the individual rights of lesbians and gay men and for formal legal equality but not for more substantive social equality. The growing recognition of human rights for lesbians and gay men rests on a long history of struggle. The equality rights section of the Canadian Charter of Rights and Freedoms could be used to allow for more human rights protection for lesbians and gay men, and this included restraining and eventually turning back the security campaigns against queers. Even though the military and the RCMP fought vociferously to lessen the impact of these equality provisions on their institutional relations, they were eventually forced to abandon their overt practices of discrimination. We detail the military and RCMP rejection of equality rights and show how, eventually, thanks to legal and social struggles, they were forced to end their official practices.

Nonetheless, CSIS can still deny security clearances to closeted gay men and lesbians or to those who have relationships with people in the closet on the grounds that they are vulnerable to blackmail. The use of the social relations of the closet against those who engage in same-gender sex continues as a security practice against queers. Informal discrimination also continues within the military and in the public service regarding security clearance levels.

In the crucial period leading up to the implementation of the equality rights section of the Charter of Rights and Freedoms, Gays of Ottawa tried to get state funding to investigate legal discrimination against gay men and lesbians. In its 1982 brief to the Special Parliamentary Committee on Equality Rights, GO stated that it had submitted a proposal to the Department of Justice "to share costs to research and develop legal studies on the various laws affecting Lesbians and Gay Men. To our knowledge, it was the only application of its kind. The application was denied. Through the Access to Information Act we learned the reasons for the rejection. Apparently, the information might be 'conducive to laying the groundwork for a political campaign by the gay community.'" The government did not want this funding used to push forward sexual orientation protection as an equality rights issue. It should be noted that, at this time, it was not yet officially clear that Section 15 of the Charter had any bearing on sexual orientation.[1]

The expansion of gay and lesbian community formation, the growth of gay and lesbian activist movements, and challenges to national security practices within the public service and the military set the stage for the undermining of the national security war on queers. In this context, Section 15 of the Charter created a more favourable terrain for struggles for human rights.[2] Laws could now be challenged on constitutional grounds if they conflicted with the equality rights section of the Charter, and various levels of government were supposed to bring their human rights legislation into line with this section. Not surprisingly, this steered struggles in a legal rights direction and away from other forms of organizing.

While the equality rights section of the Charter of Rights and Freedoms has been very useful for some legal struggles, other sections have been used to justify continuing discrimination and the exploitation of capitalist social relations.[3] For example, workers' struggles and substantive forms of social equality are not as protected by Section 15 as are individual and formal equality rights. Critiquing the Charter from a feminist perspective, Judy Fudge made the following comment: "once again Canadian feminists are confronted with the gulf between formal, and often merely symbolic, legal equality and substantive, material inequality for women."[4]

Section 15 prohibited discrimination against a number of groups but did not specifically mention prohibition of discrimination based on sexual orientation. By the late 1970s, "sexual orientation" had replaced "sexual preference" as a way of officially covering the sexualities of gay men, lesbians, and bisexuals. As a generic term, "sexual orientation" includes hegemonic sexuality (i.e., heterosexuality) as well as subordinated sexualities like homosexuality and

From Exclusion to Assimilation

bisexuality. Considered immutable and intrinsic, the concept of sexual orientation presents a number of difficulties for social constructionist approaches to sexuality. Nonetheless, the Charter was written in an open-ended fashion, which allowed gay and lesbian activists and their lawyers to argue that sexual orientation protection could and should be read into it.[5] This had an important impact on struggles against discrimination in the military and RCMP, further undermining the national security war on queers.

In 1986, the federal Conservative government, in response to a 1985 report of the Special Parliamentary Committee on Equality Rights regarding the impact of Section 15, stated that the courts would interpret it as including sexual orientation protection. The military and the RCMP, however, were adamantly opposed to the implications of equality rights for their organizations. Despite this government "commitment," it took another ten years of struggles and costly court battles before sexual orientation protection was finally added to the Canadian Human Rights Act as the Conservative government and then the Liberal government stalled and delayed. The Liberal government enacted this protection after years of lesbian/gay activism, pressure from the Canadian Human Rights Commission, and the 1995 Egan/Nesbitt decision.[6] One of the main reasons for this delay was the opposition of the military and RCMP hierarchy as well as that of moral conservatives within the Tory and Liberal Parties. A number of provinces secured this protection in a more timely manner, but these changes had no immediate implications for the federal public service or the military and RCMP.[7]

The achievement of sexual orientation protection in human rights legislation did not end discrimination. It meant that individuals who experienced discrimination based on sexual orientation could make a complaint to a provincial or a federal human rights commission. Many of these human rights commissions have faced funding cuts and have developed arbitrary criteria for deciding which cases not to pursue.[8] Human rights commissions, established to help people facing discrimination, can become yet another obstacle. Nonetheless, over the last twenty-three years, there has been remarkable progress on basic human rights protection for lesbians, gays, and bisexuals within the Canadian state, and this has had a significant impact on national security campaigns, the public service, and even, finally, on the military and the RCMP.

This major change in legal protection occurred not only in the context of the actions of the lesbian and gay movements and human rights supporters but also in that of a lessening of dependence on the heterosexual familial construct within capitalist and state relations. In the military and the RCMP, an investment in the ideology of heterosexual masculinity, and heterosexuality more generally, translated into a stronger opposition to the implications of equality rights for gay men and lesbians. The military and RCMP hierarchies fought against these pressures and changes as they saw any tolerance of homosexuality as a threat to the fabric and stability of their institutions. They viewed gay men and lesbians in their ranks as a basic challenge to their operational effectiveness and efficiency.

These transformations led to an uneven and limited moral deregulation of queer sexualities on the part of state agencies.[9] Although no longer as strictly regulated by state laws and policing, queer sexual practices are still regulated through market forces, professional agencies and policies, and within popular culture. Popular cultural production still enshrines heterosexuality as the norm, while opening up more ghettoized social spaces for queers and normalizing only certain images of queer lives.[10]

From the 1990s on, basic human rights protection has extended to spousal benefits and family recognition rights, and this has had implications for the military. At the same time, there has been a limited recriminalization of consensual gay men's sexualities, a continuing but uneven escalation of sexual censorship against queer erotic materials, and major informal practices of exclusion and discrimination in the military and RCMP/CSIS.[11]

In the contemporary period, queer people live a contradiction. On the one hand, our individual formal and abstract human rights are now increasingly recognized; on the other hand, our relationships often remain stigmatized and our sexualities and our desires are still censored, criminalized, and hated. This dilemma exists because same-gender eroticism does not have substantive social equality with normalized heterosexuality. One of the problems with the "rights" perspective is that it accepts existing social forms and argues simply for the inclusion of queers. Lesbian and gay rights are focused on integrating with heterosexual-dominated institutional relations rather than on challenging heterosexual hegemony – on being included in existing forms of the family, marriage, and the military rather than on challenging the inequalities and oppressions within these relations.

As Patrick Barnholden commented with reference to the massive April 25, 1993, gay and lesbian march on Washington, DC, which focused on lesbian and gay entry into the US military,

> This single issue organizing seems predicated on the very assimilationist assumption of simply letting us into the military without any major transformation of its militarist, racist, sexist and heterosexist organization. This shifted the

From Exclusion to Assimilation

political focus of the event in a much more integrationist direction where the more transformative aspects of our liberation movements were not highlighted. American patriotism seemed overwhelming in much of the military ban discussion and actions as some lesbian and gay vets marched in military formation wearing their military uniforms ... There were some marchers who did try to call into question the role of the US military. Lavender Vets for Peace, for instance, marched under a banner of "We demand the right to love, not the right to kill." Others wore anti-military t-shirts and the Prairie Fire Organizing Committee [a left-wing anti-racist group] put out a poster of a bearded man in drag under the words "Not every boy wants to be a soldier."[12]

Integration into heterosexist social forms represents a critical but also limiting form of social transformation – one that leads to the incorporation and accommodation of the subversive potential of queer liberation within existing institutional relations. While we have made major progress in our battle for human rights, oppression and heterosexual hegemony remain. Still, this progress played an important part in undermining the national security campaigns against queers and in transforming official policies in the military and RCMP/CSIS.

Given the implementation of Section 15 of the Charter and the shift of much gay/lesbian activism towards formal equality rights, I tended by the mid-1980s to move into areas of queer activism that had little to do with formal equality. I became active in the Canadian Committee against Customs Censorship, fighting the seizures of queer books and publications, and, later, in AIDS treatment activism in AIDS ACTION NOW! In these areas the continuing substantive inequality and oppression, including state policies facing queers and other people, could be more specifically addressed.

The three-year delay in the implementation of Section 15 of the Charter of Rights and Freedoms gave governments time to review their legislation and to seek changes to bring it into line with the equality rights section. A federal discussion paper on the equality provisions raised a number of issues related to the military, including whether women should be able to serve in combat positions and whether homosexuality should be acceptable within the military. The section on sexual orientation focused entirely on the military and is composed of armed forces arguments in defence of its exclusionary position. To justify present discriminatory practices, military officials emphasized that Canada's military policy was consistent with military policies in Britain, the

United States, and West Germany. The familiar arguments included the illegality of homosexuality in other countries, the "disruptive" effect of homosexuals on "the efficiency of the forces" in a situation "where personal privacy is most difficult," the possibility of "physical attacks" on homosexuals, and the belief that homosexuals "are at greater risk of subversion by authorities of foreign countries" and are thus subject to "blackmail."[13] The discussion paper insisted that the foregoing arguments made queers "impossible to place ... in security sensitive positions." Other reasons for exclusion included "the significance of a cohesive force, adherence to majoritarian values and public image."[14] Clearly, the armed forces and the federal Tory government did not intend to use the Charter as a vehicle to change exclusionary policies in the military.

On March 5, 1985, the House of Commons Standing Committee on Justice and Legal Affairs set up the Special Parliamentary Committee on Equality Rights to deal with the equality issues raised by the implementation of Section 15. This committee, which included Svend Robinson as its NDP member, heard many deputations from gay and lesbian groups across the country, all of which challenged national security and exclusionary policies. Robinson described to us how the committee work began to shift the dynamic of struggle in favour of equality rights for gays and lesbians:

> We finished the report *Equality for All* in '85 and held hearings across the
> country. What I just remember so vividly from those hearings was [that] that
> was really probably the first time on the public record that people spoke out
> strongly on the issue of both the RCMP and the Canadian Armed Forces and
> the committee met with people from the RCMP. I still remember meeting in a
> hotel room in Toronto in a very clandestine manner with ... an officer in the
> RCMP who I arranged for the committee to hear from behind closed doors,
> because that was obviously what he insisted on at that time, and just how
> moved the committee was. They were blown away by his evidence. Then Darl
> Wood ... from Nova Scotia who appeared before the committee there, and
> again it was just great. She is eloquent, powerful, and there were others as well,
> as I recall. And that committee, which was dominated by Conservatives re-
> member, ... that committee was so moved by the evidence we heard that it
> unanimously and again very directly said, "End these policies" ... And that was,
> I think, a major breakthrough at that point because the military and the RCMP
> were fighting tooth and nail against these changes. (July 30, 2002)

Blair Johnston worked on GO's submission as well as on other briefs dealing with equality rights during this period. He described some of these:

[There was the brief for] the Equality [for All] group in '85, and I wrote ...
stuff for the Secretary of State because they were looking at equality issues and
they didn't have gay rights down as an equality issue to merit any attention
because it wasn't developed enough. So, I wrote a brief that was about three-
quarters of an inch thick, with all kinds of references. I pulled together a lot of
material in a very short period of time, and sent it into them saying, "What do
you mean not matured? There are many more studies and you just contact us
and we'll send you as many studies as you want." We didn't have anymore
studies, but the issue was to get it on the agenda for a meeting that the minister
was planning in six months. And it did get on the agenda. That was the whole
issue – to get the issue on the agenda. This is how a bureaucracy works. You
can play at the senior level as much as you want, but anything that a minister
decides is often submerged in tonic by the bureaucracy. Unless you have something bubbling up from the bottom as well. (February 1, 2001)

GO raised concerns over the issue of discrimination against lesbians and gay
men in federal employment, including specific concerns about the policies of
the RCMP and the Canadian Armed Forces:

In the particular case of the policies of the RCMP and the Canadian Forces, their
policies on "occupational requirements" is derived in a completely backward
manner. From an examination of Canadian Forces' policy letters (1977 through
1982) and the RCMP Aide-Memoire (presented to the Committee earlier) we
can see that both organizations have created a stereotype of the typical homosexual. They have invested this creature with alleged characteristics. They have
then compared their creation to a series of selected criteria for employment and
concluded that the mythical homosexual fails on all counts. Their conclusion is
then expanded to apply to each and every Lesbian and Gay Man. By coining the
new term "bona fide occupational impediments," they have attempted to disguise
a blatant act of wholesale discrimination which has no justification in fact or
reality.[15]

GO identified the new ideological conceptualization of homosexuals as an
occupational impediment (which was part of the broader concept of operational effectiveness) as central to the military and RCMP arguments for
continuing their exclusion policies. It also took up the security issue, criticizing
"an earlier witness [who] introduced anecdotal material concerning the alleged
security risk that all Gay Men and Lesbians pose to military and national security. We expect this Committee to firmly reject such excuses on the grounds of

the circular Catch-22 argument used and the example of the many Lesbians and Gay men who presently hold security clearances to the highest level in the Public Service."[16] By highlighting the progress some gays and lesbians made in the public service, GO undermined military and RCMP arguments against queer members. It also pointed out how the Criminal Code continued to discriminate against gay men and lesbians, including through higher age of consent laws and the bawdy-house legislation.

Based on many submissions and months of deliberation and struggle, *Equality for All*, the report of the Special Parliamentary Committee on Equality Rights, was tabled on October 25, 1985. A series of recommendations argued that sexual orientation protection should be part of Section 15 and that such protection should be added to the Canadian Human Rights Act. The report also suggested that "the Canadian Armed Forces and the RCMP bring their employment practices into conformity with the Canadian Human Rights Act as amended to prohibit discrimination on the basis of sexual orientation."[17] It emphasized official military policy leading to the exclusion of gays and lesbians and stated: "[The RCMP] has no formal written policy on homosexual members, although a draft *aide-mémoire* setting out the rationale for not knowingly recruiting or retaining homosexual members was tabled with the Committee. When a member of the RCMP is discovered to be homosexual, the member is discharged." The report referred to stories and experiences of

a number of former members of the Canadian Armed Forces, who had served in the Forces for years, apparently without problem, but were released for only one reason – their sexual orientation. They described the arbitrary, grossly insensitive treatment to which they were subjected as part of the investigation of their personal lives. They were detained in isolated conditions for many hours and subjected to intensive interrogation about their activities and those of others.[18]

After going through the standard military objections to the inclusion of lesbians and gay men, the report concluded,

The arguments do not justify the present policies. They are based on the stereotypical view of homosexuals that assumes them to be dangerous people imposing their sexual preference on others. They also give undue weight to the presumed sensitivities of others. Finally, the blackmail argument is a circular one – if sexual orientation were not a factor in employment, the main reason for any such vulnerability of homosexuals would disappear. If a foreign power, or anyone else, wants to subvert a Canadian, they would use whatever blandishments appear most compellingly to that particular individual; in this regard, heterosexuals are just as vulnerable as homosexuals.[19]

The arguments mobilized by GO and other gay and lesbian activists had an impact on the committee, and Svend Robinson pushed them forward from inside the committee. No doubt, they prompted those opposed to equality rights for queers to begin changing their stance regarding blackmail. The authors of *Equality for All* argued as follows:

> [I]f the Canadian Armed Forces and the RCMP still wish to justify their policies with respect to homosexuals, the place for them to do so is before a Human Rights Tribunal established under the Canadian Human Rights Act. It would be up to them to persuade a tribunal that their policy was based on a bona fide occupational requirement. However, this Committee has not heard evidence justifying such an exemption from the Act.[20]

This would draw the military and the RCMP into the human rights arena, forcing them to try to prove their occupational requirement claims under human rights legislation.

Security clearances and homosexuality also fell within the committee's inquiry:

> Cabinet Directive 35, adopted in the early 1960s, sets out criteria for granting security clearances. Among the grounds upon which access to confidential information could be denied is a "character defect," such as "illicit sexual behaviour," that may make a person susceptible to blackmail or coercion. The government of Canada has Cabinet Directive 35 under active review: it is expected that replacement guidelines on security clearances will be issued shortly. The arguments about blackmail made with respect to members of the Canadian Armed Forces and the RCMP apply equally to this area.[21]

The authors recommended that "the federal government security clearance guidelines covering employees not discriminate on the basis of sexual orientation." How far this position went is not clear, but it pointed in a useful direction. They also called for uniform age of consent laws, with no distinction based on sexual orientation.[22]

On March 4, 1986, the government tabled *Toward Equality,* its response to the report of the Special Parliamentary Committee on Equality Rights. Regarding sexual orientation protection, *Toward Equality* provided the following general statements:

> The Government recognizes that the issue of sexual orientation addresses some of the most difficult moral and religious concerns of Canadians. There is no simple manner of reconciling deeply felt views. Though fully cognizant of the social dilemmas that the issue raises, the Government is committed to the principle that all Canadians have an equal opportunity to participate as fully as they can in our society ... The Government believes that one's sexual orientation is irrelevant to whether one can perform a job or use a service or facility. The Department of Justice is of the view that the courts will find that sexual orientation is encompassed by the guarantees in section 15 of the Charter. The Government will take whatever measures are necessary to ensure that sexual orientation is a prohibited ground of discrimination in relation to all areas of federal jurisdiction.[23]

By foregrounding moral and religious concerns, government officials invoked a political debate regarding homosexuality – one that continues in contemporary disagreements over same-sex marriage. Constructing these issues in moral ways detracts from the ability to view them as fundamental to human rights and equality rights. Although Charter protection of sexual orientation was conceded, successive governments actively fought this provision. Only when court victories began to take place was Ottawa forced to enact human rights legislation for gay men and lesbians.

While reiterating its commitment to equality rights, the federal government also affirmed "the requirement of the Armed Forces to be operationally effective in the interests of national security," thus echoing arguments made by the military.[24] This language provided justification for the military's continued opposition to equality rights for lesbians and gay men even while Section 15 could be used to argue for protection for gays and lesbians.

In his comments, Justice Minister John Crosbie stated: "Sexual orientation is not a ground for denial of a security clearance," adding that "the criteria applied are loyalty to Canada and reliability." Crosbie did not note that, under Cabinet Directive 35, homosexuality was a prime consideration in determining a person's reliability. In his formulation, being gay or lesbian did not make one a security risk; however, being unreliable *because* one was homosexual did. Here we see how, in national security discourse, "unreliability" came to be associated with homosexuality. This was one more way in which discrimination continued to be organized.[25]

THE MILITARY AND RCMP OPPOSE EQUALITY RIGHTS: FROM BLACKMAIL TO OPERATIONAL EFFECTIVENESS

The military and the RCMP continued to adamantly oppose equality rights for queers. As early as 1982, the Canadian Armed Forces asked the federal government for an exemption from certain sections of the Charter of Rights and Freedoms, citing, among other reasons, the need to exclude homosexuals.[26] A key component of these arguments was the notion that queers interfered with the operational effectiveness of hierarchical and patriarchal forms of organization. This position developed in response to the growing visibility of gay men and lesbians and our struggles against the national security regime. Operational effectiveness was coded with heterosexuality and intimately linked to notions of the defence of national security. This conceptualization was generalized in the military and RCMP responses to equality rights.

The RCMP and Equality Rights: Queers as a Management Problem

On May 1, 1985, when he appeared before the Special Parliamentary Committee on Equality Rights, Svend Robinson again confronted Commissioner Simmonds over RCMP opposition to the inclusion of queers. When asked about the impact of equality rights on the RCMP, Simmonds stated:

> As the member says, there is a new reality since April 17 [when Section 15 came into effect] ... but the reality of attitudes has not really changed that much. So you have a management problem in the light of the new reality. [Since our last discussion]... I have drawn together ... what I called a position on homosexual recruitment and members in the police. Based on the findings during the course of putting this together internally to the outfit, I think I must tell you that the aversion to it – and it might be discriminatory as all get out – within police ranks is extraordinarily high. Therefore it causes you a lot of problems in managing the organization.[27]

Simmonds' use of the word "aversion" to describe RCMP members' response to homosexuality is especially interesting given the use of aversion therapy to try to cure queers of their sexual desires. Simmonds also clearly constructed homosexuals in the RCMP not so much as a national security problem but as a management problem. In May 1985, the RCMP presented the document entitled "RCMP Policy in Respect of Homosexual Conduct" to the Special Parliamentary Committee on Equality Rights.[28] Some parts of this vociferously anti-queer text read,

> In the case of homosexuals, it is the considered view of the Commissioner and authorities in the RCMP, that such persons, because of their sexual orientation, create a number of serious problems for the RCMP which militate against their employment. RCMP policy in respect of homosexuals is, and remains, that they are not knowingly engaged or retained in the RCMP as peace officers ... These problems are specified as ... Homosexuality presents a bona fide operational impediment in that it is not possible to fully utilize homosexuals to meet the exigencies of the RCMP ... The presence of homosexuals at isolated postings, in communal life in barracks, on board ship, in the field and other situations where personal privacy is most difficult or impossible, unfortunately always has the potential of leading to physical confrontation toward the homosexual if he should in any way attempt to thrust his tendencies on other members. To permit homosexuals in the Forces would adversely affect the operational efficiency of the RCMP.[29]

There are a number of arguments developed here. First, the claim that homosexuality is a bona fide operational impediment and that it adversely affects the operational efficiency of the RCMP is connected to the idea that queers interfere with the operational efficiency of the military. Second, the lack of a private realm argument is once again mobilized against homosexuals. This argument is reminiscent of military responses to the 1957 Wolfenden Report (see Chapter 4) and the 1969 Criminal Code reform. Finally, the homosexual is positioned as the culprit who attempts to "thrust" his tendencies on other members.

In other parts of the document, the maintenance of discipline among RCMP ranks becomes associated with the need to exclude homosexuals. In this discourse, the notion that what is acceptable in civilian society may not be acceptable within the RCMP is intended to lend credibility to the idea that homosexuals must be excluded in order to maintain discipline and to avoid damage to morale:

> Discipline is essential in a police force and a hierarchical rank structure is essential to the maintenance of discipline required to respond without question

on occasions. This requirement for a highly disciplined and structured Force, and for the maintenance within a closed society of a lifestyle acceptable to the vast majority of its members inevitably results in some restriction of personal freedoms. Certain practices which may be tolerated in civilian society may have to be barred in order to meet police requirements. Homosexuality falls within this category and is one such practice ... To engage or retain known homosexuals would do grave damage to morale in the RCMP and, for that reason alone, such a course of action is unacceptable.[30]

The authors argue that the RCMP, being a closed society, must exclude homosexuals. Indeed, the document makes connections between the undesirability of homosexuals and issues of security:

Experience has shown that homosexuals are at greater risk of being subverted by authorities of foreign countries whose interests are inimical to those of Canada and her allies. Such persons are, either directly or indirectly, subject to blackmail. Even if a homosexual is entirely open about the matter and thereby reducing the risk of direct blackmail, he is still a security risk indirectly because of the involvement of a partner "who may not have come out of the closet" or because the member's propensity may be exploited. Experience, over the years, has demonstrated a degree of vulnerability to blackmail. Prevailing social attitudes make it imprudent to place homosexuals in security sensitive positions.[31]

Empirical evidence is neither offered nor needed since, in this security discourse, homosexuality, blackmail, and security risk are linked together as a matter of "common sense."[32] Despite the work of the gay and lesbian movements, the relations of the closet continued to serve as a way to target homosexuals. To reinforce their argument, under a section entitled "Moral Disapproval," the authors of the RCMP document offer this statement: "The RCMP encourages and enforces a strict compliance to the accepted moral standards. The mere fact that homosexuality is not a criminal offence when committed in private between consenting adults (over 21) does not involve moral approval of that conduct, and conduct may be scandalous and disgraceful without committing a criminal offence. Consequently, the Force does not wish to employ or retain those males and females who engage in homosexuality."[33] Like the military, the RCMP associated homosexuality with "scandalous and disgraceful conduct." Positioning homosexuality in this moral fashion while insisting that queers posed challenges to operational requirements, RCMP officials believed they could distance themselves from the legal and constitutional obligations set out by the Charter of Rights and Freedoms and the Human Rights Act. The RCMP could claim, then, that the Charter does "not proscribe sexual orientation as a prohibited ground of discrimination." Further, "even if [it did prohibit] discrimination on the ground of sexual orientation, it is the RCMP view that such prohibition would not apply to the RCMP in light of the bona fide occupational requirement which can be demonstratably justified in a free and democratic society."[34] Embracing a heterosexist perspective, the RCMP argued that the specific character of the force rendered it immune from equality rights for queers.

Hate Propaganda: GO's Response to the RCMP's Aide-Mémoire

The GO brief to the Special Parliamentary Committee on Equality Rights highlighted the RCMP's explicit heterosexist discourse: "Perhaps the most extreme and worrisome example is provided by the RCMP *aide-mémoire* and statements from Commissioner Simmonds about the discomfort of Canada's police forces. As a caution you should be aware that with respect to gay men and lesbians, the McDonald Royal Commission on RCMP activities concluded in 1981 that the Force 'had poor analytical capability.'"[35] The GO document focused on how the RCMP position paper manipulated the stereotype of the dangerous homosexual by emphasizing certain words and phrases:

> The focus of the Aide Memoire [sic] is the fabrication of a stereotypic (male) homosexual. He and his employment is constructed as a "subversive," "unwholesome," "disruptive" presence, who would "thrust his tendencies," "do grave damage," "undermine leadership," "inflict (his) views," "cause additional stress" and "solicit" a "socially abhorrent" relationship with "scandalous," "disgraceful," and "unusual behavioural traits" generating "repugnance," "loss of faith and trust" and other unspecified "dangers." The author exploits the stereotypic image of the homosexual as a child or youth molester.[36]

The authors of the GO brief argued that the RCMP was deliberately using inflammatory language and images to incite fear and loathing of queers. Moreover, they describe the RCMP position paper as hate propaganda:

> The document ignores and contradicts Canadian Human Rights Commission polls which indicate public acceptance of Gay and Lesbian members ... In this document we have the homosexual monster, a Frankenstein who thrusts, solicits,

From Exclusion to Assimilation

damages and inflicts his dangers on the uncomfortable RCMP policy drafter. Frankly, through the skilled use of innuendo and direct misrepresentation, the author has generated an incredible piece of hate propaganda ... To put this RCMP policy statement into a human perspective we would encourage each member of the Committee to read the document carefully and insert their own name whenever we are referred to ... We sincerely hope that this offensive piece of hate propaganda is withdrawn with apologies.[37]

Undeterred, in 1985 Simmonds reiterated that the RCMP would not knowingly hire gay Mounties. Due to intense political pressure, an apparent shift in this policy took place the following year.[38] In April 1986, Solicitor General Beatty outlined the new RCMP official position on homosexuals within the Force, positing that, if gay men and lesbians were out, they could join. When, before the House of Commons Justice Committee, NDP Member of Parliament Ian Waddell asked Beatty about the government's policy on gays and lesbians, he responded: "Homosexuality per se would not be a bar to entering the RCMP." His deputy, Fred Gibson, added, "Homosexuality, sexual preference, is not a legitimate ground for discrimination." When Waddell asked Gibson whether open gays and lesbians could join the RCMP, Gibson replied: "If there was no relevance to the job he was being asked to do in his sexual orientation that is right. For example, whether a person was a homosexual or a heterosexual, if his activities made him subject to blackmail, and if he was going to be in a position of trust, this could perhaps deny him a security clearance." Beatty explained that, when an individual is a homosexual and admits it publicly, there is no bar to entry because "in that case an individual would not be backmailable." In response, Waddell insisted that these comments proved that no policy change had taken place.[39]

CSIS followed the RCMP's general trend. In a 1986 response to *Equality for All*, CSIS announced that it would continue to reject homosexuals seeking security clearance for public service employment. One of the key activities that CSIS took over from the RCMP was the investigation of homosexuals who were working for the federal government. Craig McDermott of CSIS told the *Ottawa Citizen* that an out homosexual "can't be put under any duress (blackmailed) and therefore could be potentially hired."[40] The emphasis here is on "potentially."

The Military: Queers as Hindering Operational Effectiveness
Shortly after the equality rights section came into effect, a military spokesperson

asked the House of Commons Justice Committee whether the Charter prohibited discrimination against gay men and lesbians in the military. Colonel G.L. Waterfield, deputy judge-advocate, argued that it was not clear to the military whether sexual orientation protection was included in the equality rights section of the Charter. Daniel Mainguy, vice-chief of defence staff, reiterated the military's position that the armed forces would not knowingly hire homosexuals and would "release" members or employees who were found to be homosexuals. The military claimed that closeted homosexuals were a security risk and that those who were open about their sexuality created discomfort among those with whom they shared living quarters.[41] The military came to rely less on blackmail and direct security concerns and more on showing how out homosexuals disrupted its operational efficiency.

The chief of the defence staff formed the Military Charter Task Force to respond to *Toward Equality*. The areas explored included the employment of women in the military, sexual orientation, mandatory retirement, physical and medical employment standards, and the recognition of common-law relationships. The operational effectiveness of the military was the focal point of the task force's response to equality rights. In its report on the purpose and characteristics of military forces, the task force emphasizes the need for discipline, obedience, and following the proper chain of command. It comments: "the National Defence Act incorporates a Code of Service Discipline that subjects CF [Canadian Forces] members to laws and types of trial that do not apply to the rest of society." And it specifies important differences between the hierarchical and patriarchal organization of the military and that of the rest of society. It also points to the lack of a distinct private realm in the military, the continuing significance of physical strength (thus adversely affecting women's entry into the military), and the importance of cohesion and morale.[42]

The task force reiterates, based on CFAO 19-20, that people "who commit sexually abnormal acts or homosexual acts are neither enrolled nor retained," and it also cites the government's perspective that equality rights in the military must be consistent with its being "operationally effective in the interests of national security." While pointing to the "broad and vague" character of sexual orientation, the task force defines it as "lesbianism and male homosexuality."[43] In investigating the military's "social environment," it insists that anti-gay, anti-lesbian attitudes "unavoidably carry over from society at large into the CF, and may not be alterable." It also points to the "widespread and deeply-held aversion to homosexuality in Canada." This wholesale acceptance of bigotry and prejudice is then linked with the military's operational effectiveness in order to solidify the argument against the employment of homosexuals. Predictably, the task force concludes that the presence of gay men and lesbians undermines military cohesion and morale.[44]

In an attempt to garner evidence for its conclusions regarding the disruptive nature of homosexuals, the task force offers information from an internal military study, which demonstrates "that the number of homosexual cases of sexual assault is ... proportionally four times higher than that for heterosexual cases of sexual assault."[45] It uses this suspect study to argue that these numbers would increase if gay men and lesbians were let into the military. In relation to the right to privacy, it raises the usual concerns around the lack of a private realm, especially in isolated posts, barrack life, on ships, and in common ablution and shower facilities.[46]

The military task force report operates from the standpoint of heterosexual hegemony, thus privileging the "rights" of heterosexual members. It follows that the conceptualization of operational effectiveness assumes and defends the heterosexist and hegemonic character of the military. The task force's argument also rests on a construction of homosexuals as people "who receive sexual stimulation from bodily contacts with people of the same sex," thus building on the idea of homosexuals as sex-crazed. Clearly, homosexuals are sexualized in ways that heterosexuals are not.[47]

Policies of other Western countries "limit[ed] the employment of homosexuals in their armed forces. Those that may be culturally most similar to Canada, the United States and the United Kingdom, ha[d] policies of total exclusion that have recently been revealed and confirmed."[48] At the same time, the military in a number of European countries, including the Netherlands (1974), Denmark (1979), and Sweden (1984), had already abolished their exclusionist policies.[49]

Fear of AIDS: The Mobilization of Medical/Health Fears

The Military Charter Task Force also employed a form of medical discourse in its effort to discredit homosexuals. At the core of this discourse is the connection between homosexual "deviance" and the diseased body. The task force's report reinforces this discourse with statements such as "adverse medical implications could be expected from a policy of employing homosexuals" and "male homosexuals are the largest and highest risk group for AIDS."[50] The term "high-risk group" was harshly criticized by gay and AIDS activist groups. The term was taken from epidemiology, but its meaning was shifted in mass media and professional discourses, with groups such as gay men being constructed as a risk to the general population. This was a result of the homosexualization of AIDS, which was an early part of the social organization of knowledge regarding AIDS. Obviously, it built on earlier discourses of homo-sexuals as national, social, and sexual dangers. AIDS activists attacked the discourse of risk groups by emphasizing risk *activities,* in which anyone could engage. The idea of safe sex was directed at changing people's erotic practices. One major piece of wisdom acquired through safe sex organizing was the knowledge that, once again, many men who engaged in sexual activities with other men did not see themselves as gay, homosexual, bisexual, or queer. Because these men did not view themselves as homosexual or queer, they often rejected safe sex organizing and education that was directed towards these groups.[51]

Given the heterosexist character of the military, the notion that homo-sexuals alone posed a medical risk fuelled the arguments for excluding them. The task force report argues that "employing homosexuals in the CF could be followed by an increase in sexually-transmitted diseases which would generate additional costs for screening programs, HB vaccine, and patient treatment."[52] According to this logic, not only did homosexuals pose a disease risk but they were also expensive.

The task force report mentions only two options for balancing equality rights and operational efficiency, but these are conceived as prohibitive and were not intended to be taken seriously. The first option is a provision to separate gay men and lesbians and heterosexual men and women, effectively creating four sets of accommodation and hygiene facilities. Of course, the report goes on to point out that this would be impossible on a submarine or a warship. The other option involves the partial employment of homosexuals but only in areas where they would not disrupt the operational efficiency of the military. Again, the report adds that this option would interfere with the military's "flexibility in assignment," thus undermining its "practical feasibility."[53] We need hardly add that it fails to provide an option based on challenging heterosexism within the military and supporting equality rights for lesbians and gay men.

Homosexuality as an Active Characteristic
The document produced by the Military Charter Task Force also develops a rather peculiar analysis of race in relation to homosexuality. It categorizes racial differences as a "passive characteristic" (apparently more easily addressed within the military) as opposed to homosexuality, which constitutes an "active characteristic." We can contrast its claim of the passive character of "race" (by which it seems to refer exclusively to people of colour) with the very active accounts of racism and white supremacy within the Canadian military – for instance, during the 1992-93 Somalia mission. Lawrence Braithwaite, a black

member of the Reserve Forces in the early 1990s, remembered being called "boy" by some white members, whereas Asian men were often called "gooks." He also remembered one black officer being referred to as "N.O.," which stood for "nigger officer." Further, he reported seeing many "Keep Canada Canadian" pins that depicted Sikhs in RCMP uniforms with a slash through them. When Braithwaite was posted to a new base, the first words he heard were "Black people are evil."[54]

According to the task force report, "The adverse reactions to homosexuals are not similarly rooted in the passive characteristic but rather arise from the active character of their sexual proclivity, which is the cause of heterosexuals' aversion."[55] In other words, the active character of homosexuality causes problems for heterosexuals, a notion that builds on earlier concepts of homosexuals as a sexual danger and more recent pre-AIDS and AIDS constructions of gay men as sexually active and even predatory. Ultimately, the end logic of this discourse sexualizes the gay man as aggressive rather than as effeminate or passive.[56] Even though heterosexual-identified men engage in most of the sexual violence in our society, they are not, as a group, constructed as a sexual danger – at least not in this fashion.

The report concludes, "Homosexuals are excluded [from the military] because their active characteristic precludes acceptance, to the detriment of cohesion and morale, as a result of which their presence is prejudicial to military effectiveness." It goes on to say: "The consequences to Canada of changing the present policy would be a diminished capability to provide for national security. For all members of the CF, the reduction in operational capability would increase the risks to them of being killed, wounded, or captured should they be committed to battle." Finally, "[The] presence of homosexuals in the CF would be detrimental [to] ... discipline, leadership, recruiting, medical fitness, and the rights to privacy of other members; the overall effect of the presence of homosexuals would be a serious decrease in the operational effectiveness of the CF. It is recommended that the current policy of not employing homosexuals in the Canadian Forces be continued as a reasonable limitation within the meaning of section 1 of the Canadian Charter of Rights and Freedoms."[57]

Although national security certainly remains essential to the task force's argument, given that operational effectiveness is central to its vision of national security, blackmail, especially regarding out queers, moves into the background. This task force report, which maintains and broadens military opposition to the inclusion of gay men and lesbians, also exposes the internal contradictions of military policy.

POST-CHARTER STRUGGLES AND ASSIMILATION IN THE MILITARY

The Military Response to Equality Rights

In February 1986, following the Military Charter Task Force, military members were no longer obligated to report to their commanding officers if they suspected that another member was homosexual. Anti-gay, anti-lesbian military policies, however, remained official until October 1992. A partial shift in policy occurred in 1988 as a result of the equality rights section of the Charter of Rights and Freedoms and the struggles and legal challenges initiated by gay and lesbian members purged from the military.

The new policy mandated the release of a member if "the member acknowledged his or her homosexuality and the Department of National Defence considered the member to be homosexual." If the "member desired to be released from the Canadian Forces" and did not "object to being released under item 5(d) to QR&O 15.01 ... the release was effected as soon as administratively possible." If, however, the member did not wish to "be released under item 5(d), he or she was retained in the Canadian Forces during this 'interim policy' period." In this situation, "certain career restrictions applied," including no promotions, no career courses, and no re-engagement with or extension of career plan.[58] Individuals who insisted on remaining in the armed forces would not be automatically forced out; however, they would not be promoted, would lose their security clearance, and would not be "re-engaged" once their contract was terminated. In other words, career paths were frozen or placed in limbo.[59] This policy modified the implementation and enforcement of CFAO 19-20 but did not supersede it. It was a compromise position and, as such, maintained exclusionary and discriminatory practices. It also exposed the contradictions in the regulations.

Increasing Challenges to Exclusionary Policies

Dany Pelletier, a sergeant in the Canadian Airborne Regiment, said that his sexuality was discovered in 1989, after he was transferred to Edmonton. He was given a choice of resigning with an "honourable discharge" or being "kicked out." He chose to quit.[60] Pelletier recalled how, that same year, a corporal who had admitted to being gay had his security clearance revoked and was then asked to submit a "voluntary release." He refused and took the military to the Federal Court of Canada, which forced the return of his security clearance.[61]

In September 1990, a special external review initiated by former Ontario judge René Marin concluded that there was "no reason whatsoever" for the military's counter-intelligence unit to single out homosexuals for investigation. This was because "SIU has no role in investigating the private sexual lives of serving members except insofar as these activities, homosexual or otherwise, may be a factor in a security investigation."[62] Although the spirit of this ruling had the potential to help queers in the military, the use of the phrase "may be a factor in a security investigation" meant that the investigation of homosexuals was still a legitimate security practice.

In 1990, the Security Intelligence Review Committee (SIRC) ruled that military policy was unconstitutional and ordered the rehiring of a former air force lieutenant who had been forced to quit because she was a lesbian. This case was brought forward by a woman who appealed to SIRC, an all-party committee that heard appeals by any government employees who had been fired, demoted, or transferred "by reason only of the denial of the security clearance." The military argued against this individual's right to appeal the "separate decision" regarding the loss of her security clearance because she had been purged for being a lesbian, which "demonstrated disregard for security regulations and apparent strong loyalty to members of the homosexual community." As we have seen, this counter-positioning of loyalty to other lesbians versus loyalty to heterosexual national security was a consistent feature of the national security campaigns against lesbians and gay men. The military released her "because of her admitted homosexual activities contrary to Canadian Forces' policy."[63]

After informing his commanding officer that he was gay, Joshua Birch, a member of the Canadian Armed Forces from 1985 until April of 1990, was told that, "effective immediately, he would no longer be eligible for promotions, postings, or further military career training." Birch was released on "medical grounds." He was unable to seek redress as sexual orientation had not yet been included in the Canadian Human Rights Act. Birch took the case to the Ontario court and, on September 23, 1991, Judge McDonald announced that the lack of protection for lesbians and gay men under the Human Rights Act was unconstitutional.[64] A series of legal struggles, and growing resistance in the ranks, was propelling this question forward and weakening the ability of the military to retain its anti-gay, anti-lesbian policies.

Prime Minister Mulroney cancelled initial plans to allow lesbians and gay men into the Canadian Armed Forces. An announcement to this effect was made to members of the Conservative caucus on October 9, 1991.[65] This announcement, however, was struck down the next day, following intense backbench opposition. Despite this, military officials and most Tory Members of Parliament were resigned to an eventual change. Yet, John de Chastelain, chief of defence staff, said that these changes would not prevent the military from refusing to tolerate any "sexual misconduct which can be demonstrated to have a disruptive effect on operational effectiveness."[66] While these discussions were taking place, military policy regarding homosexuality was being challenged as a violation of equality rights in five separate legal actions by former or current military members, the most significant of which was that of Michelle Douglas.

Michelle Douglas: The Winds of Change

Michelle Douglas took the government to court to challenge the military ban on queers. She had joined the Canadian Armed Forces in 1986. By March of that year, she was a top graduate in her platoon and came second in a class on military police training. Two months later, she received a top secret security clearance and became a member of the SIU, the division of the forces that investigates sabotage, espionage, and homosexuality. In 1988, the SIU initiated an investigation into her sexuality after she formed a close relationship with another "suspected lesbian." She was called in for questioning, at which point she initially denied her lesbianism. As she put it, "I knew that saying I was a lesbian would mean that [my job] was no longer available to me."[67] After two months of interrogation, she identified herself as a lesbian and, having lost her security clearance, was transferred to Canadian Forces Base Toronto as a protocol officer.

Later, she was asked to take a lie-detector test as part of her interrogations to determine whether she might be a security risk. During the investigation, two male members of the SIU took her to a room in Toronto's Constellation Hotel and grilled her about her friendships. This defied military policy, which stipulated that a female member must be present for the interrogation of a woman member of the military, and was one of the reasons why SIRC decided that improper procedures had been used. These officers displayed a significant interest in Douglas' sexual activities. She was shown photos of other officers and asked to identify them as gay men and lesbians. She wanted to fight her expulsion, but it "was difficult on a number of levels" as she had not yet come out to her family.[68]

In 1990, Douglas filed a wrongful dismissal suit against the armed forces. Her identification as a lesbian and the removal of her security clearance were obviously connected. SIRC ordered that she be rehired and that her rank and security clearance be reinstated. SIRC reprimanded the SIU for its improper conduct, stating: "Douglas was taken to a hotel room under false pretences and grilled by two officers who showed an 'intense prurient interest' in her sexual activities."[69] However, the government appealed the ruling.

In October 1992, the case was settled quickly by the Supreme Court of Canada. Federal lawyers conceded that, given Section 15 of the Charter of Rights and Freedoms, this discrimination could not be justified.

> I wrote a legal affidavit for this case, stating that other government departments and agencies had allowed lesbians and gay men to be employees without any disastrous consequences. This was used to suggest that there would be no major consequences in the military of such a change either. As an incredibly significant case and legal victory, it proved to be a very real defeat for national security and military anti-homosexual policies and practices.

As Kenneth Cancellara, a lawyer representing the Defence Board, stated: "We eventually decided we really didn't have any evidence to put in that would justify the policy."[70] The judge signed a consent order, and the Department of National Defence announced the end of this discriminatory policy. The judgment stated that the Canadian Forces' 1988 Interim Reply on Homosexuality policy, which we mentioned earlier, violated the equality provisions of the Charter. The military agreed to pay Douglas $100,000 for the discrimination she suffered while enlisted, plus court costs. It also announced plans for settlement offers in the four other similar lawsuits still before the courts.[71]

Douglas was ecstatic about the decision: "This is not only a great day for me, but it's a win for all gays and lesbians in Canada and in the Canadian Armed Forces. It's something I fought for a long time. It's been a long road, a difficult road at times, but I'm thrilled today."[72] She went on: "[The] Forces are clearly the last bastion. The change in terms of making this a positive work environment will take time, I know that. But we have the court's authority to do it now." Douglas believed that the rank and file in the military were far more accepting of homosexuality than were the military elite: "Among my peers I never had any difficulty. I don't think there's any question that it's an old boys network at the highest level. And now we are seeing a change."[73]

In reference to this historic victory for gay and lesbian equality, Svend Robinson offered these comments: "The Michelle Douglas decision was the biggest victory in personal terms, and often, when I look back on these twenty-three years, there is a lot of frustration, but there have been times when I feel I've been able to make a big difference ... We were able to work together along with Clay Ruby [the lawyer] of course ... This decision meant a lot to me after fighting for so damn long and the committees and so on. To finally get to follow that through and to have them cave was sweet" (July 30, 2002). But there were still those who spoke out in opposition to these changes. Halifax West Member of Parliament Howard Crosby stated that he was very concerned about the rights of heterosexual troops who would be forced to share accommodations with homosexuals, reiterating earlier military arguments. Retired brigadier general Allan McLellan, formerly in charge of adjusting armed forces policy to conform to the Charter, said that allowing gays openly in the military could damage morale, ultimately costing the lives of soldiers.[74]

Gay and lesbian activists hailed this decision as a major victory that needed to be pushed further. Tom Warner of the Coalition for Lesbian and Gay Rights in Ontario commented: "The policy is a step forward but it also has to be accompanied by changes in basic attitudes. There's still an incredible amount of homophobia in the forces. It's going to be a brave individual who comes out and decides to announce his or her sexual orientation."[75] Robinson commented that the hundreds of lesbians and gay men who lost their jobs in the armed forces should receive financial compensation for the damage done to their careers.[76] The military hierarchy worked hard to contain and limit the repercussions of this decision.

ASSIMILATING THE MILITARY HOMOSEXUAL

In response to the Douglas decision, the DND issued several announcements. Applicants to the forces or members who declared their homosexuality or engaged in homosexual activity would no longer be treated differently from heterosexual applicants or members. No immediate change in the provision of accommodations or mess arrangements was made. At this time, the family status of lesbian and gay couples was still not recognized, and they were not able to occupy married quarter accommodations or to designate their partners for pension purposes. The announcement stated that homosexual military members were permitted to go on foreign military training and duty, including to countries where homosexuality was still considered a crime; however, this was not always communicated within the military. The conduct of homosexuals when in uniform was expected to conform to the same standards as were demanded of heterosexual members. Consequently, a new order was issued addressing inappropriate or criminal sexual behaviour committed by either heterosexual or homosexual members. The former could no longer choose to refuse to share accommodation with the latter, and those who refused to work with homosexual members were seen as demonstrating a failure to adapt to military requirements.[77]

The message sent to all CF units, however, did not describe the new policy but, rather, focused on the cancellation of the old one.[78] While it was acknowledged that some members might have difficulties with this decision, changing attitudes, legislation, and evolving government policies were cited as reasons for it. Directions to senior commanders placed limits on the organizational changes required by the policy revision. The CF had to honour the Charter, and professional duty required members to comply. "Proper" behaviour became the organizing principle of this new stance, not a broader education within the ranks or a shift in practices regarding lesbians and gay men.[79] In her explication and critique of the early impacts of this shift in the military, Rosemary Park offers the following insights: "There was no expectation or demand made of members to alter their own personal views regarding homosexuality. Rather, the method for promoting policy change was to answer specific questions relating to members' behaviours with clear uncompromising answers ... The CF sought to limit the policy's impact by predicting that little would change for most members. This reassurance was given in part because few were expected to come forward and declare their homosexual orientation."[80] According to Park, the military leadership adopted a specific approach to lesbians and gay men: "[It subscribed] to a particular model for introducing the presence of known homosexuals and managing the display of homosexual affectionate and sexual behaviour. Homosexuals will be assimilated using an approach best described as 'benign neutrality.' Specifically, the CF has not endorsed homosexuality but rather has said it should not matter ... The Canadian military has sought to reduce the uniqueness of the incoming homosexual group, i.e. homosexuals are no different. To the extent possible, homosexual members are officially invisible, i.e., unknown."[81]

Park contrasts this with another possible approach, which would have included "an organizational endorsement of ... homosexuality as an alternative or accepted sexual orientation." She points out that, with the military "approach of indifference, there is also no plan to educate members about the subject. The sexual subtext underlying the military culture, and working and living conditions, will remain heterosexual ... A distinction can be made between the CF approach, which seeks to downplay the key characteristic defining the known homosexual, and an approach that respects the defining characteristic." Park refers to the efforts to introduce CF servicewomen into formerly all-male units, which "showed the difficulties of trying to dismiss gender and treat women as if they were 'men in drag.'"[82] In contrast, Park stresses that "women's chances of successful integration into a unit occurred when their military status as women was recognized and valued. Because the approach seeks to mask the presence of homosexuals and homosexual behaviour in the CF, it will be the person himself or herself who will self-identify ... There will be no active organizational support for the member who does self-identify."[83] She pinpoints the assimilationist character of this approach: "The model suggests that incoming homosexuals will be assimilated into the larger heterosexual group as long as the homosexual member accepts the dominant heterosexual world view and does not cause others to think differently ... On the other hand, if incoming homosexuals decide to highlight differences or reject dominant heterosexual culture, the CF will not provide strong organizational support."[84] If lesbians and gay men are too visible or active with their sexuality, they will receive no support from the military hierarchy. Park argues that a successful integration strategy would have involved ensuring that "both the dominant group already in place and the incoming group [were] mutually valued for their respective characteristics and contributions."[85]

Park insists that, since homosexuals face a form of social discrimination that often results in our being hated and despised, and since military policy does not confront this, the CF strategy "only partially acknowledges the homosexual member's presence ... [and] that a full integration may not be possible." This approach would likely result in only "a minimal acceptance of known homosexuals in the CF." Clearly, the change in military regulations had not been based on a policy "that fully accept[ed] and endorse[d] homosexuals and homosexuality on an equal plane with the more dominant heterosexual orientation."[86] The policies of the military in response to the Douglas decision attempted to maintain the heterosexual (and heterosexist) character of the military while creating a limited space for the assimilated lesbian or gay military member who did not challenge the overall heterosexual organization of the armed forces.

Formal and informal practices of discrimination against lesbian and gay members of the military continued. The 1992 decision concentrated on whether lesbians and gay men could be members of the military. It affirmed that, in a formal sense, they could be; but it did not bring about the substantive institutional changes that would make the military a safe and comfortable place for them. In response to the 1992 decision, one gay man who publicly declared his homosexuality was cut out of everyday conversation. He then experienced homophobic remarks and verbal harassment. He was chased and hunted by some military men, who uttered such charming comments as "We're gonna fuckin' get you! You're fuckin' dead."[87] Despite military policies against harassment, these heterosexist practices keep many members of the military living a double life and remaining firmly in the closet. A lesbian member of the military

From Exclusion to Assimilation

pointed out, incorrectly, that, despite the new policy, restrictions remained in place: "We heard that you were not allowed to be posted to Europe or the United Nations. You were basically not allowed to go anywhere outside Canada if you declared your homosexuality."[88] Lesbians and gay men were considered single when posted to a new base, even if they were in a relationship. This had signifi-cant financial and emotional implications. Separate married quarters were not allocated to single people, and if they did not want to live in the barracks, they were forced to rent off the military base or purchase a house, both of which were expensive propositions. Some lesbians found innovative unofficial ways around these restrictions. Since the military usually covered the cost of moving members (and their heterosexual partners), one lesbian military member's partner moved all her own furniture and personal effects into her partner's apartment, enabling her to claim them as her own. The military thus assumed the costs of moving these two women's belongings, even though this was con-trary to military regulations.[89]

Immediately following the 1992 decision, gay and lesbian members were refused the same spousal financial support and travel rights (to be with their partners) that were available to common-law heterosexual couples.[90] There was no official recognition of the damage done to people's careers in the past and no official apology or offers of compensation. However, since 1996, the partners of gay and lesbian service members can be officially recognized within the military as "same sex dependants" and can therefore have access to benefits afforded to common-law heterosexual partners. Like common-law different-gender couples, members claiming same-gender partner status were "required to sign a statutory declaration that they had been in a relationship for a min-imum of one-year. The wording of the statutory declaration officially labels the relationship gay or lesbian. In other words, gay military women and their part-ners have to state and sign a declaration either in front of a lawyer or their com-manding officer that they are in a 'lesbian relationship.'"[91] To exercise spousal benefits or travel rights, one must publicly come out and identify the character of one's relationship to military authorities, thereby exposing oneself and one's partner to informal practices of discrimination and harassment. The conse-quences for same-gender couples of doing this within the confines of a hetero-sexist institution are very different from those for heterosexual common-law couples.

In a situation of continuing formal, and especially informal, discrimination, some refused to out themselves and their partners through such declarations. One lesbian interviewed by Lynne Gouliquer responded to this policy as follows: "I have never written that I am in a homosexual relationship. Why should I?

Heterosexuals don't have to claim that they are heterosexual. I shouldn't have to go in and say that my partner is a female."[92] Gouliquer, referring to lesbians in the military whom she interviewed in the 1990s, adds, "[The]wording of the declaration signified to these women that the military is still interested in their sexuality to the point of documenting it. Not one of the gay servicewomen interviewed has declared officially that they are lesbian. Given the military's history of chastising homosexuality, it is little wonder that lesbian servicewomen hesitate."[93]

In 1997, the CF informed its members that special application for same-gender benefits would be accepted. Each of these claims would be approved on a case-by-case basis at the DND. It also stated that a same-sex partner was a "dependant," not a "spouse." One of the women whom Gouliquer interviewed responded: "There is less discrimination against gays, but there is still some discrimination to get rid of – paper wise, and stuff. Like right now they are emphasizing that your same-sex partner is your dependant and not your spouse. There is a big difference between spouse and dependant."[94] "Dependant" carries with it the patriarchal construction of the wife and children as the dependants of a male wage earner. This has a particular sexist and heterosexist impact on the civilian partners of military members. For example, the support provided to a wife or the female heterosexual partner of a heterosexual male military member was not provided for the lesbian partners of military members. The military insisted upon documentation for anyone requesting same-sex status, while preserving its basic heterosexual institutional character. In this context, by the late 1990s some lesbians opted not to come out officially to the military hierarchy but, rather, to affirm their same-sex relationships to co-workers, supervisors, and commanders. Whereas some official military policies have changed dramatically, social practices have not, and informal discrimination continues against gay and lesbian members of the military and their partners.

Didi Khayatt's work on the impact of sexual orientation protection on human rights legislation helps to illuminate the relation between changes in official policies and the continuing daily social practices of discrimination. Although formal human rights protection was granted under human rights legislation to gay and lesbian teachers in Ontario, everyday discrimination did not decrease.[95] Similarly, major changes in the official military exclusion policy did not lead to the end of discrimination and oppression in the military. It did, however, open up new possibilities for gay men, lesbians, and bisexuals in the military.

Many people who had been previously purged from the military continued to demand an apology and compensation. In 1993, the Gay and Lesbian Organization of Veterans (GLOV), composed of people who had been purged from the military as well as other veterans, wrote two letters to the minister of national defence expressing concerns over the treatment of gays and lesbians prior to 1992. It prepared a brief for the Senate hearing on veterans' affairs in the mid-1990s. In the 1993 response it received from Minister of National Defence Tom Siddon, GLOV was told: "As you are certainly aware, there is no longer any restriction on homosexuals serving in the Canadian Forces." While this was formally accurate, there was still discrimination in terms of partners, spousal rights, and informal practices. In 1993, GLOV was told that the military had no plans to address the discrimination that had occurred prior to 1992.[96]

Since 1992, lesbian and gay members of the military have been granted housing rights and family status for lesbian and gay couples. Furthermore, profound changes, including same-gender marriages, have occurred. For example, in 2005, the media reported the Canadian military's "first gay wedding" at the Greenwood military base in Nova Scotia. The marriage was conducted by a United Church minister because the base chaplain was Anglican and could not officiate. This union followed the 2003 introduction of matrimonial guidelines in the military.[97] These important extensions of the rights of lesbian and gay members of the military have been built on the constraints of the policy of limited inclusion, and there still has been no major challenge to the heterosexist relations that continue to prevail in the military.

Personnel shortages and the need for more recruits, including for the military occupation of Afghanistan, led to armed forces recruitment efforts at some of the larger lesbian and gay pride events. In 2008, the military focused its efforts on the pride parade in Toronto; however, given concerns over human rights violations where the armed forces were serving – notably Haiti and Afghanistan – the Hamilton Pride Committee asked it not to participate.[98] The Hamilton committee also referred to a recent immigrant who had experienced abuse at the hands of the military in their country and who did not wish it to be present at pride events. Although these changes indicate limited forms of assimilation and tolerance within the military, many informal discriminatory practices against lesbians and gays persist.

The 1992 change established a major difference between Canada and the United States with regard to policy pertaining to homosexuals in the military. In 1993, there was an attempt to alter US military policies, which resulted in what is popularly (mis)understood as the "Don't Ask, Don't Tell" policy. Widely seen as a compromise, this maintained US military anti-homosexual policies, which prohibited homosexuals in the ranks but restricted what could be asked of recruits and military members. They could no longer be asked direct questions about their sexuality; at the same time, if they declared their homosexuality, or were discovered to be involved in same-gender sexual acts, they could be discharged from the military. This has actually established a new regime within the military, which focuses on the surveillance of activities and speech that might be an indication of a homosexual "propensity."[99] In the United States, more than eleven thousand people have been discharged since "Don't Ask, Don't Tell" was implemented in 1994. The rate of discharges slowed with the 2003 invasion and occupation of Iraq and the need for more military bodies.[100] It was only in 2000, as a result of four dismissed gay service personnel having taken their case to the European Court of Human Rights, that lesbians and gay men could now be members of the armed forces in the United Kingdom.[101]

STATE MANAGEMENT OF SECURITY INFORMATION: "IN THE NATIONAL INTEREST"

In 1994, the Treasury Board issued a text on security information and administration regarding the coordination of national security practices that guided security policies until the new anti-terrorist legislation in 2001.[102] A critical examination of this text reveals that the national security practices of the 1990s built on and modified earlier security practices. Under this policy, because of its jurisdiction over the public service, the Treasury Board became the governing body for security information. The document in question deals with regulations for classifying and managing security information. Its "policy objective" is to "ensure the appropriate safeguarding of all sensitive information and assets of the federal government." Defining the procedures for determining "threats and risks," it sets out the division of labour and courses of action for managing security information. These include risk management, and they make visible the text-mediated character of security and security information. The policy covers the entire public service, including the Canadian forces, the RCMP, and CSIS, and details the control of access to information and the need to "limit access to classified information and assets to those whose duties require such access and who have a security clearance at the appropriate level."[103] Security clearance levels are still critical to the management of security information, and various reliability checks are to be carried out to determine who can have access to security information.

Key to the construction of national security is the notion of national interest. This is evident in the Treasury Board text's classification of information "as sensitive when its unauthorized disclosure or other compromise could reasonably be expected to cause injury to the national interest"; its insistence that security assessments are to be arranged for "any individual whose duties or tasks require access to essential individuals or installations critical to the national interest"; and its definition of "Classified Information" as "information related to the national interest."[104]

Documents are now to be classified as "confidential, secret, or top secret."[105] "Secret" is the level of classification "that applies to information or assets when compromise could reasonably be expected to cause serious injury to the national interest"; "top secret" applies to information "when compromise could reasonably be expected to cause exceptionally grave injury to the national interest." The text draws on the definition of "subversive or hostile activities" in the Access to Information Act:

> espionage against Canada or any state allied or associated with Canada ... activities directed toward the commission of terrorist acts ... activities directed toward accomplishing government change within Canada or foreign states by the use of or the encouragement of the use of force, violence or any criminal means ... activities directed toward gathering information used for intelligence purposes that relates to Canada or any state allied or associated with Canada ... and activities directed toward threatening the safety of Canadians, employees of the Government of Canada or property of the Government of Canada outside Canada.[106]

These terms and conditions provide a wide-ranging definition of subversion, which could easily cover civil disobedience and direct action forms of protest and/or support for Third World national and social liberation movements. Security is constructed through a set of text-based rules and regulations, and national security is performed and accomplished through following these rules and regulations.

SECURITY CLEARANCES, OUTING, AND CONTINUING PROBLEMS IN THE PUBLIC SERVICE

Problems with security investigations in the public service persist, as do obstacles to promotion. Promotion to higher security levels still entails a rigorous security check that extends to asking questions of relatives, friends, neighbours, landlords, and others. As part of such investigations, an individual's sexuality may be revealed to others by security operatives. Discrimination continues to be organized against out lesbians and gay men because, even if they are out at work, they may not be out to all friends and family members. The same holds true for their partners. Effectively, security checks can lead to people being outed – people who have good reasons for staying in the closet and/or who do not define themselves as lesbian or gay.

Alice told us that she eventually left her job in the public service because she feared the consequences a security investigation would have had for her and her partner (March 12, 1994). According to Alice, "When you start working for the civil service anywhere you have what is called a routine security clearance. They check for a criminal record and that is it. No questions are asked and it is easy to pass." However,

> After a few years they had rewritten my job description and realized I had never passed an actual security clearance. It wasn't a higher-level security clearance or because they changed the job description. It was because when I came into the position it really didn't have a job description, and it took them two years to get through all the paper work. I should have had the security clearance right after I started ... So they gave me these forms to fill out. On the forms they ask you to fill out they don't ask you if you are gay; and if you didn't know any better you would think these forms were bizarre, but you wouldn't immediately think this was an invasion of privacy. They want to know where you have lived for the past ten years and the names and addresses of all your immediate family ... They want to know the names and addresses of people you have lived with, which clearly presents a problem for gay people who are either closeted or their partners are. It's a lot of detail. They do actually go and talk to people. One cousin of mine had CSIS at her door asking about her neighbours. (March 12, 1994)

Alice described how the fact that her partner was not out to her parents created major dangers:

> In my situation my partner is an only child and her parents are in their seventies and they would have a heart attack, and it is just impossible to envision someone from CSIS going up and asking questions and stating that their daughter's girlfriend was gay. I got along really well with my boss, and she said to me that someone asked her directly if her employees were gay or if she knew if they were gay. She ha[d] been approached at first about an ex-employee who had changed departments ... and needed a new security clearance, and they came back to his ex-boss to find out if he was gay or not. She told me that I could expect them to ask her [questions regarding the security clearance investigation]. She knew I was gay and it wasn't a problem with the people I worked with. If they had just been asking my family I wouldn't have cared less, but

they would also ask questions about my partner and talk to her relatives. (March 12, 1994)

Alice described how these policies continue to discriminate against those whose partners are not in a position to be out:

You can say that it is not the security clearance itself, there is nothing coercive or shady about it. My problem, and where I think they are setting out to find gay people, is that they have hugely inflated the security clearances that are needed for jobs ... By making security clearances not related to the position it means that anyone trying to get into a position of any authority or any salary is being forced to undergo these massive security clearances. So it becomes a no-win situation for homosexuals. If you say you are gay, they will then go and ask people if you are gay. This might be no problem if you have no one in your immediate family or are out to them or your lover's [family]. They can't fire you because you are gay. You haven't lied, everything is fine. But then everyone who reads your record now knows that you are gay. You may not always have the same boss, you may one day have a boss who doesn't like gay people. You may be surrounded by co-workers who don't like gay people. If you are an out gay person it may or it may not concern you ... [However,] if, for any reason, you are closeted and you don't say you are gay, if you don't want people to know but they go and find out, then it becomes a real problem because you have a secret from your family or your co-workers, which is deemed to be a security risk. What kind of security risk really doesn't matter since anything that is secretive about your life can make you into a security risk. Basically, what this means is that, as a gay person, you are either forced out of the closet ... or you have to leave.

Security investigations still rely on the social relations of the closet. And, therefore, employment discrimination can still be organized around questions of security. As Alice pointed out, "[They] still use national security as an excuse to identify people" (March 12, 1994).

Security clearances remain central to how discrimination continues to be organized in the public service. As Alice explained: "Security clearances are completely divorced from what the job actually involves. In the same way that you inflate job descriptions, you inflate security levels. Inflating what people actually do through security clearance levels" (March 12, 1994). The level of security work people do can be exaggerated so that it then requires a higher-level security clearance. For example, in Alice's case, "Part of rewriting my job description was to allow them to get a certain level of employee. Higher level positions require higher-level security clearances." Thus, we see the melding of security levels and job classifications. This continues the problems referred to in the McDonald Commission report, where it is noted that "far too many security investigations have been done" and that "there has been a tendency for government departments and agencies to transfer what should normally be considered personnel staffing responsibilities to the security investigative agency. Field investigations incorporate the checking of an applicant's credentials. In many instances it has become the practice to designate positions as requiring a high-level security clearance where there was not even an indirect link to classified information."[107]

Alice described the impact that security clearance can have on lesbians and gay men in the public service:

> An interesting thing is how many people have left the public service because they didn't know if they could pass [the security clearance] and how many people have stayed in the public service with gay stamped on their file and have experienced discrimination as a result of that. All I can tell you is what people who have been approached have been asked. In both cases, they have been asked if a person is gay. I was lucky because my boss said to me that she could stall [on the security clearance]. No one in the entire department where I worked was in a position to give away national secrets. (March 12, 1994)

Others were not so lucky. According to Alice, "[I did not] know anyone who refused to fill out the [security] form. If you refused to fill out the form you would be fired. People would probably decide to quit [rather than undergo a security investigation of this sort]." Referring to one woman who was out in the public service, she said: "One of the reasons she left the government was because she never got the promotion she was promised. I have absolutely no doubt that she didn't get it because she was gay" (March 12, 1994).

Obviously, there are still pervasive heterosexist social practices against queer people. For many gay men, lesbians, and bisexuals, continuing forms of heterosexism mean that they still live a double life and are still subjected to the relations of the closet.

CONTINUING OFFICIAL DISCRIMINATION: FOCUS ON THE CLOSETED HOMOSEXUAL

Social struggles, equality rights, and the use of the Charter led to growing acceptance for homosexuals in most areas of employment. The arguments for operational effectiveness put forward by the military and the RCMP were undermined, and the focus reverted to the security problems presented by individuals who were still closeted or who lived with people who were. In 1992, Svend Robinson wrote a letter to CSIS asking for clarification as to whether "an individual who was gay or lesbian may be denied a security clearance if they remained in the closet." Ray Protti of CSIS replied:

> I wish to assure you that CSIS' policy is in no way ambiguous. The issue here is not one of sexual orientation but of vulnerability to blackmail or coercion. When Service investigators learn that an individual applying for a security clearance is unable, or unwilling to be open about his/her sexual orientation, even to family members, the Service will advise the Departmental Security Officer (DSO) of the potential vulnerability of this individual ... In providing this information, the Service recognizes that choosing to "remain in the closet" does not automatically imply a vulnerability. It is, however, an aspect of the question of a security clearance which requires clarification. Upon an assessment of potential vulnerability, the Service recommends the DSO interview the applicant to discuss these vulnerabilities and therefore, lessen the possibility of blackmail and coercion.[108]

This systematized the policy built up in the late 1980s and early 1990s in response to the affirmation of equality rights and the growing visibility of gay men and lesbians, with the security focus shifting towards closeted lesbians and gay men or those whose partners might be in the closet. The security forces continue to use the social practices of heterosexism against closeted people who engage in same-gender sex. They continue to code living in the closet with security and blackmail concerns rather than dealing with the social pressures that might lead people to employ this strategy in order to avoid social discrimination. They also do not understand that some individuals who engage in same-gender sex do not see themselves as lesbian, gay, or even bisexual and, therefore, do not "come out" publicly. These people are not living in the closet; rather, they are constructing their sexual life and their identifications in a different fashion. The rigid and exclusive binary classifications of heterosexual/homosexual do not encompass all people's experiences. Sexuality is far more fluid than such binaries allow.

The focus on the closeted homosexual who has something to hide defined the CSIS response to our 1998 research report. Brian K. Smith interviewed a representative from CSIS for CBC Radio News regarding this report. The program started out as follows: "[The research report] demanded a government apology for a Cold War campaign aimed at known and suspected homosexuals.

The researchers say thousands of Canadians mainly in the public service were subjected to scrutiny and treated as security risks because of their sexual orientation." The program continued, "But as Brian K. Smith reports, clearance can still be denied to someone who hides his or her sexual orientation: It is now the Canadian Security Intelligence Service that conducts security clearance checks ... CSIS says the agency no longer looks for evidence of homosexuality but it can still be a factor." The CSIS spokesperson then stated: "Any behaviour whether it be someone's financial situation, criminal record, sexual life style – it all depends on the individual. I mean if the individual is very comfortable with their situation and if it is something that is known to their employers then they are not going to be subject to coercion or blackmail." The story concluded, "The authors of today's study are not happy that some federal authorities still believe homosexuals are candidates for blackmail forty years after the campaign against them began."[109]

This CSIS policy was also recounted in a *Globe and Mail* article that said that CSIS recruits were directly asked to identify their sexual orientation. In an article on CSIS and its security screenings for potential members, Jeff Sallot points out that the policies had changed since the 1980s:

> And what if a person happens to be gay? Perhaps nothing better illustrates how things have changed than the issue of sexual preference. In the old days the RCMP Security Service devoted a lot of time and energy to weeding homosexuals out of the federal public service. They were felt to be open to blackmail and thus potential security risks. Blackmail is still a concern, but sexual orientation isn't an issue, Mr Elcock [i.e., CSIS director Ward Elcock] said, as long as it is declared. During the year-long recruitment process, the service encourages candidates to put all aspects of their personal lives "in context."[110]

Again, we see a security focus on the undeclared homosexual.

The RCMP also asked recruits if they were gay or lesbian. In the *Ottawa Citizen*, RCMP staff sergeant Normand Nadeau, who held a top administrative position with the force at its New Brunswick headquarters in Fredericton, commented: "This is a question that is black-and-white in the security interview. It is common knowledge to everybody that has gone through the interview. It is departmental policy."[111] The article continued, "Although the senior Mountie denied that the RCMP automatically rejects gays, he defended the policy of determining a potential recruit's sexual orientation as necessary to protect against the possibility that a gay officer could be blackmailed into revealing secrets. 'This is a federal department, and our members have to deal with top secret files on a regular basis and are made aware of privileged information,' Nadeau said. 'We want to make sure there is no compromise.'"[112]

In 2001, the RCMP policy of viewing closeted homosexuals as security threats was still very much alive. It came to light because of a complaint from a New Brunswick man who claimed that the RCMP refused to hire him because it thought he was gay. Daniel Maillet alleged that an RCMP investigator asked a colleague if he (Daniel) was homosexual, saying to him: "It doesn't matter if he is a homosexual, he'll just have to admit it."[113] Many legal and human rights experts agreed that the RCMP should not be asking whether possible recruits were gay and that doing so was specifically prohibited under the Canadian Human Rights Act. In 2001, Svend Robinson called for the solicitor general to order an end to this practice.[114]

By the end of the 1990s, the national security campaigns continued to rely on the social relations of the closet, and, albeit in a more limited sense, homosexuality remained a "national security risk." The national security campaign against queers had been constrained and shifted as a result of social and legal struggles, but it could still construct participation in queer sex, when hidden, as a security risk.

POLICY VERSUS PRACTICE

In 2002, Svend Robinson summed up the progress achieved to date and, in doing so, made an important distinction between policy and practice:

> I have not had any issues drawn to my attention for certainly several years. I have had no one contact me from the Canadian Armed Forces or the RCMP or CSIS with respect to harassment or discrimination ... That is obviously a very good sign, given the fact that people are well aware of the fact that I raised these issues in the past and I know that the policies on paper are clearly non-discriminatory. Now, what's happening in practice, I'm not sure ... Does the national military college in Kingston actually proactively encourage an atmosphere that encourages diversity and celebrates diversity and makes it clear that any type of harassment is out of bounds and not acceptable? ... How are same-sex couples treated in the military? ... This is where we always have to make a distinction – the laws look great, policies are great, but there is often a huge gap between laws and policies and the daily reality of people's lives, and I expect that both the RCMP and the military are still places in which it is not comfortable at all to be out. I assume that is the case, but on paper the laws are there to support those who are out. In recruitment, again, I think a good

question is: "Are there types of affirmative outreach by either the military or the RCMP?" I doubt it, and just recently you may have heard the RCMP in British Columbia were told that they couldn't participate in uniform in the [Vancouver lesbian and gay] Pride celebration. Just one example – if a member of the RCMP was involved in a same sex relationship. Now, my understanding is that they are treated identical to a common-law heterosexual partner, and any suggestion to the contrary I would want to know about and would want to challenge it. And it would be challenged successfully. There are a number of cases in the recent years where I have had lesbian members; I think it is probably exclusively lesbian members, of the RCMP, who have had issues around their partners. But those issues have been solved positively ... in terms of transfer and so on. I have no evidence that there has been any explicit discrimination on the basis of sexual orientation for either the RCMP or the Canadian Armed Forces and CSIS. (July 30, 2002)

Robinson's observations confirm significant advances in formal legal rights despite the continuation of unofficial discrimination.

During the 1980s, major campaigns against queers continued in the military and the RCMP and CSIS. Social struggles and broader social changes, the continuing growth of lesbian and gay organizing, and the ability to use the equality rights section of the Charter of Rights and Freedoms undermined these national security campaigns and forced the military and RCMP to shift their strategy from blackmail-based arguments to the queer threat to operational effectiveness. By the 1990s, the growing public visibility of queer networks and community formation weakened these national security campaigns, eventually ending them, at least at the formal level. This led to the military's move to assimilation and containment as a way of maintaining heterosexual hegemony while allowing for the existence of lesbians and gay men as members.

Although the specific official Canadian war on queers has abated, the legacy of this war against sexual deviance and for heterosexual hegemony continues. This is particularly evident in the practices of the current national security wars on dissent and the so-called war on terror. We now turn to exploring the links between these differing national security campaigns and the necessity for continuing queer opposition to national security.

From Exclusion to Assimilation

From the Canadian War
on Queers to the War on Terror
Resisting the Expanding National Security State

On July 28, 2003, I was arrested with more than two hundred other people in Montreal and charged with participating in an "unlawful assembly." All six members of the Sudbury affinity group I was part of were arrested. We were surrounded by riot police banging their shields, even though we had simply been talking with other activists in the "green" zone far away from where earlier actions had taken place. Earlier that morning hundreds of us had confronted the mini-ministerial meeting of the World Trade Organization (WTO) in downtown Montreal. This was the same WTO that had been successfully protested against in Seattle in 1999, adding impetus to the growth of a global justice movement. Thousands of protestors also confronted the WTO at its meetings in Cancun, Mexico, that September. That protest, coupled with a revolt of delegates from many "Third World" countries, led to the collapse of the meeting and that round of international trade negotiations.[1]

I was placed in a police van after having plastic handcuffs tied very tightly around my wrists, which had been placed behind my back. Despite the pain caused by these handcuffs, we were in fairly high spirits. We started to sing the Queen song "We Will, We Will, Rock You!" as loudly as we could while trying to rock the police van. Before we were taken away, others outside the van heard us and joined in.

At the police station we were processed and our backpacks and other possessions were taken away, including my glasses, which meant I could hardly see. The cell was very cold and most of us had no blankets as we tried sleeping on the concrete floor. We were told there were no more blankets. We decided to refuse to cooperate with the authorities, such as by not responding when they read out our names. As a result, they gave us more blankets to try to get us to cooperate.

I was not released until late the next afternoon, after more than twenty-eight hours in custody and only after having bail posted for me. In addition, I had to agree to a series of denials of my democratic rights, including being barred from downtown Montreal where the summit was going on until the WTO meetings were over; that I could not protest on private property without the permission of the owner; that I could not protest on any public land or property unless it was "legal" and "peaceful"; and that I could not wear a mask or hide my face by any means while protesting.

The intent of this mass arrest was to keep us off the streets until after the WTO meetings were over, thus severely limiting the other protests that had been planned. I thought that they would drop the charges against us shortly after the WTO meeting was over. Instead, they proceeded to try to convict us on unlawful assembly charges. When our defence lawyers asked for the evidence against us, they were not given much. The Crown argued that they could not divulge large parts of the evidence because to do so would disclose the identities of their informers and agents in the activist movements in Montreal. When the Crown and the police continued to refuse to disclose this evidence to the defence lawyers, the judge stayed the charges against us.

How did it come to pass that defence of the WTO became part of the defence of Canadian national security and that global justice protesters became enemies of the nation-state, requiring such a high level of police action? Why were demonstrators denied basic rights and constructed as security threats? The same questions can be asked of other police actions, such as the pepper-spraying of students at the Asia Pacific Economic Co-operation (APEC) meetings in 1997 at the University of British Columbia or the building of the "security" fence and the massive amounts of tear gas lobbed at protesters in Quebec City in 2001 in defence of the Free Trade Area of the Americas (FTAA), which would have extended and intensified the terms of the North American Free Trade Agreement (NAFTA) across the Americas. This defence of the new international alliances entered into by the Canadian state is linked to the interstate agreements that informed earlier national security campaigns, including the campaign against queers. It is also a consequence of the shifting context of national security in the era of neoliberalism and capitalist globalization, where attempts to build and defend regional and global forms of organization designed to extend

From the Canadian War on Queers to the War on Terror

the power of capital over our lives have become central to the defence of Canadian "national security."[2]

What are the connections between these events and the war on queers detailed in this book? In our view, there are many. One obvious link is the use of informers and police infiltration of movements organizing for social change. Trying to protest against secret and undemocratic meetings at which decisions are made that will detrimentally affect many people's lives and strengthen the power of corporations over the needs of poor and working-class people gets defined as subversive and as requiring police action. Police surveillance and the use of informers are common practices in the current national security campaigns against the global justice movement and against people identified as Arab or Muslim as well as other racialized people. As we began working on this conclusion, we heard the revelations about the Sûreté du Quebec's (Quebec's provincial police force) use of provocateurs, with the probable cooperation of the RCMP, at an August 2007 demonstration in Montebello, Quebec, against the Security and Prosperity Partnership (SPP) between the Canadian, Mexican, and American governments.[3] The SPP further extends NAFTA into areas of security, border policing, and economic integration.[4] This is an example of how police practices such as those used in surveillance campaigns against queers at the height of the Cold War continue. Defining some segments of society as subversive and using informants as a security strategy are as much a part of organizing the defence of the nation-state now as they were in the past.

Another link is that both the war on queers and the current wars on dissent and "terror" are organized not simply through the arbitrary actions of individual security or police officials but through policies, regulations, and official texts used to coordinate people's actions against threats defined as being in opposition to the national interest. In the war on queers, this was organized through the notion of character weakness and, more concretely, through the attempts to shift alleged and suspected homosexuals into a confirmed category. Once placed in this category, individuals could be purged, demoted, and denied security clearances. In the current national security campaigns, at international summits in Canada some people are designated as internationally protected persons (see below); the notion of subversion has been expanded to cover various forms of protest; and the so-called war on terror has spawned new anti-terrorist legislation, national security certificates, and other texts and policies. National security was textually mediated in the campaigns against queers and continues to be textually mediated in the current war on terror. Information on individuals and secret lists of people identified as possible subversives and terror suspects are kept, updated, and expanded.[5]

There are major continuities *and* discontinuities between the national security campaigns against queers and the current national security campaigns against global justice and anti-poverty protesters and against people identified as Arab and Muslim. While targets have shifted and new enemies have been created, many of the same tactics (including surveillance, interrogations, and the collection of names), with new and different technologies (including video surveillance, computer technology, pepper spray, and tasers), are being used. Rendition and national security certificates are also being deployed.

Above all, national security persists as an ideological practice. The focus in the Canadian war on queers was on sexuality and gender deviance framed within a defence of heterosexual hegemony. National security operated as a means of sexual regulation. The focus of the current campaigns is on defence of capitalist social relations and of "Western" and "white" power and "civilization." These current campaigns are deeply racialized, and they have or do depict queers, direct action protesters, and people of colour as counterpoised to the nation and national security. These groups are transformed into "others," into threats to the nation, and are excluded from citizenship rights as well as from human and democratic rights. The flexible parameters of subversion, now increasingly expanding to include definitions of terrorism, are extended to cover these groups. Heterosexuals, supporters of capitalism, and white Christian–identified people are produced as being at the centre of Canada. Thus, national security, as in the war on queers, continues to be based on the exclusion of "others" and the inclusion of the normalized. It persists as an ideological practice posing crucial questions regarding *which* nation and *whose* security are being defined and defended. National security continues to operate in our historical present as a device for both including and excluding people.

Thousands of people were directly affected by anti-homosexual national security campaigns from the late 1950s through the 1990s. Individuals lost their jobs and careers. People were followed, phones were tapped, and homes were broken into. Some were interrogated, forced to inform on others, and to undergo lie-detector tests. Many were denied security clearances. No apology has been forthcoming, and no compensation has been offered to those whose lives were devastated by this state action.

Despite the devastation to careers and lives, many queers refused to cooperate and tried to resist. Friendships and queer associations were put before national security as defined by the RCMP and the government. Solidarity was found in the expansion of overt queer networks and the development of queer talk and camp cultures and, later, in the emergence of queer movements and organizing. This provided the social and material basis for queer resistance, which, in turn, altered the ground upon which the security regime operated and, at times, forced it to alter its tactics and strategy (see Chapter 6).

With the emergence of the lesbian and gay liberation movements, the national security regime itself became a target of queer activism. The involvement of left activists in queer organizing also led to extensive RCMP surveillance of gay and lesbian organizing across the Canadian state. The RCMP confronted queers who were now proclaiming the need to get "out of the closets" and "into the streets."

By the late 1970s, the war on queers in the public service began to abate, but it continued at full intensity within the military, the RCMP, and CSIS. Due to the equality rights section of the Canadian Charter of Rights and Freedoms, years of legal and political organizing by queer activists and their lawyers began to lead to formal legal rights victories. Even though the military and the RCMP fought hard against the ending of their exclusionary policies, by the late 1980s and early 1990s the writing was on the wall, and these policies were officially eliminated. In response, the military leadership attempted to manage and restrict the presence of queers in its ranks by creating a limited space for the assimilated lesbian and gay man and making no effort to challenge heterosexual hegemonic relations. Queers were tolerated as long as we did not challenge the overall heterosexist character of the military.

This strategy dovetailed with a broader performance of respectability and responsibility within parts of the mainstream gay and lesbian movements and community, which, in turn, led towards a strategy of integration within (as opposed to transformation of) existing social forms of the military, the family, marriage, and even national security. Consequently, some queers (mostly but not entirely middle-class white men) can now claim membership in the Canadian nation and can even be supporters of national security. Lisa Duggan and others have referred to this as "homonormativity," a politics that emerges in the context of neoliberalism and that "does not contest dominant heteronormative assumptions and institutions but upholds and sustains them."[6]

At the same time that this integration is taking place, other queers are being excluded as too queer, too irresponsible, and not respectable enough to be part of this nation. Certain more "respectable" middle-class queers are coming to be invested in the defence of national security, even against other queers, and are supporting campaigns against sex workers, people living in poverty, and those identified as Arab or Muslim.[7] This group forgets the historical experience of the Canadian war on queers and comes to "otherize" some queers, people of colour, and various groups seen as security threats. In other words, it embraces the standpoint of the national security state. We reject this respectable queer support for national security campaigns. It is our hope that this book reminds people of the past, of the continuing heterosexist character of Canadian state formation and national security practices, and of how queers have been constructed as national security risks.

State responses to the recommendations we made in our 1998 preliminary report, which asked for an official apology and a clear commitment that such campaigns would never be repeated, have been limited and uneven. No apology has been forthcoming. The government responded by suggesting that these concerns had already been addressed in the McDonald Commission report, which clearly did not address most of the concerns we raised in 1998 and certainly did not address the further concerns raised in this book. We asked for a commission of inquiry to investigate the security campaigns against not only lesbians and gay men but also other groups. This was to include those purged from the military and was to address "determining how compensation for those whose careers and lives were destroyed by the security campaigns can be best allocated." We also recommended, especially given the university and professional connections with the fruit machine research, an investigation into the "involvement of universities and especially university professors with this type of research."[8] Sadly, there is no progress to report.

In 2002, Svend Robinson outlined reasons for governmental reluctance (especially of the then governing Liberal Party) on these matters:

It's really quite unacceptable that people in positions of political leadership don't understand the impact policies have in human terms on people. It would be decent and honourable just to recognize that, and as long as they remain silent that kind of stain remains. I think those folks who were subjected to these [national security campaigns] should not only be entitled to apologies but of course to compensation as well ... But part of the whole thing is the Trudeau idea of justice in our own time. He was totally resistant to this kind of compensation or apologies to Japanese Canadians, the internment of Japanese Canadians, and a whole range of other issues. I debated that with Trudeau ... and basically his position was: we do justice in our own time. And we can't rewrite history, and I suspect Chrétien is very much along the same wavelength. Remember it was Mulroney who finally did the honourable thing for Japanese Canadians. It wasn't the Liberals. I suspect that part of it is the notion that if we open up the doors to these people then others will come forward in respect to other historical injustices; when they feel that, in the context of the times, these policies were acceptable. Of course, that is deeply offensive because we acknowledge today that these policies are inhumane and gave rise not just to anguish and in some cases death but also they resulted in a huge number of dedicated and outstanding people in public life losing their jobs. I mean, both at the individual human level but also at the national level, it is critically important that there be an acknowledgment and an apology. (July 30, 2002)

To reopen these issues in 2009 raises troubling questions for both past and current national security practices and policies. In other jurisdictions, however, there has been progress on compensation questions. In the United Kingdom, for instance, the European Court of Human Rights decision regarding purged military members created the conditions for people to apply for compensation.[9]

Our report also called for an end to all continuing forms of discrimination regarding security clearances and security clearance investigations, including ending outing people. Although this is less likely to happen today, closeted lesbians and gay men continue to be a focus of these investigations, and the potential for being outed to family and friends is still present. We called for full human rights for lesbian and gay members of the public service, the military, and the RCMP, including spousal and family recognition rights. Although some changes, such as same-gender marriage rights, have been granted, delays and obstacles persist (see Chapter 11). When contacted in 2003, both the military and the RCMP claimed that they had no specific policies concerning homosexuals, they treated all members equally, and they were bound by the Canadian Human Rights Act, which prohibits discrimination on the basis of sexual orientation.[10] Of course, this is only on the official and formal level. We know that informal practices of discrimination persist in these institutions and that inclusionary policies are largely based on assimilating lesbians and gay men into heterosexual-dominated institutions. We also called for full equality for transgender people, but no such policy has been established.

We made recommendations for the release of more security documents and for archival reorganization to expedite the location and release of security information. We called for an end to the use of certain sections of the Access to Information Act to prevent the release of national security information.[11] The construction of secret texts and the denial of access to them is part of the social organization of forgetting as it pertains to the national security wars against queers. Although more documents have been released as a result of individual requests, nothing has been done on this front.

Finally, we asked for government funding for lesbian, gay, and bisexual archives and history projects.[12] These important repositories, such as the Canadian Gay and Lesbian Archives in Toronto and the Quebec Gay Archives in

Montreal, are still largely maintained through the work and dedication of queer community activists and volunteers. It is through initiatives like this that our historical memory is produced and maintained. The time has arrived for major public funding initiatives to support the work done by these queer activists so that the histories of Canadian and Québécois lesbians, gay men, bisexuals, two-spirited, and trans people, and critical sexual histories more generally continue to be preserved. Recording and preserving our pasts is essential to maintaining our visibility and presence now and in the future.

NEW TARGETS, NEW ENEMIES

Capitalist Globalization and National Security

During the early Cold War and the Keynesian welfare state, the basic framework for the operation of capital and the containment of working-class and social struggles was the nation-state. But this was increasingly undermined both by global struggles in the 1960s and 1970s and by developments within capitalism.

Third World revolts for national and social liberation; student and youth revolts; a rash of working-class insurgencies in Canada, the United States, and, especially, in France and Italy; and the re-emergence of anti-racist, feminist, and lesbian and gay liberation movements resulted in a crisis for Keynesian social and economic approaches.[13] From the vantage point of capital, social and economic policies informed by Keynesian theories provided too much power to working-class, poor, and other oppressed people. It was in response to these struggles that leading sections of capital shifted their economic, social, and political strategies, which, in turn, affected national security.

The new strategic orientation articulated in response to these global struggles was variously named as monetarism, neoliberalism, and capitalist globalization.[14] This new approach has a number of features. First, it is defined by a central struggle to reduce social expenditures that were going to poor and working-class people, and it launched a major assault on unions, working-class people, and poor people around the world. Tearing apart the sources of collective power that workers had developed in the mass production factory system heralded the emergence of post-Fordism and lean production.[15] These are attempts to reassert the profit rates and power of capital at the expense of working-class people. Second, it is defined by various new attempts to colonize the global commons through commodifying common lands, water, seeds, and various genetic materials, with devastating impact on poor farmers in many countries in the global South.[16] Coupled with this is the extension

From the Canadian War on Queers to the War on Terror

of the commodification and commercialization of people's lives in wealthier countries, where labour at the point of consumption, often done by women, becomes more central to the production of capitalist relations.[17] Third, it requires a more global orientation on the part of capital, moving beyond the boundaries of the nation-state as barriers to investment and the movement of capital are weakened around the world. This requires a double-sided transformation of nation-state relations: regulation of capital is weakened but, at the same time, the more disciplinary aspects of state relations against workers and the poor are intensified.

Given the worldwide social and economic disruptions caused by the development of capitalist globalization, we see increases in migration and refugee flows from the global South to the global North. This has led to tougher immigration legislation, which attempts to keep poorer people of colour out of the North, and this has often produced an intensification of racism. At the same time, the cheap labour of people of colour was not only needed in the South but also increasingly drawn to the North, including in illegal and very precarious forms.[18] The increasing presence of those racialized as "other" in the North leads to the portrayal of these people as threats.

Capitalist globalization includes the development of, among others, the World Bank, the International Monetary Fund, the WTO, the G-8, the failed Multi-Lateral Agreement on Investment, APEC, NAFTA, the failed FTAA, and now the SPP to create global and regional forms of organization that facilitate the power of capital and weaken that of working-class and poor people. Meetings occur and decisions are made in undemocratic backroom negotiations between state and business leaders, and they provoke major forms of hardship and turmoil around the world, not to mention the militarization of responses to resulting popular revolts.

Neoliberalism and capitalist globalization, what the Zapatistas refer to as the Fourth World War against poor, oppressed, working-class, and indigenous people, has generated forms of struggle and resistance in many parts of the world.[19] On January 1, 1994, the Zapatistas in southern Mexico rose in rebellion against NAFTA and the devastation it would cause to poor and indigenous people in Mexico.[20] Unlike many left rebellions in the global South, that of the Zapatistas has tried to welcome gender and sexual diversity.[21] Their revolt helped to generate a wave of global struggle against neoliberalism and capitalism. In 1999, this erupted in the streets of Seattle in protests against the WTO, and it continued in various protests at summits in Genoa (2001), Quebec City (2001), Cancun (2003), Heiligendamm (2007), and London (2009). By making these secret meetings public and visible, these protests proved to be highly disruptive of efforts to facilitate the power of global capital. In response, there were major security mobilizations against global justice movements.[22]

In some areas of the globe, especially in parts of the Arab and Islamic world, the democratic and radical left has either been wiped out by state repression or rendered ineffective.[23] Here the forces of resistance to Western influence, or what has been popularized as the McDonaldization of the world, often take an Islamic form. At times, this response is fundamentalist in character, such as with al Qaeda or the Taliban (which were previously allied with the United States in the war on the Soviet Union in Afghanistan).[24] As Tariq Ali suggests, this has generated a clash of fundamentalisms: Western, pro-capitalist, Christian-identified fundamentalism is set against various forms of Islamic fundamentalism.[25]

Fundamentalism is the reassertion of a fundamental, or pure, religion, culture, or identity against other, supposedly inferior, cultures, religions, or identities. It involves a fixed and ahistorical approach to the world that removes culture, religion, and identity from their social and historical contexts and from any relation to class and social struggles. It argues that, for instance, only one particular sexuality is truly Christian, Islamic, Hindu, or Jewish. Obviously, these fundamentalist approaches are anti-queer. As Klein and others have pointed out, neoliberalism is based on a fundamentalist reading, defence, and reimposition of capitalist relations.[26] We return to the problems with fundamentalism later.

National Security from APEC to Quebec City

Indigenous people in what is now called Canada have always experienced a heavy security response to their struggles, from Kenora, Grassy Narrows, Kanesatake, and Kahnawake, to Ipperwash and the murder of Dudley George, to Gustafsen Lake, to the current struggles at Six Nations near Caledonia and in Brantford, Tyendinaga, and the Lac Barrière Algonquin Community.[27] Most often, but not always, white protesters are addressed in a less repressive fashion than are indigenous protesters. This shifted to an extent in the fall of 1997, when the campus at the University of British Columbia became the site of an APEC meeting. Activist groups among students and in the community were put under RCMP surveillance. When the meeting started, major violations of people's democratic rights occurred, along with the publicized use of pepper spray against young demonstrators engaged in non-violent direct action. There was a popular outcry against this repression, and an RCMP Public Complaints Commission (PCC) was established to look into police actions.

The mobilization of national security at the APEC summit involved the RCMP defending foreign leaders who were the target of protest, including Indonesian dictator Suharto, and the APEC process itself. It became clear that "Canadian" national security was defined by the Canadian state's commitment to APEC as one vehicle for capitalist globalization and by Canadian state and corporate support for Suharto and repressive regimes. And so the RCMP defended Suharto, the other foreign leaders, and their undemocratic secret meetings. The designation of Suharto and others as internationally protected persons (IPPs) under the Canadian Criminal Code and the 1973 Convention on the Prevention and Punishment of Crimes against Internationally Protected Persons led to their protection becoming part of Canadian national security.[28]

The RCMP PCC inquiry became a long, drawn out legal process in which the concerns of the protesters were marginalized. Although the eventual report criticized the RCMP's "incompetence" and poor planning, its basic security operations were defended.[29] The use of pepper spray, which was controversial in 1997, has now been normalized as part of the repertoire of police action against global justice and anti-poverty protesters. Their arsenal of pain also includes plastic and rubber bullets, tear gas, and tasers. In June 2000, pepper spray was used against global justice activists protesting the FTAA, and more than fifty protesters were arrested at the meetings of the Organization of American States in Windsor.[30]

CSIS responded to the protests in Seattle and their spillover into Canada with a specific report on the rise of the "anti-globalization" movement. It stated that people had the right to "lawful assembly," but this also meant that bodies such as the WTO had the right "to assemble and express their views." CSIS cautioned against the "tyranny of small groups, minorities, or even majorities, to prevent the exercise of such rights by trying to shut down meetings as unacceptable in a democracy."[31] Despite the undemocratic and often secret character of the summits furthering capitalist globalization, CSIS defined national security as defending these events from people organizing in the streets.

CSIS also comments on the anti-globalization movement in its 2000 report. Global justice protesters are constructed as a security threat since they are organized and are "able to identify and publicize targets, solicit and encourage support, establish dates, recruit, raise funds, share experiences, accept responsibilities, arrange logistics, and promote goals" and because they "share a mutual antipathy for multinational corporate power. Large corporations with international undertakings stand accused of social injustice and unfair labour practices, as well as a lack of concern for the environment, management of natural resources and ecological damage." CSIS continued its arguments against the anti-globalization movement by pointing to its stance against capitalism: "underlying the anti-globalization theme is criticism of the capitalist philosophy, a stance promoted again by left-of-centre activists and militant anarchists." In this formulation, simply opposing capitalist social relations is enough to make one a risk to national security. According to CSIS, "Circumstances have also promoted the involvement of fringe extremists who espouse violence, largely represented by Black Bloc anarchists and factions of militant animal rights and environmental activists."[32] Anarchist activists, who are an important part of global justice organizing, are specifically targeted. They are associated with "violence," with no explication of anarchism as an approach that challenges state hierarchy and domination. Instead, CSIS relies on mainstream media associations of anarchism with disorder and violence.[33] In this context, dissent is increasingly read by officials, and the mainstream media, not only as subversion but also as terrorism. In June 2000, the police responded to a militant anti-poverty demonstration with a major attack when they cleared Queen's Park in Toronto of protesters. Following this, the level of police surveillance and policing of actions organized by the Ontario Coalition against Poverty (OCAP) increased significantly, with some authorities identifying OCAP as a terrorist organization due to its direct action anti-poverty work. OCAP activist John Clarke was charged with a series of offences, including "incitement to riot," because of his participation in organizing the Queen's Park demonstration. In 2001, a Crown attorney labelled John Clarke as a "terrorist" for an action involving a mock eviction of then Ontario Cabinet minister Jim Flaherty, who was responsible for the evictions of many people living in poverty across the province.[34]

The largest security mobilization against global justice protesters took place at the Summit of the Americas, which was held to discuss the FTAA, in Quebec City in April 2001. Here police used tear gas (5,192 canisters in a forty-eight-hour period, which peaked at a rate of 30 canisters per minute), pepper spray, and rubber and plastic bullets (903), injuring at least one hundred protesters and arresting more than four hundred people.[35] The police were authorized to use lethal force against protesters if they were perceived as posing a danger to any of the state leaders gathered at the summit or to the police. The police guide offered five different levels of force, but only the second level was used. It authorized the police to use plastic bullets and tear gas, which they did, with very damaging consequences.[36]

In defence of the security "Wall of Shame" and the meetings of state and corporate leaders, the police engaged in major forms of violence against protesters, especially when activists were successful in pulling down the security barrier. Unfortunately, government officials and much of the mainstream media labelled the limited and targeted destruction of corporate property and the breaches of the security fence as instances of violence. This deflected attention from the far more profound police violence as well as the violence generated daily by the poverty, homelessness, and hardship that permeate capitalist social relations. Despite police violence and some of the mainstream media coverage, activists were successful in disrupting the start of the meetings, exposing their secrecy and drawing attention to problems with the FTAA.[37]

Before the summit, the police infiltrated a small group of activists known as Germinal, who focused on opposing the Wall of Shame and incited it to engage in more militant actions. Two days before the meetings started, the members of the group were arrested, and the police portrayed them to the media as terrorists.[38] The most serious charges were dropped, and, in the end, none of those arrested were sentenced to prison time. This security police tactic is also being used in the context of the war on terror.

Svend Robinson made a complaint against the police operation in Quebec City to the Commission for Public Complaints against the RCMP (CPC). His complaint stipulated that he and others were "fired on by members of the RCMP Riot Squad" and that he himself was hit with a rubber bullet. The CPC operates by receiving a complaint and then forwarding it to the RCMP for initial investigation. As could have been predicted, Robinson was not satisfied with the RCMP report and requested a review by the CPC. This review also left Robinson unsatisfied. In the CPC's interim and final reports, the official mandate for police action was justified by the need to protect IPPs and the security threat supposedly posed by the demonstrators.

As Katherine Moreau points out in her critical analysis of the CPC response, "the 'security' of these IPPs ... was placed above the individual rights of the demonstrators in the name of 'national security.'"[39] The CPC reports take up the basic standpoint of the RCMP and national security against global justice protesters. This is organized, in particular, through "the identification of the delegates and world leaders as 'Internationally Protected Persons' ... Identifying and categorizing these people as IPPs is an organizational accomplishment that works to presuppose the RCMP's mandated action to protect/defend these individuals' 'security.'"[40] In the end, though the CPC found that the police should have issued clearer warnings regarding the use of tear gas and force (citing an incident of tasering as "inappropriate"), the RCMP's basic actions were defended.[41] As is usually the case, official complaint bodies embrace police and national security standpoints. This is a common feature of the operation of official discourse.[42]

In May 2001, following the Quebec City protests, the RCMP created a new unit, known as the Public Order Program, which was to be a "centre of excellence" for dealing with protests. This involved various police forces agreeing to share information on crowd-control techniques and on how to improve the use of "non-lethal defensive tools" such as pepper spray, tear gas, and rubber bullets.[43] This new unit was part of the criminalization of protest, and one of its tasks was to develop tactics for inflicting pain on demonstrators. Among the groups then under RCMP and CSIS surveillance were the Raging Grannies, Amnesty International, and United Church members. Some of these made it onto federal "threat assessment" lists, along with groups more commonly seen as terrorist. The boundaries between forms of civil disobedience/direct action protest, on the one hand, and terrorism, on the other, became blurred. Among other things, this led to attacks on free speech in the academic world. Before the Quebec City protests, for instance, University of Lethbridge professor Tony Hall was questioned by security police regarding an article he had written that was critical of the effect of free trade agreements on indigenous peoples. Hall was also involved in organizing an alternative summit for indigenous peoples.[44]

National Security, Racialization, and the War on Terror

The connections between the Canadian war on queers and the current national security war on terror are numerous, and they illustrate the historical and ideological legacy of national security discourse and practice. Space and scope limit our ability to present a comprehensive analysis of these connections, but we now highlight some of them.

"Terror," understood broadly, refers to the infliction of violence and death for the purpose of generating fear. Terrorism, used in social, political, national, or religious conflicts, is a strategy based on the killing or injuring of civilians with the intention of generating panic. In this sense, terrorism can be used by states, groups, and/or individuals. In the West, however, the social construction of knowledge regarding terrorism has a much more limited character, focusing mostly on individual or group forms. Although this definition of terrorism has been linked to "rogue" states such as those comprising the so-called Axis of Evil, the focus is on individuals and groups. It should be kept in mind, of course, that, being an elastic and ideological term, "terrorism," like "national security," can have its meaning shifted and expanded.

The social construction of terror and terrorism has a threefold character. First, within official Western discourse, the terror and terrorism perpetrated by

From the Canadian War on Queers to the War on Terror

Western states (e.g., the massive terror inflicted on the Vietnamese people) is not seen as such. The daily violence inflicted on people in Iraq and Afghanistan by the United States (and the Canadian military in Afghanistan) is not defined by Western governments and the mainstream media as terrorism. The generation of terror in people's lives, which Naomi Klein points to as being central to capitalism (especially fundamentalist neoliberalism), is not addressed as terror.[45] Instead, the label of terrorism is relegated to the actions of non-state groups who are opposed to the interests of Western governments and corporations (e.g., "suicide bombers," the Palestinian resistance, the Iraqi insurgency, and the Taliban in Afghanistan). The social and historical reasons behind why these groups might be engaging in these acts are not addressed. This construction of terrorism precludes the naming of American and Canadian military actions as terrorist.

Second, in the emergence of terrorism studies in the academic world and among a generation of Western experts, there is a focus on the individual psychology of terrorists, thus further separating their actions from broader social, historical, and political relations.[46] As Puar and Rai show, these constructions resemble those of queer people as psychopathic or as suffering from mental illness.[47] The embodiment of terrorism in the individual means that the problem of terrorism (and therefore the blame) is connected not to political, economic, or social policies but, rather, to the actions of "sick" or "evil" individuals. Terrorism becomes something that is not engaged in by Western states and militaries and that has far more of a psychological than a political basis. The terrorist is a seemingly irrational and monstrous individual.[48]

Third, terrorists are racialized. This process rests on earlier forms of "otherization" and racism directed towards Arabs and Muslims but intensifies it.[49] In the current war on terror discourse, Western governments, the news media, and popular cultural production generate images of the terrorist as a person of colour, with a special focus on men who are Arab or Muslim. As Edward Said pointed out when the Oklahoma City bombing took place in 1995, it was immediately assumed by officials and the media to be the work of Islamic terrorists.[50] This, of course, was not the case, but this association is even stronger since the September 11, 2001, attacks on the World Trade Center and the Pentagon. From the perspective of the Western orientalist gaze, the term "terrorist" is racially and culturally coded as Arab or Islamic. Orientalism, for Edward Said, involves the construction, in the western European–derived imagination, of people in the Middle East, or the Arab and Islamic worlds, as sharing some essential common characteristics and as being "other" to those in the more advanced West. It is rooted in a history of colonialism and imperialism.[51] One of the more recent deployments of Orientalism has been the construction of the Islamic terrorist. In it, Muslims epitomize this image of the terrorist, which, in turn, helps to organize racism and racial profiling against Arab- and Islamic-identified people.

The national security campaigns against Arabs and people identified as Muslims did not begin with September 11, 2001. The racialization and other-ization, including those directed at Palestinians resisting the occupation of their land, have a long history. It should be noted that, in university campuses across the Canadian state, there have been various clampdowns on anti-war activism and pro-Palestinian organizing.[52] During the 1991 Gulf War, racialization grew in Canada and led to heightened surveillance of and discrimination against Palestinians, Iraqis, Iranians, and others. This included CSIS conducting intimidating interviews with more than five hundred Arab Canadians and showing them photos that had been taken at anti-war demonstrations and other places for identification purposes.[53] The practice of interviewing people and showing them photos in an attempt to identify gay men and lesbians was key to the national security campaigns against queers as well. These earlier practices have now been intensified. CSIS regularly conducts "interviews and interrogations with hundreds of Arabs and Muslims across Canada at their work places, homes and in the vicinity of local mosques."[54] This leads to fear and intimidation and can put people's employment in jeopardy – yet another parallel with the war on queers.

The Bush regime quickly used the 9/11 attacks to its benefit, moving against the people of Afghanistan and setting its sights on invading Iraq. The message conveyed by the Bush regime was "Either you are with us, or you are with the terrorists."[55] The Canadian state was pressured to join in this war on terror, and Ottawa quickly proposed new anti-terrorist legislation.

People who criticized the basis of this war on terror or suggested alternatives other than lining up with the Bush regime came under attack. In October 2001, Sunera Thobani, a former president of the National Action Committee on the Status of Women (NAC), gave a talk in which she criticized US war moves. She stated: "From Chile to El Salvador, to Nicaragua, the path of US foreign policy is soaked in blood." Criticizing Canadian state attempts to support these war moves, she remarked: "Pursuing American corporate interest should not be in Canada's national interest." She also criticized Canadian state attempts to turn against "the enemy within – immigrants and refugees."[56] Thobani, who had been vilified as an "immigrant" when she was NAC president, now faced calls for her dismissal from her teaching position at the University of British Columbia. In addition, a police investigation was launched based on her supposedly having "incit[ed] hatred against an identifiable group [Americans]." Fortunately, a quick global defence campaign for Thobani was mobilized to defend her academic freedom and freedom of speech.[57] As a result, nothing ever came of this.

In the aftermath of 9/11, Canadian state officials moved quickly to introduce and pass new anti-terrorism legislation in an attempt to harmonize relevant legislation with that of the United States and other Western powers as well as for its own domestic reasons regarding perceived internal threats. On October 15, 2001, Justice Minister Anne McClellan introduced Bill C-36, the new omnibus anti-terrorism legislation. At its centre, this legislation included an expansive definition of terrorism, which could potentially cover civil disobedience and/or direct action protests organized by anti-poverty or global justice activists.[58] This led to a major outcry from supporters of civil liberties and human rights. In response to this criticism, some limited modifications were made to the legislation before it was passed.[59] However, major problems remain.[60] This legislation provides the security police with a far more public state mandate for the war on terror than they ever had for the war on queers. The security campaigns against queers were much more secretive and, though based on Cabinet directives, were administered through Security Panel directives and the actions of the RCMP and security officials.

There are multiple aspects to the Canadian national security war on terror, and we cannot trace them all here. We limit ourselves to three: rendition, national security certificates, and terrorism-related charges against Muslim-identified men in the Toronto area. Rendition is the practice of seizing a person in one country and moving her/him to another for the purposes of interrogation, torture, or prosecution. The most infamous example of this involves Canadian citizen Maher Arar, who, in 2002, was interrogated by FBI and immigration officials in New York City, held in custody for twelve days, and then flown to Jordan, where he was shackled and chained.[61] He was then driven to Syria and tortured for nearly a year until he was finally released. Following an official inquiry, it is now clear that this rendition was initiated and sustained by RCMP officers who gave false information about Arar to US security officials. CSIS passed questions to Syrian officials during Arar's incarceration, and the information he provided under torture was then given back to CSIS, who, in turn, passed it on to other Canadian authorities.[62]

Following 9/11, Canadian officials instructed the RCMP to share security information with US security agencies. In April 2002, US security officials were provided with copies of twenty-six hard-drives, hundreds of compact disks, and thousands of RCMP-seized documents. Further to this, a copy of the RCMP's SUPERText database was given to US agencies.[63] Again, as in the war on queers, we see major interactions between Canadian and American security officials and the sharing of security information.

Arar is one of a number of individuals who have gone public with stories of rendition and torture. Others are Abdullah Almalki, Ahmad El Maati, and Muayyed Nureddin and Benamar Benatta. In a 2008 report from a federal government inquiry into what happened to Almalki, El Maati, and Nureddin, former Supreme Court judge Frank Iacobucci found that the RCMP, CSIS, and the Department of Foreign Affairs had contributed to the torture of these three men in Syria through sharing unsubstantiated and inflammatory information about them with foreign intelligence and police agencies.[64]

Benamar Benatta, who was illegally transferred by the Canadian government to the United States and held for five years by US authorities, is calling for a public review of his case. Benatta, an Algerian refugee claimant, was handed over to the Americans on September 12, 2001. Canadian officials wrongfully identified Benatta as a suspect in the 9/11 terrorist attacks, based solely on prejudiced suspicions: he was a Muslim man who knew something about airplanes. Without a hearing, without legal counsel, and without the benefit of proceedings in his first language (French), Benatta was unceremoniously driven over the border in the back of a car and handed over to US officials. In the United States, he was imprisoned and held in conditions that the United Nations Working Group on Arbitrary Detention considered to be torture. Although cleared by the FBI in November, 2001, of any connection to terrorism, he spent nearly five years in detention. On July 20, 2006, Benatta was finally allowed to return to Canada and has resumed his claim for asylum.[65]

The national security certificate procedure is part of the security provisions of immigration legislation. In June 1992, amidst fears mobilized against growing numbers of poor people of colour who were trying to get into Canada, Bill C-86 introduced new security provisions to the Immigration Act. Thus, terrorism became a new category of security inadmissibility. The term "terrorism" was not defined, nor were concepts such as the "security of Canada" or "membership in an organization engaged in terrorism." These were left to ministerial discretion.[66] As part of a broader social process, these reforms led to the increased targeting of migrants and to the construction of migrants of colour as "outsiders" and "threats."

Bill C-86 gave CSIS further powers related to security assessments of migrants, especially regarding terrorism. As a result, certain refugee communities found themselves increasingly under CSIS surveillance. Through promises of the prompt resolution of their status applications and/or threats regarding what might happen to their files should they refuse to cooperate, some refugees were coerced into informing on community members.[67] As we have seen, in the Canadian war on queers, the RCMP was able to use the criminalization and stigmatization of homosexuality to coerce some gays to inform on others.

Following 9/11 and the passage of the anti-terrorist legislation in 2001, in 2002 the immigration system was overhauled yet again, with the passage of Bill C-11. As the People's Commission on Immigration "Security" Measures points out, this "reframed migrants without Canadian citizenship, including Permanent Residents, under the new category of 'foreign nationals.' It also introduced mandatory detention of non-Permanent Residents named in a security certificate, on information provided by CSIS, before any judicial review whatsoever of the allegations. This has meant years of detention for refugees such as Mohamed Harkat, who spent two years in an Ottawa jail before the certificate was even reviewed by a judge."[68] So far, only a small number of security certificates have publicly surfaced, but Professor Sharryn Aiken estimates that "hundreds of non-citizens are caught up in the web of immigration security measures."[69]

So far, national security certificates have been used against five Muslim-identified men: Mahmoud Jaballah, Mohammad Mahjoub, Hassan Almrei, Mohamed Harkat, and Adil Charkaoui. All but Almrei have been released from custody, most with very stringent home arrest conditions.[70] They were held at the Kingston Immigration Holding Centre, a $3.2 million facility within Millhaven Penitentiary specifically constructed for security certificate detainees. After a series of hunger strikes for basic health and living conditions at what came to be dubbed "Guantánamo North," on February 23, 2007, a Supreme Court decision challenged the heart of Canada's secret trials, deeming the security certificate procedure to be unconstitutional. The Supreme Court gave the government one year to respond to the decision before the law would be nullified. All five detainees remain under house arrest or in indefinite detention, under threat of deportation and possible torture.

The Conservative government introduced new security certificate legislation in the fall of 2007, which passed with Liberal Party support in 2008. This is based on the "special advocate" model (whereby a special advocate, but not the detainee, is allowed access to the "secret" information used against the detainee) and continues the injustice of security certificates while further entrenching the use of secrecy in the immigration and justice systems. The government also states that it considers information acquired using torture as unreliable; however, there is no way of ensuring that security information from other countries, including the United States, has not been tainted by torture. This provides a minor reform but holds the main features of the security certificate procedure in place: it places arbitrary power in the hands of spy agencies and politicians; it replaces precise charges with vague concepts; it relies on secret suspicions, profiling, and association instead of evidence; and it has no end except deportation to torture.[71] It assumes that Muslim immigrants are potential "threats to national security."[72] As in the war on queers, the construction of secrecy surrounding these cases makes them far more difficult to organize against while, at the same time, excluding these people from the fabric of the Canadian nation. Most recently, in an attempt to restore credibility, CSIS has ordered a review of these national security certificate cases after a Federal Court judge criticized the agency for withholding lie-detector tests that cast doubt on a key informant in the effort to deport Mohamed Harkat.[73]

Two highly publicized "anti-terrorist" mass arrests of Muslim men in the Toronto area demonstrate the character of the Canadian state's war on terror. In a joint RCMP/Immigration Canada operation initiated in 2003 and known as Project Thread, twenty-four South Asian men were arrested under suspicion of posing a security threat. The RCMP claimed it had a "van-load" of evidence to substantiate its charges. The mainstream media coverage included claims that an "Al Qaeda sleeper cell" had been uncovered. The evidence actually consisted of "the fact that the men lived in 'clusters' of 4 to 5 people, had a minimal standard of living, that one man had a picture of an airplane on his wall, the possession of pictures of 'strategic landmarks' (e.g. a photo of the men in front of the CN Tower) and the fact that all but one were from Punjab province in Pakistan, which was described as 'noted for Sunni extremism.'"[74] Within a week, all charges were dropped and the RCMP declared there was no reason to think there was any link to terrorism. However, the mainstream media did not give this nearly the same coverage as was accorded the earlier accusations of terrorism. The men had all been students of a business school and were on student visas; however, they were left stranded when the school closed, rendering their visas invalid. This led to their being detained for up to five months on immigration charges. While in detention, they were interrogated by intelligence officers about their political beliefs and religious practices. Friends contacted by the detainees were later visited by security police. The men experienced racist abuse and insults in detention, being called "Al Qaeda" and "Taliban." They were also threatened with being sent to Guantánamo Bay if they did not cooperate.[75]

In June 2006, four hundred state security officers staged pre-dawn raids on the outskirts of Toronto and arrested eighteen Canadian Muslim men, mostly in their late teens and early twenties, who were charged with various offences related to terrorism. Canadian officials claimed that these arrests were "the largest anti-terror operation in recent history." *Maclean's* portrayed this as "home-grown terror," and the media attempted to generate a moral panic against "Muslim extremism." The media produced divisions between "good" and "bad" Muslims, and the accused were presumed to be guilty before anything was proven in court.[76]

Infiltrated by a police informer who was paid half a million dollars, this group of men was arrested as part of a sting operation based on the work conducted by a police agent who had been paid at least $300,000 and who helped set up a training camp for the accused. Three of the eighteen have now had their charges stayed and have been quietly released. New allegations that the police informant provided the ammunition used for target practice at the alleged "terrorist training camp" have also come to light.[77] In September 2008, a seventeen-year-old Muslim was the first of those charged to be convicted under the anti-terror law mentioned earlier. In large part, this was due to the low standard of proof required under this legislation. The government is not required to prove that the alleged terrorist took part in or even knew of an alleged plot: it has to prove only that he or she participated in the "terrorist" group and contributed directly or indirectly to enhancing its abilities.[78] This practice of having security forces infiltrate groups of Islamic radicals and then getting them to engage in more militant actions so that they can be arrested and charged with being terrorists has also taken place in England and the United States.[79]

State of Exception and the Rule of Law

Fetishizing 9/11 as "new" and "different" leads to decontextualizing the war on terror, removing it from the history of earlier national security campaigns. It encourages us to see only the exceptional in the current situation and not the continuities with past national security campaigns. This has prompted some theorists and activists to interpret the war on terror as a "state of exception" in which the regular rule of law has been suspended. This results in an important focus on the "sexualized" torture at the Abu Ghraib prison in Iraq, on Guantánamo, on rendition, on Canada's detention practices and national security certificates, and on the erosion of civil rights.[80] It is crucial to examine these horrors, but in response to them it is sometimes suggested that eliminating this state of exception and restoring the rule of law would end them. In connection with the war on queers, this is very much how the McDonald Commission responded to the RCMP's dirty tricks (see Chapter 10). This approach was inadequate then, and it is inadequate now.

"State of exception" is an expression used by jurist and legal philosopher Carl Schmitt and adopted in the work of Italian political theorist Giorgio Agamben. For Agamben, the modern operation of power is based on an almost permanent state of exception in which the regular rule of law is suspended, as it was in the Nazi concentration camps. A central image in this view is the camp, and in this context we are no longer so much citizens as detainees. The central form of power becomes the state of exception, and the rule of law exists only in this context.[81] Although this captures something crucial about the mobilization of national security in the war on terror, it can prevent us from seeing how the deployment of national security measures is rooted in the "normal" relations and routine operations of power and the rule of law. As political and cultural theorist Michael Hardt suggests in a critique of Agamben's work, "My hesitation with this view is that by posing the extreme case of the concentration camp as the heart of sovereignty it tends to obscure the daily violence of modern sovereignty in all its forms. It implies, in other words, that if we could do away with the camp, then all the violence of sovereignty would also disappear."[82] As we suggest, doing away with the violence of the national security state requires a very broad social transformation – one that challenges the social roots of racializing, colonizing, capitalist, and state relations and the rule of law that helps to organize them.

GENDERS AND SEXUALITIES IN THE WAR ON TERROR: ANOTHER WAR FOR MASCULINITY AND HETEROSEXUALITY

In the war on terror, national security has major gender and sexuality dimensions. We therefore need to look at national security and war through a feminist lens – a lens that shows us the ways that racialized, gendered, sexual, and class relations mutually construct each other. The constant generation of fear upon which the war on terror is based reinforces patriarchal security and military agencies as the "protectors" of women in the West. The myth that women can ensure their safety by relying on men's protection, which both disempowers women and makes them vulnerable to male violence, has long been criticized by feminists.[83] Feminist theorist Iris Marion Young, in examining the "dual face of security forms, those that wage war outside a country and conduct surveillance and detention inside," points out that, in the US context, "democratic values of due process, separation of powers, free assembly, and holding powerful

From the Canadian War on Queers to the War on Terror

actors accountable come into danger when leaders mobilize fear and present themselves as protectors."[84] Often these protectors are the same men and institutions that have both ignored and been responsible for widespread sexual and other forms of violence against women, in both the past and the present. The militarization of security and defence policies and the mobilizations surrounding wars and occupations in Afghanistan and Iraq have contributed to a contested and at times contradictory shift towards a state-supported, aggressive, and violent form of masculinity and patriotism.[85] Wars and patriotism (based on defence of the "nation") often reinforce patriarchal notions of women, the idea being that women's importance lies in being mothers of soldiers or members of patriotic families who support the troops that work against the objectives of women's liberation.[86] For Western women involved in combat in Iraq and Afghanistan, there are widespread problems associated with rape, other forms of violence, and sexism in what continue to be male-dominated organizations. Never mind the problems associated with being part of an occupation army.[87]

In the current war on terror, especially regarding the occupation of Afghanistan, Western military interventions are often justified through an ahistorical and essentialist use of women. State officials, the mainstream media, and even some liberal feminists often argue that American and Canadian troops are there to "help" Afghan women and that Islam is the main danger for women in the region.[88] As Sunera Thobani puts it, this denies what Afghan women themselves have been saying and doing:

> And it's really interesting to hear all this talk about saving Afghan women. Those of us who have been colonized know what this "saving" means. For a long time now, Afghan women, and the struggles they were engaged in, were known here in the West ... And rightfully many of us were in solidarity with them. At that time Afghan women were fighting and struggling against the Taliban. They were condemning the Taliban's particular interpretation of Islam. Afghan women, Afghan women's organizations were on the front lines of this. But what did they become in the West? In the West they became nothing but poor victims of this bad, bad religion, and of these backward, backward men. The same old colonial construction. The women were in the front lines but we did not take the lead from them then. We could see them more as victims, only worthy of our pity. And today, even in the United States, people are ready to bomb these same women, seeing them as nothing more than collateral damage. You see how quickly the world can change on you. And I say that we take the lead from the Afghan women. They fought back against the Taliban, and when they were fighting back they said that it is the United States that is putting the regime in power.[89]

The Revolutionary Association of the Women of Afghanistan (RAWA), one of the women's organizations to which Thobani refers, opposes the US invasion and occupation of Afghanistan, along with the Canadian military occupation. This occupation placed in power and continues to defend the warlords that the Taliban had earlier defeated but who are equally invested in the oppression of women. RAWA opposes both occupation and Islamic fundamentalism.[90]

Far from liberating them, war and occupation made the situation worse for women in Afghanistan and Iraq. As French feminist Christine Delphy stresses, we need to be very critical of arguments about war and occupation "helping" women in countries like Afghanistan and Iraq:

> The "liberation of Afghan women" calls on values which appear to be progressive but they only appear to be, for on closer examination, they consist of a more or less conscious belief in the West's "mission." We only consider ourselves to have such a mission because we consider ourselves to be the carriers of "civilization" ... The action of Western powers in the non-Western world relies on the opinion of the public whose vision of the world has hardly changed in depth since the end of colonisation. The belief in Western superiority is intact. This more or less stated racism is today allied with a type of paternalistic compassion, their combination produces a potentially very dangerous ideology for non-Westerners and more generally for all dominated groups, for it provides justification for military intervention.[91]

The ideology of saving women is hypocritical as war and occupation actually make the lives of women far worse, often intensifying the impact of Islamic fundamentalism on their lives (especially in Iraq) and perpetuating a paternalistic and sexist approach to them that is rooted in the colonizing and imperialist practices of the past. The war on terror is not helping women in Afghanistan or Iraq; on the contrary, it is reinforcing in the global North a form of legitimized aggressive, violent, and racialized patriotic masculinity that works against women. The mobilization of the war on terror also undercuts global feminist organizing, especially as it tries to get Western women to support military campaigns that harm women in other parts of the world.

Since it has a heterosexual (and heterosexist) character, this production and defence of an aggressive patriotic masculinity is also detrimental to most queer people. Consider two main features of this form of masculinity in relation to sexuality and queerness among men. First, in the context of this aggressive heterosexual patriotism, there are attempts to emasculate the Islamic "terrorist" by turning him into a "fag." Based on constructing Islamic and Arab men as monolithically heterosexual, the assumption is that accusing them of being queer is devastating since it entails emasculation and effeminization.[92] This assumption has little to do with the actual diversity of the social organization of gendered sexualities and eroticism in the Arab and Islamic worlds, "whose ontological structure is not based on the hetero-homo binary."[93] It does, however, contribute to constructing Muslim and Arab queers and others who engage in same-gender eroticism as being outside their communities and outside of Islam, which has a major impact on Muslim and Arab queers in the Middle East, the West, and elsewhere.

Second, in Orientalist and heterosexist constructions, the "terrorist monster" can be conceptualized and sexualized as queer. This is based on earlier Orientalist images of the Middle East, which associated the Arab and Islamic worlds with decadence, as well as on the diverse range of same-gender erotic practices linked to Arab and Islamic cultures (although not named as homosexual, gay, lesbian, bisexual, or queer).[94] The latter tends to associate Arabs and Muslims per se with decadence and queerness, again denying the diversity of gender and erotic practices among these peoples.

The abuse and violence directed against fags and especially queers of colour

> not only suggests that if you're not for the war, you're a fag, it also incites violence against queers and specifically queers of colour. And indeed, there have been reports from community-based organizations throughout New York City that violent incidents against queers have increased. So on the one hand, the United States is being depicted as feminist and gay safe by this comparison with Afghanistan, and on the other had, the US state, having experienced a castration and penetration of its capitalist masculinity offers up narratives of emasculation as appropriate punishment for bin Laden, brown-skinned folks, and men in turbans.[95]

In 2001, when someone scrawled "Hijack This Fags" on a US Navy bomb aboard the USS *Enterprise,* mainstream lesbian and gay rights groups complained about the anti-gay character of this nationalist rhetoric; however, they did not challenge the broader racist war campaign that is producing this violent heterosexual masculinity.[96] Some queers are seen as patriotic "gay heroes" and are incorporated into the narrative of the heterosexual-dominated war on terror, as are those who participated in saving people after the collapse of the Twin Towers.[97] The gay right in the United States came out in favour of bombing Afghanistan, with Andrew Sullivan promoting a "gender patriotism" involving "butching up and femme-ing down to preserve the virility of the nation."[98] Yet other queers are associated with terrorism, an association that is often colour-coded. In the United States, all this has been carried out under a regime that was overtly hostile to gay and lesbian rights and a military from which visible queers are still officially excluded.

Islamic fundamentalism comes in a number of different forms, as does Christian fundamentalism, but most are hostile to women's rights and feminism and also to homosexuality, which is often depicted as an effect of Western culture, despite the indigenous same-gender erotic practices in these societies. Fundamentalist Islam constructs these practices as being outside Islam, even though there are many Muslims who engage in same-gender eroticism. On the other side, ruling forces in the West also construct Islamic and Arab cultures as monolithically heterosexual in character (now often seen as a sign of their backwardness) and codes gays and lesbians with whiteness, allowing no place for queer Muslims and Arabs. It is ironic that Western conservatives and right-ists of various shades, who have been hostile to queers for decades, are now championing sexual freedom – but apparently only in the Arab and Islamic worlds. In this discourse, Islam is portrayed as much more hostile to queers than are Christianity and Judaism, despite the intense opposition of fundamentalist Christians and Jews to queers.[99]

There is considerable evidence that situations for women and for those who engage in same-gender desires in Iraq has worsened considerably since the invasion and occupation, with the rise of Islamic fundamentalist currents both within the insurgency and among those who support the US occupation. This is especially the case with the Grand Ayatollah Ali al-Sistani, the chief spiritual leader of Iraqi Shia Muslims, who, in 2005, issued a fatwa (a decision or judgment) urging death for homosexuals, which has led to the assassination of people identified as gay. When gays went to US occupying authorities in Baghdad's Green Zone requesting protection, they were treated with contempt and derision.[100]

The situation is even more complicated in Palestine under Israeli occupation. Some Western gays have misguidedly looked to Israel as a "Western haven" for gay men and lesbians in the Middle East, especially in the context of recent efforts by the Israeli state to rebrand itself as "gay-friendly" and the campaigns against queer solidarity with Palestinians.[101]

What this overlooks is the Israeli history of opposition to same-gender desire, especially from right-wing Jewish fundamentalists, which, at times, has broken out in anti-queer violence. It also overlooks the fact that the freedoms of Jewish citizens of Israel are built on the expulsion and occupation of the Palestinians.[102]

From the Canadian War on Queers to the War on Terror

In Palestine, the situation for those engaged in same-gender eroticism can be difficult, even though there are also many Palestinian activists who are involved in promoting gender and sexual diversity. The occupation and the eclipsing of the more left resistance movements, such as the Popular Front for the Liberation of Palestine, have led to the rise of Islamic-identified movements such as Hamas, which Israeli authorities initially allowed to flourish since it was seen as a counterweight to the more democratic left groups in the resistance. Islamic-identified movements generally position themselves against homosexuality, arguing that it is "un-Islamic" or a "Western import," thus denying the experiences and even the existence of queer Muslims. This can create a difficult situation for Palestinians who engage in same-gender eroticism. As Blair Kuntz points out,

> What is less documented is Israel's own role in creating homophobia in Palestinian society through the blackmailing of gay Palestinians. As with Palestinian children, recruiting Palestinian gays as collaborators is part and parcel of Israel's policy to maintain control over Palestinian territory. The Israeli secret police often exploit gay Palestinians by coercing them into working undercover to gather information about other Palestinians. Those accused of being collaborators are at risk of stigmatization, exclusion, and occasionally retaliation. Gays identified as collaborators stigmatize gay men in general, and collaborators of all stripes are shown little mercy, especially when they are connected to serious incidents leading to the death of other Palestinians. Thus, if gays meet a violent end it is not clear whether they are killed because they are gay or because they are seen as informers.[103]

The practice of blackmailing queers is familiar, given what we know about the Canadian campaigns against queers. The war on terror and the wars and occupations in Afghanistan and Iraq are not leading to an increase in acceptance and space for those engaging in same-gender desire or for lesbian and gay rights. If anything, they are making the situations worse by fanning the flames of Islamic fundamentalism and strengthening those forces, both in the Middle East and in the West, that define same-gender eroticism as un-Islamic.

As has been mentioned, the war on terror is generating a racialized heterosexual masculinist patriotism in the global North that, among others, is directed against queers, especially against queers of colour. Efforts of some mostly white middle-class queers to identify with this heterosexual patriotism are not creating more space for queer people; rather, they are narrowing the space that is available for other queers while giving more power to the campaigns against people of colour. There are even some currents within Western gay organizing that argue that, on a global scale, the main danger facing queers today is Islamic fundamentalism.[104] As Puar and Rai write, the attempt on the part of some white middle-class queers to integrate themselves into Canadian/American patriotism and national security policies operates to

> delimit and contain the kinds of responses that LGBTQ (lesbian, gay, bisexual, transgender, queer) communities can articulate in response to September 11. If we are to resist practically the "war effort" and the US/Them and "you're either with us or against us" rhetoric, we must disarticulate the ties between patriotism and cultural and sexual identity. We must pose questions which allow us to construct practical solidarities with domestic and international communities and movements. If [some strands of liberal] Western feminism have been complicit with certain forms of imperial and nationalist domination, how can feminists of color in the United States [and Canada] as well as "Third World" feminists (such as RAWA) undermine and displace these dominant agendas? If certain forms of queer and progressive organizing remain tied to forms of nationalist and imperial domination, how can queers of color both here and across the globe disrupt the neat folding in of queerness into narratives of modernity, patriotism and nationalism?[105]

There are no easy answers. Another path needs to be developed – one that resists both heterosexual masculinist patriotism and the fundamentalisms that drive both capitalist globalization and Islamic fundamentalism. In doing this, we need to reject the coding of gay and queer as white, the West as queer-friendly, and all Muslims as heterosexual. We need to learn from, rather than deny the agency of, queer Muslims and other queers of colour.[106]

BEYOND NATIONAL SECURITY AND FUNDAMENTALISM: FOR A DIFFERENT WORLD

This brings us back to George Bush's, "Either you are with us, or you are with the terrorists." We reject this binary and point instead to various social movements that are against all forms of fundamentalism, war, and occupation, and that support democracy and the liberation of women and queer people.[107] In rejecting the terror of both "Global Capital" and "Fundamentalist Terrorism," these approaches push beyond this binary to develop a global alternative

From the Canadian War on Queers to the War on Terror

rooted in universal justice, anti-war, and anti-occupation movements as well as in those towards democracy, feminism, anti-racism, and queer liberation.[108] When more than 10 million people mobilized against the impending invasion and occupation of Iraq on Febraury 15, 2003, this provided a powerful sense of the real basis for this alternative striving for a world with a peace based on social justice.[109] We also get a sense of this other possible world in the revolt of the Zapatistas and in the global justice protests in Seattle, Quebec City, Genoa, Cancun, and, most recently, against the G-8 in Germany and the World Bank/IMF in London.[110] Rather than choosing power over other people, which dominates in state and capitalist organizing, we can build on our power to do, which provides a creative basis to remake the world.[111]

Central to this is a rejection of the ideology and practice of national security. Rather than allying with the national security of national capitalist and state agencies and their projects for strengthening global capital (and the fundamentalist responses this has generated in parts of the world), we need to develop solidarity with the millions of people who are fighting for social justice, the elimination of racism, poverty, exploitation, and militarism in all its forms, and the liberation of women and queers. This solidarity needs to be based on rejecting the Orientalist and otherizing practices that are at the heart of the war on terror and, more broadly, of national security itself. Breaking down these boundaries and barriers necessitates learning from the "other." As Edward Said suggested, one way to end the Israeli occupation of Palestine and to find a just solution for the Palestinian people is for Israelis to become the other.[112] In this process of learning from and taking up the position of the other, we are transformed, and we move far beyond the boundaries of all nation-states and fundamentalisms (which are based on exclusion).

In relation to Afghanistan and Iraq, this means ending the occupations and providing help for those, like RAWA, who support democracy and an end to oppression and exploitation. Western proponents of queer liberation need to provide support for those defending and building on indigenous practices of same-gender eroticism (and, in societies with more than two genders, it is even more complex than this) and critical sexual politics within countries in the global South. There is no static "true" culture, religion, or sexuality. We are part of history and we are all being constantly transformed by what we learn from the people with whom we interact and from those we love, need, and desire. In this sense, social difference is not something to spark fear and otherization but, rather, something to be celebrated and embraced.[113] Given the transformations that have been brought about through capitalist globalization, there is no possible return to the mythologized security offered by the nation-state. Instead, we need a global approach, a new internationalism, that is not based on exploitation and oppression.

Agency and Resistance

The queer resistance to the Canadian war on queers documented in this book makes us optimistic that a better world is possible. In the 1960s, restrained by national security, social surveillance, stigmatization, and heterosexism, queer people were still able to talk back to and even make fun of the security police. In the late twentieth century, the public and visible actions of our movements and communities undermined the basis of the national security campaigns. By the late 1990s, we had put an end to the main aspects of these campaigns against us, even though national security remains a major problem for many queers.

In the current context of the national security wars against political dissent, we also see how people's actions can make a difference. The large anti-war mobilizations against the Iraq war, especially in Quebec, played an important part in keeping Canadian troops out of that war, even though Canadian corporate and state support for it was significant.[114] More recently, people organizing to challenge the legitimacy of the national security certificates and wide-ranging anti-terrorist legislation created the basis for important legal and political challenges, forcing the government to respond.

We are never simply victims or people without agency. We have the power to act, to do, and to create. We can subvert and undo national security and move towards a world in which there are no "others" and in which we can appreciate and celebrate the differences between people. This is the world we need and desire.

Appendix
Index of Interviews

This is an index of the interviews that we conducted and used for this book. It does not include interviews conducted by other people that are referenced in the notes.

Albert was purged from the civil service in the late 1960s, when his homosexuality was discovered due to his involvement in a court case. (October 19, 1993)

Alice left her job in the public service because of the potential consequences of a security investigation for her and her partner, who was not out to her family at the time. (March 1994)

Andrew worked as a civilian employee for the Department of Defence in the 1980s. (December 19, 1994)

Barbara lived in Ottawa in the 1970s and 1980s. She was a public servant who was involved in the Trent Homophile Association in the mid-1970s. (July 14, 1997)

Barry Deeprose, a public servant, was involved with Gays of Ottawa and then with Pink Triangle Services in Ottawa. (February 21, 1995)

Bernie was purged from the navy in the early 1980s. He had been in the militia and army before he was in the navy. (June 27, 2001)

Blair Johnston was involved with Gays of Ottawa in the 1980s. He previously served in the military, although he was not out at that time, and then worked in External Affairs. (February 1, 2001)

Bob was interrogated by the RCMP in the late 1950s, when he lived in Ottawa. (October 14, 1994)

Brenda Barnes was a member of the military reserves in the 1980s. She left the military in 1989 to work in community radio and in lesbian/gay activism. (May 15, 2005)

Brian Drader wrote *The Fruit Machine,* a dramatization of the special project research and the anti-queer security campaigns. (January 16, 1998)

Brian Waite was an organizer for Toronto Gay Action and a member of the League for Socialist Action in the early 1970s. (July 27, 2000)

Bruce Somers was involved in the gay scene in Victoria in the late 1950s; he was the first president of the Association for Social Knowledge in Vancouver, Canada's first gay rights group; and in Ottawa in the mid-1960s he was involved with the Canadian Council on Religion and the Homosexual. (June 10, 1994)

Charles Hill was a gay activist who moved to Ottawa in the early 1970s. He played an active role in Gays of Ottawa. (February 20, 1995)

David, who was not a civil servant, was involved in gay networks in Ottawa in the 1960s. He was caught up in the security campaigns when a friend gave his name to the RCMP during a park sweep. (May 12, 1994)

The Honourable David Fulton served as federal justice minister and attorney general of Canada from 1957 to 1962. (May 17, 1996)

David Garmaise was a member of Gays of Ottawa and the main spokesperson for the National Gay Rights Coalition in Ottawa in the 1970s. (May 13, 2000)

Dorothy Kidd was involved in the New Tendency, the Toronto Wages for Housework Committee, and Wages Due Lesbians in the 1970s. (July 5, 2008)

Doug Sanders was centrally involved with the Association for Social Knowledge in Vancouver in the 1960s. (June 10, 1994)

Ellen Skinner is the sister of John Robert MacPherson, who killed himself after being forced out of the closet when the military purged him in 1973. (June 16, 1999)

Frank Letourneau was purged from the navy in Halifax in 1970. (December 7, 2008)

Fred, an ex-RCMP officer, worked in the character weaknesses subdivision of the Directorate of Security and Intelligence of the RCMP in Ottawa from 1967 to 1969. (October 21, 1994)

George Hislop was involved with the Community Homophile Association of Toronto in the 1970s. He died in October 2005. (August 1996)

Hank became a public servant in the late 1960s. He was put under surveillance by an RCMP officer who had been discovered to be homosexual and who was then forced to investigate Hank in order to secure a workable service record. (February 20, 1995)

Harold was purged from the navy in the late 1950s. He had been stationed on the west coast but was purged when stationed in Ottawa. (February 21, 1994)

Hector Mackenzie is a historian whose work focuses on the Department of External Affairs. (September 26, 1999)

Herbert Sutcliffe was about to be appointed as a Canadian officer working at the Pentagon in 1962 when he was identified as a homosexual and purged from his position. He died in 2003. (March 1, 1996)

Jake was a graduate student in the 1960s. He later became an employee of the National Film Board. (May 21, 1995)

Jim Egan was Canada's first gay activist. He died in 2000. (January 5, 1998)

Joan lived with Sue in Halifax in the period 1969-70, when many lesbians were purged from the navy. She eventually found employment in the public service. (February 23, 1996)

John Grube fled Victoria following the security investigations after the murder of Aaron Jenkins and later conducted his own historical research on the emergence and development of the Toronto gay men's community. He died in April 2008. (March 1, 1996)

John Sawatsky, a journalist, provided the first public account of the RCMP security campaigns against gays and the fruit machine, in *Men in the Shadows*. (January 4, 1996)

John Wilson was an early gay activist involved in Toronto Gay Action and then the Gay Alliance towards Equality. He was a member of the League for Socialist Action in the early 1970s. (May 25, 2000)

Josh was a member of the Revolutionary Marxist Group. He was a non-citizen who was involved in gay activism. (December 12, 2000)

Lois came under RCMP surveillance in the 1950s because of her relationship with a US left-wing woman. As a result of this investigation, her husband was forced to resign from the Department of National Defence. (February 22, 1995)

Marie Robertson was involved in Gays of Ottawa and was one of the founders of the Lesbian Organization of Ottawa Now. (July 15, 1999)

Marielle joined the army in 1976. She was promoted to corporal and was stationed on the west coast, where in 1981 she was discovered to be a lesbian, investigated, and dismissed. (March 11, 1998)

Marty lived in Victoria in the late 1950s. He worked as staff at the naval base and, later, in a military psychiatric ward in Halifax. (May 19, 1996)

Marvin was implicated in the RCMP's national security campaigns in the late 1950s/early 1960s. After RCMP interrogations and threats, he left Ottawa. (May 1998)

Merv worked in the navy during the 1950s. He worked with Aaron Jenkins as a pay writer and was a friend of both Jenkins and Leo Mantha. (January 12, 1998)

Michael had been a civilian military employee. He then left the civil service and was interrogated by the RCMP in the 1960s. (July 15, 1994)

Morgan was a seaman at the time of Aaron Jenkins' murder. He was one of the first men on the scene after being awakened by Aaron's screams. He lived in Toronto during the 1960s. (October 22, 1994)

Nathan was a high-ranking RCMP officer in the 1950s and 1960s. (July 22, 1999)

Patrick is a gay man who lived in Ottawa in the 1950s. (July 1994)

Paul-François Sylvestre worked for the secretary of state in the 1970s. He got caught up in the Ottawa "vice" investigation in the mid-1970s. He is the author of *Propos pour une libération (homo) sexuelle* and other books. (January 2, 1996)

Peaches Latour, a French Canadian drag performer and hair stylist, was questioned by the RCMP in the 1960s. He was involved in the Ottawa/Hull gay scene in the 1950s and 1960s. (August 31, 1994)

Peter was a gay security officer who, in the 1960s, worked for a firm in Montreal that was involved in military production for NATO. (July 20, 1995)

Pierre was a public servant involved in gay organizations in Ottawa in the early 1980s. He was declared redundant when his department was reorganized. (May 31, 1998)

Robert worked in the Department of External Affairs in the late 1960s and early 1970s. He also served with the Canadian delegation at the United Nations in New York. (October 10, 1996)

Robin Metcalfe was an activist with Gay Alliance for Equality in Halifax in the 1970s and 1980s. (August 10, 2006)

Sam worked for the Department of External Affairs in the 1950s. He left his DEA position in 1958 because he feared being identified as a threat to national security. (October 9, 1998)

Shawn, who was not a civil servant, was posted overseas in Rangoon, Burma, with a development agency. His contract was terminated in the 1960s after he was exposed as a homosexual. (July 20, 1995)

Simon lived in Victoria and participated in the underground gay scene that existed there during the 1950s. (May 16, 1996)

Steve worked in the Department of External Affairs as a class 1 foreign service officer. He was purged in 1969. (June 27, 1998)

Sue was in the militia in Halifax. She was purged in the 1960s for being a lesbian. (February 23, 1996)

New Democratic Party Member of Parliament Svend Robinson was the first openly gay member of Parliament. He played an instrumental role in the struggle against national security policies and for changes to military policies that barred gay men and lesbians from the armed forces. (July 30, 2002)

Tom Warner is a long-time gay activist. In the 1970s, he was involved in the Gay Alliance towards Equality in Toronto and the Coalition for Gay Rights in Ontario. He is the author of *Never Going Back: A History of Queer Activism in Canada*. (July 15, 1999)

Notes

PREFACE: NATIONAL SECURITY WARS - THEN AND NOW

1   Among others, see Gloria Galloway, "Ottawa Settles with Arar," *Globe and Mail*, January 26, 2007, A1, A6; see also the editorial "The Compensation Canada Owes Arar," *Globe and Mail*, January 26, 2007, A16. See also Maher Arar, "A Personal Account," *Z Net*, October 31, 2006, http://www.zmag.org/znet/viewArticle/2855; Webb, *Illusions of Security*, 9-24; and Thobani, *Exalted Subjects*, 244-46.
2   See People's Commission on Immigration "Security" Measures, "Final Report"; Razack, *Casting Out*.
3   For example, a Crown attorney labelled John Clarke, an organizer with the Ontario Coalition against Poverty, as a "terrorist" in 2001. See Jane Gadd, "Activist Called Terrorist," *Globe and Mail*, June 30, 2001, A17. On the global justice movement as a threat to national security, see CSIS, "Report No. 2000/08" and "2000 Public Report." Thanks to A.K. Thompson for drawing these texts to our attention. On the scream of refusal that is at the basis of global justice activism, see Holloway, *How to Change the World without Taking Power*, 1: "When we write and when we read it is easy to forget that the beginning is not the word, but the scream. Faced with the mutilation of human lives by capitalism, a scream of sadness, a scream of horror, a scream of anger, a scream of refusal: NO."
4   Kinsman and Gentile, with the assistance of Heidi McDonell and Mary Mahood-Greer, *"In the Interests of the State."*
5   On the use of the term "fag," see George Smith, "The Ideology of 'Fag.'"
6   On cutting out operations, see D. Smith, *Texts, Facts, and Femininity*, 30-43. See also George Smith, "The Ideology of 'Fag.'"
7   In the United States, leftist and ex–Communist Party members were centrally involved in the formation of the Mattachine Society in the early 1950s, which was the first attempt at bringing together a homophile organization. At the height of the Cold War frenzy against communists and ex-communists, more conservative group members later turfed out these leaders. See D'Emilio, *Sexual Politics, Sexual Communities*, 57-91. Left-wing activists were also centrally involved in the formation of gay liberation fronts after the Stonewall riots in New York City in 1969 and in the formation of the Gay Liberation Front in London, England. For some of the connections between the left and gay activism in Toronto in the 1970s, see Deborah Brock, "Workers of the World Caress: An Interview with Gary Kinsman on Gay and Lesbian Organizing in the 1970s Toronto Left," *Left History*, http://www.yorku.ca/lefthist/online/brock_kinsman.html.
8   On this use of the concept "historical present," see Weeks, *Sexuality and Its Discontents*, 5-10. Our use of this concept differs from Weeks' in that we are not looking at a history of relatively ungrounded discourses of sexuality but, rather, at a history of official discourses that operated as actively organizing practices and relations and that, to some extent, continue to participate in the organizing of the present. We attempt to use historical data in a non-ideological fashion, always making certain that they are socially grounded.
9   See Kinsman's *The Regulation of Desire*; "Gays and Lesbians"; "Challenging Canadian and Queer Nationalisms"; and "The Canadian Cold War on Queers."
10 For a critical analysis, see Kinsman, "Challenging Canadian and Queer Nationalisms."

11   Brenda Crossman, "Harm Is the New Indecency Test, Supreme Court Okays Sex Clubs, Orgies," *Xtra!* (Toronto), January 5, 2006, 9.

12   On anti-queer violence, see Janoff, *Pink Blood*.

13   See Laroque, *Gay Marriage*.

14   On the same-gender marriage struggle, see Laroque, *Gay Marriage;* Lahey and Alderson, *Same-Sex Marriage;* and Young and Boyd, "Losing the Feminist Voice?"

15   For more critical approaches, see Young and Boyd, "Losing the Feminist Voice?"; Sears, "Is There Sex after Marriage?" 38-39, and "Can Marriage Be Queer?"; Barnholden, "Does the 'Straight' Jacket of the Family Fit You?"; M. Warner, "Beyond Gay Marriage," 81-147; Lehr, *Queer Family Values;* Kinsman, "Don't Get Me to the Church on Time"; Kinsman, *The Regulation of Desire,* especially 228-34, 308-17, 398-402; Kinsman, "Responsibility as a Strategy of Governance"; and Warner, "Fighting the Anti-Queer Right-Wing." See also Chauncey, *Why Marriage?* for a useful historical analysis of the same-sex marriage debates in the United States. This book exaggerates the egalitarian changes that have taken place in marriage law and relations and is weak on the radical queer critique of the "normalization" of marriage.

16   See Kinsman, "Responsibility as a Strategy of Governance."

17   See Alan Sears, "The Opening and Commodification of Gay Space: Queer in a Lean World." *Against the Current* 89 (November-December 2000), http://www.solidarity-us.org/node/965, and "Queer Times?"; Kinsman, "Responsibility as a Strategy of Governance" and "Gays and Lesbians." See also Hennessy, *Profit and Pleasure.*

18   See Sears, "Is There Sex after Marriage?"

19   On state formation, see Corrigan and Sayer, *The Great Arch.* See also Kinsman, "Challenging Canadian and Queer Nationalisms."

CHAPTER 1: QUEERING NATIONAL SECURITY, THE COLD WAR, AND CANADIAN HISTORY

1   "David" is a pseudonym, as are most of the names of the people we interviewed. A fictionalized and dramatized version of David's account is included in Nancy Nicol's *Stand Together,* a film about the history of lesbian and gay organizing in Ontario. Parentheses at the end of interview extracts indicate the date the interviews took place. Participants identified by first name only indicates a pseudonym used to protect her or his confidentiality. In some cases, we have obscured specific dates and locations that could lead to identification. A few individuals have given us permission to use their first names. Full names are actual names that we have received permission to use. All interviews were conducted by Gary Kinsman, by Gary Kinsman and Patrizia Gentile, or by Patrizia Gentile, unless otherwise referenced. See the Appendix for a list of people interviewed for this research. For the 1950s and 1960s, we interviewed thirty-six gay or bisexual men and ten lesbians who were either directly affected by the security campaigns or who had direct knowledge of them.

      As general references for this book, see Kinsman, "'Character Weaknesses' and 'Fruit Machines'"; *The Regulation of Desire;* "'Inverts,' 'Psychopaths' and 'Normal' Men"; "The Textual Practices of Sexual Rule"; "Challenging Canadian and Queer Nationalisms"; "Constructing Gay Men and Lesbians as National Security Risks, 1950-70"; "National Security as Moral Regulation"; and "The Canadian Cold War on Queers." See Gentile, "Searching for 'Miss Civil Service' and 'Mr. Civil Service'" and "'Government Girls' and 'Ottawa Men.'" And see Kinsman and Gentile, with the assistance of Heidi McDonell and Mary Mahood-Greer, *In the Interests of the State.*

2   In Canada, all same-gender sexual acts between men were criminalized until 1969.

3   Canadian Security Intelligence Service (CSIS), Access to Information Request (AIR) 91-088, Directorate of Security and Intelligence (DSI) (RCMP) annual reports from 1960 to 1967-68. For 1967-68, see p. 33. Wherever possible, we mention the specific archives or department in which we found

documents. In the event that archival information, reference numbers, or access request numbers are not available, we indicate that the document is in the possession of the authors.

4　CSIS, AIR 91-088, DSI Annual Report, 1967-68. In the 1960s, the RCMP used these three categories to organize and document the results of their investigations and surveillance strategies. The goal was to move people from the "suspected" and "alleged" columns into the "confirmed." See Chapter 4.

5　Dean Beeby reports that almost two-thirds of all individuals in the RCMP lists were not employed by the federal government. See Dean Beeby, "Mounties Staged Massive Hunt for Gay Men in the Civil Service," *Globe and Mail*, April 24, 1992; "RCMP Hoped 'Fruit Machine' Would Identify Homosexuals," *Globe and Mail*, April 24, 1992; and "RCMP Was Ordered to Identify Gays: Only Carrying Out Cabinet Policy," *Globe and Mail*, April 25, 1992. Beeby based this estimate on the RCMP DSI report for 1961-62, which states that the index of the character weaknesses section contains the names of 850 federal government employees and "over 2,000 known or suspected homosexuals who are not known to be employed by the government." Beeby reduced this proportion of government to non-government names to a third. Personal communication from Dean Beeby.

6　For an initial critical analysis of these texts, see Kinsman, "'Character Weaknesses' and 'Fruit Machines.'" See also Robinson and Kimmel, "The Queer Career of Homosexual Security Vetting in Cold War Canada," which proposes a less critical investigation of the security purges.

7　CSIS, AIR 92-008, Appendix A, "Homosexuality within the Federal Government Service – Statistics." J.M. Bella, Director of Security and Intelligence, to the RCMP Commissioner, "Homosexuality within the Federal Government Service," April 29, 1960.

8　Ibid., 2, 4.

9　CSIS, AIR 91-088, R.B. Bryce, memorandum for the Prime Minister and the Minister of Justice, "Security Cases Involving Homosexuality," January 26, 1961, 2.

10　CSIS, AIR 91-088, DSI Annual Report, 1961-62, 22.

11　On the importance of an active sense of agency in developing liberationist social theory, see the work of Bannerji, especially "But Who Speaks for Us?"

12　As Bologh suggests, "ideology refers to all forms of knowledge that are divorced from their conditions of production (their grounds)." Bologh, *Dialectical Phenomenology*, 19. On ideology, see also the work of D. Smith, including, *The Everyday World as Problematic; The Conceptual Practices of Power; Texts, Facts, and Femininity; Writing the Social;* and *Institutional Ethnography*. See also Bannerji, including *Thinking Through* and her articles on the ideological construction of India, especially "Beyond the Ruling Category to What Actually Happens" and "Writing 'India,' Doing Ideology."

13　On heterosexual hegemony, see Kinsman, *The Regulation of Desire*, especially 6-7 and 37-40. The notion of hegemony we are using, expanding, and transforming comes from the work of Antonio Gramsci. See Gramsci, *Selections from the Prison Notebooks*. At the same time, there are limitations to the notions of hegemony and counter-hegemony as they are still too state-centred and, in relation to social power and social transformation, can carry with them statist political projects. See Day, *Gramsci Is Dead*.

14　Thanks to Dan O'Meara, who, at a conference on security questions at Laurentian University, March 6, 2008, raised concerns over our use of the term "war." We also employ this term as the Zapatistas do when they speak of the neoliberal "Fourth World War" against poor, indigenous, and working-class people around the world. See Subcommandante Marcos of the Zapatistas, "The Fourth World War," *In Motion Magazine*, http://www.inmotionmagazine.com/auto/fourth.html; "Between the Satellite and the Microscope"; and "The Machinery of Ethnocide." See also *The Fourth World War* (film); and El Kilombo Intergalactico, *Beyond Resistance: Everything*.

15　See Kinsman, "Challenging Canadian and Queer Nationalisms."

16　On transgender and transsexual struggles and experiences, see V. Namaste, *Invisible Lives;* Irving, "Contested Terrain of a Barely Scratched Surface"; "Trans Politics and Anti-Capitalism"; and "Normalized Transgressions." See also Fausto-Sterling, *Sexing the Body*.

17 On doing gender, see Kessler and McKenna, *Gender*.

18 Jagose, *Queer Theory*, 72-126.

19 See Kinsman, "Queerness Is Not in Our Genes"; Brookley, *The Rhetoric and Power of the Gay Gene*; and Fausto-Sterling, *Sexing the Body*.

20 See Kinsman, "The National Security Campaign against Gay Men and Lesbians"; and Kinsman and Gentile, *"In the Interests of the State."*

21 See Foucault's *Discipline and Punish* and *The History of Sexuality*; and D. Smith, *Writing the Social*.

22 CSIS, AIR 91-088, D.F. Wall, memorandum to the Security Panel, "Security Cases Involving Character Weaknesses, with Special Reference to the Problem of Homosexuality," May 12, 1959, 12-13. This document was one of the first declassified in 1992. Journalist Dean Beeby of Canadian Press obtained a series of Security Panel and RCMP documents relating to the anti-homosexual security campaigns of the late 1950s and 1960s through the Access to Information Act. See note 5 for the previously mentioned Canadian Press stories by Dean Beeby.

23 See Kinsman, *The Regulation of Desire*, especially 148-54, 183-92; and "Official Discourse as Sexual Regulation."

24 CSIS, AIR 91-088, Don Wall, "Security Cases Involving Character Weaknesses, with Special Reference to the Problem of Homosexuality," May 12, 1959; Hillenkoetter is quoted in this memo, pp. 7-9. Hillenkoetter is also quoted in Robinson and Kimmel, "The Queer Career of Homosexual Security Vetting," 331-32. For more information on the anti-homosexual campaign in the US State Department, see Johnson, "Homosexual Citizens" and *The Lavender Scare*.

25 Hewitt, *Spying 101*, 53-54.

26 R.G. Waldeck, "Homosexual International," *Human Events*, 29 September 1960, 453-56.

27 "Dialogism" and its variants (such as "dialogical") were central terms used by Russian literary theorist M.M. Bakhtin to illustrate how "everything means, is understood, as part of a greater whole – there is constant interaction between meanings, all of which have the potential of conditioning others." See Holquist, ed., *The Dialogic Imagination*, 426-27. In analyzing Bakhtin, David McNally sees dialogism as the idea that individuals come into being in and through their embodied communicative interaction with others. He stresses the social and historical character of the body in Bakhtin's work, often obscured in poststructuralist and postmodern readings of this thinker. See McNally, *Bodies of Meaning*, 124-29.

28 See Kealey, "Spymasters, Spies, and Their Subjects"; Scher, *The UnCanadians*; Whitaker and Marcuse, *Cold War Canada*; and Iacovetta, *Gatekeepers*.

29 For a broader analysis, however, see Kinsman, Buse, and Steedman, *Whose National Security?*

30 An excerpt from an article originally published in *US News and World Report*, a magazine read by US federal civil servants. See *Civil Service News*, "How Canada Fights Spies: Security of State Is Put before That of Individual," April 1956, 5.

31 Canada, *House of Commons Debates* (October 25, 1963), 4049. The Bill of Rights, Canada's first piece of legislation formally protecting Canadians' rights, was established under the Diefenbaker government in 1960.

32 On John Sawatsky, see his *Men in the Shadows*, 124-37. On Dean Beeby, see his "Mounties Staged Massive Hunt" and "RCMP Hoped 'Fruit Machine' Would Identify Homosexuals."

33 On textual mediation, see D. Smith's work, including *Texts, Facts, and Femininity*; *The Everyday World as Problematic*; and *The Conceptual Practices of Power*. See also her *Institutional Ethnography*.

34 On Jim Egan, see his *Challenging the Conspiracy of Silence* and *Jim Egan: Canada's Pioneer Gay Activist*; and Kinsman, *The Regulation of Desire*, 167-69, 190-92. See also *Jim Loves Jack* (film). And see Jim Egan, "Most Fantastic Witch-Hunt since Inquisition Was Followed by Dismissal of Homosexuals by the Hundreds from US Government Offices," *Justice Weekly*, March 13, 1954, 13; and his "Persecution of Homosexuals Gets Blamed for Their Increased Activity in Public," *Justice Weekly*, April 3, 1954, 13.

35 On aspects of this approach, see Campbell and Manicom, eds., "Introduction," in *Knowledge, Experience, and Ruling Relations*, 7-9; see also D. Smith, *Institutional Ethnography*.

36 On this rupture between ruling discourse and lived experience, see D. Smith, *The Everyday World as Problematic*, 49-60.

37 On the methodological and theoretical use of "experience" in this book, see Campbell and Manicom, eds., *Knowledge, Experience, and Ruling Relations*, 7-10; and D. Smith, *Institutional Ethnography*. See also Hennessy, *Profit and Pleasure*, 17-22; and Wood, *Democracy against Capitalism*, 96-97. Reification is the social process through which social relations between people become relations between things. On reification, see Lukacs, *History and Class Consciousness*. On the related notion of fetishism, see Holloway, *How to Change the World without Taking Power*.

38 See D. Smith, *Texts, Facts, and Femininity*, 86-119.

39 See D. Smith, *The Everyday World as Problematic*, 78-88.

40 An effort has been made to preserve the indexical (context-dependent) and reflexive (mutually determined) character of these oral historical accounts.

41 On some of the dilemmas of conducting oral historical work, including the ethical decision-making process, see Fernie, "Talking Forbidden Love," 67-68.

42 On the monologic voice, see Holquist, *The Dialogic Imagination*, 426-27; and McNally, *Bodies of Meaning*, 124-29.

43 D. Smith, *Texts, Facts, and Femininity*, especially 120-58.

44 See Bérubé and D'Emilio, "The Military and Lesbians during the McCarthy Years"; Meyer, *Creating GI Jane*; and Kinsman, *The Regulation of Desire*, especially 181-83, 359-60. Also on women and the military, see Enloe, *Does Khaki Become You?* and "Heterosexist Masculinity in the Military"; and Pierson, *"They're Still Women After All."*

45 This account comes from the preliminary research interviews conducted for the wonderful film *Forbidden Love*. We thank Lynne Fernie and Aerlyn Weissman for their permission to use it in our research.

46 Harold, "A Case History, with Observations," 1960-61. In the possession of the authors.

47 See Kinsman's *The Regulation of Desire*, especially 148-54, 181-83, 359-60, and his "Official Discourse as Sexual Regulation," 56-102.

48 Ashante Infantry, "Herbert Sutcliffe, 86: Faced Up to Anti-Gay Bias, Dismissed from Armed Forces for Being Homosexual," *Toronto Star*, September 3, 2003. See also the video, directed by Jose Torrealba, based on Paul Jackson's research, *Open Secrets*, in which Sutcliffe and his partner are interviewed.

49 The term "outing" is a contemporary expression for describing what the security regime was doing. On outing, see Gross, *Contested Closets*; and Kinsman, "Outing and the Dismantling of 'the Closet.'"

50 We spoke to Fred (a former RCMP officer in the Character Weaknesses Section of the DSI) about his work activities, to the Honourable Davie Fulton, who was minister of justice from 1957 to 1962, to a deputy minister of justice, and to three other people involved in the administration and governance of either the DEA or the RCMP. We conducted fifty-three research interviews for the 1950s and 1960s with people who were directly affected, had direct knowledge of the campaigns based on their participation in them, or had previously conducted research on the security regime. We also touch on the intersection of historical sociological work on the national security campaigns with the emergence of lesbian/gay networks in Ottawa and elsewhere. Our research overlaps with Ottawa social history, union and working-class history (including the emergence of associations and the formation of unions), and broader questions of Canadian state formation. We also engage with questions of historical and social memory and past and present forms of queer politics and organizing. On state formation, see Corrigan and Sayer, *The Great Arch*.

51 McNally, *Bodies of Meaning*, 191 (emphasis in original).

52 On memory and the social organization of forgetting, see Corrigan and Sayer, *The Great Arch*, 195; Dunbar-Ortiz, "The Opposite of Truth Is Forgetting"; K. Ross, *May '68 and Its Afterlives*; Radstone and Hodgkin, *Regimes of Memory* and its companion volume *Contested Pasts*. See also Gentile, "Capital Queer: Social Memory and Queer Place(s) in Cold War Ottawa," in *Remembering Place, Placing Memory*, edited by James Opp and John Walsh (UBC Press, forthcoming).

53 See Corrigan, *Social Forms/Human Capacities*, for a fuller development of this notion of human capacities and their social and historical character. We also draw on unorthodox readings of Marxism that do not produce workers as passive victims of capital but, rather, emphasize the active agency of workers in resisting and transforming capital and oppression. See H. Cleaver, *Reading Capital Politically*; Dyer-Witheford, *Cyber-Marx*, 62-90; and Kinsman, "The Politics of Revolution."

54 As quoted in McNally, *Bodies of Meaning*, 195. On how reification takes place in the writing of sociology and within sociological theory, see D. Smith, *Writing the Social*, 45-69.

55 This is the underlying assumption in Whitaker and Marcuse, *Cold War Canada*. This assumption is also present in Whitaker and Hewitt, *Canada and the Cold War*.

56 See McNally, *Another World Is Possible*, 204-66.

57 Kinsman, Buse, and Steedman, *Whose National Security?* especially 2-5, 278-85.

58 Many different theories of the social character of social formations such as the USSR have been put forward. The view we find most persuasive is that these societies were bureaucratic class societies of a new type, in which, after the initial revolutionary period, a new bureaucratic ruling class came to rule through the Communist Party and state relations, and mobilized Marxism-Leninism as a dominant ideology to obscure the oppression and the exploitation of workers and peasants. Although they were not capitalist in character, these societies based themselves on the exploitation of the working class and peasantry, and were in no way socialist or communist. On this and other approaches, see Mochover and Fantham, *The Century of the Unexpected;* some of the writings of C.L.R. James, who develops a state capitalist analysis of the Soviet Union, including James, Dunayevskaya, and Lee, *State Capitalism and World Revolution;* and James, Lee, and Chaulieu, *Facing Reality*.

59 See, for instance, Kolko and Kolko, *The Limits of Power*.

60 See Smith and Smith, "Re-organizing the Job-Skills Training Nexus," which captures the shift from Keynesianism to neoliberalism in one area. See also H. Cleaver, *Reading Capital Politically*, especially 27-28, 156-57; and Negri, *Books for Burning*, 1-50.

61 On the social construction of whiteness, see Frankenburg, *White Women, Race Matters;* Roedigger, *The Wages of Whiteness* and *Towards the Abolition of Whiteness*. See also McClintock, *Imperial Leather*. Hennessy, *Profits and Pleasure*, 51-52, points out that McClintock's critical analysis is limited when it comes to lesbian and queer experience.

62 See Anti-Capitalist Convergence of Montreal (CLAC), *An Anarchist Attack on Global Governance;* Kinsman, "Mapping Social Relations of Struggle," especially 144-54; and McNally, *Another World Is Possible*. See also Ali, *Bush in Babylon;* Solomon and Erlich, *Target Iraq;* and Moores, ed., *The New Imperialists*. On the global food crisis, see Caffentzis, "Starvation Politics." On Iran, while we oppose imperialist attacks, we fully support Iranian movements for democracy, workers' rights, women's rights, and rights for sexual and gender minorities.

63 See Bérubé, *Coming Out under Fire*. On the Canadian context, see Kinsman, *The Regulation of Desire*, 148-57; and Jackson, *One of the Boys*. On daycare centres during and after the war years, see Prentice, ed., *Changing Child Care*. On Bérubé, see also Gary Kinsman, "Allan Bérubé: Queer Working-Class Historian, 1946-2007," *Against the Current* 135 (July-August 2008), http://auto_sol.tao.ca/node/3109.

64 M.L. Adams, *The Trouble with Normal*. For the US experience, see Meyerowitz, *Not June Cleaver*. For a different view, see May, *Homeward Bound*. Also see Canaday, *The Straight State*.

65 Weinberg, *Society and the Healthy Homosexual*. On the limitations of conceptualizing homophobia as a psychological problem that obscures the way in which it is shaped through broader social relations, see Kinsman, *The Regulation of Desire*, 33.

66 M.L. Adams, *The Trouble with Normal*. See also Brock, ed., *Making Normal*.

67 Corrigan, "On Moral Regulation." See also Valverde, *The Age of Light, Soap, and Water;* Strange and Loo, *Making Good;* and Brock, *Making Normal*.

68 J. Katz, *The Invention of Heterosexuality;* M.L. Adams, *The Trouble with Normal;* and Kinsman, "National Security as Moral Regulation."

69 Grace and Leys, "The Concept of Subversion and Its Implications," 62-63 (emphasis in original).

70 On collecting categories, see Corrigan, "On Moral Regulation." See also his collection, *Social Forms/ Human Capacities*.
71 On cutting-out operations, see D. Smith, *Texts, Facts, and Femininity*, 30-43.
72 See Kinsman, Buse, and Steedman, *Whose National Security?*
73 The Popular Front for the Liberation of Palestine, Hamas, Hezbollah, the Kurdistan Workers Party, the Colombian ELN, and many others are on the Canadian state's list of terrorist organizations. See the Canadian Legal Information Institute, S.I/2004-155, Schedule, http://www.canlii.org/ca/regu/si2004-155/part318082.html. See also *Canada Gazette*, 137, 10, November 14, 2003, http://canadagazette.gc.ca/archives/p2/2003/2003-11-14-x/html/sor-dors365-eng.html. On anti-poverty activists, see Jane Gadd, "Activist Called Terrorist," *Globe and Mail*, June 30, 2001, A17. The activist labelled a terrorist by the Crown attorney was John Clarke, an organizer with OCAP.
74 See Engelstein, "Soviet Policy toward Male Homosexuality."
75 On Trotskyism, see Thompson and Lewis, *The Revolution Unfinished?* On the SWP, see Kinsman, "From Anti-Queer to Queers as 'Peripheral'"; Thorstad, ed., *Gay Liberation and Socialism;* and Forgione and Hill, eds., *No Apologies.*

CHAPTER 2: QUEER HISTORY AND SOCIOLOGY FROM BELOW

1 Reflexivity is the process of mutual determination and is part of the accomplishment of any social process. On reflexivity, see Garfinkel, *Studies in Ethnomethodology*. See also George Smith, "Political Activist as Ethnographer." On some of the problems with mainstream sociological theory, see D. Smith, *Writing the Social*. We adopt a reflexive or mutually determined epistemological (theory of knowledge) perspective and an ontological (how the social is produced) perspective that views the social world as being produced through the social practices of people within historical constraints. On epistemology and ontology, see also Frampton et al., eds., *Sociology for Changing the World*.
2 Thompson, *The Making of the English Working Class*. See also E. Wood, *Democracy against Capitalism*, especially 13, 49-107.
3 In opposition to processes of reification, Thompson affirmed that "class is a relationship and not a thing" and that class "is a historical phenomenon. I do not see class as a 'structure' nor even as a 'category,' but as something which ... happens ... in human relationships." Thompson, *The Making of the English Working Class*, 9-10.
4 See McNally, *Another World Is Possible*, 267-398. On developing opposition from below and to the left, see the Zapatista Army of National Liberation, "Sixth Declaration of the Lacandon Jungle"; and El Kilombo Intergalactico, *Beyond Resistance*. See also Holloway, *How to Change the World without Taking Power.*
5 On autonomist Marxism, see H. Cleaver, *Reading Capital;* Dyer-Witheford, *Cyber-Marx*, 62-90; and Kinsman, "The Politics of Revolution."
6 See D. Smith, *The Everyday World as Problematic.*
7 On text-mediated social organization, see D. Smith's, *Texts, Facts, and Femininity*, especially 120-58; "Textually Mediated Social Organization"; and *Writing the Social*. On institutional ethnography, see Campbell and Manicom, eds., *Experience, Knowledge, and Ruling Relations;* and D. Smith, *Institutional Ethnography*. On institutional ethnography, see also D. Smith, *The Everyday World as Problematic*, 151-79; Devault, "Institutional Ethnography"; and Campbell and Gregor, *Mapping Social Relations.*
8 See George Smith, "Policing the Gay Community"; "Political Activist as Ethnographer"; and "The Ideology of 'Fag'"; Khayatt, *Lesbian Teachers* and "Compulsory Heterosexuality"; Kinsman, *The Regulation of Desire;* and O'Brien and Weir, "Lesbians and Gay Men inside and outside Families."
9 See Kinsman, "The Textual Practices of Sexual Rule," 80-95.
10 D. Smith, *Texts, Facts, and Femininity*, 86-119.
11 See Kinsman, "Mapping Social Relations of Struggle," 136.

12 Foucault's *Discipline and Punish; The History of Sexuality;* and *Power/Knowledge.*

13 See Foucault's *Discipline and Punish* and *The History of Sexuality.*

14 The doctor's position in power and knowledge relations generally grants her or him the power to diagnose and prescribe based on the medical gaze. Forms of disciplinary knowledge are at the same time claims to power and knowledge in which power is constructed through knowledge and knowledge is constructed through power relations. This conflation of power and knowledge can put liberatory knowledge projects in question. See D. Smith, especially *The Conceptual Practices of Power,* 70, 79-80. See also D. Smith, *Writing the Social,* 96-130.

15 For an effective use of Foucault's approach to investigating the technologies of surveillance, see Maynard, "Through a Hole in the Lavatory Wall." Maynard also grounds these surveillance technologies in social relations and practices. Also on the technologies and analysis of surveillance, see Hier and Greenberg, eds., *Surveillance.*

16 Foucault often understood discourse more as statements than as text-mediated social practices. He does not explicate how people situated in different social locations produce discourse as a social accomplishment. For instance, in *The History of Sexuality,* vol. 1, he suggests that "the homosexual" emerges off the pages of medical discourse out of the very statements classifying a new type of sexual being (42-44). On the contrary, we view the emergence of the homosexual *and* the heterosexual as a complex coming together of the opening up of new social spaces and the transformation of social relations within capitalism, the seizure and expansion of these spaces by queer people, and the responses to this by sexual policing and regulation. See Kinsman's "Capitalism and Industrialization" and *The Regulation of Desire,* 50-52. Our book explores social practices/relations, whereas Foucault's work is sometimes limited by a discourse reductionism, which confines the social world to the terrain of discourse alone. See Weir, "Studies in the Medicalization of Sexual Danger"; and Fine, *Democracy and the Rule of Law,* 189-202. Using Foucault's work produces an ontological difficulty, as neither power nor discourse is clearly constructed through the social practices of people. It almost seems as if power and discourse produce themselves and are not the social accomplishments of people in historical and social contexts. We view discursive practices as a process of social organization that always depends on and relates to extra-discursive relations. Discourse is always social and is always produced by people. Although Foucault generates major insights and is especially useful in critically addressing the technologies and strategies of social surveillance and normalization, its tendency towards discourse reductionism poses significant limitations. See Fine, *Democracy and the Rule of Law,* 189-202. We use Foucault's insights to read discourse and power as social accomplishments. What is produced socially can also be transformed collectively by people. Foucault is much less useful when it comes to learning from and analyzing oral historical or first-hand accounts (which are neglected in his studies). Foucault's work on governmentality – which focuses on how power operates across public-private boundaries, on how terrains become governable, and on practices of self-formation – is also useful for our investigation. At the same time, although national security has a lot to do with self-formation and self-surveillance – and involves the collaboration of groups outside state relations, including churches and the media – it is also state-focused and organized. See the work of Michel Foucault, including "On Governmentality." See also Burchell, Gordon, and Miller, eds., *The Foucault Effect;* Game and Johnson, eds., *Foucault's New Domains;* Dean, "A Social Structure of Many Souls," and *Critical and Effective Histories.* On extra-state organization of national security, see Maurutto, "Private Policing and Surveillance of Catholics."

17 On queer theory, see Sedgwick, *Epistemology of the Closet;* Butler, *Gender Trouble;* M. Warner, ed., *Fear of a Queer Planet;* Seidman, ed., *Queer Theory/Sociology;* Jagose, *Queer Theory;* Hennessy, "Queer Theory, Left Politics" and *Profit and Pleasure;* McIntosh, "Queer Theory and the War of the Sexes"; K. Namaste, "'Tragic Misreadings'"; and V. Namaste, *Invisible Lives.*

18 Sedgwick, *Epistemology of the Closet,* 1. Eve Kosofsky Sedgwick died on April 12, 2009. See http://dukeupress.typepad.com/dukeupresslog/2009/04/eve-kosofsky-sedgwick-19502009.html.

19　See D. Smith, *Writing the Social*, 96-130; McNally, "Language, History and Class Struggle" and *Bodies of Meaning*.

20　Poststructuralism is a broad theoretical approach that no longer accepts structuralist forms of analysis (in which the social is determined through social structures). Rather than focusing on unitary structures, poststructuralists stress fragmentation and difference. We view postmodernism as a general space or mood that combines a number of shared themes. On social and political terrains, the general assumption is that we are in a new period and are moving beyond "modernity" and the classic analysis of capitalism. An emphasis is placed on language and discourse in both poststructuralism and postmodernism and, often, on the importance of 'psychoanalytical and literary deconstructive theory as well. In general, the subject – or subject positions – is seen as constituted through discourse.

21　Sedgwick, *Epistemology of the Closet*.

22　See Sayer, ed., *Readings from Karl Marx*, 7-10, and many other collections of Marx's writings, including his *Early Writings*, 421-23. See also Bannerji, *Thinking Through*.

23　See D. Smith, *Writing the Social*, 29-44; and H. Cleaver, *Reading Capital Politically*, 31-77.

24　Some of the resources for this view of historical materialism are Holloway, *How to Change the World without Taking Power*; Sayer, *Marx's Method* and *The Violence of Abstraction*; Bologh, *Dialectical Phenomenology*; Rubin, for his emphasis on social forms and social relations in *Essays on Marx's Theory of Value*; Haug's comments on Marxism, especially in *Beyond Female Masochism*; H. Cleaver, *Reading Capital Politically*; Dyer-Witheford, *Cyber-Marx*; the work of Bannerji and D. Smith; and Hennessy, *Profit and Pleasure*. Also see Holloway, Matamoros, and Tischler, eds., *Negativity and Revolution*, and Floyd, *The Reification of Desire*.

25　On dialectics, see Ollman, *Dance of the Dialectic*; Bannerji, *Thinking Through*; Holloway's use of dialectical theorizing in *How to Change the World without Taking Power*; and Holloway, Matamoros, and Tischler, eds., *Negativity and Revolution*.

26　For instance, as Marx writes in the *Grundrisse*, in a capitalist society the moment of production needs to be mediated and realized through the moment of consumption. Without production there would be no consumption. See Marx, *Grundrisse*, 90-94; and also Bannerji, *Thinking Through*, especially 49-51, 66-67.

27　Bannerji, *Thinking Through*.

28　The lack of a social mediational analysis is one of the limitations of the path-breaking article by Robinson and Kimmel, "The Queer Career of Homosexual Security Vetting," 319-45.

29　Kinsman, Buse, and Steedman's *Whose National Security?* moves beyond this standard view, 2-5.

30　Previous analyses of the national security campaigns against queers were based either on interviews with RCMP officers or an analysis of declassified texts. For example, in *Men in the Shadows*, Sawatsky relies on interviews with RCMP officers. Robinson and Kimmel rely on a critical reading of the national security texts, putting them in the historical context of developing Canadian security regime polices. Their article is important in that it draws attention to this under-documented and under-theorized period in Canadian history.

31　D. Smith, *Texts, Facts, and Femininity*, 120-58.

32　For earlier work on these topics, see Kinsman, "'Character Weaknesses' and 'Fruit Machines'"; and Robinson and Kimmel, "The Queer Career of Homosexual Security Vetting." See also Sawatsky's *Men in the Shadows*, 111-40, and *For Services Rendered*; R. Whitaker's, "Origins of the Canadian Government's Internal Security System, 1946-52" and *Double Standard*; Whitaker and Marcuse, *Cold War Canada*; Girard, "From Subversion to Liberation" and "Gays, Lesbians and the Legal Process since 1945." See also Scher, *The UnCanadians*; and Hannant, *The Infernal Machine*.

33　McDonnell's "Finding Security in the Archives" and "The Experience of a Researcher in the Maze." It is our position that all of these documents, including the blanked-out material contained in them, should be released for texts generated before 1990, at the very least.

34   See D. Smith's *Texts, Facts, and Femininity,* 120-58, 209-24, and *Institutional Ethnography.*
35   D. Smith, *Writing the Social,* 157. On ideological codes, see D. Smith, *Writing the Social,* especially 157-71, 172-94.
36   At the same time, we have difficulties with Smith's suggestion that ideological codes are analogous to "genetic codes" since that suggests they are automatic and self-generating and cannot be disrupted. See D. Smith, *Writing the Social,* 159. We want always to hold onto the possibilities for subversion and avoid the reification of human social practices.
37   This is also a problem with approaches derived from Foucault (personal conversation with Lorna Weir, June 1996). This could also limit work inspired by institutional ethnography. See Frampton et al., *Sociology for Changing the World,* 258-59.
38   See D. Smith, "Sociological Theory."
39   See Plummer, "Homosexual Problems."
40   See M. Warner, *Fear of a Queer Planet;* and Butler, *Gender Trouble.* Heteronormativity has now been extended to homonormativity. On the latter, see Duggan, *The Twilight of Equality?*
41   See Kinsman, *The Regulation of Desire,* 33-34.
42   See Robinson and Kimmel, "The Queer Career of Homosexual Security Vetting."
43   Ibid., 321.
44   Ibid., 342.
45   "Prepolitical activities are social acts of resistance that have not yet crystallized into political institutions as opposed to isolated individual acts of resistance." See Kennedy and Davis, *Boots of Leather, Slippers of Gold,* 390n3.
46   Robinson and Kimmel, "The Queer Career of Homosexual Security Vetting," 345.
47   See D. Smith, *Writing the Social.*
48   On the sociological problem of generalization and institutional relations as generalizers of local experience, see D. Smith, *The Everyday World as Problematic,* 154-67. The generalized character of social organization is a feature of social organization itself.
49   A critical part of doing research involves learning more about the social settings we are exploring – that is, learning the methods members of a setting use to accomplish those settings and learning from their insiders' knowledge. As we learn more about how the setting is put together, we ask different and more revealing questions. The researcher's active involvement also shapes and helps to produce the research context and the knowledge generated. On reflexivity, see Garfinkel, *Studies in Ethnomethodology.*
50   On questions of memory in relation to doing oral histories, see Fernie, "Talking Forbidden Love," 59-60. See also Dunbar-Ortiz, "The Opposite of Truth Is Forgetting"; K. Ross, *May '68 and Its Afterlives;* Radstone and Hodgkin, *Regimes of Memory,* and its companion volume *Contested Pasts.*
51   McNally, *Bodies of Meaning,* 124-29; and D. Smith, *Writing the Social,* 96-130.
52   D. Smith faced a somewhat similar dilemma in researching mothering and schooling. She describes pressures to shift from the standpoints of mothers and their work in relation to schooling in the home to those of school-defined relevancies. See D. Smith, *The Everyday World as Problematic,* especially 156-57, 185-87, 188-90. See also D. Smith, *Writing the Social,* 157-71; and Griffith and Smith, *Mothering for Schooling.*
53   On bracketing, see Garfinkel, *Studies in Ethnomethodology.* We also had some difficulties in locating people and in talking to them. One person involved in the security regime declined an interview request, citing poor health and an unwillingless to focus on "bad memories."
54   See D. Smith, *The Everyday World as Problematic,* 151-79, and *Institutional Ethnography.*
55   See D. Smith, *The Everyday World as Problematic,* 166-67.
56   Ibid., 161-75; Dalla Costa and James, *The Power of Women;* and Federici, *Wages against Housework.*
57   We develop these three features of institutional ethnography throughout this book but in no way claim to accomplish an extensive institutional ethnography of the security regime. We hope that others will take on this project using the insights and suggestions developed here.

58 See Whitaker and Marcuse, *Cold War Canada;* Hannant, *The Infernal Machine;* and Kinsman, Buse, and Steedman, *Whose National Security?*

59 The 1981 McDonald Commission report also highlighted these external and internal dimensions: "In our mind there is more than just an internal need for a security intelligence agency. Canada's international alliances require that it be able to assure its allies, with whom it participates in common defence arrangements, that it has a sound system of internal security. Allied countries will not entrust Canadian officials and political leaders with secret information unless Canada has in place effective structures and procedures for detecting and preventing foreign espionage. Similarly, Canada is a signatory to a number of international agreements providing for cooperation in combating terrorism." See Canada, Royal Commission of Inquiry into Certain Activities of the Royal Canadian Mounted Police, *Second Report: Freedom and Security under the Law,* 1:41 (hereafter the McDonald Commission). All references to the McDonald Commission are drawn from the *Second Report,* volumes 1 and 2.

60 See Kinsman, Buse, and Steedman, *Whose National Security?*

61 On the construction of the nation and nationalism, see Enloe, *Does Khaki Become You?* and *Bananas, Beaches and Bases;* and Parker et al., eds., *Nationalisms and Sexualities.*

62 Canada, Treasury Board, *Treasury Board Manual,* C-6. In the possession of the authors.

63 Moran, "The Uses of Homosexuality," 155.

64 Harold's text, 17. The text produced by Harold is in the possession of the authors.

65 Kinsman, Buse, and Steedman, *Whose National Security?* especially 2-5, 278-85.

66 Canada, *Report of the Royal Commission on Security* (Mackenzie Commission), 8.

67 See Geoffrey Smith's "National Security and Personal Isolation" and "Commentary: Security, Gender, and the Historical Process."

68 Cited in Robinson and Kimmel, "The Queer Career of Homosexual Security Vetting," 325-26, quoting from Library and Archives Canada (LAC), Privy Council Office (PCO), series 18, vol. 103, file S-100-M, Security Panel Meeting, April 6, 1948.

69 See Kinsman, *The Regulation of Desire,* 107-200.

70 Moran, "The Uses of Homosexuality," 166.

71 See PCO, AIR 885078, "Revised Terms of Reference for General Inquiry into Security Procedures," attached to "Memorandum for the Security Panel, General Inquiry into Security Methods and Procedures," May 12, 1966, cover letter by D.F. Wall, Secretary, "Memorandum for the Cabinet: General Inquiry into Security Methods and Procedures," May 12, 1966.

72 Mackenzie Commission, 1.

73 Ibid., 28.

74 Ibid., 27-44.

75 On cutting-out operations, see D. Smith, *Texts, Facts, and Femininity,* especially 30-32, 43.

76 Collecting categories are the official mandated concepts through which a series of unrelated practices are combined so that they can be regulated together through common administrative classifications. Our use of collecting categories comes from Corrigan's work, specifically his "On Moral Regulation" and *Social Forms/Human Capacities.*

77 For example, coding "Canadian" as white, or in the measures deployed against Japanese Canadians in the Second World War, or in the current campaigns against Arabs and Muslims in the context of the war on terror. See Iacovetta, "Making Model Citizens"; and R. Whitaker, *Double Standard.* On more recent developments, see Wright, "Against Illegality." See also Bannerji, *The Dark Side of the Nation;* Sharma, *Home Economics;* and Thobani, *Exalted Subjects.*

78 On this, see Puar, *Terrorist Assemblages.*

79 Mackenzie Commission, 45, s. 119. See also Whitaker, *Double Standard.*

80 See Sears, "To Teach Them How to Live" and "Before the Welfare State."

81 See Wright, "Against Illegality," and the concluding chapter of this book.

82 On state formation as an ideological project, see Corrigan and Sayer, *The Great Arch,* 7-9.

83   See Anderson, *Imagined Communities.*

84   See Sears, *A Good Book: In Theory,* 48.

85   See Kinsman, Buse, and Steedman, "How the Centre Holds – National Security as an Ideological Practice." The expression itself comes from Mercedes Steedman.

86   Mackenzie Commission, 9, s. 26.

87   "Performative" refers to a language or speech act that performs an act rather than simply making a statement. On performative, see D. Smith, *Writing the Social,* 107-9.

88   Mackenzie Commission, 36, s. 100.

89   See Kinsman, "'Character Weaknesses' and 'Fruit Machines.'"

90   See Hannant, *The Infernal Machine.* In the United States, this transition took place earlier in the 1950s. Johnson's *The Lavender Scare* notes that this loyalty/unreliability discourse had earlier roots but really started to develop in the early 1950s.

91   Department of External Affairs (DEA), AIR A-2321, Security Sub-Panel minutes, July 8, 1958, 4.

92   Mackenzie Commission, 36, s. 98.

93   See Kinsman, *The Regulation of Desire,* especially 148-54, 181-92, and "Official Discourse as Sexual Regulation."

94   Chauncey, *Gay New York.*

95   Kinsman, *The Regulation of Desire,* 173; Kinsman and Gentile, *"In the Interests of the State,"* 38-49.

96   For instance, consider this excerpt from a Security Panel text: "By exercising fairly simple precautions, homosexuals are usually able to keep their habits hidden from those who are not specifically seeking them out." From CSIS, AIR 91-088, D.F. Wall, Memorandum to the Security Panel, "Security Cases Involving Character Weaknesses, with Special Reference to the Problem of Homosexuality," May 12, 1959, 12-13.

97   In his early writings in the 1950s, Jim Egan pointed out that the anti-gay laws and social stigmas against homosexuals created the basis for the blackmail of some homosexuals. See, for instance, Egan, "Parliamentary Legislative Committee Ignored This Letter from Homosexual Suggesting Changes in Criminal Code," *Canada's Pioneer Gay Activist,* 83-84. The Association for Social Knowledge (ASK) used this potential for blackmail as an argument for homosexual law reform in the 1960s. See Kinsman, *The Regulation of Desire,* 230-48.

98   Moran, "The Uses of Homosexuality." The account in the next few paragraphs derives from our reading of the Moran text. Moran's approach is influenced by the work of Jacques Derrida and Michel Foucault. Like many influenced by postmodernism and poststructuralism, he tends to focus too much on ideas and discourse disconnected from social practices. Part of our project is to give Moran's insightful work a firmer and more materialist social and historical grounding. When we refer to Britain or the British, we are largely referencing English influence, and we understand that Wales and Scotland are distinct nations that have been historically dominated by England. See Corrigan and Sayer, *The Great Arch.*

99   On Burgess, see also Sommer, "Anthony Blunt and Guy Burgess."

100   Moran, "The Uses of Homosexuality," 154.

101   Kinsman, *The Regulation of Desire,* 148-54; and Jackson, *One of the Boys.* On the US experience, see Bérubé, *Coming Out under Fire.*

102   Moran, "The Uses of Homosexuality," 155.

103   CSIS, AIR 91-088, D.F. Wall, "Minutes of the 68th Meeting of the Security Panel," October 6, 1959, 5.

104   Moran, "The Uses of Homosexuality," 169n4. Here Moran refers to Jeffry Weeks' *Coming Out.*

105   Moran, "The Uses of Homosexuality," 158.

106   See Kinsman, *The Regulation of Desire,* 157-224. See also Chenier, "Stranger in Our Midst" and her book based on this work, *Strangers in Our Midst.*

107   Moran, "The Uses of Homosexuality," 158, 166.

108   This is explored in relation to the practices of sexual regulation more generally in Kinsman, *The Regulation of Desire.*

109 Moran, "The Uses of Homosexuality," 156.

110 Ibid., 156-57.

111 Ibid., especially 157-58, 161.

112 Ibid., 149-50.

113 Ibid., especially 149-50, 165-66.

114 On the critique of multiculturalism, see Ng, "Multiculturalism as Ideology"; and Bannerji, *Thinking Through* and *The Dark Side of the Nation*. See also Puar, *Terrorist Assemblages*.

CHAPTER 3: THE COLD WAR AGAINST QUEERS

1 Hewitt, *Spying 101,* 58.

2 We have spoken to more gay men than lesbians. We interviewed seven women who were affected by the campaigns in the 1950s and 1960s, and we have access to three other similar interviews with lesbians.

3 Starnes, *Closely Guarded,* 184.

4 See Kinsman, *The Regulation of Desire,* 148-212.

5 See Whitaker and Hewitt, *Canada and the Cold War,* 154-56; and Palmer, *Canada's 1960s,* 80-105.

6 Terry, "Momism and the Making of the Treasonous Homosexuals" and *An American Obsession,* 315-21.

7 See Kinsman, *The Regulation of Desire,* 192-98.

8 Terry, "Momism and the Making of the Treasonous Lesbian," 10. May, *Homeward Bound,* 96-97, offers a brief discussion on momism. See also Johnson, *The Lavender Scare,* 95-96.

9 On Strecker's work, see Terry, "Momism and the Making of the Treasonous Homosexuals." Also see Strecker, *Their Mother's Sons;* and Strecker and Lathbury, *Their Mother's Daughters.*

10 See M.L. Adams, *The Trouble with Normal,* 158-65; and B. Ross, "Destaining the (Tattooed) Delinquent Body."

11 M.L. Adams, *The Trouble with Normal,* quoting from A.G. McDougall, "Judgement Re: *Women's Barracks,*" November 22, 1952, Archives of Ottawa (AO), RG 4-32, 1953, no. 830. On this case and the context surrounding it, see M.L. Adams, "Margin Notes."

12 See Kinsman, *The Regulation of Desire.*

13 Sawatsky, *Men in the Shadows,* 126n1. See also Canadian Security Intelligence Service (CSIS), AIR 91-088, J. Bordeleau, Assistant Commissioner, Director, Security and Intelligence, RCMP, to D.F. Wall, January 25, 1963, 1.

14 Archibald, *Sex and the Public Service,* 14.

15 Ibid.

16 Office of Equal Opportunities for Women, *The Employment of Women in the Public Service of Canada,* 1.

17 Archibald, *Sex and the Public Service,* 17. By the 1950s, more than 80 percent of women employed by the civil service were concentrated in administrative support staff positions, working as secretaries, typists, clerks, and stenographers. In 1961, the renewed Civil Service Act did not forbid discrimination on the basis of sex. This act clarified that the term "civil service" applied only to those employees hired under the Civil Service Act and that "public service" included employees of departments and agencies listed in Schedule A of the Public Service Superannuation Act. "Public service" is, therefore, a broader term than "civil service," and we use it unless we are referring more specifically to the civil service.

18 Ibid., 18.

19 Henkenhaf, "Women in the Canadian Federal Civil Service during World War II."

20 Lynch, "Ottawa Hostel," 278. The Terrace was a two-storey building complex with sleeping quarters, cafeteria, tuck shop, lounge area, and large main hall. It was located on Sussex Street and Lady Grey Drive, across the street from Major's Hill Park (where the National Art Gallery now stands). The Laurentian Hills, the view one saw through the cafeteria windows, were the inspiration behind the

residence's name. See Inglis, "Laurentian Terrace," 200. Originally built as temporary wartime housing, it lasted as a residence managed by various government institutions until 1964.

21 Canada, *House of Commons Debates* (June 4, 1942), 3059. In a long speech delivered to the War Appropriation Committee in 1942, Mr. Coldwell made this plea: "I urge the minister [Minister of Finance Ilsley] and the government to give consideration to this problem which so nearly affects the lives of a large number of young people in this city, particularly those who may in after years be the wives of the men who will return from overseas and become the mothers of the future generations of Canadians." Ibid., 3058. See also Philips, "The Government Girl," 25.

22 On regimes of rationality, see D. Smith, "Whistling Women."

23 These points are raised and developed in useful ways in Greenberg, *The Construction of Homosexuality*, 434-54.

24 See Pringle, *Secretaries Talk;* and Witz and Savage, eds., *Gender and Bureaucracy* for more on bureaucracy, gender, and power.

25 For recent work on women war workers, see Keshen, *Saints, Sinners, and Soldiers*, especially 145-71.

26 On the social construction of femininity as a discourse and social practice, see D. Smith, *Texts, Facts, and Femininity*, 159-208.

27 See May, *Homeward Bound*, for more on the idealization of women and the family in the 1950s and the integration and consumption of those ideals in American mass culture. For a Canadian example, see Strong-Boag, "Home Dreams."

28 Pringle, *Secretaries Talk*, 94; see also Witz and Savage, eds., *Gender and Bureaucracy* and Canaday, *The Straight State.*

29 For a history of these beauty contests, see Gentile, "Searching for 'Miss Civil Service' and 'Mr. Civil Service.'"

30 The *RA News* was the official organ of the Recreational Association, an organization established for federal government employees. The executive of the Recreational Association Centre initiated the Miss Civil Service pageants to help boost morale. The *RA News* attempted to enforce this ideal on all female civil servants via articles and numerous advice columns on dating and marriage, all of which contributed to defining the heterosexual "typical government girl" and, by extension, the heterosexual "typical government man." This ideal was a counterpoint to the new lesbian and gay threat.

31 Bérubé and D'Emilio, "The Military and Lesbians during the McCarthy Years," 760.

32 Enloe, *Does Khaki Become You?* 138; Pierson, *"They're Still Women After All."*

33 Enloe, *Does Khaki Become You?* 141, 212.

34 For more on the "lesbian threat" in the US military, see Meyer, *Creating GI Jane*, especially 148-78.

35 Ibid., 149-50.

36 Hannon, " ... Deemed Necessary to Discriminate ...," 19.

37 D'Emilio, *Sexual Politics, Sexual Communities*, 28.

38 Keshen, *Saints, Sinners, and Soldiers*, 182-83.

39 D'Emilio, *Sexual Politics, Sexual Communities;* and Bérubé, "Marching to a Different Drummer," 390.

40 Bérubé and D'Emilio, "The Military and Lesbians," 761.

41 The hunt for lesbians in the US military led to the purging of thousands of women. According to a 1957 US Navy report, detection for homosexual activity in the navy was "much higher for the female than the male," even though "homosexual activity is difficult to detect." Ibid., 760.

42 Jackson, *One of the Boys*, 22.

43 D'Emilio, *Sexual Politics, Sexual Communities*, 44.

44 Bérubé and D'Emilio, "The Military and Lesbians," especially 760, 762-63.

45 For Canadian examples, see Jackson, *One of the Boys.*

46 Alcorn reported that "it would appear that he is definitely a homosexual of the feminine type. He has already been guilty of offences and may continue to be involved in further difficulties. I do not believe

anything would be gained by attempting to continue this man in the Navy and would recommend his discharge on administrative grounds." Library and Archives Canada (LAC), Navy personnel file N-23682, Aaron H. Jenkins, D.E. Alcorn, MD, consultant's report," D.E. Alcorn, MD, consultant's report, July 17, 1957. See Hustak, *They Were Hanged*, 100-1. Earlier in 1956, Jenkins had been diagnosed as "immature, highly effeminate and emotionally unstable." See LAC, Navy personnel file N-23682, Aaron H. Jenkins, G. Arsenault, "Personnel Selection Report," June 29, 1956.

47 Hustak, *They Were Hanged*, 101.

48 See Chauncey's "Christian Brotherhood or Sexual Perversion?" and *Gay New York*. There is a great deal in Chauncey's work on the connections of class, sexuality, and gender in the formation of gay cultures.

49 On the social and historical roots of the use of "fairy" in relation to men who had sex with other men, see Chauncey, *Gay New York*, 47-63. Fairies were part of a pre-homosexual form of gender and sexual organization and culture within working-class life that came to inform, and overlap with, "gender invert" notions of homosexuality.

50 See Terry, "Theorizing Deviant Historiography" and "Anxious Slippages between 'Us' and 'Them.'" See also Kennedy and Davis, *Boots of Leather, Slippers of Gold*.

51 See I. Young, *Global Challenges*.

52 Moran, "The Uses of Homosexuality," 160-61.

53 In the sexological and medical discourse of the 1950s, the notion of the homosexual began to be separated from notions of gender inversion and to be defined according to a difference in sexual orientation. See Kinsman, *The Regulation of Desire*, 200.

54 CSIS, AIR 91-088, W.H. Kelly, Assistant DSI, Memorandum and Paper, "Top Secret," August 9, 1961, 2.

55 See Kinsey et al., *Sexual Behavior in the Human Male* and *Sexual Behavior in the Human Female*. For commentary on Kinsey, see Chauncey, *Gay New York*, 70-74; and Kinsman, *The Regulation of Desire*, 158-60.

56 CSIS, AIR 92-008, F.R. Wake, "Memorandum for D.F. Wall: Security Risks – Homosexual," 1 (emphasis in original).

57 CSIS, AIR 91-088, W.H. Kelly, Assistant DSI, Memorandum and Paper, "Top Secret," August 9, 1961, 3-4.

58 On cogency, see Kinsman, "The Textual Practices of Sexual Rule."

59 See the interview with George Marshall in *Two*, July-August 1966, 12.

60 See Enloe, *Does Khaki Become You?* 11-13.

61 Goffman, *Asylums*, xiii-xiv. This can also be related to Foucault's use of "complete and austere institutions," in *Discipline and Punish*, 231-56.

62 See Kinsman, *The Regulation of Desire*, especially 53-54, 99-100.

63 See Bérubé, *Coming Out under Fire*. For Canada, see Kinsman, *The Regulation of Desire*, 148-57.

64 Jackson, *One of the Boys*, 22.

65 Feasby, ed., *Official History of the Canadian Medical Services*, vol. 2, *Clinical Subjects*, 85-86. The following references are based on this text as well as on vol. 1, *Organizations and Campaigns*.

66 See Kinsman, *The Regulation of Desire*, especially 53-54, 98-100.

67 See Weir, "Studies in the Medicalization of Sexual Danger," 256-74. Much of this section is also based on Kinsman, *The Regulation of Desire*, 150-54.

68 See Kinsman, *The Regulation of Desire*, 151; and E. Freedman, "Uncontrolled Desires."

69 In *One of the Boys*, Jackson argues that many people were affected by anti-homosexual regulations during the Second World War. We suggest that more were affected, especially when we consider the thousands discharged under the broader anti-psychopath provisions.

70 E. Freedman, "Uncontrolled Desires," 213.

71 Feasby, ed., *Official History of the Canadian Medical Service*, 2:85-86.

72 *Physical Standards and Instructions for the Medical Examination of Recruits*, 1943, 62. In the possession of the authors. See also Jackson, *One of the Boys*, 114.

73 Feasby, *Official History of the Canadian Medical Service*, 2:84; Jackson, *One of the Boys*, 114.
74 Feasby, *Official History of the Canadian Medical Service*, 2:85.
75 Once a diagnosis of psychopathic personality with abnormal sexuality was applied, the psychiatrists graded the individual so that he (or she) could be discharged from the service: "Under the PULHEMS system of personality classification [which is what they used], the final category measured the soldier's stability, S, on a five-point scale. Under a grading of 5, the individual was deemed unfit for any military service. Homosexuals were to be graded S5 and discharged as a matter of course." Feasby, *Official History of the Canadian Medical Service*, 2:86. Jackson, *One of the Boys*, 114.
76 This applies to Kinsman's earlier work in *The Regulation of Desire*, in which he tends to imply a direct relation between the medical regulatory texts and what happened to homosexuals in the Canadian military during the Second World War. This initial study needs elaboration, following Jackson's work, by using first-hand accounts of those who were affected by these regulations. Using first-hand accounts would allow for a more grounded sense of the impact of the regulations in people's lives. See Kinsman, *The Regulation of Desire*, 151-54.
77 See ibid., 154-57.
78 Quoted in Canada, *Report of the Royal Commission on the Criminal Law Relating to Criminal Sexual Psychopaths*, 8.
79 Moral panics are defined by Stan Cohen as follows: "A condition, episode, person or group of persons emerges to become defined as a threat to societal values and interests; its nature is presented in a styl-ized and stereotyped fashion by the mass media: the moral barricades are manned by editors, bishops, and politicians and other right-thinking people; socially accredited experts pronounce their diagnoses and solutions ... Sometimes the panic is passed over and forgotten, but at other times it has a more serious and long-term repercussion and it might produce changes in legal and social policy or even in the way in which societies conceive themselves." See Cohen, *Folk Devils and Moral Panics*, 9. Un-fortunately, "moral panic" is overused in the literature to the point that it seems self-generating. We locate and ground moral panics in social and institutional relations actively constructed between the media, the police, the courts, "citizens' groups," professional experts, and state agencies. These relations combine in different ways in different panics.
80 See Kinsman, *The Regulation of Desire*, 183-98. See also Chenier, "The Criminal Sexual Psychopath in Canada" and her book *Strangers in Our Midst*.
81 E. Freedman, "Uncontrolled Desires," 213. The unproblematized use of "paedophilia" in this quota-tion presents some difficulties. This term was a sexological invention generalized in the 1950s. It was supposed to refer to an erotic interest in pre-pubescent young people but often included adolescents as well. It usually did not focus on sexual assaults and sexual violence within households and fam-ilies and did not cover fathers who raped their daughters. See Kinsman, *The Regulation of Desire*, 198-200.
82 None of the twenty-three men sentenced as criminal sexual psychopaths from 1948 to 1955 was a father of, or related to, those assaulted or harassed. See the *Report of the Royal Commission on the Criminal Law Relating to Criminal Sexual Psychopaths*. For more on this, see Kinsman, *The Regulation of Desire*, 183-92.
83 See Kinsman, *The Regulation of Desire*, 183-92.
84 See Girard, "Gays, Lesbians and the Legal Process since 1945," 94.
85 See George Smith, "Political Activist as Ethnographer."
86 See Committee on Homosexual Offences and Prostitution, *Report of the Committee on Homosexual Offences and Prostitution* (Wolfenden Report).
87 Kinsman, *The Regulation of Desire*, 213-78.
88 We wish we knew what "living on the avails of homosexualism" meant. Girard, "From Subversion to Liberation," 11.
89 Ibid., 15-16.
90 See Johnson, *The Lavender Scare*.

91 Despite important victories on the immigration front, problems continue to arise for queer people attempting to immigrate into Canada. For instance, acting on the belief that he is not gay, the Immigration and Refugee Board has denied Alvaro Orozco refugee status in Canada. The board is trying to deport him to Nicaragua, where he will face harassment as an openly gay person. See Julia Garro, "Alvaro Orozco Denied Status: Set to Be Deported Oct. 4," *Xtra!* (Toronto), September 14, 2007.

92 On the violence of abstraction, see Sayer, *The Violence of Abstraction;* and Bannerji, *Thinking Through.*

93 See Kinsman, *Whose National Security?* For an excellent account of a progressive union's fight against racism and heterosexism, and how this union was torn apart by the Cold War national security campaigns in the United States, see Allan Bérubé's wonderful work, recounted in Scarlett C. Davis, "No Race Baiting, Red-Baiting, or Queer Baiting: The Marine Cooks and Stewards Union Knew Differences Are Small, Solidarity Is Key," *Dispatcher,* February 1997, 6-7. Bérubé died in late 2007. See Gary Kinsman, "Allan Bérubé: Queer Working-Class Historian, 1946-2007," *Against the Current* 135 (July-August 2008), http://auto_sol.tao.ca/node/3109.

94 On the involvement of gay leftists in the early Mattachine Society in the United States, see D'Emilio, *Sexual Politics, Sexual Communities,* 57-91. In Canada, Doug Sanders, a central figure throughout most of the history of the Association for Social Knowledge in Vancouver in the 1960s, was also a spokesperson for the Committee to Aid American War Objectors.

95 On the English experience, see also Shepherd, "Gay Sex Spy Orgy"; and Moran's "The Uses of Homosexuality" and *The Homosexual(ity) of Law.* On the US experience, see also R. Cleaver, "Sexual Dissidents and the National Security State, 1942-1992."

96 The interview comes from the Lesbians Making History Collective, "People Think That Didn't Happen in Canada," 84. The same Lois appears in Fernie and Weissman's *Forbidden Love* (film). On the Rosenberg case, see Robert Meeropol, "The Rosenberg Case," Rosenberg Fund for Children, April 1, 2002, http://www.rfc.org/case.htm.

97 On the connections between the CIA, the FBI, and the RCMP, see Hewitt, *Spying 101,* 159-60.

98 This quote comes from *Civil Service News,* "How Canada Fights Spies: Security of State Is Put before That of Individual," 4.

99 While many authors date the beginnings of the development of the Canadian national security regime to the late 1940s following the Gouzenko affair and the royal commission set up regarding it, Larry Hannant locates the formative period earlier. Hannant traces the beginnings to a response to the threat of communists after the First World War and efforts to conduct surveillance on communists in the unions. This included the 1931 initiation of the fingerprinting of civil service recruits in order to exclude criminals. This led to the development of security files and surveillance, which extended into the factories during the war effort and affected the armed forces and the merchant marine. National security practices in the postwar years were built on earlier campaigns against the left, the Communist Party, and the trade unions. See Hannant, *The Infernal Machine.* On the origin and historical development of the Canadian security regime, see also Whitaker and Marcuse, *Cold War Canada;* and the series edited by Kealey and Whitaker, *RCMP Security Bulletins.*

100 Igor Gouzenko defected from the Soviet Embassy in Ottawa in 1945 with documents incriminating the USSR in organizing a Canadian spy ring. This provoked a royal commission and the development of the Security Panel. See Whitaker and Hewitt, *Canada and the Cold War,* 13-22. More generally, see Whitaker and Marcuse, *Cold War Canada,* especially 27-110, 161-87; and R. Whitaker, "Origins of the Canadian Government's Internal Security System, 1946-1952."

101 McDonald Commission, 1:89-90. The initial terms of reference were "to advise on the coordination of the planning, organization and execution of security measures which affect government departments and, [sic] to advise on such other security questions as might be referred to it." See PCO, AIR 853057, Letter to Commander J.G. Wright, Executive Secretary, Joint Security Committee, Department of National Defence, from D. Beavis, Secretary of the Security Sub-Panel, December 11, 1964, 2.

102 PCO, AIR 853057, Letter to Commander J.G. Wright, Executive Secretary, Joint Security Committee, Department of National Defence, from D. Beavis, Secretary of the Security Sub-Panel, December 11, 1964.

103 McDonald Commission, 1:89-90. One important exception was in relation to the collection of intelligence regarding supporters of Quebec independence and sovereignty. "In the summer of 1967, the Security Panel encouraged the RCMP to make a much greater effort to keep the government informed about the separatist movement in Quebec – its democratic and constitutional manifestations as well as its terrorist manifestations, and its connection with foreign interference activities." Canadian national security clearly constructed Québécois independence and/or sovereignty movements as profoundly threatening.

104 All unattributed page references in this section on the Security Panel and the Security Sub-Panel are to the letter to Commander Wright from Beavis, December 11, 1964, 4.

105 CSIS, AIR 91-088, W.H. Kelly, "Memorandum for File," June 8, 1961. The Character Deviate Committee of the Security Panel is mentioned in this document.

106 McDonald Commission, 1:89-90.

107 Ibid.

108 Ibid., 85-86.

109 See Witz and Savage, eds., *Gender and Bureaucracy,* 16.

110 Quoted in Whitaker and Marcuse, *Cold War Canada,* 183.

111 On this, see Hannant, *The Infernal Machine.*

112 This formulation of "loyalty-security discourse" is used by Terry in "Momism and the Making of the Treasonous Lesbian," 3.

113 There is a clear relation between this language and the conceptualization of homosexuals as sexual psychopaths. This interview is in *Two,* July-August 1966: 12. The quotes in the rest of this paragraph are from this interview.

114 Ibid.

115 Privy Council Office (PCO), AIR 864001, Security Panel, Robert Bryce, "Security of Information in the Public Service of Canada," November 1956, Preface.

116 Ibid.

117 McDonald Commission, 1:85.

118 PCO, AIR 864001, Security Panel, Robert Bryce, "Security of Information in the Public Service of Canada," November 1956, 4.

119 Ibid., 5.

120 Ibid., 7.

121 According to this manual, extracts have the same classification level as does the document from which they are taken, and the level also refers to how the information was obtained. If the information was obtained at a higher security level, it would also be classified at that level. These classifications, it was noted, could and did change over time. Ibid., 8.

122 Ibid., 25.

123 Ibid., 26.

124 Ibid., 50.

125 Robinson and Kimmel, "The Queer Career of Homosexual Security Vetting," 322.

126 Confidential security clearances required "a fingerprint and subversive indices check." See PCO, AIR 853057, D.F. Wall, "Memorandum for the Security Panel: Security Investigations at the Universities," April 24, 1964, Appendix B, "Character Investigations (A) Security Screening – Applicants and Employees of Public Service." All quotes in this paragraph are from this text.

127 Ibid.

128 These extracts were reprinted as "How Canada Fights Spies" in the *Civil Service News,* but were originally published in the *US News and World Report,* a right-wing US publication.

129 Ibid.
130 Ibid.
131 Ibid.
132 Ibid.
133 Ibid.
134 See Gidney, "Under the President's Gaze."
135 Dates for the US purge against homosexuals are taken from Johnson, *The Lavender Scare.*
136 Johnson, "Homosexual Citizens"; see also Johnson, *The Lavender Scare.*
137 Moran, "The Uses of Homosexuality."
138 Sawatsky, *Men in the Shadows,* 126n2.
139 McDonald Commission, 2:782.
140 On the earlier emergence of notions of moral or character failings in security regime discourse and practice, see Hannant, *The Infernal Machine.*
141 McDonald Commission, 2:782. This text takes up the standpoint of national security. There is no evidence offered to justify their comment about homosexuals in Canadian government employ being compromised by Soviet agents.
142 Robinson and Kimmel, "The Queer Career of Homosexual Security Vetting," 331.
143 McDonald Commission, 2:795.
144 LAC, Robert Bryce, interviewed by Jim Littleton, sound recording, ISN, 61905, C09276(1), 1887-0259/031, October 22, 1980.
145 Ibid.
146 Ibid.
147 LAC, Don Wall, interviewed by Donald Brittain, sound recording, ISN 61917, CO9276(2), C9277, October 23, 1980.
148 See Robinson and Kimmel, "The Queer Career of Homosexual Security Vetting," 324.
149 See Girard, "From Subversion to Liberation." See also Robinson and Kimmel, "The Queer Career of Homosexual Security Vetting," 328; Cabinet Directive 24, October 16, 1952, cited from the McDonald Commission, 2:782, and CSIS, AIR 92-008, Carl Betke and S.W. Horrall, "From Royal Commission on Espionage to Royal Commission on Security, 1946-1966," from "Canada's Security Service: An Historical Outline, 1864-1966."
150 Robinson and Kimmel, "The Queer Career of Homosexual Security Vetting," 329. The authors cite Department of External Affairs (DEA) file 50207-40, Cabinet Directive 29, "Security Screening of Government Employee," December 21, 1955.
151 CSIS, AIR 91-088, D.F. Wall, "Minutes of the 68th Meeting of the Security Panel," October 6, 1959, 5.
152 Sawatsky, *Men in the Shadows,* 124.
153 The following is in the possession of the authors: D.F. Wall, minutes of "The 17th Meeting of the Security Sub-Panel: A Security Case in the Department of Defence Production," March 20, 1956 (March 22, 1956), 5-6. There was also a 1956 case of an inebriated RCAF civilian employee who passed low-grade information to a Soviet official. The incident was not thought serious, and G.F. Frazer of the Privy Council Office argued that, on the whole, character weaknesses were less sensitive than were subversive threats. See Robinson and Kimmel, "The Queer Career of Homosexual Security Vetting," 329.
154 Robinson and Kimmel, "The Queer Career of Homosexual Security Vetting," 331.
155 DEA, AIR A-2321, G.F. Frazer, Secretary, Memo to the Security Panel, "Security Cases Involving Character Weaknesses," July 2, 1958, 1.
156 This suggests that some Security Panel members subscribed to the form of limited tolerance for closeted elite homosexuals that Moran describes for the English situation. See Moran, "The Uses of Homosexuality."
157 CSIS, AIR 92-008, Carl Betke and S.W. Horall, "From Royal Commission on Espionage to Royal Commission on Security," 1978.

158 Ibid.

159 Ibid.

160 Beeby refers to the incident when he writes, "The RCMP Security Service knew of at least one clerk at the Canadian embassy in Moscow who was photographed by the KGB in a homosexual encounter in the 1950s and was pressed to cooperate. The clerk confessed and was fired, but the Mounties feared repetition of the episode." See Dean Beeby, "Mounties Staged Massive Hunt for Gay Men in the Civil Service," *Globe and Mail*, April 24, 1992, A1-A2. The RCMP itself reported that "in 1958 this Force was called upon to investigate a government employee who the Russian Intelligence Service ... had attempted to compromise while he was serving in Moscow. The attempt was based on a threat to expose the employee's homosexual activities. The attempt failed because the employee reported the entire matter to his superior and was returned to Canada [text whited out]. Through this cumulative effect our present investigation of homosexuals was commenced." See CSIS, AIR 91-088, W.H. Kelly, Assistant DSI, Memorandum and Paper, "Top Secret," August 9, 1961, 2.

161 Sawatsky, *For Services Rendered*, 172-73. Unless otherwise cited, the following account draws on this source.

162 Starnes, *Closely Guarded*, 67.

163 See Sawatsky, *Men in the Shadows* and his *For Services Rendered*, 175-77. See also Loos, "The Unexplained Demise of Diplomat John Watkins," 9.

164 On Watkins, see also McLeod, *Lesbian and Gay Liberation in Canada*, 12-13; Beeby and Kaplan, eds., *Moscow Dispatches*; and I. Adams, *Agent of Influence*.

165 See I. Adams, *Agent of Influence*, 225-26.

166 Ian Adams, in *S: Portrait of a Spy*, mentions an unnamed Canadian ambassador in Moscow who was entrapped in a homosexual encounter by the KGB. In the second edition (1981), he reveals that this person was Watkins. David Martin, in *Wilderness of Mirrors*, reveals that Watkins had been the target of attempted blackmail by the Soviet secret service and that he died while being questioned by the RCMP. Chapman Pincher, in *Their Trade in Treachery*, names the ambassador as Watkins and reveals that he died suddenly during interrogation by the RCMP. In *Men in the Shadows*, Sawatsky provides the first detailed non-fictionalized account of this incident. Later, Adams wrote a historical novel entitled *Agent of Influence*, based on John Watkins. See I. Adams, *Agent of Influence*, 223-33.

167 Loos, "Watkins Death Probe Seeks New Evidence," 13-14, and "Mounties Cleared in Watkins Inquest," 12.

168 Starnes, *Closely Guarded*, 67-68.

169 CSIS, AIR 91-088, W.H. Kelly, Assistant DSI, Memorandum and Paper, "Top Secret," August 9, 1961, 2.

170 See DEA, AIR A-2321, G.F. Frazer, "Security Cases Involving Character Weakness," July 8, 1958; and CSIS, AIR 91-088, D.F. Wall, Secretary of the Security Panel, "Security Cases Involving Character Weaknesses, with Special Reference to the Problem of Homosexuality," May 12, 1959.

171 LAC, Navy personnel file N-9190, Leo A.J. Mantha, "Leo Mantha-Okalla Jail, BC," March 9, 1959. A thorough biography of Leo Mantha's life has yet to be written; however, for more information on Mantha, see Hustak's *They Were Hanged*, 97-114. On Mantha and Jenkins and the purge campaign, see also Steele and Tomzack, *Legal Memory* (film).

172 LAC, Navy personnel file N-9190, Leo A.J. Mantha, "Leo Mantha-Okalla Jail, BC," March 9, 1959. At the same time, we have to read these psychological and psychiatric accounts of Mantha and Jenkins critically and as active parts of the attempt to construct them as a homosexual problem.

173 Hustak writes that Mantha was a regular at a bar at the Empress Hotel in Victoria, which he referred to as "the rendezvous for a discreet circle of homosexuals in the military." See Hustak, *They Were Hanged*, 103.

174 LAC, Navy personnel file N-9190, Leo A.J. Mantha, W. Leslie, MD, consultant's report, February 3, 1956. See Hustak, *They Were Hanged*, 103.

175 LAC, Navy personnel file N-9190, Leo A.J. Mantha, "Leo Mantha-Okalla Jail, BC," March 9, 1959.

176 The provisional diagnosis given to Mantha was that of "personality disorder with alcohol and sexual deviation." See LAC, Navy personnel file N-9190, Leo A.J. Mantha, "Case History," signed by Sgt. Lt. Lyden, RCN, February 3, 1956. Dr. W. Leslie recommended discharge, and in his consultant's report wrote that "this man is accused of sexual deviation in his ship" and that "he gives a long history of extreme conflict over homosexual tendencies which he recognizes as socially unacceptable and feels very shameful. So long as he does not drink he can control them, although they still make themselves felt from time to time." See LAC Navy personnel file N-9190, Leo A.J. Mantha, W. Leslie, MD, consultant's report, February 3, 1956.

177 This builds on the notion of homosexuality as a form of psychopathology, suggesting that it was still accepted within military discourse and that it shaped the context within which homosexuals were problematized in the national security campaigns. See Hustak, *They Were Hanged*, 10. This disease, or syndrome, known as "homosexual panic," was named by Dr. Edward J. Kempf. See Kempf, "Homosexual Panic" and "Enlightened ... Sublimation of the Abnormal."

178 LAC, Navy personnel file N-23682, Aaron H. Jenkins, "Personnel Selection Record," signed by G. Arsenault, June 29, 1956.

179 Ibid.

180 LAC, Navy personnel file N-23682, Aaron H. Jenkins, "Divisional Record Sheet, 1957-1958."

181 LAC, Navy personnel file N-23682, Aaron H. Jenkins, D.E. Alcorn, MD, consultant's report, July 18, 1957.

182 LAC, Navy personnel file N-23682, Aaron H. Jenkins, D.E. Alcorn, MD, consultant's report, November 1, 1957.

183 Ibid.

184 See Renwick, "No Fury Like a Homosexual Scorned," 32. See also Pat Johnson, "Forty Years Ago Today, Leo Mantha Was the Last Man to Be Hanged in British Columbia," *Vancouver Courier*, April 28, 1999, 1.

185 Renwick, "No Fury Like a Homosexual Scorned," 50.

186 LAC, RG 13 c1, vol. 1774, "Leo Mantha File," court transcripts, 527; also quoted in Johnson, "Forty Years Ago Today," 1.

187 As quoted in Johnson, "Forty Years Ago Today," 1.

188 Ibid.

189 Male police officers would act as though they were sexually available in order to entrap other men into initiating a sexual approach.

190 John Grube died on April 21, 2008. See James Dubro, "John Grube, Proud Life, May 23, 1930 – April 21, 2008," *Xtra!* (Toronto), May 8, 2008.

191 See Kinsman, *The Regulation of Desire*, 160-61.

192 This was rooted in PCO, AIR 853117, R.B. Bryce, Memorandum for the Cabinet, "Security Screening of Government Employee, December 19, 1955." See CSIS, AIR 91-088, D.F. Wall, "Security Cases Involving Character Weaknesses, with Special Reference to Homosexuality, May 12, 1959."

193 CSIS, AIR 91-088, D.F. Wall, "Security Cases Involving Character Weaknesses, with Special Reference to Homosexuality, May 12, 1959."

194 CSIS, AIR 91-088, R.B. Bryce, "Memorandum for the Prime Minister and the Minister of Justice, Security Cases Involving Homosexuality," December 19, 1960 (2nd version). Probably referring to the same case, the RCMP reported that "there is one case on file where an attempt was made to compromise a Canadian government employee." See CSIS, AIR 91-088, DSI Report, 1959-60, Part 2, Security Branch A, Appendix G, "Appendix to Annual Report on Homosexuality among Federal Government Employees," 42.

195 CSIS, AIR 91-088, D.F. Wall, "Security Cases Involving Character Weaknesses, with Special Reference to Homosexuality, May 12, 1959."

196 CSIS, AIR 91-088, D.F. Wall to Commissioner C.E. Rivett-Carnac, "Minutes of the 68th Meeting of the Security Panel, October 20, 1959."

197 Ibid., 5.

198 PCO, AIR 864001, Cabinet Directive No. 35, "Security in the Public Service of Canada," December 18, 1963.

199 Robinson and Kimmel, as mentioned in the last chapter, hold that those opposed to a broader national security campaign against gay men and lesbians adopted a "liberal" position. See Robinson and Kimmel, "The Queer Career of Homosexual Security Vetting."

200 On this, see *Report of the Committee on Homosexual Offences and Prostitution* (Wolfenden Report). On the Wolfenden Report and its impact in Canada, see Kinsman, *The Regulation of Desire*, 213-24.

201 This refers to a general prohibition, implied in Security Panel directives, on directly interviewing alleged homosexuals presently in the civil service. The police also wanted the decision regarding when departments should be provided with information about homosexuals in their ranks left to the RCMP's discretion and noted: "We would also appreciate clarification on whether or not we should provide the department concerned with information on a homosexual who is not employed on duties having access to classified material." These quotes come from LAC, CSIS, AIR 91-088, Appendix C, "RCMP Request for Terms of Reference," May 1960; CSIS, AIR 91-088, "Meeting to Consider Reports of Mr. Don Wall and Dr. F.R. Wake on the Problem of Character Weaknesses in the Government Service," brief on reports attached, March 4, 1963.

202 CSIS, AIR 91-088, "I" Directorate Annual Report, 1959-60, report of the Directorate, Appendix G, "Appendix to Annual Report on Homosexuality among Federal Government Employees," 42.

203 Ibid.

204 Starnes, *Closely Guarded,* 54.

205 See George Smith, "Policing the Gay Community," on the social organization of policing. See also his "Political Activist as Ethnographer."

206 See Kinsman, *The Regulation of Desire,* especially 148-57, 181-83.

207 CSIS, AIR 91-088, "A Special Meeting of a Quorum of the Security Panel: Minutes," June 24, 1960 (issued July 26, 1960).

208 Ibid., 2.

209 Ibid.

210 Ibid., 4.

211 Ibid.

212 CSIS, AIR 91-0088, R.B. Bryce, "Memorandum for the Prime Minister and Minister of Justice: Security Cases Involving Homosexuality," December 19, 1960 (1st version).

213 Ibid., January 26, 1961 (2nd version).

214 Ibid., December 19, 1960 (1st version).

215 Ibid.

216 Ibid., January 26, 1961 (2nd version). Notice how the RCMP raises the criminalization of homosexuality in its support for extending the campaign to encompass all government workers.

217 PCO, AIR 864001, Cabinet Directive No. 35, "Security in the Public Service of Canada," 74. PCO, AIR 864001, R.G. Robertson, Secretary to the Cabinet, "Memorandum for Deputy Ministers and Heads of Agency, Revised Cabinet Directive on Security," December 27, 1963, 1.

218 PCO, AIR 864001, Cabinet Directive No. 35, "Security in the Public Service of Canada."

219 PCO, AIR 864001, R.G. Robertson, Secretary to the Cabinet, "Memorandum for Deputy Ministers and Heads of Agency, Revised Cabinet Directive on Security," December 27, 1963, 1. The McDonald Commission report also emphasized this point: "One change it made was to require greater frankness in dealing with employees whose reliability or loyalty was in doubt. Further it provided procedures for reviewing such cases both within the responsible department or agency and, if necessary, by a Board of Review composed of three of the Deputy Ministers who served on the Security Panel." McDonald Commission, 2:783.

220 PCO, AIR 864001, Cabinet Directive No. 35, "Security in the Public Service of Canada."

CHAPTER 4: SPYING AND INTERROGATION

1   The McDonald Commission stated that the DND "has an obvious responsibility for the security of Canada in terms of the protection of Canadian sovereignty and contributing to world peace, it also has a number of functions which relate to the internal security of Canada and to intelligence. The security and intelligence components of the Department report to the Director General of Security and Intelligence." See McDonald Commission, 1:130. The McDonald Commission also pointed out that, "while it uses its own Special Investigation Unit to conduct inquiries on the personal reliability of applicants for positions in the Canadian Armed Forces, it relies heavily on the RCMP for information about the criminal record of applicants or their participation in subversive activities ... Actual or suspected security incidents particularly where espionage, subversion, sabotage or arson is a possibility, are investigated by the Department's Special Investigative Unit and, if there is evidence to suggest that any of these acts have been committed, the RCMP is informed. The Special Investigation Unit also maintains a Police and Security Liaison Programme under which it combines information obtained from the RCMP and other police forces with information from open sources." See McDonald Commission, 1:87-88.

2   This is based on two accounts, an interview conducted with Harold on February 21, 1994, and his written account from 1960-61 (which we refer to as his text) entitled "A Case History, with Observations 1960-1961," which is in the personal possession of the authors. He identified a Security Agency A and a Security Agency B. In 1994, Harold clarified that Agency A was Naval Intelligence and Agency B was the RCMP. The quotes from Harold in this section, unless otherwise specified, are from Harold's text, 5, 9-13, 15-17, 19, and 23.

3   This is also suggested by Steele and Tomczak in *Legal Memory* (film). Harold is depicted by one of the actors in this film under a different pseudonym.

4   Gibson, *Get Off My Ship*, 358-59.

5   See Axel Otto Olson's testimony at a private session of the Royal Commission on the Criminal Law Relating to Criminal Sexual Psychopaths, Montreal and Toronto, commencing February 6, 1956. See Report of Private Session, Osgoode Hall, Toronto, February 13, 1956, 137-47. Also see Olson, "1956: The Royal Commission on the Criminal Law Relating to Criminal Sexual Psychopaths," 8-9.

6   George Chauncey argues that the relations of the closet were actively constructed in response to the emergence of open same-gender erotic cultures. See Chauncey, *Gay New York*.

7   These are far more than just cultural phenomena. Eve Sedgwick suggests this in her *Epistemology of the Closet*. The distinction between living in the closet and living a double life is limited but significant. See Chauncey, *Gay New York*, 375n9.

8   In the 1950s and 1960s in the United States, Canada, and western Europe, the homophile movement consisted of people who argued for more tolerance and understanding for homosexuals. Homophile groups were mostly composed of homosexuals.

9   This 1989 account comes from the preliminary research interviews conducted for Fernie and Weissman's film *Forbidden Love*. We thank Lynne Fernie and Aerlyn Weissman for their permission to use this account here.

10 See Wolfenden Report. On the Wolfenden Report and its impact in Canada, see Kinsman, *The Regulation of Desire*, 212-87, "The Textual Practices of Sexual Rule," 87-92, and "Wolfenden in Canada."

11 See Kinsman, *The Regulation of Desire*, "Official Discourse as Sexual Regulation," and "Wolfenden in Canada."

12 There may have been a more general problem with pensions for people discharged from the military. Sutcliffe did get an honourable discharge and still experienced threats and problems when he attempted to receive his pension. A military official said to him: "All I can say is that we will not give you your pension money back, we will keep it. And in time to come you will get your pension" (March 1, 1996).

13 In his autobiography, Sutcliffe also suggests that he was told by the director of military intelligence: "You have been fingered by an Ottawa youth who visited your apartment some time ago," Sutcliffe,

Herbert Frederick Sutcliffe, 157. For more on Sutcliffe, see "Addendum: Will the Real Herbert Frederick Sutcliffe, MBE, CD, Please Stand Up (or Come Out of the Closet and Be Frank)" located at the CLGA.

14   Sutcliffe, *Herbert Frederick Sutcliffe,* 157-58.

15   This account comes from the preliminary research interviews conducted for Fernie and Weissman's *Forbidden Love* (film). All the quotes from Yvette are from these interviews.

16   See Leznoff, "The Homosexual in Urban Society."

17   The CCRH was a mid-1960s homophile group in Ottawa that tried to develop more understanding and tolerance of homosexuality within the churches. See Kinsman, *The Regulation of Desire,* 238-39.

18   See Johnson's "Homosexual Citizens" and *The Lavender Scare.*

19   See Mackenzie, "Purged ... from Memory," 384. Information has also been drawn from an August 12, 1999, letter to Gary Kinsman from Mackenzie and from a September 26, 1999, interview. See also Robinson and Kimmel, "The Queer Career of Homosexual Security Vetting," 335.

20   August 12, 1999, letter to Gary Kinsman from Mackenzie and a September 26, 1999, interview. See also Mackenzie, "Purged ... from Memory."

21   Department of External Affairs (DEA), AIR A-2321, G.F. Frazer, "The 28th Meeting of the Security Sub-Panel," July 8, 1958, 3.

22   Sawatsky, *For Services Rendered,* 173.

23   Bill Crean held this position before Starnes, who was followed by Hamilton Southam. See Starnes, *Closely Guarded,* 91.

24   Ibid., 93.

25   Ibid., and 106.

26   CSIS, AIR 91-088, D.F. Wall, "Minutes of the 68th Meeting of the Security Panel," October 6, 1959, 5.

27   Starnes, *Closely Guarded,* 92.

28   For some of his rather non-traditional views on the origins of the Cold War, see Holmes, "Moscow 1947-1948." See also Holmes, *The Shaping of Peace;* and Mackenzie, "Purged ... from Memory," 376. For more on John Holmes, see Chapnick, *Canada's Voice.*

29   In Dean Beeby, "RCMP Was Ordered to Identify Gays," *Globe and Mail,* April 25, 1992. Beeby remembers hearing the rumour that Holmes was gay when he (Beeby) was a graduate student at the University of Toronto in the early 1980s.

30   Starnes, *Closely Guarded,* 53.

31   Ibid., 54.

32   Ibid., 70.

33   Goreham, "The Fruit Machine: Homosexual Victimization."

34   On this general context, see Kinsman, *The Regulation of Desire,* 257-64. See also *History's Courtroom: The Bedrooms of the Nation* (documentary) on the George Everett Klippert case.

35   Blair Fraser, "How We Check on Loyalty," *Maclean's,* January 15, 1952, 5, 44.

36   DEA, AIR A-2321, G.F. Frazer, "The 28th Meeting of the Security Sub-Panel," July 8, 1958, 3.

37   PCO, AIR 853057, memorandum for the Security Panel: "Security in Canadian Defence Industry," with a cover letter from Don Wall, August 27, 1964. The "Security in Canadian Defence Industry" was also mentioned in PCO, AIR 853057, D.F. Wall to Mr. Robertson, memorandum for Mr. Robertson, June 3, 1964.

38   On ASK, see Kinsman, *The Regulation of Desire,* 230-48.

39   LAC, Don Wall, interviewed by Donald Brittain, sound recording, ISN 61917, CO9276(2), C9277, October 23, 1980.

40   For other journalistic accounts, see S. Katz, "RCMP," 13-15, 32-41; and Sawatsky, *Men in the Shadows.*

41   S. Katz, "RCMP," 13. Katz also wrote relatively liberal articles on homosexuals in Toronto. See Katz, "The Homosexual Next Door," 10-11, 28-30, and "The Harsh Facts of Life in the 'Gay' World," 18, 34-38. On these, see Kinsman, *The Regulation of Desire,* 251-52.

42   S. Katz, "RCMP," 32.

43   Ibid., 38.

44   Hewitt, *Spying 101*, 23.
45   Ibid., 23-24. "By the mid 1970s branches were often called 'Ops' or Operations ... In 'D' Branch there were desks for labour, Trotskyism ('Trots'), Maoism, the New Left and 'alternative societies.'" See ibid., 37. Institutions also had their own designation codes. Hewitt reports that the University of Waterloo was D-909-3-E-5. F Branch looked after files, and K Branch, in which Don Wall had served, was the research branch. L Branch was created in the early 1970s to deal with informants and to centralize control of the recruitment and handling of "sources." See ibid., 35.
46   Ibid., 29.
47   Sawatsky, *Men in the Shadows*, 125-26.
48   CSIS, AIR 91-088, I Directorate Annual Report, 1959-60, Report of the Directorate, Appendix G, "Appendix to Annual Report on Homosexuality among Federal Government Employees," 42-45; Sawatsky, *Men in the Shadows*, 125-27.
49   See Sawatsky, *Men in the Shadows*, 127-28. See also CSIS, AIR 91-088, Directorate of Security and Intelligence, Annual Report, 1963-64, 31.
50   Sawatsky, *Men in the Shadows*, 126n2. Regarding a shift from "top secret" to "secret" in communication regarding the "current investigation to identify homosexuals employed in and by the Federal Government" and classification of "D939-7-GEN" files, see J.R.W. Bordeleau, Chief Superintendent, DSI, "Re: Security Screening of Government Employees – Character Weaknesses," February 22, 1962. This document is in the possession of the authors.
51   Hewitt, *Spying 101*, 36.
52   On this, see Donner, *Protectors of Privilege*, 3.
53   In Dean Beeby, "RCMP Was Ordered to Identify Gays," *Globe and Mail*, April 25, 1992.
54   On police use and development of photography, see McCoy, "Activating the Photographic Text."
55   But see also Hewitt, *Spying 101*, 192n4: "For the sake of simplicity, Security Service will be used throughout this article, as will the term *source*, since this word, as opposed to 'informer' or 'informant,' was the one used by the Mounted Police." In our view, "source" has a more neutral ring to it, and "informant" more clearly captures the power/knowledge relations involved in RCMP surveillance work.
56   CSIS, AIR 92-008, J.M. Bella, Director of Security and Intelligence, memo to the Commissioner, "Homosexuality within the Federal Government Service," April 29, 1960, 6.

CHAPTER 5: THE FRUIT MACHINE

1   CSIS, AIR 91-088, F.R. Wake, "Report on Special Project," December 19, 1962.
2   Hannant, *The Infernal Machine*.
3   Ibid., 41-61.
4   Sawatsky, *Men in the Shadows*, 133.
5   Ibid., 133-36. Sawatsky mentions one particular RCMP officer "who coined it the fruit machine."
6   Wake, "Report on Special Project."
7   CSIS, AIR 92-008, Carl Betke and S.W. Horrall, "From Royal Commission on Espionage to Royal Commission on Security, 1946-1966," 1978.
8   CSIS, AIR 92-008, J.M. Bella, Director of Security and Intelligence, Memo to the Commissioner, "Homosexuality within the Federal Government Service," April 29, 1960, 6. Note the RCMP use here of the criminalization of homosexual sexual practices.
9   CSIS, AIR 91-088, C.W. Harvison, RCMP Commissioner, "Re: Meeting to Consider Reports of Mr. Don Wall and Dr. F.R. Wake on the Problem of Character Weaknesses in the Government Services," Directorate of Security and Intelligence, March 4, 1963. Appendix A, "A Summary of the Salient Points in 'United States Security Procedures': A Report by the Secretary of the Security Panel," 1-5, is attached to the document cited at the beginning of this note.
10   CSIS, AIR 91-088, W.H. Kelly, Assistant, Directorate of Security and Intelligence, "Top Secret," June 8, 1961.

11 LAC, Don Wall, interviewed by Donald Brittain, sound recording, ISN 61917, CO9276(2), C9277, October 23, 1980.

12 All information regarding Wake's personal and professional life was taken from documents obtained from University Archives, Carleton University. We thank university archivist Patti Harper for her assistance in locating these documents.

13 See Canada, *Report of the Royal Commission on the Criminal Law Relating to Criminal Sexual Psychopaths;* and Kinsman, "Official Discourse as Sexual Regulation," 99-298, and *The Regulation of Desire,* 183-92.

14 Archives of Ontario (AO), Mental Health Division, RG 29, vol. 305, file 435-3-5, part 1, Mental Health – Ont., 1949-58. We thank Elise Chenier for this reference.

15 CSIS, AIR 91-088, R.B. Bryce, "Letter to Commissioner C.W. Harvison," December 20, 1960, 1. In the same text, in addition to Wake, Bryce mentions that Cameron recommended other local medical experts whose names were blacked out by CSIS for our reading pleasure. One of these was a psychiatric advisor to the Department of Veteran Affairs; the other was a psychiatrist with a private practice in Ottawa. He also recommended Dr. R.G. Ratz, director of the Medical Advisory Services in the Department of National Health and Welfare, for a "public service point of view."

16 On psychological knowledge as a crucial part of social administration, see Rose, *The Psychological Complex.*

17 See documents from University Archives, Carleton University, on Wake and the Carleton psychology department.

18 E. Herman, "The Career of Cold War Psychology," 54.

19 Ibid.

20 Some of his presentations and publications include Wake, "Normal Aggression and Delinquency" (speech and article by the same name); Wake, Beattie, and King, "Physical Cruelty in Male Juvenile Delinquents" and "A Comparison of Physical Cruelty in Rural and Urban Delinquent Boys"; and Beattie and Wake, "Suggestibility in Delinquents" and "Physical Cruelty." Elise Chenier has a commentary on the context of "Normal Aggression and Delinquency" in "Stranger in Our Midst" and *Strangers in Our Midst.*

21 Robinson and Kimmel report that "a Search of *Psychological Abstracts* (1950-70) reveals that his published research was mainly concerned with juvenile delinquency and physical cruelty." See Robinson and Kimmel, "The Queer Career of Homosexual Security Vetting," 339n57.

22 From discussions with some members of the Carleton psychology department in 1994-95.

23 Neville Hamilton, "Teenage Church Course Answers Questions That Can't Be Asked; They're Lifting the Curtain on Sex Secrecy," *Ottawa Journal,* February 5, 1965, 1, 21. This quote is from page 21.

24 CSIS, AIR 92-088, F.R. Wake, Memorandum for D.F. Wall, "Security Risks – Homosexual," 1961-62.

25 CSIS, AIR 91-088, Dr. F.R. Wake, "Report on Special Project," December 19, 1962.

26 Jennifer Terry, personal correspondence to Gary Kinsman, July 9, 1996.

27 CSIS, AIR 91-088, Dr. F.R. Wake, "Report on Special Project," December 19, 1962, 18.

28 On psychology as part of social administration and on psychological testing, see Rose, *The Psychological Complex.* On psychological testing in Canada, see Kinsman, *The Regulation of Desire,* 160-61. See also Brown, "Security by Exclusion."

29 See contributions in Amrine, "The 1965 Congressional Inquiry into Testing."

30 See Terry, "Anxious Slippages between 'Us' and 'Them'"; "Theorizing Deviant Historiography"; and *An American Obsession.*

31 See Kinsman, "Queerness Is Not in Our Genes," especially 267-68, 271-74.

32 On the CCRH, see Kinsman, *The Regulation of Desire,* 238-39.

33 Regarding the Palmer sweat test, Dean Beeby points out that Wake referenced R.A. McCleary, who, in 1953, had measured changes in hand sweat by using crystals that changed colour with greater amounts of moisture. See Beeby, "RCMP Hoped 'Fruit Machine' Would Identify Homosexuals," *Globe and Mail,* April 24, 1992, A2. See also R.A. McCleary, "Palmer Sweat as an Index of Anxiety," *School of Aviation*

Medicine, Project No. 21, 1207-0004, Report No. 1, October 1953. McCleary's project is listed in Dr. Wake's bibliography, attached to his "Report on Special Project." The span of attention test was constructed to test for homosexuality in 1956 by clinical psychologist Harold S. Zamansky of Northeastern University.

34 CSIS, AIR 91-088, Dr. F.R. Wake, "Report on Special Project," December 19, 1962. Wake included three sets of M/F tests in the report. The first set included forty-eight statements, the second set thirty-eight statements, and the third set sixty statements.

35 Ibid., 14.

36 Ibid., Appendix A, "Word Association List," 1-3.

37 Many, but not all, of these words appear in Rodgers, *Gay Talk* (previously published as *The Queen's Vernacular*).

38 Wake used the phrase "neutral words."

39 CSIS, AIR 91-088, Dr. F.R. Wake, "Report on Special Project," December 19, 1962, 12.

40 On their work, see Hess and Polt, "Pupil Size as Related to Interest Value of Visual Stimuli."

41 See ibid. and Hess and Polt, "Pupil Size in Relation to Mental Activity during Simple Problem Solving." Their research was supported by a grant from the Social Sciences Research Committee of the University of Chicago and by Interpublic, New York. See Chenier, "Stranger in Our Midst," 9, and *Strangers in Our Midst*.

42 We are very grateful to Dean Beeby for allowing us access to the interviews he conducted with Wake on April 22 and 23, 1992.

43 CSIS, AIR 91-088, Dr. F.R. Wake, "Report on Special Project," December 19, 1962, 12. Clearly, there are no neutral value-free pictures.

44 On physique photos that ostensibly focus on the non-erotic beauty of the male body and how they came to be used and elaborated upon by gay men, see Waugh, "A Heritage of Pornography"; "Photography, Passion and Power"; and "Gay Male Visual Culture in North America during the Fifties." See also Waugh, *Hard to Imagine*, 176-283; and Miller, "Beefcake with No Labels Attached," 33.

45 CSIS, AIR 91-088, Dr. F.R. Wake, "Report on Special Project," December 19, 1962, 12 (emphasis in original).

46 Ibid., 12-13.

47 Hess, Seltzer, and Shlien, "Pupil Response of Hetero- and Homosexual Males to Pictures of Men and Women" (unpublished article).

48 Here, Hess and Polt refer to their article in *Science* 1960, but see also Hess, Seltzer, and Shlien, "Pupil Response of Hetero- and Homosexual Males," 1. We thank Elise Chenier for bringing this reference to our attention.

49 These quotes are all from Hess, Seltzer, and Shlien, "Pupil Response of Hetero- and Homosexual Males," 1-2.

50 Ibid., 2. Notice the use here of "overt homosexuals" as distinct from "covert homosexuals." This distinction was developed by Maurice Leznoff and drew on class divisions, which were related to how out these gay networks were. See Kinsman, *The Regulation of Desire*, 161-65; and Leznoff, "The Homosexual in Urban Society."

51 Hess, Seltzer, and Shlien, "Pupil Response of Hetero- and Homosexual Males." Notice the difference in language here from that used in Wake's report. It is an amalgamation of the Kinsey Report's notion of "sexual outlet" (on this term, see Kinsman, *The Regulation of Desire*, 158-60) and the conceptualization of heterosexual that was then emerging in response to the demarcation of a homosexual sexual orientation. On this emergence, see J. Katz, *The Invention of Heterosexuality*.

52 Hess, Seltzer, and Shlien, "Pupil Response of Hetero- and Homosexual Males," 1-2.

53 Ibid., 4-5.

54 Ibid., 5.

55 Ibid., 5-6.

56 Ibid., 7.

57 CSIS, AIR 91-088, Dr. F.R. Wake, "Report on Special Project," December 19, 1962, 17.
58 See J. Katz, *The Invention of Heterosexuality*, 83-166.
59 CSIS, AIR 91-088, Dr. F.R. Wake, "Report on Special Project," December 19, 1962, 17.
60 Ibid.; PCO, AIR 9293070, D.F. Wall, Minutes, "A Meeting of Special Group of the Security Panel Held in the Office of the Minister of Justice," February 28, 1963, and Robinson and Kimmel, "The Queer Career of Homosexual Security Vetting," 341.
61 This was an American journal dedicated to the study of psychophysiology, the branch of psychology concerned with the physiological bases of psychological processes. See Lawless and Wake, "Sex Differences in Pupillary Response to Visual Stimuli," 568. We thank Elise Chenier for this reference.
62 Ibid.
63 Ibid.
64 Ibid.
65 Brian Drader's play *The Fruit Machine: A Play on Gay History* has been performed in Toronto, Winnipeg, and Vancouver. It combines the history of the security campaigns against gay men and the fruit machine research, with a story about coming out. See also a short film by Wrik Mead entitled *Fruit Machine* and the sections from it that were used in Nancy Nicol's *Stand Together* (film).
66 In his study, Sawatsky reports that recruits for the "normal" control group were told that this "was an experiment to measure stress." See Sawatsky, *Men in the Shadows*, 136.
67 CSIS, AIR 91-088, Dr. F.R. Wake, "Report on Special Project," December 19, 1962. These are listed in Appendix C, which deals with masculinity/femininity tests. Some of them are included in Drader's *The Fruit Machine*. Included in Appendix C is one entitled "Northern California No. B4567." These statements are much more specific, and the research subject is asked to respond "strongly agree," "agree," "not sure," "disagree," or "strongly disagree" to each of them; all revolve around fighting and arguments. They include the following: "A boxing or wrestling match is more exciting when it's a real grudge fight, and the fighters are really mad at each other"; "It is perfectly natural for boys to want to fight sometimes"; and "Sometimes an actual fight is the only way to settle an argument." Brian Drader, interviewed by Gary Kinsman, Vancouver, British Columbia, January 16, 1998.
68 CSIS, AIR 91-088, J. Bordeleau, Assistant Commissioner, Director, Security and Intelligence, RCMP, to D.F. Wall, January 25, 1963, 1.
69 Sawatsky, *Men in the Shadows*, 133.
70 CSIS, AIR 91-088, Dr. F.R. Wake, "Report on Special Project," December 19, 1962, 17.
71 Interviews with F.R. Wake by Dean Beeby, April 22, 1992, and April 23, 1992.
72 Dean Beeby, "Mounties Staged Massive Hunt for Gay Males in Civil Service," *Globe and Mail*, April 24, 1992, A2. This is based on CSIS, AIR 91-088, Directorate of Security and Intelligence Annual Report, 1964-65.
73 CSIS, AIR 91-088, Directorate of Security and Intelligence Annual Report, 1965-66, 33.
74 CSIS, AIR 91-088, Directorate of Security and Intelligence Annual Report, 1966-67, 27.
75 Sawatsky, *Men in the Shadows*, 136.
76 Brett, *Cold Dark Matter*. See also the review by Mike Gillespie, "Mind over Matter," *Ottawa Citizen*, February 20, 2005, C12.
77 Los Angeles, Model E-AR-400, CWM 1990189-001. The technology measures muscular reactions. Supposedly, an upsurge on the dial occurs when the question asked is painful or causes stress. The technology was linked to measuring the amount of sweat produced in response to particular questions. It is in this area that there are some connections with aspects of the fruit machine research. See "E-Meter," *Wikipedia*, http://en.wikipedia.org/wiki/E-meter.
78 Ibid.
79 Richard Burnett, "Bugs for PM: Three Dollar Bill," *Montreal Hour*, March 30, 2006. The catalogue at the War Museum's archives suggests that this object is "an early example of a lie-detector kit. Used by Canadian security officers to aid in determining the sexual orientation of people, fearing the leaking of secrets through blackmail." Information regarding the donor is restricted.

1   Canadian Security Intelligence Service (CSIS), Access to Information Request (AIR) 91-088, Director-ate of Security and Intelligence Annual Report, 1962-63, 19.

2   Ibid., 30.

3   On camp cultural formation, see Kinsman, *The Regulation of Desire,* 226-27.

4   See Kinsman, "National Security as Moral Regulation."

5   Here, we are making connections with the social historical work of E.P. Thompson on "history from below." See Thompson, *The Making of the English Working Class.* Although this work needs to address race, gender, sexuality, and other oppressions, we suggest that there is much that is productive in using this approach to make sense of the contested relations of morality and ethics. See Chapter 2 on our use of Thompson's work. See also Weeks, *Sexuality and Its Discontents* and *Invented Moralities.* Although this work is very insightful, links to class and class struggle are needed. Mariana Valverde pinpoints distinctions between morality and ethics in a commentary on the feminist sex debates of the early 1980s: "While the term 'morality' suggests both rigidity and individualism, the term 'ethics' is more suited to the kind of approach that feminists need. Ethics connotes reasoning about values and actions; it connotes discussion and community. Ethics also suggests the development of guidelines, and not so much the drawing up of a rigid code that would substitute for the process of reasoning and discus-sion." See Valverde, *Sex, Power, and Pleasure,* 203-4.

6   Based on Gary's discussion with Peaches Latour, August 31, 1994. Prostitutes also frequented the Chez Henri. On Peaches Latour, see Marchand, "A Peach of a Gal among Roses and Thorns: Peaches Latour Recounts Joys and Sorrows of Drag," *Capital Xtra!* Pride Guide, July 1999, 8.

7   Blaine Marchand interviewed Norman Dahl and George Wilkes. See Marchand, "Memory Lane: Gatineau River Summers Were a Gay Experience," *Capital Xtra!* August 22, 1997, 29.

8   Literature on gay and queer space is growing. See, among others, Bell and Valentine, eds., *Mapping Desire;* and Ingram, Bouthillette, and Retter, eds., *Queers in Space.*

9   On the purging of "communist" unions from the official labour movement in the 1950s and 1960s, see the experience of Mine Mill, explored in Steedman, Suschnigg, and Buse, *Hard Lessons.*

10   On the postal workers, see Bruno, "Not the Same Old Place"; and Hunt, "No Longer Outsiders."

11   PCO, AIR 853057, "Minutes of the 76th Meeting of the Security Panel Held in the Privy Council Committee Room, East Block, September 23, 1964," completed on October 27, 1964, 3-4.

12   PCO, AIR 885078, Memorandum for the Security Panel, "Hearings in Relation to Dismissals on Secur-ity Grounds," November 29, 1967, 6.

13   PCO, AIR 907106, G.F Frazer, Acting Secretary, "Minutes of the 80th Meeting of the Security Panel, December 8, 1967," December 20, 1967.

14   CSIS, AIR 91-088, Directorate of Security and Intelligence Annual Report, 1963-64.

15   Hewitt, *Spying 101,* 107.

16   DEA, AIR A-2321, "The 28th Meeting of the Security Sub-Panel: Security Cases Involving Character Weaknesses," July 8, 1958, 4.

17   See Fadel, "Homosexual Offences in Ottawa." His study is based on police and court records. Fadel examines cases only in which there was clear consent (meaning he does not look at indecent assault charges) and that did not involve younger people. The offence of gross indecency was central to the long history of the criminalization of homosexual sex in Canada; it applied to oral sex and was abol-ished in 1988.

18   Ibid., 65-66, 68.

19   Ibid., 82-83.

20   On dangerous sexual offenders, see Kinsman, *The Regulation of Desire,* especially 183-92, 257-64. See also Chapter 3 in this book.

21   See also Grube, "Queens and Flaming Virgins."

22 Personal communication to Gary Kinsman from Elise Chenier, May 6, 1995. On the Continental, see Chenier, "Rethinking Class in Lesbian Bar Culture."

23 See Kennedy and Davis, *Boots of Leather, Slippers of Gold;* Nestle, "Butch-Femme Relationships," and more generally her *A Restricted Country;* Weissman and Fernie, *Forbidden Love* (film); and B. Ross, "Destaining the (Tattooed) Delinquent Body."

24 For a more detailed analysis of this law reform process, see Kinsman, *The Regulation of Desire,* 213-78, and "Wolfenden in Canada."

25 Wolfenden Report, 89.

26 Davies, "Sexual Taboos and Social Boundaries," 1051.

27 Crane, *Gays and the Law,* 187.

28 In the mid-1960s, Vancouver postal clerk George Victor Spencer was discovered collecting information for the USSR. The Conservative opposition attacked the Pearson government for mishandling the case, creating pressure for an official commission to investigate security matters. McDonald Commission, 2:784.

29 Ibid.

30 Mackenzie Commission, 36, s. 100.

31 Ibid.

32 See Kinsman, *The Regulation of Desire,* 246-47; and Doug Sanders, Association for Social Knowledge, "Submission to the Royal Commission on Security," February 29, 1968 (in the possession of the authors). The following quotes are all from this text.

33 On Hooker's work, see D'Emilio, *Sexual Politics, Sexual Communities,* 141; and Kinsman, *The Regulation of Desire,* 178, 247.

34 Sanders, "Submission to the Royal Commission on Security," 2.

35 Sanders, quoted in Kinsman, *The Regulation of Desire,* 264.

CHAPTER 7: THE CAMPAIGN CONTINUES IN THE 1970S

1 Kinsman, *The Regulation of Desire,* 213-87.

2 Ibid., 182-83, 358-60.

3 Ibid., 288-93.

4 Ibid.; and B. Ross, *The House That Jill Built,* 3-56.

5 D'Emilio, *Sexual Politics, Sexual Communities,* 223-39.

6 See Kinsman, "Gays and Lesbians: Pushing the Boundaries," especially 221-39, and *The Regulation of Desire,* 212-409; Sears, "Queer Times?"; and Alan Sears, "The Opening and Commodification of Gay Space: Queer in a Lean World," *Against the Current* 89 (November-December 2000), http://www.solidarity-us.org/node/965.

7 Trudeau stated this in response to questions on security asked earlier by Erik Nielsen (Progressive Conservative, Yukon). See "Homosexuals Unstable, Kept from Secrets: PM," *Toronto Star,* July 12, 1973, 77; and McLeod, *Lesbian and Gay Liberation in Canada,* 131.

8 Pierre Elliott Trudeau, letter to the editor, *GO INFO,* June 1980, 10-11. Dated 4 February 1978, the letter suggests that, in this area, the Canadian state would enforce anti-homosexual laws of other countries.

9 On this, see Gilmartin, "We Weren't Bar People"; Chamberland, "Remembering Lesbian Bars"; Davis, *Boots of Leather;* and Chenier, "Tough Ladies and Troublemakers."

10 *Body Politic,* "Threatened with Expulsion from Military," 1.

11 Ibid.

12 Wheeler, "Unfit for Service," 30.

13 Ibid., 32.

14 Hannon, " ... Deemed Necessary to Discriminate ...," 19.

15   This reference is drawn from a letter from Tom Siddon, minister of national defence, to A. Simon Korman, spokesperson for Gay and Lesbian Organization of Veterans (GLOV), dated September 24, 1993, appended to "Brief: Gay and Lesbian Organization of Veterans," written by Tim Reid, president of GLOV, about 1995. In the possession of the authors.

16   Ibid.

17   *Body Politic,* "Threatened with Expulsion from Military," 1.

18   Ibid.

19   See "Homosexuality – Sexual Abnormality Investigation, Medical Examination and Disposal," Canadian Forces Administrative Order 19-20, 1976. The document may be obtained by consulting Canada, Department of National Defence, *Charter Task Force: Final Report,* vol. 2, *Annexes to Charter Task Force: Final Report,* specifically Part 4, "Sexual Orientation."

20   Wheeler, "Unfit for Service," 29.

21   Enloe, *Does Khaki Become You?* 143.

22   Our account of Cameron's purge from the military is based on an interview conducted by Gerald Hannon and published in the *Body Politic.* See Hannon, " ... Deemed Necessary to Discriminate ...," 10, 19.

23   On the use of lie-detector tests, see Bunn, "Euphoric Security."

24   The story broke on the front page of the *Kitchener-Waterloo Record* in May during a visit with her parents. The story also ran in the *Globe and Mail.*

25   Hannon, " ... Deemed Necessary to Discriminate ...," 10.

26   Ibid., 10, 19.

27   Ibid., 19.

28   Ibid.

29   See the *Body Politic,* "Threatened with Expulsion from Military," 1. On Barbara Thornborrow, see T. Warner, *Never Going Back,* 142-43. Thornborrow is also interviewed in Nicol's *Stand Together* (film).

30   See interview with Barbara Thornborrow in Nicol's *Stand Together* (film).

31   See B. Freeman's interview with Barbara Thornborrow, "Private Goes Public," 13. Much of our account of Thornborrow's experience is based on this interview and the *Body Politic*'s article, "Threatened with Expulsion from Military," 1.

32   See B. Freeman "Private Goes Public," 13.

33   Ibid.

34   Thornborrow, in Nicol's *Stand Together* (film).

35   See B. Freeman "Private Goes Public," 13.

36   Ibid.

37   See the *Body Politic,* "Canadian Human Rights Act," 1.

38   See also T. Warner, *Never Going Back,* 142-43, 144-45 (on John Damien), and 145-46 (on Doug Wilson).

39   See the *Body Politic,* "Threatened with Expulsion from Military," 1.

40   See B. Freeman, "Private Goes Public," 13.

41   "Military's Sexual Policy 'Stupidity,' Lesbian Says," *Globe and Mail,* March 1, 1985, 5.

42   Darl Wood, "Interrogation: Trapped and Alone," quoted in Wheeler, "Unfit for Service," 32.

43   Ibid.

44   His account is from the 1995 GLOV document entitled "Brief of the Gay and Lesbian Organization of Veterans, Policy of the Day," in the possession of the authors. The rest of the quotes regarding Reid's experiences come from this source.

45   Also appended to the Gays of Ottawa brief "Cleaning Up the Acts: Selected Equality Issues Affecting the Gay and Lesbian Minority – A Brief to the House of Commons Sub-Committee on Equality Rights from Gays of Ottawa, July 16, 1985," are letters from National Defence on reasons for purging gay and lesbian personnel. In the possession of the authors. See the letter from R.H. Falls, admiral, to R.G.L. Fairweather, chief commissioner, Canadian Human Rights Commission, "Extracts from a Letter by

Admiral R.H. Falls, Chief of the Defence Staff, to the Canadian Human Rights Commission, July 26, 1979."

46 On the Turret, see T. Warner, *Never Going Back,* 166.

47 Thanks to Robin Metcalfe for this (August 10, 2006).

CHAPTER 8: "GAY POLITICAL ACTIVISTS" AND "RADICAL LESBIANS"

1 See Denis LeBlanc and John Duggan in Nicol's *Stand Together* (film).

2 On the early gay liberation movement in Canada, see T. Warner, *Never Going Back,* 61-95.

3 Although some important aspects of this project are found in this chapter, readers wanting a more comprehensive history of lesbian, gay, and queer activism should look at Tom Warner's *Never Going Back.* This book is a major step forward in the history of queer organizing in Canada. Written by a long-time gay liberation activist who participated in much of what he writes about, the book is a rich resource; however, it is limited by its inability to adequately address class relations and the link between queer oppression and capitalism. See Kinsman, "Never Going Back." Other sources for histories of lesbian and gay activism in the 1970s include B. Ross, *The House That Jill Built*; M. Smith, *Lesbian and Gay Rights in Canada*; Sylvestre, *Les homosexuels s'organisent*; Jackson and Persky, eds., *Flaunting It!*; McLeod, *Lesbian and Gay Liberation in Canada*; and Higgins, *De la clandestinité à l'affirmation.*

4 Library and Archives Canada (LAC), Canadian Security Intelligence Service (CSIS), RG 146, vol. 3050, file "Gay Alliance towards Equality – Toronto," Ottawa "D" Ops to Montreal "D" Ops re: National Gay Rights Coalition (NGRC), June 21, 1976, 240.

5 Hewitt, "Information Believed to Be True," especially 191-228. See also his book *Spying 101.*

6 Rebick reclaims the word "radical" in *Imagine Democracy.*

7 On ATIP, see Badgley, "Researchers and Canada's Public Archives"; and McDonell, "The Experiences of a Researcher in the Maze." We first became aware of the possibility of gaining access to documents pertaining to this surveillance when Hewitt, who was researching the national security campaigns on university campuses across the country, sent Kinsman RCMP reports he had received under Access to Information regarding the Community Homophile Association of Toronto (LAC, RG 146, vol. 3115, file "Community Homophile Association Toronto, Ont.," ATIP Request 98-A-00085). This was supplemented by our own Access to Information requests, which have yielded the release of more than 438 pages (out of 752 possible pages) on surveillance of gay and lesbian groups in the 1970s. This is probably only a small fraction of what exists in the RCMP records now maintained by CSIS. Many have large portions blanked out, suppressing important parts of the RCMP surveillance campaign. We were denied access to the remaining pages due to exemptions for security reasons. We gained access to files on nine groups: LAC, RG 146, vol. 3042, file "Gay Activists Alliance (Vancouver, BC)"; the generic vol. 3049, file "Canadian Gay Liberation Movement"; vol. 3049, file "Gay Liberation Movement – University of Waterloo"; vol. 3121, file "Gays of Ottawa"; vol. 3054, file "University of Western Ontario Homophile Association"; vol. 3050, file "Homosexual Liberation Front, Montreal, Quebec"; vol. 3050, file "Gay Alliance towards Equality – BC"; vol. 3195, file "National Gay Rights Coalition"; and vol. 3050, file "Gay Alliance towards Equality – Toronto." Since there are two groups called Gay Alliance towards Equality (GATE) reported on in these documents, we refer to GATE Vancouver as GATE-V (all references to GATE-V are from RG 146, vol. 3050, file "Gay Alliance towards Equality – BC") and GATE Toronto as GATE-T. We also requested information on a series of other gay and lesbian organizations but received none. In a few cases, we were able to gain access to information on these groups in the files of other gay/lesbian associations. For example, we found some information on the *Body Politic* under GATE-T, information on Toronto Gay Action (TGA) was included under GATE-T (since GATE grew out of TGA), and some information on the Coalition for Gay Rights in Ontario (CGRO) was also included in the GATE-T file. This may be because GATE-T played an important part in initiating CGRO. We did not receive any information for our requests regarding Saskatoon Gay Action, Toronto Gay Youth, Unitarian Universalist Gays, York University Homophile Association, Queen's

University Homophile Association, Trent University Homophile Association, the Homophile Reform Association, the Lesbian Organization of Ottawa Now, the Lesbian Organization of Toronto, the Association for Social Knowledge, and the Canadian Council on Religion and the Homosexual. We were given information only from files that were directly mentioned in the finding aid for RG 146.

8   Hewitt, *Spying 101*, xii.

9   LAC, RG 146, vol. 3049, file "Canadian Gay Liberation Movement"; Kirk Makin and Lorne Slotnick, "After the Raids, Two Years Later, Gay Community Remains Bitter," *Globe and Mail*, February 10, 1983, 35-36.

10 This report on various gay groups appears in the files of a number of the associations to which we were able to gain access as it mentions several different organizations. It is entitled "Re: National Gay Rights Coalition (NGRC) Canada" and is dated June 21, 1976. In most copies, the Introduction is entirely blanked out. In the National Gay Rights Coalition file copy, however, we can make out some of the text, which reads, "This is in reply to Montreal Security Service Request [blanked out] Requiring Information on Gay Activities And Organizational Assessment." See LAC, RG 146, vol. 3195, file "National Gay Rights Coalition, Canada," 23. In the report located in the GATE-T file, the Introduction is entirely blanked out. See LAC, RG 146, vol. 3050, file "GATE-T," 238. The reports include a very interesting formulation: "the following is a brief outline of gay organizations of security service interest." This is preceded by a discussion of the new "gay political activists," implying that only some gay groups are of security service interest.

11 LAC, RG 146, vol. 3049, file "Gay Liberation Movement – University of Waterloo," February 7, 1974, 63.

12 Hewitt, *Spying 101*, 219n3.

13 In the United States, surveillance of the New Left and the Black Panther Party led the FBI into the gay and lesbian movements. In England, surveillance work and conspiracy charges against some members of the London-based Gay Liberation Front (GLF) were premised on associations between some activists in GLF and the Angry Brigade, which was a small left-wing group that engaged in sporadic attacks upon the establishment. See L. Robinson, "When Is a Scene a Conspiracy?" See also L. Robinson, "Three Revolutionary Years" and her book *Gay Men and the Left in Post-War Britain*. On the London GLF, see Power, *No Bath but Plenty of Bubbles*.

14 Hewitt, *Spying 101*, 15.

15 On the mass media, see Fishman, *The Manufacturing of News*; and George Smith, "Media Frames," 279-83. See also George Smith, "Political Activist as Ethnographer," 63-64, on how media accounts have to be deconstructed twice to uncover both the official knowledge upon which they are based and the way this is presented within journalistic discourse.

16 LAC, RG 146, vol. 3050, file "GATE-T," January 18-19, 1975, 249, 250. Articles from the *Old Mole* (249) and *Labour Challenge* (276). Also in 1976, the RCMP report prepared for the Montreal Security Service discussed CGRO, which suggests that the police were monitoring its activities. The report includes the following statement regarding CGRO: "This group was active in the last provincial election quizzing candidates on their position on gay rights. Furthermore, this group organized two demonstrations at Queen's Park. One had 300 and the other had 50 participants. Both were to demand increased gay rights. Significantly, CGRO has the same telephone number as the Gay Alliance towards Equality and so it can be assumed that GATE has controlling interest in the Group" (239). Here, we learn more of how RCMP detective skills operate: RCMP members notice that GATE, a gay political activist group, and CGRO share a phone number, and this leads them to conclude that GATE controls CGRO. At the same time, GATE-T did initiate the conference that led to the formation of CGRO. On CGRO, see T. Warner, *Never Going Back*, 149-52. CGRO later became the Coalition for Lesbian and Gay Rights in Ontario (CLGRO). In 2009, CLGRO folded, after three decades of lesbian and gay rights militancy. See Krishna Rau, "CLGRO to Shut Down after 30 Years of Leadership, Group's Absence Will Leave Huge Gap in Sex-Positive Activism," *Xtra!* (Toronto) January 30, 2009, http://www.xtra.ca/public/National/CLGRO_to_shut_down_after_30_years_of_leadership-6191.aspx.

17 See Hewitt, *Spying 101*, especially 138-41, for more on the Key Sectors program. On the reorganization of the RCMP and reference to the changing role of D Branch or D Ops, see p. 141.

18 LAC, RG 146, vol. 3050, file "GATE-T," "Trends in Unaligned Marxists and Pressure Groups in Toronto," August 18, 1976.

19 Hewitt, *Spying 101*, 119.

20 "Trends in Unaligned Marxists and Pressure Groups in Toronto," August 18, 1976.

21 LAC, RG 146, vol. 3050, file "Homosexual Liberation Front, Montreal, Quebec," Report by the Montreal Security Service on the Comité Québécois contre la guerre en Indochine, 7. The report also details the participation of the Groupe marxiste révolutionnaire in the demonstration, on pp. 6-7. See also RG 146, vol. 3050, file "GATE-T," "Re: International Day of Protest Re: United States Action in Vietnam November 6th, 1971 – Canada," 338. Security surveillance of peace and anti-war activism continued through the 1980s and 1990s and, in new forms, in the twenty-first century. A Canadian Press article stated: "Peace groups across Canada were infiltrated and spied upon for years in the 1980s by the RCMP and later the Canadian Security Intelligence Service, documents obtained under freedom of information legislation show." See Canadian Press, "Mounties Spied on Peaceniks, Left-Wing Organizations Infiltrated by RCMP, CSIS," *Halifax Herald*, July 30, 2000. This surveillance continued in the 1990s, directed at the global justice movement. See David Pugliese and Jim Bronskill, "Criminalizing Dissent, Keeping the Public in Check," *Ottawa Citizen*, August 18, 2001, A1, A5.

22 See D'Emilio, *Sexual Politics, Sexual Communities*, 223-39.

23 Justice Minister John Turner delivered this report to Cabinet in April 1971. Jerry Rubin and Abbie Hoffman founded the Youth International Party in the United States, and a group was set up in Vancouver. It attempted to link counter-cultural hippies with more political aspects of New Left, anti-war, and youth organizing, also known as Yippies. The Vancouver Liberation Front, similar to the Yippies, attempted to link the local hippie scene with New Left political organizing. The Communist Party of Canada (Marxist-Leninist) was the main Maoist group across the Canadian state at this time. Its main leader was Hardial Bains. Larger Maoist groups, like En Lutte (In Struggle) and the Workers Communist Party, emerged in Quebec later in the 1970s.

24 Peter O'Neil, Yvonne Zacharias, and Frances Bula, "Former Premier, Mayor Assassins' Targets: W.A.C. Bennett, Campbell Named in RCMP Report," *Vancouver Sun*, June 19, 2002.

25 Tom Sandborn, "Tales of a Paranoid State: Cabinet Documents Label Gay Activists Dangerous," *Xtra! West*, June 27, 2002, 15.

26 The statement that they received little support undermines the significance of their involvement. See LAC, RG 146, vol. 3050, file, "GATE-V," report prepared for D Branch regarding "protests and demonstrations against the Prime Minister and Canadian Government – federal elections," September 26, 1972.

27 LAC, RG 146, vol. 3115, file "Community Homophile Association Toronto, Ont.," O Division, Toronto, August 7, 1973, "Re: Composite Report on the University of Toronto (U of T), Toronto, Ontario (Key Sectors Education)," 5-7.

28 Hewitt, *Spying 101*, 180-81.

29 Ibid., 189, which references 269n45.

30 See Pender, "The Gaze on Clubs, Native Studies, and Teachers at Laurentian University, 1960s-70s," 111-13. Pender's research is based on his "Mounties on Campus." References to the surveillance of Native studies at Laurentian are based on the following document: LAC, RG 146, vol. 3199, file 95-A-00094, 284-92. With regard to the focus on AIM and its connections from 1969 on, see LAC, RG 146, vol. 94, file 94-A-00057, "Red Power-Canada," February 26, 1969.

31 LAC, RG 146, vol. 3050, file "GATE-V," 63-66. Rosie Douglas, then prime minister of Dominica, died in 2000. To his last days, he refused to criticize the student protest at Sir George Williams University, which he viewed as a justified protest against racist discrimination.

32 Among others, see Palmer, *Canada's 1960s*, 284-86.

33 Hewitt, *Spying 101*, 151.

34 According to Don McLeod, the Trent Homophile Association emerged out of a lesbian group known as the Women in September 1976. McLeod, *Lesbian and Gay Liberation in Canada*, 240.

35 For instance, there is a report on a rally at the University of Waterloo, October 8, 1975, regarding the Green Paper on immigration. See LAC, RG 146, vol. 3049, file "Gay Liberation Movement – University of Waterloo," 61. With regard to this question, there appears to have been more general surveillance of gay groups across the country as there is also a report on a Gays of Ottawa protest, which was to be held in 1974 in front of the office of Manpower and Immigration in Ottawa: "This Group is demanding that they be allowed to meet with the Minister of Immigration officials. [blanked out] advised that he would like the Ottawa City Police advised of this forthcoming demonstration." See LAC, RG 146, vol. 3121, file "Gays of Ottawa," dated June 11, 1974, 38. See also McLeod, *Lesbian and Gay Liberation*, 247; T. Warner, *Never Going Back*, 142; and Kyper, "'A Member of the Prohibited Class of Persons.'"

36 LAC, RG 146, vol. 3195, "Re: National Gay Rights Coalition (NGRC)," June 21, 1976.

37 LAC, RG 146, vol. 3050, "GATE-V," June 12, 1973.

38 On Trotsky, see E. Mandel, *Trotsky as Alternative*; and Trotsky's *The Revolution Betrayed* and *History of the Russian Revolution*.

39 See Trotsky, *The Revolution Betrayed*.

40 On the Cuban Revolution and gays and lesbians, see A. Young, *Gays under the Cuban Revolution*; Arguelles and Rich, "Homosexuality, Homophobia and Revolution"; and Lumsden, *Machos, Maricones, and Gays*. For more recent developments, see Michael Voss, "Castro Champions Gay Rights in Cuba," BBC News, Havana, March 27, 2008, http://news.bbc.co.uk/2/hi/americas/7314845.stm.

41 LAC, RG 146, vol. 3050, file "GATE-T," "Re: National Gay Rights Coalition (NGRC)," 238.

42 See Carroll, ed., *Organizing Dissent*; Weir, "Social Movement Activism in the Formation of Ontario New Democratic Party Policy on Abortion, 1982-1984"; and Frampton et al., eds., *Sociology for Changing the World*.

43 LAC, RG 146, vol. 3050, file "GATE-T," "Re: National Gay Rights Coalition (NGRC)," 240.

44 LAC, RG 146, vol. 3050, file "GATE-T," excerpts from "The Gay Movement in Canada," *LSA/LSO Discussion Bulletin*, Toronto, June 1972, 263-64. On TGA, see also T. Warner, *Never Going Back*, 67.

45 LAC, RG 146, vol. 3050, file "GATE-T," John Wilson, "Marchers Demand Full Rights for Gays," *Labour Challenge*, September 13, 1971, 340.

46 Ibid. The use of the clenched fist salute also points to a clear relation to the Black Power movement, the New Left, and to other social movements.

47 Canadian Gay and Lesbian Archives (CGLA), Community Homophile Association of Toronto (CHAT) file, Toronto, n.d. (emphasis in original).

48 LAC, RG 146, vol. 3115, file "Community Homophile Association Toronto, Ont.," RCMP surveillance report on the Ottawa demonstration, "Protests and Demonstrations Ottawa, Ontario." This slogan was also used in the first issue of the *Body Politic: Gay Liberation Newspaper*, November-December 1971, found in LAC, RG 146, vol. 3050, file "GATE-T," 312.

49 Wilson, "Marchers Demand Full Rights For Gays," 340.

50 See the August 28th Gay Day Committee, "We Demand." This document is in the possession of the authors. An edited version is included in Jackson and Persky, *Flaunting It!* 217-20.

51 Ibid.

52 CLGA, file, "A Draft of a Brief to Be Sent to the Federal Government," June 16, 1971 (revised). The specific formulations and the order of the demands differ in this earlier version. The reference in this version to the 1969 *Report of the Royal Commission on Security* states: "[This report] recommends denial of promotion and dismissal from top government posts for homosexuals creating a climate of fear for homosexual civil servants. Our inquiries concerning implementation of these recommendations and of RCMP surveillance of homosexuals in Ottawa have not been answered by the Solicitor General's Office," 1.

53 McLeod, *Lesbian and Gay Liberation in Canada*, 51, 58.

54 August 28th Gay Day Committee, "We Demand."

55 Ibid.

56 Ibid. (emphasis in original).

57 Ibid.

58 Ibid.

59 LAC, RG 146, vol. 3115, file "Community Homophile Association Toronto, Ont." The heading of the document is "RE: League for Socialist Action Forums, Ontario." O Division, Toronto Security Intelligence Branch (SIB), August 23, 1971, 50-53; and also in LAC, RG 146, vol. 3050, file "GATE-T," RCMP Toronto Detachment, Security Intelligence Branch (SIB), August 23, 1971, 357-59.

60 LAC, RG 146, vol. 3050, file "GATE-T," from Officer i/c D Branch, Security Service, to Officer i/c VIP, Security Section (H-439), "Protests and Demonstrations – Ottawa," 355, 356: "The TGA has invited all the Gay Groups and individuals across the country to join the march. [blanked out] the Gay Liberation Movement (Trotskyist infiltrated) ... will join in the demonstration."

61 LAC, RG 146, vol. 3050, file "GATE-T," action request, "Your Info! Demonstration Planned for Parliament Hill, August 28, 1971, A Div," 365; and RCMP transit slip, August 17, 1971, 389.

62 LAC, RG 146, vol. 3115, file "Community Homophile Association, Toronto, Ont.," document prepared by A Division of Ottawa SIB, September 8, 1971, "Protests and Demonstrations, Ottawa, Ontario," 46-48. The same report is included in RG 146, vol. 3050, file "Homosexual Liberation Front, Montreal, Quebec," 130-32.

63 LAC, RG 146, vol. 3050, file "Homosexual Liberation Front, Montreal, Quebec," 130.

64 LAC, RG 146, vol. 3115, file "Community Homophile Association Toronto, Ont.," 46.

65 Ibid., 47.

66 Ibid. In this released document, much of the relevant information is blanked out for "security reasons." In our 1998 research report, we requested that these documents be fully released so that a clearer analysis of these campaigns could be developed. See McDonell, "Finding Security in the Archives" and "The Experiences of a Researcher in the Maze." See also the "Motion regarding ATIP Recommendations," passed at the Whose National Security? Conference, in Kinsman, Buse, and Steedman, eds., *Whose National Security?* 212.

67 LAC, RG 146, vol. 3115, file "Community Homophile Association, Toronto, Ont," document prepared by A Division of Ottawa SIB, September 8, 1971, "Protests and Demonstrations, Ottawa, Ontario," 46-48. The same report is included in RG 146, vol. 3050, file "Homosexual Liberation Front, Montreal, Quebec," 130-32. Under "Investigator's Comments," we could read only a few observations. After a blanked-out section, we read, "May a copy of this report be forwarded to 'O,' 'K' and 'D' Divisions for information purposes." This is a specific request for this document to be sent to RCMP security services in southern Ontario/Toronto. On K Ops, see Hewitt, "Information Believed to Be True," 200.

68 D. Smith, *Texts, Facts, and Femininity,* 136.

69 Wilson, "Marchers Demand Full Rights for Gays," 34. An article in the RCMP file on GATE-V, taken from the *Georgia Straight,* also reports on the demonstration. This article indicates that there were twenty demonstrators and a hundred spectators. Four members of GATE are reported to have spoken, criticizing federal legislation regarding homosexuals. The speakers included Ellen Woodsworth, "who spoke of some of the problems encountered by lesbians in their everyday lives." See Rick Doucet, "Out of the Closets and into the Streets," *Georgia Straight,* August 31-September 3, 1971, included in LAC, RG 146, vol. 3050, file "GATE-V," 184.

70 LAC, RG 146, vol. 3050, file "GATE-V," Vancouver Security Service, "Gay Alliance Towards Equality – Vancouver, BC," September 10, 1971, 179-80.

71 LAC, RG 146, vol. 3050, file "GATE-V," "Gay Liberation Demonstration, Vancouver BC, 28 August 1971," Vancouver RCMP, Division E, Special L, September 3, 1971, 188-89.

72 Ibid., 189. L Branch was formed in the early 1970s to address issues relating to informants. See Hewitt, *Spying 101,* 25. This certainly suggests that the RCMP had informants in the Vancouver gay and lesbian scene.

73   LAC, RG 146, vol. 3050, file "GATE-T," 278-335. Handwritten on the promotional letter for the *Body Politic,* 12 August, 1971, is "For your files, of interest," 277.
74   LAC, RG 146, vol. 3050, file "Homosexual Liberation Front, Montreal, Quebec" reports where one could purchase the *Body Politic* in Montreal, 92-93. There was also discussion of whether the RCMP should receive the *Body Politic.* See RG 146, vol. 3050, file "GATE-T," 275-76; and a clipping from the *Edmonton Journal* on their legal case from the Edmonton Security Service (217).
75   Higgins, *De la clandestinité à l'affirmation,* 113. Warner suggests that the FLH was formed earlier, in late 1970, directly in response to the police raids and closure of gay establishments under the War Measures Act. See T. Warner, *Never Going Back,* 66-67.
76   Higgins, *De la clandestinité à l'affirmation,* 113-16. Unless otherwise indicated, this account of the FLH is based on Higgins and on McLeod, *Lesbian and Gay Liberation in Canada,* 65-66. The RCMP file also includes the rules and regulations of the FLH. See LAC, RG 146, vol. 3050, "Homosexual Liberation Front, Montreal, Quebec," C Division, 104-22.
77   LAC, RG 146, vol. 3050, file "Gay Alliance Towards Equality – BC," clipping, *Labour Challenge,* July 26, 1971. Another RCMP document notes that several organizations were present at this demonstration, including the FLH, the women's action movement, the Ligue socialiste ouvrière (the Quebec wing of the LSA), and the Ligue des jeunes socialistes (the Quebec wing of the Young Socialists). The information is also in a Montreal document prepared by C Division on June 8, 1971, "Protests and Demonstrations against Confederation – July 1st Québec," RG 146, vol. 3050, "Homosexual Liberation Front, Montreal, Quebec," 134. The manifesto is also included.
78   Hewitt, *Spying 101,* 156.
79   Ibid., 124.
80   Kinsman, "From Anti-Queer to Queers as 'Peripheral.'" See also Thorstad, "Homosexuality and the American Left"; and L. Smith, "Looking Backward."
81   McLeod, *Lesbian and Gay Liberation in Canada,* 73.
82   See L. Smith, "Looking Backward."
83   See also Waite, "A Strategy for Gay Liberation," 221-23. On the development of the rights strategy in the gay movement during these years, see M. Smith, *Lesbian and Gay Rights in Canada,* 41-50; and T. Warner, *Never Going Back,* 68-75.
84   See Sethna, "High-School Confidential."
85   These references are to a brief article in the *Body Politic* on Brian Mossop's purgation from the Communist Party of Canada (dated by the RCMP as December-January 1977). According to this article, the Communist Party's *Tribune* picked up the story of Mossop's expulsion. See Gibson, "Communist Party Expels Gay Activist," 5; LAC, RG 146, vol. 3195, file "National Gay Rights Coalition," 3. On Brian Mossop's account of his experience, see "Gay and Socialist, or Some Reflections of a Commie Fag," 49-51.
86   See League for Socialist Action/Ligue socialiste ouvrière, *Gay Liberation in Canada.*
87   See document collection, Thorstad, *Gay Liberation and Socialism* and "Homosexuality and the American Left."
88   Flood, "The Movement: Gay Liberation Is That Important," 24. The resignation letter is dated November 7, 1974.
89   Walker, "LSA Line 'Inadequate,' Gay Activist Resigns," 6-7.
90   The International Socialists, formed in 1975, also came to support gay/lesbian liberation, although not always an autonomous gay and lesbian movement. It arrived on the scene later and does not appear in any of these RCMP documents. On the early history of the International Socialists, see Bakan and Murton, "Origins of the International Socialists." By the early 1980s, some of the Marxist-Leninist groups, especially En Lutte/In Struggle, were beginning to move towards support for gay/lesbian liberation. See Gay/Lesbian Caucus of In Struggle, "Our Resolution for In Struggle's 4th Congress," 6-7.

91 The New Tendency published five issues of the *Newsletter* in 1973 and 1974. Articles included workplace organizing, workers autonomy perspectives, the refusal of work, and community struggles. The group also distributed a series of other publications, including translations of materials from the Italian radical left such as *Italy: New Tactics and Organization: With a Canadian Introduction,* produced by the International Workers Solidarity Committee, in conjunction with the Community Resource Centre in Windsor and distributed by the Labour Education Project in Toronto, about 1972; Adriano Sofri of Lotta Continua, *Beyond Trade Unionism and Vanguardism: Organizing for Workers' Power,* Community Resource Centre (Windsor) and the *Newsletter,* c. 1973; and *Autonomous Struggles and the Capitalist Crisis, A Workers' Autonomy Pamphlet,* the *Newsletter,* c. 1973. On the Windsor Labour Centre and Windsor Gay Unity, see *Out of the Driver's Seat: Marxism in North America Today,* 1974, especially 9-13. This pamphlet outlines the political perspective of the Windsor-based labour centre in the wake of its 1974 divisions. Issues explored include the nature of the working class, women in the working class, gay liberation, and student struggles. This material is all from Kinsman's new research on the New Tendency and the autonomist left in the Canadian context in the 1970s.

92 *Labour Challenge,* 26 July 1971, 191.

93 LAC, RG 146, vol. 3115, file "Community Homophile Association Toronto, Ont.," O Division, Toronto SIB, dated August 23, 1971, 50-53. See also LAC, RG 146, vol. 3050, file "GATE-T" (TGA), RCMP, Toronto Detachment, SIB, August 23, 1971, 357-59. References to the RCMP report on this forum come from the GATE-T document.

94 This quote was taken from LAC, RG 146, vol. 3050, file "GATE-T" (TGA), RCMP, Toronto Detachment, SIB, August 23, 1971, 357-59.

95 McLeod, *Lesbian and Gay Liberation in Canada,* 74.

96 LAC, RG 146, vol. 3042, file "Gay Activists Alliance (Vancouver, BC)," 114.

97 It may be the case that specific requests regarding the surveillance of the LSA would get significantly more documents.

98 In LAC, RG 146, vol. 3050, file "GATE-T," 262-67, section entitled "Gay Movement in Canada." We also see this focus on the relation between CHAT and the TGA in the 1972 composite report on the University of Toronto and its section on the University of Toronto Homophile Association. Page 256 remarks that the UTHA has ties with CHAT and the TGA: "the Toronto Gay Action is a more militant homosexual group, with a purely male membership, and is an advocate of Gay Liberation. The University of Toronto Homophile Association takes a middle position between these two groups and it is suspected that members of the Homophile Association hold dual membership in either CHAT or the Toronto Gay Action" (23). Again, we see a major interest in the relation between CHAT and the TGA, with the latter being constructed as a militant group that supports gay liberation.

99 This would include, among others, Bannon, "Some Further Notes on Gay Liberation"; Bannon and Bennet, "A Perspective on Gay Liberation"; Flood, "For a Full (Not Limited) Intervention in Gay Liberation"; and Notte and MacKenzie, "Towards Gay Liberation."

100 LAC, RG 146, vol. 3049, file "Gay Liberation Movement – University of Waterloo," Division O, "Subdivision Toronto, Detachment Niagara Falls," 69, 88-90, 98. References in this paragraph come from this document. The LSO/LJS support for the gay liberation movement is also listed in the RCMP file on the FLH (to which we gained access). See LAC, RG 146, vol. 3050, file "Homosexuals Liberation Movement, Montreal, Quebec," in "Investigator's Comments," April 21, 1972, 95-99.

101 On the Keable Commission, see Parent, "Remembering Federal Police Surveillance in Québec." See also Dowson, *Ross Dowson v. the RCMP,* 7.

102 Dowson, *Ross Dowson v. the RCMP,* 30.

103 Hewitt, *Spying 101,* 191.

104 On the declaration of the War Measures Act, see, among others, Parent, "Remembering Federal Police Surveillance in Québec," 242- 43.

105 Dowson, *Ross Dowson v. the RCMP.* Dowson, born in 1917, was a leading figure in the Canadian Trotskyist movement from the 1940s through to the early 1970s. He was a leading activist in the LSA

and, later, the Forward group (also known as the Socialist League), which he formed when he felt that the LSA was moving away from its historic position of winning the NDP over to socialism and was becoming too critical of Canadian nationalism. Ross Dowson died in 2002, following an immobilizing stroke in 1988. See Hiebert, "Obituary: Ross Dowson."

106 Dowson, *Ross Dowson v. the RCMP*, 30. The RWL and other Trotskyist groups were still under CSIS surveillance in 1988. On this, see Hewitt, *Spying 101*, 207.

107 Dowson, *Ross Dowson v. the RCMP*, 53.

108 Ibid., 55.

109 Ibid., 26.

110 Ibid.

111 Ibid., 25, 52-56.

112 Ibid., 57-58.

113 Ibid., 6.

114 Ibid., 9. Also on the surveillance of Waffle events and activities, see Hewitt, *Spying 101*, 135.

115 The Old Mole evolved from a broader radical student group based at the University of Toronto towards a more clearly Trotskyist-defined group. See "Statement of the Political Committee, Revolutionary Marxist Group," *Old Mole* (Toronto), July-August 1973, 3.

116 For a rather one-sided critique of this slowness, see Maurice Flood's contribution to "Proposition from the Left: A Gay Activist Says 'No, Thank You,'" 15. Although he correctly criticizes the RMG's publication the *Old Mole* for its lack of coverage of the gay liberation movement, he neglects to acknowledge that even these small articles were the result of the struggles of gays and lesbians within the RMG.

117 This was printed as part of Flood, "Proposition from the Left," 14, 25. See also interview by Deborah Brock with Kinsman, "Workers of the World Caress: An Interview with Gary Kinsman on Gay and Lesbian Organizing in the 1970s Toronto Left." *Left History*, http://www.yorku.ca/lefthist/online/brock_kinsman.html.

118 See Revolutionary Marxist Group, *Women's Liberation*.

119 Josh went on: "In any case, I was gone within a year as non-citizens were frozen in place in government jobs anyways. They introduced rules where non-citizens could not receive any further promotions but would not be dismissed" (December 12, 2000).

120 The RWL, like the US SWP, broke away from Trotskyism in the 1980s to move in the direction of support for Castroism and relatively uncritical support for the Cuban revolution. The RWL was renamed the Communist League, which continues to exist. Among the documents we received with the heading "Re: Canadian Trotskyist Movement" was the "monthly report for February 1978 on the Ligue Ouvrière Révolutionnaire (LOR) [blanked out] and the Groupe Socialiste des Travailleurs du Québec (GSTQ)" because it contains a brief mention of a "public meeting for the gay liberation movement." See LAC, RG 146, vol. 3050, file "Homosexuals Liberation Front, Montreal, Québec."

121 See Forgione and Hill, eds., *No Apologies*; and Kinsman, "From Anti-Queer to Queers as 'Peripheral.'"

122 See Tendency Z, "Declaration of Tendency Z," 1-11; Gary, Amy, Natalie, "We May Not Be Witches but We Sure Have Been Burned," our resignation letter from the RWL, March 8, 1980, at the *Left History* site, http://www.yorku.ca/lefthist/online/doc_pages/witches1.html; and Deborah Brock, "Workers of the World Caress: An Interview with Gary Kinsman on Gay and Lesbian Organizing in the 1970s Toronto Left," *Left History*, http://www.yorku.ca/lefthist/online/brock_kinsman.html. On critiques of Leninism, see Rowbotham, "The Women's Movement and Organizing for Socialism"; Kinsman, "Vladimir Lenin"; and Bonefeld and Tischler, eds., *What Is to Be Done?*

123 The theory of permanent revolution holds that, in dependent or underdeveloped countries, given the global character of capitalism, which prevented development for the Third World, revolutionary movements would need to link the bourgeois-democratic demands of the revolution to anti-capitalist and working-class social transformation. The revolutionary process therefore did not conform to stages

(first the bourgeois-democratic stage and then the working-class socialist stage) but, rather, had a permanent character. This approach can be applied in other areas as well. Uneven and combined development is tied into this perspective and points to how the global character of capitalism leads to both situations of underdevelopment and more advanced capitalist relations within the same social formations. For instance, in Czarist Russia, feudal peasant-based relations were combined with more modern capitalist relations and proletarianization in major cities. This created the basis for the process of permanent revolution. See Thompson and Lewis, *The Revolution Unfinished;* Trotsky, *The Permanent Revolution and Results and Prospects;* and Michael Löwy, "The Marxism of Trotsky's 'Results and Prospects,'" International Viewpoint, http://www.internationalviewpoint.org/spip.php?article1118.

124 On the problems with this statist orientation, see Holloway, *How to Change the World without Taking Power.*
125 For some useful explications and critiques of Trotskyism, see Thompson and Lewis, *The Revolution Unfinished;* Rowbotham, "The Women's Movement and Organizing for Socialism"; and Keefer, "Marxism, Anarchism, and the Genealogy of 'Socialism from Below.'"
126 On GATE-T, the RCMP report that it was formed in 1974 and grew out of Toronto Gay Action. It also reports that GATE "was the organizing force behind the campaign to support [blanked out – John Damien] who was fired as a racing steward for the Ontario Racing Commission because he was homosexual. This has been the major issue in the gay community over the last year. The current president of GATE is [blanked out]." See LAC, RG 146, vol. 3050, file "GATE-T."
127 On the editorial and the picket, see McLeod, *Lesbian and Gay Liberation in Canada,* 188-89.
128 LAC, RG 146, vol. 3050, file "GATE-T," 251.
129 Ibid.
130 On John Damien and his struggle, see M. Smith, *Lesbian and Gay Rights in Canada,* 51-52.
131 LAC, RG 146, vol. 3050, file "GATE-T," 244.
132 On the RMG's involvement in lesbian and gay struggles, see also B. Ross, *The House That Jill Built,* especially 123-24, 253n65, and 286n22.
133 See the *Body Politic* editorial, "On Diversity and Diversion," and the RMG Lesbians and Gays (letter to the editor), "Conference Coverage Unfair," the *Body Politic.* See also the letter from Pat Leslie of the Other Woman, "Conference Coverage," the *Body Politic.* For an early critique from the RMG's gay caucus of the *Body Politic,* see RMG Lesbians and Gays, "RMG Indicts the Body Politic."
134 The Marxist Institute of Toronto was established in 1973 as a broad-based Marxist educational society. A split produced the New Marxist Institute, and the Marxist Institute became the Toronto Liberation School in 1975.
135 LAC, RG 146, vol. 3050, file "GATE-T," 235, 237.
136 Chris Bearchell died in 2007. On the series, see Mossop, "Lecture Series Examines Sexism," 7. Eli Zaretsky was the author of "Capitalism, the Family and Personal Life," 69-125. This was later published as a small book (same title) by Pluto Press (London) in 1976.
137 LAC, RG 146, vol. 3050, file "GATE-T," 243.
138 See McLeod, *Lesbian and Gay Liberation in Canada,* 228-29.
139 On the Gay Marxist Study Group, see also B. Ross, *The House That Jill Built,* 286n22.
140 See Guard, "Women Worth Watching"; and Steedman, "The Red Petticoat Brigade."
141 See Dean Beeby, "RCMP Eyed Women's Groups as 'Subversives' – Papers," *Daily News,* October 12, 1993, 10.
142 See Sethna and Hewitt, "Staging Protest." For more on the Abortion Caravan, see Rebick, *Ten Thousand Roses,* 35-46.
143 See Laura Fraser, "Surveillance 'Kind of Eerie': MacNeil," *Halifax Chronicle Herald,* August 6, 2008, A1-A2. Fraser's piece is based on Steve Hewitt and Christabelle Sethna's "Sweating and Uncombed."
144 See also Hewitt and Sethna, "Sweating and Uncombed."
145 LAC, RG 146, vol. 3050, file "GATE-T," July 28, 1971, 385. TGA becomes part of GATE-T files.

146 LAC, RG 146, vol. 3121, file "Gays of Ottawa," 34; and McLeod, *Lesbian and Gay Liberation in Canada,* 244.

147 There is a need for more research on the surveillance of the feminist movement. Christabelle Sethna and Steven Hewitt have now embarked on an exploration of the national security investigations of feminist groups. See their "Staging Protest"; and Hewitt and Sethna, "Sweating and Uncombed."

148 For the development of the theoretical perspective behind this campaign, see Dalla Costa and James, *The Power of Women and the Subversion of the Community;* and Federici, *Wages against Housework.* See also an account that develops this perspective in relation to autonomist Marxism in H. Cleaver, *Reading Capital Politically,* 71-74.

149 Personal communication in 2001 between Gary Kinsman and Angela Miles, who was involved very early on in Wages for Housework organizing in Toronto, and from an interview Gary conducted with Dorothy Kidd on July 3, 2008. Kidd was also involved in the Wages for Housework campaign and in Wages Due Lesbians.

150 LAC, RG 146, vol. 3050, file "GATE-T," Unaligned Marxist and Pressure Groups, "Toronto Wages for Housework Committee," 227.

151 Ibid., 225.

152 Personal communication between Gary Kinsman and Boo Watson, 2000.

153 Agger, "Address to the March 11 Cutbacks Rally," 6. See also Agger and Wyland, "Wages Due Lesbians," 57-62; and Wages Due, "Lesbian Autonomy and the Gay Movement," 8.

154 See Wyland, *Motherhood, Lesbianism and Child Custody.* On Wages Due, see B. Ross, *The House That Jill Built,* 53-54. See also Arnup, "Lesbian Mothers and Child Custody"; W. Gross, "Judging the Best Interests of the Child"; Arnup, ed., *Lesbian Parenting;* and Stone, "Lesbian Mothers Organizing," 198-208.

155 LAC, RG 146, vol. 3050, file "GATE-T," Unaligned Marxist and Pressure Groups, "Toronto Wages for Housework Committee," 227. Dorothy Kidd points out that "single" must refer to not having a relationship with a man, since most of the women in WD were involved in relationships with women. Personal communication, June 6, 2009.

156 See D. Smith, *Texts, Facts, and Femininity,* 159-208.

157 On performances of lesbianism in relation to gender, see B. Ross, *The House That Jill Built,* and her "Destaining the (Tattooed) Delinquent Body"; Nestle, "Butch-Femme Relationships"; Kennedy and Davis, *Boots of Leather, Slippers of Gold;* and Weissman and Fernie, *Forbidden Love* (film). Comments on the unfeminine appearance of feminists seem to have been common in RCMP reports from the early 1970s. See also Sethna and Hewitt, "Staging Protest"; and Hewitt and Sethna, "Sweating and Uncombed."

158 LAC, RG 146, vol. 3050, file "GATE-T," Unaligned Marxist and Pressure Groups, "Toronto Wages for Housework Committee," 225.

159 On one response from a lesbian involved in GATE-T to the activities of Wages Due Lesbians, see Bearchell, "The Wages of Disunity," 19.

160 LAC, RG 146, vol. 3050, file "GATE-T," Unaligned Marxist and Pressure Groups, "Toronto Wages for Housework Committee," 225.

161 Ibid., 230.

162 Ibid.

163 See T. Warner, *Never Going Back,* 180-81, for more on LOON, and especially 75 and 87 for information on GO.

164 In Nicol, *Stand Together* (film).

165 Neil Herland, "Marching Forward, 25 Years of Lesbian and Gay Activism in Ottawa," *Capital Xtra!* June 28, 1996, 2.

166 RG 146, vol. 3054, file "University of Western Ontario Homophile Association," London Security Service document to Toronto 2 "D" OPS – prepared on July 6, 1977, 5-6.

167   LAC, RG 146, vol. 3054, file "University of Western Ontario Homophile Association." The RCMP also conducted surveillance of and collected announcements of gay dances and meetings held by the University of Western Ontario Homophile Association and the Homophile Association of London Ontario (HALO). Regarding one dance at the University of Western Ontario, the RCMP report reads, "Discreet observations of the above building revealed that [whited out]." See page 12 of this document. HALO dances were also monitored (ibid., 10).

168   See Keck, "Making Work." We dedicate this section to Jennifer Keck, a social activist and professor of social work at Laurentian University, who died of cancer-related disorders in June 2002.

169   See Smith and Smith, "Re-organizing the Job-Skills Training Nexus," 174-76. On the development of Keynesianism as a strategy of capital, see H. Cleaver, *Reading Capital Politically.*

170   Keck, "Making Work," 177.

171   On CHAT, see T. Warner, *Never Going Back,* 59-60; and the CGLA, CHAT file (for instance, see *Back Chat,* 1971: 1). CHAT received a grant of $9,000, which ran from June through September 1971, to help educate people about homosexuality. The OFY grant paid the salaries of nine people, most of whom were university students, for a thirteen-week summer period. A clipped article from the *Toronto Star* was entitled "Homosexuals Win Federal Grant for Service Work," 23 August, 1971, CHAT files, p. 56. See also Andrea Merry, "Homosexuals Win Federal Grant for Service Work," *Toronto Daily Star,* August 10, 1971, 49, also in the CHAT files. See also McLeod, *Lesbian and Gay Liberation in Canada,* 70.

· 172   In March 1972, CHAT was awarded a grant of $14,602 under Canada Manpower's LIP. The funding was to operate CHAT's twenty-four-hour information and counselling telephone service. Also included in the RCMP files on CHAT was a 1973 article entitled "Homosexual Group Awarded Another LIP Grant." According to this article, CHAT received another grant of $24,072 under the Trudeau government's LIP program. CHAT had also received LIP grants totalling $30,000 the year before to establish a "a crisis intervention and information service for disoriented homophiles."

173   LAC, RG 146, vol. 3050, file "GATE-T," LSA document, 1972, 226.

174   Keck, "Making Work," 200.

175   Ibid., 201-2.

176   This includes a letter to the editor of the *Toronto Star* (April 13, 1972) from George Hislop, as president and director of CHAT, about police surveillance and entrapment. See LAC, RG 146, vol. 3115, file "Community Homophile Association Toronto, Ont." There is also an article referencing CHAT: David Scott, "Police and Homosexuals Co-operate to Stop Offences in Parks, Subways," *Toronto Star,* April 6, 1972, 41. The released RCMP files also include a report on the demonstration during gay pride week on August 26, 1972 (Secret, D Branch, 25-08-72, RE: Community Homophile Association of Toronto). This report mentions an article from *Labour Challenge,* August 21, 1972, regarding the pride demonstration held at Queen's Park on August 26, 1972. This report gives us insight into RCMP monitoring work and the course of action the RCMP followed to link this work with that of the local police forces. The RCMP shared information about the demonstration with local police so that the latter could prepare for it.

177   RG 146, vol. 3042, file "Gay Activists Alliance (Vancouver, BC)." The project description reads, "the purpose of the project is to establish the community centre to be known as the Open Doors which will contain community service offices and social facility especially towards the homosexual minority, but always open to all," 119. See also a memo entitled "Re: Dept. of Manpower and Immigration, Penetration of Local Initiatives Program, Canada." It is also stated that, "in view of the people involved as well as the nature of some of the applications, it is suggested that careful examination be afforded the following cases prior to final approval of the grants," 118. See also McLeod, *Lesbian and Gay Liberation in Canada,* 59, 95-97.

178   See McLeod, *Lesbian and Gay Liberation in Canada,* 96-97.

179   LAC, RG 146, vol. 3049, file "Gay Liberation Movement – University of Waterloo," 64.

180 Quoted in the first issue of the *Body Politic*, "Vancouver Gay Liberation," 2; on the GLF and GATE-V, see McLeod, *Lesbian and Gay Liberation in Canada*, 54, 69.

181 LAC, RG 146, vol. 3050, file "GATE-V," Vancouver Security Service (Division E), December 20, 1972, 99. As Hewitt points out, having RCMP members enrolled in university classes on which they also conducted surveillance was one way of circumventing the prohibition against the recruitment of human sources on campuses. See Hewitt, *Spying 101*, 215-16.

182 LAC, RG 146, vol. 3050, file "GATE-V," Vancouver Security Service (Division E), December 20, 1972. Clippings from these various newspapers and gay newsletters are included in this file.

183 See T. Warner, *Never Going Back*, 74, 146; and M. Smith, *Lesbian and Gay Rights in Canada*, 53-55.

184 LAC, RG 146, vol. 3050, file "GATE-V," prepared for D Branch regarding GATE, June 12, 1973, 79.

185 See Kinsey et al., *Sexual Behavior in the Human Male* and *Sexual Behavior in the Human Female*.

186 LAC, RG 146, vol. 3050, file "GATE-V," prepared for D Branch regarding GATE, June 12, 1973, 79.

187 Ibid., 80.

188 LAC, RG 146, vol. 3050, file "GATE-V," transit slip (date, April 26, 1975). The request is handwritten: "Would you please provide us with an assessment of this organization suitable for 'A' Ops briefing purposes." This quotation comes from the same document cited at the beginning of the note in a document titled "Response to April 24, 1975 Transit Slip: Organizational Assessment Form Prepared on May 28, 1975."

189 LAC, RG 146, vol. 3050, file "GATE-V," "Response to April 24, 1975 Transit Slip: Organizational Assessment Form Prepared on May 28, 1975."

CHAPTER 9: SEXUAL POLICING AND NATIONAL SECURITY

1 See Walker, "David Garmaise and the NGRC," 9.

2 LAC, RG 146, vol. 3121, file "Gays of Ottawa," Ottawa Security Service report, June 23, 1976 (includes "Attn. Montreal 'D' Ops").

3 On moral panics, see Cohen, *Folk Devils and Moral Panics*, 9. We do not see moral panics as an explanation of a social process but, rather, as a way of investigating social relations.

4 Dayman, "Ottawa." This section is based on this article, unless otherwise cited.

5 There are some similarities here with the social organization of the attempted moral campaign to clean up Toronto's Yonge Street. See Kinsman, *The Regulation of Desire*, 336-38.

6 Dayman, "Ottawa."

7 See the *Body Politic* editorial, "Justice Canadian-Style," 2. Interestingly, the term "white slavery," used in the social purity movement in the late nineteenth and early twentieth centuries to refer to young white women drawn into prostitution, appeared in one of these headlines. On this, see Kinsman, *The Regulation of Desire*, 111-17.

8 See Jackson and Persky, "Victories and Defeats," 229.

9 *Body Politic*, "Justice Canadian-Style," 2.

10 On this, see George Smith, "The Ideology of 'Fag.'" On outing, see L. Gross, *Contested Closets*.

11 George Smith, "The Ideology of 'Fag.'"

12 *Body Politic*, "Justice Canadian-Style," 2.

13 See McLeod, *Lesbian and Gay Liberation in Canada*, 208-11; and Hannon, "Anatomy of a Sex Scandal," 10-11.

14 Sylvestre, *Propos pour une libération (homo)sexuelle*, 20-21.

15 McLeod, *Lesbian and Gay Liberation in Canada*, 216, 219, and 222.

16 In the context of the GO protests, NDP MPP Michael Cassidy (Ottawa Centre) wrote to Ontario's solicitor general asking for an explanation of the double standard involved in charging gay clients of prostitutes with more serious crimes (such as gross indecency and buggery) than heterosexual clients (who were usually charged as "found ins"). Organized through the Criminal Code, the continuing

criminalization of consensual same-gender sex led to more intensive sexual policing of gay sex, which continued to be viewed as more obscene than heterosexual sex. And the higher age of consent for homosexual activities made it possible to lay many of these charges. The *Body Politic* called on its readers to demand "an impartial inquiry into the Ottawa police department's method of handling this investigation." See the *Body Politic*, "Justice Canadian-Style," 2. These demands were rejected, with Tory premier Bill Davis declaring that "a public inquiry would serve no purpose." See McLeod, *Lesbian and Gay Liberation in Canada*, 208-9.

17 Sylvestre is referring to his first book, *Propos pour une libération (homo)sexuelle,* published in 1976.

18 LAC, RG 146, vol. 3115, file "Community Homophile Association Toronto, Ont.," "RE: National Gay Rights Coalition (NGRC), June 21, 1976." This text appears only in the file released from the Community Homophile Association of Toronto that we received from Steve Hewitt. In others, it is as follows: "This is in reply to Montreal Security Service Request [blanked out] Requiring Information on Gay Activities." See page 23 in LAC, vol. 3195, file "National Gay Rights Coalition," Montreal D OPS, "Unaligned Marxist and Pressure Groups RE: National Gay Rights Coalition (NGRC)."

19 In the lead-up to the 2010 Vancouver Winter Olympics, a social cleansing of poor and homeless people in the Vancouver area and violations of the rights of indigenous nations who have not ceded their land are under way. See the websites of the Anti-Poverty Committee, Vancouver, Coast Salish Territory, http://apc.resist.ca/; and No 2010 Olympics on Stolen Native Land, http://www.no2010.com/.

20 Sylvestre, *Les homosexuels s'organisent,* 140.

21 See S. Russell, "The Offence of Keeping a Common Bawdy-House"; and Trollope, "Bawdy Politics, Baths and the Bawdy House Laws," 9.

22 See George Smith, "Policing the Gay Community" and "Political Activist as Ethnographer." The bawdy-house law was used in the raid on Katacombes in Montreal in 1994, when 175 men were initially charged as found-ins, and also in the raid on the Remington's bar in Toronto in 1996. All of the charges arising from the raid on Remington's were dropped, except for those against the management. See Donovan Vincent, "Gay Club's Manager Convicted," *Toronto Star,* December 14, 1999, B5; and Pavelich, "The Bijou Raid," 23-24. In late 2002, the Calgary police raided Goliath's Sauna and Texas Lounge. They arrested thirteen people on charges of being found-ins and two employees as keepers of a common bawdy house. See EGALE Canada, "The State Has No Place in the Bathhouses of the Nation." Press release, December 18, 2002, http://www.egale.ca/index.asp?lang=E&menu= 1&item=100. In 2005, a Supreme Court decision regarding a swingers' club in Montreal modified the interpretation of "indecency" under the Criminal Code to focus on the question of harm. On this, see Brenda Crossman, "Harm Is the New Indecency Test: Supreme Court of Canada Okays Sex Clubs," *Xtra!* (Toronto), January 5, 2006, 9. This applied to different-gender consensual erotic acts in a "private" club. It does not appear that this decision covers sex between men in bars and bathhouses, given the greater "indecency" legally and socially constructed around same-gender erotic acts between men, and it would clearly not cover consensual erotic acts between men in a park or public washrooms.

23 This account is based on McLeod, *Lesbian and Gay Liberation in Canada,* especially 201-3, 243, 245, and 246-47; Higgins, *De la clandestinité à l'affirmation,* 122; and Sylvestre, *Les homosexuels s'organisent,* 141.

24 Jackson and Persky, "Victories and Defeats," 230; Sylvestre, *Les homosexuels s'organisent,* 142; *Body Politic,* "Olympic Crackdown," August 1976, 1.

25 Higgins, *De la clandestinité à l'affirmation,* 125.

26 *Body Politic,* "Olympic Crackdown," 1, and *Body Politic,* "The Police and the Press," 17.

27 This account is based on Sylvestre, *Les homosexuels s'organisent,* especially 125, 140, and 142; *Body Politic,* "The Police and the Press," 17; Higgins, *De la clandestinité à l'affirmation,* 125. For the Toronto bath raids, see Fleming, "The Bawdy House 'Boys,'" 109.

28 *Body Politic,* "The Police and the Press," 17.

29   Sylvestre, *Les homosexuels s'organisent,* 140.

30   Jackson and Persky, "Victories and Defeats," 231; Sylvestre, *Les homosexuels s'organisent,* 144; *Body Politic,* "Olympic Crackdown," 1. See also T. Warner, *Never Going Back,* 107-8.

31   *Body Politic,* "The Police and the Press," 17.

32   See M. Smith, *Lesbian and Gay Rights in Canada;* and T. Warner, *Never Going Back,* 108, 149.

33   *Body Politic,* "RCMP Investigates Gay Movement," 7; Sylvestre, *Les homosexuels s'organisent,* 142. Later that month, three Metro Toronto police officers emerged from the apartment of a member of the Body Politic collective while he was at work. He was never officially told of the visit. *Body Politic,* "Olympic Crackdown," 1.

34   Higgins, *De la clandestinité à l'affirmation,* 126; Sylvestre, *Les homosexuels s'organisent,* 143; and *Body Politic,* "Olympic Crackdown," 1.

35   This was a conference initiated by the CGRO entitled "Lesbians in the Gay Movement." See Coalition for Lesbian and Gay Rights in Ontario, *Speaking Out, Forcing Change,* 2.

36   Sylvestre, *Propos pour une libération (homo)sexuelle,* 114-15; *Body Politic,* "Olympic Crackdown," 1.

37   Ibid.

38   CGLA (Toronto), NGRC file, "NGRC/CNDH News Release, May 27, 1976," 1-2.

39   *Body Politic,* "Olympic Crackdown," 1, and "The Police and the Press," 17.

40   Jackson and Persky, "Victories and Defeats," 231-32; and Trollope, "Bawdy Politics," 9.

41   *Body Politic,* "Olympic Crackdown," 17.

42   LAC, RG 146, vol. 3195, file "National Gay Rights Coalition," "Re: Security Screening – Character Weakness (Homosexual), November 2, 1976," signed by M.S. Sexsmith.

43   See McLeod, *Lesbian and Gay Liberation in Canada,* 105; and T. Warner, *Never Going Back,* 76-77.

44   See LAC, RG 146, vol. 3115, file "Community Homophile Association Toronto, Ont." "RCMP Division O, October 27, 1972, Detachment, Toronto Security Service re: Community Homophile Association of Toronto – CHAT – Toronto, Ontario." This document listed the following ten organizations: GATE-V, CHAT, the *Body Politic,* Toronto Gay Action, Toronto Gay Youth, Gay Alliance for Equality-Halifax, Saskatoon Gay Action, Gays of Ottawa, FLH-Montreal, and the Canadian Gay Activist Alliance-BC. LAC, RG 146, vol. 3115, file "Community Homophile Association of Toronto," clipping from *Labour Challenge* written by Joe Young, "Gay Map Cross-Country Actions," c. 1973; M. Smith, *Lesbian and Gay Rights in Canada,* 48, 58. At the meeting, GATE-T reported that the NDP was the most sympathetic of the major political parties but that it still had a long way to go. Much of the Ontario NDP caucus still refused to take a publicly supportive stand.

45   LAC, RG 146, vol. 3121, file "Gays of Ottawa," from A Section, subdivision of Ottawa Security, "Report on Clipping of an Article from the *Ottawa Citizen* on the National Gay Election Coalition, September 24, 1973."

46   LAC, RG 146, vol. 3121, file "Gays of Ottawa," "Homosexuals: An Oppressed Minority," n.d.; LAC, RG 146, vol. 3121, file "Gays of Ottawa," legal fact sheet, n.d.

47   See also T. Warner, *Never Going Back,* 154-59.

48   LAC, RG 146, vol. 3121, file "Gays of Ottawa," clipping from the *Ottawa Citizen,* "Homosexuals Demand Rights." On the NGRC and the renamed Canadian Lesbian and Gay Rights Coalition, see M. Smith, *Lesbian and Gay Rights in Canada,* 58-66. At the same time, Smith's account is inadequate on two grounds: first, her discussion of the important struggle over and the controversies regarding lesbian participation focuses on the 50 percent lesbian control policy that was adopted at the Saskatoon conference in 1977 and repealed at the Halifax conference in 1978; second, her treatment of the inter-related rupture of the Saskatoon Gay Community Centre and the NGRC/CLGRC in 1978-79 is incomplete. See T. Warner, *Never Going Back,* 154-59.

49   LAC, RG 146, vol. 3050, file "GATE-T," RCMP A Division, "Re: Gay Alliance Towards Equality (GATE) Toronto, Ontario, July 2, 1975."

50   Ibid.

51 An RCMP document provides a brief description of the NGRC, produced specifically in response to the Montreal Security Service request. See LAC, RG 146, vol. 3050, file "GATE-T," "To Montreal D Ops re: National Gay Rights Coalition (NGRC) Canada, June 21, 1976."

52 Mary Trueman, "Mounties Don't Want Files Opened," *Globe and Mail*, October 5, 1976, 1.

53 This quote is taken from a letter written by David Garmaise as president of NGRC to Nadon, dated October 6, 1976. See LAC, RG 146, vol. 3195, file "National Gay Rights Coalition." The same document includes a copy of a letter sent to David as an acknowledgment of receipt to Commissioner Nadon, October 13, 1976; a copy of David's letter to Nadon, October 6, 1976; a copy of David's letter to Fox, October 5, 1976; a copy of David's letter to Ron Basford, October 5, 1976, regarding the inclusion of homosexuality in the Canadian Human Rights Act.

54 LAC, RG 146, vol. 3195, file "National Gay Rights Coalition, Canada" clipping, "RCMP Bias: Homosexuals Asking for Equal Job Treatment," *Globe and Mail*, October 7, 1976.

55 Jim Young, Doug Wilson, and John Foster, "1984: James Bond Comes to Ottawa," *Rites* (Toronto), July-August 1984, 14.

56 McLeod, *Lesbian and Gay Liberation in Canada*, 247-48.

57 LAC, RG 146, vol. 3195, file "National Gay Rights Coalition," transit slip, October 7, 1976, regarding National Gay Rights Coalition. In same file, see also transit slip to Inspector Godfrey, A Ops, from D Ops, informing Godfrey that the information would "no doubt be of interest to your section," October 19, 1976.

58 LAC, RG 146, vol. 3195, file "National Gay Rights Coalition," June 28, 1976.

59 LAC, RG 146, vol. 3195, file "National Gay Rights Coalition," "Re: Security Screening – Character Weakness (Homosexual), November 2, 1976," signed by M.S. Sexsmith. This document was sent to the officers in charge of A, C, D, E, F, H, K, and O divisions, the NCOs in charge of L, J, and B divisions, and security officers in B, D, E, F, H, I, J, L operations and foreign services.

60 Ibid., Sexsmith to M. Cassidy, carded as Annex A, February 1976. This letter also contains Paragraph 100 of the *Report on the Royal Commission on Security*.

61 LAC, RG 146, vol. 3195, file "National Gay Rights Coalition," clipping, Lawrence Martin, "Gay Group Claims RCMP Is Unfair to Homosexuals," *Globe and Mail*, August 23, 1977.

62 Ibid.

63 On Wilson, see Korinek, "The Most Openly Gay Person."

64 This raises the question of "burn out," a problem that continues to plague volunteer-based social movement activism, which lacks the social and financial resources of the RCMP and the Canadian state. For some commentary on this, see Plyler, "How to Keep On Keepin On."

65 LAC, RG 146, vol. 3049, file "Canadian Gay Liberation Movement," "Canadian Gay Liberation Movement – From the Alberta Area Command of Operations of the RCMP." This mentioned the article on the upcoming conference published in the *Body Politic;* it also reported the involvement of the Gay Community Centre of Saskatoon, with Doug Wilson as the contact person, to "Ott 3 Attn: 'A' and 'D' OPS. Info to Calgary, Vancouver, Winnipeg, Regina, Toronto, Montreal, Ottawa, Halifax and the Saskatoon Security Service; from NCO I/C 'A' Operations, Alberta Area Command, PLS ACK TKS OTT ACK TKS." On the copy we received, someone later wrote "of no interest" (either on 30/6/77 or 78/10/06). In the same volume and file, see also "Report from the Saskatoon Security Service to Ottawa and Other Security Service Divisions across the Country," dated June 22, 1977. One report reads, "no further info is available at this time. Any info available from other sections would be appreciated."

66 LAC, RG 146, vol. 3049, file "Canadian Gay Liberation Movement," "Report from the Saskatoon Security Service to Ottawa D Ops," July 29, 1977, 40-43. It was actually just the Young Socialists.

67 Ibid. Monitoring work included the clipping of an article from the University of Saskatchewan student newspaper, the *Sheaf,* in the same file.

68 LAC, RG 146, vol. 3195, file "National Gay Rights Coalition," "Re: National Gay Rights Coalition Canada" – transit slip, October 7, 1976.

69 LAC, RG 146, vol. 3195, file "National Gay Rights Coalition," to Montreal D OPS, OTT 3, Unaligned Marxist and Pressure Groups, "Re: National Gay Rights Coalition (NGRC)," June 21, 1976, 23.

70 LAC, RG 146, vol. 3195, file "National Gay Rights Coalition," "Re: National Gay Rights Coalition Canada," transit slip, October 7, 1976.

71 See B. Ross, *The House That Jill Built,* 155-58. See also Hollibaugh, "Sexuality and the State," in which she is interviewed by Ehrensaft and Milkman.

72 See B. Ross, *The House That Jill Built,* 158-60.

73 See the *Body Politic,* "*TBP* Raided and Charged," 8. On the Toronto protests against Bryant and the raid on the *Body Politic,* see Nicol, *Stand Together* (film); and T. Warner, *Never Going Back,* 134-37. For the discussion and debate around the article "Men Loving Boys Loving Men" and the police raid and charges, see Hannon, "Men Loving Boys Loving Men"; Bebout, Bearchell, and Wilson, "Another Look"; M. Smith, *Lesbian and Gay Rights in Canada,* 68; and B. Ross, *The House That Jill Built,* 165-70.

74 On LOOT and BEAVER (Better End to All Vicious Erotic Repression), see B. Ross, *The House That Jill Built,* 133. On BEAVER, see also Brock, *Making Work, Making Trouble,* especially 41, 61, and 161. See also LAC, RG 146, vol. 3050, file "GATE-T," no title, 208-14. References to the Anita Bryant protests and gay and lesbian groups are found on page 3. The author of this document refers to "Wages to Lesbians" instead of "Wages Due" (see page 214).

75 International Women's Day began early in the twentieth century as a day of support and solidarity for working-class women, and its theme was bread and roses. Bread signified the need for more resources and an end to poverty; roses symbolized the need for a better quality of life. See Egan, Gardner, and Persad, "The Politics of Transformation."

76 The major current within radical feminism emerging out of the experiences of organizing against men's violence against women tended, understandably, to prioritize questions of gender and patriarchal power. Radical feminists considered men's involvement to be an impediment to deepening the feminist struggle. Socialist feminists were more often involved in reproductive rights campaigns and in supporting union women's struggles, addressing the intersections of class and gender. They were therefore more open than were radical feminists to male participation in aid of the feminist struggle. On WAVAW, see B. Ross, *The House That Jill Built,* especially 113, 152, 177-78, and 183-88.

77 LAC, RG 146, vol. 3050, file "GATE-T," 214. The repeated use of "Wages to Lesbians" rather than "Wages Due" suggests the same informant/agent wrote up the surveillance on the anti-Bryant organizing.

78 See B. Ross, *The House That Jill Built,* 176-84.

79 Hannon, "Making Gay Sex Dirty."

80 See Hannon, "Raids, Rage and Bawdyhouses"; McCaskell, "The Bath Raids and Gay Politics"; George Smith, "Policing the Gay Community"; and Kinsman, "Mapping Social Relations of Struggle." See also Nicol, *Stand Together* (film); and T. Warner, *Never Going Back,* 109-12.

81 See CBC News, "Toronto Police Spied on Gay Community in 1980s: Report," May 17, 2007, http://www.cbc.ca/canada/toronto/story/2007/05/17/spy-gay-community.html; CBC News, "Ex-Head of Police Oversight Board Outraged over Wiretaps," May 18, 2007, http://www.cbc.ca/canada/toronto/story/2007/05/16/eng-report.html.

82 See *Action!* "McMurtry Strikes Again: Gays Smeared."

83 See CBC News, "Toronto Police Spied on Gay Community" and "Ex-Head of Police Oversight Board Outraged"; and *Xtra* staff, "Under Police Surveillance: Maloney on How He Learned He Was Being Watched," xtra.ca, May 18, 2007, http://www.xtra.ca/public/National/Under_police_surveillance-3059.aspx.

CHAPTER 10: CONTINUING EXCLUSION

1 On the resiliency of official discourse, see Kinsman, "The Textual Practices of Sexual Rule."

2 See Grace and Leys, "The Concept of Subversion and Its Implications."

3   See Dowson, *Ross Dowson v. the RCMP*.

4   On official discourse and commissions of inquiry, see Burton and Carlen, *Official Discourse;* Ashforth, "Reckoning Schemes of Legitimation" (although at times his notion of power/knowledge relations, borrowed from Foucault, needs to be more grounded in social relations and practices); and D. Smith, *The Conceptual Practices of Power,* 101-4. See also Kinsman, "Restoring Confidence in the Criminal Justice System."

5   We say "public" here since not all the proceedings of the commission are published and available to researchers.

6   Canada, Royal Commission of Inquiry into Certain Activities of the Royal Canadian Mounted Police, *Second Report: Freedom and Security under the Law,* 2:688 (hereafter the McDonald Commission).

7   Grace and Leys, "The Concept of Subversion and Its Implications," 76. This, in part, may represent internal conflicts within the workings of the commission.

8   McDonald Commission, 1:45. On the contributions and the limitations of the rule of law, see Fine, *Democracy and the Rule of Law.* See also Corrigan and Sayer, "How the Law Rules?"; and Pashukanis, *Law and Marxism.* On the importance to critical analysis of the social form of law and its connection to state relations and the significance of not fetishizing these, see Holloway, *How to Change the World without Taking Power.*

9   On these points, see Fine, *Democracy and the Rule of Law,* especially 7-9, 175.

10 For more on how commissions of inquiry, such as royal commissions, work to resolve crises of legitimacy, see Burton and Carlen, *Official Discourse;* and Ashforth, "Reckoning Schemes of Legitimation."

11 This can be seen as an instance of what George Smith describes as "recursion": the procedures are re-formed while the same social form is retained. See George Smith, "Political Activist as Ethnographer."

12 Letter from Lawrence MacCauley, PC, Member of Parliament, to Gary Kinsman, January 6, 1999. There is a similar letter from Lawrence MacCauley to Member of Parliament Svend Robinson with the same date. We received a much more supportive and encouraging letter from John Hucker of the Canadian Human Rights Commission, July 23, 1998. Letters in the possession of the authors.

13 Another briefing note produced for the solicitor general states: "All files opened solely on the basis of an individual's sexual orientation have subsequently been destroyed." Under "Background," it refers to the release of our research report and to the fact that, in 1981, "the Commission of Inquiry Concerning Activities of the Royal Canadian Mounted Police otherwise known as the McDonald Commission examined the issue of security clearance investigations of homosexuals and recommended the end of the systematic collection of information on homosexuals and recommended that the existing files be reviewed and destroyed if they did not fall within the guidelines for opening and maintaining files." Solicitor general briefing note, September 8, 1998, in the possession of the authors.

14 It is also argued that "all of the activities of the RCMP Security Service were closely examined by the McDonald Commission. The Enquiry was thorough and painstaking and that government [of the day] took the action it deemed appropriate ... The McDonald Commission recommended that files which were opened concerning this investigation be destroyed." Ibid.

15 See Canada, *House of Commons Debates* (April 27, 1992), 9713-14; and "PM Denounces 1960s Purge of Homosexual Civil Servants," *Globe and Mail,* April 28, 1992.

16 In Britain, the Ministry of Defence apologized to all servicemen and servicewomen who experienced discrimination before the ban on homosexuality was finally lifted after a challenge in the European Court of Human Rights in 2000. The Ministry of Defence has also committed itself to paying compensation to those lesbians and gay men who were persecuted. See Michael Evans, "We're Sorry MoD Tells Gay Victims of Persecution," *London Times,* June 28, 2007, 24.

17 The recommendations in the research report included an official apology; a commission of inquiry; that all continuing forms of discrimination regarding security clearances and security clearance procedures be eliminated; full human rights for lesbians, gay men, bisexuals, and transgender people, including spousal and family recognition rights; archival reorganization to facilitate research on the

security campaigns; and support for lesbian, gay, and bisexual history projects. See Kinsman and Gentile, *"In the Interests of the State,"* 145-46.

18 McDonald Commission, 2:794-95.

19 Ibid., 794.

20 Ibid., 795.

21 Ibid.

22 Ibid.

23 The following quotes are from the McDonald Commission report, 2:782, 784-85, unless otherwise noted.

24 Ibid., 807.

25 Ibid.

26 According to the commission, "Perhaps the most important weakness of CD-35, however, is the lack of an effective and independent appeal mechanism." This was a major weakness; however, from the standpoints of those directly affected by the national security campaigns, there were many others as well. See McDonald Commission, 2:786. The report also points out that CD-35 was a confidential document until declassified in 1978 during the course of the commission's public hearings. See McDonald Commission, 2:806.

27 McDonald Commission, 2:786, 788.

28 Ibid., 788.

29 Ibid., 800-1.

30 Ibid., 788.

31 Ibid.

32 Ibid.

33 See Loos, "Mounties Await Policy on Destruction of Files," 10; and Young, Wilson, and Foster, "1984," 14. The McDonald Commission reported the 800,000 figure for 1977. About half of the RCMP Security Service resources were then devoted to "counter-subversion." See McDonald Commission, 1:72, 518. In February 1988, the solicitor general stated that, since the McDonald Report, the service had reduced the number of people investigated by the former counter-subversion branch by 95 percent. Closed files were supposedly destroyed or sent to the National Archives of Canada. See Grace and Leys, "The Concept of Subversion and Its Implications," 253n32. This section is largely based on Young, Wilson, and Foster as well as Grace and Leys.

34 Grace and Leys, "The Concept of Subversion and Its Implications," 80.

35 M. Mandel, "Freedom of Expression and National Security," 206.

36 See P. Russell, "The Proposed Charter for a Civilian Intelligence Agency," especially 327-28.

37 Orr, "Challenging '50s-Style Mounties," 20.

38 Ibid.

39 See P. Russell, "The Proposed Charter"; Young, Wilson, and Foster, "1984," 14; and "Big Brother Is Watching," *Pink Ink* (Toronto), August 1983, 8.

40 Grace and Leys, "The Concept of Subversion," 80.

41 Ibid., 80-81.

42 See Young, Wilson, and Foster, "1984," 15.

43 See Grace and Leys, "The Concept of Subversion"; and Young, Wilson, and Foster, "1984," 14-15.

44 Grace and Leys, "The Concept of Subversion."

45 Ibid., 73, 253n35.

46 Ibid., 75.

47 Ibid.

48 Lawrence MacCauley, PC, Member of Parliament, to Gary Kinsman, January 6, 1999.

49 "Alleged Anti-Gay Security Campaign," Corley/Security and Intelligence, 957-5274, September 8, 1998. In the possession of the authors.

50 Canadian Security Intelligence Service Act, RSC 1985, c. C-23, s. 2.

51   See Wheeler, "Unfit for Service," 29.
52   Defence Minister Tom Siddon, Director General Information, response to query: "Sexual Abnormal-
     ity – Canadian Forces," August 24, 1982. Appended to "Brief: Gay and Lesbian Organization of
     Veterans" (hereafter GLOV brief), written by Tim Reid, President of GLOV, c. 1995. In the possession
     of the authors.
53   Wheeler, "Unfit for Service," 29.
54   GLOV brief.
55   John Duggan to the Honourable J. Gilles Lamontagne, Minister of National Defence, June 5, 1982. In
     the possession of the authors.
56   Ibid.
57   Ibid.
58   R.L. Lacroix, Executive Assistant to the Honourable J. Gilles Lamontagne, Minister of National Defence,
     to John Duggan, July 9, 1982. In the possession of the authors.
59   Wheeler, "Unfit for Service," 30-31.
60   Rowe, "Another Soldier's Story," 44.
61   See Razack, Dark Threats and White Knights.
62   Colin Leslie, "On Guard for Thee: Members of the Airborne 'Beat the Shit' Out of Gay Soldiers,"
     Capital Xtra! November 17, 1995, 13.
63   Razack, Dark Threats and White Knights, 70. Commissioned for the Somalia Inquiry, anthropologist
     Donna Winslow based her study on interviews with fifty members of the Airborne Regiment.
64   Ibid.
65   Ibid., 71. See also Theweleit, Male Fantasies, vol. 2, Male Bodies.
66   See Gouliquer, "Negotiating Sexuality," 259-60.
67   Ibid., 259-60.
68   "Lesbian 'Clique' Dismissed at Top-Secret Military Base," Globe and Mail, February 28, 1985, 8.
69   Ibid.
70   Doucette, "'Hard Core' Lesbians," 4.
71   "Forces Deny Security Caused Women's Firing," Toronto Star, March 1, 1985, A8.
72   Ibid.; Fulton, "Halifax Fights Lesbian Purge," 4; and Doucette, "'Hard Core' Lesbians," 4.
73   Some of the women fired from Shelburne later dismissed their military lawyer for releasing informa-
     tion to the media without their consent. See Fulton, "Halifax Fights Lesbian Purge," 4.
74   "Military's Sexual Policy 'Stupidity,' Lesbian Says," Globe and Mail, March 1, 1985, 5.
75   See Fulton, "Halifax Fights Lesbian Purge," 4.
76   Ken Belanger, Chairperson, Civil Rights Committee, Gay Alliance for Equality, Halifax, letter printed
     in Rites (Toronto), April 1985, 5.
77   Ibid.
78   See Gouliquer, "Negotiating Sexuality," 260.
79   Doucette, "'Hard Core' Lesbians," 4.
80   "Forces Firm on Ban on Homosexuals," Globe and Mail, March 6, 1985, 9.
81   The tape was made six months after Sirard was discharged from the Canadian Armed Forces. All
     references to his experience come from a transcription of the September 14, 1982, tape recording in
     the possession of the authors.
82   The Turret was a building on Barrington Street that, in 1977, was leased by the Gay Alliance for Equal-
     ity, who wanted to turn it into a community centre. In 1982, it became Rumours and moved to
     Granville Street (Robin Metcalfe, August 10, 2006).
83   Tom Siddon letter, GLOV brief, Annex A. In the possession of the authors.
84   Canadian Forces Administrative Order 19-20 (hereafter CFAO 19-20) 1976. This document can be
     found in Canada, Department of National Defence, Charter Task Force: Final Report, vol. 2, Annexes
     to Charter Task Force: Final Report, specifically Part 4, "Sexual Orientation."
85   Ibid.

86 Quoted from Siddon, response to query, "Sexual Abnormality – Canadian Forces," August 24, 1992. In the possession of the authors.

87 The key text mandating these investigations was CFAO 19-20. It stipulated that, when suspected homosexuality was reported, "the CO [commanding officer] shall investigate the report in whatever manner he deems appropriate. In making the investigation, he should make use of a medical officer (MO) and if necessary, the military police or any other means at his disposal ... If the investigation tends to substantiate the report, the CO shall: a. call in the local Special Investigation Unit (SIU) to investigate further, and b. when the MO so recommends, refer the subject to psychiatric examination ... When the investigations ... indicate with reasonable certainty that a member of the CF is a homosexual, or has a sexual abnormality, the CO shall forward the investigation report, with copies of the medical and the SIU reports, to NDHQ [National Defence Headquarters] ... When forwarding the report, the CO, the base commander where applicable, and the command headquarters shall make appropriate recommendations."

88 Ibid.

89 Ibid.

90 In the answers forwarded by Tom Siddon to the 1993 GLOV brief and questions, we are told that, "if military members were released as a result of homosexual activity which did not, of itself, contravene the Criminal Code of Canada, the assigned release item would have been 5 (d)." See GLOV brief, Annex A, 5. In the possession of the authors.

91 One was in the *Toronto Star* and the other in the *Toronto Sun*. See "Sex Discrimination in Forces Opposed," *Toronto Star*, May 26, 1982. There was also an article in *Le Droit* entitled "L'armee et la discrimination," May 26, 1982. See also "Gay OK in Our Armed Forces, Ottawa," *Toronto Sun*, May 26, 1982.

92 *Proceedings of the Standing Committee on Justice and Legal Affairs*, December 2, 1982, 111:17.

93 *Proceedings of the Standing Committee on Justice and Legal Affairs*, April 12, 1984, 111:14.

94 Ibid.

95 Ibid. Also in response to Robinson, Simmonds stated: "My position at the present time is that the nature of the organization, what the force is, our perception of the public expectation, and so on, is such that we do not knowingly hire people of that persuasion." Ibid., 14:14, 14:23.

96 Bob Kaplan to Svend Robinson, January 18, 1984, 1. In the possession of the authors. The 1963 Cabinet Directive (CD-35) continues as a ruling text regarding national security.

97 Bob Kaplan to Svend Robinson, March 29, 1984, 1. In the possession of the authors.

98 This 1983 letter, which came to us via our research, is in the possession of the authors.

99 Stephen Bindman, "Gay Sues Govt. over Dismissal from RCMP," *Ottawa Citizen*, April 16, 1986, A1, A2; "Gay Mountie's Lawsuit to Proceed," *Ottawa Citizen*, February 26, 1987, A5; Stephen Bindman, "Out-of-Court Deal Gets Gay Man His Mountie Badge Back," *Ottawa Citizen*, July 19, 1988, A1, A2. See also the editorial "Justice Delayed," *Ottawa Citizen*, July 21, 1988; and "Gay Mountie Reinstated," *Globe and Mail*, July 7, 1988, A5.

100 See Bindman, "Gay Sues Govt."; "Gay Mountie's Lawsuit to Proceed"; and Bindman, "Out-of-Court Deal."

101 See Bindman, "Gay Sues Govt."; "Gay Mountie's Lawsuit to Proceed"; and Bindman, "Out-of-Court Deal." See also "Justice Delayed" and "Gay Mountie Reinstated."

CHAPTER 11: FROM EXCLUSION TO ASSIMILATION

1 GO remarked: "On comparable grounds, federal funding was denied to the Faculty of Law of Laval University for a conference on homosexuality and justice." Gays of Ottawa, "Cleaning Up the Acts: Selected Equality Issues Affecting the Gay and Lesbian Minority – A Brief to the House of Commons Sub-Committee on Equality Rights from Gays of Ottawa, July 16, 1985" (hereafter GO brief), 4. In the possession of the authors.

2   See D. Herman, *Rights of Passage*, 26-29; Rayside, *On the Fringe*, 105-39; M. Smith, *Lesbian and Gay Rights in Canada;* and Lahey, *Are We "Persons" Yet?* See also T. Warner, *Never Going Back,* 192-96.

3   On the limitations of the Charter, see M. Mandel, *Charter of Rights and the Legalization of Politics in Canada;* Fudge and Glasbeek, "The Politics of Rights"; and Fudge, "The Public/Private Distinction." On the limitations of even a positive Supreme Court Charter decision regarding the collective bargaining rights of public-sector workers, see Tucker, "Constitutionalizing the Right to Bargain" and "The Constitutional Right to Bargain Collectively."

4   Fudge, "The Public/Private Distinction," 487.

5   For a perceptive early analysis regarding the open-ended character of the list in Section 15 and how it includes protection of the rights of lesbians and gay men, see Jefferson, "Gay Rights and the Charter."

6   See Rayside, *On the Fringe,* 105-39. See Sanders, "Constructing Lesbian and Gay Rights," especially 103, 108, 123, and 127.

7   See Rayside, *On the Fringe;* D. Herman, *Rites of Passage,* 33-37; M. Smith, *Lesbian and Gay Rights in Canada;* and Kinsman, "Gays and Lesbians," 227-31. See also T. Warner, *Never Going Back.*

8   For instance, while working at a Loeb grocery store in Sudbury in the mid-1990s, Mary Ross experienced discrimination because she was a lesbian, even though this was prohibited in Ontario. On arbitrary technical grounds, the Ontario Human Rights Commission (OHRC) did not pursue Ross' initial human rights complaint: it was officially received by the commission more than six months after the discrimination had forced her to go on disability leave. Later, even though Ross reached a settlement with the corporation owning the store, the OHRC refused to address this discrimination.

9   Alan Sears, "The Opening and Commodification of Gay Space: Queer in a Lean World," *Against the Current,* November-December 2000, http://www.solidarity-us.org/node/965. See also Hennessy, *Profit and Pleasure.*

10 On this, see Kinsman, "Constructing Sexual Problems."

11 On this paragraph, see Kinsman, "Gays and Lesbians," especially 228-34, 236-38.

12 Patrick Barnholden, "Not Every Queer Wants to Be a Soldier," *Halifax Gazette,* May 1993, 5.

13 Kinsman, "The Charter and Us," 4-5.

14 Ibid.

15 Their submission was called "Cleaning Up the Acts: Selected Equality Issues Affecting the Gay and Lesbian Minority," 6.

16 Ibid., 7.

17 Canada, Special Parliamentary Committee on Equality Rights, Sub-Committee of the Standing Committee on Justice and Legal Affairs, *Equality for All,* 30.

18 Ibid., 30, 31.

19 Ibid., 31.

20 Ibid.

21 Ibid.

22 Ibid., 32.

23 Canada, Special Parliamentary Committee on Equality Rights, *Toward Equality,* "Sexual Orientation," 2.

24 Canada, Department of National Defence, *Charter Task Force: Final Report,* vol. 2, 1, quoting from *Toward Equality.*

25 Greg Watson, "Security Service Says Policy on Homosexuals Unchanged," *Ottawa Citizen,* March 5, 1986, A1, A16.

26 Trow, "Forces Fight Rights," 15.

27 *Body Politic,* "Queer-Free and Proud of It," 19.

28 See "Draft RCMP Policy Statement on Employment of Gay Men and Lesbians," presented to the Special Parliamentary Committee on Equality Rights, May 1985, by RCMP commissioner Simmonds. This document is the same as the "Aide-Mémoire: RCMP Policy in Respect of Homosexual Conduct," included in the GO brief. In the possession of the authors.

29 "Aide-Mémoire: RCMP Policy in Respect of Homosexual Conduct," 1.

30 Ibid., 2.

31 Ibid., 3.

32 See "RCMP: No Queers Please," *Rites*, July-August 1985, 4. Under the heading "Hierarchical Rank Structure," the RCMP aide-mémoire argues that "discipline requires a strict and hierarchical rank structure in the RCMP, which places leaders in a dominant position ... This could create a unique problem pertaining to the use of rank or position to impose or solicit a homosexual relationship upon a subordinate. This is a particularly unwholesome situation where the subordinate is a youthful member of the RCMP, an auxiliary or a summer student. Apart from being socially abhorrent, this would undermine leadership, authority and respect between the ranks, and adversely affect the Force's chain of command." This builds on the image of the homosexual as a sexual predator, danger, or threat, especially in relation to young people, and overlays this with the image of the homosexual as a child/ youth molester. Under "Illegality" is written, "Not only is homosexual activity illegal in some of the countries of the world ... but is also illegal in Canada, when involving persons under the age of 21 with or without their consent or when committed in public places. Consequently, as a number of members of the RCMP are under 21 years, the Force has a duty to exercise great care so as not to unnecessarily expose them to dangers in this regard. There is also the problem of communal living in barracks, on ships, or in patrol cabins. These are clearly not private places, and any homosexual acts committed in such places would in fact be criminal offences. Notwithstanding that certain homosexual activity is not a criminal offence, it may still constitute an offence in the RCMP under Sec. 25, disgraceful conduct, or Sec. 26, conduct unbecoming, of the RCMP Act. These offences are contained in the Code of Conduct which forms part of the RCMP Act, an Act of the Parliament of Canada." "Aide-Mémoire: RCMP Policy in Respect of Homosexual Conduct," 4. This operates, as in the military, under the Queen's Regulations and Orders, so that an act that is not criminal under Canadian law can, under the RCMP Act, result in a discharge. From "Draft RCMP Policy Statement on Employment of Gay Men and Lesbians."

33 "Aide-Mémoire: RCMP Policy in Respect of Homosexual Conduct," 5.

34 Ibid., 6.

35 GO brief, 10.

36 Ibid.

37 Ibid., 10-11.

38 Greg McIntyre, "Gay Hiring 'Disgusts' Mounties," *Vancouver Province*, March 2, 1986.

39 "Beatty Outlines Policy for 'Gay' RCMP Recruits," *Guelph Daily Mercury*, April 21, 1986.

40 Greg Watson, "Security Service Says Policy on Homosexuals Unchanged," *Ottawa Citizen*, March 5, 1986.

41 "Forces Ask If Charter Applies to Homosexuals," *Toronto Star*, April 26, 1985, A17.

42 *Charter Task Force: Final Report*, vol.1, Part 4, "Sexual Orientation," 1, 6.

43 Ibid., 1, 2, 4.

44 Ibid., 4.

45 Ibid., 9.

46 The task force argued: "It is almost impossible for members to lead a private social life. This close physical contact could stimulate homosexual advances and, conversely, these same conditions could raise the sensitivity of other members to the presence of homosexuals ... To force heterosexual members to sleep and shower next to homosexuals under the conditions described above would obviously be a further intrusion on their life-style ... While heterosexual members appear to have no trouble accepting the close physical proximity and physical contact that are unavoidable in military life, they appear to recoil from members who receive sexual stimulation from bodily contacts with people of the same sex. As the conditions cannot be changed, the reaction appears to be to shun or expel the homosexual." See ibid., 10.

47 See Foucault, *The History of Sexuality*, vol. 1.

48   *Charter Task Force: Final Report,* vol. 1, Part 4, "Sexual Orientation," 11.
49   See Gade, Segal, and Johnson, "The Experience of Foreign Militaries."
50   *Charter Task Force: Final Report,* vol. 1, Part 4, "Sexual Orientation," 13, 15.
51   On the problems with "risk groups," see Patton, *Sex and Germs* and *Inventing AIDS;* Treichler, *How to Have Theory in an Epidemic;* and Kinsman, *The Regulation of Desire,* 347-55.
52   *Charter Task Force: Final Report,* vol. 1, Part 4, "Sexual Orientation," 16.
53   Ibid., 18-19.
54   Braithwaite, "Armed and Dangerous," 13-14.
55   *Charter Task Force: Final Report,* vol. 1, Part 4, "Sexual Orientation," 19.
56   See Kinsman, *The Regulation of Desire,* 333-36.
57   *Charter Task Force: Final Report,* vol. 1, Part 4, "Sexual Orientation," 20-21.
58   GLOV brief, Annex A, 7-8. In the possession of the authors.
59   Eleanor Brown, "Canadian Forces Surrender: Court Decision Opens Gates for Lesbian and Gay Soldiers," *Xtra!* (Toronto), October 30, 1992, 15.
60   Braithwaite, "Armed and Dangerous," 13-14.
61   Stephen Bindman, "Military to Lift Ban on Homosexuals," *Ottawa Citizen,* October 10, 1991.
62   Ibid.
63   Ibid.; and "Court Allows Woman's Appeal of Security Clearance Denial," *Ottawa Citizen,* March 31, 1990.
64   Bindman, "Military to Lift Ban on Homosexuals"; Syms, "Mulroney Backtracks after Canadian Military Changes Anti-Gay Policy," 6.
65   Syms, "Mulroney Backtracks after Canadian Military Changes Anti-Gay Policy," 6.
66   Ibid.
67   Peter Hays, "Military Drops Gay Ban as Key Trial Begins," *Daily News,* October 28, 1992; John Kennedy, "Lesbian Soldier Was Hooked Up to Lie Detector and Asked about Sex," *Capital Xtra!* November 17, 1995, 13.
68   See Kennedy, "Lesbian Soldier Was Hooked Up to Lie Detector," 13; Gouliquer, "Negotiating Sexuality," 261.
69   See Thomas Claridge and Geoffrey York, "Forces Agree to End Anti-Gay Policies: Ottawa Pays Former Officer $100,000 to Settle Rights Suit," *Globe and Mail,* October 28, 1992, A1, A11; Eleanor Brown, "Canadian Forces Surrender," 15; "Court Allows Woman's Appeal of Security Clearance Denial," *Ottawa Citizen,* March 31, 1990; Syms, "Mulroney Backtracks," 6; and Bindman, "Military to Lift Ban."
70   See Rob Ferguson, "Lesbian Ex-Soldier Wins Discrimination Case: Landmark Ruling Forces Military Policy Change," *Chronicle Herald,* October 28, 1992.
71   See Sanders, "Constructing Lesbian and Gay Rights," 118.
72   Hays, "Military Drops Gay Ban."
73   Brown, "Canadian Forces Surrender," 15; Hays, "Military Drops Gay Ban."
74   Hays, "Military Drops Gay Ban."
75   Ferguson, "Lesbian Ex-Soldier Wins Discrimination Case."
76   Claridge and York, "Forces Agree to End Anti-Gay Policies," A1, A11.
77   We rely in this section on Park, "Opening the Canadian Forces to Gays and Lesbians," 172-73.
78   Ibid., 173.
79   Ibid.
80   Ibid., 173-74.
81   Ibid., 173.
82   Ibid., 175.
83   Ibid.
84   Ibid., 176.

85 Ibid. Although we strongly agree with Park's critique of the assimilationist policies and practices in the military in relation to lesbians and gay men, we question whether the goal is instead a form of integration into the military that accepts the value and differences of lesbians and gay men. Although this is to be preferred to an assimilationist approach, we suggest a more profound transformation of military relations is required, one that contests the very social form of the military and challenges its disciplinary character and the ideologies of "national defence" and "national security."

86 Ibid., 177.

87 Rowe, "Another Soldier's Story," 9, 45.

88 See Gouliquer, "Negotiating Sexuality," 261-62.

89 Ibid.

90 This information is drawn partly from an interview as well as correspondence with a man in the navy in 1994-95 in Halifax.

91 See Gouliquer, "Negotiating Sexuality," 263.

92 Ibid.

93 Ibid., 263-64.

94 Poulin, "The Military Is the Wife and I Am the Mistress"; Gouliquer, "Negotiating Sexuality," 270.

95 See Khayatt's "Legalized Invisibility" and *Lesbian Teachers*.

96 Siddon, responding to a question from GLOV, wrote, "It is my understanding that the Special Investigations Unit (SIU) did not have any separate written policies, regulations, directives or guidelines on their dealings with gays and lesbians. They were also told that there are no plans to set up an inquiry or otherwise address the issue of the treatment of homosexuals in the military prior to the cancellation of CFAO 19-20." From the GLOV brief letter, Annex A, 6.

97 See "Canadian Forces Sees First Gay Wedding," *Globe and Mail*, June 14, 2005.

98 Dale Smith, "Canadian Forces Invited to Capital Pride, But Not Hamilton," *Capital Xtra!* July 16, 2008.

99 See, in particular, Halley's *Don't*, upon which we rely here, for a very interesting critique of the partially progressive appearance of the 1993 policy revisions. See also Herek, Jobe, and Carney, eds., *Out in Force*. On the US military, see also Shilts, *Conduct Unbecoming*.

100 See "Former President Jimmy Carter Calls for Repeal of Gay Ban," statement of Aaron Belkin, Director, Michael D. Palm Center, University of California, Santa Barbara, May 17, 2007, http://www.palmcenter.org.

101 Purged military members in the UK can also apply for compensation. See Evans, "We're Sorry MoD Tells Gay Victims of Persecution," 24.

102 Canada, Treasury Board, *Treasury Board Manual*. All quotes in this section are from this text. Authority for the policy comes from "a government decision" and from Section 7 of the Financial Administration Act. This policy is related to other legislation, including the Access to Information Act, the Canadian Security Intelligence Service Act, the Canada Labour Code, the Criminal Code, the Official Secrets Act, the Privacy Act, a number of public service acts, and the Queen's Regulations and Orders (in the military). Here, we see the text-mediated character of the construction of national security. In the possession of the authors.

103 Ibid., 3.

104 Ibid., 2.

105 Ibid., Appendix A, "Classifying and Designating Information."

106 Access to Information Act, RSC 1985, c. A-1, s. 15 (2)(a).

107 McDonald Commission, 2:788.

108 Ray Protti to Svend Robinson, March 2, 1992. In the possession of the authors.

109 Brian K. Smith, CBC News, Ottawa. Excerpt from CBC Radio News, April 14, 1998.

110 Jeff Sallot, "The Spy Masters' Talent Hunt Goes Public," *Globe and Mail*, June 22, 1999, A2.

111 David Stonehouse, "Aspiring Mounties Asked: Are You Gay? RCMP Says Policy Prevents Blackmail, Protects Secrets," *Ottawa Citizen*, December 3, 2001.

112 Ibid.

113 Ibid.

114 David Stonehouse, "Aspiring Mounties Asked: Are You Gay?" and David Stonehouse, "MP Angered by RCMP's Gay Question to Recruits: Svend Robinson Says 'Irrelevant' Practice Should End Immediately," *Ottawa Citizen*, December 7, 2001.

CHAPTER 12: FROM THE CANADIAN WAR ON QUEERS TO THE WAR ON TERROR

1 On the Seattle protests against the WTO, see *This Is What Democracy Looks Like* (film). On the Cancun protests against the WTO, see *Km. 0 (Kilometer Zero)* (film). See also Kinsman, "Mapping Social Relations of Struggle." On the protests and arrests in Montreal, see Ken Hechtman, "Riot Post-Mortem, What Went Wrong for Protestors on Monday Morning," *Montreal Mirror*, July 31-August 6, 2003, http://www.montrealmirror.com/ARCHIVES/2003/073103/news3.html.

2 For the purposes of brevity, we are using language that can easily be read as reifying or fetishizing capital. However, capital is not a thing but, rather, a social relation between people based on capitalists' appropriation of the new value produced by paid and unpaid workers. On our use of capital, see H. Cleaver, *Reading Capital Politically;* Holloway, "Capital Moves." On a critique of fetishism, see Holloway, *How to Change the World without Taking Power.*

3 See CBC News, "Police Admit Going Undercover at Montebello Protest," cbc.ca, August 24, 2007, http://www.cbc.ca/news/yourview/2007/08/police_admit_going_undercover.html.

4 On the Security and Prosperity Partnership Agreement, see the website for No One Is Illegal (Vancouver), http://noii-van.resist.ca/. Also see the official SPP website at http://www.spp.gov.

5 CBC News, "RCMP Slammed for Storing Secret Files on Canadians," CBC News, February 13, 2008.

6 Duggan, *The Twilight of Equality?* 50. Although this critique of homonormativity is quite insightful, further investigation of its historical and social bases is needed. In initiating this project, the "Queer Futures" special issue of *Radical History Review,* edited by Kevin P. Murphy, is quite useful. At the same time, the theorizing of homonormativity is based on that of heteronormativity. This emphasis on normativity is limited since queer oppression is about far more than norms and normalization. The connections between homonormativity and class relations also need further exploration.

7 On this, see Puar, *Terrorist Assemblages.* For an earlier period and support for campaigns against sex workers and people living in poverty, see Kinsman's *The Regulation of Desire;* "Gays and Lesbians"; and "Challenging Canadian and Queer Nationalisms."

8 See Kinsman and Gentile, *"In the Interests of the State,"* 145.

9 See Michael Evans, "We're Sorry MoD Tells Gay Victims of Persecution," *London Times,* June 28, 2007, 24.

10 Dan Irving contacted the military and the RCMP on our behalf. He heard back from Paul Villeneuve of the military and talked to Chief Officer Roger Brown of the RCMP. E-mail communication from Dan Irving, September 8, 2003.

11 Especially the use of Sections 13-1A, 13-1B, 15-1, and 21 of the Access to Information Act. On the problems with these sections, see McDonnell, "Finding Security in the Archives"; McDonell "The Experiences of a Researcher in the Maze"; and Badgley, "Researchers and Canada's Public Archives." On the use of Access to Information, also see Huey, "Subverting Surveillance Systems."

12 See Kinsman and Gentile, *"In the Interests of the State,"* 145-46.

13 On this global cycle of struggle, see H. Cleaver, *Reading Capital Politically,* 24-28.

14 Ibid., especially 27-28; and Dyer-Witheford, *Cyber-Marx,* 72-90. See also Klein, *The Shock Doctrine.* Klein insightfully reports on the origins of neoliberalism, although she often uses other terms to describe it. Klein's insights, however, are limited by a commitment to a return to a Keynesian welfare state rather than to a broader critique of capitalist social relations. For critiques of Klein's *Shock Doctrine,* see Hardt, "Capitalism"; and Calnintsky, "Of Capital and Compromise."

15 See Sears, *Re-Tooling the Mind Factory*.

16 See McNally, *Another World Is Possible*, 2nd ed.

17 See Dyer-Witheford, *Cyber-Marx*, 91-129.

18 See Wright, "Against Illegality"; and Ng, "Exploring the Globalized Regime of Ruling from the Standpoint of Immigrant Workers." See also Sharma, *Home Economics*.

19 See Marcos, "The Fourth World War," *In Motion Magazine*, http://www.inmotionmagazine.com/auto/fourth.html; "Between the Satellite and the Microscope"; and "The Machinery of Ethnocide." See also Big Noise, *The Fourth World War* (film); and El Kilombo Intergalactico, *Beyond Resistance*.

20 Among others, see McNally, *Another World Is Possible*, 2nd ed., 5-8; Marcos, "First Declaration from the Lacandon Jungle"; Mentinis, *Zapatistas;* and El Kilombo Intergalactico, *Beyond Resistance*. On the political impact of the Zapatistas in Canada and the US, see Khasnabish, *Zapatismo beyond Borders*.

21 See Zapagringo blog, "Zapatismo and Queer Struggles," *Zapagringo*, http://zapagringo.blogspot.com/.

22 See McNally, *Another World Is Possible*, 2nd ed.; Notes from Nowhere, eds., *We Are Everywhere;* and Harvie et al., eds., *Shut Them Down!*

23 See Ali, *The Clash of Fundamentalisms*, 114-53.

24 On the history and development of the Taliban, see Rashid, *Taliban, Militant Islam, Oil and Fundamentalism in Central Asia*.

25 See Ali, *The Clash of Fundamentalisms*.

26 Klein traces some of the roots of this capitalist fundamentalism in *Shock Doctrine*, especially 49-71.

27 See Alfred and Lowe, "Warrior Societies in Contemporary Indigenous Communities"; Keefer, "The Six Nations Land Reclamation," "Declaring the Exception," and his Gord Hill interview "The Tradition of Resistance"; and Pasternak, "'They're Clear-Cutting Our Way of Life.'" CSIS also spied on indigenous protesters in 2007. See Stewart Bell, "Aboriginal Protests Watched by CSIS," *National Post*, June 26, 2008.

28 See Okafor, "The 1997 APEC Summit and the Security of Internationally Protected Persons"; and Pearlston, "APEC Days at UBC." On struggles against APEC, see also Choudry, "NGOs, Social Movements and Anti-APEC Activism." Suharto, fortunately, was toppled from power by his own people in a student-initiated revolt in May 1998.

29 Canada, Commission for Public Complaints against the RCMP, *APEC – Commission Interim Report*, 2001. Jaggi Singh, one of the people arrested during the protests, said, "This report will go down in history as one of the most expensive door stops ever." Nicolaas Van Rijn, "PM's Role Ignored, Say Protestors," *Toronto Star*, August 7, 2001, A6.

30 Windsor Peace Committee, *Windsor OAS Days of Action*.

31 CSIS, "Report No. 2000/08: Anti-Globalization – A Spreading Phenomenon." Thanks to A.K. Thompson for drawing this to our attention.

32 CSIS, "2000 Public Report," August 12, 2001. Thanks to A.K. Thompson for drawing this to our attention.

33 See McNally, *Another World Is Possible*, 1st ed., 244-49; Talon, "Anarchy in Seattle and Quebec City"; and Day, "The Man with the Hissing Bomb."

34 See Jane Gadd, "Activist Called Terrorist," *Globe and Mail*, June 30, 2001, A17. On OCAP, see its website, http://www.ocap.ca/; and Shantz, "Fighting to Win."

35 See Moreau, "Criminals, Hooligans, Violence," 3. See also Swift, *No-Nonsense Guide to Democracy*, 11; and Chang et al., *Resist!*

36 See Mark MacKinnon and Barrie McKenna, "Use of Lethal Force Was an Option: Officers Authorized to Use Extreme Tactics on Protestors in Guidelines Issued for Summit," *Globe and Mail*, April 25, 2001, A7.

37 On the Quebec City protests, see Chang et al., *Resist!* See also Notes from Nowhere, eds., *We Are Everywhere*, 336-51. These protests contributed to the undermining of the FTAA and the eventual blocking of the FTAA negotiations at the meetings in Mar Del Plata, Argentina, in 2005.

38 See the A-Infos website, http://www.ainfos.ca/. See also People's Commission on Immigration "Security" Measures, "Final Report."

39 Moreau, "Criminals, Hooligans, Violence," 78.

40 Ibid., 79.

41 Ibid., 87. Moreau's analysis is much more detailed than is summarized here.

42 On official discourse, see Burton and Carlen, *Official Discourse;* and Ashforth, "Reckoning Schemes of Legitimation."

43 See Hewitt, *Spying 101,* 217; and David Pugilese and Jim Bronskill, "In the Crossfire: Right to Peaceful Protest under Siege, Critics Say," *Sudbury Star,* August 25, 2001, B10.

44 Pugilese and Bronskill, "In the Crossfire," B10.

45 Klein, *The Shock Doctrine.* Also see Teeple, "Towards a Theory of Terrorism."

46 See Puar and Rai, "Monster, Terrorist, Fag," 125; and Puar, *Terrorist Assemblages,* 51-56. There are also other currents in terrorism studies. For instance, in *Dying to Win,* Pape argues that the motivation for suicide bombers is often nationalism. Louise Richardson argues that terrorists can be quite "normal" and are not "crazy." See Richardson, *What Terrorists Want.*

47 Puar and Rai, "Monster, Terrorist, Fag," 121-25.

48 Ibid. In contrast, the film *V for Vendetta* may provide some ways of grasping why "terrorism" could be a possible political strategy.

49 See Razack, *Casting Out;* and Thobani, *Exalted Subjects.*

50 See Sut Jhally and Sanjay Talreja's *Edward Said: On Orientalism* (film).

51 Said, *Orientalism.* In cultural studies, Orientalism is often not situated within broader class, gender, racial, sexual, and other relations. See the work of Bannerji, including "Writing 'India,' Doing Ideology" and "Beyond the Ruling Category to What Actually Happens." We try to use "Orientalism" in a more materialist and socially grounded fashion.

52 Boyko, "Students and the Fight for Free Speech in Canada." Prohibitions on student activism in support of Palestine and the anti-war movement have taken place at Concordia, York, and McMaster Universities, among others. See the Solidarity for Palestinian Human Rights website, http://www.sphr.org/v3/. Also see Liisa Schofield, "Exposed: University of Toronto Suppresses Pro-Palestinian Activism," rabble.ca, February 18, 2009, http://rabble.ca/news/exposed-university-toronto-suppressed-pro-palestinian-activism; and Judy Rebick and Alan Sears, "Memo to Minister Kenney: Criticism of Israel Is Not Anti-Semitism," rabble.ca, March 1, 2009, http://www.rabble.ca/news/memo-minister-kenney-criticism-israel-not-anti-semitism.

53 See Kashmeri, *The Gulf Within.*

54 Sephan Christoff, "Spies at Work: CSIS Questioning of Canadian Muslims Threatens Their Jobs," *Montreal Mirror,* April 16, 2007.

55 George W. Bush, "Address to a Joint Session of Congress and the American People," September 20, 2001, http://www.whitehouse.gov.

56 Thobani, "It's Bloodthirsty Vengeance," 91-92.

57 See Hawthorne and Winter, *After Shock,* 16.

58 The definition included activity "with the intention of intimidating the public, or a segment of the public, with regard to its security, including its economic security, or compelling a person, a government or a domestic or international organization to do or to refrain from doing any act." The "terrorist" act must fall under a list of possible actions, including "to cause substantial property damage" or "to cause serious interference with or serious disruptions of an essential service, facility, or system ... other than as a result of lawful advocacy, protest, dissent or stoppage of work." Daniels, "Introduction," 9. Also see Rollings-Magnusson, "Buying Security with Freedom."

59 The word "lawful" was deleted from the definition of terrorist activity. This allowed various protest activities (whether lawful or not) that did not cause harm to people to avoid being categorized as terrorism. An interpretive clause was also added to clarify that the expression of political, religious, or

ideological beliefs is not a terrorist activity unless it constitutes conduct that meets the accepted definition.

60 See Thobani, *Exalted Subjects*, 219, 348n6. As an illustration of the problems this legislation (which allows the RCMP to take terrorist suspects into custody for up to forty-eight hours with no charges or warrant) created for social movement activists, consider the following. In September 2007, under the anti-terrorist legislation, the RCMP took into custody a group of nomadic Navajo Indians en route to support the indigenous quarry protest near Deseronto. Twenty-eight members of the tribe were on their way to Deseronto in nine vehicles, with ten horses in tow, to show support for the struggle of the Tyendinaga Mohawks when stopped on Highway 41. See Samantha Craggs, "Arrest of Native Caravan under Anti-Terrorism Act," *Belleville Intelligencer,* September 18, 2007.

61 See Maher Arar, "A Personal Account," *Z Net,* October 31, 2006, http://www.zmag.org/znet/viewArticle/2855; Webb, *Illusions of Security,* 9-24; and Thobani, *Exalted Subjects,* 244-46.

62 Webb, *Illusions of Security,* 9-24; Thobani, *Exalted Subjects,* 244-46; and People's Commission on Immigration "Security" Measures, "Final Report."

63 Webb, *Illusions of Security,* 10-11.

64 Jim Brown, "Canada Contributed to Torture: Arab-Canadians Were Mistreated in Syrian Jail," *Sudbury Star,* October 23, 2008, A7.

65 For the press release, see the website of the Benatta Coalition for a Public Review, http://benamarbenatta.com/.

66 See Aitken, "Of Gods and Monsters." See also People's Commission on Immigration "Security" Measures, "Final Report." Also see Wilkinson, "Are Human Rights Being Jeopardized in Twenty-First Century Canada?"

67 People's Commission on Immigration "Security" Measures, "Final Report."

68 Ibid. The security certificate process is set in motion when the minister of citizenship and immigration and the solicitor general of Canada, at the request of CSIS, sign a certificate naming an individual as a threat to national security. A Federal Court judge reviews certificates, but the standard of proof is "reasonable grounds to believe." This standard is not as rigorous as the criminal law equivalent of "beyond all reasonable doubt." Detainees and their lawyers are not given access to information against the former, and key terms, including "national security," "terrorism," and "membership," remain undefined. The certificate then becomes a deportation order, with no regard given to whether the individual might be tortured if deported.

69 Ibid. Also see Wilkinson, "Are Human Rights Being Jeopardized in Twenty-First Century Canada?"

70 Michelle Shephard, "Gitmo North's Last Prisoner in Limbo after 6 Years," *TheStar.com,* September 5, 2007. Also see Diab, *Guantánamo North.*

71 Neigh, "National Security Certificates."

72 Razack, *Casting Out.*

73 Tonda MacCharles, "Key Polygraph Tests Withheld, Canada's Spy Agency Moves to Restore its Credibility after 'Inexcusable' Mistake before Federal Court," *Toronto Star,* June 6, 2009, A6. The case against Adil Charkaoui is also crumbling, with the government admitting it has no credible evidence it is willing to put forward in court. See Thomas Walkom, "Six Years in Legal Labyrinth," *Toronto Star,* August 26, 2009, www.thestar.ca/comment/columnists/article/686404.

74 People's Commission on Immigration "Security" Measures, "Final Report."

75 Ibid.

76 See Razack, *Casting Out,* 3-4; Stephan Christoff, "The Roots of Rage: Terror and Repression in Canada," *Dominion,* July 16, 2006, http://www.dominionpaper.ca/opinion/2006/07/16/the_roots_.html. See also the Concerned Individuals against a Rush to Judgment statement, http://auto_sol.tao.ca/node/2137; Robert Fisk, "What Is the Term 'Brown-Skinned' Doing on the Front Page of a Major Canadian Daily?" June 10, 2006, http://auto_sol.tao.ca/node/2157; and Harsha Wallia, "Responding to the Toronto 'Terror' Arrests," *Z Net,* June 13, 2006, http://www.zmag.org/znet/viewArticle/3721.

77 Thomas Walkom and Anonymous, "Toronto's Alleged Terrorist Ring: Eye of the Storm," *Toronto Star,* April 6, 2008, A1, A7-A9; Colin Freeze and Omar El Arrad, "Terror Informant Wanted $14 Million: Police Reportedly Paid Him at Least $500,000," *Globe and Mail,* February 2, 2007, A1, A6; and Ian MacLeod, "'Toronto 18' Terror Suspects Posed Little Danger: Analyst," *Ottawa Citizen,* March 6, 2008. See also Thomas Walkom, "Bizarre Allegations about Toronto 18: Unorthodox Decisions Are Raising Questions about Crown's Case," *Toronto Star,* September 25, 2007.

78 See Isabel Teotonio, "Toronto 18 Trial: Youth Becomes Canada's First Convicted Terrorist," *Toronto Star,* September 26, 2008, A1, A6; Thomas Walkom, "Terror Verdict Bad News for Rest of Toronto 18," *Toronto Star,* September 26, 2008, A6; and Walkom, "Canada's Terrorist Shoplifter," *Toronto Star,* May 27, 2009, http://www.thestar.com/comment/columnists/article/640862.

79 See Paul Craig Roberts, "Desperate for Terror Arrests: FBI Turns to Entrapment," *AntiWar.com,* June 7, 2005, http://www.antiwar.com/roberts/?articleid=6237.

80 On the sexualization of torture at Abu Ghraib and how this operates to decontextualize the torture from the broader racializing power relations of the military-prison complex, see Puar, *Terrorist Assemblages,* 79-113; and Razack, *Casting Out,* 59-80.

81 See Agamben's *State of Exception* and *Homo Sacer.* See also "Indefinite Detention," in Judith Butler, *Precarious Life.* Puar also develops some useful critiques of Agamben's approach in *Terrorist Assemblages.*

82 Michael Hardt, interviewed by Dumm, "Intermezzo," 166-67. See also Michael Hardt, interviewed by Kinsman, "From the Perspective of Resistance," 77-78.

83 See, among others, Stanko, *Intimate Intrusions,* especially 86-102, and her *Everyday Violence.*

84 I. Young, *Global Challenges,* especially 118 and, more generally, 117-39.

85 See Thobani, "The 'War on Terror' and the Crisis of American Masculinity."

86 See Hawthorne and Winter, *After Shock.*

87 See World Net Daily, "In the Military: Raping America's Female Soldiers – Are US Armed Forces Prepared to Deal with Predators in the Ranks?" *World Net Daily,* August 21, 2008, http://www.worldnetdaily.com/index.php?fa=PAGE.view&pageid=72922; and Yochi J. Dreazen, "Rate of Sexual Assault in Army Prompts an Effort at Prevention," *Wall Street Journal,* October 3, 2008.

88 See Puar, *Terrorist Assemblages,* 7.

89 Thobani, "It's Bloodthirsty Vengeance," 94.

90 RAWA, widely known, has access to the Western media but there are other women's organizations in Afghanistan as well. On RAWA, see its statements collected in Hawthorne and Winter, *After Shock.* Visit RAWA's website, http://www.rawa.org/, for more on RAWA, especially its communiqué on Universal Human Rights Day, December 10, 2007. See also Justin Podur, "The NATO Occupation and Fundamentalism: An Interview with Miriam of RAWA," *Z Net,* August 14, 2008, http://www.zmag.org/znet/viewArticle/18429.

91 Delphy, "A War for Afghan Women?" 343-44.

92 For instance, Puar and Rai report that, shortly after the 9/11 attacks, posters appeared in Manhattan depicting turbaned caricatures of bin Laden, who was being penetrated anally by the Empire State Building, and the words "The Empire Strikes Back" or "So You Like Skyscrapers, Huh, Bitch?" See Puar and Rai, "Monster, Terrorist, Fag," 126. The misogyny is very clear. Individuals could also gain access to a website on which they could torture Osama bin Laden to death, the last act of torture being sodomy. Also generated was the gender-dependent "black humour," which included making bin Laden have a sex change operation and forcing him to live in Afghanistan as a woman. There are major racializing, sexist, and heterosexist subtexts here (ibid., 125-26). This section is influenced by both the Puar and Rai article and Puar's detailed analysis in *Terrorist Assemblages.* Puar is able to develop a creative analysis by bringing together social practices not usually assembled for this purpose. Despite the major insights in this article and book, both are limited by the layers of hyper-discourse one has to negotiate in order to retrieve them. See Karl Kersplebedeb, "Jasbir Puar's Homonationalism Talk: A Real Disappointment," *sketchy thoughts,* November 6, 2008, http://sketchythoughts.blogspot.

com/2008/11/jasbir-puars-homonationalism-talk-real.html. Unfortunately, Puar's work lacks a more materialist social and historical grounding. This section of our chapter attempts to provide a basis for moving in this direction.

93 Massad, *Desiring Arabs*, 40.

94 See Murray and Roscoe, *Islamic Homosexualities*; B. Whitaker, *Unspeakable Love*; and especially Massad, *Desiring Arabs*, and the controversies it has generated. For a respectful but also critical review of Massad's book, see Peter Drucker, "Arab Sexualities," review of *Desiring Arabs*, by Joseph Massad, *Against the Current* 137 (November-December 2008), http://www.solidarity-us.org/node/1962. See also Gary Kinsman, "Different Rainbows: Third World Queer Liberation," review of *Different Rainbows*, by Peter Drucker, *Against the Current* 96 (January-February 2002), http://www.solidarity-us.org/node/1031; and Drucker, *Different Rainbows*. While recognizing erotic diversity, we also need to avoid the Orientalist reading of "Eastern" *ars erotica* in contrast to a "Western" *scientia sexualis* as produced in Foucault's *The History of Sexuality*, vol. 1. For a critique of this, see Puar, *Terrorist Assemblages*, 74-76.

95 Puar and Rai, "Monster, Terrorist, Fag," 126.

96 Ibid., 127; and Puar, *Terrorist Assemblages*, 43.

97 For instance, see "The Gay Heroes of the Terrorist Tragedy," *Advocate*, October 23, 2001. This attempt to construct homosexual patriotism can also be seen in the reproduction of an ad from the Human Rights Campaign "Millions for Marriage" headlined "The Terrorists Killed People Not Because They Were Gay or Straight – but Because They Were Americans," in Murphy, ed., "Queer Futures," 125. See also Puar, *Terrorist Assemblages*, 41-43.

98 Puar, *Terrorist Assemblages*, 43.

99 Ibid., 13.

100 See Doug Ireland, "UN: Human Rights Report Confirms Iraqi Gay Killings," http://auto_sol.tao.ca/node/2505.

101 On this, see Haneen Maikey and Jason Ritchie, "Queers for Palestine: A Response to an Article in the Advocate," April 28, 2009, Upping the Anti website, http://uppingtheanti.org/node/3276; Andrew Brett, "Pro-Israel Lobbyists Threaten Funding for Toronto's Gay Pride," rabble.ca, May 27, 2009, http://www.rabble.ca/blogs/bloggers/andrew-brett/2009/05/pro-israel-lobbyists-threaten-funding-torontos-gay-pride; and Andrew Brett, "Pride Toronto Stands Its Ground against Pro-Israel Lobbyists," rabble.ca, May 31, 2009, http://www.rabble.ca/blogs/bloggers/andrew-brett/2009/05/pride-toronto-stands-its-ground-against-pro-israel-lobbyists.

102 Puar, *Terrorist Assemblages*, 16-20.

103 Blair Kuntz, "'Queer' as a Tool of Colonial Oppression: The Case of Israel/Palestine," *ZMag*, August 13, 2006, http://www.zmag.org/znet/viewArticle/3391.

104 Puar, *Terrorist Assemblages*, 19.

105 Puar and Rai, "Monster, Terrorist, Fag," 130.

106 Puar, *Terrorist Assemblages*.

107 Sandoval, *Methodology of the Oppressed*.

108 Petchesky, "Phantom Towers."

109 For a visual and musical account of the February 15, 2003, protests, see System of a Down's music video "Boom."

110 See Notes from Nowhere, eds., *We Are Everywhere*.

111 Holloway, *How to Change the World without Taking Power*.

112 See Jhally and Talreja's *Edward Said* (film).

113 See Corrigan, *Social Forms/Human Capacities*.

114 See Fenton, "Canada in Iraq."

Bibliography

ARCHIVAL SOURCES

Archives of Ontario, Toronto
Mental Health Division, RG 29

Canadian Lesbian and Gay Archives, Toronto
Community Homophile Association of Toronto (CHAT) files
National Gay Rights Coalition (NGRC) files

Carleton University Archives, Ottawa
Frank Robert Wake files

Library and Archives Canada, Ottawa
Robert Bryce, interviewed by Jim Littleton, sound recording, ISN 61905, C09276(1), 1887-0259/031, October 22, 1980
Canadian Security Intelligence Service (CSIS), RG 146
Don Wall, interviewed by Donald Brittain, sound recording, ISN 61917, CO9276(2), C9277, October 23, 1980

OTHER SOURCES

Abdo, Nahla. "Eurocentrism, Orientalism, and Essentialism: Some Reflections on September 11 and Beyond." In *After Shock: September 11, 2001: Global Feminist Perspectives*, edited by Susan Hawthorne and Bronwyn Winter, 408-29. Vancouver: Raincoast Books, 2003.
Action! "McMurtry Strikes Again: Gays Smeared." *Action! Publication of the Right to Privacy Committee* 1, 3 (1981).
Adams, Ian. *Agent of Influence: A True Story*. Toronto: Stoddart, 1999.
–. *S: Portrait of a Spy*. Toronto: Gage Publishing, 1977.
Adams, Mary Louise. "Margin Notes: Reading Lesbianism as Obscenity in a Cold War Courtroom." In *Love, Hate and Fear in Canada's Cold War*, edited by Richard Cavell, 135-58. Toronto: University of Toronto Press, 2004.
–. *The Trouble with Normal: Postwar Youth and the Making of Heterosexuality*. Toronto: University of Toronto Press, 1997.
Agamben, Giorgio. *Homo Sacer: Sovereign Power and Bare Life*. Translated by Daniel Heller-Roazen. Stanford: Stanford University Press, 1998.
–. *State of Exception*. Chicago: University of Chicago Press, 2005.
Agger, Ellen. "Address to the March 11 Cutbacks Rally." *Body Politic*, June 1976, 6.
Agger, Ellen, and Francie Wyland. "Wages Due Lesbians." *Quest* 5, 1 (1979): 57-62.
Aitken, Sharryn. "Of Gods and Monsters: National Security and Canadian Refugee Policy." *Revue Québécoise de droit international* 14, 1 (2001): 8-36.

Alfred, Taiaiake, and Lana Lowe. "Warrior Societies in Contemporary Indigenous Communities." *Upping the Anti* 2 (January 2006): 82-102.

Ali, Tariq. *Bush in Babylon: The Recolonization of Iraq*. London: Verso, 2003.

–. *The Clash of Fundamentalisms: Crusades, Jihads and Modernity*. London: Verso, 2003.

Amrine, Michael. "The 1965 Congressional Inquiry into Testing: A Commentary." *American Psychologist* 20, 11 (1965): 859-70.

Anderson, Benedict. *Imagined Communities*. London: Verso, 1983.

Anti-Capitalist Convergence of Montreal (CLAC). *An Anarchist Attack on Global Governance*. Montreal: Anti-Capitalist Convergence of Montreal, 2002.

Archibald, Kathleen. *Sex and the Public Service*. Ottawa: Queen's Printer, 1970.

Arguelles, Lourdes, and B. Ruby Rich. "Homosexuality, Homophobia and Revolution: Notes towards an Understanding of the Cuban Lesbian and Gay Male Experience." *Signs* 9, 4 (1984): 683-99.

Arnup, Katherine. "Lesbian Mothers and Child Custody." In "Sexuality and the State," edited by Ian Lumsden, special issue, *Atkinson Review of Canadian Studies* 1, 2 (1984): 35-40.

–, ed. *Lesbian Parenting: Living with Pride and Prejudice*. Charlottetown: Gynergy Books, 1995.

Ashforth, Adam. "Reckoning Schemes of Legitimation: On Commissions of Inquiry as Power/Knowledge Forms." *Journal of Historical Sociology* 1, 1 (1990): 1-22.

August 28th Gay Day Committee. "We Demand." In *Flaunting It! A Decade of Gay Journalism from the Body Politic*, edited by Ed Jackson and Stan Persky, 217-20. Vancouver/Toronto: New Star Books/Pink Triangle Press, 1982.

Badgley, Kerry. "Researchers and Canada's Public Archives: Gaining Access to Security Collections." In *Whose National Security? Canadian State Surveillance and the Creation of Enemies*, edited by Gary Kinsman, Dieter K. Buse, and Mercedes Steedman, 223-28. Toronto: Between the Lines, 2000.

Bakan, Abbie, and Philip Murton. "Origins of the International Socialists." *Marxism: A Socialist Annual* 4 (2006): 55-65.

Bannerji, Himani. "Beyond the Ruling Category to What Actually Happens: Notes on James Mill's Historiography in the History of British India." In *Knowledge, Experience, and Ruling Relations*, edited by Marie Campbell and Ann Manicom, 49-64. Toronto: University of Toronto Press, 1995.

–. "But Who Speaks for Us?" Chap. 3 in *Thinking Through: Essays on Feminism, Marxism and Anti-Racism*. Toronto: Women's Press, 1995.

–. *The Dark Side of the Nation: Essays on Multiculturalism, Nationalism, and Gender*. Toronto: Canadian Scholar's Press, 2000.

–. *Thinking Through: Essays on Feminism, Marxism and Anti-Racism*. Toronto: Women's Press, 1995.

–. "Writing 'India,' Doing Ideology." *Left History* 2, 2 (1994): 5-17.

Bannon, John. "Some Further Notes on Gay Liberation." *League for Socialist Action/Ligue socialiste ouvrière Discussion Bulletin 1972* 10, 24 (1972).

Bannon, John, and Brian Bennet. "A Perspective on Gay Liberation." *League for Socialist Action/Ligue socialiste ouvrière Discussion Bulletin 1972* 10, 2 (1972).

Barnholden, Patrick. "Does the 'Straight' Jacket of the Family Fit You?" *New Socialist* 4, 3 (1999): 22-23.

Bearchell, Chris. "The Wages of Disunity." *Body Politic*, September 1977, 19.

Beattie, K.L., and F.R. Wake. "Physical Cruelty: A Review of the Literature." *Canadian Psychologist* 5a, 4 (1964): 233-44.

–. "Suggestibility in Delinquents." *Canadian Journal of Corrections* 2 (April 1965): 157-72.

Bebout, Rick, Chris Bearchell, and Alexander Wilson. "Another Look." In *Flaunting It! A Decade of Gay Journalism from the Body Politic*, edited by Ed Jackson and Stan Persky, 166-74. Vancouver/Toronto: New Star Books/Pink Triangle Press, 1982.

Beeby, Dean, and Bill Kaplan, eds. *Moscow Dispatches: Inside Cold War Russia*. Toronto: James Lorimer, 1987.

Bell, David, and Gill Valentine, eds. *Mapping Desire: Geographies of Sexualities*. London: Routledge, 1995.

Bérubé, Allan. *Coming Out under Fire: The History of Gay Men and Women in World War Two*. New York: Free Press, 1990.

–. "Marching to a Different Drummer: Lesbian and Gay GIs in World War II." In *Hidden from History: Reclaiming the Gay and Lesbian Past*, edited by Martin Duberman, Martha Vicinus, and George Chauncey, 383-94. New York: Meridian, 1990.

Bérubé, Allan, and John D'Emilio. "The Military and Lesbians during the McCarthy Years." *Signs* 9, 4 (1984): 759-75.

Body Politic. "Canadian Human Rights Act, No Rights for Gays." June 1977, 1, 9.

–. "Justice Canadian-Style." May-June 1975, 2.

–. "Olympic Crackdown." August 1976, 1, 17.

–. "On Diversity and Diversion." October 1976, 2.

–. "The Police and the Press." August 1976, 17.

–. "Queer-Free and Proud of It: The Mounties Recruit Only the Best, and That Doesn't Include the Likes of You." July 1985, 19.

–. "RCMP Investigates Gay Movement." June 1976, 7.

–. "TBP Raided and Charged." February 1978, 8-9.

–. "Threatened with Expulsion from Military: Lesbian Goes Public." June 1977, 1.

–. "Vancouver Gay Liberation." November-December 1971, 2.

Bologh, Roslyn Wallach. *Dialectical Phenomenology: Marx's Method*. Boston/London: Routledge and Kegan Paul, 1979.

Bonefeld, Werner, and Sergio Tischler, eds. *What Is To Be Done? Leninism, Anti-Leninist Marxism and the Question of Revolution Today*. Aldershot: Ashgate, 2002.

Boyko, Ian. "Students and the Fight for Free Speech in Canada." In *Disciplining Dissent: The Curbing of Free Expression in Academia and the Media*, edited by William Bruneau and James L. Turk, 165-70. Toronto: James Lorimer, 2004.

Braithwaite, Lawrence. "Armed and Dangerous: A Gay Soldier on Misogyny, Homophobia, and Racism in the Canadian Armed Forces." *Rites* (Toronto), November-December 1991, 13-14.

Brett, Alex. *Cold Dark Matter*. Toronto: Dundurn Group, 2005.

Brock, Deborah, ed. *Making Normal: Social Regulation in Canada*. Toronto: Thomson Nelson, 2003.

–. *Making Work, Making Trouble: Prostitution as a Social Problem*. Toronto: University of Toronto Press, 1998.

Brookley, Robert Alan. *The Rhetoric and Power of the Gay Gene: Reinventing the Male Homosexual*. Bloomington and Indianapolis: Indiana University Press, 2002.

Brown, Ralph. "Security by Exclusion: Identifying Risky People." Chap. 11 in *Loyalty and Security: Employment Tests in the United States*. New Haven: Yale University Press, 1968.

Bruno, Walter. "Not the Same Old Place: Openly Gay in the Post Office." In *Flaunting It!* edited by Ed Jackson and Stan Persky, 76-79. Vancouver/Toronto: New Star Books/Pink Triangle Press, 1982.

Bunn, Geoff. "Euphoric Security: The Lie Detector and Popular Culture." In *Whose National Security? Canadian State Surveillance and the Creation of Enemies*, edited by Gary Kinsman, Dieter K. Buse, and Mercedes Steedman, 201-10. Toronto: Between the Lines, 2000.

Burchell, Graham, Colin Gordon, and Peter Miller, eds. *The Foucault Effect: Studies in Governmentality*. Chicago: University of Chicago Press, 1991.

Burton, Frank, and Pat Carlen. *Official Discourse*. London: Routledge and Kegan Paul, 1979.

Butler, Judith. *Gender Trouble: Feminism and the Subversion of Identity*. New York: Routledge, 1990.

–. *Precarious Life: The Powers of Mourning and Violence*. London: Verso, 2004.

Caffentzis, George. "Starvation Politics: From Ancient Egypt to the Present." *Turbulence: Ideas for Movement* 4 (July 2008): 15-17.

Calnintsky, David. "Of Capital and Compromise." *Upping the Anti* 6 (May 2008): 167-74.

Campbell, Marie, and Fran Gregor. *Mapping Social Relations*. Toronto: Garamond Press, 2002.

Campbell, Marie, and Ann Manicom, eds. *Knowledge, Experience, and Ruling Relations: Explorations in the Social Organization of Knowledge*. Toronto: University of Toronto Press, 1995.

Canada. *Report of the Royal Commission on Security*. Ottawa: Queen's Printer, 1969.

–. *Report of the Royal Commission on the Criminal Law Relating to Criminal Sexual Psychopaths*. Ottawa: Queen's Printer, 1958.

Canada. Commission for Public Complaints against the RCMP. *APEC – Commission Interim Report*. Ottawa: 2001. http://www.cpc-cpp.gc.ca/prr/rep/phr/apec/apec-intR-index-eng.aspx.

Canada. Department of National Defence. *Charter Task Force: Final Report*. 2 vols. Ottawa: Department of National Defence, 1986.

Canada. Parliament. House of Commons. Sub-Committee on Equality Rights. *Toward Equality: The Response to the Report of the Parliamentary Committee on Equality Rights*. Ottawa: Communications and Public Affairs, Department of Justice, 1986.

Canada. Royal Commission of Inquiry into Certain Activities of the Royal Canadian Mounted Police. *Second Report: Freedom and Security under the Law*. 2 vols. Ottawa: Supply and Services, 1981.

Canada. Special Parliamentary Committee on Equality Rights, Sub-Committee of the Standing Committee on Justice and Legal Affairs. *Equality for All*. Ottawa: Supply and Services, 1985.

Canada. Treasury Board. *Treasury Board Manual: Information and Administrative Management Component, Security*. Ottawa: Treasury Board, 1994.

Canaday, Margot. *The Straight State: Sexuality and Citizenship in Twentieth-Century America*. Princeton: Princeton University Press, 2009.

Carroll, William K., ed. *Organizing Dissent: Contemporary Social Movements in Theory and Practice*. Toronto: Garamond Press, 1997.

Chamberland, Line. "Remembering Lesbian Bars: Montreal 1955-1975." In *Canadian Women: A Reader*, edited by Wendy Mitchinson, Paula Bourne, Alison Prentice, Gail Cuthbert Brundt, Beth Light, and Naomi Black, 352-79. Toronto: Harcourt Brace, 1996.

Chang, Jen, Bethany Or, Eloginy Tharmendran, Emmie Tsumura, Steve Daniels, and Darryl Leroux, eds. *Resist: A Grassroots Collection of Stories, Poetry, Photos and Analyses from the Quebec City FTAA Protests and Beyond*. Halifax: Fernwood, 2001.

Chapnick, Adam. *Canada's Voice: The Public Life of John Wendell Holmes*. Vancouver: UBC Press, 2009.

Chauncey, George. "Christian Brotherhood or Sexual Perversion? Homosexual Identities and the Construction of Sexual Boundaries in the World War One Era." In *Hidden from History: Reclaiming the Gay and Lesbian Past*, edited by Martin Duberman, Martha Vicinus, and George Chauncey, 294-317. New York: Meridian, 1990.

–. *Gay New York: Gender, Urban Culture, and the Making of the Gay Male World, 1890-1940*. New York: Basic Books, 1994.

–. *Why Marriage? The History Shaping Today's Debate*. New York: Basic Books, 2004.

Chenier, Elise. "The Criminal Sexual Psychopath in Canada: Sex, Psychiatry, and the Law at Mid-Century." *Canadian Bulletin of Medical History* 20, 1 (2003): 75-101.

–. "Rethinking Class in Lesbian Bar Culture: Living 'the Gay Life' in Toronto, 1955-1965." *Left History* 9, 2 (2004): 85-118.

–. "Stranger in Our Midst: Sex, Psychiatry, and the Law in Postwar Canada." PhD diss., Queen's University, 2001.

–. *Strangers in Our Midst: Sexual Deviance in Cold War Canada*. Toronto: University of Toronto Press, 2008.

–. "Tough Ladies and Troublemakers: Toronto's Public Lesbian Community, 1955-1965." MA thesis, Queen's University, 1995.

Choudry, Abdul Aziz. "NGOs, Social Movements and Anti-APEC Activism: A Study in Power, Knowledge and Struggle." PhD diss., Concordia University, April 2008.

Civil Service News. "How Canada Fights Spies: Security of State Is Put before That of Individual." April 1956, 3-4.

Cleaver, Harry. *Reading Capital Politically.* Oakland: AK Press/Antitheses, 2000.

Cleaver, Richard. "Sexual Dissidents and the National Security State, 1942-1992." In *A Certain Terror: Heterosexism, Militarism, Violence and Change,* edited by Richard Cleaver and Patricia Myers, 171-208. Chicago: Great Lakes Region American Friends Service Committee, 1993.

Coalition for Lesbian and Gay Rights in Ontario. *Speaking Out, Forcing Change: A Short History of CLGRO.* Toronto: CLGRO, 2000.

Cohen, Stan. *Folk Devils and Moral Panics.* London: MacGibbon and Kee, 1972.

Committee on Homosexual Offences and Prostitution. *Report of the Committee on Homosexual Offences and Prostitution.* New York: Stein and Day, 1963.

Corrigan, Philip. "On Moral Regulation." *Sociological Review* 29, 2 (1981): 313-37.

–. *Social Forms/Human Capacities: Essays in Authority and Difference.* London: Routledge, 1990.

Corrigan, Philip, and Derek Sayer. *The Great Arch: English State Formation as Cultural Revolution.* Oxford: Blackwell, 1985.

–. "How the Law Rules? Variations on Some Themes in Karl Marx." In *Law, State and Society,* edited by B. Fryer, 21-53. London: Croom Helm, 1981.

Crane, Paul. *Gays and the Law.* London: Pluto Press, 1982.

CSIS (Canadian Security Intelligence Service). "2000 Public Report." August 12, 2001. CSIS. http//: www.csis-scrs.gc.ca/pblctns/nnlrprt/2000/rprt2000-eng.asp.

–. "Report No. 2000/08: Anti-Globalization – A Spreading Phenomenon." August 22, 2000. CSIS. http:// www.csis-scrs.gc.ca/pblctns/prspctvs/200008-eng.asp.

Cunningham, Frank, Sue Findlay, Marlene Kadar, Alan Lennon, and Ed Silva, eds. *Social Movements/ Social Change: The Politics and Practice of Organizing.* Toronto: Between the Lines/Socialist Studies, 1990.

Dalla Costa, Mariarosa, and Selma James. *The Power of Women and the Subversion of the Community.* Bristol: Falling Wall Press, 1972.

Daniels, Ronald J. "Introduction." In *The Security of Freedom: Essays on Canada's Anti-Terrorism Bill,* edited by Ronald J. Daniels, Patrick Macklem, and Kent Roach, 3-18. Toronto: University of Toronto Press, 2001.

Daniels, Ronald J., Patrick Macklem, and Kent Roach, eds. *The Security of Freedom: Essays on Canada's Anti-Terrorism Bill.* Toronto: University of Toronto Press, 2001.

Davies, Christie. "Sexual Taboos and Social Boundaries." *American Journal of Sociology* 87, 5 (1982): 1032-63.

Day, Richard. *Gramsci Is Dead: Anarchist Currents in the Newest Social Movements.* Toronto: Between the Lines, 2005.

–. "The Man with the Hissing Bomb: Anarchism and Terrorism in the North American Imagination." Paper presented at "Human Conditions Series: 2nd Annual International Multidisciplinary Conference on 'Terror,'" Laurentian University, Barrie, Ontario, May 3, 2008.

Dayman, Ron. "Ottawa: Police and Press Lies End in Death." *Body Politic,* May-June 1975, 1, 6.

Dean, Mitchell. *Critical and Effective Histories: Foucault's Methods and Historical Sociology.* London: Routledge, 1994.

–. "'A Social Structure of Many Souls': Moral Regulation, Government and Self-Formation." *Canadian Journal of Sociology* 19, 2 (1994): 145-68.

Delphy, Christine. "A War for Afghan Women?" In *After Shock: September 11, 2001: Global Feminist Perspectives,* edited by Susan Hawthorne and Bronwyn Winter, 333-47. Vancouver: Raincoast Books, 2003.

D'Emilio, John. *Sexual Politics, Sexual Communities: The Making of a Homosexual Minority in the United States, 1940-1970.* Chicago: University of Chicago Press, 1983.

Devault, Marjorie L. "Institutional Ethnography: A Strategy for Feminist Inquiry." In *Liberating Method, Feminism and Social Research,* edited by Marjorie L. Devault, 46-54. Philadelphia: Temple University Press, 1999.

Diab, Robert. *Guantánamo North: Terrorism and the Administration of Justice in Canada.* Halifax: Fernwood, 2008.

Donner, Frank J. *Protectors of Privilege: Red Squads and Police Repression in Urban America.* Berkeley: University of California Press, 1990.

Doucette, Joanne. "'Hard Core' Lesbians Given the Boot." *Rites* (Toronto), April 1985, 4.

Dowson, Ross. *Ross Dowson v. the RCMP: A Vivid Episode in the Ongoing Struggle for Freedom of Thought and Social Justice in Canada.* Foreword by Clayton Ruby. Toronto: Forward, 1980.

Drader, Brian. *The Fruit Machine: A Play on Gay History.* Toronto: Playwrights Guild of Canada, 1995.

Drucker, Peter. *Different Rainbows.* London: Gay Men's Press, 2000.

Duggan, Lisa. *The Twilight of Equality? Neoliberalism, Cultural Politics and the Attack on Democracy.* Boston: Beacon, 2003.

Dumm, Thomas L. "Intermezzo: The *Theory & Event* Interview: Sovereignty, Multitudes, Absolute Democracy: A Discussion between Michael Hardt and Thomas L. Dumm about Hardt's and Negri's *Empire.*" In *Empire's New Clothes: Reading Hardt and Negri,* edited by Paul A. Passavant and Jodi Dean, 163-73. New York: Routledge, 2004.

Dunbar-Ortiz, Roxanne. "The Opposite of Truth Is Forgetting." *Upping the Anti* 6 (Spring 2008): 47-58.

Dyer-Witheford, Nick. *Cyber-Marx: Cycles and Circuits of Struggle in High Technology Capitalism.* Chicago: University of Illinois Press, 1999.

Egan, Carolyn, Linda Lee Gardner, and Judy Vashti Persad. "The Politics of Transformation: Struggles with Race, Class, and Sexuality in the March 8th Coalition." In *Social Movements/Social Change: The Politics and Practice of Organizing,* edited by Frank Cunningham, Sue Findlay, Marlene Kadar, Alan Lennon, and Ed Silva, 20-47. Toronto: Between the Lines/Socialist Studies, 1988.

Egan, Jim. *Challenging the Conspiracy of Silence: My Life as a Canadian Gay Activist.* Compiled and edited by Donald W. McLeod. Toronto: Canadian Lesbian and Gay Archives/Homewood Books, 1998.

–. *Jim Egan: Canada's Pioneer Gay Activist.* Compiled and edited by Robert Champagne. Toronto: Canadian Lesbian and Gay History Network, 1987.

El Kilombo Intergalactico. *Beyond Resistance: Everything – An Interview with Subcommandante Insurgente Marcos.* Durham: Paperboat Press, 2008.

Engelstein, Laura. "Soviet Policy toward Male Homosexuality: Its Origin and Historical Roots." In *Gay Men and the Sexual History of the Political Left,* edited by Gert Hekma, Harry Oosterhuis, and James Steakley, 155-78. New York/London: Harrington Park/Haworth Press, 1995.

Enloe, Cynthia. *Bananas, Beaches and Bases: Making Feminist Sense of International Politics.* London: Pandora, 1989.

–. *Does Khaki Become You? Militarization and Women's Lives.* London: Pluto, 1983.

–. "Heterosexist Masculinity in the Military." *Sojourner* 18, 10 (1993): 2-4.

–. "Masculinity as a Foreign Policy Issue." In *After Shock: September 11, 2001: Global Feminist Perspectives,* edited by Susan Hawthorne and Bronwyn Winter, 284-89. Vancouver: Raincoast Books, 2003.

Fadel, Alec. "Homosexual Offences in Ottawa, 1950 to 1967: The Medicalization of the Legal Process." Master's thesis, Concordia University, 1994.

Fausto-Sterling, Anne. *Sexing the Body: Gender Politics and the Construction of Sexuality.* New York: Basic Books, 2000.

Feasby, W.R., ed. *Official History of the Canadian Medical Services, 1939-1945.* Vol. 1, *Organizations and Campaigns.* Ottawa: Ministry of National Defence/Queen's Printer, 1956.

–. *Official History of the Canadian Medical Services, 1939-1945.* Vol. 2, *Clinical Subjects.* Ottawa: Ministry of National Defence/Queen's Printer, 1953.

Federici, Silvia. *Wages against Housework.* London: Power of Women Collective/Falling Wall Press, 1975.

Fenton, Anthony. "Canada in Iraq: Dedication to the War of Terror." *New Socialist* 62 (2007): 26-27.

Fernie, Lynne. "Talking Forbidden Love: An Interview with Lynne Fernie – Interview by Terry Goldie." In *In a Queer Country: Gay and Lesbian Studies in the Canadian Context,* edited by Terry Goldie, 50-68. Vancouver: Arsenal Pulp Press, 2001.

Fine, Bob. *Democracy and the Rule of Law: Liberal Ideas and Marxist Critiques.* London: Pluto Press, 1984.

Fishman, Mark. *The Manufacturing of News.* Austin: University of Texas Press, 1980.

Fleming, Thomas S. "The Bawdy House 'Boys': Some Notes on Media, Sporadic Moral Crusades, and Selective Law Enforcement." *Canadian Criminology Forum* 3 (Spring 1981): 101-15.

Flood, Maurice J. "For a Full (Not Limited) Intervention in Gay Liberation." *League for Socialist Action/Ligue socialiste ouvrière Discussion Bulletin 1972* 10, 16 (1972).

–. "The Movement: Gay Liberation Is That Important." *Body Politic,* November-December 1974, 24.

–. "Proposition from the Left: A Gay Activist Says 'No, Thank You.'" *Body Politic,* September-October 1974, 14, 25.

Floyd, Kevin. *The Reification of Desire: Toward a Queer Marxism.* Minneapolis: University of Minnesota Press, 2009.

Forgione, Steve, and Kurt T. Hill, eds. *No Apologies: The Unauthorized Publication of Internal Discussion Documents of the Socialist Workers Party (SWP) Concerning Lesbian/Gay Male Liberation, 1975-1979.* New York: Lesbian/Gay Rights Monitoring Group, 1980.

Foucault, Michel. *Discipline and Punish: The Birth of the Prison.* New York: Vintage, 1979.

–. *The History of Sexuality.* Vol. 1, *An Introduction.* New York: Vintage, 1980.

–. "On Governmentality." *Ideology and Consciousness* 6 (1979): 5-21.

–. *Power/Knowledge.* Edited by C. Gordon. New York: Pantheon, 1980.

Frampton, Caelie, Gary Kinsman, A.K. Thompson, and Kate Tilleczek, eds. *Sociology for Changing the World: Social Movements/Social Research.* Halifax: Fernwood, 2006.

Frankenburg, Ruth. *White Women, Race Matters: The Social Construction of Whiteness.* Minneapolis: University of Minnesota Press, 1993.

Freedman, Estelle. "'Uncontrolled Desires': The Response to the Sexual Psychopath, 1920-1960." In *Passion and Power: Sexuality in History,* edited by Kathy Peiss and Christina Simmons, 199-225. Philadelphia: Temple University Press, 1989.

Freeman, Barbara. "Private Goes Public." *Body Politic,* July-August 1977, 13.

Fudge, Judy. "The Public/Private Distinction: The Possibilities of and the Limits to the Use of the Charter to Further Feminist Litigation." *Osgoode Hall Law Journal* 25, 3 (1987): 485-554.

Fudge, Judy, and Harry Glasbeek. "The Politics of Rights: A Politics with Little Class." *Social Legal Studies* 1 (1992): 45-70.

Fulton, Anne. "Halifax Fights Lesbian Purge." *Rites* (Toronto), April 1985, 4.

Gade, Paul A., David R. Segal, and Edgar M. Johnson. "The Experience of Foreign Militaries." In *Out in Force: Sexual Orientation in the Military,* edited by Gregory M. Herek, Jared B. Jobe, and Ralph M. Carney, 106-30. Chicago: University of Chicago Press, 1996.

Game, Mike, and Terry Johnson, eds. *Foucault's New Domains.* London: Routledge, 1993.

Garfinkel, Harold. *Studies in Ethnomethodology.* Englewood Cliffs: Prentice-Hall, 1967.

Gay/Lesbian Caucus of In Struggle, "Our Resolution for In Struggle's 4th Congress." *In Struggle* 9, 25 (1982): 6-7.

Gentile, Patrizia. "Capital Queer: Social Memory and Queer Place(s) in Cold War Ottawa." In *Remembering Place, Placing Memory,* edited by James Opp and John Walsh. Vancouver: UBC Press, forthcoming.

–. "'Government Girls' and 'Ottawa Men': Cold War Management of Gender Relations in the Civil Service." In *Whose National Security? Canadian State Surveillance and the Creation of Enemies,* edited by Gary Kinsman, Dieter K. Buse, and Mercedes Steedman, 131-41. Toronto: Between the Lines, 2000.

–. "Queen of the Maple Leaf: A History of Beauty Contests in Twentieth-Century Canada." PhD diss., Queen's University, 2006.

–. "Searching for 'Miss Civil Service' and 'Mr. Civil Service': Gender Anxiety, Beauty Contests, and Fruit Machines in the Canadian Civil Service, 1950-1973." Master's thesis, Carleton University, 1996.

Gibson, David. "Communist Party Expels Gay Activist." *Body Politic,* November 1976, 5.

Gibson, E. Lawrence. *Get Off My Ship.* New York: Avon, 1978.

Gidney, Catherine. "'Under the President's Gaze': Sexuality and Morality at a Canadian University during the Second World War." *Canadian Historical Review* 82, 1 (2001): 36-54.

Gilmartin, Katie. "We Weren't Bar People: Middle-Class Lesbian Identities and Cultural Space." *GLQ: A Journal of Lesbian and Gay Studies* 3, 1 (1996): 1-51.

Gindin, Sam. "Socialism with Sober Senses: Developing Worker's Capacities." *Socialist Register 1998* 34 (1998): 75-101.

Girard, Philip. "From Subversion to Liberation: Homosexuals and the Immigration Act, 1952-1977." *Canadian Journal of Law and Society* 2, 1 (1987): 1-27.

–. "Gays, Lesbians and the Legal Process since 1945." Unpublished paper, 1985. In the possession of the authors.

Goffman, Erving. *Asylums: Essays on the Social Situation of Mental Patients and Other Inmates.* Garden City/New York: Doubleday/Anchor Books, 1961.

Goreham, Richard. "The Fruit Machine: Homosexual Victimization." Research report for possible film project, May 12, 1995. In the possession of the authors.

Gouliquer, Lynne. "Negotiating Sexuality: Lesbians in the Canadian Military." In *Women's Bodies, Women's Lives: Health, Well-Being and Body Image,* edited by Baukje Miedema, Janet M. Sheppard, and Vivienne Anderson, 254-76. Toronto: Sumach Press, 2000.

Grace, Elizabeth, and Colin Leys. "The Concept of Subversion and Its Implications." In *Dissent and the State,* edited by C.E.S. Franks, 62-85. Toronto: Oxford University Press, 1989.

Gramsci, Antonio. *Selections from the Prison Notebooks.* Edited and translated by Quintin Hoare and Geoffrey Nowell Smith. New York: International, 1971.

Greenberg, David F. *The Construction of Homosexuality.* Chicago: University of Chicago Press, 1988.

Griffith, Alison I., and Dorothy E. Smith. *Mothering for Schooling.* New York: Routledge Falmer, 2005.

Gross, Larry. *Contested Closets: The Politics and Ethics of Outing.* Minneapolis: University of Minnesota Press, 1993.

Gross, Wendy. "Judging the Best Interests of the Child: Child Custody and the Homosexual Parent." *Canadian Journal of Women and the Law* 3, 1 (1989): 18-32.

Grube, John. "Queens and Flaming Virgins: Towards a Sense of Gay Community." *Rites* (Toronto), March 1986, 14-17.

Guard, Julie. "Women Worth Watching: Radical Housewives in Cold War Canada." In *Whose National Security? Canadian State Surveillance and the Creation of Enemies,* edited by Gary Kinsman, Dieter K. Buse, and Mercedes Steedman, 73-88. Toronto: Between the Lines, 2000.

Halley, Janet E. *Don't: A Reader's Guide to the Military's Anti-Gay Policy.* Durham: Duke University Press, 1999.

Hannant, Larry. *The Infernal Machine: Investigating the Loyalty of Canada's Citizens.* Toronto: University of Toronto Press, 1995.

Hannon, Gerald. "Anatomy of a Sex Scandal: What Happened in Ottawa." *Body Politic,* June 1976, 10-11.

–. " … Deemed Necessary to Discriminate …" *Body Politic,* September 1977, 10, 19.

–. "Making Gay Sex Dirty." *Body Politic,* May 1981, 8-9.

–. "Men Loving Boys Loving Men." In *Flaunting It!* edited by Ed Jackson and Stan Persky, 146-74. Vancouver/Toronto: New Star Books/Pink Triangle Press, 1982.

–. "Raids, Rage and Bawdyhouses." In *Flaunting It!* edited by Ed Jackson and Stan Persky, 273-94. Vancouver/Toronto: New Star Books/Pink Triangle Press, 1982.

Hardt, Michael. "Capitalism: The Violence of Capital." *New Left Review* 48 (November-December 2007): 153-60.

Harvie, David, Keir Milburn, Ben Trott, and David Watts, eds. *Shut Them Down! The G8, Gleneagles 2005 and the Movement of Movements.* Leeds/Brooklyn: Dissent!/Autonomedia, 2005.

Haug, Frigga. *Beyond Female Masochism: Memory-Work and Politics.* London: Verso, 1992.

Hawthorne, Susan, and Bronwyn Winter, eds. *After Shock: September 11, 2001: Global Feminist Perspectives.* Vancouver: Raincoast Books, 2003.

Henkenhaf, Heidi J. "Women in the Canadian Federal Civil Service during World War II." Master's thesis, Memorial University, 1994.

Hennessy, Rosemary. *Profit and Pleasure: Sexual Identities in Late Capitalism.* New York: Routledge, 2000.

–. "Queer Theory, Left Politics." *Rethinking Marxism* 7, 3 (1994): 85-111.

Herek, Gregory M., Jared B. Jobe, and Ralph M. Carney, eds. *Out in Force: Sexual Orientation and the Military.* Chicago: University of Chicago Press, 1996.

Herman, Didi. *Rights of Passage: Struggles for Lesbian and Gay Equality.* Toronto: University of Toronto Press, 1994.

Herman, Ellen. "The Career of Cold War Psychology." *Radical History Review* 63 (Fall 1995): 52-85.

Hess, Eckhard H., and James M. Polt. "Pupil Size as Related to Interest Value of Visual Stimuli." *Science* 132, 3423 (1960): 349-50.

–. "Pupil Size in Relation to Mental Activity during Simple Problem Solving." *Science* 143, 3611 (1964): 1190-92.

Hess, Eckhard H., A.L. Seltzer, and J.M. Shlien. "Pupil Response of Hetero- and Homosexual Males to Pictures of Men and Women: A Pilot Study." *Journal of Abnormal Psychology* 70 (June 1965): 165-68.

–. "Pupil Response of Hetero- and Homosexual Males to Pictures of Men and Women." University of Indiana, Kinsey Institute Archives, unpublished article.

Hewitt, Steve. "'Information Believed to Be True': RCMP Security Intelligence Activities on Canadian University Campuses and the Controversy Surrounding Them, 1961-71." *Canadian Historical Review* 81, 2 (2000): 191-228.

–. *Spying 101: The RCMP's Secret Activities at Canadian Universities, 1917-1997.* Toronto: University of Toronto Press, 2002.

Hewitt, Steve, and Christabelle Sethna. "'Sweating and Uncombed': Canadian State Security, the Indochinese Conference and the Feminist Threat, 1968-1972." Paper presented at the Canadian Historical Association, University of British Columbia, Vancouver, May-June 2008.

Hiebert, Ken. "Obituary: Ross Dowson." *New Socialist* 35 (2002): 33.

Hier, Sean P., and Josh Greenberg, eds. *Surveillance: Power, Problems, and Politics.* Vancouver: UBC Press, 2009.

Higgins, Ross. *De la clandestinité à l'affirmation: pour une histoire de la communauté gaie montréalaise.* Montreal: Comeau and Nadeau, 1999.

Hollibaugh, Amber, "Sexuality and the State: The Defeat of the Briggs Initiative and Beyond – Interview by Diane Ehrensaft and Ruth Milkman." In *My Dangerous Desires: A Queer Girl Dreaming Her Way Home,* edited by Amber L. Hollibaugh, 43-61. Durham: Duke University Press, 2000.

Holloway, John. "Capital Moves." In *Revolutionary Writing: Common-Sense Essays in Post-Political Politics,* edited by Werner Bonefeld, 161-69. New York: Autonomedia, 2003.

–. *How To Change the World without Taking Power: The Meaning of Revolution Today*. London: Pluto Press, 2005.

Holloway, John, Fernando Matamoros, and Sergio Tischler, eds. *Negativity and Revolution: Adorno and Political Activism*. London: Pluto Press, 2009.

Holmes, John W. "Moscow 1947-1948: Reflections on the Origins of My Cold War." In *Nearly Neighbours: Canada and the Soviet Union: From Cold War to Detente and Beyond*, edited by J.L. Black and Norman Hillmer, 41-55. Kingston: Ronald P. Frye, 1989.

–. *The Shaping of Peace: Canada and the Search for World Order, 1943-1957*. 2 vols. Toronto: University of Toronto Press, 1979-82.

Holquist, Michael, ed. *The Dialogic Imagination: Four Essays by M.M. Bakhtin*. Austin: University of Texas Press, 1981.

Huey, Laura. "Subverting Surveillance Systems: Access to Information Mechanisms as Tools of Counter-Surveillance." In *Surveillance: Power, Problems, and Politics*, edited by Sean P. Hier and Josh Greenberg, 219-35. Vancouver: UBC Press, 2009.

Hunt, Gerald. "No Longer Outsiders: Labor's Response to Sexual Diversity in Canada." In *Laboring for Rights: Unions and Sexual Diversity across Nations*, edited by Gerald Hunt, 10-36. Philadelphia: Temple University Press, 1999.

Hustak, Alan. *They Were Hanged*. Toronto: Lorimer, 1987.

Iacovetta, Franca. *Gatekeepers: Reshaping Immigrant Lives in Cold War Canada*. Toronto: Between the Lines, 2006.

–. "Making Model Citizens: Gender, Corrupted Democracy, and Immigrant Reception Work in Cold War Canada." In *Whose National Security? Canadian State Surveillance and the Creation of Enemies*, edited by Gary Kinsman, Dieter K. Buse, and Mercedes Steedman, 154-67. Toronto: Between the Lines, 2000.

Inglis, E.L. "Laurentian Terrace." *Civil Service Review* (June 1943): 200.

Ingram, Gordona Brent, Anne-Marie Bouthillette, and Yolanda Retter, eds. *Queers in Space: Communities, Public Places, Sites of Resistance*. Seattle: Bay Press, 1997.

Irving, Dan. "Contested Terrain of a Barely Scratched Surface: Exploring the Formation of Alliances between Trans Activists and Labour, Feminist and Gay and Lesbian Organizing." PhD diss., York University, 2005.

–. "Normalized Transgressions: Legitimizing the Transsexual Body as Productive." *Radical History Review* 100 (Winter 2008): 38-59.

–. "Trans Politics and Anti-Capitalism." *Upping the Anti* 4 (2007): 63-75.

Jackson, Ed, and Stan Persky, eds. *Flaunting It! A Decade of Gay Journalism from the Body Politic*. Vancouver/Toronto: New Star Books/Pink Triangle Press, 1982.

–. "Victories and Defeats: A Gay and Lesbian Chronology, 1964-1982." In *Flaunting It!* edited by Ed Jackson and Stan Persky, 224-43. Vancouver/Toronto: New Star Books/Pink Triangle Press, 1982.

Jackson, Paul. *One of the Boys: Homosexuality in the Military during World War II*. Montreal and Kingston: McGill-Queen's University Press, 2004.

Jagose, Annamarie. *Queer Theory: An Introduction*. New York: New York University Press, 1996.

James, C.L.R., Raya Dunayevskaya, and Grace Lee. *State Capitalism and World Revolution*. Detroit: Facing Reality, 1969.

James, C.L.R, Grace Lee, and Pierre Chaulieu. *Facing Reality*. Detroit: Berwick, 1974.

Janoff, Douglas V. *Pink Blood: Homophobic Violence in Canada*. Toronto: University of Toronto Press, 2005.

Jefferson, James E. "Gay Rights and the Charter." *University of Toronto Law Review* 43, 1 (1985): 256-77.

Johnson, David K. "'Homosexual Citizens': Washington's Gay Community Confronts the Civil Service." *Washington History* 6, 2 (1994-95): 45-97.

–. *The Lavender Scare: The Cold War Persecution of Gays and Lesbians in the Federal Government*. Chicago: University of Chicago Press, 2004.

Kashmeri, Zuhair. *The Gulf Within: Canadian Arabs, Racism and the Gulf War.* Toronto: James Lorimer, 1991.

–. "When CSIS Calls: Canadian Arabs, Racism, and the Gulf War." In *Whose National Security? Canadian State Surveillance and the Creation of Enemies,* edited by Gary Kinsman, Dieter K. Buse, and Mercedes Steedman, 256-63. Toronto: Between the Lines, 2000.

Katz, Jonathon Ned. *The Invention of Heterosexuality.* New York: Dutton.

Katz, Sidney. "The Harsh Facts of Life in the 'Gay' World." *Maclean's,* March 7, 1964, 1995, 18, 34-38.

–. "The Homosexual Next Door." *Maclean's,* February 22, 1964, 10-11, 28-30.

–. "RCMP: Inside Canada's Secret Police." *Maclean's,* April 20, 1963, 13-15, 32-41.

Kealey, Greg. "Spymasters, Spies, and Their Subjects: The RCMP and Canadian State Repression." In *Whose National Security? Canadian State Surveillance and the Creation of Enemies,* edited by Gary Kinsman, Dieter K. Buse, and Mercedes Steedman, 18-33. Toronto: Between the Lines, 2000.

Kealey, Greg, and Reg Whitaker. *RCMP Security Bulletins.* St. John's: Canadian Committee on Labour History.

Keck, Jennifer. "Making Work: Federal Job Creation Funding in the 1970s." PhD diss., University of Toronto, 1995.

Keefer, Tom. "Declaring the Exception: Direct Action, Six Nations and the Struggle in Brantford." *Upping the Anti* 7 (October 2008): 111-28.

–. "Marxism, Anarchism, and the Genealogy of 'Socialism from Below.'" *Upping the Anti* 2 (January 2006): 58-81.

–. "The Six Nations Land Reclamation." *Upping the Anti* 3 (November 2006): 135-67.

–. "The Tradition of Resistance, on Indigenous Anti-Colonialism" (interview with Gord Hill). *Upping the Anti* 5 (October 2007): 61-71.

Kempf, Edward J. "Enlightened ... Sublimation of the Abnormal." In *Gay American History: Lesbians and Gay Men in the USA,* edited by Jonathan Ned Katz, 391-93. New York: Thomas Y. Crowall, 1976.

–. "Homosexual Panic." In *Gay American History: Lesbians and Gay Men in the USA,* edited by Jonathan Ned Katz, 372-74. New York: Thomas Y. Crowall, 1976.

Kennedy, Elizabeth Lapovsky, and Madeline D. Davis. *Boots of Leather, Slippers of Gold: The History of a Lesbian Community.* New York: Routledge, 1993.

Keshen, Jeffery A. *Saints, Sinners, and Soldiers: Canada's Second World War.* Vancouver: UBC Press, 2004.

Kessler, Suzanne J., and Wendy McKenna. *Gender: An Ethnomethodological Approach.* Chicago: University of Chicago Press, 1978.

Khasnabish, Alex. *Zapatismo beyond Borders: New Imaginations of Political Possibility.* Toronto: University of Toronto Press, 2008.

Khayatt, Didi Madiha. "Compulsory Heterosexuality: Schools and Lesbian Students." In *Experience and Ruling Relations: Studies in the Social Organization of Knowledge,* edited by Marie Campbell and Anne Manicom, 149-63. Toronto: University of Toronto Press, 1995.

–. "Legalized Invisibility: The Effect of Bill 7 on Lesbian Teachers." *Women's Studies International Forum* 13 (1990): 185-93.

–. *Lesbian Teachers: An Invisible Presence.* Albany: State University of New York Press, 1992.

Kinsey, Alfred, Wardell Pomeroy, and Clyde Martin. *Sexual Behavior in the Human Female.* Philadelphia: W.B. Saunders, 1953.

Kinsey, Alfred, Wardell Pomeroy, Clyde Martin, and Paul Gebhard. *Sexual Behavior in the Human Male.* Philadelphia: W.B. Saunders, 1948.

Kinsman, Gary. "The Canadian Cold War on Queers: Sexual Regulation and Resistance." In *Love, Hate, and Fear in Canada's Cold War,* edited by Richard Cavell, 108-32. Toronto: University of Toronto Press/Green College Thematic Series, 2004.

–. "Capitalism and Industrialization." In *Encyclopedia of Lesbian, Gay, Bisexual and Transgendered History in America.* Vol. 1, edited by Marc Stein, 192-95. Detroit: Charles Scribner's Sons, 2004.

–. "Challenging Canadian and Queer Nationalisms." In *In a Queer Country: Gay and Lesbian Studies in the Canadian Context*, edited by Terry Goldie, 209-34. Vancouver: Arsenal Pulp Press, 2001.

–. "'Character Weaknesses' and 'Fruit Machines': Towards an Analysis of the Anti-Homosexual Security Campaign in the Canadian Civil Service." *Labour/Le Travail* 35 (Spring 1995): 133-61.

–. "The Charter and Us," *Rites* (Toronto), April 1985, 4-5.

–. "Constructing Gay Men and Lesbians as National Security Risks, 1950-70." In *Whose National Security? Canadian State Surveillance and the Creation of Enemies*, edited by Gary Kinsman, Dieter K. Buse, and Mercedes Steedman, 143-53. Toronto: Between the Lines, 2000.

–. "Constructing Sexual Problems: 'These Things May Lead to the Tragedy of Our Species.'" In *Power and Resistance: Critical Thinking about Canadian Social Issues*, edited by Les Samuelson and Wayne Antony, 101-15. Halifax: Fernwood, 2007.

–. "Don't Get Me to the Church on Time: Ending Social Discrimination against Same-Sex and Other Relationships." Summary of brief to the Justice and Human Rights Committee Review on Questions Relating to Same-Sex Marriage, 2003.

–. "From Anti-Queer to Queers as 'Peripheral': The Socialist Workers Party, Gay Liberation, and North American Trotskyism, 1960-1980." Paper presented at "History of American Trotskyism" conference, New York City, September 2000.

–. "From the Perspective of Resistance" (interview with Michael Hardt). *Upping the Anti* 5 (October 2007): 77-78.

–. "Gays and Lesbians: Pushing the Boundaries." In *Canadian Society: Meeting the Challenges of the Twenty-First Century*, edited by Dan Glenday and Anne Duffy, 212-46. Don Mills, ON: Oxford University Press, 2001.

–. "How the Centre Holds – National Security as an Ideological Practice." In *Whose National Security? Canadian State Surveillance and the Creation of Enemies*, edited by Gary Kinsman, Dieter K. Buse, and Mercedes Steedman, 278-85. Toronto: Between the Lines, 2000.

–. "'Inverts,' 'Psychopaths' and 'Normal' Men: Historical Sociological Perspectives on Gay and Heterosexual Masculinities." In *Men and Masculinities: A Critical Anthology*, edited by Tony Haddad, 3-35. Toronto: Canadian Scholars' Press, 1993.

–. "Mapping Social Relations of Struggle: Activism, Ethnography, Social Organization." In *Sociology for Changing the World*, edited by Caelie Frampton, Gary Kinsman, A.K. Thompson, and Kate Tilleczek, 133-56. Halifax: Fernwood, 2006.

–. "National Security as Moral Regulation: Making the Normal and the Deviant in the Security Campaigns against Gay Men and Lesbians." In *Making Normal: Social Regulation in Canada*, edited by Deborah Brock, 121-45. Toronto: Thomson Nelson, 2003.

–. "The National Security Campaign against Gay Men and Lesbians." *Canadian Dimension* 32, 5 (1998): 13-15.

–. "Never Going Back: A History of Queer Activism in Canada." Review of *Never Looking Back*, by Tom Warner. *New Socialist* 39 (2003): 35.

–. "Official Discourse as Sexual Regulation." PhD diss., OISE/University of Toronto, 1989.

–. "Outing and the Dismantling of 'the Closet.'" Review of *Contested Closets: The Politics and Ethics of Outing*, by Larry Gross. *Lesbian and Gay Studies Newsletter* 21, 2 (1994): 37-38.

–. "The Politics of Revolution: Learning from Autonomist Marxism." *Upping the Anti* 1, 1 (2005): 41-50.

–. "Queerness Is Not in Our Genes: Biological Determinism versus Social Liberation." In *Making Normal: Social Regulation in Canada*, edited by Deborah Brock, 262-84. Toronto: Thomson Nelson, 2003.

–. *The Regulation of Desire: Homo and Hetero Sexualities*. Montreal: Black Rose, 1996.

–. "'Responsibility' as a Strategy of Governance: Regulating People with AIDS and Lesbians and Gay Men in Ontario." *Economy and Society* 25, 3 (1996): 393-409.

–. "'Restoring Confidence in the Criminal Justice System': The Hughes Commission and Mass Media Coverage – Making Homosexuality a Problem." In *Violence and Social Control in the Home*,

Workplace, Community and Institutions, edited by Atlantic Association of Sociologists and Anthropologists, 211-69. St. John's: ISER Press, Memorial University of Newfoundland, 1992.

–. "The Textual Practices of Sexual Rule: Sexual Policing and Gay Men." In *Knowledge, Experience, and Ruling Relations: Studies in the Social Organization of Knowledge,* edited by Marie Campbell and Ann Manicom, 80-95. Toronto: University of Toronto Press, 1995.

–. "Vladimir Lenin: Socialism from Below." *New Socialist* 3, 2 (1998): 10.

–. "Wolfenden in Canada: Using and Moving beyond the Text in Struggles for Law Reform." Paper presented at "Wolfenden 50" conference, London, June 2007.

Kinsman, Gary, Dieter K. Buse, and Mercedes Steedman, eds. *Whose National Security? Canadian State Surveillance and the Creation of Enemies.* Toronto: Between the Lines, 2000.

Kinsman, Gary, and Patrizia Gentile, with the assistance of Heidi McDonell and Mary Mahood-Greer. *"In the Interests of the State": The Anti-Gay, Anti-Lesbian National Security Campaigns in Canada – A Research Report.* Sudbury: Laurentian University, 1998.

Klein, Naomi. *The Shock Doctrine: The Rise of Disaster Capitalism.* Toronto: Knopf Canada, 2007.

Kolko, G., and J. Kolko. *The Limits of Power: The World and United States Foreign Policy, 1945-1954.* New York: Harper and Row, 1972.

Korinek, Valerie. "'The Most Openly Gay Person for at Least a Thousand Miles': Doug Wilson and the Politicization of a Province, 1975-1983." *Canadian Historical Review* 84, 4 (2003): 517-50.

Kyper, John. "'A Member of the Prohibited Class of Persons ...' or, My Modest Contribution to the Queering of Canada." *Left History* 13, 2 (2008): 151-61.

Lahey, Kathleen. *Are We 'Persons' Yet? Law and Sexuality in Canada.* Toronto: University of Toronto Press, 1999.

Lahey, Kathleen, and Kevin Alderson. *Same-Sex Marriage: The Personal and the Political.* Toronto: Insomniac Press, 2004.

Laroque, Sylvain. *Gay Marriage: The Story of a Canadian Social Revolution.* Toronto: James Lorimer, 2006.

Lawless, James C., and F.R. Wake. "Sex Differences in Pupillary Response to Visual Stimuli." *Psychophysiology* 5, 5 (1969): 568.

League for Socialist Action/Ligue socialiste ouvrière. *Gay Liberation in Canada: A Socialist Perspective.* Toronto: Vanguard, 1977.

Lehr, Valerie. *Queer Family Values: Debunking the Myth of the Nuclear Family.* Philadelphia: Temple University Press, 1999.

Lesbians Making History Collective. "People Think That Didn't Happen in Canada." *Fireweed* 28 (Spring 1989): 84.

Leslie, Pat. "Conference Coverage." *Body Politic,* November 1976, 2, 20.

Leznoff, Maurice. "The Homosexual in Urban Society." Master's thesis, McGill University, 1954.

Loos, Bill. "Mounties Await Policy on Destruction of Files." *Body Politic,* April 1983, 10.

–. "Mounties Cleared in Watkins Inquest." *Body Politic,* September 1982, 12.

–. "The Unexplained Demise of Diplomat John Watkins." *Body Politic,* October 1981, 9.

–. "Watkins Death Probe Seeks New Evidence." *Body Politic,* June 1982, 13-14.

Lukacs, Georg. *History and Class Consciousness.* London: Merlin, 1968.

Lumsden, Ian. *Machos, Maricones, and Gays: Cuba and Homosexuality.* Philadelphia: Temple University Press, 1996.

Lynch, Charles I. "Ottawa Hostel." *Civil Service Review* (September 1942): 278-81.

Mackenzie, Hector. "Purged ... from Memory: The Department of External Affairs and John Holmes." *International Journal: Canadian Institute of International Affairs* 59, 2 (2004): 375-86.

Mandel, Ernest. *Trotsky as Alternative.* London: Verso, 1995.

Mandel, Michael. *Charter of Rights and the Legalization of Politics in Canada.* Rev. ed. Toronto: Thompson Educational, 1994.

—. "Freedom of Expression and National Security." *University of Western Ontario Law Review* 23, 2 (1985): 205-9.

Marcos, Subcommandante Insurgente. "Between the Satellite and the Microscope." In *Ya Basta! Ten Years of the Zapatista Uprising: Writings of Subcommandante Insurgente Marcos,* edited by Žiga Vodovnik, 445-82. Oakland: AK Press, 2004.

—. "First Declaration from the Lacandon Jungle." In *Ya Basta! Ten Years of the Zapatista Uprising: Writings of Subcommandante Insurgente Marcos,* edited by Žiga Vodovnik, 643-45. Oakland: AK Press, 2004.

—. "The Machinery of Ethnocide." In *Ya Basta! Ten Years of the Zapatista Uprising: Writings of Subcommandante Insurgente Marcos,* edited by Žiga Vodovnik, 449-463. Oakland: AK Press.

Martin, David. *Wilderness of Mirrors: Intrigue, Deception, and the Secrets That Destroyed Two of the Cold War's Most Important Agents.* Guilford, CT: Lyons Press, 2003.

Marx, Karl. *Early Writings.* Introduced by Lucio Colletti. Translated by Rodney Livingstone and Gregor Benton. New York: Vintage, 1975.

—. *Grundrisse.* Translated by Martin Nicolaus. New York: Penguin, 1974.

Massad, Joseph. *Desiring Arabs.* Chicago: University of Chicago Press, 2007.

Maurutto, Paula. "Private Policing and Surveillance of Catholics: Anti-Communism in the Roman Catholic Archdiocese of Toronto, 1920-60." In *Whose National Security? Canadian State Surveillance and the Creation of Enemies,* edited by Gary Kinsman, Dieter K. Buse, and Mercedes Steedman, 37-54. Toronto: Between the Lines, 2000.

May, Elaine Tyler. *Homeward Bound: American Families in the Cold War Era.* New York: Basic Books, 1998.

Maynard, Steven. "Through a Hole in the Lavatory Wall: Homosexual Subcultures, Police Surveillance, and the Dialectics of Discovery, Toronto, 1890-1930." *Journal of the History of Sexuality* 5, 2 (1994): 207-42.

McCaskell, Tim. "The Bath Raids and Gay Politics." In *Social Movements/Social Change: The Politics and Practice of Organizing,* edited by Frank Cunningham, Sue Findlay, Marlene Kadar, Alan Lennon, and Ed Silva, 169-88. Toronto: Between the Lines/Socialist Studies, 1988.

McCleary, R.A. "Palmer Sweat as an Index of Anxiety." *School of Aviation Medicine,* Project No. 21, 1207-0004, Report No. 1, October 1953.

McClintock, Anne. *Imperial Leather: Race, Gender and Sexuality in the Colonial Context.* New York: Routledge, 1995.

McCoy, Liza. "Activating the Photographic Text." In *Knowledge, Experience, and Ruling Relations: Studies in the Social Organization of Knowledge,* edited by Marie Campbell and Ann Manicom, 181-92. Toronto: University of Toronto Press, 1995.

McDonnell, Heidi. "The Experiences of a Researcher in the Maze." In *Whose National Security? Canadian State Surveillance and the Creation of Enemies,* edited by Gary Kinsman, Dieter K. Buse, and Mercedes Steedman, 223-32. Toronto: Between the Lines, 2000.

—. "Finding Security in the Archives." In *"In the Interests of the State": The Anti-Gay, Anti-Lesbian National Security Campaign in Canada,* by Gary Kinsman and Patrizia Gentile, with the assistance of Heidi McDonell and Mary Mahood-Greer, 147-50. Sudbury: Laurentian University, 1988.

McIntosh, Mary. "Queer Theory and the War of the Sexes." In *Activating Theory: Lesbian, Gay and Bisexual Politics,* edited by Joseph Bristow and Angela R. Wilson, 30-52. London: Lawrence and Wishart, 1993.

McLeod, Donald. *Lesbian and Gay Liberation in Canada: A Selected Annotated Chronology, 1964-1975.* Toronto: ECW Press/Homewood Books, 1996.

McNally, David. *Another World Is Possible: Globalization and Anti-Capitalism.* 1st ed. Winnipeg: Arbeiter Ring, 2002.

—. *Another World Is Possible: Globalization and Anti-Capitalism.* 2nd ed. Winnipeg/Monmouth, Wales: Arbeiter Ring/Merlin Press, 2006.

–. *Bodies of Meaning: Studies on Language, Labor, and Liberation.* Albany: State University of New York Press, 2001.

–. "Language, History and Class Struggle." In *In Defence of History: Marxism and the Postmodern Agenda,* edited by Ellen Meiksins Wood and John Bellamy Foster, 26-42. New York: Monthly Review, 1997.

Mentinis, Mihalis. *Zapatistas: The Chiapas Revolt and What It Means for Radical Politics.* London: Pluto Press, 2006.

Meyer, Lisa. *Creating GI Jane: Sexuality and Power in the Women's Army Corps during World War II.* New York: Columbia University Press, 1996.

–. "Creating G.I. Jane: The Regulation of Sexuality and Sexual Behaviour in the Women's Army Corps during World War II." *Feminist Studies* 18, 3 (1992): 581-601.

Meyerowitz, Joanne. *Not June Cleaver: Women and Gender in Postwar America, 1945-1960.* Philadelphia: Temple University Press, 1994.

Miller, Alan. "Beefcake with No Labels Attached." *Body Politic,* January 1983, 33.

Mochover, Moshe, and John Fantham. *The Century of the Unexpected: A New Analysis of Soviet Type Societies.* London: Big Flame, 1979.

Moores, Colin, ed. *The New Imperialists: Ideologies of Empire.* Oxford: Oneworld, 2006.

Moran, Les. *The Homosexual(ity) of Law.* London: Routledge, 1996.

–. "The Uses of Homosexuality: Homosexuality for National Security." *International Journal of Sociology and the Law* 19 (1991): 149-70.

Moreau, Katherine. "Criminals, Hooligans, Violence: A Case Study and Discursive Analysis of the Criminalization of Political Dissent." Master's thesis, Laurentian University, 2006.

Mossop, Brian. "Gay and Socialist, or Some Reflections of a Commie Fag." *Canadian Dimension* 14, 7 (1980): 49-51.

–. "Lecture Series Examines Sexism." *Body Politic,* June 1976, 7.

Murphy, Kevin P., ed. "Queer Futures." Special issue, *Radical History Review* 100 (Winter 2008).

Murray, Stephen, and Will Roscoe. *Islamic Homosexualities: Culture, History and Literature.* New York: New York University Press, 1997.

Namaste, Ki. "'Tragic Misreadings': Queer Theory's Erasure of Transgender Subjectivity." In *Queer Studies: A Lesbian, Gay, Bisexual and Transgender Anthology,* edited by Brett Beemyn and Michele Elisason, 183-203. New York: New York University Press, 1996.

Namaste, Viviane K. *Invisible Lives: The Erasure of Transsexual and Transgendered People.* Chicago: University of Chicago Press, 2000.

Negri, Antonio. *Books for Burning: Between Civil War and Democracy in 1970s Italy.* London: Verso, 2005.

Neigh, Scott. "National Security Certificates: Organizing against Secret Trials in Canada." Paper presented at "Canadian Security into the 21st Century: (Re)Articulations in the Post-9/11 World," Laurentian University, Sudbury, Ontario, March 5, 2008.

Nestle, Joan. "Butch-Femme Relationships: Sexual Courage in the 1950s," in *A Restricted Country.* Ithaca: Firebrand, 1987.

–. *A Restricted Country.* Ithaca: Firebrand, 1987.

Ng, Roxana. "Exploring the Globalized Regime of Ruling from the Standpoint of Immigrant Workers." In *Sociology for Changing the World: Social Movements/Social Research,* edited by Cailie Frampton, Gary Kinsman, A.K. Thompson, and Kate Tilleczek, 174-208. Halifax: Fernwood, 2006.

–. "Multiculturalism as Ideology: A Textual Analysis." In *Knowledge, Experience, and Ruling Relations,* edited by Marie Campbell and Ann Manicom, 35-48. Toronto: University of Toronto Press, 1995.

Notes from Nowhere, eds. *We Are Everywhere: The Irresistible Rise of Global Anticapitalism.* London: Verso, 2003.

Notte, Randy, and Ian MacKenzie. "Towards Gay Liberation." *Young Socialists/Ligue des jeunes socialistes Discussion Bulletin* 8, 5 (1972).

O'Brien, Carol-Ann, and Lorna Weir. "Lesbians and Gay Men inside and outside Families." In *Canadian Families: Diversity, Conflict, and Change,* edited by Nancy Mandell and Ann Duffy, 111-39. Toronto: Harcourt Brace, 1995.

Office of Equal Opportunities for Women. *The Employment of Women in the Public Service of Canada: Mandate for Change.* 1st ed. Ottawa: Queen's Printer, 1973.

Okafor, Obiora Chinedu. "The 1997 APEC Summit and the Security of Internationally Protected Persons: Did Someone Say 'Suharto'?" In *Pepper in Our Eyes: The APEC Affair,* edited by Wes Pue, 185-96. Vancouver: UBC Press, 2000.

Ollman, Bertell. *Dance of the Dialectic: Steps in Marx's Method.* Urbana and Chicago: University of Illinois Press, 2003.

Olson, Alex Otto. "1956: The Royal Commission on the Criminal Law Relating to Criminal Sexual Psychopaths." Edited and introduced by Robert Champagne, *Rites* (Toronto), November 1986, 8-9.

Orr, Kevin. "Challenging '50s-Style Mounties." *Body Politic,* November 1983, 20.

Palmer, Bryan D. *Canada's 1960s: The Ironies of Identity in a Rebellious Era.* Toronto: University of Toronto Press, 2009.

Pape, Robert A. *Dying to Win: The Strategic Logic of Suicide.* New York: Random House, 2005.

Parent, Madeleine. "Remembering Federal Police Surveillance in Québec, 1940s-70s." In *Whose National Security? Canadian State Surveillance and the Creation of Enemies,* edited by Gary Kinsman, Dieter K. Buse, and Mercedes Steedman, 235-45. Toronto: Between the Lines, 2000.

Park, Rosemary E. "Opening the Canadian Forces to Gays and Lesbians: An Inevitable Decision but Improbable Reconfiguration." In *Gays and Lesbians in the Military: Issues, Concerns, and Contrasts,* edited by Wilbur J. Scott and Sandra Carson Stanley, 165-79. New York: Aldine de Gruyter, 1994.

Parker, Andrew, Mary Russo, Doris Sommer, and Patricia Yaeger, eds. *Nationalisms and Sexualities.* New York: Routledge, 1992.

Pashukanis, E. *Law and Marxism.* London: Pluto Press, 1983.

Pasternak, Shiri. "'They're Clear-Cutting Our Way of Life': Algonquins Defend the Forest." *Upping the Anti* 8 (May 2009): 125-41.

Patton, Cindy. *Inventing AIDS.* New York: Routledge, 1990.

–. *Sex and Germs: The Politics of AIDS.* Boston: South End Press, 1985.

Pavelich, Greg. "The Bijou Raid: The Battle for Queer Space." *New Socialist* 5, 4 (1999): 23-24.

Pearlston, Karen. "APEC Days at UBC: Student Protests and National Security in an Era of Trade Liberalization." In *Whose National Security? Canadian State Surveillance and the Creation of Enemies,* edited by Gary Kinsman, Dieter K. Buse, and Mercedes Steedman, 267-77. Toronto: Between the Lines, 2000.

Pender, Terry. "The Gaze on Clubs, Native Studies, and Teachers at Laurentian University, 1960s-70s." In *Whose National Security? Canadian State Surveillance and the Creation of Enemies,* edited by Gary Kinsman, Dieter K. Buse, and Mercedes Steedman, 110-20. Toronto: Between the Lines, 2000.

–. "Mounties on Campus: The Social Construction of National Security Risks." Honours essay, Laurentian University, 1997.

People's Commission on Immigration "Security" Measures. "Final Report." http://www.peoplescommission.org.

Petchesky, Rosalind. "Phantom Towers: Reflections on the Battle between Global Capital and Fundamentalist Terrorism." In *After Shock: September 11, 2001: Global Feminist Perspectives,* edited by Susan Hawthorne and Bronwyn Winter, 348-63. Vancouver: Raincoast Books, 2003.

Philips, A. "The Government Girl." *Maclean's,* January 15, 1953.

Pierson, Ruth Roach. *"They're Still Women After All": The Second World War and Canadian Womanhood.* Toronto: McClelland and Stewart, 1986.

Pincher, Chapman. *Their Trade in Treachery*. New York: Bantam Books, 1981.

Plummer, Kenneth. "Homosexual Problems: Some Research Problems in the Labelling Perspective of Homosexuality." In *The Making of the Modern Homosexual*, edited by Kenneth Plummer, 53-75. London: Hutchinson, 1981.

Plyler, Jen. "How to Keep On Keepin On: Sustaining Ourselves in Community and Social Justice Struggles." *Upping the Anti* 3 (November 2006): 123-34.

Poulin, Carmen. "'The Military Is the Wife and I Am the Mistress': Partners of Lesbians in the Canadian Military." *Atlantis* 26, 1 (2001): 65-76.

Power, Lisa. *No Bath but Plenty of Bubbles: An Oral History of the Gay Liberation Front, 1970-73*. London: Cassell, 1995.

Prentice, Susan, ed. *Changing Child Care: Five Decades of Child Care Advocacy and Policy in Canada*. Halifax: Fernwood, 2001.

Pringle, Rosemary. *Secretaries Talk: Sexuality, Power and Work*. London: Verso, 1988.

Puar, Jasbir K. *Terrorist Assemblages: Homonationalism in Queer Times*. Durham: Duke University Press, 2007.

Puar, Jasbir K., and Amit S. Rai. "Monster, Terrorist, Fag: The War on Terrorism and the Production of Docile Patriots." *Social Text* 20 (3 72) (2002): 121-24.

Pue, Wes, ed. *Pepper in Our Eyes: The APEC Affair*. Vancouver: UBC Press, 2000.

Radstone, Susannah, and Katherine Hodgkin. *Contested Pasts: The Politics of Memory*. London: Routledge, 2007.

—. *Regimes of Memory*. London: Routledge, 2007.

Rashid, Ahmed. *Taliban, Militant Islam, Oil and Fundamentalism in Central Asia*. New Haven: Yale University Press, 2001.

Rayside, David. *On the Fringe: Gays and Lesbians in Politics*. Ithaca: Cornell University Press, 1998.

Razack, Sherene. *Casting Out: The Eviction of Muslims from Western Law and Politics*. Toronto: University of Toronto Press, 2008.

—. *Dark Threats and White Knights: The Somalia Affair, Peacekeeping, and the New Imperialism*. Toronto: University of Toronto Press, 2004.

Rebick, Judy. *Imagine Democracy*. Toronto: Stoddart, 2000.

—. *Ten Thousand Roses: The Making of a Feminist Revolution*. Toronto: Penguin, 2005.

Renwick, Nancy. "No Fury Like a Homosexual Scorned: Murder, Mental Illness and Shifting Perceptions of Homosexuality in Canada, 1958-1959." Master's thesis, Concordia University, 1999.

Revolutionary Marxist Group. *Women's Liberation*. RMG Document Series No. 1. Toronto: RMG, 1976.

Richardson, Louise. *What Terrorists Want: Understanding the Enemy*. New York: Random House, 2006.

RMG Lesbians and Gays. "Conference Coverage Unfair." *Body Politic*, November 1976, 20.

—. "RMG Indicts the Body Politic." *Body Politic*, November 1974, 3, 24.

Robinson, Daniel J., and David Kimmel. "The Queer Career of Homosexual Security Vetting in Cold War Canada." *Canadian Historical Review* 75, 3 (1994): 319-45.

Robinson, Lucy. *Gay Men and the Left in Post-War Britain: How the Personal Got Political*. Manchester: Manchester University Press, 2007.

—. "Three Revolutionary Years: The Impact of the Counter Culture on the Development of the Gay Liberation Movement in Britain." *Cultural and Social History* 3, 4 (2006): 445-71.

—. "When Is a Scene a Conspiracy?" Paper presented at "New World Coming: The Sixties and the Shaping of Global Consciousness," Queen's University, Kingston, Ontario, June 13, 2007.

Rodgers, Bruce. *Gay Talk: A (Sometimes Outrageous) Dictionary of Gay Slang*. New York City: Paragon Book, 1979.

Roedigger, David. *Towards the Abolition of Whiteness: Essays on Race, Politics, and Working-Class History*. London: Verso, 1994.

—. *The Wages of Whiteness: Race and the Making of the American Working Class*. London: Verso, 1993.

Rollings-Magnusson, Sandra. "Buying Security with Freedom: The Vulnerability of Human Rights in the Post 9/11 Era." In *Anti-Terrorism: Security and Insecurity after 9/11,* edited by Sandra Rollings-Magnusson, 83-101. Halifax: Fernwood, 2009.

Rose, Nikolas. *The Psychological Complex: Psychology, Politics, and Society in England, 1869-1939.* London: Routledge and Kegan Paul, 1985.

Ross, Becki L. "Destaining the (Tattooed) Delinquent Body: The Practices of Moral Regulation at Toronto's Street Haven, 1965-1969." *Journal of the History of Sexuality* 7, 4 (1997): 561-95.

–. *The House That Jill Built: A Lesbian Nation in Formation.* Toronto: University of Toronto Press, 1995.

Ross, Kristin. *May '68 and Its Afterlives.* Chicago: University of Chicago Press, 2002.

Rowbotham, Sheila. "The Women's Movement and Organizing for Socialism." In *Beyond the Fragments,* edited by Sheila Rowbotham, Lynn Segal, and Hillary Wainwright, 121-55. London: Merlin Press, 1979.

Rowe, Michael. "Another Soldier's Story." *Fab National* 9 (Spring 1998): 42-47.

Rubin, I.I. *Essays on Marx's Theory of Value.* Montreal: Black Rose Books, 1982.

Russell, Peter H. "The Proposed Charter for a Civilian Intelligence Agency: An Appraisal." *Canadian Public Policy/Analyse de politiques* 9, 3 (1983): 326-37.

Russell, Stuart. "The Offence of Keeping a Common Bawdy-House." *Ottawa Law Review* 14, 2 (1982): 270-313.

Said, Edward. *Orientalism.* New York: Vintage, 1979.

Sanders, Doug. "Constructing Lesbian and Gay Rights." *Canadian Journal of Law and Society* 9, 2 (1994): 99-143.

–. "Submission to the Royal Commission on Security." Unpublished document, February 29, 1968. In the possession of the authors.

Sandoval, Chela. *Methodology of the Oppressed.* Minneapolis: University of Minnesota Press, 2000.

Sawatsky, John. *For Services Rendered.* Toronto: Doubleday, 1982.

–. *Men in the Shadows: The RCMP Security Service.* Toronto: Totem Books, 1983.

Sayer, Derek. *Marx's Method: Ideology, Science, and Critique in Capital.* Harvester, NY: Humanities, 1983.

–, ed. *Readings from Karl Marx.* London: Routledge, 1989.

–. *The Violence of Abstraction.* Oxford: Basil Blackwell, 1987.

Scher, Len. *The UnCanadians: True Stories of the Blacklist Era.* Toronto: Lester, 1992.

Sears, Alan. "Before the Welfare State: Public Health and Social Policy." *Canadian Review of Sociology and Anthropology* 32, 2 (1995): 169-88.

–. "Can Marriage Be Queer?" *New Socialist* 29 (2001): 31-33.

–. *A Good Book, in Theory: A Guide to Theoretical Thinking.* Peterborough: Broadview Press, 2005.

–. "Is There Sex after Marriage?" *New Socialist* 53 (2005): 38-39.

–. "Queer Times?" *New Socialist* 3, 3 (1998): 12-13, 25.

–. *Re-Tooling the Mind Factory: Education in a Lean State.* Aurora, ON: Garamond Press, 2003.

–. "'To Teach Them How to Live': The Politics of Public Health from Tuberculosis to AIDS." *Journal of Historical Sociology* 5, 1 (1992): 61-83.

Sedgwick, Eve Kosofsky. *Epistemology of the Closet.* Berkeley: University of California Press, 1990.

Seidman, Steven, ed. *Queer Theory/Sociology.* Cambridge, MA/Oxford, UK: Blackwell, 1996.

Sethna, Christabelle. "High-School Confidential: RCMP Surveillance of Secondary School Student Activists." In *Whose National Security? Canadian State Surveillance and the Creation of Enemies,* edited by Gary Kinsman, Dieter K. Buse, and Mercedes Steedman, 121-28. Toronto: Between the Lines, 2000.

Sethna, Christabelle, and Steven Hewitt. "Staging Protest: The Abortion Caravan, Feminist Guerilla Theatre and RCMP Spying on Women's Groups." Paper presented at "New World Coming: The Sixties and the Shaping of Global Consciousness," Kingston, Ontario, June 14, 2007.

Shantz, Jeff. "Fighting to Win: The Ontario Coalition against Poverty." In *We Are Everywhere: The Irresistible Rise of Global Anticapitalism*, edited by Notes from Nowhere, 464-71. London: Verso Press, 2003.

Sharma, Nandita. *Home Economics: Nationalism and the Making of "Migrant Workers" in Canada.* Toronto: University of Toronto Press, 2006.

Shepherd, Simon. "Gay Sex Spy Orgy: The State's Need for Queers." In *Coming On Strong: Gay Politics and Culture*, edited by Simon Shepherd and Mick Wallis, 213-30. London: Unwin Hyman, 1989.

Shilts, Randy. *Conduct Unbecoming: Gays and Lesbians in the US Military.* New York: Fawcett Columbine, 1994.

Smith, Dorothy E. *The Conceptual Practices of Power: A Feminist Sociology of Knowledge.* Toronto: University of Toronto Press, 1990.

–. *The Everyday World as Problematic: A Feminist Sociology.* Toronto: University of Toronto Press, 1987.

–. *Institutional Ethnography: A Sociology for People.* Lanham, NY: Alta Mira, 2005.

–. "Sociological Theory: Writing Patriarchy into Feminist Texts." In *Feminism and Sociological Theory*, edited by Ruth Wallace, 34-64. New York: Sage, 1989.

–. *Texts, Facts, and Femininity: Exploring the Relations of Ruling.* London: Routledge, 1990.

–. "Whistling Women: Reflections on Rage and Rationality." In *Fragile Truths: Twenty-Five Years of Sociology and Anthropology in Canada*, edited by William Carroll, Linda Christiansen-Ruffman, Raymond Currie, and Deborah Harrison, 207-26. Ottawa: Carleton University Press, 1992.

–. *Writing the Social: Critique, Theory, and Investigations.* Toronto: University of Toronto Press, 1999.

Smith, Dorothy E., and George Smith. "Re-organizing the Job-Skills Training Nexus: From 'Human Capital' to 'Human Resources.'" In *Education for Work, Education as Work: Canada's Changing Community Colleges*, edited by Jacob Muller, 171-96. Toronto: Garamond, 1990.

Smith, Geoffrey S. "Commentary: Security, Gender, and the Historical Process." *Diplomatic History* 18, 1 (1994): 79-90.

–. "National Security and Personal Isolation: Sex, Gender, and Disease in the Cold-War United States." *International History Review* 14, 2 (1992): 307-37.

Smith, George. "The Ideology of 'Fag': The School Experience of Gay Students." *Sociological Quarterly* 39, 2 (1998): 309-35.

–. "Media Frames: How Accounts Are Produced and Read." *Fuse* 6, 5 (1983): 279-83.

–. "Policing the Gay Community: An Inquiry into Textually Mediated Social Relations." *International Journal of the Sociology of Law* 16 (1988): 163-83.

–. "Political Activist as Ethnographer." In *Sociology for Changing the World: Social Movements/Social Research*, edited by Caelie Frampton, Gary Kinsman, A.K. Thompson, and Kate Tilleczek, 44-70. Halifax: Fernwood, 2006.

Smith, Lee. "Looking Backward: The SWP and Gay Liberation, 1970-1973." In *Gay Liberation and Socialism: Documents from the Discussions on Gay Liberation inside the Socialist Workers Party (1970-1973)*, edited by David Thorstad, 108-13. New York: Thorstad, 1976.

Smith, Miriam. *Lesbian and Gay Rights in Canada: Social Movements and Equality Seeking, 1971-1995.* Toronto: University of Toronto Press, 1999.

Solomon, Norman, and Reese Erlich. *Target Iraq: What the News Media Didn't Tell You.* New York: Context Books, 2003.

Sommer, Fred. "Anthony Blunt and Guy Burgess: Gay Spies." In *Gay Men and the Sexual History of the Political Left*, edited by Gert Helma, Harry Oosterhuis, and James Steakley, 273-93. New York/London: Harrington Park Press/Haworth Press, 1995.

Stanko, Elizabeth A. *Everyday Violence.* London: Pandora, 1990.

–. *Intimate Intrusions: Women's Experiences of Male Violence.* London: Routledge and Kegan Paul, 1985.

Starnes, John. *Closely Guarded: A Life in Canadian Security and Intelligence.* Toronto: University of Toronto Press, 1998.

Steedman, Mercedes. "The Red Petticoat Brigade: Mine Mill Women's Auxiliaries and the 'Threat from Within,' 1940s-70s." In *Whose National Security? Canadian State Surveillance and the Creation of Enemies,* edited by Gary Kinsman, Dieter K. Buse, and Mercedes Steedman, 55-71. Toronto: Between the Lines, 2000.

Steedman, Mercedes, Peter Suschnigg, and Dieter K. Buse. *Hard Lessons: The Mine Mill Union in the Canadian Labour Movement.* Toronto: Dundurn Press, 1995.

Stone, Sharon Dale. "Lesbian Mothers Organizing." In *Lesbians in Canada,* edited by Sharon Dale Stone, 198-208. Toronto: Between the Lines, 1990.

Strange, Carolyn, and Tina Loo. *Making Good: Law and Moral Regulation in Canada, 1867-1939.* Toronto: University of Toronto Press, 1997.

Strecker, Edward A. *Their Mother's Sons: The Psychiatrist Examines an American Problem.* Philadelphia: J.B. Lippincott, 1946.

Strecker, Edward A., and Vincent T. Lathbury. *Their Mother's Daughters.* Philadelphia: J.B. Lippincott, 1956.

Strong-Boag, Veronica. "Home Dreams: Women and the Suburban Experiment in Canada, 1945-1960." *Canadian Historical Review* 65, 2 (1984): 154-83.

Sutcliffe, H.F. "Herbert Frederick Sutcliffe, MBE, CD: An Autobiography." Unpublished autobiography. Toronto, 1981. In holdings of Canadian Lesbian and Gay Archives (Toronto).

Swift, Richard. *The No-Nonsense Guide to Democracy.* Toronto: Between the Lines, 2002.

Sylvestre, Paul-Francois. *Les homosexuels s'organisent.* Montreal: Éditions Homeureux, 1979.

–. *Propos pour une libération (homo)sexuelle.* Montreal: Les Éditions de l'Aurore, 1976.

Syms, Shawn. "Mulroney Backtracks after Canadian Military Changes Anti-Gay Policy." *Rites* (Toronto), November-December 1991, 6.

Talon, Dennis J. "Anarchy in Seattle and Quebec City: 'Violent Anarchist' as an Ideological Code in the Mainstream Print Media." Honours essay, Laurentian University, 2007.

Teeple, Gary. "Towards a Theory of Terrorism." In *Anti-Terrorism: Security and Insecurity after 9/11,* edited by Sandra Rollings-Magnusson, 32-58. Halifax: Fernwood, 2009.

Tendency Z. "Declaration of Tendency Z." *RWL/LOR Discussion Bulletin* 3, 7 (1979): 1-11.

Terry, Jennifer. *An American Obsession: Science, Medicine, and Homosexuality in Modern Society.* Chicago: University of Chicago Press, 1999.

–. "Anxious Slippages between 'Us' and 'Them': A Brief History of the Scientific Search for Homosexual Bodies." In *Deviant Bodies,* edited by Jennifer Terry and Jacqueline Urla, 129-69. Bloomington: Indiana University Press, 1995.

–. "Momism and the Making of the Treasonous Lesbian." Paper presented at the Canadian Historical Association, Montreal, Quebec, August 26, 1995.

–. "Momism and the Making of Treasonous Homosexuals." In *"Bad" Mothers: The Politics of Blame in Twentieth-Century America,* edited by Molly Ladd-Taylor and Lauri Umansky, 169-90. New York: New York University Press, 1998.

–. "Theorizing Deviant Historiography." *Differences* 3, 2 (1991): 55-74.

Theweleit, Klaus. *Male Fantasies.* Vol. 2, *Male Bodies: Psychoanalyzing the White Terror.* Minneapolis: University of Minnesota Press, 1987.

Thobani, Sunera. *Exalted Subjects: Studies in the Making of Race and Nation in Canada.* Toronto: University of Toronto Press, 2007.

–. "It's Bloodthirsty Vengeance." In *After Shock: September 11, 2001: Global Feminist Perspectives,* edited by Susan Hawthorne and Bronwyn Winter, 91-96. Vancouver: Raincoast Books, 2003.

–. "The 'War on Terror' and the Crisis of American Masculinity." Paper presented at "Human Conditions Series: 2nd Annual International Multidisciplinary Conference on 'Terror,'" Laurentian University, Barrie, Ontario, May 2-3, 2008.

Thompson, E.P. *The Making of the English Working Class.* Harmondsworth: Penguin Books, 1968.

Thompson, Paul, and Guy Lewis. *The Revolution Unfinished? A Critique of Trotskyism*. Liverpool: Big Flame, 1977.

Thorstad, David, ed. *Gay Liberation and Socialism: Documents from the Discussions on Gay Liberation inside the Socialist Workers Party (1970-1973)*. New York: Thorstad, 1976.

—. "Homosexuality and the American Left: The Impact of Stonewall." In *Gay Men and the Sexual History of the Political Left*, edited by Gert Hekma, Harry Oosterhuis, and James Steakley, 319-49. New York: Harrington Park Press, 1995.

Treichler, Paula. *How to Have Theory in an Epidemic: Cultural Chronicles of AIDS*. Durham: Duke University Press, 1999.

Trollope, Paul. "Bawdy Politics, Baths and the Bawdy House Laws." *Body Politic*, April 1977, 9.

Trotsky, Leon. *History of the Russian Revolution*. London: Pluto Press, 1977.

—. *The Permanent Revolution and Results and Prospects*. New York: Pathfinder Press, 1972.

—. *The Revolution Betrayed*. New York: Merit, 1965.

Trow, Robert. "Forces Fight Rights." *Body Politic*, May 1982, 15.

Tucker, Eric. "The Constitutional Right to Bargain Collectively: The Ironies of Labour History in the Supreme Court of Canada." *Labour/Le travail* 61 (2008): 151-80.

—. "Constitutionalizing the Right to Bargain: How Much of a Victory?" *New Socialist* 62 (2007): 16-17.

Valverde, Mariana. *The Age of Light, Soap, and Water: Moral Reform in English Canada, 1885-1925*. Toronto: McClelland and Stewart, 1991.

—. *Sex, Power, and Pleasure*. Toronto: Women's Press, 1985.

Wages Due. "Lesbian Autonomy and the Gay Movement." *Body Politic*, August 1976, 8.

Waite, Brian. "A Strategy for Gay Liberation." In *Flaunting It! A Decade of Gay Journalism from the Body Politic*, edited by Ed Jackson and Stan Persky, 221-23. Vancouver/Toronto: New Star Books/Pink Triangle Press, 1982.

Wake, F.R. "Normal Aggression and Delinquency." *Bulletin of the Maritime Psychological Association* 8 (1959): 50-59.

—. "Normal Aggression and Delinquency." Speech before the Maritime Psychological Association, Halifax, September 17, 1959.

Wake, F.R., Kathleen L. Beattie, and Audrey J. King. "A Comparison of Physical Cruelty in Rural and Urban Delinquent Boys." *Canadian Psychologist* 7a, 3 (1966): 209-12.

—. "Physical Cruelty in Male Juvenile Delinquents." *Canadian Psychologist* 6a, 3 (1965): 241-45.

Walker, Merv. "David Garmaise and the NGRC: After a Turbulent Year One, an Informal Talk with an Informal Man." *Body Politic*, November 1976, 9.

—. "LSA Line 'Inadequate,' Gay Activist Resigns." *Body Politic*, March 1977, 6-7.

Warner, Michael. "Beyond Gay Marriage." Chap. 3 in *The Trouble with Normal: Sex, Politics, and the Ethics of Queer Life*. Cambridge, MA: Harvard University Press, 1999.

—, ed. *Fear of a Queer Planet*. Minneapolis: University of Minnesota Press, 1993.

Warner, Tom. "Fighting the Anti-Queer Right-Wing: Interview by Gary Kinsman." *New Socialist* 45 (2004): 32-34.

—. *Never Going Back: A History of Queer Activism in Canada*. Toronto: University of Toronto Press, 2002.

Waugh, Tom. "Gay Male Visual Culture in North America during the Fifties: Emerging from the Underground." *Parallelogramme* 12, 1 (1986): 63-67.

—. *Hard to Imagine: Gay Male Eroticism in Photography and Film from Their Beginnings to Stonewall*. New York: Columbia University Press, 1996.

—. "A Heritage of Pornography." *Body Politic*, January 1983, 29-33.

—. "Photography, Passion and Power." *Body Politic*, March 1984, 29-33.

Webb, Maureen. *Illusions of Security: Global Surveillance and Democracy in the Post-9/11 World*. San Francisco: City Lights, 2007.

Weeks, Jeffrey. *Coming Out*. London: Quartet, 1977.

–. *Invented Moralities: Sexual Values in an Age of Sexual Uncertainty*. New York: Columbia University Press, 1995.

–. *Sexuality and Its Discontents*. London: Routledge and Kegan Paul, 1985.

Weinberg, George. *Society and the Healthy Homosexual*. New York: Anchor Books, 1973.

Weir, Lorna. "Social Movement Activism in the Formation of Ontario New Democratic Party Policy on Abortion, 1982-1984." *Labour/Le travail* 35 (Spring 1995): 163-93.

–. "Studies in the Medicalization of Sexual Danger: Sexual Rule, Sexual Politics." PhD diss., York University, 1986.

Wheeler, Glen. "Unfit for Service." *Body Politic*, March 1983, 29-32.

Whitaker, Brian. *Unspeakable Love: Gay and Lesbian Life in the Middle East*. Berkeley: University of California Press, 2006.

Whitaker, Reginald. *Double Standard: The Secret History of Canadian Immigration*. Toronto: Lester and Orpen Dennys, 1987.

–. "Origins of the Canadian Government's Internal Security System, 1946-52." *Canadian Historical Review* 65, 2 (1984): 154-87.

Whitaker, Reginald, and Steve Hewitt. *Canada and the Cold War*. Toronto: James Lorimer, 2003.

Whitaker, Reginald, and Gary Marcuse. *Cold War Canada: The Making of a National Insecurity State, 1945-1957*. Toronto: University of Toronto Press, 1994.

Wilkinson, Lori. "Are Human Rights Being Jeopardized in Twenty-First Century Canada? An Examination of Immigration Policies Post 9/11." In *Anti-Terrorism: Security and Insecurity after 9/11*, edited by Sandra Rollings-Magnusson, 102-24. Halifax: Fernwood, 2009.

Windsor Peace Committee. *Windsor OAS Days of Action: The Criminalization of Dissent*. Windsor: Windsor Peace Committee, 2001.

Witheford, Nick Dyer. *Cyber-Marx, Cycles, and Circuits of Struggle in High-Technology Capitalism*. Urbana and Chicago: University of Illinois Press, 1999.

Witz, A., and M. Savage, eds. *Gender and Bureaucracy*. Oxford: Blackwell, 1992.

Wood, Ellen Meiksins. *Democracy against Capitalism: Renewing Historical Materialism*. Cambridge: Cambridge University Press, 1995.

Wright, Cynthia. "Against Illegality: New Directions in Organizing by and with Non-Status People in Canada." In *Sociology for Changing the World: Social Movements/Social Research*, edited by Caelie Frampton, Gary Kinsman, A.K. Thompson, and Kate Tilleczek, 189-208. Halifax: Fernwood, 2006.

Wyland, Francie. *Motherhood, Lesbianism and Child Custody*. Bristol: Falling Wall Press, 1977.

Young, Allen. *Gays under the Cuban Revolution*. San Francisco: Grey Fox Press, 1981.

Young, Claire, and Susan Boyd. "Losing the Feminist Voice? Debates on the Legal Recognition of Same-Sex Partnerships in Canada." *Feminist Legal Studies* 14, 2 (2006): 213-40.

Young, Iris. *Global Challenges: War, Self-Determination and Responsibility for Justice*. London: Polity Press, 2007.

Young, Jim, Doug Wilson, and John Foster. "1984: James Bond Comes to Ottawa." *Rites* (Toronto), July-August 1984, 14-15.

Zapatista Army of National Liberation. "Sixth Declaration of the Lacandon Jungle." In *The Other Campaign/La otra campaña*, by Subcommandante Marcos, 60-147. San Francisco: City Lights, 2006.

Zaretsky, Eli. *Capitalism, the Family and Personal Life*. London: Pluto Press, 1976.

–. "Capitalism, the Family and Personal Life." *Socialist Revolution* 13-14 (January-April 1973): 69-125.

FILMS AND DOCUMENTARIES

Edward Said: On Orientalism. DVD. Produced and edited by Sut Jhally and Sanjay Talreja. Northampton, MA: Media Education Foundation, 1998.

Forbidden Love. VHS. Directed by Aerlyn Weissman and Lynne Fernie. Ottawa: National Film Board of Canada, 1993.

The Fourth World War. DVD. Directed by Rick Rowley. New York: Big Noise Films, 2003.

Fruit Machine. Film. Directed and produced by Wrik Mead. Toronto: Canadian Filmmakers Distribution Centre, 1998.

History's Courtroom: The Bedrooms of the Nation. Film. Toronto: Leading Cases Productions Limited/ Screenlife Productions Limited, 2002.

Km. 0 (Kilometer Zero). DVD. Directed by Juan Luis Iborra and Yolanda García Serrano. Philadelphia: TLA Entertainment Group, 2003.

Jim Loves Jack: The James Egan Story. VHS. Directed by David Adkin. David Adkin Productions, 1996. Distributed by Vtape, Toronto.

Legal Memory. VHS. Directed and written by Lisa Steele and Kim Tomczak. Legal Memory Inc., 1992. Distributed by Vtape, Toronto.

Open Secrets. VHS/DVD. Directed by Jose Torrealba. Ottawa: National Film Board of Canada, 2003.

Stand Together. VHS. Directed and produced by Nancy Nicol. Toronto: Intervention Video Inc., 2002. Distributed by Vtape, Toronto.

This Is What Democracy Looks Like. DVD. Directed by Jill Friedberg and Rick Rowley. New York: Big Noise Films/Independent Media Centre, 2000.

V for Vendetta. DVD. Directed by James McTeigue. Burbank, CA: Warner Bros., 2005.

Index

Note: "(f)" after a page number indicates a figure

Glassco Commission report. *See Report of the Royal Commission on Government Organization and Management of the Public Service*

globalization. *See* capitalist globalization

Green Paper, 252

Grube, John, 105, 198, 213, 482n190

heterosexual hegemony, 5-6, 24, 29-31, 33, 48, 55, 57, 59, 60, 253-54, 338, 340, 394-95, 407, 428

Higgins, Ross, 271-72, 312

Hill, Charles, 257(f), 259, 261, 267, 302-3, 309-10

Hillenkoetter, Roscoe, 8

Hislop, George, 256, 259, 261, 267, 276, 295-96, 335

historical materialism. *See* Marx, Karl

history from below. *See* Thompson, E.P.

Holmes, John, 50, 94-95, 131, 135-38, 140

homonormativity, 433

Homophile Association of London Ontario (HALO), 294

homophobia, 24, 33, 34-35, 350-51, 414, 455

homosexual personality, 9, 48-49, 175-76

homosexual screening program (RCMP): background, 3; categorization, 3-4; in the DEA 108, 131-33; and resistance, 194-95. *See also* character weakness

"homosexual vice-ring," 304-10

homosexuality: as active characteristic, 408-9; and class, xv, 8-9, 21, 49, 52, 63, 65, 75, 94-95, 130-31, 141, 227, 291-92, 431, 433, 455-56; as dangerous, 8-9, 42, 72-75, 168-69, 238-39, 398-99, 404-5 (*see also* dangerous sexual offender); and gender stereotypes, 33, 62, 64-68, 177-78, 180-81, 226, 365, 397, 404-5 (*see also* femininity; gender inversion; masculinity); as management problem in military, 401-5; medical discourses on, 56, 68-72, 89-90, 98-101, 214, 231, 377, 407-9; overt vs covert, 130-31, 141-42, 156, 169, 180, 198-99, 205, 432-33 (*see also* closet; relations of; double life); psychological/psychiatric discourses on, 33, 48, 55-56, 64-75, 89-90, 98-101, 106-7, 169-76, 184-85, 214, 218, 377-80; scientific/technological detection, 112, 122, 168-71, 175-84, 188-90 (*see also* fruit machine);

as security threat (*see* blackmail; character weakness). *See also* criminalization of sexuality; fag; lesbians, lesbian invisibility; sexual orientation

Homosexuels pour un Québec Libre, 271

Human Rights Act (Canada), 230, 237, 298-99, 324, 327-29, 393, 398-99, 403-4, 411, 427, 435

institutional ethnography. *See* Smith, Dorothy

International Women's Day, 289, 330-32, 357, 508n75

internationally protected person, 431, 439, 441

Jackson, Paul, 69

Jenkins, Aaron, 65, 97-107. *See also* Mantha, Leo; Royal Canadian Navy, purges in

Johnson, David K., 86, 93-95, 131, 136, 140

Johnston, Blair, 116, 222-23, 226-37, 319-20, 365, 388-89, 396-97

Keable Commission. *See* Commission d'enquête sur des opérations policières en territoire québécois

Kemp's disease, 98-99

Kidd, Dorothy, 289-91, 293

Kinsey Report, 66, 218, 299

Klippert, George Everett, 215. *See also* law reform

Krever Commission. *See* Royal Commission of Inquiry into the Confidentiality of Health Records in Ontario

Latour, Peaches, 118, 130-31, 163, 200-1

Laurentian Terrace, 59, 61

law reform: Criminal Code (1969), 215, 219-22, 231, 260-65, 302, 316, 333, 341; Trudeau's statement, 215, 219-20, 222-23; Wolfenden Report, 74, 121-22, 215-27, 402. *See also* Klippert, George Everett; *Report of the Royal Commission on Security* (Mackenzie Commission report)

League for Socialist Action (LSA), 244, 246, 250, 254, 256-59, 265-66, 268, 270, 272-83, 296-301, 313, 329. *See also* Ligue socialiste ouvrière; Operation Checkmate

left movements/organizing: conflicts re gay and lesbian liberation, 272-75, 281-82, 285; new left, 244, 248, 277-78, 287; subversion, 24-25, 244, 246-47, 272, 274, 279-80,

obligations, 46, 80-84; and the social construction of secrecy, 43; and subversive threats, 41; and the war on terror, xv, 23. *See also* gendered relations; *Report of the Royal Commission on Security* (Mackenzie Commission report)

national security certificates, xi, 431-32, 446-49, 458

nationalism. *See* "cutting out" operations

neoliberalism, 430-31, 433, 436-38. *See also* capitalist globalization

New Democratic Party (NDP), xiv, 250, 278-80, 326, 339, 396, 405. *See also* Robinson, Svend

New Marxist Institute, 286-87. *See also* Gay Marxist Study Group

New Tendency, 275, 289-90, 499*n*91

normality, the social making of, xv-xvi, 5, 23-24, 29, 394, 432

North Atlantic Treaty Organization (NATO), 46, 80, 83-84, 94, 140-41, 147-48, 351. *See also* national security, as ideological practice; national security, and NATO/ tripartite obligations

Official Secrets Act, 84, 241

Olson, Axel Otto, 120, 218

Olympics (Montreal, 1976) 245-46, 293, 302, 311(f), 310-17

Operation Checkmate, 278

operational efficiency, 349-51, 394, 397, 400-3, 405-9, 425

Opportunities for Youth, 295-97

orientalism, 443-44

Other Woman collective, 285, 501*n*133

Ottawa sex scandal. *See* "homosexual vice-ring"

outing, 18, 305-6, 371-77, 388, 421-24, 435. *See also* military, outing/threats of outing

Palmer sweat test, 177-78. *See also* fruit machine; homosexuality, scientific/ technological detection

police: attitudes towards homosexuality, 158; blackmail, 119-20, 195; and demonstrations, 257-58, 283-84, 311(f), 312-13, 333-35, 429-30, 440-42; entrapment, 125, 152-53, 206, 212, 295, 315-16; informants, 206, 210-11, 431, 449; Montreal, 245-46, 271-72, 310-17, 333; Ottawa/Hull, 1-2, 88, 144-45, 152-54, 206, 210-13, 302-10,

314-17, 333 (*see also* Morality Squad); raids, 104, 127, 211-13, 270-71, 302-17, 330-32, 333-35; and RCMP investigations, 19-20, 88, 145, 149-51, 153-54, 210-13, 245-46, 302, 310, 333; surveillance, 1-3, 53, 57, 101-4, 124-27, 152-54, 197, 206, 243, 245-46, 261, 296, 302-17, 431, 440-42; Toronto, 20, 120, 211, 213-14, 313-14, 330-35, 440; Victoria, 101-4, 106, 126-27; violence/harassment, 120, 153-54, 211, 213-14, 260, 305-6, 314-15, 322, 333-35, 440-42. *See also* criminalization of sexuality

polygraph. *See* homosexuality, scientific/ technological detection

power/knowledge relations. *See* Foucault, Michel

Privy Council Office (PCO), 77-78, 114(f), 176, 326, 339, 347-48

psychopath/psychopathic personality, 7-9, 48-49, 69-73, 443. *See also* criminal sexual psychopath; homosexuality, medical discourses on

Puar, Jasbir, 443, 456, 521*n*92

Public Complaints Commission, 438-39

public service. *See* civil service

pupillary response test, 174, 177, 178-84, 189. *See also* fruit machine; homosexuality, scientific/technological detection

queer space, 48-50, 60-63, 197-98, 200-8, 241-42, 263, 357, 394, 455-56. *See also* gay and lesbian networks

queer talk, 12, 208

queering: historical materialism, 30-31; national security campaigns, 22

racialized patriotic masculinity, 452-53

RCMP surveillance: active surveillance vs monitoring, 247-48, 294, 329-33; challenges to, 323-39, 337-39, 341-42, 344, 387-89; of civil service employees, 3-4, 18-20, 54-55, 80-85, 92-97, 108-9, 130-47, 158-59, 165-67, 194-95, 220-26, 333; dirty tricks (*see* Commission d'enquête sur des opérations policières en territoire québécois); entrapment, 19-20; of federal grant applicants (*see* Local Initiatives Program); gathering names of homosexuals, 2-3, 36, 40, 95, 101-7, 117-18,

homosexuality and character defect/weakness, 47-48, 82, 109-10, 217, 218-19, 222-23, 318, 322-23, 340-48, 385, 405, 421-27; investigations, 76, 80-81, 84-85, 140-41, 142, 145-46, 309-10, 324-26, 385-87, 389, 391, 421-23; and the military, 115-16, 124, 193-94, 241, 263-64, 349-50, 355, 360-61, 371-77, 382, 397-401, 410-12; procedures, 46-47, 78, 80-86, 107, 169-70; for women, 58-59, 61

Security Panel: construction of homosexuality as security threat, 7-9, 47-48, 50, 82-83, 89-93, 97, 107-13, 121, 132, 168-70, 173-75, 182, 187-88; history of, 7, 10, 77-79; and the "liberal position," 34-36; organization of, 42-43, 46, 77-79; and the RCMP, 77-79, 90-93, 97, 107-13, 135-36; and unions, 209-10. *See also* fruit machine; Wall, Don

sex deviates, 17, 55, 62, 72, 84, 110, 114(f), 115, 120, 170, 216-17, 223, 230-31, 239, 264, 379. *See also* homosexuality, medical discourses on; military, policy of disposal of sex deviates

sexual abnormality, 231-32, 349, 371, 378

sexual deviance, 23, 24, 70, 216, 231, 407, 428, 432

sexual orientation: detection of, 175, 185, 189; discourses on, 64, 66-68; and human rights legislation, 237, 240, 286, 298-99, 313, 317, 322-24, 327-29, 330, 391-420; McDonald Commission recommendations re, 339-48; military policies re, 337-38, 357-58, 363-64, 391-420

Shelburne purges. *See* lesbians, in military

Siddon, Tom, 231, 347, 369-70, 419

Sirard, Stephane, 364-69, 371-78, 380-82

Smith, Dorothy, 28-29, 32, 268-69

Smith, George, xiii, 306

social organization of national security, 10-11, 43, 85, 93

Socialist Workers Party (SWP), 25, 273-74, 282

Somers, Bruce, 102-4, 131, 148, 176, 206-7

Special Investigations Unit (SIU): challenges to, 410-14; interrogation/investigation, 231, 233-34, 236, 238, 240, 354-56, 365-66, 370-72, 377, 382-84, 412; and military purges, 231-42, 348-49, 354-77, 382-84, 410-14; tactics, 357, 359-60, 368; use of

sexually explicit questions, 156-57, 348-49, 368-70

Special Parliamentary Committee on Equality Rights, 393, 398, 400, 402

Special Project. *See* fruit machine

Starnes, John, 54, 95-96, 109-10, 133-35, 137-39, 170, 279

state of exception, 449-50

Stiles, James, 387-88

subversion: discourses of, 24-25; 346-47; 420-21; dissent as, 250, 278, 345-47, 431, 440; and homosexuality, 3, 49, 91, 396; and left organizing, 247, 274, 287, 294; and terrorism, 11, 25, 337, 420-21, 431-32, 440-42

surveillance: fingerprinting, 77, 84, 114(f), 147, 168, 252; and resistance, 1-2, 4, 6, 191-99, 210, 241-42 (*see also* resistance); technologies of, 29, 138-39, 142, 150, 161, 166, 168, 171, 175-76, 178-83, 188-90, 432; of universities, 8, 86, 148, 246, 250-52, 261, 272, 274, 277, 294, 297, 438, 444-45. *See also* police, surveillance; RCMP surveillance; Special Investigations Unit

Sutcliffe, Herbert, 17-18, 38, 123-26, 161-62, 484n12

Sylvestre, Paul-François, 308-10, 312

Tendency Z, 282-83, 500n122

terrorism/terrorist: and "cutting out" operations, 445-49; racialization of, 45, 443-44, 452-54; social construction of, 442-44, as subversion, 11, 25, 337, 420-21, 431-32, 440-42. *See also* war on terror

Terry, Jennifer. *See* momism

Thompson, E.P., 27-28, 490n5

Thornborrow, Barbara, 232-33, 236-38, 327-29, 368-69. *See also* Cameron, Gloria

Toronto Gay Action (TGA), 249, 253, 256, 259-61, 266, 269-70, 273, 276, 288

Toronto Wages for Housework Committee, 288-93

Toronto Women's Caucus, 276, 287-88

Toward Equality, 400-1, 406

Trent Homophile Association, 252

Trotskyist movement and "infiltration," 248, 254-55, 266-67, 271-73, 275, 277, 280-83, 286, 298, 300-1. *See also* left movements/organizing; Socialist Workers Party unions: and the civil service, 57, 224; lack of support for gays and lesbians, 285, 389-90; and the national security regime, 25, 34, 77, 209-10, 279-80, 287, 300, 329, 436

University of Toronto Homophile Association (UTHA), 250, 261, 295

Vancouver Gay Sisters, 269

Waffle movement. *See* New Democratic Party (NDP)

Wages Due Lesbians, 290-95

Waite, Brian, 256, 258, 260-61, 270, 272-76, 296, 300

Wake, F.R., 35, 66-67, 114(f), 168-90. *See also* Canadian Council on Religion and the Homosexual; fruit machine; Royal Commission on the Criminal Law Relating to Criminal Sexual Psychopaths (McRuer Commission)

Wall, Don, 7-9, 78, 90, 97, 107, 113, 158, 170-71. *See also* Security Panel

war on terror, xi-xii, xv, 5, 23, 429-32, 442-58

Warner, Tom, 313-14, 414

Watkins, John, 95-97

We Demand. See August 28th Gay Day Committee

Weeks, Jeffrey, 50

Wilson, John, 257-60, 258(f), 267, 269, 273-74, 276, 300, 327-28, 329

Wolfenden Report, 34, 74, 121, 215-17, 219, 402

Women Against Violence Against Women (WAVAW), 331-32

women's/feminist movement, 57, 271, 285, 287-95, 330-32, 502*n*147

Wood, Darl, 238-41, 357, 368-69, 396

World Trade Organization (WTO), 429-30, 437-39

Young Socialists (YS), xiii, 244, 247, 250, 254, 256, 258, 270, 272-75, 277-80, 288, 297-98, 300-1

Zapatistas, 437, 457, 464*n*14

Zufelt, Warren, 306-7, 315

Printed and bound in Canada by Friesens

Set in Machine, Meta and Minion by Artegraphica Design Co. Ltd.

Copy editor: Joanne Richardson

Proofreader: Deborah Kerr

Cartographer: Eric Leinberger